RODALE'S
ILLUSTRATED ENCYCLOPEDIA OF
PERENNIALS

RODALE'S
ILLUSTRATED ENCYCLOPEDIA OF
PERENNIALS

ELLEN PHILLIPS *and* C. COLSTON BURRELL

RODALE

RODALE

WE **INSPIRE** AND **ENABLE** PEOPLE TO IMPROVE
THEIR LIVES AND THE WORLD AROUND THEM

Printed in the United States of America on acid-free
∞, recycled paper ♻

Book design by Christina Gaugler

Photo credits can be found on page 689.

We're always happy to hear from you. For questions
or comments concerning the editorial content of this
book, please write to:

Rodale Book Readers' Service
33 East Minor Street
Emmaus, PA 18098

Look for other Rodale books wherever books are
sold. Or call us at (800) 848-4735.

For more information about Rodale Organic Living
magazines and books, visit us at
www.organicgardening.com

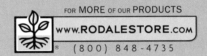

FOR **MORE** OF OUR **PRODUCTS**
WWW.RODALESTORE.COM
(800) 848-4735

Library of Congress Cataloging-in-Publication Data

Phillips, Ellen.
  Rodale's illustrated encyclopedia of
perennials / Ellen Phillips and C. Colston Burrell.
    p.   cm.
  Includes bibliographical references and index.
  ISBN 0–87596–898–8 hardcover
  ISBN 0–87596–899–6 paperback
  1. Perennials.   2. Perennials—Encyclopedias.
I. Title: Illustrated encyclopedia of perennials.   II.
Burrell, C. Colston.   III. Rodale Press.
IV. Title.
SB434.P48   2004
635.9'32'03—dc22   2003025409

Distributed in the book trade by St. Martin's Press

4 6 8 10 9 7 5 3   hardcover
4 6 8 10 9 7 5 3   paperback

CONTENTS

ACKNOWLEDGMENTS

We would like to acknowledge the hundreds of thousands of perennial lovers—the gardeners, plant breeders, nursery owners, professors, garden designers, landscapers, and other enthusiasts—whose use of and praise for our original encyclopedia has made this second edition possible.

We would like to thank our own teachers, influences, and gardening friends and colleagues, as well as those great writers past and present who have shared their passion for plants and gardening and have been such an inspiration. We'd like to acknowledge our debt to the gifted garden designers, illustrators, and photographers who've contributed so much to the beauty and delight of the present edition: designers Edith R. Eddleman, Tracy DiSabato-Aust, Stephanie Cohen, Ann Lovejoy, Lauren Springer, and Nancy McDonald; illustrators Elayne Sears and Frank Fretz; and photographers Pam Harper, Ken Druse, Richard Felber, Tom Gettings/Rodale Images, Rob Cardillo, and Matthew Benson. Special thanks to Tony Avent of Plant Delights Nursery for lending his expertise to the encyclopedia section and to Nancy Ondra for providing plant identifications for the photos.

Finally, to our editor, Chris Bucks, book designer, Chris Gaugler, photo editor, Robin Hepler, and copy editor, Sarah S. Dunn, for working so hard to make the book a success—and somehow managing to maintain their enthusiasm for the project to the last—a huge thank-you.

HOW TO USE THIS BOOK

Welcome to *Rodale's Illustrated Encyclopedia of Perennials!* We've designed this book to be used in many ways, depending on your needs as a gardener. Whether you're a design novice wondering how to put plants together and make them look good or an expert looking for the latest cultivars, you can find what you need. It's easy! Here are a few highlights:

Looking for design advice? Turn to Part I, "Designing the Perennial Garden," beginning on page 1. Chapter 1, "Designing with Perennials," tells you how to use perennials in garden design and provides expert tips on how to create your own designs.

Want a garden design by a famous garden designer? Chapter 4, "A Gallery of Garden Designs," presents seven gardens created especially for this book by some of the most talented perennial designers in this country. Turn to page 83 and take a look!

Need some quick inspiration? Chapter 3, "Perennial Combinations," takes you on a photo tour of beautiful flower and foliage combinations for every taste and site. Start the tour now by turning to page 64.

In search of autumn color? Plants for wet sites? Fabulous foliage? Chapter 2, "Perennial Flower Finder," lists perennials for special needs and special conditions. You'll find what *you* need beginning on page 39.

What about *growing* all those plants? Part II, "Growing Perennials," beginning on page 155, covers all the basics—and beyond. You'll find easy-to-use directions on preparing your soil—irrigating and fertilizing, making and using compost and other soil amendments—to get your perennials off to the best possible start. There's also a chapter on safe, effective pest, disease, and weed control using the latest organic techniques.

How do you know what will grow for you? Chapter 7, "Climate Considerations," tells you how to size up your garden's climate, determine your hardiness zone, and take advantage of your yard's microclimates to grow plants you probably think you can't. Find it all beginning on page 156.

Just looking for a few good plants? You'll find hundreds to choose from in Part III, "The Perennial Encyclopedia," beginning on page 265. Plants are in alphabetical order. Each entry describes the plant genus, garden-worthy species, varieties and cultivars to look for, how to grow it, and how to use it in your garden—where to site it, what to grow it with, and design tips to help you make sure it looks great.

We hope this overview has whetted your appetite—there's much, much more inside. Investigate for yourself and see what you learn. Make sure you have fun—with the book, and with your plants—along the way. We want you to enjoy using *Rodale's Illustrated Encyclopedia of Perennials* as much as we enjoyed writing it!

PART I

DESIGNING THE PERENNIAL GARDEN

DESIGNING WITH PERENNIALS

Two things tend to intimidate gardeners when they're thinking about putting in a perennial garden: the number of perennials to choose from, and the mystique that surrounds garden design. You may want to throw up your hands and say, "I'm not an expert! What do I know about designing gardens?" In this chapter, we'll tell you how to decide which perennials will meet your needs, and we'll take the mystery out of garden design. By breaking it down into simple steps that are easy to follow and fun to think about, we'll have you doing garden design in no time—and loving the way your new garden looks!

WAYS TO APPROACH DESIGN

Think of garden design as a series of plant combinations. When you're combining plants, there are two sets of considerations you need to think about. The first set relates to the appearance of the plants: when they bloom, what color they are (flower color *and* foliage color), how big they get, and what they look like—the form and texture of their foliage and flowers. The second set relates to the habits of the plants: what conditions they prefer (sun or shade, a wet or well-drained site, highly fertile or average soil), how fast they grow, how long they live, and how much ongoing maintenance they require to keep them performing their best.

For a garden design to look good, you have to use plants that grow well together and that will grow well on your site. Stunted, dying, or unkempt plants will ruin a design, no matter how gorgeous it looked on paper. If you have a site in full sun with good drainage, choose classic border perennials like peonies, irises, day-lilies, and delphiniums. If you want to put a perennial garden under shade trees, choose woodland wildflowers and shade-tolerant plants like hostas. Don't try to force peonies to thrive in deep shade or woodland phlox to flourish in full sun—they won't, and your garden's appearance will suffer as much as the plants you're trying to grow.

This book makes it easy to find out which growing conditions perennials prefer. Each plant entry in the encyclopedia section, beginning on page 265, includes a "How to Grow" section that provides concise information on sun and shade, mois-ture and fertility, and other preferred conditions.

When you put together lists of plants you'd like to use, check the encyclopedia entries to make sure they'll grow well to-gether. The entries also discuss how fast the plants grow, if they're especially long- or short-lived, and how much maintenance (like staking, division, and deadheading) they need.

What slows down most gardeners is the first set of considerations—when the plants bloom, what color they are, how big they get, and what they look like. In this chapter, we'll deal with each of these in detail so you can choose and combine plants with confidence. If you'd like to use tried-and-true combinations instead of making your own, you'll find combina-tions galore in Chapter 3, "Perennial Combinations."

DESIGNING BY BLOOM SEASON

One of your first considerations should be bloom season. When do you want your flowers to bloom? If you're home from the last spring frost through the first fall frost, you'll probably want your garden to pro-vide enjoyment during the entire growing season. But there are reasons you might want to focus your garden's show on one or two seasons.

If you love one season best, you could design your garden so the flowers will peak during that season. A lush display in spring, followed by more modest color through summer and fall, might be exactly right for the person for whom "garden" and "spring" are nearly the same word.

If you're at home in spring and fall but gone for part of the summer, you'll want to design a garden that blooms when you're there and requires minimal maintenance when you're not. Or if you live in a climate where summers are searing (or extremely humid), you might not want to be out in the garden until temperatures drop again in fall. On the other hand, a northern or West Coast garden can really come into its glory in summer, and you might want to focus your bloom peak so it falls during the hotter months.

Another reason to focus your attention on one or two seasons is if your garden is small. When you don't have a lot of space, a lush display in one season may look better than one or two plants in bloom at any given time. Remember that there are tricks you can use to extend bloom or color into other seasons, like planting spring-blooming bulbs with later-blooming perennials or adding some ornamental grasses for fall and winter color.

Spring Flowers

Spring is the most welcome season to many gardeners because the garden returns to life after its winter rest. We're eager to see any color—even green looks fresh and new—and the first blooms take on the excitement of an event. Now is the time for the little bulbs—snowdrops, species irises, glory-of-the-snow, crocuses—and the hellebores, the Christmas and Lenten roses (*Helleborus niger* and *H.* ×*hybridus*), with their beautiful deep-green fingered foliage.

After the first flush of color from the bulbs, spring-blooming perennials take over. Some front-of-the-border perennials that bloom as brightly as bulbs are perennial candytuft (*Iberis sempervirens*), rock cresses (*Arabis*), basket-of-gold (*Aurinia saxatilis*), and especially moss phlox (*Phlox subulata*), with its matlike form and an almost electric range of white, purple, sulfur yellow, pink, blue, and lavender. These plants like full sun and good drainage, making them excellent candidates for growing in rock gardens.

Signs of spring. A drift of 'Frans Purple' creeping phlox (*Phlox stolonifera* 'Frans Purple') sets off the variegated hosta foliage and draws the eye to this simple combination.

Spring beauty. The jewellike colors of bleeding hearts, primroses, and Spanish bluebells (*Hyacinthoides hispanica*) light a shady path.

As the larger bulbs—tulips, daffodils, fritillarias, and bulbous irises—signal the end of late frosts and the start of the vegetable growing season, midspring perennials come into their own. Old-fashioned bleeding heart (*Dicentra spectabilis*) bears sprays of pink-and-white or all-white heart-shaped flowers over equally graceful blue-green foliage. Columbines (*Aquilegia*) produce ferny foliage and wiry stems that hold trembling clusters of spurred flowers in every color. Alumroots (*Heuchera*) send up airy sprays of tiny pink, white, green, or red flowers; some, like 'Palace Purple' small-flowered alumroot (*H. micrantha* var. *diversifolia* 'Palace Purple'), are grown for their showy foliage alone.

Grecian windflower (*Anemone blanda*) and poppy anemone (*A. coronaria*) start the anemone season with bursts of color in white, pink, blue, violet, and scarlet; other species will bloom in both summer and fall. And ornamental onions (*Allium*) bear their cheerful globes or flat heads of star-shaped white, pink, lavender, rose, purple, or yellow flowers on sturdy stems over strap-shaped or tubular green foliage.

As spring moves toward summer, many of our most-loved perennials come into their own. Bearded, Siberian, and Japanese irises bloom in every color of the rainbow except true red. Their foliage adds structural interest to the garden even when they're not blooming, and Siberian iris (*Iris sibirica*) also has handsome seedpods. Single, semidouble, and double peonies in white, red, pink, and coral bloom on elegant shrubby plants; their foliage often turns an attractive copper or burgundy in fall.

Spring in bloom. Native wildflowers and garden classics—trilliums, hellebores, and purple-flowered corydalis (*Corydalis edulis*)—mix with seemingly casual abandon in this beautiful combination.

False indigoes (*Baptisia*) bear sprays of blue, cream, or white pealike flowers and beautiful blue-green foliage, and they also have attractive blue-black seedpods. Late spring is also the beginning of astilbe season. Astilbes (*Astilbe ×arendsii*) are wonderful perennials for partially shaded sites with moist soil; their ferny foliage and red, pink, white, peach, or cream plumes mix well with hostas and true ferns.

The delightful low-growing pinks (*Dianthus*) produce flat single or double, often fragrant flowers over mats of blue-green or gray-green foliage. Pinks are perfect for the front of the border in a well-drained, sunny site; they're also great for rock gardens. Many have petals with fringed edges as though they had been cut with pinking shears; this gives them their common name, though in fact many are also pink in color (others are white, red, coral, or maroon). And don't forget oriental poppies, with huge papery blooms in shades of red, scarlet, orange, peach, pink, and white. Plant poppies where other plants can fill in when their foliage dies back in summer. Choose any or all of these classic perennials to carry your garden show into early summer.

Summer Splendor

To make sure your garden can take the heat and not look tired after the excitement of spring, include these reliable perennials for nonstop color all summer long.

Daylilies (*Hemerocallis*) bloom in every color except white and blue. Choose a selection of daylilies to bloom from June through August, or plant reblooming cultivars like 'Happy Returns' and 'Stella de Oro' for bloom from June through October.

Garden phlox (*Phlox paniculata*) is a mainstay of the summer border, blooming in white, orange, pink, lavender, red, and violet, often with a contrasting eye. Yarrows (*Achillea*) are also superb summer perennials, with ferny foliage and showy, flat-topped blooms in white, cream, buff, yellow, pink, salmon, and cherry red.

Coneflowers (*Rudbeckia* and *Echinacea*) are showy, reliable summer-blooming perennials, bearing big daisy flowers in shades of orange, yellow, mauve, and white. If you want more summer daisies, try sturdy yellow-flowered lance-leaf coreopsis (*Coreopsis lanceolata*), feathery yellow *Coreopsis verticillata* 'Moonbeam', or pink-flowered *Coreopsis rosea*. Add more white to your daisy palette with Shasta daisies (*Leucanthemum*) and feverfews (*Tanacetum*).

For a cooler look, choose common lavender (*Lavandula angustifolia*), catmints (*Nepeta*), and Russian sage (*Perovskia atriplicifolia*). The bushy forms, blue to lavender colors, and spiky flowerstalks of this summer-blooming trio contrast beautifully with daisies. The large, showy Frikart's aster (*Aster ×frikartii*) continues the lavender-blue theme with its prolific flowering and long bloom period.

Moving toward summer. The delicate, foamy blooms of tiarella complement the bolder forms of 'Yellow Present' tulips, 'Astrosanguineum' ornamental rhubarb (*Rheum palmatum* 'Astrosanguineum'), great Solomon's seal (*Polygonatum biflorum* var. *commutatum*), along with the foliage of black cohosh (*Cimicifuga racemosa*) and columbine meadow rue (*Thalictrum aquilegifolium*) in this late-spring combination.

The bold shapes of summer. The globes of flowering alliums play off the spires of foxgloves in this delightful early summer border. The gardeners have used gray foliage (such as artemisias and lamb's ears) and a hot pink color scheme to tie the border together. A rhododendron echoes the bold pink of the perennials.

Give your summer garden some height with the majestic spires of delphiniums and foxgloves (*Digitalis*). Delphiniums bear blue, white, lavender, and violet flowers, while foxgloves are pink, mauve, yellow, cream, and white. And don't forget the tall, lovable hollyhocks (*Alcea rosea*), synonymous for many gardeners with childhood summers.

You can choose single or double-flowering cultivars in every color but blue and green.

Closer to the ground, butterfly weed (*Asclepias tuberosa*) and crocosmia (*Crocosmia ×crocosmiiflora*) make a fiery summer show in shades of red, scarlet, orange, and yellow. Two plants that are handsome enough to be grown for their foliage alone—hostas (*Hosta*) and geraniums (*Geranium*)—are also summer bloomers. The spires of hostas bear lilac or white bell-shaped flowers, some of which are fragrant, while the geraniums produce numerous single flowers in sometimes startling shades of pink, violet, blue-violet, maroon, and magenta.

Many of the sages (*Salvia*) also bloom in summer, with showy spikes of blue, white, red, lavender, and violet. And don't neglect the beautiful bellflowers (*Campanula*), verbenas (*Verbena*), speedwells (*Veronica*), and balloon flower (*Platycodon grandiflorus*).

There are dozens of others that make summer a glorious season in your perennial garden. Summer bulbs like gladioli (*Gladiolus*), cannas (*Canna ×generalis*), and dahlias (*Dahlia pinnata* hybrids) are garden staples. The problem isn't finding something that will bloom in summer, but choosing from the wealth of summer-blooming perennials that are available.

An Autumn Blaze

Fall is one of the great highlights of the gardening season. For many gardeners, it is the high point of the year: The air feels crisp and bracing after summer's heat and

The colors of summer. The cool blues of 'May Night' salvia and Serbian bellflower (*Campanula poscharskyana*) balance the orange-and-yellow cones of red-hot poker and the yellow of 'Moonshine' yarrow in this cheerful garden. The low-growing campanulas pool onto the stone edging at the front of the border and set off the upright forms of the salvia and red-hot poker.

Summer contrasts. The dark foliage and steel blue flowers of willow blue star (*Amsonia tabernaemontana*) are a perfect foil for the riot of orange flowers of 'Lady Stratheden' avens (*Geum* 'Lady Stratheden') and the yellow-variegated foliage of sedum (*Sedum alboroseum* var. *mediovariegatum*) in this border.

humidity, and the sky is such a clear blue it looks azure. Other colors seem more intense, too—the beige of grasses and deep-green of evergreens set off the brilliant reds, scarlets, oranges, and yellows of deciduous trees and shrubs. In the perennial garden, you can echo these colors. Mix in lilac, violet, and blue to cool the blaze.

The autumn show really begins in late summer, when the green buds of sedums like 'Autumn Joy' (*Sedum* 'Autumn Joy') and 'Vera Jameson' (*S.* 'Vera Jameson') open to reveal cotton candy-pink flowers. Boltonias (*Boltonia asteroides*) are covered with hundreds of tiny white or pink daisies. Garden mums (*Chrysanthemum* ×*morifolium*) begin their long bloom season, presenting a wealth of single, semidouble, and double

daisylike flowers in every color but blue and green. Joe-Pye weeds (*Eupatorium* spp.) bear large, airy clusters of red-violet flowers on bold shrubby plants that can reach 7 feet tall. And many species of aster join Frikart's aster (*Aster* ×*frikartii*) in a collage of lilac, violet, pink, white, and cherry red.

As temperatures drop, fall-blooming anemones produce bright but delicate-looking white, pink, rose, or mauve flowers on tall, wiry stems. Choose Japanese anemones (*Anemone* ×*hybrida* and *A. tomentosa*) for autumn bloom; their foliage is unusually handsome, holding its own in the garden in spring and summer. (This is also true of chrysanthemum foliage—mums make beautiful green cushions, competing with peonies for the "Best Perennial Foliage Award.")

Fall bloom continues with the goldenrods (*Solidago*), which add bright yellow flames to the garden. Their height and upright blooms contrast nicely with the daisy flowers and mounded forms of mums and asters. There are also low-growing cultivars for the front of the border: Calamint (*Calamintha nepeta*) covers itself with tiny bluish white flowers and has minty foliage as a bonus.

Don't overlook the pleasure of foliage in the autumn garden. As the season progresses, many peony cultivars turn bronze or wine-red; the foliage of evening primroses (*Oenothera*) also turns brilliant colors, from hot pink through maroon; and some alumroots (*Heuchera*) develop red patterns on their foliage.

Ornamental grasses are stars of the autumn garden; many bear spectacular flower heads that remain showy on the plant well into winter. Grasses also add structure to the garden, contrasting with the compact mounds of other autumn bloomers.

Round out your fall display with crocuses, autumn crocus (*Colchicum autumnale*), and other small fall-blooming bulbs.

Winter Interest

For gardeners in most of the country, winter is a rest period—the garden rests, dormant under mulch or snow, and we rest, taking a break from outdoor gardening. In those parts of the Deep South and West Coast where the growing season continues from fall through spring, gardening goes on as usual, and garden beauty takes care of itself. But for those of

Flowers for fall. A snowstorm of white blooms brightens this fall garden. Boltonia, 'Frosty Morn' sedum, and white gaura (*Gaura lindheimeri*) hold pride of place.

us in areas that have winter freezes, it takes planning to give a garden winter interest. After all, just because we're not working in the garden doesn't mean we can't see it. A tidy mound of mulch might not look too bad, but a little forethought can assure a more pleasing vista for us and some needed nourishment for overwintering birds.

Three things take on new prominence in the winter garden: seedheads, stems, and foliage. The seedheads and stems of ornamental grasses are often brightly colored—

Adding grasses. The fountaining form of the variegated miscanthus creates a dramatic backdrop for 'Becky' Shasta daisies.

yellow, orange, red, or purple—as winter begins, bleaching to a range of beige, wheat, and off-white as the season progresses. Grasses add structure to the winter garden—a structure they're more likely to keep if you stake or tie them upright before winter arrives.

There are also a number of perennials that will hold their showy seedheads well into winter if you don't "tidy up" and cut them off. Keep your pruners away from yarrows (*Achillea*), false indigos, (*Baptisia*), Siberian iris (*Iris sibirica*), blackberry lily (*Belamcanda chinensis*), grapeleaf anemone (*Anemone vitifolia*), purple coneflower (*Echinacea purpurea*), and blackeyed Susans (*Rudbeckia*). It's surprising how much the silhouettes of these perennials can add to a winter bed.

Winter interest is even easier in a mixed border. You can use open-growing trees with interesting bark like 'Heritage' river birch (*Betula nigra* 'Heritage') along with shrubs like Siberian dogwood (*Cornus alba* 'Siberica'), which has red twigs, and winterberry (*Ilex verticillata*), which is covered with bright red fruit in fall and winter. Evergreens like dwarf mugo pine (*Pinus mugo* var. *mugo*) and boxwoods (*Buxus*) are also valuable for adding structure, color, and texture.

COLOR CONSIDERATIONS

The first thing most gardeners ask about a new perennial is "What color is it?" Color catalogs are so popular because

The power of repetition. This double border uses mirror-imaging to create a garden of great beauty. Color, height, and form echo each other across the path, serving to draw the eye down the path to take in the entire view. Purple-leaved sand cherry trees (*Prunus ×cistena*) back both sides of the border, adding another unifying element.

they let you see exactly what you're getting (if the catalog color is printed well). As you peruse the encyclopedia section of this book, you'll probably find yourself looking at the photos and taking away an impression of color.

Fragrance may be more memorable, but color is more important to most gardeners—and most of the general population as well. Given how central color is in our lives and how much of it we see every day, it's surprising how intimidated people are by it. How many times have you heard or even said, "I'm just no good with color"? This is usually untrue; there aren't that many people whose wardrobes make us cringe. But there are definitely some people who seem to have a flair for choosing and mixing colors. These lucky gardeners can create eye-catching combinations time after time; they seem to have an instinctive appreciation of color harmony.

Your color sense may not be instinctive, but here's a secret: You can learn to combine colors just as beautifully as anyone. There are a few simple color techniques that are easy to learn and easy to use. Read the next few pages, play with the color wheel, then take your wheel and turn to the encyclopedia section on page 265. Choose a color combination, and flip through until you find photos of perennials with those flower colors. A little practice will give you a lot of confidence. Then take your show on the road. The next time you're passing a garden and see a color

Working with white. Don't mistake white for a neutral color! Though your eye may first be drawn to the gold of the gloriosa daisies, when you look at this picture, you'll see that the whites, including Shasta daisies, feverfew (*Tanacetum parthenium*), and white foxgloves, are equally bright.

combination you like, try to decide why the colors work. If you can't think on the spot, note down the colors and review "Using the Color Wheel" on page 18. Don't forget to jot down foliage colors—they can be the key that makes the combination work.

A Color Glossary

What's the difference between a hue, shade, tint, and tone? What are hot, cool, and neutral colors? Before we start talking about how to use color, let's review what these terms mean. Then you can mix shades of blue with the best of them.

Hue. Hue is simply another word for color. Red, blue, and green are hues.

Shade. A shade is a color that has been darkened by adding black. Olive green is a shade of green; mustard is a shade of yellow; indigo is a shade of blue.

Tint. A tint is a color that has been lightened by adding white. Sea green is a tint of green; primrose yellow is a tint of yellow; sky blue is a tint of blue.

Tone. A tone is a color that has been dulled by adding gray. The "country colors" are good examples: colonial blue, old rose, putty. Dull doesn't mean boring in this context; it means less bright.

Temperature. Colors convey a feeling of temperature. Fire colors—red, orange, and yellow—are warm; water colors—blue, green, and violet—are cool. Hot pink is also considered a warm color, while pale pink and gray are considered cool colors. To remember the difference between warm and cool colors, think of fall foliage (warm) and Easter pastels (cool).

Neutral. Cream, beige, black, tan, brown, silver, and gray, in their many tints, shades, and tones, are considered neutral colors. They are not "true" or rainbow colors from the color wheel, they're peacemakers that "go with everything" and unify clashing colors. In the garden, green can also function as a neutral color.

Combining Colors

When you combine colors in the garden, you have to create a balance between unity and boredom. The fewer colors you use, the more unified the garden looks, but the more likely it is that it will end up looking uninteresting. The more colors you use, on the other hand, the harder it is to give the garden any feeling of unity or restfulness. Fortunately, there are ways you can balance both these extremes to create a pleasing color scheme that's both exciting and unified.

If you're not using many flower colors—if, for example, you're designing a color theme garden like the ones on page 78, or you want a garden that combines blue, yellow, and pink flowers—you can add color through foliage. Plants with purple, gray-green, silver, or variegated leaves can perk up the color scheme without drawing attention away from the flowers.

You can also work with hot and cool colors very effectively in a limited-color garden. If you're using cool colors like blue and lavender, add sparks of excite-

ment with a hot color like red; if you're using hot colors like scarlet, orange, and yellow, add a few bursts of azure or sky blue. You'll be surprised at how easily this technique can put the life back into a border.

If you want to use a lot of different flower colors, you run the risk of providing so many points of interest that it's impossible to see the garden as a whole—it loses its focus. Keep this from happening by tying the bed or border together with clumps of repeating color—it will separate the groups of mixed colors so they're easier to take in, as well as give the eye something to rest on between bursts of color.

If you want to shift colors or combine clashing colors like orange and purple, you

Using yellow. Three yellow accents set the tone in this garden view: a golden-leaved hosta, creamy yellow foxgloves, and golden columbine (*Aquilegia chrysantha*). The starry columbine flowers, heavy foxglove spires, and bold, massive hosta foliage create strong visual contrast.

An exuberant mixed border. This gardener has wisely used an informal mix of annuals, perennials, and biennials to offset the formality of the path and closely clipped hedge. The rich palette of color and texture includes Russian sage, monkshoods (*Aconitum*), cleome (an annual), hollyhocks (biennials), threadleaf coreopsis (*Coreopsis verticillata*), artemisia, and 'Betty Prior' rose.

Cooling things down. Spires of blue and white refresh the eye in this garden. Blue delphiniums dominate the back of the bed, while blue cranesbills, pink beard-tongue, 'Dawn to Dusk' catmint (*Nepeta* 'Dawn to Dusk'), 'Fascination' Culver's root (*Veronicastrum* 'Fascination'), and goat's rues (*Galega*) hold the front of the bed.

can do this most effectively by separating them with neutral colors. To do this, use plants with gray-green, green, or silver foliage, or ones with cream or chartreuse flowers. White is also technically neutral, but pure white functions in the garden as a primary color—it's bold, bright, and dominant. Use pure white to make a cool color impact, but use off-white (like cream) to work as a neutral in the garden.

Designers' Color Tips

Garden designers have quite a few color tricks up their sleeves. Here are some tried-and-true techniques you can use to create pleasing effects and give your garden a more unified, less haphazard look.

- If you want to make part of a garden bed (or the entire bed) appear closer, fool the eye by using warm colors, which seem to advance toward the viewer; if you want it to look farther away, choose cool colors, which seem to recede.

- Gertrude Jekyll, who popularized the British perennial border, liked to use the full color spectrum in her designs. She'd begin a border with restful, cool colors, lead up to exciting, warm colors, then end with cool colors to balance the border and the viewing experience.

- Include plants in your border that bloom at different times but in the same color. You'll have a color memory through the bloom season to remind you of what was in bloom earlier and what's still to come.

- Instead of toning down a strong color with a neutral, use a softer tint of the same color. For example, try using the soft primrose-yellow of 'Moonbeam' coreopsis (*Coreopsis verticillata* 'Moonbeam') to tone down the clear, primary yellow of sundrops (*Oenothera fruticosa*).

(continued on page 20)

USING THE COLOR WHEEL

Use the color wheel to create foolproof color combinations in your own garden. Match flower (or foliage) colors to the colors on the wheel, then combine them in one or more of the following ways. Remember to choose perennials that will be in bloom at the same time.

Trace the color wheel and shapes below, or use a photocopier to enlarge them. Then, using the wheel and shapes, try all of these ways to come up with winning combinations.

• Choose a color on the wheel, then look at the colors on either side of it. Blue, blue-green, and blue-violet are adjacent colors. You can use them together or add more variety by extending the color range to the next two colors as well—in this case, green and violet.

• Position a ruler across the middle of a color block on the color wheel—it will also cross the center of the color on the opposite side of the wheel. These are comple-

mentary colors: Blue and orange, red and green, and blue-violet and yellow-orange are examples. Combinations using these colors are vibrant and exciting—in fact, the pure colors in combination can seem almost to pulsate. You can enjoy this effect but tone down the brightness by using variations of the colors: peach and blue instead of orange and blue, for example. Use a whole range of blues and oranges to add interest and variety.

The color wheel. Use the color wheel to find color combinations that work well together. If you want to take more of the guesswork out of this process, trace or copy the color wheel and use markers, crayons, or colored pencils to fill in each section with the appropriate color. Then cut out a square, rectangle, equilateral triangle, and isosceles triangle in the same scale as your color wheel. Place the shapes in the middle of the wheel and rotate them to see which colors they connect. Pick out the color combinations you like best.

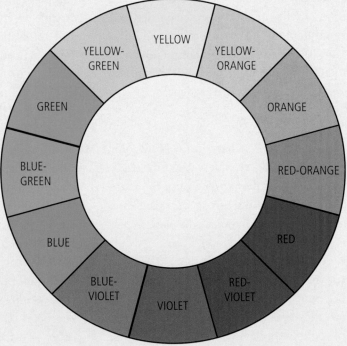

- Draw an equilateral triangle or position a triangle cutout in the center of the color wheel, and the three colors it connects form a triad—green, orange, and violet; or blue-green, yellow-orange, and red-violet, for example. Watch what happens when you add small quantities of an adjacent color (like adding blue to the second triad).
- Draw an isosceles triangle or position an isosceles triangle cutout on the color wheel to form another kind of triad.

By putting the top point of your isosceles triangle on yellow, you'll see that the two bottom points fall on blue-violet and red-violet. You can imagine this color combination using 'Moonshine' yarrow (*Achillea* 'Moonshine'), 'Johnson's Blue' cranesbill (*Geranium* 'Johnson's Blue'), and red valerian (*Centranthus ruber*).

- Draw a square or position a square cutout in the center of the color wheel, and the four colors it connects form a tetrad—one example includes green, yellow-orange, blue-violet, and red. Tetrads are pleasing in themselves, and you can add light and dark variations of the four colors for more diversity.
- Draw a rectangle or position a rectangular cutout on the color wheel, and it will connect two sets of complementary colors, like yellow and violet with orange and blue. Rotate the rectangle for additional harmonious combinations.

Color Drifts

Color drifts are a natural concept: Nature tends to plant in groups. You seldom see a single black-eyed Susan by a roadside or just one oxeye daisy in a field. Instead, you'll find groups of daisies or a whole drift of trout lilies or violets under the trees. Garden designers have taken this concept out of the wild and moved it into the garden.

Using color in drifts is a concept that artists employ, too—especially when they create abstract paintings, simplifying a scene until it is entirely shape and color. You can try this technique for yourself. Put tracing paper over any photo in this book (even any of the photos of borders), and fill in the areas where each species is planted as drifts of color: for example, white for spires of delphiniums, green for ornamental grasses, magenta for low spires of lythrum, yellow-green for lady's-mantle, and so on, until the entire picture is filled in. You'll have a clear idea from the resulting "art" how these colors work together. You can also see if you'd prefer a smaller block of red or magenta, or a different combination of colors.

Planting in drifts unifies a perennial garden by reducing the hodgepodge effect of many individual plants. It's especially effective in large borders, where single plants might get lost. If you have a small garden or are a plant collector at heart, consider planting in clumps rather than drifts—groups of three, five, or seven of the same perennial. You'll get some of the benefits of drift planting, like unified blocks of color and form, without sacrificing diversity.

STRUCTURING THE GARDEN

Structure gives a garden its shape. From fall, when your perennials go dormant, until they're well up in spring, your garden's structure comes from things like the fence in back of the border, the path, the bricks edging your raised beds, and the trunk and branches of the Japanese maple or the old boxwood at one end of the border. These permanent elements are effective all year; they mark the shape of your garden. In discussions of design, they are often called the "bones" of the garden. Like the bones of a skeleton, they provide a framework for the plants that flesh out the garden in the growing season.

Structure also keeps the garden interesting when your perennials aren't blooming. If your garden is snow-covered most of the winter, it could blend into the lawn from fall to spring. But if snowfall in your area is sporadic or nonexistent, you'll have just a mulch-covered mound during the dormant months unless you plan for some structural elements. A fence or wall will define the garden, as will an edging to your bed. A path keeps the eye moving past the empty beds.

Evergreen and deciduous trees and shrubs will add color and interesting branch shapes

Going for green (and white). If you've ever doubted garden colorists' claims that "green is a color," consider this border, which features many shades of green foliage with white flowers to create a bicolor theme.

and bark texture. If you choose carefully, you can grow trees and shrubs with brilliant fall and winter berries, as well as some that flower early in spring when the garden show is just beginning.

If you have a mixed border, you can put shrubs and small trees in the border itself; even if your border or bed isn't big enough, you can still work them in. Plant a large shrub, small tree, or group of small shrubs at one or both ends of the bed—or behind it. Or site your border next to or in front of an existing tree or shrub to add a visual framework for your garden. If you do decide to plant trees or shrubs, make sure their mature size won't be too large for your needs. Consider mature spread as well as height. Don't let your trees or shrubs cast your once-sunny border into gloom.

You can also add structure to a winter garden with herbaceous plants that keep last year's stems, seedheads, or foliage through winter. Ornamental grasses and some perennials, including coneflowers (*Rudbeckia* and *Echinacea*), will stand over winter. (For others, see "Winter Interest" on page 11.)

Foliage impact. A good mix of foliage will carry a perennial garden even when it's not in bloom. Here, golden creeping Jenny (*Lysimachia nummularia* 'Aurea'), the glossy round leaves of bergenia, spiny bear's-breech (*Acanthus spinosus*) foliage, aruncus, crambe, and a purple-leaved heuchera create an outstanding combination.

Garden Structures

You can also add structure to your garden with permanent or semipermanent accessories. A bench or table helps define the garden area. So does an arbor, gate, or trellis. A fountain, sculpture, or sundial—even a gazing ball—lets you and your visitors know that they are in your garden. These accessories provide visual cues that remind anyone who sees them of gardens, just as a watering can and wheelbarrow do. Most remain in the garden year-round, continuing to provide these cues even when the plants themselves are invisible.

Suit your accessories to your site: Keep them in scale with your garden size. Don't put a giant park bench beside a tiny bed or use a small statue to anchor a 100-foot border. (Small garden art can be included in a large border to provide interest and

surprise, but then it functions more like a plant than a structure.) Unless you're designing a sculpture garden, a few accessories are enough: Keep the focus on your plants.

Don't forget that the most important piece in any garden is a bench or chair, and make sure you have a comfortable seat in easy view of your perennials. The closer the seat, the more likely that you can enjoy the garden's fragrance, as well as the butterflies and other visitors that share your appreciation of it. You won't be working in the garden all the time (although the seat also provides a convenient resting place between weeding bouts); part of the time you should be just looking.

By giving yourself a good vantage point, you can think about design and plant combinations at your leisure—what looks good now, what you'd like to move or try next season, or what might perk up the color scheme in one part of the planting. And, of course, a bench or old-fashioned swing is the perfect place to show off your garden to friends and family.

Form and Height

Once your perennials are up, they add structure to the garden with their different forms and heights. The shrubby form of a peony or upright form of a bearded iris shapes the garden. So do the tall spires of a delphinium or black snakeroot (*Cimicifuga racemosa*), or the spiny bulk of bear's-breeches (*Acanthus*).

Unlike most trees and shrubs, a perennial's form and height can change when it blooms: Plants that grow in low rosettes like foxgloves (*Digitalis*) or mulleins (*Verbascum*) can send up very tall bloom spikes; grasslike plants like ornamental onions (*Allium*) can suddenly produce huge globes of starry blooms like a display of fireworks. A lily, which is tall and thin in bloom, may suddenly become quite short when you deadhead it after its flowers fade.

Some perennials, like old-fashioned bleeding hearts (*Dicentra spectabilis*) and oriental poppies (*Papaver orientale*), have a great presence in the garden when they bloom in spring but then go dormant in summer and disappear completely. Learn the growth habits of perennials you're considering for your garden by looking them up in the encyclopedia section.

Working with Form

Think about the basic forms of perennials as you consider using them. What would this form look attractive with? Where should you use it? How many plants do you need for the form to make an impact? Perennials can have these basic forms: creeping or prostrate, mounded, weeping, round, vase-shaped, oval upright, pyramidal, upright, and columnar. These shapes provide design keys when you think about combining plants in your garden.

You can use a plant with a distinctive form to tie a border together by repeating the plant—or groups of the plant—along the length of the border. Siberian iris (*Iris sibirica*) produces attractive grasslike clumps of narrow sword-shaped leaves, for example, and its distinctive form helps

A white border. In this garden, the spires of foxgloves and delphiniums seem to point to the explosion of white from roses, lamb's ears, white-flowered red valerian, fleabane (*Erigeron karvinskianus*), and mock orange.

A color-theme border. Reds, blues, and purples set the tone of this bold border, which is backed by purple-leaved trees and shrubs, including purple-leaved sand cherries (*Prunus* ×*cistena*) and plums, *Rosa glauca,* and purple-leaved barberries. In the border, catmint, alliums, violet sage (*Salvia nemorosa*), and dianthus flowers echo the purple hues of the foliage, while roses explode in cerise and red.

hold a border together when clumps are repeated along the length of the border. You can also echo the shape of one perennial with another that has a similar form, or provide contrast by using a perennial of different but complementary form. For example, intersperse clumps of ornamental grasses with Siberian irises. You can also change the form of a plant by pruning, shearing, or staking. Pruning can reduce overall height and ranginess; shearing can create a more compact, rounded shape; and staking can hold up plants that would normally weave through their neighbors.

Working with Height

How you use height in your garden depends on the shape of your bed or border and whether you can see it from the front only or from both front and back. If you can see the bed or border from the front only (for example, if it's planted in front of a wall or hedge), place the tallest perennials in back, the next tallest in the middle, short perennials in the front, and prostrate perennials as an edging.

If you can see the back as well as the front (for example, in an island bed or a bed that borders a driveway with lawn on the other side), plant the tallest perennials in the center of the border, with plants of descending height on either side. Whether you can see one or both sides, don't be too rigid about these height gradations or you'll end up with a row planting. For a more relaxed look, pull some taller plants out toward the middle of the border and some midheight perennials toward the edges.

Some perennials are tall but airy, creating a see-through effect in the garden. Plants like Japanese anemone (*Anemone* ×*hybrida*) and Brazilian vervain (*Verbena bonariensis*) have slender bloom stalks that give a clear view of the plants behind them. Treat these plants as if they were shorter: Put them in the middle of the border so you'll have plants behind them to form a backdrop. And here are two final height tricks: In places where you see a sudden need for a taller plant, add quick height with tall annuals like spider flower (*Cleome hasslerana*), or tuck in containers of upright plants. (Just make sure the container plants look attractive and not outlandish in the border!)

TEXTURE IN THE GARDEN

Texture means several things in the garden. One is the effect foliage and flower shape and size have on the way a plant looks—is it bold-, medium-, or fine-textured? Plants with large, solid leaves, like hostas (*Hosta*) and ligularias (*Ligularia*), are usually bold-textured. Plants with intermediate foliage, like Siberian iris (*Iris sibirica*) or evening primroses (*Oenothera*), are medium-textured. And plants with delicate, ferny or threadlike foliage, like columbines (*Aquilegia*) and pinks (*Dianthus*), are fine-textured.

Flower shape and size can change the texture of a plant while it's in bloom. The

Mixing textures. This combination gets its charm from the play of fine and coarse textures—the feathery blue oat grass (*Helictotrichon sempervirens*) and Russian sage, clouds of sea lavender (*Limonium latifolium*), and delicate winecups (*Callirhoe involucrata*) against the coarser daisies of purple coneflowers and furry lamb's ears. Note how the gardener has also played shades of purple against pink.

graceful sprays of alumroots (*Heuchera*) are fine-textured, while the foliage is medium-textured; the thimble-shaped blooms of foxgloves (*Digitalis*) are medium-textured, while the foliage is bold-textured. Plant habit can also affect overall texture. While the individual leaves of hardy cranesbills are fine- to medium-textured, the overall effect of their dense, matlike clumps is bold.

Surface Texture

Texture also refers to the appearance of leaf, flower, and stem surfaces. Are the leaves shiny like peonies, felted like lamb's ears (*Stachys byzantina*), or matte (a dull, powdered finish) like 'Autumn Joy' sedum (*Sedum* 'Autumn

Joy')? Leaves can be veined like alumroots (*Heuchera*), smooth like irises, or ribbed like hostas. And flower petals can be shiny like evening primroses (*Oenothera*), satiny like daylilies, or papery like poppies.

When you're combining perennials, vary the textures of foliage and flowers. The eye

Making the most of foliage texture. A 'Heritage' birch anchors this enticing mix of perennials with striking foliage, including fragrant variegated Solomon's seal (*Polygonatum odoratum* var. *pluriflorum* 'Variegatum'), the yellow-and-blue leaves of *Iris pallida* 'Variegata', and white-flowered dianthus.

quickly tires of many shiny-leaved plants together, refusing to take in differences between individual plants unless their colors are very different. The same is true of felted leaves, papery petals, and so on. The same look repeated over and over again becomes boring. Just as you contrast height and form to make a pleasing border, use textures to make your garden more interesting and inviting. The exception is when you're using perennials as an architectural feature, like a row of peonies or hostas. In that case, you want to create an overall impression and don't want individual plants calling attention to themselves.

Advanced Texture Techniques

Try these tips for putting texture to work in your garden. Color can create an impression of texture: the darker the color, the heavier or bolder the texture; the paler the color, the lighter or finer the texture. You can see this for yourself with a white, pale blue, or pale yellow bearded iris cultivar and a dark-violet, navy, or burgundy cultivar. Or look at a plant of purple-leaved common bugleweed (*Ajuga reptans* 'Atropurpurea') next to silver- variegated 'Silver Beauty' (*A. reptans* 'Silver Beauty').

If you put a perennial with bold texture in front of one with finer texture, you'll create an illusion of depth in your garden: Bold textures look closer, while fine textures look farther away. (Make a narrow border look deeper by using this technique!)

Expanding your options. Don't forget vines when planning your beds! They're an easy way to bring beauty up to eye level, as with this glorious combination of climbing rose and 'Hagley Hybrid' clematis.

NARROWING YOUR PLANT CHOICES

With such a wealth of plants to choose from, how do you narrow your selection to manageable proportions? A good place to start is with your garden journal. Think about where you plan to put your garden and about how big you want it to be. Will the garden get full sun, or is it in partial or full shade? Does the soil stay moist, or is it especially dry? Jot down the answers to these questions. You'll have the most attractive, low-maintenance garden if you grow plants that are well suited to your conditions. If you plan to site your garden in full sun, avoid plants that need shade, and vice versa.

Next, turn to the USDA Plant Hardiness Zone Map on page 162 and find your hardiness zone. If you live in Zone 4, you'll be wasting money if you buy plants that are hardy only as far north as Zone 6.

If a plant can't stand up to your area's hot, humid summers, you're wasting your time on it. Think about your garden's color scheme, too—if you're using a limited range of colors, you can narrow your choices to plants with those flower or foliage colors. And don't forget bloom season. If you want a garden that blooms in spring and fall, choose perennials with that in mind.

Go outside and look at the site where you'd like to have your garden. About how high would you like the tallest plants to grow? (This can vary widely, depending on whether you'd like to see over the border to the lawn, block a distracting view, or reach a certain point on a wall or fence.) Then you can limit your plant choices to ones that don't exceed your maximum height.

Finally, avoid plants you don't like. If you've never liked lilies, choose something else, even if lilies suit your conditions. You can always add them later if you grow to appreciate them.

How Books and Catalogs Can Help

When you've noted down the various criteria for narrowing your plant choices—light and moisture requirements, hardiness zone, color scheme, and height limit—you're ready for the next stage in the selection process. It's time to read about potential candidates for your garden, check out their descriptions and growth requirements, and look at color photos that show their flowers and habit.

If you have favorite perennials you'd like to include, start with them. Turn to the encyclopedia section of this book, beginning on page 265, and look up each plant. If it meets your criteria, add it to the list of "approved perennials" for your garden. If it fails, jot down why: Notes such as "must have moist shade" will serve as a reminder, and you won't have to look it up again later. This will also give you a record to refer to if you plan a second garden in an area with different conditions.

Then, skim over the other entries, adding plants that look promising. Don't get carried away—remember that most perennials look best in groups, so you'll need several of each. An initial list of 20 to 40 different plants should be ample to start; you'll probably narrow it down even more when you begin working with your design.

You can also use mail-order nursery catalogs as a starting place in the selection process, skimming through the photos and

Made in the shade. A bold use of foliage dominates this shady bed, with blue-leaved and variegated hostas' heavy, rounded forms set off by the delicate fronds of Japanese painted ferns (*Athyrium niponicum* var. *pictum*), the white-speckled foliage of 'Herman's Pride' lamiastrum (*Lamiastrum galeobdolon* 'Herman's Pride'), and the upright clumps of Siberian iris. The gardener mixed in shade-tolerant shrubs like the hydrangea at the back of the bed and annual impatiens in front to add flower color. Look closely and you'll also see hellebore flowers peeking over the leaves of the blue hosta.

Levels of interest. From the large stone planter at ground level to the yellow-leaved black locust tree (*Robinia pseudoacacia* 'Friesia'), this gardener has put something to catch the eye at every level. Yellow-leaved 'Margarita' ornamental sweet potato vine (*Ipomoea batatas* 'Margarita') carpets the ground, while fiery 'Bednall Beauty' dahlias glow beneath double yellow dahlia flowers. Airy Brazilian vervain (*Verbena bonariensis*) and fountain grass (*Pennisetum alopecuroides*) lighten the look.

noting the most appealing. Catalogs let you compare what's available; they often carry different species and cultivars, so order several for a good selection. You'll find addresses for catalogs in "Resources" on page 686. You can also use catalogs when you finalize your garden design (see "Bringing Your Design to Life" on page 36 to learn how), and of course, you can use them when you're ready to buy plants, so don't be shy about sending for them.

Every book and magazine article that discusses perennials and perennial gardening can provide you with ideas for choice plants and for good designs and plant combinations. You'll find a selection of books about perennials and related gardening topics in "Suggested Reading" on page 685.

Avoiding Pitfalls

The best way to avoid mistakes when selecting plants is to use common sense. Stick to plants that are easy to grow and suit your conditions; leave finicky perennials to the connoisseur. Start with colors that you like in combinations you find pleasing. (For example, you may enjoy purple flowers and white flowers, but a purple-and-white flower may be overwhelming.) Base your garden on what you know you'll love; later experiment with confidence, knowing that even if a plant turns out to be a disappointment, most of the garden will look great.

One common pitfall that's easy to avoid is ignoring duration of bloom. Make sure you take into account how long a perennial blooms and what it will look like before and after flowering. Many perennials have a relatively short bloom season—2 or 3 weeks—but make up for their brevity with attractive buds, foliage, or seedheads. Others have a long bloom season, while still others bloom for a short time, then disappear completely until the following year.

By checking length of bloom, you won't end up planting a stand of oriental poppies, then watching in horror as the plants go dormant in summer and leave you with bare ground where they had been. You can enjoy your poppies, but you'll know to interplant them with other perennials that will fill the gaps, or overplant them with annuals that will bloom from summer to frost. If you have a small garden, you may need a long bloom season from your perennials because you won't have room for a lot of plants that provide a succession of

A garden with everything. The deep colors of purple *Rosa glauca* foliage, purple-leaved heucheras, red-flowered daylilies, and purple Johnny-jump-ups are brightened by clumps of golden hakone grass (*Hakonechloa macra* 'Aureola').

bloom; make sure you choose long-blooming species and cultivars.

Wild-Collected Plants: A Conservation Issue

Because wildflowers and other native plants are enjoying renewed popularity in perennial gardens, some unscrupulous nurseries are digging plants up in the wild and offering them for sale. Some of these plants are endangered, and their sale is often illegal. Reputable nurseries propagate the wildflowers and other native plants they sell; as a responsible gardener, you should buy only nursery-propagated plants. Here are some ways to tell the difference.

- Beware of the phrase "nursery-grown." It doesn't necessarily mean that a plant is nursery-propagated; instead, it may have been collected in the wild, then grown on at the nursery for a season or two. (Also make sure you're not purchasing invasive plants. For a list of invasive exotic species, see "Don't Grow These!" on page 63.)
- Wildflowers that take a long time to propagate, like trilliums, trout lilies, and other spring woodland wildflowers, are often wild-collected. Don't buy them unless you're sure they're nursery-propagated.
- You should expect to pay the same price for a nursery-propagated wildflower as you would for any other perennial; beware of inexpensive plants or quantity discounts on wildflowers.

- Don't buy wildflowers that look like they were just dug from the ground and stuck in pots. Watch for battered or wilted leaves and plants that are too big for their pots but not potbound.

DRAWING YOUR OWN DESIGN

When you've considered your site and what you want to plant on it, it's time to start drawing a design. The first step is to draw a rough sketch of your yard and its major features so you can experiment with different garden shapes, sizes, and placement.

Once you've decided on a location, size, and shape for your garden, decide if you want it to follow a recognized style—formal or informal, cottage or colonial—or if you'd just like a pleasing combination of perennials.

The next step is to make a bubble diagram of the garden, drawing the bed to scale on graph paper and sketching in the shapes of the plants you've chosen. With your bubble diagram in hand, you can refine the plan until you think it's perfect. Then cut photos of the plants from catalogs and paste or tape them onto the diagram to make sure your design will look as beautiful as you hope.

We'll take you through all these steps on the next few pages. As you work, don't be afraid to revise your design as often as you want. After all, it's a lot easier to move plants with a pencil than with a shovel!

On-Site Design

Start your design process by taking your garden journal out in the yard. Draw a

A rich mix. Informal boxwood hedges encircle white-flowered Siberian irises and blue columbines. A bench, flanked by hostas, hardy geraniums, and more Siberian iris, allows the gardener to enjoy the view.

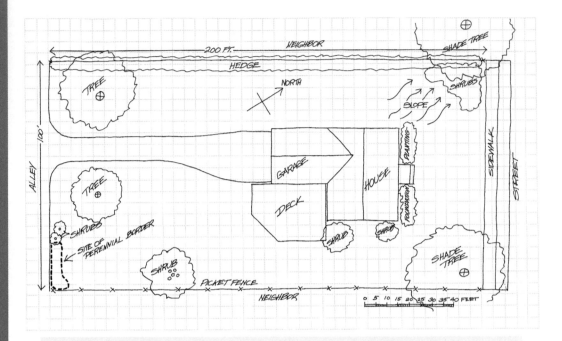

Drawing a base map. A simple base map of your property is valuable every time you want to make a design change. Try to draw the elements to scale, starting with an outline of the yard and proceeding to the house and other major features. Add your yard's dimensions, any low or high points, a north arrow, and any other relevant information (wet areas, rocks, and so on). Then sketch in potential perennial beds or borders with a dashed line.

base map of your yard in your journal. First, sketch in the yard's shape, adding dimensions in feet for each side. (If you have an existing survey of your property, you might want to start with it. Just trace over the survey and use the traced copy to note the features of your property.) Indicate what surrounds the yard on each side (a road, neighbor's yard, creek, park, and so on). Draw an arrow pointing north so you'll know which way your garden is facing. If you have a slope on your property, add arrows on that part of the map;

the arrows should point toward the low spot, in the direction of the slope.

Next, fill in the yard's features. Start with the house, trying to draw it roughly to scale. (*Rough* is the key word for all these shapes—the size and position of these features are much more important than their appearance.) Add the garage and driveway next if you have them, then any paths and other outbuildings. Draw in patios, decks, large shade trees, water features, hedges, and other major features. Add existing gardens, shrubs, large clumps of flowers, and lawn furniture, including benches and arbors.

Once you think the map looks fairly accurate, make photocopies of it or use tracing paper to position perennial gardens. If you already have an idea of where you'd like the garden to go, sketch it to scale on a copy of your map and see how it looks. If you're unsure or want to experiment, try as many sizes, shapes, and positions as you feel like drawing.

When you've decided on a garden bed or border, take your garden map outside and check the sketch against reality. If you want to get a more graphic view, lay a hose on the grass to outline the proposed bed or border, or cover it with a sheet of weighted black plastic to block out the space and shape. For a small garden, weighted newspapers would also work.

Don't forget exposure: Have you sited your garden under trees or where the house or a neighbor's house or wall will shade it, or is it in the open, where it will have full sun all day? If *where* the garden is matters most to you, choose plants that will suit the exposure you've selected; if *what* you're planting matters more, site the garden where your favorite plants will get the exposure they prefer.

Making a Bubble Diagram

Once you know what size and shape you'd like your perennial garden to be, you can draw it as a bubble diagram. (It's called a

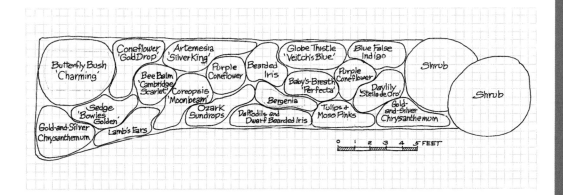

Making a bubble diagram. When you have an idea of the size and shape of your garden, draw its outline to scale on graph paper (1 inch on paper to 1 foot of ground is a good scale for most gardens). Use a pencil so you can "move" things around easily, and don't be afraid to make changes. Then draw in circles or "bubbles" to represent your perennials, making the scale of each bubble match the mature width of the plant. Write in the plant name, color, and bloom season in each bubble if you have room so you can see at a glance how good the combinations are likely to look.

bubble diagram because you draw in the plants as bubble-like blobs.) You'll need some graph paper and a list of the perennials you'd like to plant. First, draw the shape of your bed or border to scale on a piece of graph paper. A good scale to begin with is 1 inch on paper equals 1 foot of garden space. If you're planning a really large garden, use 1 inch equals 2 or 3 feet. Be sure to note on the graph paper what scale you're using.

Now you're ready to position your plants. To visualize your garden, refer to your list of plants. Read the descriptions of the plants in the encyclopedia section, beginning on page 265, and note down the mature height, flower and foliage color, bloom season, and length of bloom for each plant. Think about which plants will look best together.

Refining the Design

Take your finished bubble diagram and plant list, and look at your design. Will the plant combinations you've made for the garden work well together? Have you remembered to include plants like bulbs, annuals, and ornamental grasses to enrich your plant palette? Will the garden be in bloom when you want color most? If the design works on paper, take it outside and review it where you plan to put the garden. Do the heights, colors, and textures still work? Have you inadvertently designed a pink garden to go in front of your orange brick wall?

Don't be afraid to modify your design. If you need inspiration before adding the finishing touches, refer to Chapter 4, "A Gallery of Garden Designs," to see how professionals do it. Borrow any ideas or combinations that appeal or work for your site. Once you have added the finishing touches and smoothed out the rough spots, you can make a last check by "bringing your design to life."

Bringing Your Design to Life

An easy way to see what your dream garden will look like is to design it on paper with catalog cutouts. You'll need the list of perennials you'd like to plant, your bubble diagram on graph paper, tracing paper, and mail-order perennial catalogs.

Now you're ready to arrange the plants in your paper garden. To visualize your garden, refer to your bubble diagram and your list of plants. Using the size and height information for guidance, draw a profile of the garden by placing a sheet of tracing paper over the graph paper.

Use the bubble diagram on your graph paper as an outline, and draw the shapes of the plants you plan to use on the tracing paper. Draw spikes, mounds, lumps, and mats as appropriate, keeping the heights and widths in scale with the other perennials. When you've outlined the clumps of perennials on your tracing paper, make three copies so you'll have outlines for spring, summer, and fall. Save the original

A design reality check. To make sure your paper garden really works, put a sheet of tracing paper over your bubble diagram. Using the bubbles as a guide, draw in the shapes of your plants—shrubby, spiky, mounded, and so forth. Make a copy for each bloom season. To see if the colors really work well together, find color photos of all the perennials in your design. Cut out strips of each perennial, and position them on the design according to bloom season, with spring-blooming plants on one copy, summer-blooming on another, and so on.

drawing in case you want to change the design later.

Next, use your list of perennials to find photos of each one in mail-order catalogs. Cut out the catalog pictures, clipping a 1 by 2-inch strip of each plant. (This is a good size to get a clear idea of the impact the color will have in that part of the garden. The size of the cutout doesn't need to relate to the scale of your design.) Refer to the encyclopedia section again for bloom season, and arrange the strips of catalog photos for spring-blooming perennials in the appropriate places on one diagram; do the same for summer and fall (and winter, if appropriate). Then you can see for yourself if the colors, shapes, and sizes look right.

If you don't like your combinations, rearrange them, or try perennials or cultivars that have different flower colors. When the design looks like what you had in mind, you can make a more permanent record by pasting or taping the cutouts down on paper. If you can't find photos of some of the plants, fill them in on the appropriate diagram with colored pencils or crayons that match their flower colors.

Remember that your design is really just a starting point. When you're working on a garden design, it's important to bear in mind that your medium is plants, which can be moved easily and are very forgiving. You're not sculpting in stone. As you begin to look more closely at other people's gardens, at garden designs like the ones in Chapter 4, and at the perennial combinations in Chapter 3, you'll find plant combinations and other elements you'd like to include in your design. Don't be afraid to change it. Change is one of the best-kept secrets of successful design. You'll learn more about changing your garden in Chapter 6, "Growing with the Design."

Need more inspiration, or perhaps a jump-start after all this talk about garden design? In Chapter 2, "Perennial Flower Finder," you'll see at-a-glance lists of the best perennials for certain garden conditions, bloom seasons, flower colors, and more. And in Chapter 3, "Perennial Combinations," you'll find a wealth of beautiful perennial combinations that are guaranteed to give you gardening fever!

2

PERENNIAL FLOWER FINDER

This is a chapter of lists—lists that make it easy for you to see at a glance how to put perennials together. If you want to create a blue color-theme garden or just need a perennial that will add a touch of blue to your garden, turn to the list of blue-flowered perennials on page 43. You can look almost all the plants up in our perennial encyclopedia, beginning on page 265. Needless to say, these lists aren't meant to be exhaustive—there will always be many, many more perennials to choose from—but there are enough here to give you a strong start. You can't go wrong with these garden-worthy perennials!

Skim through the lists. Do you need perennials for clay soil, for shade, for full sun? Perennials to attract butterflies or hummingbirds? Drought-tolerant perennials? Flowers that are easy-care? Plants that can take wet feet? Think about what you want, and also see what appeals to you as you look at the lists. You might start out wanting a garden of red-flowered perennials, then decide you'd like a hummingbird garden instead because many hummingbird favorites have red flowers and you'd get the pleasure of the comical little buzzers as well. (Actually, hummingbird enthusiasts call the little birds "hummers," not "buzzers," but since they buzz loudly as they dart and hover, I can't help but call them that.) Enjoy yourself!

The lists in this chapter, as the title implies, focus on perennials. For other plants that grow well with perennials, see our perennial encyclopedia, which starts on page 265. If, after looking at our lists, you find you're hungry for more, then you're ready for Chapter 3, "Perennial Combinations," where you'll see some of our recommendations in action. There are also some excellent perennial books that are organized in much the same way we've organized these lists—grouping perennials together by similar features. If this format appeals to you, look for Larry Hodgson's *Perennials for Every Purpose* and coauthor Cole Burrell's *Perennial Combinations* for in-depth discussions of plants with similar characteristics.

Let's get started!

Note: An asterisk (*) indicates a tender perennial, such as sweet potato vine, which is usually grown as a container plant in cold climates. We've included these to help round out your color palette.

PERENNIALS BY FLOWER COLOR

Most of us play favorites when it comes to color. That's why color-theme gardens are so popular. If you love blue, white, and yellow, you might decide to plant a border featuring one, two, or all three flower colors. Perhaps you planted a bed that blooms in soft shades of lavender and gold, and now you feel that it needs a little pizzazz—maybe a touch of magenta or deep red. In these lists, you'll find perennials arranged by bloom color, so you can quickly check your choices for any given color.

Remember that many perennials have several—or even lots of—flower colors (irises, columbines, lupines, and chrysanthemums spring to mind), so you'll find them on many of these lists. When you don't expect a perennial to bloom in a certain color—for example, a near-white-flowered daylily—we'll give you the cultivar name as well as the genus or species. Otherwise, once you have your list in hand, turn to "The Perennial Encyclopedia," beginning on page 265, to find which species or cultivars are recommended.

White or Cream

Alstroemeria spp. (alstroemerias)
Aster spp. (asters)
Astilbe spp. (false spireas)
Astrantia spp. (masterworts)
Campanula spp. (bellflowers, harebells)
Chrysanthemum spp. (chrysanthemums)
Convallaria majalis (lily-of-the-valley)
Delphinium spp. (delphiniums)

Campanula

Dianthus spp. (pinks, carnations)
Dicentra spp. (bleeding hearts)
Digitalis spp. (foxgloves)
Echinacea spp. (coneflowers)
Gaura lindheimeri (white gaura)
Geranium spp. (geraniums, cranesbills)
Gypsophila paniculata (baby's-breath)
Hedychium coronarium (butterfly ginger)
Hemerocallis cvs., such as 'Gentle
    Shepherd' (daylilies)
Iberis spp. (candytufts)
Iris spp. (irises)
Lamium maculatum cvs., such as 'White
    Nancy' (spotted dead nettle)
Leucanthemum maximum (Shasta daisy)
Leucojum spp. (snowflakes)
Lilium spp. (lilies)
Paeonia spp. (peonies)
Papaver spp. (poppies)
Penstemon spp. (beardtongues,
    penstemons)

Phlox spp. (phlox)
Salvia spp. (sages)
Sanguinaria canadensis (bloodroot)
Tiarella spp. (foamflowers)
Tradescantia spp. (spiderworts)
Trillium spp. (trilliums)
Verbena spp. (verbenas, vervains)
Viola spp. (violets, violas)

Pink

Alstroemeria spp. (alstroemerias)
Armeria maritima (sea pink)
Astilbe spp. (false spireas)
Astrantia spp. (masterworts)
Bletilla striata (Chinese ground orchid)
Campanula spp. (bellflowers, harebells)
Chrysanthemum spp. (chrysanthemums)
Delphinium spp. (delphiniums)
Dianthus spp. (pinks, carnations)
Dicentra spp. (bleeding hearts)
Digitalis spp. (foxgloves)
Echinacea spp. (coneflowers)

Armeria

Epimedium spp. (fairy wings)
Eupatorium spp. (Joe-Pye weeds, bonesets)
Geranium spp. (geraniums, cranesbills)
Iris spp. (irises)
Lamium maculatum cvs., such as 'Pink Pewter', 'Beacon Silver' (spotted dead nettle)
Lilium spp. (lilies)
Lobelia spp. (lobelias)
Monarda spp. (bee balms, bergamots)
Oenothera speciosa (showy evening primrose)
Paeonia spp. (peonies)
Papaver spp. (poppies)
Phlox spp. (phlox)
Salvia spp. (sages)
Thalictrum spp. (meadow rues)
Verbena spp. (verbenas, vervains)

Red and Scarlet

Aquilegia spp. (columbines)
Astilbe spp. (false spireas)
Astrantia spp. (masterworts)
Canna spp. (cannas)
Chrysanthemum spp. (chrysanthemums)
Coreopsis 'Limerock Ruby' ('Limerock Ruby' corepsis)
Crocosmia spp. (crocosmias, montbretias)
Dianthus spp. (pinks, carnations)
Gaillardia spp. (blanket flowers)
Hemerocallis spp. (daylilies)
Heuchera cvs. (alumroots, coral bells)
Lilium spp. (lilies)
Lobelia spp. (lobelias)
Monarda spp. (bee balms, bergamots)
Paeonia spp. (peonies)

Lobelia

Papaver spp. (poppies)
Persicaria amplexicaule (mountain fleece flower, mountain knotweed)
Salvia spp. (sages)
Silene spp. (campions, pinks)
Spigelia marilandica (Indian pink)
Veronica spicata (spike speedwell)

Purple, Lilac, Mauve, and Maroon

Agapanthus spp. (lilies of the Nile, African lilies)
Allium spp. (ornamental onions)
Alstroemeria spp. (alstroemerias)
Aquilegia spp. (columbines)

Aster spp. (asters)

Astrantia spp. (masterworts)

Callirhoe involucrata (purple poppy mallow)

Campanula spp. (bellflowers, harebells)

Chrysanthemum spp. (chrysanthemums)

Delphinium spp. (delphiniums)

Digitalis spp. (foxgloves)

Echinacea spp. (coneflowers)

Eupatorium spp. (Joe-Pye weeds, bonesets)

Geranium spp. (geraniums, cranesbills)

Hemerocallis cvs., such as 'Plum Perfect' (daylilies)

Iris spp. (irises)

Knautia macedonica (knautia)

Lavandula spp. (lavenders)

Liatris spp. (gayfeathers, blazing-stars)

Liriope spp. (lilyturfs)

Lobelia spp. (lobelias)

Monarda spp. (bee balms, bergamots)

Nepeta spp. (catmints, nepetas)

Papaver spp., such as *P. orientale* 'Patty's Plum', *P. somniferum* 'Lauren's Grape' (poppies)

Phlox spp. (phlox)

Salvia spp. (sages)

Tradescantia spp. (spiderworts)

Verbena spp. (verbenas, vervains), such as *Verbena bonariensis* (Brazilian vervain)

Vernonia spp. (ironweeds)

Veronica spp. (speedwells)

Viola spp. (violets, violas)

Blue

Agastache foeniculum, such as 'Blue Fortune' (fragrant anise hyssop)

Amsonia spp. (blue stars, amsonias)

Aster spp. (asters)

Baptisia australis (blue false indigo)

Brunnera macrophylla (Siberian bugloss, forget-me-not)

Campanula spp. (bellflowers, harebells)

Ceratostigma plumbaginoides (plumbago)

Clematis spp. (clematis)

Corydalis flexuosa (blue fumeroot)

Delphinium spp. (delphiniums)

Iris spp. (irises)

Linum perenne (blue flax)

Lobelia spp. (lobelias)

Meconopsis spp. (meconopsis)

Muscari spp. (grape hyacinths)

Phlox divaricata (wild blue phlox, woodland phlox)

Agapanthus

Phlox

Phlox paniculata cvs., such as 'Blue
  Paradise' (garden phlox)
Platycodon grandiflorus (balloon flower)
Pulmonaria saccharata (Bethlehem sage)
Salvia spp. (sages)
Stokesia laevis (Stokes' aster)
Tradescantia spp. (spiderworts)
Verbena spp. (verbenas, vervains)
Veronica spp. (speedwells)

Yellow

Achillea spp. (yarrows)
Alstroemeria spp. (alstroemerias)
Aquilegia spp. (columbines)
Aurinia saxatilis (basket-of-gold)
Canna spp. (cannas)
Chrysanthemum spp. (chrysanthemums)
Chrysogonum virginianum (goldenstar,
  green-and-gold)
Coreopsis spp. (tickseed, coreopsis)

Crocosmia spp. (crocosmias, montbretias)
Digitalis spp. (foxgloves)
Doronicum spp. (leopard's banes)
Epimedium spp. (fairy wings,
  barrenworts)
Euphorbia polychroma (cushion spurge)
Hemerocallis spp. (daylilies)
Iris spp. (irises)
Kniphofia spp. (torch lilies, red-hot
  pokers)
Ligularia spp. (ligularias, groundsels)
Lilium spp. (lilies)
Lysimachia vulgaris (yellow loosestrife)
Oenothera spp. (evening primroses)
Paeonia spp. (peonies)
Papaver spp. (poppies)
Primula auricula (auricula primrose)
Ranunculus spp. (buttercups)
Rudbeckia spp. (black-eyed Susans,
  coneflowers)
Solidago spp. (goldenrods)
Viola spp. (violets, violas)

Hemerocallis

Chrysanthemum

Peach, Orange, and Coral

Agastache spp. (anise hyssops)
Alstroemeria spp. (alstroemerias)
Asclepias tuberosa (butterfly weed)
Canna spp. (cannas)
Chrysanthemum spp. (chrysanthemums)
Crocosmia spp. (crocosmias, montbretias)
Diascia vigilis (twinspur, diascia)
Eremurus spp. (foxtail lilies, desert-candles)
Gladeolus spp. (gladioli, sword lilies)
Hedychium spp. (ginger lilies, garland lilies)
Hemerocallis spp. and cvs. (daylilies)
Iris spp. (irises)
Kniphofia spp. (torch lilies, red-hot
     pokers)
Lilium spp. (lilies)
Paeonia spp. (peonies)
Papaver spp. (poppies)
Schizostylis coccineus (crimson flag)
Zephyranthes spp. (rain lilies)

Green and Chartreuse

Chrysanthemum spp. (chrysanthemums)
Euphorbia spp. (spurges, euphorbias)
Helleborus spp. (hellebores), especially
     H. foetidus (stinking hellebore)
Iris spp. (irises)
Kniphofia spp. (torch lilies, red-hot
     pokers)
Sedum spp. (stonecrops, sedums). *Note:*
     Most sedum flower heads mature to
     white, pink, red, maroon, or rust, but
     they remain green for a very long time
     first, giving the presence of green
     flowers in your garden until they
     color up.

Euphorbia

"Black"

Alcea rosea 'Nigra' (black hollyhock)
Aquilegia cvs., such as 'Black Barlow'
    (columbines)
Geranium phaeum var. *phaeum*
    (mourning widow hardy geranium)

Helleborus cvs. (hellebores)
*Ipomoea barbatus 'Blackie' and 'Ace of
    Spades' (sweet potato vine)
Iris spp. (irises)
Tulipa cvs. (tulips)
Viola cvs. (Johnny-jump-ups, pansies)

PERENNIALS FOR LONG BLOOM

Unlike annuals, perennials don't bloom nonstop from planting to frost because they need to put most of their energy into their roots so they'll live through the winter and have the strength to come up the following spring. Some perennials bloom for only a week or two, then the show's over until next year. Luckily for gardeners, other perennials bloom for weeks on end. (Others, like most ornamental grasses, bear showy plumes of flowers that turn into long-lasting seedheads.) If you enjoy a good show, choose from this list.

Acanthus spp. (bear's breeches)
Achillea spp. (yarrows)
Agastache spp. (anise hyssops)
Alchemilla spp. (lady's-mantles)
Armeria spp. (thrifts)
Aster spp. (asters)
Bergenia spp. (bergenias, winter begonias)
Calamintha nepeta (calamint)
Callirhoe spp. (winecups, poppy mallows)
Campanula spp. (bellflowers, harebells)
Canna spp. (cannas)
Centranthus ruber (red valerian)
Coreopsis spp. (tickseeds, coreopsis)

Achillea

Corydalis spp. (corydalis, fumeroots)
Dianthus spp. (pinks, carnations)
*Diascia vigilis (twinspur)
Digitalis spp. (foxgloves)
Echinacea spp. (coneflowers)
Echinops spp. (globe thistles)
Euphorbia spp. (spurges, euphorbias)
Gaura lindheimeri (white gaura)
Geranium spp. (geraniums, cranesbills)
Gypsophila spp. (baby's-breaths)
Helianthus spp. (sunflowers)
Helleborus spp. (hellebores, Christmas roses, Lenten roses)
Hemerocallis spp. (daylilies)
Kalimeris pinnatifida (Mongolian aster)
Liatris spp. (gayfeathers, blazing-stars)
Limonium spp. (sea lavenders, statices)
Lysimachia spp. (loosestrifes)
Malva spp. (mallows)

Nepeta spp. (catmints)
Oenothera spp. (evening primroses)
Penstemon spp. (beardtongues, penstemons)
Perovskia atriplicifolia (Russian sage)
Persicaria amplexicaule (mountain fleece flower)
Phygelius ×*rectus* (cape fuchsia)
Platycodon grandiflorus (balloon flower)
Rudbeckia spp. (black-eyed Susans, coneflowers)
Salvia spp. (sages)
Saponaria officinalis (bouncing bet)
Scabiosa spp. (pincushion flowers)
Stachys coccinea (scarlet sage)
Thalictrum spp. (meadow rues)
Tradescantia spp. (spiderworts)
Verbena spp. (verbenas, vervains)
Veronica spp. (speedwells)

*tender perennial

PERENNIALS BY SEASON

Knowing what perennials bloom when can be especially helpful when you're planning your garden. Maybe you want plants in bloom in every season, or you're trying to add color at a specific time—fall, for example—because you realize that you've planted all spring and summer bloomers. If you have a summer home, you may want to design a bed that blooms in a single season so you can enjoy the color while you're there. (Of course, some perennials bloom from one season into the next; these lists capture the season when the plants bloom longest.) We haven't included spring-blooming bulbs or summer-blooming grasses here, but check these lists for other seasonal showstoppers.

Spring-Flowering

Amsonia spp. (blue stars, amsonias)
Aquilegia spp. (columbines)
Aurinia saxatilis (basket-of-gold)
Cerastium tomentosum (snow-in-summer)
Chrysogonum virginianum (goldenstar, green-and-gold)
Corydalis spp. (corydalis, fumeroots)

Aquilegia

Crocus spp. (crocuses)
Dicentra spp. (bleeding hearts)
Epimedium spp. (fairy wings, barrenworts)
Helleborus spp. (hellebores, Christmas
    roses, Lenten roses)
Iris spp. (irises)
Lamium maculatum (spotted dead nettle)
Oenothera speciosa (showy evening
    primrose)
Paeonia spp. (peonies)
Primula spp. (primroses, cowslips)
Trillium spp. (trilliums)

Summer-Flowering

Achillea spp. (yarrows)
Alstroemeria spp. and hybrids
    (alstroemerias)
Anemone ×*hybrida, A. tomentosa*
    (Japanese anemones)
Asclepias tuberosa (butterfly weed)
Aster spp. (asters)

Calamintha nepeta (calamint)
Callirhoe involucrata (purple poppy
    mallow)
Ceratostigma plumbaginoides (plumbago)
Coreopsis spp. (tickseed, coreopsis)
Crocosmia ×*crocosmiiflora* (crocosmia)
Digitalis spp. (foxgloves)
Echinacea spp. (coneflowers)
Eupatorium spp. (Joe-Pye weeds, bonesets)
Geranium spp. (geraniums, cranesbills)
Heliopsis spp. (oxeyes)
Hemerocallis spp. (daylilies)
Heuchera spp. (alumroots, coral bells)
Kalimeris spp. (Mongolian asters,
    Japanese asters)
Kniphofia spp. (torch lilies, red-hot pokers)

Kniphofia

Leucanthemum maximum (Shasta daisy)
Liatris spp. (gayfeathers, blazing-stars)
Lilium spp. (lilies)
Linaria vulgaris (toadflax)
Lobelia spp. (lobelias)
Monarda spp. (bee balms, bergamots)
Nepeta spp. (catmints, nepetas)
Oenothera spp. (evening primroses)
Penstemon spp. (beardtongues, penstemons)
Platycodon grandiflorus (balloon flower)
Prunella grandiflora (large-flowered self-heal)
Rudbeckia spp. (black-eyed Susans, coneflowers)
Scabiosa spp. (pincushion flowers)
Tanacetum parthenium (feverfew)
Tradescantia spp. (spiderworts)
Veronica spp. (speedwells)

Fall-Flowering

Aconitum spp. (monkshoods)
Anemone hupehensis (Chinese anemone)
Aster spp. (asters)
Boltonia asteroids (boltonia)
Chelone lyonii (pink turtlehead)
Chrysanthemum ×*morifolium* (garden chrysanthemum)
Cimicifuga simplex (Kamchatka bugbane)
Colchicum spp. (colchicums, meadow saffrons)
Coreopsis spp. (tickseeds, coreopsis)
Cyclamen hederifolium (ivy-leaf cyclamen)
Hedychium spp. (ginger lilies, garland lilies)
Helenium spp. (sneezeweeds, Helen's flowers)

Tricyrtis

Helianthus spp. (sunflowers)
Kirengeshoma spp. (yellow bells, wax bells)
Leucanthemum nipponicum (Nippon daisy)
Lycoris spp. (spider lilies, surprise lilies)
Lysimachia vulgaris (yellow loosestrife)
Patrinia scabiosafolia (patrinia)
Physostegia virginiana (obedient plant)
Salvia spp. (sages)
Sedum spp. (stonecrops, sedums)
Solidago spp. (goldenrods)
Tricyrtis spp. (toad lilies)

Winter Interest

Acanthus spp. (bears-breeches)
Achillea spp. (yarrows)
Arum spp. (arums)
Asarum spp. (wild gingers)
Aster spp. (asters)
Astilbe spp. (false spireas)
Baptisia spp. (false indigos, wild indigos)
Bergenia spp. (bergenias, winter begonias)

Cyclamen coum (hardy cyclamen)
Echinacea spp. (coneflowers)
Eupatorium spp. (Joe-Pye weeds, bonesets)
Ferns
Galanthus spp. (snowdrops)
Helleborus spp. (hellebores, Christmas roses, Lenten roses)
Hibiscus spp. (rose mallows, hibiscus)
Hosta spp. (hostas)
Lespedeza spp. (bush clovers)
Lilium formosanum (Formosa lily)
Ornamental grasses
Rudbeckia spp. (black-eyed Susans, coneflowers)
Vernonia spp. (ironweeds)

PERENNIALS WITH SHOWY FOLIAGE

Attractive foliage can hold its own with flowers in the perennial garden, providing interest when plants aren't in bloom, complementing or contrasting with flower color, or enhancing a color-theme bed. Foliage can brighten shady gardens and cool down sunny ones, create tropical effects in temperate gardens, or weave a tapestry of colorful groundcover under other plantings. Some plants have such showy foliage that they can stand alone as specimen plants. Foliage is a fact of perennial life, so why not make the most of it? The choices below will get you off to a good start.

White or Silver; Solid, Mottled, or Variegated

Ajuga reptans 'Silver Carpet' ('Silver Carpet' common bugleweed)
Artemisia spp. (artemisias, wormwoods)
Arum italicum 'Pictum' ('Pictum' Italian arum)
Asarum spp. (wild gingers)
Athyrium niponicum 'Pictum' ('Pictum' Japanese lady fern)

Carex morrowii 'Variegata' (variegated morrow sedge)
Cerastium tomentosum (snow-in-summer)
Heuchera americana cvs. (alumroots, rock geraniums)
Hosta cvs., such as 'Patriot' (hostas)
Lamium maculatum cvs., such as 'White Nancy', 'Beacon Silver' (spotted dead nettles)

Arum

PERENNIALS TO ATTRACT BIRDS AND BUTTERFLIES

Birds and butterflies add delight to any garden—and they're easy to attract. Rather than fussing with messy hummingbird "nectar," grow plants that produce real nectar that hummingbirds love! With a little planning, you can grow flowers to attract the little jewel-bright birds all season, from the first columbines of spring through fall's last hibiscus flowers. Fuchsias in pots or hanging baskets add a romantic appeal and are major hummingbird attracters, as is the old-fashioned trumpet vine (*Campsis radicans*) (but beware—it likes to ramble!). Butterflies like flat flower heads that they can land on comfortably, and their larvae—caterpillars—enjoy the leaves of certain plants like milkweeds. Tuck a shallow dish with pebbles and a little water among your perennials to give the butterflies their own water fountain, or make a discreet mud hole for them by watering a small patch of bare ground—they love the nutrients in mud and will congregate there by the dozen. Plants with showy seedheads not only look good in fall and winter when not much else is going on in your garden, they also provide much-needed nourishment to migrating and overwintering songbirds. Include some of each—nectar plants, seed-bearing plants, and butterfly plants—in your garden for a triple treat!

NECTAR PLANTS FOR HUMMINGBIRDS

Aquilegia spp. (columbines)
Delphinium spp. (delphiniums)
Fuchsia spp. (fuchsias)
Heuchera ×*brizoides* (hybrid coral bells)
Hibiscus spp. (rose mallows, hibiscus)
Kniphofia hybrids (torch lilies, red-hot pokers)
Lilium spp. (lilies)
Lobelia spp., especially *L. cardinalis,* cardinal flower (lobelias)
Monarda spp. (bee balms, bergamots)
Penstemon spp. (beard-tongues, penstemons)
Phlox spp. (phlox)
Salvia spp. (sages)
Verbena spp. (verbenas, vervains)

SEED-BEARING PLANTS FOR SONGBIRDS

Centaurea spp. (cornflowers, knapweeds)
Coreopsis spp. (tickseeds, coreopsis)
Echinacea spp. (coneflowers)
Helianthus spp. (sunflowers)
Heliopsis spp. (oxeyes)
Liatris spp. (gayfeathers, blazing-stars)
Panicum virgatum (switchgrass)
Rudbeckia spp. (black-eyed Susans, coneflowers)
Silphium spp. (rosinweeds, compass plants)

BUTTERFLY FAVORITES

Agastache spp. (anise hyssops)
Asclepias spp., especially A. *tuberosa,* butterfly weed, and A. *incarnata,* swamp milkweed (milkweeds)
Aster spp. (asters)
Echinacea spp. (coneflowers)
Erigeron spp. (fleabanes)
Eupatorium spp. (Joe-Pye weeds, bonesets)
Gaillardia ×*grandiflora* (blanket flower)
Helianthus spp. (sunflowers)
Lobelia spp. (lobelias)
Monarda spp. (bee balms, bergamots)
Phlox spp. (phlox)
Scabiosa spp. (pincushion flowers)
Silphium spp. (rosinweeds, compass plants)
Solidago spp. (goldenrods)
Stokesia laevis (Stokes' aster)
Verbena spp. (verbenas, vervains)
Vernonia spp. (ironweeds)
Veronica spp. (speedwells)

Liriope spicata 'Silver Dragon' ('Silver Dragon' creeping liriope)

Miscanthus sinensis 'Caberet', 'Cosmopolitan' (variegated Japanese silver grasses)

Phalaris arundinacea cvs., such as 'Feesey's Variety' (ribbon grass)

Polygonatum odoratum 'Variegatum' (variegated Japanese Solomon's seal)

Pulmonaria spp. (lungworts, Bethlehem sages)

Sedum cvs., such as 'Frosty Morn' (stonecrops, sedums)

Stachys byzantina (lamb's ears)

Vinca spp. and cvs., such as *V. minor* 'Ralph Shuggart' (vincas, periwinkles)

Yucca filamentosa 'Variegata' (variegated Adam's needle)

Gold or Chartreuse; Solid or Variegated

Acanthus mollis 'Hollard's Gold' ('Hollard's Gold' bear's-breeches)

Agastache 'Golden Jubilee' ('Golden Jubilee' anise hyssop)

Arachnoides simplisior 'Variegata' (variegated holly fern)

*Canna ×generalis 'Bengal Tiger' ('Pretoria') ('Bengal Tiger' canna)

Carex elata 'Aurea' (Bowles' golden sedge), *C. dolichostachya* 'Kaga Nisiki' (Kaga brocade sedge), *C. morrowii* 'Goldband' ('Goldband' morrow sedge)

Dicentra spectabilis 'Gold Heart' ('Gold Heart' old-fashioned bleeding heart)

*tender perennial

Carex

Filipendula ulmaria 'Aurea' (European queen of the meadow)

Geranium 'Ann Folkard' ('Ann Folkard' geranium)

Hakonechloa macra 'Aureola', 'All Gold' (golden hakone grass, Japanese fountain grass)

Heliopsis helianthoides 'Loraine Sunshine' ('Loraine Sunshine' oxeye)

Heuchera 'Amber Waves' ('Amber Waves' coral bells)

Hosta cvs., such as 'Gold Standard', 'Tokudama', 'Sum and Substance' (hostas)

*Ipomoea batatas 'Margarita' ('Margarita' sweet potato vine)

Iris variegated selection s such as *I. ensata* 'Variegata', (variegated Japanese iris), *I. pallida* 'Aureo-Variegata' (variegated sweet iris)

Lamium maculatum 'Aureum' ('Aureum' spotted dead nettle)

Ligularia tussilaginea 'Aureomaculata' (leopard plant)

Liriope muscari 'Pee Dee Gold Ingot' (blue lilyturf)

Lysimachia nummularia 'Golden Globe' ('Golden Globe' creeping Jenny); *L. clethroides* 'Geisha' ('Geisha' gooseneck loosestrife)

Miscanthus sinensis 'Strictus' ('Strictus' Japanese silver grass)

*Pelargonium cvs. (zonal geraniums)

Phlox paniculata 'Goldmine' and others (garden phlox)

*Solenostemon scotellarioides cvs. (coleus)

Tanacetum vulgare 'Isla Gold' ('Isla Gold' tansy)

Tradescantia 'Blue and Gold' ('Blue and Gold' spiderwort)

Tricyrtis formosana 'Gates of Heaven' ('Gates of Heaven' Formosa toad lily)

Veronica repens 'Sunshine', *V. prostrata* 'Aztec Gold' (harebell speedwells)

Helictotrichon

Yucca 'Golden Sword', 'Color Guard' (variegated yuccas)

Blue or Gray-Blue

Achillea 'Moonshine' ('Moonshine' yarrow)

Corydalis flexuosa, *C. ochroleuca* (blue and white fumeroots)

Crambe maritima (sea kale)

Dicentra cvs. (bleeding hearts)

Festuca cinerea, such as 'Elijah Blue', 'Skinner's Blue', 'Solling' (blue fescue)

Helictotrichon sempervirens (blue oat grass)

Hosta cvs., such as 'Eatoi Blue', 'Krossa Regal', 'Blue Mammoth', 'Big Daddy' (hostas)

Panicum virgatum 'Heavy Metal', 'Dallas Blues' ('Heavy Metal' or 'Dallas Blues' switchgrass)

Ruta graveolens cvs., such as 'Blue Beauty', 'Blue Mound' (rues)

Yucca rostrata (beaked blue yucca)

Purple or Purple Variegations

Ajuga reptans 'Atropurpurea' or 'Purpurea' ('Atropurpurea' or 'Purpuea' common bugleweed)

Angelica gigas (Korean angelica, purple parsnip)

*Anthriscus 'Ravenswing' (cow parsley)

Aster lateriflorus 'Lady in Black' ('Lady in Black' calico aster)

Sedum

Canna ×generalis, such as 'Pink Futurity', 'King Humpert', 'Wyoming', 'Australia', 'Intrigue', 'Pacific Beauty' (cannas)
Colocasia esculenta 'Black Magic' ('Black Magic' elephant ear)
Corydalis flexuosa 'Purple Leaf' ('Purple Leaf' blue fumeroot)
Dahlia 'Bednall Beauty', 'Yellow Hammer', 'Bishop of Llandaff' (dahlias)
Eupatorium rugosum 'Chocolate' ('Chocolate' white snakeroot)
Geranium pratense 'Midnight Reiter' ('Midnight Reiter' meadow cranesbill)
Heuchera cvs., such as 'Palace Purple', 'Cathedral Windows', 'Velvet Night' (alumroots, coral bells)
Ipomoea batatas 'Blackie', 'Black Heart' ('Blackie' and 'Black Heart' sweet potato vines)
Lysimachia ciliata 'Atropurpurea' ('Atropurpurea' fringed loosestrife)
*tender perennial

Persicaria microcephala 'Red Dragon' ('Red Dragon' knotweed)
Polemonium yezoense 'Purple Rain' ('Purple Rain' Jacob's ladder)
Ricinus communis (castor bean)
Sedum 'Matrona', 'Vera Jameson' ('Matrona' and 'Vera Jameson' sedums)
Solenostemon scotellarioides cvs. (coleus)

Glossy

Ajuga reptans (common bugleweed)
Asarum europaeum (European wild ginger)
Astilbe spp. (false spireas)
Bergenia cordifolia (heart-leaved bergenia)
Chelone spp. (turtleheads)
Colchicum spp. (colchicums, meadow saffrons)

Asarum

Darmera peltata (umbrella plant)

Epimedium spp. (fairy wings, barrenworts)

Helleborus spp. (hellebores, Christmas roses, Lenten roses)

Heuchera micrantha var. *diversifolia* 'Palace Purple' ('Palace Purple' alumroot)

Hosta spp. (hostas)

Liriope muscari (blue lilyturf)

Pachysandra spp. (pachysandras, spurges)

Paeonia spp. (peonies)

Phygelius spp. (cape fuchsias, cape figworts)

Polystichum spp. (holly ferns, sword ferns)

Stokesia laevis (Stokes' aster)

Specimen

Acanthus spp. (bear's-breeches)

Angelica spp. (angelicas, archangels)

Aralia spp. (spikenards)

Astilboides tabularis (astilboides)

*Canna ×*generalis* (canna)

Crambe spp. (crambes, kales)

Cyathea cooperi (lacy tree fern)

Darmera peltata (umbrella plant)

Filipendula spp. (meadowsweets, queen of the meadows)

Hedychium spp. (ginger lilies, garland lilies)

Hosta spp., such as 'Great Expectations', 'Krossa Regal', 'Sum and Substance', 'Blue Mammoth', 'Big Daddy' (large-leaved hostas)

Cyathea

Inula spp. (elecampanes, inulas)
Kirengeshoma palmata (Japanese yellow bells)
Lespedeza spp. (bush clovers)
Ligularia spp. (ligularias, groundsels)
Matteuccia struthiopteris (ostrich fern)
Miscanthus spp. (Japanese silver grasses)
Onoclea sensibilis (sensitive fern)

Osmunda spp. (flowering ferns)
Rheum spp. (rhubarbs)
Rodgersia spp. (rodgersias, Roger's-flowers)
Silphium spp. (rosinweeds, compass plants)
Symphytum ×*uplandicum* (Russian comfrey)
Telekia speciosa (telekia)
Yucca spp. (yuccas, Adam's needles)

PERENNIALS BY CARE REQUIREMENTS

If you're a busy gardener or you have extensive gardens, you probably want to look for the easy-care perennials and avoid those fussy types that require tons of coddling, primping, and other maintenance. If a perennial you're considering isn't on one list or the other, consider it to require moderate care—maybe some deadheading, watering during dry spells, cutting back, or dividing occasionally—and plant or avoid accordingly.

Easy Care

Acanthus spp. (bear's-breeches)
Aconitum spp. (monkshoods)
Actaea spp. (baneberries)
Agapanthus spp. (lilies of the Nile, African lilies)
Alchemilla spp. (lady's-mantles)
Amsonia spp. (blue stars, amsonias)
Armeria spp. (thrifts)
Aruncus spp. (goat's beards)

Astilbe spp. (false spireas)
Baptisia spp. (false indigos, wild indigos)
Bergenia spp. (bergenias, winter begonias)
Cimicifuga spp. (bugbanes, cohoshes, snakeroots)

Alchemilla

Dicentra spp. (bleeding hearts)
Dictamnus albus (gas plant)
Digitalis spp. (foxgloves)
Echinacea spp. (coneflowers)
Echinops spp. (globe thistles)
Epimedium spp. (fairy wings, barrenworts)
Eryngium spp. (sea hollies, eryngos)
Euphorbia spp. (spurges, euphorbias)
Gaura lindheimeri (white gaura)
Geranium spp. (geraniums, cranesbills)
Gypsophila spp. (baby's-breaths)
Helleborus spp. (hellebores, Christmas roses, Lenten roses)
Hemerocallis spp. (daylilies)
Heuchera spp. (alumroots, coral bells)
Hosta spp. (hostas, plaintain lilies, funkias)
Kirengeshoma spp. (yellow bells, wax bells)
Kniphofia spp. (torch lilies, red-hot pokers)
Liatris spp. (gayfeathers, blazing-stars)
Limonium spp. (sea lavenders, statices)
Lysimachia spp. (loosestrifes)
Paeonia spp. (peonies)
Papaver orientale (Oriental poppy)
Pennisetum spp. (fountain grasses)
Perovskia atriplicifolia (Russian sage)
Platycodon grandiflorus (balloon flower)
Rheum spp. (rhubarbs)
Thalictrum spp. (meadow rues)
Thermopsis spp. (bush peas, thermopsis)

Veronicastrum virginicum (Culver's root)
Yucca spp. (yuccas, Adam's needles)

Intensive Care

Delphinium cvs. (delphiniums)
Eremurus spp. (foxtail lilies, desert-candles)
Fritillaria spp. (fritillaries, checkered lilies)
Lewisia spp. (lewisias)
Lupinus cvs. (lupines)
Meconopsis spp. (meconopsis)
Penstemon spp. (beardtongues, penstemons)
Primula spp. (primroses, cowslips)

Delphinium

PERENNIALS BY PREFERRED CONDITIONS

Sun or shade. Hot or cool. Wet or dry. Like us, perennials have their preferences. Check this section to find perennials that match your garden's conditions.

Hot and Dry, Sunny

Achillea spp. (yarrows)

Agapanthus spp. (lilies of the Nile, African lilies)

Agastache spp. (anise hyssops)

Agave spp. (agaves)

Allium spp. (ornamental onions)

Anthemis tinctoria (golden marguerite)

Dianthus

Artemisia spp. (artemisias, wormwoods)

Asclepias tuberosa (butterfly weed)

Calamintha nepeta (calamint)

Callirhoe involucrata (purple poppy mallow)

Centranthus ruber (red valerian)

Chrysopsis spp. (golden asters)

Delosperma spp. (ice plants)

Dianthus gratianopolitanus (cheddar pinks)

Echinacea spp. (coneflowers)

Echinops spp. (globe thistles)

Eryngium spp. (sea hollies, eryngos)

Euphorbia spp. (spurges, euphorbias)

Festuca glauca (blue fescue)

Gaillardia spp. (blanket flowers)

Gaura lindheimeri (white gaura)

Helianthus spp. (sunflowers)

Helictotrichon sempervirens (blue oat grass)

Iris bearded hybrids (bearded irises)

Knautia macedonica (knautia)

Lavandula spp. (lavenders)

Limonium latifolium (sea lavender)

Nepeta spp. (catmints, nepetas)

Oenothera spp. (evening primroses)

Opuntia spp. (prickly pears)

Penstemon spp. (beardtongues, penstemons)

Perovskia atriplicifolia (Russian sage)

Phlomis spp. (Jerusalem sages)

Phormium spp. (phormiums, New Zealand flax)

Romneya coulteri (matilja poppy)

Coreopsis

Salvia spp. (sages)
Santolina chamaecyparissus (lavender cotton)
Schizachyrium scoparium (little bluestem)
Verbascum spp. (mulleins)
Verbena spp. (verbenas, vervains)
Veronicastrum virginicum (Culver's root)
Yucca spp. (yuccas, Adam's needles)

Moist Soil, Sunny

Agastache spp. (anise hyssops)
Alstroemeria spp. and hybrids (alstroemerias)
Amsonia spp. (blue stars, amsonias)
Anemone ×*hybrida* (Japanese anemone)
Aster ×*frikartii* (Frikart's aster)
Astrantia major (masterwort)

Baptisia spp. (false indigos, wild indigos)
Calamagrostis ×*acutiflora* (feather reed grass)
Canna ×*generalis* (canna)
Coreopsis spp. (tickseed, coreopsis)
Crocosmia ×*crocosmiiflora* (crocosmia)
Digitalis spp. (foxgloves)
Geranium spp. (geraniums, cranesbills)
Hedychium spp. (ginger lilies, garland lilies)
Helianthus angustifolius (swamp sunflower)
Hemerocallis spp. (daylilies)
Heuchera ×*brizoides* (hybrid coral bells)
Kalimeris spp. (Mongolian asters, Japanese asters)
Kniphofia spp. (torch lilies, red-hot pokers)
Lespedeza spp. (bush clovers)
Leucanthemum ×*superbum* (Shasta daisy)
Liatris spp. (gayfeathers, blazing-stars)
Molinia caerulea (purple moor grass)
Paeonia spp. (peonies)
Patrinia spp. (patrinias)
Penstemon digitalis (foxglove penstemon)
Phlox spp. (phlox)
Platycodon grandiflorus (balloon flower)
Silphium spp. (rosinweeds, compass plants)
Solidago spp. (goldenrods)
Tanacetum parthenium (feverfew)
Veronica spp. (speedwells)

Wet Soil, Sunny

Acorus spp. (sweet flags)

Alchemilla spp. (lady's-mantles)

Asclepias incarnata (swamp milkweed)

Boltonia asteroides (boltonia)

Caltha palustris (marsh marigold, cowslip)

Canna spp. (cannas)

Carex elata 'Aurea' (Bowles' golden sedge)

Chelone spp. (turtleheads)

Darmera peltata (umbrella plant)

Eupatorium spp. (Joe-Pye weeds, bonesets)

Filipendula spp. (meadowsweets, queen of the meadows)

Helenium spp. (sneezeweeds, Helen's flowers)

Hibiscus moscheutos (common rose mallow)

Iris ensata, I. pseudacorus, I. versicolor, I. virginica (Japanese iris, yellow flag iris, blue flag iris, southern blue flag iris)

Juncus spp. (rushes)

Ligularia spp. (ligularias, groundsels)

Lobelia spp. (lobelias)

Matteuccia struthiopteris (ostrich fern)

Monarda spp. (bee balms, bergamots)

Myosotis scorpioides (water forget-me-not)

Osmunda spp. (flowering ferns)

Panicum virgatum (switchgrass)

Physostegia spp. (obedient plants)

Boltonia

Rodgersia spp. (rodgersias, Roger's-flowers)

Sanguisorba spp. (burnets)

Sarracenia spp. (pitcher plants)

Stokesia laevis (Stokes' aster)

Thalictrum spp. (meadow rues)

Thelypteris spp. (river ferns, marsh ferns)

Veratrum spp. (false hellebores, Indian pokes)

Vernonia spp. (ironweeds)

Zephyranthes spp. (rain lilies)

Dry Shade

Anemonella thalictroides (rue anemone, windflower)

Aquilegia spp. (columbines)

Arum italicum 'Pictum' (Italian arum)

Carex morrowii and cvs., such as 'Variegata' (morrow sedges)

Covallaria majalis (lily-of-the-valley)

Chasmanthium latifolium (Northern sea oats)

Cyclamen

Cyclamen spp. (hardy cyclamens)

Dicentra spp. (bleeding hearts)

Dodecatheon spp. (shooting-stars)

Dryopteris spp. (shield ferns, wood ferns)

Epimedium spp. (fairy wings, barrenworts)

Euphorbia amygdaloides (wood spurge)

Helleborus spp. (hellebores, Christmas roses, Lenten roses)

Hepatica spp. (hepaticas, liverleafs, harbingers of spring)

Heuchera americana (alumroot, rock geranium)

Pachysandra spp. (pachysandras, spurges)

Polygonatum odoratum and cvs., such as 'Variegatum' (Japanese Solomon's seals)

Polystichum spp. (holly ferns, sword ferns)

Moist Shade

Aconitum spp. (monkshoods)

Actaea spp. (baneberries)

Arisaema spp. (Jack-in-the-pulpits)

Asarum spp. (wild gingers)

Astilbe spp. (false spireas)

Astrantia spp. (masterworts)

Begonia grandis (hardy begonia)

Brunnera macrophylla (Siberian bugloss, forget-me-not)

Cimicifuga spp. (bugbanes, cohoshes, snakeroots)

Corydalis lutea (golden fumeroot)

Dicentra spp. (bleeding hearts)

Ferns

Helleborus spp. (hellebores, Christmas roses, Lenten roses)

Heuchera spp. (alumroots, coral bells)

×*Heucherella alba* (white foamy bells)

Hosta spp. (hostas, plantain lilies, funkias)

Iris cristata (crested iris)

Kirengeshoma spp. (yellow bells, wax bells)

Ligularia spp. (ligularias, groundsels)

Mertensia virginica (Virginia bluebells)

Myosotis spp. (forget-me-nots)

Omphalodes spp. (navel seeds, blue-eyed Marys)

NATIVE PERENNIALS

These native Americans will add a patriotic touch to your perennial garden! If they're native to your region, you can proudly show them off to admirers and feel a glow of environmental correctness, too. (Look them up in "The Perennial Encyclopedia," starting on page 265, to find your favorites and learn where they're native.)

Amsonia spp. (blue stars, amsonias)
Aquilegia canadensis (wild columbine)
Aster spp. (asters)
Baptisia spp. (false indigos, wild indigos)
Callirhoe spp. (winecups, poppy mallows)

Calylophus serrulatus (yellow sundrops)
Chelone spp. (turtleheads)
Cimicifuga spp. (bugbanes, cohoshes, snakeroots)
Coreopsis spp. (tickseeds, coreopsis)
Echinacea spp. (coneflowers)
Eryngium yuccifolium (rattlesnake master)
Geum triflorum (prairie smoke)
Helianthus spp. (sunflowers)
Heuchera spp. (alumroots, coral bells)
Hydrastis canadensis (goldenseal)
Lobelia spp. (lobelias)
Lupinus spp. (lupines)
Mertensia virginica (Virginia bluebells)
Monarda spp. (bee balms, bergamots)

Penstemon spp. (beard-tongues, penstemons)
Phlox spp. (phlox)
Podophyllum peltatum (mayapple)
Porteranthus trifoliatus (bowman's root)
Rudbeckia spp. (black-eyed Susans, coneflowers)
Salvia spp. (sages)
Sanguinaria canadensis (bloodroot)
Scizachyrium scoparium (little bluestem)
Scutellaria spp. (skullcaps)
Sedum spp. (stonecrops, sedums)
Stylophorum diphyllum (celandine poppy)
Trillium spp. (trilliums)
Veronicastrum virginicum (culver's root)

Phlox divaricata (wild blue phlox, woodland phlox)
Polygonatum spp. (Solomon's seals)
Primula spp. (primroses, cowslips)
Pulmonaria spp. (lungworts, Bethlehem sages)
Smilacina racemosa (Solomon's plume)
Tiarella spp. (foamflowers)
Tricyrtis spp. (toad lilies)
Trillium spp. (trilliums)
Trollius spp. (globeflowers)
Uvularia spp. (bellworts, merrybells)
Viola spp. (violets, violas)

Trollius

DON'T GROW THESE!

We all grow plants from distant shores in our own gardens. The allure of exotic (nonnative) plants is inescapable. Fortunately, most of the plants we introduce into our gardens are not problematic. But from time to time, a plant adapts too well to its adopted home and spreads beyond the garden. These invasive exotic species compete with native plants for a place in the sun, altering the structure and function of the ecosystems they invade. The American Lands Alliance has identified nearly 500 invasive species across North America, many of which are perennials grown in gardens and sold by nurseries.

When an exotic begins to reproduce, it displaces a native species. Once a plant is entrenched, it begins to proliferate, growing faster, taller, or wider and shading out smaller plants. An established, mature plant can disperse hundreds—or thousands—of seeds.

Purple loosestrife is the poster child for invasive exotics, but it may be too late to control this and other firmly entrenched species like dame's rocket (*Hesperis matronalis*) and bishop's weed (*Aegopodium podagraria*). Because of the damage they do, we've not included these invasive species in the encyclopedia section of this book. Some of these plants are still being sold, despite their documented ability to degrade ecosystems. You can help by not buying these plants or, if you already have them, by digging them up and destroying them.

Not every invasive species acts the same way in all parts of the country or in all ecosystems within a region. How can you tell if a plant is going to be invasive? A few traits should raise red flags. Nonnative species, especially those bearing fleshy fruits, are at the top of the suspect list. Other indicators of potential invasiveness include: type or mode of reproduction, with plants that reproduce both vegetatively and sexually (like thistles) getting the highest invasive rating; time required to reach reproductive maturity, with annuals or early-maturing perennials getting the highest rating; and viability of seeds, with the longest-lived getting the highest invasive rating.

It's not too late to stem the tide of invasive garden escapes. Some popular ornamental plants that are becoming all too familiar in native meadows, hedgerows, and woodlots are lesser celandine (*Ranunculus ficaria*), Japanese silver grass (*Miscanthus sinensis*), and sweet autumn clematis (*Clematis terniflora*).

So do your homework and discover which plants are invasive in your region or state. Be alert to any plants thriving beyond the confines of garden beds in your own yard and around your neighborhood. If you find a plant becoming problematic, or if you want more information on invasive alien plants, contact your local native plant society or Faith T. Campbell, American Lands Alliance (phytodoer@aol.com), the Mid-Atlantic Exotic Plant Pest Council List Serve (MA-EPPC-owner@egroups.com), or the Nature Conservancy Wildland Invasive Species Program (http://tncweeds.ucdavis.edu).

REGIONALLY OR NATIONALLY INVASIVE EXOTIC SPECIES

Lords and ladies (*Arum italicum*)
Giant reed (*Arundo donax*)
Pampas grass (*Cortaderia selloana*)
Japanese knotweed (*Fallopia japonica*)
Purple loosestrife (*Lythrum salicaria, L. virgatum*)
Fountain grass (*Pennisetum setaceum*)
Periwinkle (*Vinca minor*)

3

PERENNIAL
COMBINATIONS

P utting plants together isn't quite as easy as choosing an outfit for the day—making
sure the top and bottom match and the shoes and accessories look good with the
clothes. It's more like mixing the perfect salad—a visual feast as well as a delightful
combination of flavors, textures, and fragrances. That doesn't mean it's hard, it just means
that you need to keep a few things in mind as you think about creating great combinations.
Keep your eyes open as you page through books and magazines or drive around the neighborhood—a disposable camera and a notebook are good glove-compartment companions
for your travels. (That notebook can come in handy if you're a TV garden-program ad-
dict, too.) Keep your mind open as well: That run-of-the-mill bedding plant you've turned
your nose up at for years may be exactly what you need to tie a combination together.

To make combinations that work, think about plants' flower color, foliage color, flower
texture, foliage texture, bloom season, length of bloom, and fragrance; what they look like
out of bloom, whether they have interesting seedheads or berries, and whether they die back
after bloom or in winter. And, of course, you have to take their preferred growing condi-

tions into account—sun or shade, wet or dry, tender or hardy, acidic or alkaline. Just to make things more complicated, plants grow at different rates and mature at different sizes: That sweet little wild indigo sitting demurely in its nursery pot today may take on shrublike proportions, obliterating the companion plants that looked so good with it the first couple of years.

Whew! When you put all that together, it's quite a list—but you can do it! And (here's the best part) you can cheat.

5 FAST COMBINATION STRATEGIES

Feeling faint just thinking about all the plants and possible combinations you could try? Here are five easy ways to narrow the field. Using them will build your confidence—and before you know it, you'll be heading out into the wild, wonderful world of combinations on your own. No matter how good you get, you can always come back to these simple tools when inspiration doesn't strike or you just need a jump-start.

Ready to cheat? Let's go!

Quick-combination cheating strategy #1: Just lift it. If you're paging through a garden magazine and see a combination you love, go for it! If it will work in your climate and conditions (see Chapter 7, "Climate Considerations," on page 156, if you're not sure), someone else will have done the design work for you, and you can see the results before purchasing a single plant.

Quick-combination cheating strategy #2: Try a reality check. Most nurseries sell more plants if they sell them in bloom. So as you think about promising combinations, if it's the right season for them to be in bloom, you can pull together pots of the various plants right there in the nursery and see how they look together. Add in pots of the other plants you'd like to use—the ones that aren't in bloom—and see how their foliage adds or detracts from the combination. If it doesn't look as good "in person" as you thought, you can play with other plants (you're in a nursery, after all) until you hit on a grouping that works. Before you pull out the checkbook, make sure the plants that you're grouping all need similar conditions (such as full sun and moist soil) and that you know how big they'll become.

Quick-combination cheating strategy #3: Take the tour. Going on garden tours is a great way to discover what in-the-know gardeners are growing. With notebook and camera in hand, you can zoom in on sections of garden beds that you think work particularly well and capture them for your garden. You may even see plants growing in different parts of a bed or landscape that would look fabulous if you put them together. (Remember the rule of similar growing conditions, though.) Most serious gardeners use plant labels so you can identify the plants easily, but if you don't see a label, ask—you'll probably learn not only what the plant is but also where it came from. These gardeners have gone through all the trial and error, so you can follow their lead with confidence.

Quick-combination cheating strategy #4: Do just one thing. Here's a fun game to play with combinations. If you see a combination that's ugly, challenged, or just plain wrong somehow, try to think of one change you could make that would fix it. Is one of the plants' shapes, textures, or colors not working with the rest? Is one plant overwhelming the others, or is one ridiculously small? Is there too much of one plant, too little of another? Is it the right plant but the wrong cultivar—say, wrong foliage or flower color? If you can visualize a fast fix, you may have just found yourself a fabulous combination.

Quick-combination cheating strategy #5: Forget the flowers. Blasphemy, you say? Think again. Sometime you have a combination that is *almost* perfect but needs a little oomph (maybe something brighter or bolder?), or it's just pleading for a certain color. If you can't find it in any catalog, maybe you should stop thinking flowers and start thinking garden art. Consider a silver, purple, or screaming red gazing ball tucked into your combination or rising above it on a stand; an obelisk or sculpture for height; or an interesting "found object," birdbath, or sundial. Even a striking container filled with plants that echo your combination's shape or colors can be set in among the perennials in the bed. Garden art now comes in all shapes, sizes, colors, and degrees of taste and tackiness. What you use is up to you, but whether it's from a trendy gallery or your neighbor's recycling pile, make sure it en-hances the combination and doesn't over-whelm it.

PUTTING IT ALL TOGETHER

Now let's pull together a combination so you can see how all the pieces fit. Picture a purple bearded iris. Beautiful, right? Now picture a whole bed of purple bearded iris. Boring! What to do? Your first impulse might be to mix together a group of bearded iris that bloom in different colors, but you're still looking at a mass of plants with the same shape, and that's still boring. (And just think how it will look when they've finished blooming!) Instead, picture a purple bearded iris with a purple columbine. Now you're getting somewhere! The purple of the columbine flowers echoes the bearded iris's color, but where the iris flowers are bold and massive, the delicate bells of the columbine provide a soft contrast. (Of course, if you'd like a wider array of flower colors, you can choose columbines with flower colors that create a lovely contrast to the iris blooms—bold red and red-and-yellow come to mind.) The ferny, frothy columbine foliage softens the upright swords of the bearded iris leaves, too.

The iris and columbine bloom at the same time, so you'll enjoy the combination, unlike the ones shown in some cheesy nursery catalogs we know! They're full of illustrations of combinations that never bloom together in nature—or, for that matter, in your garden!—all in glorious, eye-popping, impossible bloom at once. And if you choose an iris that has fragrant flowers—as many do, especially the older types—you'll have another source of delight every time you pass by.

You're not quite finished. Your combination looks good, but what happens when the bloom is over? Suddenly, it's boring again. To combat that, you might choose a third partner for the iris and columbine—one with foliage that contrasts with both the upright iris leaf fans and the ferny columbine foliage. A variegated hosta would work, with its giant spoons of leaves in cream and green, white and green, or chartreuse and green. It blooms later, too, extending the flower show into the summer. A small fountain-shape ornamental grass like hakonechloa would also make a nice contrast, with its delicate arching blades in green or, in the cultivar 'Aurea', chartreuse.

Starting to see the possibilities? Itching to add a fourth plant—maybe a purple-flowered aster to continue the color theme into fall? Just make sure it likes the light shade or partial sun that suits the other perennials in your combination. Now, a fifth plant: perhaps the yellow foxglove (*Digitalis grandiflora*), with its delicate stems of pale yellow flowers, rising around

A classic combo. Nothing says "perennial" like this lovely combination of pink 'Bowl of Beauty' peonies and the lavender-blue sweetpea-like blooms of false indigos (*Baptisia*). The shrubby form and foliage of both plants are as handsome as the flowers are beautiful, and each has three-season interest: Peony foliage turns gorgeous shades of red, purple, and copper in fall (depending on the cultivar); and false indigos produce striking heads of black seedpods. The flowering honeysuckle provides the perfect backdrop.

and among the other plants. (With plant combinations, as with plant groupings, odd numbers are better than even—three rather than two, five rather than four. You'll find that they'll look more natural and less contrived.) You can repeat your combination to make a bed or border, or intersperse it among other groupings, using the repetition to tie the bed together. Beautiful—congratulations!

COMBINING COLORS

For most gardeners, color is at the heart of gardening. Even plantaholics who love every nuance of leaf and stem and petal will admit (if bribed with a good plant) that they're suckers for color. But as you probably know from thinking you'd put together a great color combination (only to find that the reds clashed and the white wasn't such a great idea, after all, and where did that hideous off-magenta come from?), combining colors isn't as simple as it ought to be.

Let's talk about color the way we *see* color: all together. When you look at a combination, you see the flowers—if the plants are in bloom—but you also see the foliage and stems, buds, seedheads, berries, and so on. To make sure your combinations look really good, you should look beyond the flowers to the whole picture. We know—you're growing perennials for the flowers, aren't you? So let's talk about them first.

Color galore. Lilies, delphiniums, the yellow spires of ligularia, aconites, and flowering kale create a riot of color in this lucky gardener's yard.

Fabulous Flower Colors

Here are three quick ways to look at color: complementary, contrasting, and echoing. (For a refresher on color, see "Color Considerations" on page 12.) Complementary colors look good together without drawing too much attention—pastels, shades in the same intensity, like soft lavender with soft blue. Contrasting colors *demand* attention—a patch of blazing orange or hot pink among the lavenders and blues, for example, or flame red or purple-black with chartreuse. And echoes give contrasting forms of the same color, as in our dark purple iris/columbine example, or gradations of a color, like dark purple, lilac, mauve, and red-violet irises.

You can create combinations that use more than one of these characteristics, too, adding depth and dimension to your combinations. For example, a combination of dark pink 'Queen Alexandra' astilbe, light pink 'Erica' astilbe, and hostas provides plenty of echo—the astilbe flowers and foliage and the light and dark pink—while the hosta foliage provides a pleasing shape, texture, and color contrast to the astilbe foliage. The lavender-blue flower spikes contrast with the plumy astilbe flower spikes, while the color complements the pinks of the astilbe flowers.

Beyond Bloom

The black seedpods of wild indigo, heavy round scarlet rose hips of rugosa roses, and dense or feathery seedheads of most ornamental grasses hold their own for impact

A color-theme combo. The soft peach of spring lupines is mirrored in annual diascia (*Diascia vigilis*) at their feet. The repeating color and contrasting form makes the combination more interesting—and pleasing—than it would be if the gardener repeated both color and form.

Towers of flowers. This gardener has chosen to use one dominant flower shape (the spire) but add interest by varying the flower color. Peach foxtail lilies (*Eremurus* hybrids) glow like rockets in flight against purple delphiniums, red foxgloves, and yellow loosestrife (*Lysimachia punctata*).

against all but the most stunning flowers. Keep pods, seedheads, hips, and berries in mind when you're choosing plants for combinations—they'll extend the plants' season of interest long after flowers fade.

Then there's foliage. The bluish foliage of *Rosa glauca* and 'Blue Beauty' rue; the wine-red foliage of 'Chocolate Ruffles' heuchera, 'Husker Red' foxglove penstemon, and 'Burgundy Bliss' salvia; the silver mottling of 'Spilled Milk' and 'Polar Splash' pulmonarias; the electric chartreuse of 'All Gold' hakenechloa and 'Sunspot' heu-

cherella, with its red-centered leaves . . . foliage has its own fascination, and, thanks to dedicated breeders and tireless plant explorers, there are an infinity of forms, textures, and colors to play with.

Unlike flowers, foliage is a garden feature all season, so take special care when combining plants with colored foliage. (Playing with pots in the nursery is especially useful here. If you're planning a combination for a sunny bed, drag the pots into the sun and look at them there; for a shady combination, pull them under a shady awning or other

PLAYING WITH PERFUME

Don't overlook fragrance when planning your combinations, especially if you want as many fragrant flowers as possible. If you plant too many clashing fragrances cheek-to-jowl, on hot days your garden may smell like a stifling tearoom full of heavily perfumed Victorians. Instead, plan for certain scents to predominate in certain seasons—and keep your peonies at a respectful distance from your lilacs, your roses well away from the lilies. Remember that in certain plants, fragrances may clash even within the species or genus, and the subtle distinctions may be lost if you plant, for example, a rose garden. Space roses (or perennials) with different fragrances apart so you can enjoy the unique fragrance of each. Plants with scented foliage, like herbs and the eglantine rose, are easier to mix among plants with fragrant flowers because you usually have to brush against them to release their fragrances.

dark spot and see how they shine.) Not all colors—and not all variegations—look good together! See which ones you like, and be sure to check bloom color and think about how it will look against boldly colored or variegated foliage. Screaming orange flowers and purple foliage may not be at the top of your most-wanted list!

Turn to page 81 for our "Fabulous Foliage Combinations." Since by now you're probably dying to head for the nearest nursery, without more ado, let's start our combination tour.

Beyond bloom. Though 'Diamont' astilbe, hostas, and annual impatiens bloom in this shady garden, the rich mix of foliage and the centrally placed birdbath are really the stars of the show. Note how the gardener has put a stone in the birdbath so birds and butterflies can perch in comfort while they're drinking.

A GALLERY OF PERENNIAL COMBINATIONS

Much as we writers hate to admit it, when it comes to perennial combinations, a picture really *is* worth a thousand words. So let's take a look at what makes good combinations. We hope you use what you like, and learn from them all. Enjoy your stroll through the combination gallery.

Seasonal Combinations

If you plan combinations for every season, your garden will always look designed. If, on the other hand, you leave for Rome every summer and your garden is under a foot of snow all winter, you really see it only in spring and fall, so you might want to focus on combinations for those seasons. Or maybe you enjoy having different parts of your yard "light up" at different times of year, so you have a spring garden in the front, a summer garden out back, and a fall garden around the side. Here are some ideas for spring, summer, fall, and even winter.

Sensuous spring combinations. Enjoy the candy pastels of spring with simple but lovely combinations like these. Yellow winter aconites, lavender-pink species crocuses, and white snowdrops make a perfect picture (*above*), while purple hyacinths glow against the flowers that exemplify the color aptly known as primrose yellow (*left*).

Summer's bounty. The flames of a red salvia are cooled by waves of lavender at its feet and soft pink asters behind (*left*). Taking the opposite tack, the creator of the combination below uses red bee balm to heat up a sea of pastel yarrows in pink, white, and yellow.

Winter flowers. Mild-climate gardeners can enjoy four seasons of bloom (*below*). Here, snowdrops raise their fragile bells above the glossy evergreen foliage of bergenia, which turns purple-bronze in fall and holds its color through winter.

Autumn joy. A three-tiered combination of apricot and scarlet mums, along with purple asters (*above*) shows that daisies need never be dull.

Combinations for Sun and Shade

It's summer as we write this, and the roads are lined with sunny streetside combinations of daylilies, Shasta and oxeye daisies, black-eyed Susans, purple coneflowers, achilleas, true lilies, and coreopsis in their warm, sun-drenched shades of orange, yellow, paprika, deep red, plum, mauve-pink, and pumpkin, with the bright white of daisies and the occasional lavender-blue of Russian sage (*Perovskia atriplicifolia*) providing contrast.

Meanwhile, the shady spots under trees glow with the chartreuse and golden foliage of hostas, the brilliant hues of tender perennial coleus and impatiens, and the bold color-drenched leaves of caladiums.

Shade combinations can be as simple as a green-and-white-leaved hosta with a Japanese lady fern (*Athyrium niponicum* 'Pictum'), perhaps with a groundcover of *Lamium* 'White Nancy' and a silver- or burgundy-veined alumroot to provide textural contrast. Or they can be intricate, like this one from coauthor Cole Burrell's Virginia garden (see page 98) with its repeating yellow notes: Yellow-flowered fairy wings (*Epimedium franchetii, E. lishihchenii,* and *E. chlorandrum*) are grown as an opulent groundcover under clumps of yellow-flowered fairy-bells (*Disporum uniflorum*) and ferns; behind them, yellow-leaved old-fashioned bleeding heart (*Dicentra spectabilis* 'Gold Heart') continues the color scheme while providing foliage contrast.

A simple sun combo. Shape says it all (*below*), as yarrow's glowing yellow parasols rise above the red-violet spires of salvia.

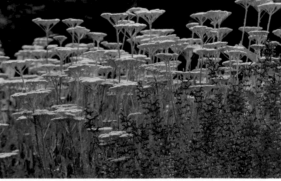

In full sun. Silver and gold brighten this summer border (*above*). The yellow flower clouds of lady's-mantle (*Alchemilla mollis*) and felted gray spikes of lamb's ears (*Stachys byzantina*) accent the front of the border, while yarrows (*Achillea*) and artemisias dominate the back.

A walk in the woods. Hostas and ferns beckon the visitor to explore this shady path (*above*). Who knows what surprises wait around the bend?

A foliage fiesta. Hostas, a potted *Heuchera,* and ferns are the stars of this shady show (*right*). The cream-and-blue foliage of the hostas makes a beautiful contrast to the red-purple of the *Heuchera* 'Chocolate Ruffles' and purple *Cryptotania japonica* 'Atropurpurea'. Hosta flowers flutter above the foliage display in orchidlike profusion.

Hot and Cool Combinations

Some people love piping hot colors, while others are drawn to cool, refreshing shades. You may find yourself in one camp or the other, or you may favor hot colors some years or seasons and cool colors in other seasons. (Or you may love both!) Hot and cool color combinations let you mix a range of colors together and still have a unifying color theme. See our warm- and cool-color garden designs on page 90 for more inspiration, but first, see what you think of these combinations.

Tropical heat. Tender perennial 'Pretoria' canna (*right*) provides a bold green-and-yellow backdrop to the red-hot flower spikes of 'Victoria' cardinal flower (*Lobelia cardinalis* 'Victoria'), which has purple-black foliage to set off the brilliant flowers. The same color contrast also plays out at ground level with a boldly variegated zonal geranium.

A garden ablaze. Yellow flames of 'The Rocket' ligularia are echoed by the red spires of showy Himalayan fleece flower (*Persicaria amplexicaule* 'Firetail') in this fiery combination (*left*).

Hot and cool. Red plays off blue in this spring mix (*left*) of tulips and forget-me-nots (*Myosotis sylvestris*).

A cool blaze of color. Soothing pastel shades run riot on this fence and arbor (*below*), as blue-lavender catmint spills over the front of the fragrant border and sets off the pink roses and lilies (*Lilium regale*) behind it. Honeysuckle (*Lonicera* ×*heckrottii*) climbs the pergola behind the fence, continuing the theme of perfumed pastel abundance.

Color Theme Combinations

If you have a favorite color, you might enjoy creating combinations that highlight that color. You can mix these single-color combos in among other plantings, spotlight a color-theme combination by growing it on its own (around the mailbox, framing a door, in a window box), or create a color-theme garden where a single color predominates an entire bed or border.

A sunny scene. Yellow sets the tone in this garden (*above*), from the trees—a yellow-leaved catalpa (*Catalpa bignonioides* 'Aurea') and European elder (*Sambucus nigra* 'Aurea') to the golden creeping Jenny (*Lysimachia nummularia* 'Aurea') at ground level. The color also comes into play with the ornamental grasses—'Bowles' Golden' sedge and porcupine grass (*Miscanthus sinensis* var. *strictus*).

A white border. At left, the silver leaves of an ornamental pear tree (*Pyrus salicifolia*) and willow (*Salix hakuro* 'Nishiki') enhance the white blooms of foxgloves (*Digitalis purpurea* 'Alba'), white-flowered red valerian (*Centranthus ruber* var. *albus*), alliums (*Allium stipitatum* 'Album'), snow-in-summer (*Cerastium tomentosum*), and camassia (*Camassia leichtlinii*).

A gray garden. Gray forms its own color theme (*left*) as the gray of woolly yarrow (*Achillea tomentosa*) and lamb's ears is echoed in the flagstones. Yarrow flowers add splashes of gold.

Stars and stripes. Spires of 'May Night' salvia rise above the stars of 'Bath's Pink' dianthus in this charming play of flower forms (*below*).

Peachy keen. In this combination (*above*), peach predominates, from the deep tones of the dianthus at the foot of the planting through the changeable hues of the yarrow at its height.

Other Theme Combinations

Themes don't have to be limited to a single color, or even to hot and cool colors. You could grow a garden in your school colors, your team colors, even your prom colors! You can combine plants with a single shape for a spiky theme or lollipop theme (though it's best to do these on a small scale—a whole bed of spikes or balls will be visually distressing). Look at these combinations for other theme ideas.

A pair of plumes. In this unconventional but imposing combination (*left*), the gardener has echoed the sunlit plumes of pampas grass (*Cortaderia selloana* 'Sunningdale Silver') with the heavy flower heads of annual amaranth. The heavy, dark foliage of the amaranth contrasts with the light, slender blades of the grass. Because both set abundant seed, the show will continue until frost.

Light and lovely. White-flowered lavender and purple veronica raise their flower spikes under the graceful globes of *Allium senescens* (*right*).

Think pink. Pink astilbes are the stars of this late-spring border (*above*), but pink-flowered roses, yarrows (*Achillea*), alumroots (*Heuchera*), and lamb's ears play key supporting roles.

Fabulous Foliage Combinations

Perennial foliage is at least as important as flowers because most perennials' bloom time is short. Foliage can look great all season, adding interest to beds whether or not in bloom. Foliage is quieter than flowers, too, making combinations restful and low-key. (Though there are exceptions—bold leaf textures and colors can scream for attention as loudly as any flower.)

A simple standout. Coral bells (*Heuchera*) create a frothy spray over this delightful combination (*above*). The delicate red-purple foliage is the perfect foil for bold variegated hosta leaves.

A foliage tapestry. Silver and purple echo each other across a rich variety of foliage shape and texture in this striking combination (*below*). The spoon-shaped leaves of 'British Sterling' lungwort (*Pulmonaria* 'British Sterling') mingle with the palm-shaped foliage of *Heuchera* 'Pewter Veil', a variegated hosta, and the delicate fronds of Japanese lady fern (*Athyrium niponicum* 'Pictum'), while under all peek the lovely purpled leaves of Labrador violets (*Viola labradorica*).

A variety of variegation. The white bell flowers of fragrant variegated Solomon's seal (*Polygonatum odoratum* var. *pluriflorum* 'Variegatum') arch over the leaves of a variegated hosta in this lovely shade combination (*left*). Feathery wild bleeding heart (*Dicentra eximia*) completes the charming picture.

Combinations for Special Places

If you have a dank, dark corner under the eaves, you may feel lucky to get even pachysandra to grow. That broiling, compacted strip along the driveway seems custom-made for crabgrass—or worse. You've been trying to get grass, or ivy, or anything to grow on the slope from the yard down to the street for so long, you're about ready to throw in the trowel and blanket the ground with crown vetch. Don't be so quick to surrender to the lowest common denominator. There really *is* an attractive, interesting combination for every situation.

For a wet site. Japanese primroses (*Primula japonica*) bloom amid the foliage of Japanese iris (*Iris ensata*) in a combination (*left*) that will provide waves of color from spring into summer. The arum at right adds foliar interest and will bear showy spikes of orange-red berries in late summer.

A wall of bloom. The yellow stars of sedum (*Sedum humifusum*) and purple stars of Serbian bellflower (*Campanula poscharskyana*) form a cheerful combination to grow on a rock wall (*right*).

Hungry for more? Coauthor Cole Burrell has written an entire book, *Perennial Combinations*, with more than 120 colorful combinations for every taste, site, and situation. See "Suggested Reading" on page 685 for even more inspiration!

4

A GALLERY
OF GARDEN DESIGNS

We know how intimidating garden design can be, especially if you're trying to do it yourself. So we've asked seven noted garden designers to create gardens designed especially for certain situations or climates.

A Classic Perennial Garden. This lovely garden, with its double beds leading to a rose-covered arbor, features a mix of favorite perennials. Page 84.

Warm- and Cool-Color Borders. Whether your taste runs to cool colors or the hot end of the spectrum, you'll find lots to love in these color-theme gardens. Page 90.

A Native Plant Garden for Sun *and* Shade. This colorful bed transitions from sun to shade and showcases the beauty and diversity of our native perennials. Page 98.

A Magical Moonlit Garden. Lovely for moon-viewing or just moonlighting, this garden's half-moon borders appeal to all the senses—especially after dark. Page 102.

A Cold-Climate Perennial Garden. Perfect for a corner of the yard, this delightful bed is anchored by a stunning purple-leaved rose bush. Page 108.

A Drought-Tolerant Garden. Where rainfall is scarce or you're looking for low maintenance, this garden provides colorful bloom from spring through fall. Page 114.

A Perennial Garden Room. Perfect for a small backyard or to create a sense of privacy, this design features matching borders enclosed by a formal hedge. Page 118.

A CLASSIC PERENNIAL GARDEN

This garden includes many of the features you'd expect from a traditional perennial garden: paired rectangular beds; a rose- and clematis-covered arbor; favorite perennials like 'Munstead' common lavender, 'David' garden phlox, and 'Goldsturm' black-eyed Susan; and repetition of key plants and flower shapes while including a wide variety of both to keep the garden beds visually stimulating. But it's got some design surprises, too.

Rather than simply repeating the plants in both beds—creating mirroring beds—designer Stephanie Cohen has chosen to create echoing beds instead. These beds have color schemes and plant forms that echo rather than duplicate each other. For example, she anchors one bed with shrubby 'Purple Smoke' false indigo and duplicates the anchoring function—but not the plants—by using bold, spiny bear's-breech in the facing bed.

By using 'Moonshine' yarrow in one bed and 'Coronation Gold' and 'Fireland' yarrows in the other, Stephanie again creates an echo. The viewer simultaneously enjoys the similarity and the difference. The lavender-blue spires of Russian sage in one bed echo the spires of true lavender in the other.

The beds also differ subtly in color scheme. The bed with the false indigos as focal points features softer colors, while the 'Coronation Gold' and 'Fireland' yarrows give the bed with the bear's-breech warmer, deeper shades of gold and red. But they're tied together by the repetition of key plants—the 'Caradonna' garden sage,

'Sweet Dreams' coreopsis, 'Walker's Low' blue catmint, 'David' garden phlox, white-flowered valerian, 'Goldsturm' black-eyed Susan, and 'Knockout' roses—for a richly colorful effect.

The Garden in Bloom

The display in this lovely garden begins in early spring with a selection of bold Triumph tulips. 'Bastagne' is a very dark red tulip—almost a blood red, with cardinal red flames and plum anthers. It grows 18 inches tall and is lightly scented. It's combined with 'Crispa' tulips, which have exotic lacy petals, and 'Swan Wings', a pure white tulip that reaches a stately 22 inches tall. 'Swan Wings', with crystalline fringed edges and black anthers, is both charming and exotic-looking. The tulips wake up the garden and prepare the viewers for the show yet to come.

In the bed that's anchored by the false indigos, the real display begins when these gorgeous bushy plants come into bloom. 'Purple Smoke' false indigo produces flowers in a mix of blue and purple sweetpea-like blooms borne in clusters. Leave them in place to mature into blue-black pods that are also ornamental. The false indigos are joined by the delicate blooms of 'King of Hearts' bleeding heart and the dark purple flower spikes of 'Caradonna' garden sage, which also has dark purple-black stems. Spring also marks the start of geranium bloom. In the bed with the bear's-breech, 'Brookside' and 'Rozanne' geraniums bloom from spring to fall, and their foliage turns beautiful shades of orange, red, and gold as cold weather arrives.

June brings the garden into summer bloom, as the 'Dortmund' climbing rose and 'Henryi' clematis begin covering the arbor with their deep red and starry white blooms, echoing the colors of the tulips in early spring. Both 'Dortmund' and the 'Knockout' roses in the beds are single

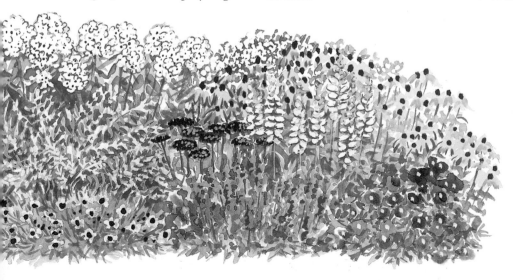

reds that will bloom into fall. The new growth on the 'Knockout' bushes is a lovely purple-red, adding to the show. Color abounds in the garden with the pale primrose yellow of 'Moonshine' yarrow, the white blooms of the valerian, the lavender of the catmint and 'Munstead' common lavender, and the airy clouds of pink baby's-breath. In late June, these are joined by 'Sweet Dreams' coreopsis, which has whitish pink flowers with red eyes. As the season progresses, the bold gold daisies of 'Goldsturm' black-eyed Susan and white panicles of 'David' garden phlox join the show, extending the colorful display into fall.

Across the path, June makes a splash with the bold gold of stately 'Coronation Gold' yarrow and the red of 'Fireland' yarrow, which changes to pink and then gold as the season progresses. The clouds of white blooms on the 'Bristol Fairy' baby's-breath echo the 'Pink Fairy' across the way. The spiny bear's-breech, with its bold foliage and unusual hooded flowers, adds color to the late June and July garden. The white flowers with their showy mauve bracts repeat the colors of the early false indigo in the facing bed. 'Blue Perfection' pincushion flower enters the show in July, joining the 'Walker's Low' blue catmint to add a cooler note to the bed.

Russian sage also comes into bloom as summer progresses and continues the show into fall, repeating the spikes of the sage and lavender. Later still, the spiky form is repeated again as the sparkling white 'Miss Manners' obedient plant comes into bloom. The lovely 'Becky' Shasta daisy blooms from late June to fall, its yellow-centered white blooms complementing the black-centered gold daisies of 'Goldsturm' black-eyed Susan.

In Another Place

If you don't have room for both beds, choose your favorite and site it anywhere your yard gets full sun—along a deck, patio, or walk, or even as a foundation planting. If your taste runs to the more traditional, choose the bed with the false indigo and lavender. If you'd like a more adventurous look, more along the lines of contemporary European garden design, plant the bed with the bear's-breech and Russian sage. You'll enjoy a colorful garden of classic perennials either way!

Expert Care Tips

Designer Stephanie Cohen reminds us that you'll get a much longer bloom season if you remember to deadhead or cut back your perennials after bloom. She notes that the 'Bachanal' and 'King of Hearts' bleeding hearts will bloom continuously from spring to fall if you keep them deadheaded. You can get 'Caradonna' garden sage to rebloom twice after its initial bloom if you deadhead it. 'David' garden phlox will also continue

LAYERS OF DELIGHT

Beauty isn't the only thing a good perennial garden can offer. This one offers a wealth of flowers for cutting, and many offer heavenly fragrance as well. As if that weren't enough, designer Stephanie Cohen chose her perennials to attract butterflies to the garden for a second tier of beauty hovering over the first!

With this garden, you can have floral bounty indoors as well as out because many of the featured flowers make wonderful cut flowers. To fill your house with bloom from late spring through fall, bring in bunches of dark purple 'Caradonna' garden sage; red

'Dortmund' and 'Knockout' roses; 'Pink Fairy' and white 'Bristol Fairy' baby's-breath; white-flowered valerian; 'Coronation Gold', 'Moonshine', and 'Fireland' yarrows; 'Munstead' common lavender; 'Goldsturm' black-eyed Susan; Russian sage; 'Becky' Shasta daisy; and 'Blue Perfection' pincushion flower as they come into bloom.

Fragrance will entice you (and your guests) to linger in the garden, and it will also come inside with your fresh-cut bouquets. Enjoy the scented medley of 'Dortmund' roses, 'Walker's Low' blue catmint, 'David' garden phlox, and Russian sage. Besides cut-

ting it for bouquets or just brushing it in the garden to release its signature scent, you can make the 'Munstead' common lavender blooms into potpourri, sachets, or lavender wands. Even the 'Bastagne' tulips are lightly scented.

Butterflies like to rest on flat flowers, so they'll be attracted to the 'Becky' Shasta daisies, 'Goldsturm' black-eyed Susan, 'Blue Perfection' pincushion flower, and all the yarrows—'Coronation Gold', 'Moonshine', and 'Fireland'. Birds—especially finches—will enjoy the seedheads of the black-eyed Susans when they ripen in fall. And you'll enjoy the lively show!

to bloom if you cut it back when the initial blooms fade.

Don't get carried away and deadhead *all* your perennials, though! The handsome blue-black seedpods of false indigos add distinction to the garden into fall, and the black-eyed Susans and yarrows will add fall and winter interest if you leave them standing.

Stephanie suggests that you make the path through the beds grass or mulch. Edge the beds if you're using grass, or it will grow into them and create a mainte-

nance headache. If you sink an edging along the sides of the beds, path maintenance is as easy as mowing. If you're starting with bare ground rather than lawn, mulch will give you a very low-maintenance path. (Just renew the mulch as needed and pull any weed seedlings that root in it.) Use natural brown mulch and let it weather to gray to match the rustic cedar arbor or pergola, which will also weather to gray, setting off the red and white of the rose and clematis flowers growing on it.

A Classic Perennial Garden

This inviting garden smells as good as it looks. Below is a list of plants included in this design. (Don't forget to underplant with groups of 'Bastagne', 'Crispa', and 'Swan Wings' Triumph tulips. Plant clusters of the same type together in what designers call "organic shapes"—kidneys, irregular ovals, amoebas, and so on—rather than in rows.) For more information on the perennial plants in this garden, see "The Perennial Encyclopedia," beginning on page 265. (*Note:* The numbers in parentheses refer to the quantity of each plant used.)

PLANTS FOR THE CLASSIC PERENNIAL GARDEN

Bed with False Indigo
1. 'Pink Fairy' baby's-breath (*Gypsophila paniculata* 'Pink Fairy') (5 plants)
2. 'Goldsturm' black-eyed Susan (*Rudbeckia fulgida* var. *sullivantii* 'Goldsturm') (6 total)
3. 'King of Hearts' bleeding heart (*Dicentra* 'King of Hearts') (5)
4. 'Walker's Low' blue catmint (*Nepeta ×faassenii* 'Walker's Low') (6 total)
5. 'Sweet Dreams' coreopsis (*Coreopsis* 'Sweet Dreams') (8 total)
6. 'Purple Smoke' false indigo (*Baptisia* 'Purple Smoke') (1)
7. 'Brookside' geranium (*Geranium* 'Brookside') (3)
8. 'Munstead' common lavender (*Lavandula angustifolia* 'Munstead') (5)
9. 'David' garden phlox (*Phlox paniculata* 'David') (3)
10. 'Knockout' rose (*Rosa* 'Knockout') (1)
11. 'Caradonna' garden sage (*Salvia nemorosa* 'Caradonna') (5)
12. 'Alba' red valerian (*Centranthus ruber* 'Alba') (4)
13. 'Moonshine' yarrow (*Achillea* 'Moonshine') (5)

Bed with Bear's-Breech
1. 'Bristol Fairy' baby's-breath (*Gypsophila paniculata* 'Bristol Fairy') (3 plants)
2. Spiny bear's-breech (*Acanthus spinosus*) (3)
3. 'Goldsturm' black-eyed Susan (*Rudbeckia fulgida* var. *sullivantii* 'Goldsturm') (5)
4. 'Bacchanal' bleeding heart (*Dicentra* 'Bacchanal') (3)
5. 'Walker's Low' blue catmint (*Nepeta ×faassenii* 'Walker's Low') (2)
6. 'Sweet Dreams' coreopsis (*Coreopsis* 'Sweet Dreams') (3)

MEET THE DESIGNER
Stephanie Cohen

Stephanie Cohen is the director of the Landscape Arboretum at Temple University, Ambler campus. She has taught classes on both herbaceous plants and perennial design for many years, is a contributing editor to *Country Living Gardener,* and was seen on QVC as the gardening diva.

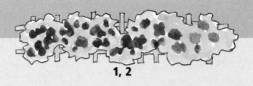

1, 2

7. 'Brookside' geranium
   (*Geranium* 'Brookside') (4)
8. 'Rozanne' geranium
   (*Geranium* 'Rozanne') (3)
9. 'Miss Manners' obedient
   plant (*Physostegia virginiana*
   'Miss Manners') (4)
10. 'David' garden phlox
    (*Phlox paniculata* 'David') (4)
11. 'Blue Perfection' pincushion
    flower (*Scabiosa caucasica*
    'Blue Perfection') (5)
12. 'Knockout' rose (*Rosa*
    'Knockout') (1)
13. Russian sage (*Perovskia
    atriplicifolia*) (5)
14. 'Caradonna' garden
    sage (*Salvia nemorosa*
    'Caradonna') (5)
15. 'Becky' Shasta daisy
    (*Leucanthemum maximum*
    'Becky') (3)
16. 'Alba' red valerian
    (*Centranthus ruber* 'Alba') (3)
17. 'Coronation Gold' yarrow
    (*Achillea* 'Coronation Gold')
    (3)
18. 'Fireland' yarrow (*Achillea*
    'Fireland') (3)

On the Arbor
 1. 'Henryi' clematis (*Clematis*
    'Henryi')
 2. 'Dortmund' climbing rose
    (*Rosa* 'Dortmund')

Bed with False Indigo

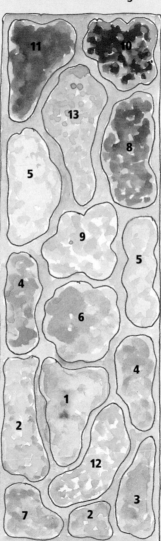

Bed with Bear's-Breech

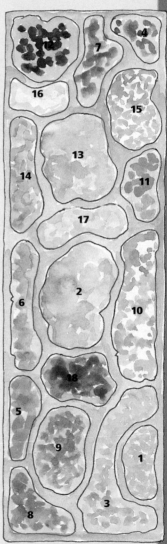

WARM- AND COOL-COLOR BORDERS

For those of us who love to play with color—and who doesn't?—designer Tracy DiSabato-Aust has created two versions of the same border, each using a different color theme. One version features warm colors; in the other, cool colors star. These exciting and ever-evolving gardens were designed using colors adjacent to each other on the color wheel. This is known as an analogous color theme, which creates color harmony.

In the warm-color border, reds, oranges, and yellows glow for a vibrant, lively effect. This border would be nice viewed from a distance, as its colors will advance. (Warm or hot colors create an optical illusion, making the plants look closer than they really are.)

In the cool-color border, blues, purples, and greens create a soothing and relaxing symphony. This border would be appropriate for an intimate or smaller garden where it can be viewed up close. (Just as the hotter colors make plants look closer, cool colors make them recede.)

These borders could be backed by a structure such as a wall or fence. On the structure, you can grow vines on a trellis to soften the vertical outline, at the same time making the best use of the vertical space and enhancing the garden's color effect.

In the warm-color border, the purple flowers of the 'Polish Spirit' clematis add a touch of tension and contrast to help intensify the yellows in the border. In the cool-color border, the yellow flowers of the 'Graham Thomas' honeysuckle complement and add the needed tension to intensify the purples and blues in that border. If you choose to back the border with a hedge, or if it doesn't have a wall or fence behind it, then an obelisk could be added if desired to support the vines.

Each border also features a piece of garden art of your choice. Have fun selecting art that will personalize your border and create an interesting focal point. Choose a durable piece to add garden interest year-round, or bring your artwork inside for the winter if you live in an area that experiences freezing weather.

Although these are predominantly herbaceous perennial borders, Tracy has included a few woody plants, as well as tropicals and some outstanding annuals. The woody plants help add structure and scale to the borders and serve to provide interesting textures, forms, and—in the case of the beautyberry and honeysuckles—even fruit for the winter. The large tropicals—the Japanese banana and 'Red Stripe' canna—add needed weight to the gardens and an exotic mood, while extending the season of interest along with the other annual plants. The peak

season of interest for the borders is summer. However, there will be excitement and interest in the gardens year-round due to the wide and varied plant palette, as well as the layering or interplanting of certain plants.

The Garden in Bloom

For early spring color, phase in bulbs as time and budget permit. In the warm garden, plant tulips such as 'Big Smile', 'Carmine Parrot', or 'Blushing Lady', or daffodils such as 'Tahiti' or 'Stratosphere' for early flower interest. In the cool border, 'Queen of Night', 'Blue Heron', or 'Black Parrot' tulips would harmonize beautifully with the color scheme. Reticulated iris (*Iris reticulata*) would be particularly nice tucked in at the feet of selected perennials or grasses for extremely early color.

In the cool-color border, the low-growing Japanese white pine and 'Albyn'

THE SCIENCE BEHIND THE DESIGN

When Tracy DiSabato-Aust designed these color theme borders, she used more than an eye for aesthetics to create their proportions. The proportions (length and width) for the borders were selected from what is known as the Fibonocci Series. These are numbers based on the Golden Mean, a rule of "ideal" proportion developed by the ancient Greeks. It is common throughout nature and has been taught in art schools for centuries. The proper placement of a piece of art in the border is also based on these principles.

Scots pine provide an evergreen backdrop for the bulbs, which will be followed by the alpine columbine. As spring progresses, the dark blue-purple Siberian iris, fragrant bearded iris, deep purple 'Caradonna' garden sage, and 'Plum Pudding' coral bells come into bloom, followed by the 'Patty's Plum' and 'Lauren's Grape' poppies, and the purple-black blooms of mourning widows. Early summer adds 'Blue Sapphire' blue flax, 'Purple Sensation' ornamental onion, and 'Komachi' balloon flower to the display. On the trellis, the creamy yellow blooms of 'Graham Thomas' honeysuckle are a perfect foil for the deep purple-red starry flowers of 'Polish Spirit' clematis. Both will bloom into fall.

In high summer, the border's bloom is dramatic, with jewel-bright 'Ruby Slippers' lobelia, 'Omega Skyrocket' Stoke's aster, the airy mauve-flowered stalks of Brazilian vervain, and the commanding purple-red blooms of 'Thomas Edison' dahlia joining the show. Stately blue-foliaged 'Heavy Metal' switchgrass is also blooming, and the exotic foliage of the Japanese banana creates a handsome counterpart to the slender leaves of the ornamental grass.

Fall adds the bright blue flowers of plumbago to the display and brightens the garden with the showy purple berries of 'Issai' purple beautyberry and the red berries of the 'Graham Thomas' honeysuckle.

In the warm-color border, a colorful foliage display follows the early bulb show. The 'Golden Sword' yuccas create a wonderful sunny foliage accent, echoing the gold-variegated foliage of the variegated aralia at the other end of the border. The unusual bronze foliage of the leatherleaf sedge adds a repeating note at the front of the border, as the 'Red Stripe' canna and 'Ruby Queen' Swiss chard provide bolder splashes of red and green. The purple foliage of the 'Purpurascens' Japanese silver grass and 'Solfatare' crocosmia along with the gold of 'Golden Spirit' smokebush contribute their glowing colors as they fill in.

The 'Fireglow' euphorbia begins the perennial bloom display, followed by the poppies, 'Little Maid' red-hot poker, purple-red 'Polish Spirit' clematis, and orange-flowered 'Orange Mandarin' honeysuckle. In summer, the garden heats up as the bright, clear yellow of 'Solfatare' crocosmia and the golden orange daisies of 'Prairie Sunset' oxeye contrast with the bold orange of the butterfly weed and the hot reds of the bee balm, sun rose, and scarlet rose mallow. In late summer, the California and corn poppies continue their orange and red display as the tiger lily and Japanese silver grass come into bloom. Fall brings the purple-tinged plumes of the Japanese silver grass into prominence; they duet with the feathery plumes of the 'Golden Spirit' smokebush as the season draws to a close.

(continued on page 96)

WARM- AND COOL-COLOR BORDERS

These paired color-theme borders are irresistible! It's fun to see how the cool-color plants replace the warm-color choices in the same basic design. Following is a list of plants included in this design. (If you choose to add them, don't forget to underplant with groups of spring bulbs—tulips, daffodils, and reticulated iris, as Tracy recommends on page 92. Plant clusters of the same type together in loose groups, rather than in rows.) For more information on the perennial plants in this garden, see "The Perennial Encyclopedia," beginning on page 265. (*Note:* The numbers in parentheses refer to the quantity of each plant used.)

PLANTS FOR THE WARM- AND COOL-COLOR BORDERS

Warm-Color Border

1. Variegated aralia (*Aralia elata* 'Aureovariegata') (1 plant)
2. 'Jacob Cline' bee balm (*Monarda* 'Jacob Cline') (1)
3. Butterfly weed (*Asclepias tuberosa*) (3)
4. 'Red Stripe' canna (*Canna* 'Red Stripe') (3 total)
5. 'Polish Spirit' clematis (*Clematis* 'Polish Spirit') (1)
6. 'Solfatare' crocosmia (*Crocosmia* ×*crocosmiiflora* 'Solfatare') (5)
7. 'Fireglow' euphorbia (*Euphorbia griffithii* 'Fireglow') (1)
8. 'Orange Mandarin' honeysuckle (*Lonicera periclymenum* 'Orange Mandarin) (1)
9. 'Purpurascens' Japanese silver grass (*Miscanthus* 'Purpurascens') (3 total)
10. Tiger lily (*Lilium lancifolium* var. *splendens*) (5)
11. Scarlet rose mallow (*Hibiscus coccineus*) (1)
12. 'Prairie Sunset' oxeye (*Heliopsis helianthoides* var. *scabra* 'Prairie Sunset') (3)
13. California poppy (*Eschscholzia californica*) (seed)
14. Corn poppy (*Papaver rhoeas*) (seed)
15. 'Turkenlouis' Oriental poppy (*Papaver orientale* 'Turkenlouis') (3)
16. 'Little Maid' red-hot poker (*Kniphofia* 'Little Maid') (5)
17. Leatherleaf sedge (*Carex buchananii*) (3 total)

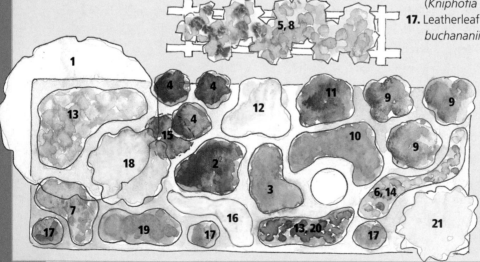

18. 'Golden Spirit' smokebush (*Cotinus* 'Golden Spirit') (1)

19. 'Fire Dragon' sun rose (*Helianthemum* 'Fire Dragon') (3)

20. 'Ruby Queen' Swiss chard (*Beta vulgaris* 'Ruby Queen') (3)

21. 'Golden Sword' yucca (*Yucca flaccida* 'Golden Sword') (3)

Cool-Color Border

1. 'Komachi' balloon flower (*Platycodon grandiflorus* 'Komachi') (5 plants)

2. 'Issai' purple beautyberry (*Callicarpa dichotoma* 'Issai') (1)

3. 'Polish Spirit' clematis (*Clematis* 'Polish Spirit') (1)

4. Alpine columbine (*Aquilegia alpina*) (3)

5. 'Plum Pudding' coral bells (*Heuchera* 'Plum Pudding') (3)

6. 'Thomas Edison' dahlia (*Dahlia* 'Thomas Edison') (3)

7. 'Blue Sapphire' blue flax *Linum perenne* 'Blau Saphir') (5)

8. 'Graham Thomas' honeysuckle (*Lonicera periclymenum* 'Graham Thomas') (1)

9. 'Perfume Counter' bearded iris (*Iris* 'Perfume Counter') (5)

10. 'Caesar's Brother' Siberian iris (*Iris sibirica* 'Caesar's Brother') (3)

11. Japanese banana (*Musa basjoo*) (1)

12. 'Ruby Slippers' lobelia (*Lobelia* 'Ruby Slippers') (3)

13. Mourning widows (*Geranium phaeum*) (3 total)

14. 'Purple Sensation' ornamental onion (*Allium hollandicum* [*aflatunense*] 'Purple Sensation') (5)

15. 'Albyn' Scots pine (*Pinus sylvestris* 'Albyn') (1)

16. Japanese white pine (*Pinus parviflora* 'Glauca') (1)

17. Plumbago (*Ceratostigma plumbaginoides*) (7)

18. 'Lauren's Grape' bread poppy (*Papaver somniferum* 'Lauren's Grape') (seed)

19. 'Patty's Plum' Oriental poppy (*Papaver orientale* 'Patty's Plum') (3)

20. 'Caradonna' garden sage (*Salvia nemorosa* 'Caradonna') (3)

21. 'Omega Skyrocket' Stokes' aster (*Stokesia laevis* 'Omega Skyrocket') (3)

22. 'Heavy Metal' switchgrass (*Panicum virgatum* 'Heavy Metal') (3 total)

23. Brazilian vervain (*Verbena bonariensis*) (5)

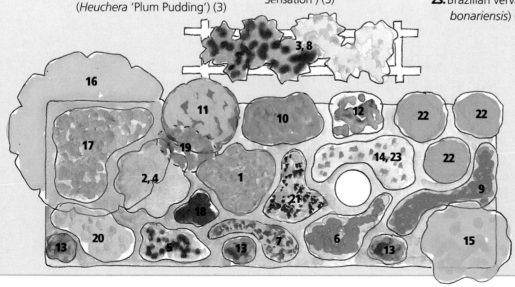

WARM- AND COOL-COLOR BORDERS (CONT.)

MEET THE DESIGNER

Tracy DiSabato-Aust

Tracy DiSabato-Aust has earned international acclaim as one of America's most entertaining and knowledgeable garden writers and professional speakers. She's frequently featured in magazines, on television, on the radio, and on the lecture circuit, and is the author of the best-selling book *The Well-Tended Perennial Garden*, as well as the recently published *The Well-Designed Mixed Garden*.

In Another Place

These colorful borders are easy to adapt. If you'd like a longer border, plant the design twice, but in mirror image, so each end is anchored with a variegated aralia (if you're planting the warm-color border) or a Japanese white pine (if you've chosen the cool-color border). Use your favorite of the two color schemes, plant one of each, or, if you'd like to try your hand at a color-theme border that features one or more of *your* favorite colors, use Tracy's design as a framework. Choose plants with flowers, foliage, and/or fruit in your chosen color that match the basic shapes, sizes, and functions of Tracy's choices in her warm- and cool-color borders. (See Chapter 3, "Perennial Combinations," for more ideas.) Have fun creating your own customized version!

Expert Care Tips

You'll need to start some of the poppies in Tracy's garden design from seed. These include the California, corn, and 'Lauren's Grape' bread poppies. You can start them indoors and transplant them to the border, or plant your perennials and shrubs, then sow the poppy seeds around them.

Some of the annuals and perennials will self-sow, enhancing the garden's free-spirited look and adding more color as the years pass. Thin as desired to prevent overcrowding and to remove volunteers that pop up where they aren't wanted.

To extend the season of interest, deadhead your perennials. Leave the grass seedheads to add late-season interest, but be warned—you'll need to pull seedlings rigorously in spring to keep them from taking over.

If you live in a cold-winter area, you'll need to dig and bring in your tropical plants (the 'Red Stripe' canna if you plant the warm-color border, and the Japanese banana if you plant the cool-color border). An easier option is to grow them in containers and sink the containers in the beds, then lift them in fall when frost threatens and bring them indoors. You can also treat them as annuals and re-place them every year—if you can bear to (we couldn't!).

The 'Golden Spirit' smokebush and 'Issai' purple beautyberry require special yearly maintenance. Cut these shrubs back heavily (a technique called coppicing or stooling), down to 4 to 6 inches above ground level about 1 month before growth begins. This will keep their size and habit manageable in the gardens, and they won't outgrow their space and over-whelm the perennials. The variegated ar-alia will send up suckers, which should be removed.

A NATIVE PLANT GARDEN FOR SUN *AND* SHADE

Most yards are a mix of trees and lawn. If you're adding a garden to a yard like this, you'll need to plan for both sun and shade in your design, as this garden does. Coauthor Cole Burrell, whose landscape design firm, Native Landscape Design and Restoration, specializes in native plants, uses native perennials lavishly in this gorgeous, dynamic garden.

The Garden in Bloom

The garden's color scheme is white and yellow, which are common colors along summer roadsides. Spring color comes from huge drifts of daffodils planted throughout. Long-blooming daffodils with a succession of flowers include 'February Gold' (yellow, early), 'Peeping Tom' (yellow, slightly later), 'W. P. Milner' (white and pale yellow, midseason), and 'Tracey' (white, midseason).

The sunny garden bed begins its main show in June, with false indigo, evening primrose, blue flag iris, and Bowman's root. July bloomers include Stoke's aster, rosinweed, Culver's root, Joe-Pye weed, and wild quinine. The peak comes in August and September with grasses, tall tickseed, sweet coneflower, azure sage, and early goldenrod, which overlap with the July bloomers. Late-season color from aromatic aster carries the garden through frost.

In the shaded bed, the main bloom times are spring and late summer. Early bloomers (with the daffodils) include wild bleeding heart, dwarf crested iris, and celandine poppy. Ferns emerge to cover the fading bulb foliage. Solomon's seal, goat's beard, and black cohosh add their white blooms to the great fern display in summer. In late summer, starry white wood aster lights up the shadows along with the purple berries of spikenard.

In Another Place

This garden would also look lovely along a path or property line, or separating the yard from the road. You can choose either bed if you'd like to create a smaller garden.

For gardeners north of USDA Plant Hardiness Zone 6, beautyberry is not hardy. A witch hazel (*Hamamelis virginiana*, hardy to Zone 4), with its yellow autumn flowers, is a good substitute.

Expert Care Tips

The best soil for this garden is moderately fertile clay, which will often become dry in summer between rains. Plants grow better with limited nitrogen, which keeps them compact and in scale with the space. (So fertilizing is another chore you can skip!) Excess nitrogen encourages lush growth that is susceptible to toppling in wind or rain. Some supplemental watering will be necessary to keep the garden attractive and blooming well late in the season.

GOING BEYOND BLOOM

Most of us still think of flowers when we think of perennials and garden design. But to be successful, a design should rely on structure—the "architectural" elements of shape and height—and on progression, as this garden does. Each season provides new focal points to capture the gardener's (and visitors') attention.

In the shaded bed, the beautyberry and spikenard add height and—like the tree trunk that's also a central element of this bed—anchor the more ephemeral perennials. The beautyberry's startling lavender-purple berries provide an unexpected surprise in late summer and complement the purple fruits of the spikenard. Throughout the growing season, the leather wood fern, interrupted fern, wild bleeding heart, and wild ginger add foliar interest under the tree's canopy.

In the sunny parts of the garden, the bushy false indigo and Joe-Pye weed serve the same function as the shrubs in the shaded bed, while the 'Color Guard' yuccas and the blue leaves of 'Dallas Blues' switchgrass create a colorful foliar display.

A NATIVE PLANT GARDEN FOR *SUN AND* SHADE

This native plant garden is as tough as it is beautiful. Below is a list of plants included in this design. (Don't forget to underplant with large groups of 'February Gold', 'Peeping Tom', 'W. P. Milner', and 'Tracey' daffodils. Some gardeners throw the daffodil bulbs to make the planting look more random and naturalized, but to prevent harm to the bulbs it's probably wisest to simply set them out in drifts of a single variety. Make sure the groupings look natural—don't set the bulbs out in rows.) For more information on the perennial plants in this garden, see "The Perennial Encyclopedia," beginning on page 265. (*Note:* The numbers in parentheses refer to the quantity of each plant used.)

PLANTS FOR THE NATIVE PLANT GARDEN FOR SUN *AND* SHADE

Sunny Bed

1. 'Color Guard' Adam's needle (*Yucca filamentosa* 'Color Guard') (9 plants)
2. Hardy ageratum (*Eupatorium coelestinum* 'Album') (4)
3. Aromatic aster (*Aster oblongifolius* 'Raydon') (9 total)
4. 'Bluebird' smooth aster (*Aster laevis* 'Bluebird') (3)
5. 'Contraband Girl' Virginia blue flag (*Iris virginica* 'Contraband Girl') (6)
6. Bowman's root (*Porteranthus trifoliatus*) (9 total)
7. Sweet coneflower (*Rudbeckia subtomentosa*) (6)
8. Culver's root (*Veronicastrum virginicum*) (2)
9. 'Cold Crick' evening primrose (*Oenothera* 'Cold Crick') (10 total)
10. 'Carolina Moonlight' false indigo (*Baptisia* 'Carolina Moonlight') (3)
11. 'Purple Smoke' false indigo (*Baptisia* 'Purple Smoke') (3)
12. Early goldenrod (*Solidago juncea*) (6 total)
13. 'Joe White' Joe-Pye weed (*Eupatorium fistulosum* 'Joe White') (1)
14. Wild quinine (*Parthenium integrifolium*) (9 total)

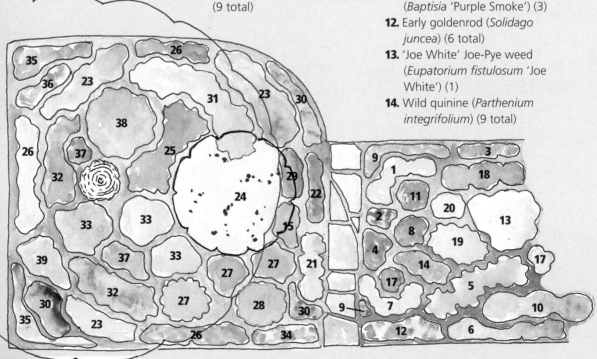

MEET THE DESIGNER

C. Colston Burrell

Cole Burrell is a garden designer, writer, photographer, and the owner of Native Landscape Design and Restoration, which is located near Charlottesville, Virginia. He is the author of *Perennial* *Combinations, Better Homes and Gardens Perennials for Today's Gardens, A Gardener's Encyclopedia of Wildflowers,* and numerous other books and articles on plants and gardening.

15. Rosinweed (*Silphium compsitum*) (3)

16. Three-leaved rosinweed (*Silphium trifoliatum*) (3)

17. Pitcher's azure sage (*Salvia azurea* var. *grandiflora*) (3)

18. 'Peachey' Stokes' aster (*Stokesia laevis* 'Peachey') (3)

19. 'Dallas Blues' switchgrass (*Panicum virgatum* 'Dallas Blues') (2)

20. Tall tickseed (*Coreopsis tripteris*) (3)

Shaded Bed

21. 'Color Guard' Adam's needle (*Yucca filamentosa* 'Color Guard') (3)

22. 'Bluebird' smooth aster (*Aster laevis* 'Bluebird') (3)

23. White wood aster (*Aster divaricatus*) (8 total)

24. Beautyberry (*Callicarpa americana*) (1)

25. Black cohosh (*Cimicifuga racemosa*) (3)

26. 'Alba' wild bleeding heart (*Dicentra eximia* 'Alba') (11 total)

27. 'Contraband Girl' Virginia blue flag (*Iris virginica* 'Contraband Girl') (3)

28. Arkansas blue star (*Amsonia hubrechtii*) (1)

29. Boltonia (*Boltonia asteroides*) (2)

30. 'Cold Crick' evening primrose (*Oenothera* 'Cold Crick') (8 total)

31. Interrupted fern (*Osmunda claytoniana*) (4 total)

32. Leather wood fern (*Dryopteris marginalis*) (7 total)

33. Goat's beard (*Aruncus dioicus*) (3)

34. Early goldenrod (*Solidago juncea*) (3)

35. Crested iris (*Iris cristata*) (6 total)

36. Celandine poppy (*Stylophorum diphyllum*) (6 total)

37. Solomon's seal (*Polygonatum biflorum*) (4 total)

38. Spikenard (*Aralia racemosa*) (1)

39. Wild ginger (*Asarum canadense*) (5)

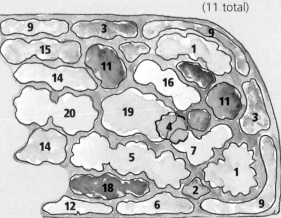

A MAGICAL MOONLIT GARDEN

This enchanting garden is beautiful by day, but is really meant to be enjoyed from sunset on. Its shape—two half-moon beds surrounding a circular terrace, with a full-moon bed behind one of the half-moons that echoes the round shape of the terrace—subtly emphasizes the moonlight theme. Designer Edith R. Eddleman has chosen perennials and accessories that light up the garden in moonlight. She chose the flower colors of lavender, lemon yellow, and white, which glow during the twilight hours of early evening.

The moon, which rises in the east and sets in the west, passes over this garden nightly and brings a magical glow to the pale blooms. It is also reflected in the circle of water within the cauldron. (Edith has chosen to convert an antique sugar-making cauldron into a water-garden focal point. If you can't find a cauldron at a flea market or antiques shop, you can substitute any large, round-mouthed container that will hold water, such as a half-barrel.)

The garden also features a tall tripod trellis capped by a stainless steel gazing ball finial. The silver gazing ball will also reflect sunlight and moonlight. Edith suggests growing a moonvine on the trellis; this annual vine bears huge white morning-glory flowers at night throughout summer and fall (until frost). If you'd rather have a more permanent vine, use 'John Clayton' honeysuckle (*Lonicera sempervirens* 'John Clayton'), which has soft yellow blooms from spring through frost. Or grow the moonvine and honeysuckle together for a stunning floral feature.

You'd expect a magical garden to be fragrant, and this one doesn't disappoint. The flowers of 'Franz Schubert' garden phlox, the night-blooming citron daylily, and the August-blooming tall white-flowered Formosa lily fill the night air with intoxicating perfume. The native white night-blooming water lily (*Nymphaea odora*) in the cauldron water garden adds its own sweet fragrance to the night.

Because the terrace has been designed around the trunk of a shade tree, portions of this south-facing garden are in deciduous shade. The leafy canopy of shade makes the terrace a pleasure to sit on during the day as well as at night. Edith recommends using irregularly shaped stones that contain mica for the terrace so it will glitter in sunlight and moonlight, enhancing the magical feeling of the garden. She suggests digging the circle of the garden 5 inches deep, then setting the stones on a bed of 4 inches of firmed sand, and filling in around them with more sand.

The sunny parts of the garden are oriented west to take advantage of backlighting by the setting sun. If you're thinking the Magical Moonlit Garden sounds like a perfect setting for romance, we think you're right!

The Garden in Bloom

Though the Magical Moonlit Garden comes into fullest bloom in summer, when it's most pleasant to sit outdoors, there is plenty of interest throughout the year. In winter, the evergreen Lenten rose, yucca, lilyturf, and Mediterranean spurge provide structure, and the Lenten rose and Mediterranean spurge also flower in winter. A beautiful selection of cream-veined Italian arum and silver-marbled 'Chameleon' arum are tucked around the large, showy hostas. And farther out is a clump of 'Heavy Metal' switchgrass, which adds great winter interest.

To enhance the entire garden in spring, underplant with a variety of small bulbs, including Tomasini's crocus (*Crocus tomasianus*) in all its color forms: white, 'Ruby Giant', 'Whitewell Purple', and 'Roseum'. Add to this patches of 'Cream Beauty' golden crocus (*Crocus chrysanthum* 'Cream Beauty'), a few clumps of narrow-foliaged narcissus (fragrant, bright yellow), early Campernelle jonquil (*Narcissus* ×*odorus* and *N.* ×*odorus* 'Flora Pleno', or cream-yellow 'Hawara'), and some blue Siberian squill, snowdrops, winter aconite, and pink-flowered 'Radar' Grecian windflower (*Anemone blanda* 'Radar').

In early spring—February where Edith gardens in Zone 7—the 'Georgia Blue' creeping veronica joins the show, quickly followed by the large, soft pink flowers of

'Enchantress' fairy wings. 'May Breeze' woodland phlox adds fragrance to the spring garden.

The pale yellow spikes of 'Carolina Moonlight' false indigo light up the spring, as will the clematis, pinks, yarrow, vervain, and verbena. Fragrance comes from the large white flowers of 'Casa Blanca' lilies.

White purple coneflowers, verbena, phlox, anise hyssop, and 'Heavy Metal' switchgrass carry the seasonal show into late summer, when the 'Joe White' Joe-Pye weed explodes in clouds of fluffy white bloom, followed by the lemon-peel yellow flowers of the sunflowers, soft lavender and white asters, pink anemones, and cream-flowered patrinia.

After frost, leave the beautiful skeletons of the Formosa lilies, 'Heavy Metal' switchgrass, and sedum. Leave up the coneflowers to provide a fall feast for visiting finches.

In Another Place

If you want a smaller garden, you could plant just the terrace garden with the two half-moons, or grow either half-moon bed by itself in a shady area. If your yard is sunny, you could plant the full-moon portion of the garden as an island bed. If you love the Magical Moonlit Garden so much that you'd like to carry the theme even farther, you can repeat the half-moon crescent

SCENTS AND SENSIBILITY

Fragrance is one of the most elusive qualities of any plant. Some fragrances, such as those of lavender or roses, are almost universally loved. But in other cases, what smells delightful to one gardener is enough to send others reeling in the opposite direction. (Marigolds and chrysanthemums tend to be two of those "love-'em-or-hate-'em" plants.) Our reactions to certain odors are based not simply on the chemicals involved but also on our memories and associations with those scents. So it's particularly important that the plants you choose for your garden should offer fragrances that you personally find appealing.

If possible, smell a fragrant plant before you buy it. You may find that the scent that your friend raves about is undetectable to your nose—or the narcissi and lilies she loves smell so overpowering they give you a headache.

You can smell some plants from hundreds of feet away, while others require you to get up close before you notice any fragrance. Many herbs, such as thyme, sage, and lemon balm, release their fragrant oils only when you rub or crush the leaves. When you are deciding which fragrant plants to grow, consider a mixture of plants with these different qualities—some strong, some subtle—so you're not overwhelmed by several powerful fragrances competing for attention.

beds elsewhere on your property to enhance your landscape.

Elements of the garden can also be changed to suit your site and taste. For example, if the tall tripod trellis seems like too much work or doesn't suit your aesthetic, you can plant another clump of 'Lemon Queen' sunflower to grow in its place.

If you garden in a cold-climate area (north of USDA Plant Hardiness Zone 7), 'Norman Beale's Blue Mist' verbena's light blue color could be replaced by Persian catmint (*Nepeta mussinii*), and you could substitute another 'Carolina Moonlight' false indigo or white wild indigo (*Baptisia alba*) for the spurge. In place of the Formosa lilies, you could use the gold band lily (*Lilium aurantium*), though it will not provide the same magnificent winter structure and probably should be staked.

Expert Care Tips

Tomasini's crocus sets seed and will gradually spread throughout the garden, creating a lovely carpet of spring color. Brazilian vervain will self-sow, so even if the plants die each year (as they are likely to in Zone 6 and certainly will in Zones 5 and colder), new seedlings will emerge in spring. Don't cut verbenas back until spring; the foliage protects the crowns through winter.

Cut down yucca bloom stalks when the flowers fade. Leave the ornamental stalks of 'Heavy Metal' switchgrass to add interest to the late fall and winter garden, then cut them down at the end of February before new growth starts. Cut the Formosa lily stalks in March. Edith notes that they'll be beautiful indoors in dried bouquets even after standing outside through winter.

You could start the annual 'White Queen' cleome and moonvine from seed, but Edith recommends starting with plants, which are readily available. After the first year, the cleome will self-sow.

Cut the 'Walker's Low' catmint back after bloom and it will rebloom in summer and look better. 'Moonbeam' coreopsis will bloom from spring to frost if you divide it every year; give spares to friends or trade them at garden-club swaps.

Leave the tripod trellis and stainless steel gazing ball out all winter, adding interest to the garden. (If you use a silver glass gazing ball instead, bring it into a protected place for winter.) The water lily should survive the winter in the cauldron, but if leaving it out makes you nervous, lift it out (in its planting basket) and set it in a frost-free place such as a utility room for the winter, moistening the basket periodically.

A MAGICAL MOONLIT GARDEN

The romantic Moonlit Garden appeals to all the senses, inviting viewers to sit and watch the sun go down—and the moon come up. Flower colors were chosen to be especially showy after dark, and many of the blooms are fragrant, perfuming the night air. Below is a list of plants included in this design. For more information on the perennial plants in this garden, see "The Perennial Encyclopedia," beginning on page 265. (*Note:* The numbers in parentheses refer to the quantity of each plant used.)

PLANTS FOR THE MAGICAL MOONLIT GARDEN

1. 'Pamina' Japanese anemone (*Anemone ×hybrida* 'Pamina') (4 total)

2. Rough anise hyssop (*Agastache rugosum*) (2)
3. 'Valerie Finnis' artemisia (*Artemisia ludoviciana* 'Valerie Finnis') (2)
4. 'Chameleon' arum (*Arum* 'Chameleon')* (4)
5. Italian arum (*Arum italicum*)*
6. Tartarian aster (*Aster tartaricus*) (3)
7. 'Wildwood Purity' hardy begonia (*Begonia grandis* 'Wildwood Purity') (3)

8. Calamint (*Calamintha nepeta*) (3)
9. 'Walker's Low' Persian catmint (*Nepeta recemosa* 'Walker's Low') (5 total)
10. Solitary clematis (*Clematis integrifolia*) (1)
11. Curlyheads (*Clematis ochroleuca*) (1)
12. 'White Queen' cleome (*Cleome hasslerana* 'White Queen')* (3)

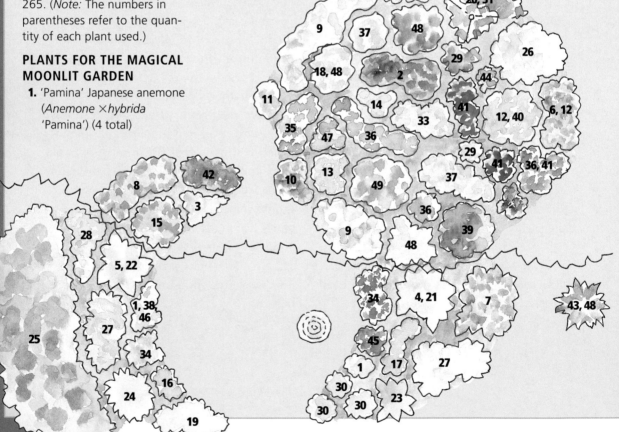

13. 'Moonbeam' coreopsis (*Coreopsis* 'Moonbeam') (3)

14. Citron daylily (*Hemerocallis citrina*) (1)

15. 'Carolina Moonlight' false indigo (*Baptisia* 'Carolina Moonlight') (1)

16. 'Enchantress' fairy wings (*Epimedium* 'Enchantress') (1)

17. 'Niveum' fairy wings (*Epimedium Youngianum* 'Nivium') (2)

18. Butterfly gladiolus (*Gladiolus papilio*)* (6)

19. 'Aureola' golden hakone grass (*Hakonechloa macra* 'Aureola') (2)

20. 'John Clayton' honeysuckle (*Lonicera sempervirens* 'John Clayton') (1)

21. 'Big Daddy' hosta (*Hosta* 'Big Daddy') (1)

22. 'Big Mama' hosta (*Hosta* 'Big Mama') (1)

23. 'Blue Cadet' hosta (*Hosta* 'Blue Cadet') (3)

24. 'Hadspen Blue' hosta (*Hosta* 'Hadspen Blue') (3)

25. 'Preziosa' hydrangea (*Hydrangea* 'Preziosa') (5)

26. 'Joe White' Joe-Pye weed (*Eupatorium* 'Joe White') (1)

27. Lenten rose (*Helleborus* ×*hybridus*) (7 total)

28. 'Casa Blanca' lily (*Lilium* 'Casa Blanca') (3)

29. Formosa lily (*Lilium formosanum*) (3)

30. 'Monroe White' lilyturf (*Liriope* muscari 'Monroe White') (3 total)

31. Moonvine (*Ipomoea alba*) (1)

32. Patrinia (*Patrinia villosa*) (2)

33. 'Franz Schubert' garden phlox (*Phlox paniculata* 'Franz Schubert') (3)

34. 'May Breeze' woodland phlox (*Phlox divaricata* 'May Breeze') (2)

35. 'Island White' pinks (*Dianthus* 'Island White') (5)

36. White-flowered purple coneflower (*Echinacea purpurea* var. *alba*) (5 total)

37. 'Matrona' sedum (*Sedum* 'Matrona') (3 total)

38. Common snowdrop (*Galanthus nivalis*)* (12)

39. Mediterranean spurge (*Euphorbia characias* var. *characias*) (1)

40. 'Lemon Queen' sunflower (*Helianthus* 'Lemon Queen') (1)

41. 'Heavy Metal' switchgrass (*Panicum virgatum* 'Heavy Metal') (6 total)

42. 'Norman Beal's Blue Mist' verbena (*Verbena* 'Norman Beal's Blue Mist') (2)

43. 'Georgia Blue' creeping veronica (*Veronica peduncularis* 'Georgia Blue') (5)

44. Brazilian vervain (*Verbena bonariensis*) (2)

45. Showy wild ginger (*Asarum splendens*) (3)

46. Winter aconite (*Eranthis hyemalis*)* (12)

47. 'Moonshine' yarrow (*Achillea* 'Moonshine') (3)

48. 'Ivory' yucca (*Yucca flaccida* 'Ivory') (4 total)

49. Night-blooming water lily (*Nymphaea odora*) (1)

* underplanted

MEET THE DESIGNER

EDITH R. EDDLEMAN

Edith R. Eddleman designs residential, commercial, and public perennial gardens. For over 20 years, she has been the designer and curator of the perennial borders at the J. C. Raulston Arboretum at North Carolina State University. She's also a well-known lecturer on perennials and garden design.

A COLD-CLIMATE PERENNIAL GARDEN

As this striking garden proves, gardeners in cold-winter areas can have beds bursting with gorgeous perennials just like their mild-weather counterparts. The trade-off for lovely cool summers—and weather that favors such classic perennials as lupines, delphiniums, peonies, and Siberian irises—is a shorter growing season. But those few months of glorious color make cold-climate gardeners appreciate their perennials all the more.

This triangular bed has been designed to be planted in a corner of a sunny yard. It can face either southeast or southwest. Plants will live longer and grow better if the site is well drained.

Although designer Nancy McDonald rightly notes that the fashion is to plant everything in groups of three or five, she prefers to plant only one of everything. As she says, this gives great variety and excitement to a garden. To make the bed more cohesive, Nancy has echoed plant colors and forms. In general, she has used flowers in the blue-purple-pink continuum, with bits of white (like garlic chives) and soft yellow (hollyhocks, scabious) here and there for accent.

Nancy likes purple-leaved plants, so she anchored the bed with one outstanding foliage shrub, *Rosa glauca*, with its lovely purple-blue-green foliage, and echoed the purple color in the perennials. "Every shrub should have a pet clematis," Nancy says, and her choice for this rose is *Clematis ×durandii*, a 5-foot non-climbing vine whose flowers stand out in an intense blue glow against the purple foliage and starry pink single flowers of the rose. You may use a different clematis, but be sure it doesn't get so large that it overwhelms the rose.

Nancy prefers plants that look nice the whole growing season, with both lovely flowers and good foliage before and after bloom. (We agree!) *Rosa glauca* in the corner of the bed is one such plant, along with Siberian irises, peonies, sedums, geraniums, 'Hopley's Purple' ornamental oregano, calico asters, and Mediterranean sea holly, a spiny perennial with an appearance that's so outlandish Nancy describes it as "clearly from another planet." She has included many of her own favorites, including 'Red Royal' Siberian iris, which she describes as an incredible red-purple, the best of that color; and 'Midnight Reiter' meadow cranesbill, with purple foliage and lavender-blue flowers.

Add bulbs to this bed with a lavish hand. Nancy uses small daffodils ('Minnow', 'Tête à Tête', 'W. P. Milner', 'Sun Disc', etc.) near the front, so the ripening summer foliage is less obtrusive. Larger daffodils can go farther back, where the big perennials will hide the foliage as it dies back. She also loves 'White Splendor' Grecian windflower (*Anemone blanda* 'White Splendor'), grape hyacinth (*Muscari latifolium*), winter aconite (*Eranthis hyemalis*), reticulated iris (*Iris reticulata*), and snowdrops (*Galanthus*), but urges you to plant what *you* love. Nancy adds, "I'd love to plant lots of small tulips, but where I live, they're just expensive deer and chipmunk food."

The Garden in Bloom

Spring in this garden belongs to bulbs, with the bright colors of rock cress (*Aubrieta deltoidea*), the pure white of candytuft (*Iberis*), and the beginning of the long Johnny-jump-up and violet (*Viola*) season. As spring warms to summer, the garden comes into its own. Siberian iris come into bloom: red-purple 'Red Royal', pale blue 'Harbor Mist', dark blue 'Dewful', blended dark and pale blue 'Super Ego', and aptly named 'Summer Sky' Siberian iris, an old but excellent cultivar with a profusion of small, delicate, sky blue flowers with white and gold. They make perfect foils for the sturdy classic double soft pink 'Sarah Bernhardt' and intense purplish pink

'Richard Carvel' Chinese peonies; both peonies are very floriferous. Late spring also brings the showy geraniums into bloom, with columbines, martagon lilies, lupines, and peach-leaved bellflower (*Campanula persicifolia*) close behind. True summer begins as the peonies' flowering ends and the soft yellow-flowered hollyhocks begin blooming.

True summer bloomers include the brilliant blue-flowered clematis, the daylilies ('Little Rainbow', named for its blooms of soft yellow, pink, and apricot; and the soft yellow 'Butterpat', both of which reliably bloom after cold nights), golden mar-guerite, white-flowered mullein with its imposing flower spikes, common lavender, dark blue 'Blue Peter' spike speedwell, Shasta daisy, white-flowered red valerian, and many others. In late summer the 'David' garden phlox starts blooming, with 'Lemon Queen' sunflower, wood betony, 'Hopley's Purple' ornamental oregano, and the starry white blooms of garlic chives coming into their own.

In fall, the reliably cold-hardy, buff pink 'Mary Stoker' and soft pink, late-flowering 'Clara Curtis' hardy garden chrysanthemums steal the show. The green-and-cream-variegated foliage of 'Frosty Morn'

Evergreen Perennials: Myth or Reality?

As you plan your garden with winter interest in mind, you may be tempted to include a lot of perennials with evergreen foliage. After all, why not have some color, even if it's only green, all year long in the perennial garden? Well, depending on where you live, a winter garden based on "evergreen" perennials can be a delight or a disappointment.

A wide variety of perennials are commonly touted as evergreens, including fairy wings (*Epimedium*), bergenias, ajugas, European wild ginger (*Asarum europaeum*), pinks (*Dianthus*), rock cresses (*Arabis*), thrifts (*Armeria*), and thymes (*Thymus*). Whether these plants are worth adding to your winter garden depends a great deal on your climate.

In general, perennials growing in mild-winter areas tend to hold their leaves longer than those in climates with cold, dry winters. Winter winds can dry out the soil and sap water from plant leaves, causing the leaves to discolor and droop. Bergenias and fairy wings, for example, often get browned and tattered by mid-winter storms and end up looking unattractive until the new leaves emerge.

If you live in an area where even evergreen trees and shrubs look ratty by winter's end, don't count on evergreen perennials to keep your garden attractive all winter. But if you grow these plants anyway for their warm-season flowers and foliage, enjoy their green leaves as long as winter winds hold off, and try some of the other tricks discussed in "Winter Interest" on page 11 to carry the show in mid- to late winter.

and the purple-leaved 'Matrona' sedums really shine, with 'Lady in Black' calico aster adding its cloud of tiny daisies above purple foliage.

In Another Place

You can also plant the Cold-Climate Perennial Garden in the L of a house. It's critical that no large trees or other buildings shade the bed because the L itself will cast as much shade as these plants can stand.

To make the bed fit wider corners or odd spaces, plant perennials in groups of two or three rather than singly. You could also repeat the bed in another corner of the yard to unify the landscape—both front corners or both back corners.

When using this design, Nancy urges you to feel free to substitute other cultivars of the plants she lists if the colors please you better. For example, the 'Lady in Black' calico aster is an outstanding purple-leaved form, but if you prefer green-leaved plants, she recommends 'Coombe Fishacre' instead. She encourages you to choose your favorite colors for the Russell hybrid lupines. Nancy prefers her own old heirloom white garden phlox to the modern, mildew-resistant 'David'. But make sure you try some of Nancy's favorite combinations, such as the gorgeous pairing of the deep blue 'Dewful' Siberian iris against the deep, deep rose pink 'Richard Carvel' Chinese peony.

Expert Care Tips

All of the plants on this map do well in USDA Plant Hardiness Zone 4. (Nancy's own winter low temperatures are -30°F to -40°F!) Nancy points out that she has excellent snow cover when the temperatures are that low. She suspects that without the snow, many of these plants would not survive. Another critical factor in winter survival is drainage. Nancy's soil is very, very sandy loam—even after she adds huge amounts of compost, she has good drainage. Plants that are native to hot, dry places, such as lavender and Mediterranean sea holly, have grown well (if slowly) in Nancy's garden for 10 years or more, but she doubts they would make it in a Zone 4 garden with clay soil and little snow. She cautions that only the common lavender listed is reliably hardy, so resist the temptation to plant other species unless you're growing them as annuals.

This garden's maintenance is straightforward. Perennials have been chosen for low maintenance—the yellow hollyhock's foliage is rust-resistant, and 'David' garden phlox resists the mildew that makes so many cultivars of this species unsightly just as they're coming into bloom. Deadhead the golden marguerite religiously for continued bloom. If you remember to deadhead the red valerian and Shasta daisy, you'll get repeat bloom!

A COLD-CLIMATE PERENNIAL GARDEN

An exception to the rule, this garden features single specimen perennials unified by a repeating color scheme rather than repeated plants. Nancy has left spaces in her design that you can fill in with a selection of perennials. To fill in the back and center of the bed, among the taller perennials, choose any combination of martagon lily (*Lilium martagon*), especially the lovely 'Album'; peach-leaved bellflower (*Campanula persicifolia*); purple toadflax (*Linaria purpurea*) in white, soft pink, or lavender; garlic chives (*Allium tuberosum*); and columbines (*Aquilegia* cultivars)—Nancy suggests 'Black Barlow' and 'Ruby Port' toward the front and the soft yellow 'Yellow Queen' farther back.

Fill in the spaces along the front of the bed with any combination you like of rock cress (*Aubrieta deltoidea*); maiden pinks (*Dianthus deltoides*), which bloom in white through deep, deep pink (Nancy's favorite is white with a deep pink eye); Johnny-jump-ups (*Viola ×tricolor*) and horned violets (*Viola cornuta*), especially 'Lorna Cawthorne', which blooms for months without deadheading; perennial candytuft (*Iberis sempervirens*); and 'Blue Sapphire' blue flax

(*Linum perenne* 'Blue Sapphire'). And don't forget to underplant the entire bed with bulbs!

Below is a list of plants used in this design. For more information on these perennial plants, see "The Perennial Encyclopedia," beginning on page 265. (*Note:* Nancy uses only one of each plant, except where noted.)

PLANTS FOR THE COLD-CLIMATE GARDEN

1. 'Lady in Black' calico aster (*Aster lateriflorus* 'Lady in Black')
2. 'Grandiflora' or 'Alba' wood betony (*Stachys officinalis* 'Grandiflora' or 'Alba')
3. 'Clara Curtis' hardy garden chrysanthemum (*C. zawadskii* var. *latilobum* 'Clara Curtis')
4. 'Mary Stoker' hardy garden chrysanthemum (*C. zawadskii* var. *latilobum* 'Mary Stoker')
5. *Clematis ×durandii*
6. Solitary clematis (*Clematis integrifolia*)
7. 'Midnight Reiter' meadow cranesbill (*Geranium pratense* 'Midnight Reiter')
8. 'Mayflower' wood cranesbill (*Geranium sylvaticum* 'Mayflower')
9. 'Album' or 'Fascination' Culver's root (*Veronicastrum virginicum* 'Album' or 'Fascination')

10. 'Becky' Shasta daisy (*Leucanthemum maximum* 'Becky')
11. 'Butterpat' daylily (*Hemerocallis* 'Butterpat')
12. 'Little Rainbow' daylily (*Hemerocallis* 'Little Rainbow')
13. Showy geranium (*Geranium ×magnificum*)
14. 'Veitch's Blue' globe thistle (*Echinops ritro* 'Veitch's Blue')
15. Yellow hollyhock (*Alcea rugosa*)
16. 'Dewful' Siberian iris (*Iris sibirica* 'Dewful')
17. 'Harbor Mist' Siberian iris (*Iris sibirica* 'Harbor Mist')
18. 'Red Royal' Siberian iris (*Iris sibirica* 'Red Royal')
19. 'Summer Sky' Siberian iris (*Iris sibirica* 'Summer Sky')
20. 'Super Ego' Siberian iris (*Iris sibirica* 'Super Ego')
21. 'Hidcote' or 'Munstead' common lavender (*Lavandula angustifolia* 'Hidcote' or 'Munstead')
22. Russell hybrids lupines (*Lupinus* Russell hybrids)
23. 'Wargrave' or 'Moonlight' golden marguerite (*Anthemis tinctoria* 'Wargrave' or 'Moonlight')
24. 'Album' nettle-leaved mullein (*Verbascum chaixii* 'Album')

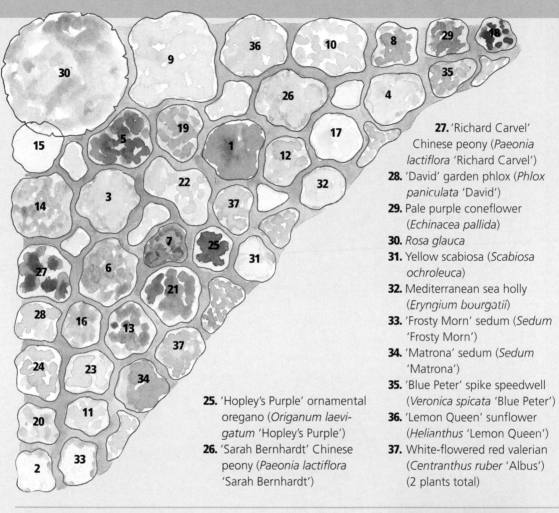

27. 'Richard Carvel' Chinese peony (*Paeonia lactiflora* 'Richard Carvel')
28. 'David' garden phlox (*Phlox paniculata* 'David')
29. Pale purple coneflower (*Echinacea pallida*)
30. *Rosa glauca*
31. Yellow scabiosa (*Scabiosa ochroleuca*)
32. Mediterranean sea holly (*Eryngium bourgatii*)
33. 'Frosty Morn' sedum (*Sedum* 'Frosty Morn')
34. 'Matrona' sedum (*Sedum* 'Matrona')
35. 'Blue Peter' spike speedwell (*Veronica spicata* 'Blue Peter')
36. 'Lemon Queen' sunflower (*Helianthus* 'Lemon Queen')
37. White-flowered red valerian (*Centranthus ruber* 'Albus') (2 plants total)

25. 'Hopley's Purple' ornamental oregano (*Origanum laevigatum* 'Hopley's Purple')
26. 'Sarah Bernhardt' Chinese peony (*Paeonia lactiflora* 'Sarah Bernhardt')

MEET THE DESIGNER
NANCY McDONALD

Nancy McDonald is a freelance writer and editor who lives and gardens in Michigan's Upper Peninsula. She's also an EMT with the local ambulance corps and a deputy sheriff for Search and Rescue.

A DROUGHT-TOLERANT GARDEN

If you garden where rainfall is sparse or watering is restricted during dry summers, this colorful garden is for you. Designer Lauren Springer chose perennials and bulbs that can stand up to full sun and drought and still bloom beautifully year after year.

Lauren's garden is a perfect example of a symmetrical bed: Its two sides almost perfectly mirror each other. This allows her to use a rich palette of plants and still create a cohesive design. The soft colors that predominate in the design and the repeating colors of the perennials further unify the bed.

The Garden in Bloom

The garden begins to awaken in early spring with graceful perennial 'Lady Jane' and 'Cynthia' tulips, along with blue grape hyacinths that emerge amid the chartreuse flowers of cushion spurge. The earliest perennials include white wall rock cress next to purple pasque flower.

Late spring and early summer are a riot of bloom, with 'Bath's Pink' pinks, cerise red valerian, blue-and-yellow 'Edith Wolford' bearded iris, and pale yellow 'Moonshine' yarrow.

High summer heat brings on the bigger perennials, including pale pink shrub mallow, soft yellow hollyhock, 'Kelwayi' golden marguerite, orange butterfly weed, and gold-and-red blanket flower.

As summer meets fall, purple poppy mallow and yellow Ozark sundrops are still going strong. They are now joined by hazy blue Russian sage and fragrant peach-flowered rock anise hyssop.

The season draws to a close as the lavender chalices of fall-flowering autumn crocus open. Good foliage enhances the floral display, with striped 'Golden Sword' Adam's needle, furry 'Silver Carpet' lamb's ear, and the blue foliage of 'Bath's Pinks' pinks as stars among the supporting players.

In Another Place

Because this garden design is so symmetrical, it's easy to adapt to smaller and larger spaces: Simply divide the design and plant half of it.

The plants in the Drought-Tolerant Garden are all hardy and adaptable to much of the United States, north into USDA Plant Hardiness Zone 5 (most into Zone 4), extending south to Zone 8. However, the plant selection is not generally well suited to the humid parts of the South—Florida, the Gulf States, or Texas.

Expert Care Tips

None of the plants in this design require more than 20 inches of moisture per year. In the sunniest, hottest climates, the garden can be planted in an east-facing exposure with morning sun and afternoon shade. Otherwise, full sun with a southern exposure is best.

The bed is 10 feet wide, which makes getting to the plants at the back challenging. Because it's designed for low maintenance, upkeep can be limited to spring cleanup and a couple of deadheading sessions a year.

FILLING IN

Often, a perennial garden can look rather bare when it's newly planted—all those dots of plants floating in a sea of soil. This makes it tempting to plant too close, with disastrous results as the plants crowd each other out and need to be moved a few years down the road. To avoid this time- and labor-intensive pitfall and still make your garden look lush quickly, fill in around your new perennials with annuals for the first season or two until the more permanent plants fill in.

Rather than using bedding annuals, which she feels retard the growth of young perennials, designer Lauren Springer recommends some favorite annuals that you can grow from seed. They'll add a lot of color and will self-sow in subsequent years. Like the perennials in her garden design, Lauren's choices are all drought-tolerant. She recommends thinning the annual seedlings to leave plenty of space for your new perennials— even if the garden does look a little sparse as a result—rather than going for instant gratification and stunted progress.

For first-season color, try these annuals:

Desert bluebell (*Phacelia campanularia*)
Annual catchfly (*Silene americana*)
Oriental larkspur (*Consolida ambigua*)
Love-in-a-mist (*Nigella damascena*)
Corsican pansy (*Viola corsica*)
California poppy (*Eschscholzia californica*)

A DROUGHT-TOLERANT GARDEN

If you want beauty, symmetry, and low maintenance, plant this easy-care perennial garden. Below is a list of plants included in this design. For more information on the perennial plants in this garden, see "The Perennial Encyclopedia," beginning on page 265. (*Note:* The numbers in parentheses refer to the quantity of each plant used.)

PLANTS FOR THE DROUGHT-TOLERANT GARDEN

1. 'Golden Sword' Adam's needle (*Yucca filamentosa* 'Golden Sword') (6 plants total)
2. Rock anise hyssop (*Agastache rupestris*) (2 total)
3. 'Citrina' basket-of-gold (*Aurinia saxatilis* 'Citrina') (2 total)
4. Blanket flower (*Gaillardia* ×*grandiflora*) (2 total)
5. Butterfly weed (*Asclepias tuberosa*) (3)
6. 'Walker's Low' blue catmint (*Nepeta* ×*faassenii* 'Walker's Low') (2 total)
7. Autumn crocus (*Crocus speciosus*) (72 total)
8. White gaura (*Gaura lindheimeri*) (6 total)
9. Common grape hyacinth (*Muscari botryoides*) (48 total)
10. Yellow hollyhock (*Alcea rugosa*) (3 total)
11. 'Edith Wolford' bearded iris (*Iris germanica* pale blue hybrid 'Edith Wolford') (23 total)

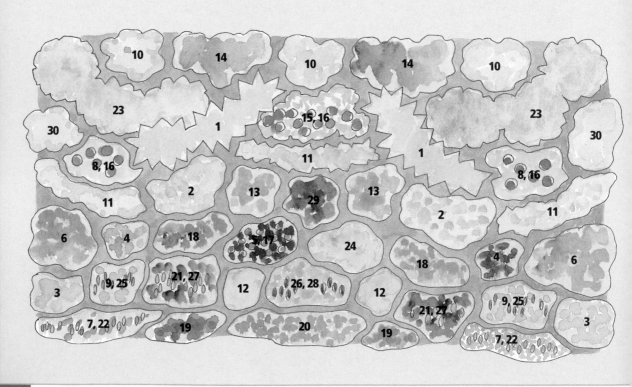

12. 'Silver Carpet' lamb's ear (*Stachys byzantina* 'Silver Carpet') (2 total)

13. 'Munstead' common lavender (*Lavandula angustifolia* 'Munstead') (2 total)

14. Shrub mallow (*Lavatera thuringiaca*) (2 total)

15. 'Kelwayi' golden marguerite (*Anthemis tinctoria* 'Kelwayi') (3)

16. Giant onion (*Allium giganteum*) (24 total)

17. Persian onion (*Allium aflatunense*) (12)

18. Oregano (*Origanum laevigatum*) (6 total)

19. Pasque flower (*Pulsatilla vulgaris*) (4 total)

20. 'Bath's Pink' pinks (*Dianthus* 'Bath's Pink') (5)

21. Purple poppy mallow (*Callirhoe involucrata*) (2 total)

22. Wall rock cress (*Arabis caucasica*) (6 total)

23. Hybrid Russian sage (*Perovskia* ×*hybrida*) (6 total)

24. Sea lavender (*Limonium latifolium*) (1)

25. Cushion spurge (*Euphorbia polychroma*) (4 total)

26. Ozark sundrops (*Oenothera macrocarpa*) (1)

27. 'Lady Jane' lady tulip (*Tulipa clusiana* 'Lady Jane') (72 total)

28. 'Cynthia' species tulip (*Tulipa clusiana* var. *chrysantha* 'Cynthia') (36)

29. Red valerian (*Centranthus ruber*) (1)

30. 'Moonshine' yarrow (*Achillea* 'Moonshine') (2 total)

MEET THE DESIGNER

Lauren Springer

Lauren Springer, an award-winning garden writer and photographer, is a contributing editor for *Horticulture* magazine and a popular speaker. Her private gardens have been featured on television and in many publications, including the *New York Times.* She designed the Watersmart and Romantic Gardens at the Denver Botanic Gardens and is author of *The Undaunted Garden.*

A PERENNIAL GARDEN ROOM

If you fantasize about creating a garden room—a private, enclosed paradise where everyday distractions disappear and you can relax in the serene company of beautiful blooms—designer Ann Lovejoy's luxuriant garden can make your dreams come true. This garden is also perfectly suited to a small yard, such as a townhouse or row house typically has: You can convert the entire yard into a private garden. No one seeing the formally trimmed bordering hedges would guess at the colorful show going on inside.

The large, stately double border offers complementary plantings in a sophisticated colorist's palette of smoky purples, strong blues, and deep reds, lightened with silvery grays, chalky yellows, and chartreuse. These beds will peak in sequential bursts of bloom from May through September or October, presenting an ongoing concert of flowers and foliage.

Each impressive bed is 40 by 20 feet, backed with an 8-foot-tall clipped privet hedge and fronted with lawn, with an inset edge paved with 1-by-2-foot stone slabs. In hot-summer regions, this garden could be placed where it received half a day of full sun. In cooler summer areas, a full day of sunlight is ideal.

Though these borders have been designed with a classic or formal look, the perennials Ann has chosen are not the usual garden stalwarts. You'll find no peonies, irises, hardy geraniums, delphiniums, foxgloves, lupines, pinks, mums, or even hellebores here. The plant partnerships in this garden emphasize the architectural qualities of the main performers, all of which hold their own from early summer into fall. Ann has chosen earlier bloomers in part for good habit, handsome foliage, and attractive seedheads, which contribute to the border's good looks through fall. Quite a few of these perennials also take on lovely fall color. Ann has kept the gardener's busy schedule in mind, choosing sturdy plants that don't need staking or excessive amounts of fertilizer and water.

Group the plants in these beds in soft triangles or wandering ribbons rather than in straight lines. Plant groundcovers so they weave into the beds and spill over onto the stone pavers for a more natural, relaxed look.

The Garden in Bloom

Because this garden's floral display really begins in late spring, much of the early-season interest is provided by the wealth of colorful foliage, which also presents a season-long feast of contrasting form and texture. The stiff gold-striped swords of the Adam's needle and spiny leaves of the sea holly; the ferny blue foliage of the rue and dusty meadow rue; the steel blue, upright stems of the oat grass and blue wild rye; the purple-leaved sedums, 'Lady in Black' calico aster, 'Bishop of Llandaff' dahlia, purple-leaved culinary sage, 'Chocolate'

white snakeroot, and 'Black Negligee' cohosh; the chartreuse foliage of the tansy and feverfew; the large copper leaves of the canna; the burgundy foliage of the 'Black Dragon' lilies and 'Crimson Butterflies' white gaura; the huge, bright red leaves of 'Red Ace' rhubarb; and the silver-grays of the lavender cotton and wormwood create an ongoing backdrop to the changing bloom display.

Bloom begins with the stout burgundy bloom spikes of 'Red Ace' rhubarb, bicolor flowers of 'Purple Smoke' false indigo, rich 'Patty's Plum' oriental poppy, soft blue Arkansas blue star, 'Cherry Bells' bellflower, and warm purple ornamental onion heads. The starry flowers of the blue star are echoed in the star-studded balls of the ornamental onions.

As spring yields to summer, the ruby red daisy flowers of 'Limerock Ruby' coreopsis, burgundy spikes of narrow-leaved gas plant, stately warm yellow wands of foxtail lily, blues of the catmints, and deep purple penstemon enrich the display.

At summer's peak, the garden is in its glory, with soft yellow 'Norwich Canary' crocosmia, lavender and soft purple coneflowers with showy orange centers, pale yellow 'Moonshine' yarrow, 'Hopley's Purple' ornamental oregano, 'Pale Yellow' Antwerp hollyhock, burgundy canna flowers, brilliant red balls of 'Bishop of Llandaff' dahlia, silver-blue spiny heads of 'Blue Ribbon' sea holly, the huge fragrant purple-and-white trumpets of 'Black

Dragon' lily, descriptively named 'Crimson Butterflies' white gaura, 'Burgundy' blanket flower, cream flower spikes of Adam's needle, airy mauve blooms of Brazilian vervain, and the chalk yellow cottonball flowers of dusty meadow rue. The seedheads of the ornamental onions and false indigos enrich the display.

As summer moves toward fall, the sedums come into bloom with heads of rose-pink, rose, and plum. The massive cream bloom clusters of the Joe-Pye weed, the copper-red daisies of 'Moerheim Beauty' sneezeweed, and the arching clear yellow sprays of 'Fireworks' rough-stemmed goldenrod command attention. The white-and-yellow button flowers of the tansy, feverfew, and lavender cotton contrast with their chartreuse and gray foliage, and the asters add their pink and purple daisies to the display.

Fall brings with it the majestic white spires of 'Black Negligee' cohosh and the soft pink daisy clouds of 'Pink Beauty' boltonia. The feathery plumes of Arkansas blue star foliage turn a glorious yellow-orange, and the privet foliage flushes a beautiful yellow-purple. As the

DEPENDABLE PERENNIALS THAT DETER DEER

While many people associate deer with the beauty and grace of natural woods and fields, gardeners in deer country—in both the East and West—have a much less benign view of these creatures. Hungry deer can decimate a planting overnight, reducing a carefully planned perennial garden to a shambles of trampled, leafless stems. If you live in an area where deer are a problem, consider trying some deer-resistant plants to discourage deer from feeding in your beds and borders.

Like insect-resistant plants, deer-resistant perennials are a good place to start in a pest-control program. If the deer (or insects) don't like the taste of your plants, they'll search elsewhere for more palatable fare and spare your plantings. If other food is scarce, of course, the deer might overcome their aversions and snack on your perennial sunflowers, but at least the animals are less likely to completely devour these distasteful (to them, not to gardeners!) plants. Some perennials that deer-plagued gardeners have reported success with include the following:

Old-fashioned bleeding heart (Dicentra spectabilis)
Columbines (Aquilegia)
Daffodils (Narcissus)
Fairy wings (Epimedium)
False spireas (Astilbe)
Foxgloves (Digitalis)
Hellebores (Helleborus)
Irises (Iris)
Lavenders (Lavandula)
Lungworts (Pulmonaria)
Ornamental onions (Allium)
Large periwinkle (Vinca major)
Sunflowers (Helianthus)
Yuccas (Yucca)

flower show fades to winter, the rich mix of foliage form and color continues to create garden interest until snow blankets the beds.

In Another Place

A garden of this size is not for the faint of heart or shallow of pocketbook. You might choose to plant a single border in a corner of the yard. If you want to reduce the size of the beds, use single plants rather than multiples, especially of the larger background perennials. If you don't want the enclosure and privacy provided by the privet hedge, back the beds in front of a fence, or plant them without a backdrop. (Of course, you could also plant them in front of a stone or brick wall or an evergreen hedge, all of which will tend to give them a more formal look.) You can also extend the size of the lawn between the beds from its present size (roughly 8 feet wide) to whatever size seems comfortable for you.

Expert Care Tips

Ann recommends getting your perennials off to a vigorous start by purchasing plants in 1-gallon pots. The exceptions are the bulbs—the ornamental onions, alliums, and lilies—and a few fast-growing perennials: Arkansas blue star, 'Silver Brocade' beach wormwood, 'Lady in Black' calico aster,

'Little Titch' catmint, 'Hopley's Purple' ornamental oregano, 'Vera Jameson' sedum, 'Aureum' feverfew, and Brazilian vervain. Purchase the bulbs dry, and the perennials in 4-inch pots. Tender perennials like the canna and 'Bishop of Llandaff' dahlia should be dug each year in cold climates and brought indoors for winter, then replanted when the soil has warmed in late spring.

For a garden this size, maintenance can be a nightmare unless you plan carefully in advance. Ann has done part of the work for you by focusing on perennials that don't need staking or huge amounts of water and fertilizer. To make maintenance manageable, a weed-suppressing mulch is a must. A thick layer of shredded leaves mixed with garden or mushroom compost creates an attractive, natural backdrop for the perennials, retains moisture, and adds just the right amount of balanced organic fertilizer as it breaks down. Replenish the mulch each fall after you clean up the garden and shred your fallen leaves (which will itself provide plenty of raw material for next year's compost!), or in spring before new growth begins.

This garden is also a perfect candidate for a drip irrigation system. With some drip systems, you can add liquid fertilizers such as liquid seaweed (kelp) to the water. (See Chapter 8, "Perennial Gardening Basics" for more on composting, fertilizing, and drip irrigation.)

A PERENNIAL GARDEN ROOM

This garden, with its wide grass path and double borders, invites you to stroll through and admire the luscious color and ever-changing show. Below is a list of plants included in this design. For more information on the perennial plants in this garden, see "The Perennial Encyclopedia" beginning on page 265. (*Note:* The numbers in parentheses refer to the quantity of each plant used.)

PLANTS FOR A PERENNIAL GARDEN ROOM

1. 'Golden Sword' Adam's needle (*Yucca filamentosa* 'Golden Sword') (3 plants)
2. 'Firebird' agastache (*Agastache* 'Firebird') (3)
3. Allium (*Allium schubertii*) (25 total)
4. Korean angelica (*Angelica gigas*) (3)
5. Rock anise hyssop (*Agastache rupestris*) (3)
6. 'Lady in Black' calico aster (*Aster lateriflorus* 'Lady in Black') (3)
7. Frikart's aster (*Aster ×frikartii*) (3)
8. 'Cherry Bells' bellflower (*Campanula* 'Cherry Bells') (6 total)
9. Arkansas blue star (*Amsonia hubrechtii*) (3)
10. 'Pink Beauty' boltonia (*Boltonia asteroides* 'Pink Beauty') (6 total)
11. Canna (*Canna australis*) (3)
12. 'Pink Elf' cape fuchsia (*Phygelius* 'Pink Elf') (1)
13. 'Little Titch' catmint (*Nepeta* 'Little Titch') (5)
14. 'Souvenir d'Andre Chaudron' Siberian catmint (*Nepeta siberica* 'Souvenir d'Andre Chaudron') (3)
15. 'Mary Stoker' chrysanthemum (Chrysanthemum 'Mary Stoker') (3)
16. 'Black Negligee' cohosh (*Cimicifuga* 'Black Negligee') (6 total)

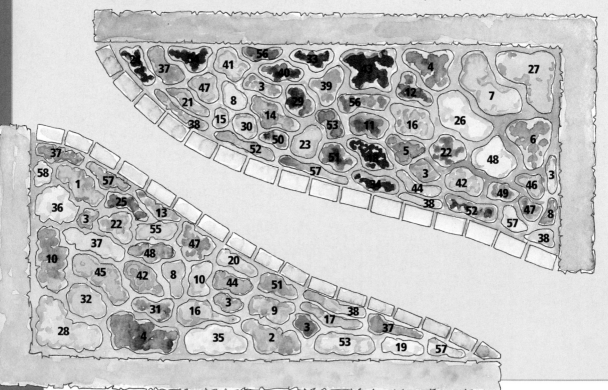

17. Tennessee coneflower (*Echinacea tennesseensis*) (5)

18. 'Limerock Ruby' coreopsis (*Coreopsis* 'Limerock Ruby') (3)

19. 'Norwich Canary' crocosmia (*Crocosmia* 'Norwich Canary') (5)

20. 'Solfaterre' crocosmia (*Crocosmia* 'Solfaterre') (5)

21. 'Bishop of Llandaff' dahlia (*Dahlia* 'Bishop of Llandaff') (5)

22. 'Purple Smoke' false indigo (*Baptisia* 'Purple Smoke') (6 total)

23. 'Aureum' feverfew (*Tanacetum parthenium* 'Aureum') (3)

24. Narrow-leaved gas plant (*Dictamnus angustifolius*) (5)

25. 'Crimson Butterflies' white gaura (*Gaura lindheimeri* 'Crimson Butterflies') (3)

26. 'Fireworks' rough-stemmed goldenrod (*Solidago rugosa* 'Fireworks') (3)

27. 'Gateway' Joe-Pye weed (*Eupatorium* 'Gateway') (3)

28. Giant kale (*Crambe cordifolia*) (3)

29. 'Red Dragon' knotweed (*Persicaria* 'Red Dragon') (3)

30. 'Margery Fish' lavender cotton (*Santolina* 'Margery Fish') (1)

31. 'Black Dragon' lily (*Lilium* 'Black Dragon') (5)

32. Foxtail lily (*Eremurus bungei*) (5)

33. 'Red Rum' tree mallow (*Lavatera* 'Red Rum') (1)

34. 'Ruby Wedding' masterwort (*Astrantia* 'Ruby Wedding') (3)

35. 'Glauca' dusty meadow rue (*Thalictrum flavum* 'Glauca') (3)

36. Mullein (*Verbascum roripifolium*) (3)

37. Blue oat grass (*Helictotrichon sempervirens*) (6 total)

38. 'Hopley's Purple' ornamental oregano (*Origanum* 'Hopley's Purple') (24 total)

39. 'Patty's Plum' oriental poppy (*Papaver orientale* 'Patty's Plum') (3)

40. 'Raven' penstemon (*Penstemon* 'Raven') (3)

41. 'Winchester Fanfare' phygelius (Phygelius 'Winchester Fanfare') (1)

42. 'Kim's Knee-High' purple coneflower (*Echinacea* 'Kim's Knee-High') (3)

43. 'Red Ace' rhubarb (*Rheum* 'Red Ace') (1)

44. 'Blue Beauty' rue (*Ruta graveolens* 'Blue Beauty') (3)

45. Russian sage (*Perovskia atriplicifolia*) (5)

46. Blue wild rye (*Elymus magellanicus*) (3)

47. 'Purpureum' culinary sage (*Salvia officinalis* 'Purpureum') (2)

48. 'Valerie Finnis' white sage (*Artemisia ludoviciana* 'Valerie Finnis') (6 total)

49. 'Blue Ribbon' sea holly (*Eryngium* 'Blue Ribbon') (3)

50. 'Matrona' sedum (*Sedum* 'Matrona') (3)

51. 'Purple Emperor' sedum (*Sedum* 'Purple Emperor') (6 total)

52. 'Vera Jameson' sedum (*Sedum* 'Vera Jameson') (7)

53. 'Chocolate' white snakeroot (*Eupatorium rugosum* 'Chocolate') (6 total)

54. 'Moerheim Beauty' sneezeweed (*Helenium* 'Moerheim Beauty') (8)

55. 'Isla Gold' tansy (*Tanacetum vulgare* 'Isla Gold') (3)

56. Brazilian vervain (*Verbena bonariensis*) (7)

57. 'Silver Brocade' beach wormwood (*Artemisia stelleriana* 'Silver Brocade') (25 total)

58. 'Moonshine' yarrow (*Achillea* 'Moonshine') (3)

MEET THE DESIGNER

Ann Lovejoy

Ann Lovejoy ranks among the country's leading garden experts and has been featured on National Public Radio and national public television. She has written more than 19 books and is a regular garden and food columnist for the *Seattle Post-Intelligencer.*

5

FROM GARDEN DESIGN TO GARDEN BED

A garden develops in three stages: design, installation, and growth. The first four chapters of this book show you how to create a garden on paper, this chapter tells you how to get the garden in the ground, and Chapter 6, "Growing with the Design," tells you what can happen as your perennials (or you, the gardener) change and grow. Though each of the stages is enjoyable, this one, making your dream garden a reality, is the most exciting. Let's get started!

PREPARING THE BED

The first step toward in-ground gardening is making your bed (or island, or border). If you're digging a garden in what is now lawn, first outline the bed with a garden hose, ground limestone, or flour. With an edging tool or a sharp spade, cut around the outline of the bed. Use the spade to cut strips of sod and roll them up for reuse or composting.

When you've removed the sod from the bed area, you're ready to work the soil.

Good soil is humus-rich and well-drained but moisture-retentive. If your grass is growing well without fertilizer and the ground drains quickly, your soil is probably average to good. Work the soil from one edge of the bed to the other with a garden fork or a shovel, breaking up clods and removing rocks, large roots, and other debris. Add soil amendments like compost and aged manure, and work it again to a fork's (or shovel's) depth. Rake the surface smooth. Then cover the bed with a light mulch like shredded leaves to prevent erosion until your plants arrive.

If your soil is heavy clay, it needs more intensive care. Making a raised bed and double-digging are two ways to improve the structure and drainage of clay soils. Adding ample organic matter will increase the humus content. If your soil is extremely sandy, treat it like average soil, but add lots of organic matter and mulch it heavily.

The time you spend improving your soil is the most important time you'll ever spend in the garden, and it will repay you over and over as your garden grows. You'll find out all about digging, double-digging, soil types, organic matter, and soil amendments in Chapter 8, "Perennial Gardening Basics."

BUYING PERENNIALS

After you've dug your garden and prepared the soil, the next step is getting your plants.

The most common way to acquire perennials is to buy them, though we discuss money-saving alternatives like seed-starting and plant swaps in "Seeds and Seedlings" on page 136, and "Plant Exchanges and Societies" on page 137.

You can buy perennials at a local nursery or garden center, where you pick out each plant yourself, load them in the car, and take them home for same-day planting. Or you can order perennials through the mail from nursery catalogs. Both ways have advantages, so most gardeners end up buying some of their plants locally and some by mail order.

Plants by Mail

There are two big advantages to mail-order shopping: convenience and selection. When you order through the mail, perennials are delivered right to your door. And mail-order nurseries offer a much larger selection than most garden centers are able to because the mail-order companies usually have large growing fields.

If you're looking for an unusual species or a particular cultivar, you'll often have the best luck by turning to a catalog. It's fun to compare catalogs, too. Many provide valuable growing tips, information on good plant combinations, entertaining plant anecdotes, and design suggestions, as well as clear descriptions and color photos of the perennials.

The drawback of mail ordering is that you can't see the plants you're buying until

How to Be a Smart Mail-Order Shopper

Mail-order shopping is a convenient way to order a large selection of perennials, but it pays to be cautious: Some mail-order nurseries are better than others. (See "Resources" on page 686 for some of our favorites.) Here's how to get the most from mail-order shopping.

- Order early for the best plant selection.
- Specify a desired shipping time so plants will arrive when you want them.
- When plants arrive, get out your plant journal and write down when you received them, from whom, and what condition they arrived in. This information will come in handy when you choose nurseries to order from the next time.
- Evaluate containerized mail-order plants just as if you were looking them over at the garden center. Don't expect perfect foliage, though—shipping often leads to broken or bruised leaves. If the plants are healthy, they'll recover quickly. Diseased foliage and insects are more serious matters; return plants that show signs of infection or infestation.
- Examine bareroot plants (the ones shipped without soil around the roots; the bare roots are usually wrapped in damp newspaper or excelsior and plastic) for pests and diseases, too. Check the roots, crowns, and stems for pests or signs of pest damage.
- If the roots of your bareroot plants are sparse or in poor condition, return the plants.
- Rewrap bareroot plants after you've inspected them, and store them in a cool place until you are ready to plant them in your garden.
- Before planting, soak the roots of bareroot plants in water for at least 1 hour.
- If you receive substandard or damaged plants and want a refund or replacement plant, you should contact the nursery immediately.
- Avoid hype and exaggerated claims. If it sounds too good to be true, it usually is. However, reputable nurseries sometimes offer collections of perennials that are excellent buys (but not *unbelievable* buys).

---

they arrive. The best way to avoid disappointment is to start with a small order from each nursery you want to try. Some nurseries ship plants in containers, some ship bareroot, and others use both techniques. Specify shipping times when ordering by mail to make sure your plants arrive when you can actually plant them. A nursery in another part of the country may not know when planting conditions will be right in your area.

At the Nursery or Garden Center

The advantages of buying perennials from a local nursery or garden center are that you can get your plants the minute you need them, and you can choose the healthiest, most attractive plants. Many garden centers also have display gardens where you can see the mature sizes and forms of the plants. The plants will be larger than those available by mail, so you'll get more "instant gratification" when you put them in the ground (although the mail-order plants usually catch up by the end of the season).

There's a hidden drawback to garden-center shopping, though—the candy-store syndrome. When you see all those wonderful plants, it's tempting to buy one of each. The best way to avoid temptation is to make a list of the plants you plan to buy, then stick to it. Otherwise, you might set out to buy five irises and return home with a carload of mixed plants that looked great in the store but not in your garden design. Another drawback is that your selection may be limited. Here are some tips for getting the most from buying plants at a garden center.

- The best selection is available in spring.
- If you want a specific color, buy a cultivar.
- Avoid plants that are visibly rootbound. Check the root systems of plants that are leggy or too large in relation to the size of the pot by gently tipping the plants out of their pots. (If roots are growing out of the bottom of the pot or you can't tip the plant out of the pot—in fact, you'd have to cut the pot to get the plant out—it's rootbound.)
- Choose plants with lush foliage and multiple stems. Avoid plants with dry, pale, or shriveled leaves.
- Check for insects on the leaves (examine both the tops and undersides) and along the stems.

At the garden center. After good soil, a good nursery or garden center can be a gardener's most valuable asset. Look for one that labels plants clearly (including cultivar name where appropriate), gives specific cultural information, and offers healthy plants.

- Plants bought in fall will look weather-beaten because they may have been sitting on a bench all summer. So don't go by appearances—check the root system. If it's in good shape, the plant is probably healthy.
- If you can't plant immediately, keep containers well watered. Check them daily.

WHEN YOUR PLANTS ARRIVE

Let's back up a minute here to stress a vital point: Dig your beds *before* your plants arrive. Don't order plants or buy them locally unless you've prepared a place to put them. You'll be rushed enough at planting time without having to start from scratch, and your plants deserve a better start than you could give them with last-minute bed-making.

Even if you've already prepared your garden bed, you still may not be able to put your perennials in the ground as soon as they arrive, especially if they're mail-order plants. More likely, you'll come home after a long day's work, with hours of chores still before you, and find them on the doorstep. You may have to wait until the next day—or even the weekend—before you can plant. Here's what to do with your plants in the meantime.

- Take mail-order plants out of the box as soon as you get them.

In the beginning. Coauthor Cole Burrell didn't have much to work with when he began designing the garden at his former home in Minneapolis. Here, he's prepared the beds for planting.

A transformation. Believe it or not, this is the same garden as on the opposite page! It's now a lush mix of perennials and complementary plants: pink turtlehead (*Chelone lyonii*), 'White Lightning' black cohosh (*Cimicifuga racemosa* 'White Lightning'), wild blue phlox (*Phlox divaricata*), 'Desdemona' bigleaf ligularia (*Ligularia dentata* 'Desdemona'), 'Halcyon' hosta, and old-fashioned bleeding heart (*Dicentra spectabilis*), with a serene seating area tucked inside for privacy. Note how the water garden at the front adds a tropical touch to this Zone 4 property, with 'Black Magic' taro (*Colocasia* 'Black Magic'), 'Variegatus' variegated sweet flag (*Acorus calamus* 'Variegatus'), and water hyacinth.

- Water container-grown plants whenever the soil dries. The smaller the pot, the more often you'll have to water.
- Set container-grown plants outside in a shaded area until you can plant them.
- If bareroot plants are wrapped in a protective material like peat or shredded wood, make sure to keep the material damp. If the plants aren't wrapped in protective material, soak the roots in lukewarm water, then cover them with moist soil or compost.
- Keep bareroot perennials in a protected place until you can plant them.
- Plant your perennials as soon as you are able to.

You'll find detailed instructions on caring for your new perennials in "What to Do Once the Plants Come Home" on page 185.

PLANTING TIME

When you're ready to plant, remove the mulch from your prepared bed. Choose an overcast day if possible, and don't plant during the heat of the day. Place container-grown plants, pots and all, on the bed where you plan to plant them. (Consult your design to make sure you're putting them in the right spots.)

You can dig the holes for as many perennials as you think you're going to plant that day, but plant only one perennial at a time. Remove it from its pot by turning the pot upside down, with one hand spread over the soil around the stem, and tap the bottom of the pot with your trowel to loosen the roots. The roots may have grown into a tangled mass. Separate them by gently pulling them apart or quartering the root ball with a knife—this will make it easier for the roots to spread through the soil, and the plant will establish itself more quickly. Remove most of the potting medium and any broken or diseased roots.

Place each container-grown perennial in the ground so that its crown is at the same depth at which it grew in the pot, or slightly higher; the soil will settle a bit over the next few weeks. Make sure you spread the roots out in the hole as you plant.

If you're planting bareroot perennials, remove the protective material from the roots, then soak the roots in a bucket of lukewarm water for 1 to 2 hours to hydrate them before planting. Again, plant one perennial at a time. Dig a large enough hole so you'll have room to spread out the roots. Prune off diseased or damaged roots. Mound up soil in the center of the hole and set the plant on top of the mound, spreading its roots out over the sides. Make sure the mound is the right size to position the plant's crown at the soil surface. Fill in the hole with soil, then firm it down.

THOSE %$#@!! LABELS

Have you heard about an evil race of slugs that sneak into your garden at night and steal all your plant labels? Well, neither have we, but it's as good an explanation as any as to why plant labels always disappear. Perhaps "always" is a bit strong. Sometimes they break instead, sometimes they appear yards from the plant they came with, and sometimes—most of the time—they just fade away. Inevitably, this is just when those knowledgeable plant friends you were hoping to impress come by and say, "What's *that* plant?" To make sure you can answer them, try these tactics.

- **Keep good notes.** Write down what you planted, where it came from, and when and where you planted it. Keep a sketch of your garden and fill in the new plant's name and location. (This is especially useful when your labels start to wander.) And keep the nursery bill (with the plant list) in your notebook with your planting notes.

- **Make more.** While you can still read the label, make several more wooden "tongue-depressor" labels and an indelible marker. When you inevitably see that the plant's name is fading fast on the original label, you can pop in a replacement.
- **Make 'em last.** If you can afford it, buy metal labels and write the names of your plants on them with a pencil, then attach them to the plants' stems. These labels should stay put, and they'll last at least as long as your plants.

One last point that's important but easy to forget: Keep the plant labels with your perennials, and stick them firmly in the ground next to each plant as you plant it. You'll find step-by-step directions for planting container-grown and bareroot perennials in "Putting in the Plants" on page 186.

AFTERCARE: A TIMETABLE

How well your plants thrive depends on the care you give them after planting. You can't just plop them in the ground and walk away. Newly planted perennials need more attention than established plants. You'll find detailed how-to information on every aspect of growing perennials in Chapter 8, "Perennial Gardening Basics." Use this care calendar to make sure you're giving your new plants what they need.

Right Away

Water. Water both bareroot and container-grown perennials as soon as you've planted them.

Cut back foliage. If the nursery hasn't already done this, cut off one-third to two-thirds of the foliage on bareroot plants; otherwise, plants will lose water through their leaves faster than their damaged roots can take it up, causing wilting. If they wilt even after you've cut them back, you probably were too tenderhearted; cut back to a few inches to give plants a chance to recover.

Mulch. Mulch your plants after watering them to maintain soil moisture and guard against wilting. Mulch will keep weeds from competing with your new plants, too. (We're not talking about bark-chip mulch here; a layer of compost or leaf mulch is more attractive and will slowly provide nutrients to the plants as it breaks down.)

Provide shade. Shade your newly planted perennials from direct sunlight until they've had a chance to recover from the shock of transplanting. If possible, cover them with a spunbonded row cover like Reemay or with shade cloth, screening, or a lath cover for the first 2 or 3 days after planting.

The First Week

Water. Your plants' primary need will continue to be water. Check at least once a day; before and after work is even better.

Check for bugs. Check your perennials daily for signs of pests and pest damage. New plants are smaller so they're particularly vulnerable to pest damage. If you find insects or damage, check in Chapter 9, "Perennial Pest and Disease Control," for the culprit and what to do about it. Remember that animals and birds can decimate a planting, too—if you see signs of their damage, protect your plants with screens or netting.

Remove shade. Gradually remove your shade cover after the first few days—ideally, leave it on only during the heat of the day, and remove it in morning and late afternoon. If you work and can't get home to move the cover, take it off completely after the third day; make doubly sure that plants are well watered and mulched.

The First Season

Water. Watering will remain critical during the first growing season. Make sure your perennials get 1 inch of water a week, from either rain or the hose.

Weed. Weeding is most important the first 2 years after planting; after that, plants will be established and large enough to shade out most weed seedlings. Mulch will help control weeds, but check for them every time you're in the garden.

Feed. If you've prepared the soil well, your perennials will grow vigorously without much more than an application of compost in the middle of the season, or compost (or manure or seaweed) tea once a month.

Monitor for insects and diseases. Continue to keep an eye out for pests and diseases and apply appropriate controls.

Stake. In the first year after planting, stake perennials like peonies and delphiniums that might have weak stems.

Disbud. If you buy bareroot late-blooming perennials (like asters and mums) in May or June, remove all their flower buds. They need to establish themselves the first growing season, not put their energy into flowering.

Deadhead. Cut off spent flower heads to keep your perennials from wasting energy by setting seed.

Move things around. If plants don't look right where you've placed them, don't be afraid to move them around. Don't move perennials in bloom. Wait until they've stopped blooming, then move them with a large soil ball around their roots; or,

mark them and their new location on a copy of your design and move them at the end of the season.

Add new plants. If you find you've left a gap in your bed that won't be filled in by the following season, add more plants to cover the bare spot.

Enjoy. Take time to appreciate the beautiful garden you've made.

PUTTING IN YOUR GARDEN OVER TIME

It's great if you can design a garden, then buy all the perennials you've included and plant them. Your garden will mature at the same rate, so it has an even, finished look. And you'll see the complete design—outdoors, growing, in full color—within one season.

But for many of us, a one-shot garden is just an ideal. For one reason or another—time, money, an unexpected trip, or other interruption to our plans—we have to implement our garden in stages. Instead of the 3 or 4 years it usually takes a perennial garden to mature, it may take ours 5 or 6. In the end, though, a multistep garden will look just like the one-shot. And you can use time-tested techniques to make sure it looks lovely every step of the way.

If you're planting your garden in stages, one of the most sensible steps is to put in the slower-growing perennials first. Perennials like peonies, oriental poppies, daylilies, blue false indigo (*Baptisia australis*), gas plant (*Dictamnus albus*), bal-

Filling in with annuals. One of the best ways to make a perennial garden look established its first season is to interplant with annuals while you're waiting for the perennials to fill in. (Many perennials take at least two growing seasons to reach flowering size.) You'll get lots of season-long color from the annuals if you keep them watered and deadheaded. In this border, annual cleome and purple-leaved perilla enhance the red color theme and add richness to the perennial palette of bee balm, garden phlox, sedum, globe thistle, and purple coneflower.

loon flower (*Platycodon grandiflorus*), Siberian iris (*Iris sibirica*), large-leaved hostas (*Hosta*), and baby's-breath (*Gypsophila paniculata*) are slow to establish. If your design includes any of these plants, start with them.

Ways to Approach a Design

Every gardener faces the problem of putting a good face on a new garden. Perennials take a long time to mature—often three or four growing seasons—and the garden can look bare or haphazard in the meantime. One way to give your new garden a fuller, more mature look is to fill in the gaps with colorful annuals while the perennials mature.

You'll be more successful if you choose annuals with the same color, form, and texture as the perennials that will grow to replace them. This designer trick will give your garden a unified look and let you try out your color scheme the first season. Snapdragons (*Antirrhinum majus*) and sweet alyssum (*Lobularia maritima*) mix especially well with perennials; use them in the front and middle of the bed or border. For height, try annuals like cleome (*Cleome hasslerana*) and cosmos (*Cosmos bipinnatus*).

A drawback is the cost of annuals. If you buy bedding plants rather than starting them from seed, annuals can cost almost as much as the least expensive perennials. A different alternative—especially if you're planning to add another bed or border in a few years—is to overplant rather than use a lot of annuals. Plant three perennials where your design calls for one, then move the two extras as plants mature. This technique gives your garden a fuller look, and you'll have good-size plants on hand when you're ready to start the new garden.

A final trick that's really effective is to plant lots of bulbs for a bright first-season show. Daffodils, species tulips, crocuses, and other "little bulbs" will make your garden sparkle in spring, while lilies will pick up the show in summer. Plant bulbs thickly—in groups, rather than singly—for a dazzling display.

When You Don't Have Time

One obvious solution to a time crunch is to plant a piece of the garden rather than trying to do it all at once. You can put in part of the bed or border each year until it's all planted. An advantage of this technique is that if you don't like part of the design, you won't have to redo the entire garden—you may have to move or replace only 3 plants rather than 30. A drawback is that each section will mature in the order you planted, so one end of the border may just be filling in when the other is peaking.

Another way to tackle the time problem is to start with the parts of your yard that will make the most impact. Put in the colorful sunny border this year, and worry about more intricate and less showy plant-

ings like the shade and bog gardens later. If your terrace is the central feature of your yard, put in a bed around it now; save the property-line border for another year.

Don't forget ongoing time concerns, too—the larger the garden, the more time it will take to weed, water, deadhead, and do other routine chores. When you're planning your bed or border, don't bite off more than you can chew.

When You Don't Have Money

If ready money is the problem rather than time—and with plant prices what they are today, planting an entire garden isn't an inexpensive undertaking—there are plenty of ways to get garden color for a minimum of cash. Here are some ideas to get you started.

- Trade plants with neighbors. Almost everybody has a little too much of something, and these "extra" plants are often fast-growing—just what you need for quick color.
- Start perennials from seed. (See "Seeds and Seedlings" on page 136.)
- Start with commonly available plants, and replace them with more choice perennials when you can afford them. For example, plant a "ditch daylily" this year, and replace it with a favorite cultivar in a couple of years. While you wait, you'll still be able to enjoy the daylily's form and flowers.
- Use fast-growing plants—spotted lamium (*Lamium maculatum*) in shade, cone-

flowers (*Rudbeckia*) and bee balm (*Monarda didyma*) in sunny areas—until you can afford to replace them with a more diverse selection. Other fast-growing perennials include mums, catmints (*Nepeta*), fringed bleeding heart (*Dicentra eximia*), and gayfeathers (*Liatris*). In a shady site, fill in with running ferns like lady fern (*Athyrium filix-femina*), New York fern (*Thelypteris noveboracensis*), and sensitive fern (*Onoclea sensibilis*).

- Start with a small garden and a limited color scheme, then expand to a larger garden with a broader color scheme when you're able.

The Nursery Bed

Creating a private nursery of their own is a fantasy for many gardeners. Make it a reality of sorts in your garden with a nursery bed, a great way to save money and protect small, vulnerable plants.

If your design calls for lots of groundcovers or other perennials that are easy to propagate, like mums, start with a plant or two of each. Then make lots of divisions or take lots of cuttings from the parent plants—many more than you would from a plant in your garden. For example, if you were dividing a daylily to replant in your garden, you might cut it into two to four divisions. For the nursery bed, you might separate and plant out every fan of leaves. After all, this isn't a display garden; a nursery bed, like a compost pile, is one of the working areas of the garden.

A nursery bed is ideal for perennial seedlings, too, since they often take 2 to 3 years to grow large enough to hold their own in the garden. Meanwhile, keeping the young plants together makes it easier to give them the care they need.

The best nursery bed is a large, open-topped coldframe because you can screen the bottom to keep voles out and shade the top with lath or screen without fear of crushing the plants. If you don't want to make a coldframe or don't think it would look right in your garden, make a raised bed for your nursery. An east-facing site in partial shade is best because it gets indirect light.

Prepare the soil for your nursery bed the same way you would for a perennial bed, but screen it to remove clods, twigs, and rocks; the soil texture should be fairly fine. Add plenty of compost or other organic matter. Use the same kind of soil in your nursery bed that the plants will eventually grow in. Don't overfeed your nursery plants or they'll grow spindly and susceptible to pest and disease attack.

The plants in your nursery bed are small and vulnerable—you'll need to protect them from sun, driving rain, and pests. Fine window screen will serve all three purposes: It provides shade, breaks the force of raindrops that could flatten seedlings, and keeps pests from reaching plants. You can also put slats or shade cloth over the bed, or protect it with wood lath. When you're siting your

HELP FOR A LARGE GARDEN

If you have a large yard—or just want a sizable garden—and you're starting from scratch, you need an excellent strategic plan or you'll quickly exceed your gardening time and budget. Another danger is that impulse planting will result in a haphazard look. Here are some tips to get your garden up and running without breaking either your back or the bank.

PLAN AHEAD

Before you begin to dig or plant, make sure you take time to consider the following points.

- Think about where you'll enjoy the garden as you plan beds and borders. What will you see from your windows? What will your neighbors see? (Remember, good gardens make good neighbors.)
- Plan a maintenance program. Site fussier plants in beds closer to the house, where it's easier to care for them, and tough, self-sufficient perennials at a distance.
- Don't site a bed or border in a high-traffic area where family and friends will be tempted to tramp through it. If some "through traffic" is unavoidable, add large, flat stepping-stones to make a convenient path.
- To eliminate hard-to-maintain areas, plant perennials and groundcovers around trees to eliminate trimming and on difficult-to-mow slopes.
- Put in permanent elements first, like a hedge or an ever-green border. They'll frame the garden or hide unattractive views. Once the trees or shrubs are growing, plant your perennials.
- Make both shady and sunny nursery beds. Don't make the beds too small—as your plants grow you'll need more space than seems likely at first.

CHOOSING PLANTS

When you're ready to pick out plants, use these tips to decide what to buy and where to plant it.

- Buy essential plants first—groundcovers, hostas, daylilies, and other basic, easy-to-move plants. Divide them regularly, and put the divisions in a nursery bed.

nursery bed, make sure it's within reach of your hose; you'll be watering often. For more on nursery beds, see "Make Your Own Nursery Bed" on page 262.

Seeds and Seedlings

If you have more time and patience than money to spend on your perennials, starting plants from seed is an excellent choice. A packet of seed is much cheaper than the equivalent number of plants (or even one plant!). In exchange for a good buy, though, you must be willing to wait. And you must limit your selection to perennials that come true from seed—mostly species, though some cultivars can be seed-grown.

In addition to simply germinating your seeds, you'll need to set up a coldframe or nursery bed to protect the seedling perennials while they grow. Seedlings require considerable care for the first season, and continuing care for the following year or two until they reach blooming size. For more on growing perennials from seed, see Chapter 10, "Propagating Perennials."

(See page 262 for more on setting up a nursery bed.) Move divisions to the garden as you're ready for them.

- Don't be afraid to invest in top-quality cultivars if you can divide or propagate them.
- For plants that resent transplanting, like peonies, false and wild indigos (*Baptisia*), and gas plant (*Dictamnus albus*), dig small sections of the future border and put these plants in where you'll eventually want them. Mulch and mow around the sections until you can dig the spaces in between and connect them.
- In a big garden, you can tolerate more invasive plants than in a small garden. Site aggressive thugs where you can mow around them—under trees or up against hedges, for example—to keep them from getting out of hand.

GETTING GOOD BUYS

To get the most greenery for your greenbacks, follow these tips.

- Save money by buying from nurseries that sell seedling-size plants, then grow them on in your nursery beds.
- Look for special packages from nurseries—group offers of daffodils, hostas, and other popular perennials. You can save money with these packages, but be aware of the trade-offs: If you buy a group of unnamed plants, don't expect cultivar quality. Plan to put them on a slope or distant area that needs color rather than in a nearby bed or border. If you buy a "named, our choice" special, you won't sacrifice quality, you just won't know exactly what you're getting.
- You can also take advantage of summer sales, when many nurseries try to sell stock quickly so that they don't have to maintain it into fall. Don't plant your bargains right away, though—it's too hard on the plants. Instead, keep the pots in a shady area near the house, where you can water them often, then plant them in fall.
- With big gardens, it's time- and cost-effective to start plants from seed. Many perennials, including species hostas and daylilies, are easy to grow if you use fresh seed.

Plant Exchanges and Societies

Plant societies like the American Rock Garden Society and the Hardy Plant Society are great sources of inexpensive seeds and plants—many have seed and plant swaps and sales. You'll find rare and unusual plants in addition to popular perennials. Societies are also excellent sources of information, and joining one is a good way to meet fellow enthusiasts. Some of the plant societies of interest to perennial gardeners are listed in "Resources" on page 686.

Botanical gardens, public gardens, and arboreta also often have plant and seed sales. Sometimes universities with horticulture programs sponsor plant sales, too. You must join plant societies to participate in their programs, but garden, arboretum, and university sales are often open to the general public. Contact your local university's horticulture department and the nearest botanical garden to see if they have plant sales. You'll enjoy the gardens, too!

Perennials from seed. If you don't have a lot of spare cash, one way to have an affordable garden is to grow most of your perennials from seed. It takes a little more time and the choices are more limited, but you can still have spectacular results. Buy plants of the cultivars you really want for quick impact, then sow easy-from-seed perennials like this combination of 'Goldsturm' black-eyed Susan and 'Monch' showy aster.

6

GROWING WITH THE DESIGN

Plants aren't predictable. They don't stay neat and tidy as they do in their nursery pots (or even the first couple of years after you plant them) while they're getting established. Just when, in year 2 or 3, your garden is filling in nicely and you're secretly harboring visions of the HGTV crew pulling into the drive, a terrible thing happens. Lamb's ears begin cropping up in the lawn. Where you thought you had lamb's ears in the garden bed, you find lamb's-*quarters*. The bleeding heart is now bigger than your car—then it vanishes for the summer, leaving a bare spot the size of a moon crater. The peonies and roses are wrestling for supremacy, and your beautiful clematis—so gorgeous only last year!—is nowhere to be seen. The adorable little hostas you tucked among your hellebores and alumroots have reached elephantine proportions, the hellebores have self-sown everywhere, and the poor alumroots—the ones that haven't been crushed to death by the massive hostas—have vanished in a sea of purple perilla. What's a gardener to do?

Plants aren't the only thing that will grow and change in your garden, either. Your tastes will change, as well. That bank of mixed daylilies that you loved as a new gardener may seem dreary and predictable 5 or 10 years down the road. Last year's hot plant—you know, the one you paid $80 for and had to fight off four other gardeners to get—doesn't look so

Keeping up appearances. A stone edging and neatly mowed grass path set off the controlled exuberance of this garden, where roses and weigela bloom above beds of flowering peonies, veronica, and forget-me-nots—and a statue draws the eye to the crossroad at the garden's heart. Edgings are especially important when beds adjoin grass because vigorous grasses are otherwise certain to invade the beds.

hot where you put it, after all. You're so sick of your yellow-and-purple border you could scream. And what were you thinking when you planted roses along the garden path? Your arms are bleeding by the time you get back to the house.

Clearly, it's time for a change. And here's a secret: It always will be. That's one of the things that makes gardening so exciting and keeps us in love with it. There will always be the next new plant to try, the next bed to make over, and the next inspiring photo, great combination, stunning container, or "in" color. Enjoy the flexibility and creativity a living garden provides—the two of you can keep on growing together.

For now, though, flexibility and creativity may not seem like much consolation when your garden's stopped looking like it was designed by Gertrude Jekyll and started looking like it was designed by Dr. Jekyll. So here are some ways to restore its mature beauty or give it a whole new look.

WHEN GOOD GARDENS GO BAD

First, take a deep breath—it's not as bad as it looks. Perennial gardens *do* grow past their best looks, usually between years 3 and 5. If the perennials in your garden don't look right or aren't growing compatibly with their neighbors, remember the gardener's most valuable design tools—a trowel and shovel. Read on for ways to bring your garden back to its best.

Divvy 'em Up

If a perennial is overflowing its bounds, look it up in "The Perennial Encyclopedia," beginning on page 265, and see if it can be divided, and whether you should divide it in spring or fall. If your plants are losing vigor—not growing or blooming the way they did a few seasons ago—they probably also need to be divided. As its name implies, this technique involves taking the plant out of the ground and splitting it into smaller pieces. Replant one of these pieces in improved soil in the original hole, and plant the rest elsewhere or give them to plant-loving friends, donate them to a church plant sale, or take them to a plant sale or swap. (But label them first, please!) The smaller pieces

usually take a season to get established, then display all the vigor of new plants. (For more on how to divide perennials, see "Divide and Multiply" on page 252.)

Move It or Lose It

Don't be afraid to move plants around, even if it's only a foot to the right or left. Unless they have a taproot, most perennials are very forgiving. Move them after bloom season, in the cooler part of the day, with a large soil ball around their roots, and water them carefully until they're reestablished. Often, moving plants will solve design problems simply and effectively. But before you reach for the spade, ask yourself three things: Is it unhappy where it is? If the growing conditions aren't right for it where you have it but are perfect in another part of the yard or garden, move it. Is it just in

A CHANGE FOR THE BETTER

Many changes in the garden are good things. Forty blooms on a mature peony are a far more spectacular sight than four on a third-year plant. Creeping perennials will spread to fill in gaps, making the plants seem to flow together in a beautiful blend of color and texture. Bulbs will multiply, forming sizable clumps.

Slow-growing perennials like peonies, oriental poppies, and blue false indigo (*Baptisia*

australis) will change predictably: As long as they're healthy, they'll just get bigger every year. Other changes are less predictable but equally delightful. The stems of perennials may weave among those of neighboring plants, so those plants may suddenly "bloom" out of season. A perennial may not be the color you expected, but the new color may work even better than the one you wanted. You may find you've

accidentally created a haven for butterflies or hummingbirds.

Other perennials may disappear from where you planted them and pop up in another part of the garden, or return from seedlings that bloom in a completely different color than the original plants. Plants grow and change as long as they live. In reality, no 2 years in the garden ever look the same—it's one of the pleasures of gardening.

the wrong place? If you simply made a design goof—its foliage or flowers weren't the color you thought they'd be, it gets too tall or short—and, now that you know it better, you think you have a better place for it, move it. And most important: Do you really like it? If you think the plant doesn't look good because (admit it) you realize

that you just don't like it, lose it. Take it to a plant sale, give it to a neighbor, or swap it for a plant you like better. Just because you planted it doesn't mean you're stuck with it.

Stop Herban Sprawl

Some perennials, like certain artemisias and peonies, are notorious for rising to luxuriant heights and then keeling over in all directions from their centers like spokes on a wheel (a phenomenon called lodging). This is, shall we say, *not* the look most gardeners had in mind when they planted them. If some of your plants have come down with a case of "herban sprawl," there are several potential cures. First, as we all know, overwatering and overfertilizing with high-nitrogen fertilizers can cause plants to shoot up quickly, forming weak stems and oversize leaves, which further weigh down the stems. If this is your problem, cut back on the watering and use a balanced organic fertilizer, or just use compost for a few years until the problem corrects itself. Plants like yarrows and artemisias that prefer poor, dry soil may lodge if they're grown in the rich, moist soil preferred by most perennials. Plants like

Keep up the good work. The designers of this garden were thinking of future maintenance when they put the stone edgings in place along these double borders. You can see that the beds are mulched to retain water and keep down weeds. The beautifully grown perennials—classics like peonies, hardy geraniums, white-flowered veronica, catmint, irises, and foxgloves—reflect the loving care they're given.

Controlled abandon. The wealth of plants in this West Coast garden may have an air of wild abandon, but not abandonment. The careful selection of plants includes a giant annual castor bean, dahlias, lavender-blue double aster, Joe-Pye weed, coleus, and Brazilian vervain, accented by the columnar purple 'Helmond Pillar' barberry (*Berberis* 'Helmond Pillar') and luxurious bloom that reveal the gardener's loving hand.

double peonies have very heavy blooms, and one good rain can send them plunging to the ground. Grow single-flowered types to avoid the problem, but if you love the doubles (and who doesn't?), discreet staking is probably the best solution. (See page 205 for more on choosing and using stakes and other plant supports.) Another potential cause is cutting back a plant that was serving as a support for the now-splayed perennial. Again, staking (or better placement) is the answer.

Control Creepy Crawlies

Groundcovering perennials are not called "covering" by accident. They tend to expand faster than an ice-cream cone on a hot sidewalk—and go a lot farther, too. If you've planted ajuga, lamium, lamb's ears, lily-of-the-valley, sweet woodruff—or, for that matter, any perennial groundcover—where it's happy, it will spread. Thymes are one of the few groundcovering plants that

(continued on page 146)

Weeds or wildflowers? This garden is a stunning example of a prairie meadow, featuring beloved native plants like purple coneflower (*Echinacea purpurea*), ragged coneflower (*Rudbeckia laciniata*), Kansas gayfeather (*Liatris pycnostachya*), cup plant (*Silphium perfoliatum*), flat-topped aster (*Aster umbellatus*), drooping coneflower (*Ratibida pinnata*), and Indian grass (*Sorghastrum nutans*).

A GARDEN LIFE CYCLE

It takes so long for a perennial garden to come into its true glory that most gardeners don't even think about what comes next. But like us, gardens grow, mature, and then start to decline. Fortunately, it's easy to rejuvenate them, as this series of illustrations shows.

The new garden. Their first season perennials are establishing themselves, so the bed will look a little bare—or at least a little green!—unless you fill in with annuals, containers, and/or garden art.

The mature garden. At its peak, the garden is a lush mix of eye-catching color and pleasing textures. Plants have filled in and are growing and blooming well but not crowding each other out.

The aging garden. You'll know your bed is past its prime when perennials crowd each other and look scraggly and overgrown, there are gaps where some plants have died out, plants stop blooming strongly, self-sown perennials begin cropping up everywhere, and/or perennials have grow too big for their space (or even the scale of the garden). It's time for remedial action!

The garden renewed. The gardener has finished the makeover, dividing overgrown perennials, removing and replacing some of the plants, trimming some back, opening more space where it's needed, and filling in as appropriate. The bed looks slightly different from the original design because the gardener is trying a few new perennials to complement the successful ones from the first round, having learned firsthand what works for him or her, and it looks even better this time.

tend to expand slowly and sweetly into ever-larger mats (creeping phlox will also do this, but on a much grander scale). That's why it's best to reserve perennial groundcovers for (as their name implies) bare patches under trees, steep exposed slopes, or other areas where you'd probably grow lawn if you could. Save your perennial beds for plants that aren't famed for the speed at which they spread, and let groundcovers shine as the wonderful lawn alternatives that they are. (Note: If you're the type of gardener who goes wild if ajuga or another groundcover begins to creep into the lawn, sullying the grass monoculture, confine your groundcovers with edgings, and root out any escapees early and often.)

Stop the Sowing Machine

Some perennials tend to self-sow with reckless abandon. Seedlings from plants like garlic chives (*Allium tuberosum*), columbines (*Aquilegia*), and coneflowers (*Rudbeckia*) may crop up all over the bed. This can be great if you enjoy taking extras to plant sales or have new beds in need of (free!) plants, but not if your perennial bed has vanished under the violets or, worse, if a thug like tansy has taken hold and shouldered out everything else. Check the individual entries in "The Perennial Encyclopedia," beginning on page 265, to see if plants you're considering self-sow, and how aggressively, or ask at your local nursery. If your garden beds are informal or you enjoy the cottage-garden style, indulge in perennials (and annuals and biennials) that self-sow and enjoy the adventure. If your beds are more formal, remember: *Caveat emptor* (Let the buyer beware),

and proceed with caution—or deadhead your perennials before they go to seed.

GROWING AS A GARDENER

Most people feel the urge to occasionally redo the house: change the paint colors or wallpaper patterns, replace the curtains, upgrade some furniture, move things around. It's interesting, it's exciting, and it's refreshing. You can try new things, or see if the way you picture something is really how it looks. You get that wonderful new-house feeling for a lot less money and trouble than it takes to move. The same is true of our wardrobes, our hairstyles, and our hobbies. Why not our gardens?

It costs a lot less to give a garden bed a makeover than it costs to redo a room. And, like your house, a garden you'll love is a garden that reflects who you are *now*—not 6 years ago when you originally planted it. We say, go for it! After all, makeovers are fun. But before you rush to rip out everything, you'll be happier if you start with . . .

The 10 Commandments of Great Garden Makeovers

You know you're not happy with your garden, but do you know why? Or what to do about it? Here's how to find out.

1. **Record what's there now.** Take pictures in every season, or whenever the garden looks strikingly different because of growth changes or plants coming into or going out of bloom. If you have a digital camera or a scanner, make color printouts.

2. **Decide what you love (or hate).** As you look at the photos, note things you dislike, things you still like, and things you don't care about either way.

3. **Ask yourself why.** Pinpoint *why* you don't like what you're looking at. Is a flower color not what you expected, does it look wrong next to its neighbors' colors, or does it bloom in the wrong season, wrecking the beautiful combination you'd hoped for? Did a plant get too big and obscure the plants around it, or not grow as big as you'd hoped, so it's hidden behind other plants or simply fails to make enough impact? Do all the flower colors have the same value (all pastels, all darks, all mid-range), does all the plants' foliage have the same texture, or are the plants all the same height? Any of these factors can make a garden bed look flat or boring. Once you can see if it's a plant, a group of plants, or the whole bed that bothers you, it will be easier to fix the problem.

4. **Look for what *isn't* there.** Ask yourself if anything's missing. Sometimes the reason a garden isn't satisfying is that there's no focal point. If a large part of the border isn't in bloom for months on end and there's no foliage or structural interest to hold the eye, it can look drab and lifeless. It's at least as important to assess what's not there as what is.

5. **Gather resources.** Pull out that pile of catalogs, magazines, books, and those all-important sticky tags, and tag plants, features, combinations, beds, and anything else that appeals to you.

6. **Connect the dots.** Sit down with your garden photos, your pile of tagged resources, and your notebook. If you're unhappy with individual plants, see if you can find replacements with the characteristics you're looking for. (It may be as easy as replacing one iris with

Finding your center. Sometimes all it takes to give a garden a new look is the right piece of art. Here, a weathered urn centers this grouping of bigleaf ligularia (*Ligularia dentata*), gold-leaved hosta, blue monkshood, 'Superba' snakeweed (*Polygonum bistorta* 'Superba'), and 'Atropurpurea' purple-leaved fringed loosestrife (*Lysimachia ciliata* 'Atropurpurea'), with a foreground of lungwort (*Pulmonaria*).

A riotous rock garden. This rock garden is easy care and colorful. Pinks (*Dianthus*) and hairy beardtongue (*Penstemon hirsutus*) flower among the rocks and gravel—a sea of pink that requires very little water.

another one in a different color.) If some new combinations would put the pizzazz back in your border, see if you can find a few good ones in your magazines, turn back to Chapter 3 for inspiration, or look in a good reference book like Cole Burrell's *Perennial Combinations*. If sameness is your garden's problem, see if adding plants with different height, flower colors and forms, or foliage size and texture would bring it back to life. A great way to do this if you're using color printouts or copies of your garden photos is to make color photocopies of (or scan and print out) the new plants and combinations or features you'd like to add, then cut and place them on the garden photo (don't cut and *paste* unless they really look good). With several copies of the garden photo, you can try a number of versions and compare them all, then see which (if any) you and your family prefer.

An eyecatching display. This late-spring garden is a blooming carpet of Allegheny foamflower (*Tiarella cordifolia*), 'Ruby Mar' bleeding heart (*Dicentra* 'Ruby Mar'), and Siberian bugloss (*Brunnera macrophylla*) against a backdrop of 'Desdemona' bigleaf ligularia (*Ligularia dentata* 'Desdemona') and 'Purple Sensation' allium (*Allium* 'Purple Sensation').

Sweet dreams are made of this. Your garden may never look like this majestic sweep of borders, grass paths, and stone steps, but if you wish it did, consider what you can do to capture its essence in your own yard. A grass path with stepping-stones? Backing your garden with a formal hedge? See Ann Lovejoy's garden design on page 118 for a hedged garden—you can recreate the feeling if not the garden itself.

A tropical touch. Hardy bananas (*Musa basjoo*), rice-paper plants (*Tetrapanax*), purple-leaved cannas, golden sedges, 'Atropurpuream' sweet Joe-Pye weed (*Eupatorium purpureum* 'Atropurpuream'), 'Giganteus' Japanese silver grass (*Miscanthus* 'Giganteus'), 'Firetail' mountain fleece flower (*Persicaria amplexicaule* 'Firetail'), and dahlias lend a tropical feel to this temperate garden.

7. **Take a reality break.** Before you get too excited about a potential makeover, stop and make sure the new plants will grow in your climate and conditions. It may look good on paper but be a disaster in the ground. The time to find this out is *before* you've sent off your check and spent a day with your spade.

8. **Know when to hold.** If everything checks out, decide where you're going to get the new plants and/or garden features, but don't rush to order them. Wait to rework your garden until spring or fall (or winter in frost-free areas), when conditions are best for planting.

9. **Know when to fold.** It's hard to believe that there's a garden alive that couldn't be made over using at least *some* of the plants that are already growing there, but if yours qualifies, don't waste more time and money trying to make things right. Decide what you'd like to try instead, dig up the plants, give them good homes (either elsewhere in your yard or with

Better think twice. Unless you have a gardening staff, a garden like this would be a maintenance nightmare. The carefully shaped shrubs, cleanly clipped grass, immaculate path, and perfect beds bespeak a level of care outside most gardeners' means.

Low maintenance, maximum impact. These hardy plants provide a stunning summer show. Deep rose-pink 'Garnet' penstemon, white spikes of red valerian (*Centranthus ruber* var. *albus*), tall pink tree mallows (*Lavatera*), blue Jacob's ladders (*Polemonium*), and 'Patty's Plum' oriental poppies entice visitors along the path.

friends or fellow plant fanatics), prepare the bed, and start over.

10. **Give it a try!** Once you've done your homework, decided what you want to do, and waited for the best time of year, get going. It's makeover time!

Ch-Ch-Changes

If your tastes have changed and your garden no longer makes you happy, you may not need a whole garden makeover—you may need to just add or remove an element. On the other hand, it may be something in your landscape that's affecting your garden pleasure— and not in a good way. Here are some things to try.

Try New Art

Maybe the costumed goose or the pink flamingo looked cute when you set it out there, but now it's giving your garden a dated look. Try something different and see what it does for your garden. An urn, a chimney pot, a birdbath, or an interesting container might be just what's needed. But before you trade in your plaster bunny for a gazing ball, consider its size and placement carefully. A gazing ball on a tall stand, a gazing ball on a short column, and a gazing ball nestled into plants at ground level create three very different effects. It might be the size of the piece: A huge

Northern lights. A cheerful mix of hostas, delphiniums, lilies, and chartreuse ferns prove that even in Alaska, the growing season is not too short for a glorious display.

sculpture in a tiny garden works only if the garden has been specifically created to set off that sculpture. Small pieces in a huge garden work only if their purpose is to add delight when a garden visitor, stooping to admire a plant, unexpectedly discovers them. Make sure the new piece fits both its place and its function.

Remember: More Is Not Better

This is a tough one, especially for those of us who are collectors, but it's almost invariably true—unless your goal is to create a botanical collection, go into the nursery business, or open a theme park. To this end, a garden gnome may be cute, but 50 garden gnomes are scary. A few colors of iris look better than a row of every color and color blend of iris ever bred. If you—we won't name names—must have absolutely every epimedium or hosta or daffodil in the world, treat them like combinations and create attractive-looking groupings or disperse them among other combinations. Consider weaving them among other perennials, or split up the collection and plant parts of it in different areas of the landscape. At all costs, avoid the monoculture look unless you're a farmer and your idea of heaven is acres and acres of corn.

Block Out Distractions

If the problem with your garden isn't the garden but the neighbor's clothesline, jungle gym, or aboveground pool right behind it, remember that good fences (or better yet, hedges) make good neighbors—and good gardens. Can't afford a fence? Set up a sturdy latticework trellis behind your garden and in front of the offending view and grow gorgeous vines. Clematis, climbing roses, morning glories, passionflower—it's the perfect opportunity to experiment with all those gorgeous vines you've been longing to grow. Perennial vines will be an extremely dominant feature when they're blooming, so combine them with the same care you'd use to put together a perennial combination, and match the flower colors to your bed's predominant colors.

Beg, Borrow, or Steal Some Color

If you like your garden most of the time but there are stretches when not much is in bloom and it could really use some color, remember the designer tricks we discussed in Chapter 1 and use one or more of them to bring your garden back to life. Fill in color gaps with long-blooming annuals, tuck in colorful containers, or add bright, sparkly art to mimic flowers (gazing balls of different sizes set at different heights might work wonders here).

Crown a New Queen

If your garden is aglow with *Rudbeckia* 'Goldsturm' only because it was the rage 10 years ago, give it a face-lift by ridding yourself of it (it will look gorgeous in your meadow garden) and replacing it with today's hot perennial. But this time, make sure you're planting it because you like it.

Dress It Up

If what once looked charming and cottagelike now looks weedy, overgrown, and unkempt, try a more formal look, with neatly arranged symmetrical beds, pleasingly ordered plants, and tidy paths and edgings.

Dress It Down

If the upkeep of a formal garden is driving you crazy or it's begun to feel cold and static over the years, reassure yourself that it's okay to take it out and go for the cottage look. Your neighbors won't hate you. (Well, okay, they probably will. But remember, they're not the ones who have to take care of it.)

Oust Ugly Plants

We know. Everybody, every magazine, every garden show, and every catalog said that this perennial was the most stunning thing this side of heaven. You bought it—for a premium price—and planted it, and . . . it's ugly. There's no way around it: No matter how you look at it, no matter what you tell yourself, it's hideous. You cringe every time you see it. You keep hoping it will just die. Trust us, it won't, so get rid of it. Dig it up, throw it out, and find a plant that you really like to put in its place. Breathe a huge sigh of relief. End of story!

Have Fun

Let's not forget this part. Maybe what's wrong with your garden is that you just tried too hard. You wanted it to look like a picture in a book or magazine, and maybe it does. But it doesn't look like *you*. As you rework it, trust your own taste and plant what you love. If you use good design principles (see Chapter 1), you can grow whatever you want. It will look good—and it will look like you. It doesn't get better than that!

PART II

Growing
Perennials

7

CLIMATE CONSIDERATIONS

Before you head for the nursery or order a single perennial, consider this: The two most common reasons for perennial plant death are failure to water plants their first season (shame, shame—not that *we'd* know anything about this), and trying to grow plants in the wrong climatic conditions. We can't help you with the first problem—well, we can tell you to use drip irrigation, mulch, and/or choose drought-tolerant plants, but we're not volunteering to water for you. But we are happy to help you avoid the heartbreak that comes from choosing the wrong plants for your area.

In this chapter, you'll learn what climate is and why it matters, what catalogs mean when they refer to hardiness zones, what heat zones are, how to determine what your garden's climate is, and how to choose plants that are adapted to your conditions. You'll also find lists of the best perennials for hard-to-please climates (like New England and the Southwest).

THE TRUTH ABOUT CLIMATE

Most people think of climate in terms of heat and cold. If your summers are hot enough to melt plastic and your winters are frost-free, you'd probably say you live in a warm climate. Alternatively, if you live in northern Vermont where, as the natives say, you have 11 months of winter and 1 month of mighty cold weather, you could say your climate was cold. Temperature extremes play an important part in determining what you can—and, more important to some gardeners, *can't*—grow. But temperatures are only a part of the climate picture.

Humidity is as important to climate as temperature. Summers may be equally hot in Arizona and Alabama, but the plants that do well in each state are radically different. Arizona plants are adapted to hot, dry summers and would rot in the foglike dampness of an Alabama August. When you're choosing plants for your perennial border, find out if they're adapted to dry areas (these are often listed as plants for xeriscapes, or drought-tolerant plants), or if they thrive in a more humid environment. Then buy the ones that match your conditions.

Snow cover is another important consideration. If you live in an area that is usually blanketed with snow all winter, you can grow plants that would die farther south if grown in a site with sporadic snow cover. Snow acts as a natural insulator, keeping the soil evenly frozen. Perennials are most likely to die over winter if the soil frequently freezes and thaws because repeated freezing and thawing action tends to heave the plants out of the ground, exposing their roots to freezing and drying out. (The other cause of perennials dying in winter is cold, wet soil, which isn't a problem if the soil stays frozen.)

Other aspects of climate that may determine what grows well for you are wind, rain, and the types of "natural disaster" conditions that make the headlines. If your garden is in an exposed site and you live in an area with high winds, your plants will face a triple threat. First, the wind beating against the unprotected plants will batter them and knock them over unless they're sturdily staked. Second, winds dry out plants and soil, so your plants will need a deep mulch and frequent watering or they may scorch. Third, winds create colder temperatures (the dreaded windchill factor), which means that your plants may be growing in a colder climate than simple geography might lead you to believe.

Rains that sheet down in torrents can also flatten your plants. If you live in an area where downpours are the norm, consider siting your garden where it gets some shelter from overhanging branches, walls, or other structures. Hailstorms can turn flowers and foliage into streamers or punch holes in leaves like a hungry caterpillar. If you live in a hail-prone area, minimize the damage by growing plants with small or fine leaves, rather than plants with large, showy (or, more likely in your case, formerly showy) leaves.

You can see that what we call "climate" is actually a complex interaction of geography and weather patterns. The way your climate is pieced together determines what you can grow—or at least imposes significant limits. By finding out what these limits are, you'll be that much closer to a garden that grows well and looks great with only routine care.

Know Your Climate Limitations

No gardener can grow every perennial (although we know quite a few who want to) because every property has its climatic limitations. Even gardeners in England envy our warm, dry summers and stunning autumns, just as we envy their mild winters and moderate summers. A Denver gardener might have a showstopping rock garden that's the envy of his Nashville friends, while he covets the beautiful border of peonies and irises that they take for granted.

What about all those "perfect" perennial gardens photographed for magazines and books? No matter how large or complicated they are, even the best gardens have only a limited selection of the many available perennials. Whenever you look at a photo of a lush, gorgeous garden, you don't see the plants the gardener tried—and failed—to grow. What you do see is the eventual success that the gardener achieved from finding out which plants grow well together in her garden's specific conditions. These site-specific conditions are referred to as the microclimate. Each microclimate is influenced by slope and aspect, walls and fences, the amount and type of vegetation such as hedges and tree canopies, and local soil conditions (for example, a gravel ridge versus a low-lying, humus-rich yard).

The secrets of perennial gardening success are learning about your particular microclimate—and it can be quite a bit different from the microclimate two blocks over—and learning about the needs of the perennials you'd like to plant. In addition to the plant lists in this chapter, the encyclopedia entries, beginning on page 265, provide growing specifics for every plant, so refer to those when considering whether a given perennial would be suitable for your garden.

Your Climate Checklist

To focus on your own climate, run through the following climate checklist. (If you don't know an answer, you can often get it by calling your local weather station or Cooperative Extension Service.) Review the results and you'll have a good idea of your yard's general climate as well as the specific conditions prevailing in different parts of the yard. Both your yard's overall climate and the climates of smaller areas in the yard are called *microclimates* because they reflect the specific conditions of small sites.

- What is the average date of your first fall frost?
- What is the average date of your last spring frost?
- Do you have winter snow cover? If so, is it constant or sporadic?

THAT WONDERFUL WEATHER LORE

One part of climate that's hard to overlook is the weather. We check the forecast in the paper and on the news at night and in the morning, and we perk up for the weather announcements on the radio. We compulsively go to Weather.com to see if conditions have changed since we last looked 15 minutes ago. We may even buy a weather radio if we commute in cold-weather areas or are concerned about frost or other calamities smiting our plants. We scan the skies and stick our arms or heads out the door to see if we'll need a jacket or an umbrella. Each of us is a sort of weather prophet, making our best guess and proceeding accordingly.

Fortunately, our ancestors have left us a rich mine of lore about the weather to help us make our guesses. For them, weather was often a matter of life and death because many made their living from agriculture or the sea. Even for those who didn't, transportation was neither as safe nor as weather-proof as it is today, so they needed a forecast they could rely on before setting out on a journey. As a result, they studied the weather closely and passed on their observations from generation to generation.

Here are some sayings that still stand the test of time. Keep them in mind the next time you're trying to decide if it will rain or if you need to water.

- "When ye see a cloud rise out of the west, straightway cometh the rain" (Luke 12:54). This refers to the fact that weather fronts usually move from west to east in the northern hemisphere.
- "Rainbow in the morning, shepherd take warning. Rainbow toward night, shepherd's delight." A morning rainbow, caused by the rising sun from the east shining on rain clouds in the west, indicates rain heading your way from the west. A rainbow seen in the evening is caused by the setting sun shining from the west on rain clouds in the east, indicating fair weather approaching from the west.
- "If the sun goes pale to bed, 'twill rain tomorrow, it is said." High cirrus clouds in the west give the setting sun a veiled look. When appearing as bands or mare's tails, they signal an approaching storm.
- "Clear moon, frost soon." Cloud cover acts like a blanket over the earth, keeping temperatures from dipping as low as they would on a clear night.

ANIMAL AND PLANT PREDICTORS

Another body of weather lore involves the appearance or behavior of plants and animals. Even today, we grow up with sayings about unusually large woolly bear caterpillars and extraplump squirrels or other hibernators being signs of a cold winter to come. Some of this lore has a basis in science. Here are some reliable weather indicators to watch for.

- "The darker the color of a caterpillar in fall, the harder the winter." This indicator has proven reliable, but we don't yet know why.
- "When the sheep collect and huddle, tomorrow will become a puddle." Sheep respond in this way to a change from a high- to low-pressure system, which often brings rain.
- "The higher the geese, the fairer the weather." High flying is a response to a high-pressure system; if geese fly low, a low-pressure system is coming, and rain with it. This saying applies to all migratory birds.
- "When the wild azalea shuts its doors, that's when winter tempest roars." Azaleas and rhododendron leaves curl up tightly when the temperature drops.

- Do you have fairly consistent rains in summer? Are some months usually dry? Which ones?
- Is your area humid all year? Very humid in summer? Is the air usually dry?
- What is each month's average high temperature in your area?
- What is each month's average low temperature in your area?
- What is each month's average precipitation in your area?
- Does your area have frequent high winds, torrential rains, dust storms, or hailstorms?
- Think about what your yard looks like. Are there exposed, open places that seem more windy than other areas? Are there low areas that get frost earlier and that seem to stay cold longer than the rest of the yard? What about hills or other high places that might suffer from windchill more than the rest of the yard, or that warm up too early and might be hit hard by late frosts?
- Do trees, hedges, walls, or fences create shady areas that tend to be cooler than the surrounding yard? Are there bright areas that heat up faster?

Record the climate information from this checklist in your garden journal. When you're tempted by a perennial you're reading about or looking at in a catalog, refer to the

Prairie profusion. Low on maintenance, high on color, this meadow-inspired seaside garden shines in summer with 'Hyperion' and purple daylilies, white gaura (*Gaura lindheimeri*), butterfly weed, lance-leaf coreopsis (*Coreopsis lanceolata*), and 'East Friesland' salvia.

journal. You'll have a good idea whether the plant will grow well in your conditions.

Fooling Mother Nature

Plants usually grow best and are healthiest when given the conditions they prefer. But sometimes you can still grow "impossible" plants—the ones that "just don't grow here"—if you are able to compensate for growing them outside their natural range.

For example, tulips need a certain amount of chilling to bloom. If you live in the Deep South, where the winters don't stay cold for the required number of weeks, your tulips will come up, but they won't bloom. You can still have blooming tulips— if you prechill the bulbs in the refrigerator every year. But you can also have beautiful bulbs like African lilies (*Agapanthus*) and crinums (*Crinum*) that would freeze and die with the first frost farther north.

Peonies also bloom better in cold-winter areas. If you're a Deep South gardener whose heart is set on peonies, the trick here is to look for cultivars that have been specially bred to do well in hotter areas. Researchers at colleges like the University of Georgia are always testing and evaluating perennials to find those that are adapted to southern conditions.

Gardeners in the North often envy the beautiful rosemary bushes that grow in southern colonial and cottage gardens. In areas where rosemary won't overwinter outdoors, you can still have stately rosemary bushes if you grow them in pots and bring them in each fall. (Agapanthus look stunning in containers, too.) You can choose ornamental pots for a formal touch, or sink the pots into the ground to make it look like the plants are growing in your garden bed. Northerners can grow many tender perennials if they are willing to overwinter them indoors, root cuttings indoors, or dig and store tender bulbs.

Remember that *where* you put a plant can help it survive, too. Chancy perennials sited in front of a south-facing wall are more likely to live through winter than similar plants in colder, exposed sites. Sometimes a well-drained site can make the difference between death and survival. For more about these and other ways to protect your plants in winter, see "Winter Protection" on page 213. Although these tactics can make a real difference, your plant selection will ultimately depend on the plants' hardiness and heat tolerance.

PLANT HARDINESS AND HARDINESS ZONES

Hardiness can mean a lot of things, from a plant's ability to withstand drought and neglect to its pest-resistance and durability. Most often, it is used to refer to cold-hardiness—the coldest temperature a plant can live through. If a plant can survive low temperatures of -10°F but will die at -11°F or below, it is considered hardy to -10°F.

Information about plant hardiness has been collected for most perennials and is readily available. For this information to be

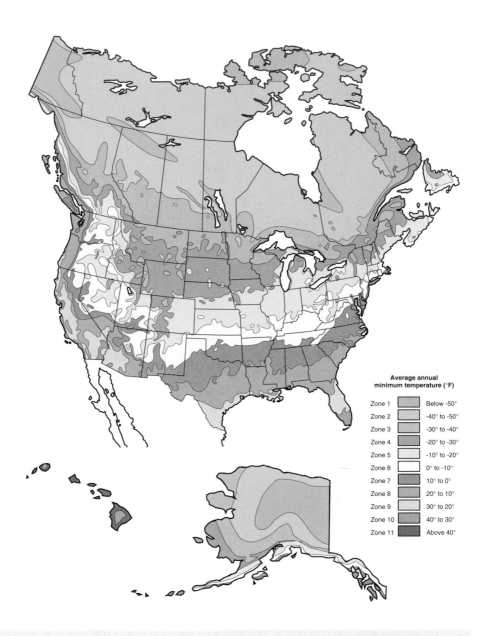

**Average annual
minimum temperature (°F)**

Zone 1	Below -50°
Zone 2	-40° to -50°
Zone 3	-30° to -40°
Zone 4	-20° to -30°
Zone 5	-10° to -20°
Zone 6	0° to -10°
Zone 7	10° to 0°
Zone 8	20° to 10°
Zone 9	30° to 20°
Zone 10	40° to 30°
Zone 11	Above 40°

USDA Plant Hardiness Zone Map. This map is recognized as the best estimator of minimum temperatures available. Look at the map to find your area, then match its color to the key on the lower right. When you've found your color, the key will tell you what hardiness zone you live in. Remember that the map is a general guide; your particular conditions may vary.

useful, you need to be able to connect it to your climate. It doesn't help to know that a perennial is hardy to -10°F if you don't know whether the temperature gets below -10°F in your area. Fortunately, plant scientists and meteorologists have gotten together and mapped North America in terms of plant hardiness, dividing it into zones. A plant hardiness zone map can tell you which hardiness zone you live and garden in.

Of course, plant zones are created from temperature averages, so some winters will be colder and others will be milder. If there's solid snow cover or your plants are buried under a heavy winter mulch, most likely no harm will be done during a colder-than-average winter; if they're exposed, a freak cold spell may kill the less hardy perennials. Gardening is a gamble, and few seasons see every plant through alive. You're just as likely to lose plants in a cool, wet winter where the soil stays damp as you are in cold snaps (many perennials don't tolerate wet feet for prolonged periods).

The USDA Plant Hardiness Zone Map

The standard hardiness map is the USDA Plant Hardiness Zone Map (see the opposite page). This map, revised in 1990 from the 1965 version, incorporates data from weather stations across North America. It accurately gives the current range of the average annual minimum temperatures for areas across the United States, Canada, and Mexico. These areas are assigned zone numbers, with the zones stretching in rough bands across the continent. Each zone represents a minimum temperature range, such as 10° to 20°F. This is the coldest it is likely to get in that area.

The USDA map divides the country into 11 plant hardiness zones. Each zone except the coldest (Zone 1) and warmest (Zone 11) is subdivided into two sections, A and B, each representing a 5°F range. This means, for example, that Emmaus, Pennsylvania, where Rodale Inc. is located, is in Zone 6B, with average winter minimum temperatures of 0° to -5°F. Gardeners in Emmaus can feel confident about planting perennials that are hardy to -5°F or below. They're on fairly safe ground planting perennials that are hardy to 0° to -5°F, but they risk losing plants to the cold if they choose plants that are not hardy to 0°F.

The hardiness zones on the U.S. mainland run only from 1 to 10. Zone 11 includes only the very warmest parts of the country, where temperatures remain above 40°F year-round, such as parts of Hawaii. Most zone maps also don't include the A and B divisions. Though the A and B divisions are more precise, the broader zones are still a useful guide and are the zones referred to in most gardening books, magazines, and catalogs. When you look up an entry in this book's encyclopedia, you'll see hardiness listed in whole zones rather than half zones.

Arnold Arboretum Zone Map

Occasionally, you'll find references to the Arnold Arboretum zone map in an old gardening book. This map was compiled by the Arnold Arboretum in Jamaica Plain, Massachusetts, and last revised in 1967. It has slightly different hardiness zones than the USDA map. However, the painstaking data collection that went into the 1990 USDA Plant Hardiness Zone Map convinced the Arnold Arboretum to switch to the USDA map. Newer references all feature the USDA zones.

Using Hardiness Zones

Here's how to use plant hardiness zones. You're looking at a perennial you'd like to grow in your garden—say, garden phlox (*Phlox paniculata*). The catalog or plant tag says the phlox is hardy to Zone 3. That means that if you live in Zone 3 or in a warmer zone (such as Zone 7), garden phlox will be cold-hardy in your area. If you live in a colder zone, garden phlox will not be reliably hardy in your area. Gardeners in colder zones should choose another phlox or a similar but hardier perennial. Moss phlox (*P. subulata*) and creeping phlox (*P. stolonifera*) are hardy to Zone 2, while woodland phlox (*P. divaricata*) and wild sweet William (*P. maculata*) are hardy to Zone 3. If you live in the southern part of Zone 3, you could take a chance on garden phlox, giving it a protected site and a heavy winter mulch. There are no guarantees, though, so try a plant or two, not a large group.

Deep South gardeners are often confronted with the opposite problem: Plants that grow well in colder areas can't take the heat. Fortunately, some catalogs and books, including this encyclopedia, give a hardiness range rather than simply listing the coldest zone a plant will grow in. If you're a southern gardener and want to grow the bold, colorful hybrid lupines (*Lupinus*), a cold-hardiness limit (Zone 3) would imply that you're on solid ground. However, a hardiness range (Zones 3 to 6) shows you that lupines won't survive the humid heat of a southern summer.

THE AHS HEAT ZONE MAP

Since heat tolerance can also determine whether perennials grow and thrive, in 1997 the American Horticultural Society (AHS) developed a second map for American gardeners, the AHS Heat Zone Map. This map also divides the country into zones that represent the average number of days per year above 86°F. There are 12 heat zones, again ranging from the coldest, Zone 1, with less than 1 day above 86°F, to Zone 12, with more than 210 days above 86°F.

As with hardiness zones, plants do well across a range of heat zones. Heat-loving perennials like lavender will thrive in drier parts of Zones 8 through 12, while perennials like delphiniums and poppies, which prefer cool summers, grow best in Zones 1 through 4. And bear in mind that hot, humid conditions have very different effects on perennials—especially mildew- and rot-prone perennials—than hot, dry conditions.

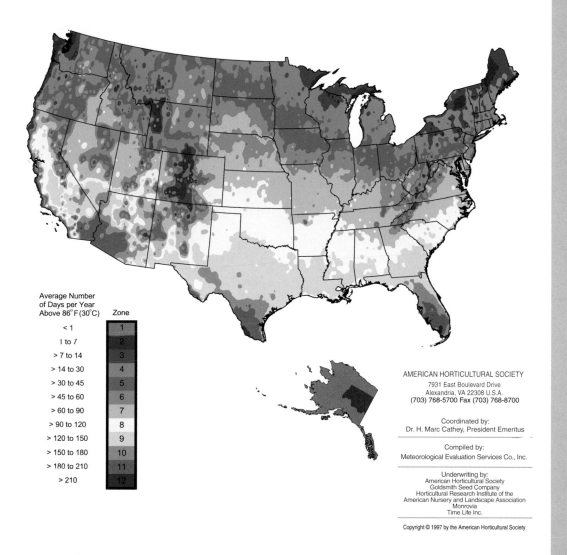

Average Number
of Days per Year
Above 86°F (30°C)   Zone

< 1	1
1 to 7	2
> 7 to 14	3
> 14 to 30	4
> 30 to 45	5
> 45 to 60	6
> 60 to 90	7
> 90 to 120	8
> 120 to 150	9
> 150 to 180	10
> 180 to 210	11
> 210	12

AMERICAN HORTICULTURAL SOCIETY
7931 East Boulevard Drive
Alexandria, VA 22308 U.S.A.
(703) 768-5700 Fax (703) 768-8700

Coordinated by:
Dr. H. Marc Cathey, President Emeritus

Compiled by:
Meteorological Evaluation Services Co., Inc.

Underwriting by:
American Horticultural Society
Goldsmith Seed Company
Horticultural Research Institute of the
American Nursery and Landscape Association
Monrovia
Time Life Inc.

The AHS Heat Zone Map. This map lets you know just how hot your area really gets. It measures the average number of days above 86°F in each zone, with Zone 1 having the least and Zone 12 the most. Just look for your region and match its color on the bar on the lower left to find your heat zone.

The book that first introduced the AHS Heat Zone Map to gardeners is *Heat-Zone Gardening* by Dr. H. Marc Cathey, who developed the concept for the American Horticultural Society when he was its president. It's a good place to turn for more information. You can also find heat zones listed in books like Larry Hodgson's *Perennials for Every Purpose*.

Unfortunately for those of us who like to keep things simple, there's more to plants' heat tolerance than daytime temperature alone. Most experts agree that it's the average *night* temperature, rather than daytime temperature, that determines whether a perennial will thrive in a given area: Nighttime temperatures determine whether a plant can convert the products of photosynthesis (sugars) into useful energy through the process of respiration. Plants unaccustomed or ill-adapted to high night temperatures "burn up" because they are never able to create usable energy from photosynthesis and are unable to grow as a result.

Because nighttime temperatures—and the interaction between day and night temperatures—are the real keys to the temperature puzzle, we have decided not to include the heat zones in the encyclopedia section. To be certain that a perennial you're considering will do well in your garden, ask the advice of staff at your local nursery, botanic garden, extension office, or garden club or society, or call a knowledgeable friend. Another way is to just try it for yourself. Plants don't read books, and the unique conditions in your garden may enable a plant to thrive despite its heat zone rating.

GARDENING ON THE EDGE

For most gardeners, plant hardiness and heat zones are good guides for what they can grow. In some parts of the country, however, special conditions like highly alkaline soil, drought, high rainfall, or high humidity are limiting factors. This is especially true of the Southwest, far North, Deep South, and Rockies.

Making the Desert Bloom

In the Southwest, humidity and rainfall are low, and watering is often restricted. It makes sense to grow perennials that don't need a lot of water, especially since what rain does fall often comes in winter rather than during the growing season. Perennials for the Southwest also have to be both heat- and cold-tolerant: Days are often scorching, while nights can drop near or below freezing.

These daunting requirements have led to the development of xeriscaping, a style of dryland gardening that uses only tough, drought-tolerant plants. For a list of perennials that grow well in southwest conditions, see "Best Perennials: A Regional Guide" on page 168. (You can also check with your local extension agent or arboretum for a broader selection.) Successful xeriscaping depends on more than plant selection. To get the most from dryland perennial gardening, give your plants a protected site: Use windscreens—either fencing or hedges—and trees, shrubs, or structures to shade your garden. Use drip irrigation, and mulch your beds.

The drier the climate, the more alkaline the soil is likely to be. If you live in near-desert conditions, your selection of plants will be fairly restricted unless you garden in raised beds with imported topsoil or lower your soil's pH. You'll find more information in "Changing Your pH" on page 177.

Perennials Southern Style

The high humidity and relentless summer heat combine to make gardening a challenge in the Deep South. While gardeners swelter in an atmosphere as inviting as a wet sleeping bag, pests and diseases thrive. In addition, southern gardeners may face heavy clay soil or thirsty sand. For perennials to grow well in the South, they must be heat-tolerant and disease-resistant. For a list of top perennials for Deep South gardens, see "Best Perennials: A Regional Guide" on page 168, or consult your local extension agent for more perennials that do well in your area.

Dr. Allan Armitage of the University of Georgia has done extensive trials to see which perennials stand up to southern conditions. He has developed the recommendations that follow, which will help you have a better garden.

- **Avoid taller cultivars.** The abundant heat and moisture and the longer growing season cause plants to grow bigger in the South, so starting with tall plants invites lots of staking. Look for short or dwarf cultivars of your favorite perennials.

Dryland gardening. Make the desert bloom in your backyard with a centerpiece of sculptural cacti and succulents—in this case, prickly pears (*Opuntia*) and euphorbias—and bright beds of threadleaf coreopsis and annual everlasting 'Strawberry Fields' globeflower (*Gomphrena globosa* 'Strawberry Fields').

- **Hold off on fertilizer.** High-nitrogen fertilizers will cause loose, lanky growth at the expense of flowers.
- **Improve your soil.** Add organic matter like compost and shredded leaves. In clay soil, organic matter increases drainage and aeration; it increases water and nutrient retention in sandy soil. For more on organic matter, see "Super Soil Amendments" on page 178.

BEST PERENNIALS: A REGIONAL GUIDE

These perennials are proven performers in their areas. Use them as the basis for a bed or border if you live in one of these challenging regions. To expand your selection, see what sells well in a good local garden center, visit a nearby botanical garden and see what they're growing, and try to find mail-order nurseries that specialize in regional plants. Experiment with other perennials and add the ones that are successful for you. In a few years, you'll have your own customized list.

Note that if only a genus name is listed (indicated by "spp." after the name), more than one species in that genus can be grown in your region, but not every species will be suitable. Similarly, hardiness zones given after the genus name will reflect the range for the genus and won't apply to every species. Look up the genus in "The Perennial Encyclopedia," beginning on page 265, to find which species you can grow.

10 FOR THE SOUTHWEST

Agastache spp. (anise hyssops): Zones 3 to 8
Artemisia spp. (artemisias, wormwoods): Zones 3 to 9
Gaillardia spp. (blanket flowers): Zones 2 to 10
Gaura lindheimeri (white gaura): Zones 5 to 9
Oenothera spp. (evening primroses): Zones 3 to 8
Penstemon spp. (beard-tongues, penstemons): Zones 2 to 9
Salvia spp. (sages): Zones 3 to 10
Verbascum spp. (mulleins): Zones 4 to 8
Verbena spp. (verbenas, vervains): Zones 3 to 10
Yucca spp. (yuccas, Adam's needles): Zones 3 to 10

10 FOR THE DEEP SOUTH

Amsonia spp. (blue stars, amsonias): Zones 4 to 10
Asclepias tuberosa (butterfly weed): Zones 4 to 9
Chrysanthemum maximum (Shasta daisy): Zones 4 to 9
Eupatorium coelestinum (hardy ageratum): Zones 6 to 10
Hedychium spp. (ginger lilies, garland lilies): Zones 7 to 11
Hemerocallis spp. and hybrids (daylilies): Zones 2 to 9
Hibiscus spp. (rose mallows, hibiscus): Zones 4 to 10
Salvia spp. (sages): Zones 3 to 10
Verbena spp. (verbenas, vervains): Zones 3 to 10
Zephyranthes spp. (rain lilies): Zones 7 to 11

10 FOR THE FAR NORTH

Anemone spp. (windflowers): Zones 2 to 9
Campanula spp. (bellflowers, harebells): Zones 2 to 8
Delphinium hybrids (delphiniums): Zones 2 to 7
Dicentra spp. (bleeding hearts): Zones 2 to 9
Eryngium spp. (sea hollies, eryngos): Zones 2 to 9
Hemerocallis spp. and cultivars (daylilies): Zones 2 to 9
Lupinus hybrids (hybrid lupines): Zones 2 to 5
Paeonia lactiflora cultivars (Chinese peonies): Zones 2 to 8
Papaver orientale (oriental poppy): Zones 2 to 10
Phlox spp. (phlox): Zones 2 to 9

10 FOR THE ROCKIES

Artemisia spp. (artemisias, wormwoods): Zones 3 to 9
Campanula spp. (bellflowers, harebells): Zones 2 to 8
Dictamnus albus (gas plant): Zones 3 to 8
Iberis sempervirens (perennial candytuft): Zones 3 to 9
Lupinus spp. (lupines): Zones 2 to 6
Nepeta spp. (catmints, nepetas): Zones 3 to 9
Penstemon spp. (beard-tongues, penstemons): Zones 3 to 9
Phlomis spp. (Jerusalem sages): Zones 4 to 9
Salvia spp. (sages): Zones 3 to 10
Veronica spp. (speedwells): Zones 2 to 8

Dr. Armitage has also found that southern gardeners can grow some perennials that traditionally do poorly in the South. The trick is to plant beautiful but heat-intolerant plants like delphiniums, lupines, and primroses in fall, enjoy their bloom the following spring and summer, then dig them up and consign them to the compost heap. If you're willing to treat them as annuals, you'll get a fine show from these finicky beauties, and you can use heat-tolerant bedding plants to fill in the gaps they leave after you pull them. This works for bulbs like tulips that need chilling, too: Simply treat them as annuals and replant each fall.

The Big Chill

Perennial gardening in the Far North presents a different challenge: winter. Temperatures far into the minuses may be the norm at night for months, often accompanied by high winds. Ice storms may coat the garden with "glass." Arctic winds may whip your fragile plants, causing breakage and dehydration. And frosts may continue to strike into June, take a month off, and start up again in August.

Fortunately, gardeners from Maine to Minnesota have a broad selection of perennials that withstand cold. For a list of some of the best, see "Best Perennials: A Regional Guide" on the opposite page. And there are a number of ways to reduce the risks and guarantee a beautiful garden display. One way is to choose perennials that bloom when frost is unlikely. If you want to plant fall-flowering perennials like chrysanthemums and asters, buy cultivars that bloom in September rather than October. On the other hand, if your heart is set on spring-flowering perennials, buy late-blooming cultivars that are likely to escape late-spring frosts.

Another way to ward off winter fatalities is to protect your plants' roots. Make sure your beds are well-drained to avoid root rot. When the ground freezes, mulch your perennials deeply to guard against frost heaving. Deep snow is an excellent insulator: Pile it on your beds to keep the soil frozen and plants protected. Site your beds in areas where they're protected from chilling, drying winds.

Rocky Mountain High

Rocky Mountain gardeners have their own distinct set of climatic conditions. They face severe winter cold and intense summer heat. As in the Southwest, humidity and rainfall are extremely low, and as in the North, wind exposure creates both windchill and serious drying. On the plus side, the benefits of high-altitude gardening are bright sunlight and well-drained, gravelly soils—perfect conditions for rock gardening. Rocky Mountain gardeners can easily grow the gorgeous alpine plants that avid rock gardeners in other parts of the country can only dream about.

If a beautiful rock garden isn't your ideal, you can create a standard perennial bed or border if you irrigate your plants—or plant a lovely xeriscape with little or no additional water. Make sure you choose plants adapted to Rocky Mountain conditions. See "Best Perennials: A Regional Guide" on page 168 for a list of some of the best, and check with the Denver Botanic Garden or your local extension agent for others. Site your garden in a sheltered location where plants will be protected from wind, use drip irrigation, and mulch your perennials. Then you can enjoy the plants and their beautiful mountain backdrop.

OTHER CONSIDERATIONS

Once you've matched your perennials to your climate, you've come a long way toward a great garden. But there are other conditions that must be met.

First, site plants where they'll get the exposure they need. Plants that prefer to grow in full sun will languish in deep shade; shade-loving plants will fry in the sun. Matching a plant's soil preferences is another way to ensure success. You'll find out what exposure specific perennials prefer, how to prepare the soil for perennials, and other cultural tactics in Chapter 8, "Perennial Gardening Basics." You can look up specific perennials' needs in the individual entries in "The Perennial Encyclopedia," beginning on page 265.

8

PERENNIAL GARDENING BASICS

Sound gardening principles are the same whether you're growing squash, shrubs, or Siberian irises. In this chapter, you'll learn how to prepare your garden, how to put in your plants, and how to take care of them once they're planted. Once you've mastered the basics, you can grow any perennial in this book. But, as with any skill, you have to start from the ground up.

Remember the name "perennial" when you're preparing a garden bed or border for these beautiful and durable plants. A clump of peonies or poppies can live for 75 years, and all perennials live for at least 3 to 5 years. So give your garden the attention it needs *before* you put in your plants.

Double vision. A vision of loveliness, in this case—the pastels of late spring and early summer: astilbes, foxgloves, hardy geraniums, delphiniums, Siberian irises, and peonies brighten the view of lucky visitors who sit on the sheltered bench. Good soil preparation has paid off in this lush garden.

SIZING UP YOUR SOIL

Good soil is the backbone of a good garden. Well-prepared soil is fluffy and loose so water, air, and nutrients can filter down easily and roots have room to stretch. You can grow a lovely garden without knowing anything about soil; all you need is good soil and sound gardening techniques, like mulching, composting, and adding organic matter to your garden beds. But if your soil is hard to work, if it drains too quickly or too slowly, or if your plants aren't as lush and healthy as they should be, you'll have a better garden if you learn a few things about soil.

Soil 101

Most people think of soil as a layer of decayed leaves, twigs, and so on, but this organic matter and the organisms that live in it really make up only 5 percent of the soil. Soil is 45 percent mineral particles—the bedrock of the earth broken down over time—and 50 percent space between particles, space that's filled with air and water. Your soil will be made of particles of whatever rocks are prevalent in your area. The reason you can't pick out the crushed limestone, granite, or sandstone is because soil particles are so small that they've lost these distinguishing characteristics.

Sand, Silt, and Clay

Soil particles are classified by particle size as either sand, silt, or clay.

Sand. The largest particle is sand, which can be seen by the naked eye and is pinhead-size or larger. Sand particles fit together loosely, leaving space for oxygen to reach plant roots for good growth. This space between particles also means that sandy soils drain quickly and don't hold many nutrients.

Silt. The next soil component is silt, which is barely visible as individual particles. Silt particles fit together more tightly, so they hold more water and nutrients while still allowing room for oxygen to get to the roots.

Clay. Clay, the smallest soil particle, can be seen individually only under a microscope. Clay can hold large amounts of water and nutrients, but the particles pack together so tightly that little air is available to plant roots.

Most soil in residential areas is loam—a combination of sand, silt, and clay. If the soil has a high percentage of sand, it is a sandy loam; a high percentage of clay is a clay loam; and so on. Unless you live on the beach, in a swamp, or on a mud slick, you won't have to garden in pure sand, silt, or clay.

Soil scientists consider the ideal garden soil to be 20 percent clay, 40 percent silt, and 40 percent sand. The sand encourages good drainage, while the clay and silt help to hold nutrients and some moisture for good root growth. But remember that this is just an ideal—there's a lot of leeway for good garden performance because different plants have different soil requirements. And adding organic matter like shredded leaves or strawy manure will bring your soil into better balance no matter what its composition is—organic matter both aerates the soil and retains water and nutrients. (For more on organic matter, see "Super Soil Amendments" on page 178.)

Simple Soil Tests

How do you know if you have good loam soil, or if you have too much clay or sand? There are simple tests—they take just a few minutes—that you can do at home to find out what kind of soil you have.

The Watering Test

This test looks at how your soil handles water. When you're watering the lawn or garden, does the water disappear so fast it looks like only the leaves have gotten wet, rather than the soil surface? And do you find that you have to water frequently to keep plants from wilting? If so, you have a lot of sand in your soil. On the other hand, if water puddles up and seems to take forever to sink into the soil, you have a high percentage of clay. Soil with very high clay content may dry and crack apart into clods or plates between rains; it also becomes sticky or very slippery when it's wet.

The Soil Ball Test

Try the soil ball test after a rain or after you water, when the soil is moist but not soggy. Take a handful of soil from the site where you want to grow perennials and squeeze it. When you open your hand, see what happens to the soil. If it crumbles apart, it's a loam. If it stays in a ball, it's basically clay. If it disintegrates easily and you can see and feel gritty little crystals in it, it's a sandy soil. And if it crumbles but feels greasy, it's silt.

The Water Jar Test

For a slightly more scientific evaluation, try the water jar test. Collect several soil samples where you want to site your flowerbed, and mix them together. Sieve or pick out any pebbles, roots, and other large debris. Put 1 cup of the mixed soil in a clear quart jar, fill the jar with water, and seal it. Then shake the jar vigorously.

Let the jar stand for 24 hours so the contents settle out, then examine the soil layers that have formed in the bottom of the jar. Don't move the jar or all the clay will float up again. (The organic particles in the soil—bits of leaves, twigs, and so on—will be lighter than the soil particles and will be floating or lying on top of the soil layers; for the purposes of this test, just ignore them.)

The largest and heaviest particles—sand—will have settled on the bottom; the medium-size and medium-weight particles—silt—will be in the middle; and the smallest and lightest—clay—will be on top. Estimate the percentage of each layer, and you can make an educated guess at your soil's texture. If you have a grease pencil, crayon, or indelible marker, you can mark off the level of each layer for easy reference.

For example, if you have a ¼-inch layer of sand, a ½-inch layer of silt, and a ¼-inch layer of clay (totaling 1 inch), your soil is 25 percent sand, 50 percent silt, and 25 percent clay.

Once you've estimated the percentages of each particle type, you can see if you have a

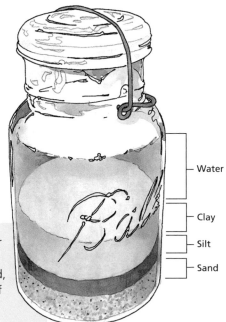

The water jar test. Put 1 cup of garden soil in a clear quart jar, fill the jar with water, seal, and shake. Leave the jar undisturbed for 24 hours, and the layers of sand, silt, and clay will settle out. By comparing the depth of the layers, you can estimate your soil's composition.

sandy loam, a silt loam, or a clay loam. Here's how to interpret the percentages.

Clay soils. Clay loams are common. If your soil has 20 to 35 percent clay and at least 45 percent sand, it's a sandy clay loam. If it's 25 to 40 percent clay and up to 20 percent sand, it's a silty clay loam. And if it's over 45 percent clay, it is classed as clay.

Sandy soils. Sandy loams are also common, with 50 to 70 percent sand. Loamy sand soils have 70 to 85 percent sand. The soil must be 85 to 100 percent sand before it can be classed as sand.

Silt soils. Silt loams, with 45 to 80 percent silt, are common in the Midwest, but high-silt soils are rare, mainly occurring on river deltas. You'd have to have 80 to 100 percent silt before the soil could be classed as silt rather than silt loam.

Professional Soil Tests

Once you've determined what type of soil you have, you may want to know what's *in* the soil. Is it phosphorus-rich? Does it have too much calcium? The best way to find out is to have your soil tested. Private soil labs and Cooperative Extension Services across the country will analyze soil samples for pH and nutrient content.

Each soil-testing service has its own procedures, so don't just send off soil; write, call, or e-mail for instructions first. You'll receive a variation of the following general directions.

Remove the surface debris from the area you plan to sample, then dig a small hole 6 inches deep. With a clean stainless-steel trowel or large stainless-steel spoon, cut a slice of soil from the side of the hole and put it in a clean plastic bucket. Take 10 to 15 samples from around the garden area, then mix them together in the bucket. Put the required amount of mixed soil in a plastic bag, then mail it and any required information in the package provided by the soil-testing service. Be sure to ask for organic recommendations.

It usually takes 4 to 6 weeks to get the results of your soil test, so give yourself plenty of time. If you're planning to put in a new flowerbed in fall, take your soil test in spring; if you want to upgrade your garden in spring, take it the previous fall. You can test for pH any time the soil isn't frozen. When the results come back, you can start collecting soil amendments to correct deficiencies and balance pH. Then you'll be ready when it's time to dig your beds.

Understanding pH

Soil pH is one of the simple mysteries of gardening: It sounds like a concept straight out of higher physics, but it's actually easy to determine and, except in extreme cases, it's easy to correct. Soil pH is a measure of the acidity or alkalinity of your soil. It's measured on a scale from 0 (highly acid) to 14.0 (highly alkaline), with 7.0, the pH of water, considered neutral. Most garden perennials grow best in soil with a pH of 6.0 to 7.0—slightly acid to neutral. Many

GET YOUR SOIL TEST HERE!

If you'd like to treat yourself and your garden to a professional soil test, here are four top-notch private labs with soil-testing services. They'll all provide you with organic recommendations so you can get your perennial garden off to a healthy start! Write or call for instructions and testing fees before sending off your soil.

You can also call your local Cooperative Extension Service about doing a soil test for you. Look them up in the phone book under the city or county government listings, then call to see what you need to do. Don't forget to request organic recommendations.

Peaceful Valley Farm Supply
P.O. Box 2209
Grass Valley, CA 95945
(916) 272-4769

Timberleaf Soil Testing Services
26489 Ynez Road, Suite C-197
Temecula, CA 92591
(909) 677-7510

Wallace Laboratories
365 Coral Circle
El Segundo, CA 90245
(310) 615-0116

Woods End Research
   Laboratory, Inc.
P.O. Box 297
Mt. Vernon, ME 04352
(207) 293-2457

woodland perennials prefer a more acid soil—pH 5.5 to 6.5.

Most perennials are flexible in their pH requirements; the problems start when soils are very acid or alkaline. Strongly acid and alkaline soils bind essential nutrients, making them unavailable to plants. The plants then exhibit deficiency symptoms, such as stunted growth or yellowed leaves. Acid soils can release heavy metals like aluminum, lead, and cadmium in harmful concentrations, as well as create an unfavorable environment for beneficial soil organisms. Alkaline soils are also often highly saline (salty), a condition toxic to plants.

Once you've determined your soil's pH, you can bring acid soils closer to neutral by adding lime, while alkaline soils may need sulfur to neutralize them. (See "Changing Your pH" on the opposite page to find out how much lime or sulfur to add.) Adding organic matter like leaves, grass clippings, or compost to your soil will level out the pH reading from either end: It raises the pH of acid soils and lowers the pH of alkaline soils. If your soil pH is mildly acidic (pH 5.5 to 6.0) to mildly alkaline (pH 7.1 to 7.8), you should be able to balance it with organic matter alone. You'll learn more about organic matter in "Super Soil Amendments" on page 178.

Checking Your Soil's pH

You can test soil pH yourself with a home soil test kit or a pH meter (both are available from garden centers and catalogs). Instead of testing, though, you might be able to guess your soil's pH by learning a little about the geology and native plants of your area. Nature preserves, parks, botanical gardens, and other public gardens often have books on the natural history of their area for sale; you can also try local colleges, libraries, and the nature and geography sections of bookstores.

If the predominant rock in your area is limestone, your soil is probably neutral to slightly alkaline; if it's sandstone or granite, you may have acid soil. If you live in an eastern woodland area where azaleas, rhododendrons, mountain laurels, blueberries, bayberries, ferns, and hemlocks are common, your soil is probably acidic; if you live in the arid Southwest, it's likely that your soil is alkaline.

Matching Plants to pH

If your soil is acidic and you'd like to keep it that way for your rhododendrons, ferns, hemlocks, and oaks, grow perennial woodland wildflowers and lilies, which prefer more acid soil, rather than garden perennials that grow best in near-neutral soil.

If your soil is alkaline and you're having a hard time lowering the pH, there are a number of lovely and popular perennials that appreciate mildly alkaline conditions, including baby's-breaths (*Gypsophila*), bearded irises (*Iris* hybrids), delphiniums, lavenders (*Lavandula*), clematis (*Clematis*), and pinks (*Dianthus*).

One way to grow favorite plants that aren't adapted to your soil's pH is to grow them in containers. You can buy or mix your own potting soil to match the plants'

CHANGING YOUR pH

If your soil is too acidic—a frequent problem in high-rainfall areas, where calcium leaches from the soil—add ground limestone, wood ashes, or bonemeal to correct the problem. Choose calcitic limestone if your soil has enough magnesium, and dolomite if your soil needs magnesium as well as calcium. To raise pH 1 point, add 5 pounds of calcitic limestone or 7 pounds of dolomite per 100 square feet. Add 6 pounds of wood ashes (instead of the limestone) per 100 square feet if you want faster results. Broadcast these materials by hand and rake them into the surface of your beds, or apply them to larger areas with a small garden spreader. If you broadcast by hand, wear gloves.

Don't get carried away when adding dolomite or wood ashes. Repeated applications of dolomite can cause an excess of magnesium, which can harm your plants, while an overdose of wood ashes will create a potassium overload. Use these materials cautiously.

If your soil is too alkaline—a particular problem in dryland areas—add powdered elemental sulfur to lower pH. To lower pH 1 point, add 1 pound of sulfur per 100 square feet. You can also add evergreen needles to the soil or use them as mulch, or work peat moss into the soil to help lower soil pH.

pH requirements. If, on the other hand, you'd like to bring your pH closer to neutral, the best time to amend the soil is when you dig your beds.

SUPER SOIL AMENDMENTS

Soil amendments benefit your garden—and your perennials—by supplying the humus that's the basis for good plant growth. Adding amendments loosens the soil so there are more spaces for air and nutrient-bearing water, increases water retention so you don't have to irrigate as often, improves drainage, and creates a favorable microclimate for beneficial soil organisms, including earthworms.

Unlike fertilizers, which provide plant nutrients without adding organic matter to the soil, the primary function of soil amendments is to improve soil structure. The phrase "soil structure" refers to the way soil particles fit together. Particles in a soil with good structure are close enough together to retain water and nutrients, but far enough apart to allow air and water to reach plant roots. When soil particles are too closely packed together, as in heavy clays, air and water can't get in; when they're too far apart, as in sands, they won't hold necessary water and nutrients long enough for plants to take them up.

Adding soil amendments balances these extremes by loosening up clay soils and adding moisture-retentive organic matter to sandy soils. Many amendments add nutrients as well, but when you're turning in shredded leaves, compost, or even manure, you're also adding organic matter to the soil. (For more on fertilizers, see "Fertilizing for Fabulous Flowers" on page 189.)

All garden soils, even good garden loams, benefit from regular additions of organic matter. You need to apply more every season because organic matter isn't stable in the soil. This essential material is constantly being broken down into humus by soil organisms. Humus binds nutrients and holds them in the soil of the root zone. To continue to give your perennials the benefits of organic matter, you must give your soil a steady supply. Fortunately, that's easy to do: Just incorporate organic matter into new beds, and add compost and mulch to established beds. (Remember that many of the same materials are used as both soil amendments and mulches, including compost and shredded leaves. They're generally considered amendments if they're worked into the soil and mulch if they're spread on top.)

The most commonly available soil amendments are compost, shredded leaves, grass clippings, hay and straw, aged manure, aged sawdust, and peat moss. You may be able to get other amendments locally, like alfalfa meal, seaweed, mushroom compost, ground corncobs, and apple pomace.

Compost and aged manure are balanced amendments and can be turned into the soil as is, at any time. Grass clippings are a good source of fast-release nitrogen, but they decompose quickly, adding little bulk

THE PERENNIAL GARDENER'S GUIDE TO ORGANIC SOIL AMENDMENTS

Organic soil amendments are the core of the perennial gardener's soil-improvement program. Choose the amendments that are most readily available to you, and turn them into the soil when you prepare your beds. Chop and compost hay, straw, and leaves first for quicker decomposition. You'll be adding humus, improving soil structure and water retention, and neutralizing pH every time you add soil amendments. Your perennials will thank you!

Organic Amendment	Average NPK Analysis	Average Application Rate per 100 sq. ft.	Comments
Compost, dry commercial	1-1-1	10 lb.	Balanced amendment; good when homemade compost is in short supply.
Compost, homemade	0.5-0.5-0.5 to 4-4-4	100 lb.	Ideal balanced amendment; add at any time.
Grass clippings, green	0.5-0.2-0.5	30 lb.	Decompose quickly, adding little bulk to soil.
Hay, weed-free	2.2-0.6-2.2	15 lb.	Add nitrogen source, such as bloodmeal, to speed breakdown.
Manure, cow (dry)	2-2.3-2.4	15 lb.	Manures add balanced nutrients to soil; dry manure won't burn plants.
Manure, horse (dry)	1.7-0.7-1.8	15 lb.	
Manure, sheep (dry)	4-1.4-3.5	5 lb.	
Manure, swine (dry)	2-1.8-1.8	15 lb.	
Oak leaves	0.8-9.4-0.1	15 lb.	Add nitrogen source, such as bloodmeal, to speed breakdown.
Peat moss	Negligible	3–6 cu. ft.	Lowers pH; do not use on acid soils.
Sawdust	Negligible	15 lb.	Add nitrogen source, such as bloodmeal, to speed breakdown.
Wheat straw	0.7-0.2-1.2	15 lb.	Add nitrogen source, such as bloodmeal, to speed breakdown.
Worm castings	0.5-0.5-0.3	10 lb.	Good soil conditioner.

to the soil. Peat, on the other hand, decomposes extremely slowly, so it will stay in the soil a long time. However, peat has a serious drawback if you live in an area where the soil is neutral to acid: It is a low-pH material and will acidify the soil if you add enough of it to have an impact on soil structure.

Shredded leaves, aged sawdust, hay, and straw need time to break down. Soil organisms use nitrogen in the decomposition process and may compete with your perennials for nitrogen if you add amendments the same season you plant. Ideally, prepare your beds in fall for spring planting, or in spring for fall planting, giving these amendments plenty of time to break down before you put in plants. If that's not possible, prepare the beds at least 6 weeks before you plant, and add a high-nitrogen fertilizer like bloodmeal or chicken manure with your soil amendments to speed decomposition. If you use sawdust, which is woody and needs a lot of nitrogen to break down, make sure it's well aged—the best sawdust will be so old it's black. (Also make sure to use sawdust that comes from wood that's not treated.) Pile fresh sawdust outside to weather until it has aged for a few seasons.

HOW TO MAKE COMPOST

Compost is the gardener's black gold—the perfect soil amendment and fertilizer. Its low nitrogen content provides the right amount of fertility for perennials. Too much nitrogen can cause weak, leggy growth that looks unattractive, flops over, and invites disease and insect invasions. If you've prepared your bed well before planting, compost is often the only fertilizer your perennials will need. Making your own compost is easy and fun, and it takes only 3 square feet of garden space.

Composting is controlled decomposition, with finished compost about halfway between fresh organic matter and humus. It works the same way as decomposition in the ground—beneficial decomposer microorganisms feed on nitrogen and carbon in the plant material, breaking it down. But because you're controlling the process, you can monitor the composting and speed it up, and because it's occurring above ground, it doesn't compete with your plants for nitrogen.

Materials for Your Pile

To make compost, just mix high-carbon and high-nitrogen materials and add air. High-carbon materials are easy to recognize: They're the fibrous ones that take a while to break down. Straw, hay, leaves, sawdust, shredded newspaper, pine needles, hedge trimmings, and the woodier parts of perennials (like old daylily flowerstalks) are all high-carbon.

High-nitrogen materials are the succulent plant materials that break down quickly, like grass clippings, fresh weeds, perennial prunings, fruits, and vegetables. Other nitrogen sources you can add to balance the compost pile are farmyard manure, bloodmeal, chicken manure, cotton-seed meal, and guano. (Because farmyard manure might be contaminated with *E. coli*, use it only in compost intended for ornamental plants, wear gloves when working with it, and wash your hands well afterward.)

You can also add kitchen scraps like eggshells, vegetable and fruit peelings, coffee grounds, and tea leaves. Don't add dog droppings or the contents of the cat's litter box, both of which may carry disease; or meat scraps, bones, or grease, which attract rodents and other scav-engers. And don't add diseased plants to your pile—throw them out. Otherwise, you might be spreading disease along with your compost.

Siting and Building the Pile

Site your compost pile in a spot close to the garden—you want the compost within easy reach. You can make a simple pile (just pile it up into a mound), or build a wire or wooden bin for your compost. While the bin is more attractive, the pile blends in better with the landscape and is easier to

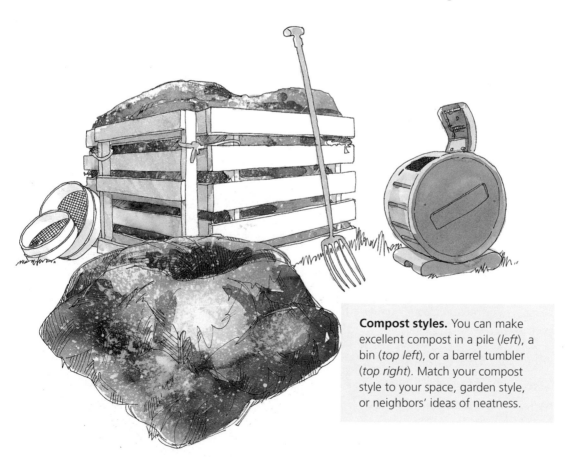

Compost styles. You can make excellent compost in a pile (*left*), a bin (*top left*), or a barrel tumbler (*top right*). Match your compost style to your space, garden style, or neighbors' ideas of neatness.

work because you aren't restricted by the walls of the bin. If your garden features formal elements such as a picket fence, you might want to make compost bins to match.

Build your pile as materials become available. Add kitchen scraps after dinner, grass clippings after you mow the lawn, and the trimmings from shrubs after you finish pruning. Sprinkle thin layers of topsoil or finished compost throughout the pile to introduce the organisms that create compost. If you have a lot of grass clippings, mix fibrous materials, like shredded newspaper or straw, with them or add small amounts to the pile at a time. Large amounts of grass clippings can pack down and exclude air. Don't make the pile too tall, either. It needs air to "cook," or heat up, and a tall pile can pack down under its own weight. When that happens, anaerobic bacteria take over and turn your would-be compost into a smelly, slimy mess. The ideal size for a compost pile is 3 feet tall and wide; when you've reached that size, just start another pile.

If you're not in a rush for compost, you can build a pile (or several) and let it compost on its own for a season. By the following year, you'll have beautiful, dark, crumbly compost with no further effort on your part.

Tricks for Quick Compost

If you need compost soon, there are tricks for speeding up the process. You can add more nitrogen, water the high-carbon layers to dampen (but not drown) them, and turn the pile every third day with a pitchfork to add more air. You can also shred or chop the high-carbon materials before adding them to the pile—the smaller the pieces, the quicker the process. All these techniques will make your pile cook faster, resulting in finished compost in as little as 3 weeks. (Remember that composting slows down in cold weather and speeds up when it's hot, so you'll get finished compost faster in hot weather.)

DIGGING AND DOUBLE-DIGGING

Gardening is digging—digging out weeds, digging up plants to move or divide, digging in soil amendments. But the biggest digging job a perennial gardener faces is making a new flowerbed or border. Yes, it's hard work, but unless you have heavy clay, digging a bed shouldn't be daunting. Just remove the sod, turn over the soil, add organic matter, settle the bed, and you're ready to plant. If you do have heavy clay soil, you can use a special technique called double-digging to improve drainage and aeration so you can have a beautiful perennial bed (see "Double-Digging" on page 184).

Digging a New Bed

Before you make a new perennial bed or enlarge a bed or border, test the moisture content of the soil. Don't dig a bed when the soil is wet—you'll destroy the soil's structure, creating clods and compaction. Don't dig when the soil is powder-dry, either; this also destroys the soil's structure and can cause erosion. The best time to work the soil is when it's slightly moist.

When you're ready to dig, mark off the area with lime, flour, stakes and string, or even a garden hose. Slice off the sod in the marked area by sliding a spade under the roots. (Sod makes great compost, or you can use it to patch sparse lawn areas.) Turn the soil to a spade or fork's depth. Add compost or other organic matter and any soil amendments, then work over the area again with your fork or spade to incorporate these materials and to break up clods. To settle the soil, water it several times.

The soil will settle on its own if you prepare the bed either in fall for spring planting or in spring for fall planting, mulch it to keep out weeds, and let it sit until planting time. This waiting period is especially important if you're turning in fresh manure because it can burn plants; let it age in the soil for 3 to 4 weeks before planting, or better yet, compost it before using.

Perennial Beds and Problem Soils

If you have a loose, friable loam soil that's easy to turn over with a garden fork or spade, digging a perennial bed is a simple job. If you don't have good soil to begin with, analyze the problem before you jump in.

Help for Sandy Soils

If you have a high-sand soil that drains too fast, water carries nutrients out of the root zone before plants can take them up. Add large amounts of organic matter (shredded leaves, strawy manure, grass clippings, compost, and so on) to improve water and nutrient retention. One benefit: The soil will be easy to work because sandy soils are generally loose.

If, on the other hand, your soil is so extremely sandy that you can't grow many of the perennials you'd like to have, you might want to consider raised beds. By creating raised beds of good topsoil and working in plenty of organic matter, you'll make a kind of giant planter for your perennials. Keep the plants watered, fed, and mulched, and your perennials will thrive.

Coping with Clay Soils

Your problem is more likely to be subsoil or heavy clay soil rather than sandy soil, though. If yours is the kind of soil that water just sits on rather than soaks into and you can bend a spade trying to dig it, make raised beds as you would for very sandy soil. (This works well with boggy soils, too, when it would cost too much to drain them.) If the soil is heavy and difficult but not impossible to work and if water does eventually soak in rather than puddling up until it evaporates, try double-digging.

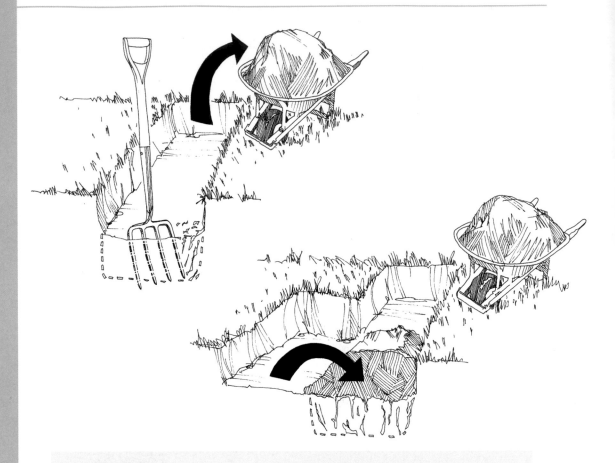

Double-digging. If you have poor or rocky soil, double-digging will improve its aeration, moisture retention, and fertility. To double-dig, mark the shape of the new bed on the ground with flour or lime and begin at one end. First, remove one spade's width and depth of soil from a strip the width of the bed, and put it into a garden cart or wheelbarrow, as shown. Next, use a garden fork to loosen the soil in the trench to the depth of the tines. Do the same in the next section of the bed, putting the soil you remove in the first trench. Continue until you've reached the end of the bed. Fill in the last trench with the soil in the cart or barrow. Finish your bed by applying compost and any other soil amendments you'd like to add, then working them into the top layer of soil with your garden fork.

Double-Digging

Double-digging is working the soil to twice the ordinary depth—two spades' depth rather than one. Double-digging is hard work, but the results are worth it—you'll turn second-class soil into first-rate beds, and you have to do it only once for each bed. As with any digging, don't double-dig when the soil is wet or bone-dry. Here's how to double-dig.

1. Mark off the area to be worked, and remove the sod as you would for normal digging (see "Digging a New Bed" on page 182).
2. Starting at one end of the bed, dig a trench across the bed that's 1 foot wide and the depth of your spade (not including the handle). Pile the soil into a wheelbarrow or garden cart.
3. When you've removed the soil from the trench, work back across the trench with a garden fork, loosening (but not removing) the soil to the depth of the tines.
4. Repeat the procedure, creating a second trench next to the first. Move the soil from the second trench into the first trench.
5. Continue trenching and replacing soil in the trenches until you reach the end of the bed.
6. Use the soil in the wheelbarrow to fill the last trench.
7. Spread organic matter and any additional soil amendments over the bed, then work them into the top 4 to 6 inches of soil.

The loosened soil and added amendments will raise the level of your bed a few inches. Note that added organic matter is critical to the success of double-digging; without it, you'll just have loosened heavy soil that will soon become compacted again.

WHAT TO DO ONCE THE PLANTS COME HOME

When you've made your beds and amended your soil, you're ready for plants. If you're not ready to plant when your perennials arrive in the mail or the minute you get home from the nursery, there are things you can do to get your perennials off to a good start even before you put them in the ground. If you've bought container-grown plants at a garden center or nursery, care is simple: Don't let them dry out (this may mean watering every day; in summer, maybe twice a day), and set them out under trees or in another place where they'll be protected from full sun until you can plant them. Try to plant them as soon as possible.

Mail-order plants may arrive in containers or bareroot. The first thing to do when you get the box is open it; get those plants into the light and out of the cramped conditions of the box. When you take out your plants, they may look slightly worse for wear. Some may be shipped dormant and look mummified. But even the most wilted or battered specimen will revive quickly with a little coddling.

Care for Container-Grown Plants

If you've ordered container-grown plants, don't be surprised if the containers are smaller than you expect: Even plants that are large when they mature are often shipped small. (This is *not* a bad thing!

Healthy, well-grown small plants will suffer less transplant shock and establish themselves faster than large plants.) The smaller the container, the more often you'll have to water. Don't put plants in small containers out in full sun; you'll stress them and bring on wilting and dehydration. Keep them in partial shade until you can plant them, and try to get them in the ground as soon as you can.

Care for Bareroot Plants

Bareroot perennials need more initial care than container-grown plants, but otherwise they'll establish themselves and grow just as vigorously. When you order bareroot plants, they usually come with the roots in peat, shredded wood, or some other protective substance. If you can plant right away, remove the protective material and soak the roots in a bucket of lukewarm water for 1 to 2 hours to rehydrate them before planting. If you must delay planting, keep the material damp (but not soggy), and keep the plants out of the sun until you can plant them. If your plants arrive without a protective covering on their roots, soak the roots to rehydrate them, then cover them with moist potting soil or compost until you can plant.

Before planting, remove all protective material from your bareroot perennials and compost it; it will wick water away from the roots, causing them to dry out, if you put it in the planting hole. Remember that bareroot perennials have less holding ca-pacity than container-grown plants, so try to get them in the ground within 3 days of their arrival. If you have to wait longer than that, pot them up until you can plant them. And don't forget to keep the labels with the plants!

PUTTING IN THE PLANTS

When you have a plan, a prepared bed, and your perennials, you're ready to plant. If you can, choose an overcast day for planting—hot sun stresses transplants. If you're planting container-grown perennials during the growing season, remember to set them out (pots and all) on the bed before you plant. Then you can make any last-minute design changes without having to dig up your plants.

Planting Container-Grown Perennials

Plant container-grown perennials a little higher than they sit in the pots if you're planting in newly prepared soil because it will settle after planting. In established beds, plant these perennials at the same level that they sit in the pots. Don't plant perennials deep or the crowns will be buried and the plants will struggle or even die.

Start small. Plant one perennial at a time rather than taking them all out of their pots and leaving them to dehydrate. And don't just grab a plant by the stem and pull it out of its pot. Instead, cover the surface of the pot with one hand, spreading your fingers over the soil on either side of the stem. Invert the pot so it's resting upside down on your hand, *then* pull off the pot. (If it doesn't pull off easily, tap or squeeze it a few times and try again. Really stubborn pots may have to be cut off.)

If the roots have filled the pot so tightly that they hold its shape once you've removed the pot or if they circle the container, gently pull them loose or quarter the root ball before planting. To quarter the root ball, take a sharp knife or trowel, turn the plant upside down, and slice the root ball into four equal sections, stopping about an inch from the top of the soil ball. Spread the quarters out in the planting hole. This will ensure that the roots grow out into the soil instead of remaining in a ball.

Planting Bareroot Perennials

Again, bareroot perennials are a bit trickier. Before you plant a bareroot perennial, cut off any dead, damaged, or diseased roots with sharp, clean scissors-style pruners or a sharp knife—dull blades will damage roots.

Mound soil in the bottom of the planting hole and spread the roots out so the crown rests on top of the mound. You'll have to tell from looking at the plant where the roots end and the crown begins. If you can see a soil line on the perennial where stems or leaf bases change from green to yellow or white, plant it at the same depth as it grew in the nursery. If not, plant it so the soil comes up to, but not

over, the crown. When you've filled in around the plant, pat the soil down firmly to create good contact between roots and soil. As with container-grown perennials, try to plant one at a time.

If you're adding plants to an established bed, dig a hole as wide as the roots are long. Try not to disturb the roots of adjacent perennials—make sure there's room for the new plant before you start digging.

Fibrous-Rooted Plants

If you're planting a fibrous-rooted perennial—one with lots of roots coming down from the crown—form a cone of soil in the center of the hole, making the cone high enough to position the crown at the surface of the soil. Snip off any damaged roots, then take the plant, turn it upside down, and shake it so the roots fall evenly on every side of the crown. Turn the plant over on top of the soil cone so that the roots spread out evenly rather than clumping. Add the remaining soil to the hole, tamp it down, and check to make sure the crown of the plant is at the right level.

Taprooted Plants

For taprooted perennials, which have one long root, you need a deep, narrow hole without a soil cone. Make this hole by inserting a trowel in the place you want your plant and pulling the trowel toward you to make a V-shaped incision. Slide the taproot into the hole, make sure the crown is at the correct level, and step on the soil beside the newly planted perennial to close the hole and tamp down the soil.

After You Plant

Whether you're planting bareroot or container-grown perennials—and no matter how many you're planting—keep the identification labels with the plants. Insert them firmly in the ground at the base of the plant, where you can find them but they'll be discreetly hidden as the plant grows. Don't lose them! Even the most detailed garden plan can't beat on-the-spot identification. (For ways to keep those pesky la-

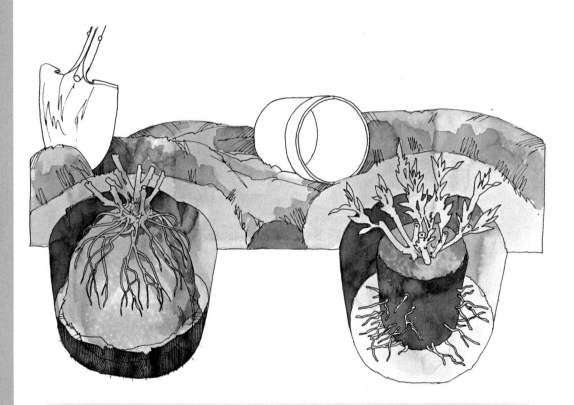

How to plant perennials. To plant a bareroot perennial (*left*), mound soil in the bottom of the planting hole and set the plant on top of the mound, spreading its roots down the sides. Fill in around the plant with soil. Plant these perennials at the same depth they grew in the nursery—don't cover the crowns. Container-grown perennials (*right*) are a snap to plant. Plant them at the same depth they sit in the pot. If the surrounding soil is loose, plant them a little high. The plant will sink when the soil settles. If the plant is rootbound, loosen the rootball before planting.

bels in place and visible, see "Those %$#@!! Labels" on page 130.)

Once your plants are in the ground, water them in thoroughly. Keep an eye on them over the next few weeks and make sure they stay watered and don't dehydrate. Otherwise, leave them alone until they start growing—don't fertilize them. They won't need additional nutrients until they're growing well. And never put fertilizer in the planting hole: It could burn the roots, and a nutrient boost is the last thing a stressed plant needs as it tries to recover from planting.

FERTILIZING FOR FABULOUS FLOWERS

Once your perennials are in the ground and growing, you can consider fertilizing them. If you've faithfully improved the soil, they may not need more than a dose of compost and a spray of liquid seaweed or compost tea to perform well all season. However, if your beds have been in place for a few years or you're growing heavy feeders like peonies, delphiniums, and phlox, fertilizers can give your perennials a needed boost. Remember, though, that it's easy to overfertilize perennials, especially with nitrogen, which causes tender, lanky growth and fewer flowers. Moderation is the key here: See what your plants need, then give it to them.

Fertilizer Basics

To get the most from fertilizing, it helps to know a bit about plant nutrition. Fertilizers

supply three major nutrients to plants: nitrogen (N), phosphorus (P), and potassium (K). If you buy a commercial fertilizer, the percentage of each of these key nutrients will be expressed as a ratio, called the NPK ratio. For example, if your bag says 1-2-2, the fertilizer contains 1 percent nitrogen, 2 percent phosphate (the form of phosphorus used by plants), and 2 percent potash (the form of potassium used by plants).

Different fertilizers have different NPK ratios, which is important because each of these major nutrients does something different for your plants. Nitrogen boosts vegetative growth—the leaves and stems. Phosphorus stimulates flower and fruit production. And potassium enhances root growth. Plants need all three of these nutrients to grow, but they may need different levels at different times: more nitrogen in springtime when growth starts, more phosphorus when they're flowering, and more potassium in fall when major root growth occurs. You can also match the NPK ratio to your soil's supply of these nutrients; for example, your soil may have enough potassium but need more nitrogen and phosphorus, so you'd want to choose a low-potassium fertilizer.

Choosing the Right Fertilizer

By knowing a fertilizer's NPK ratio, you can choose the best combination for your plants. For example, if you need to add a high-nitrogen fertilizer, you could choose bloodmeal, with a 10-0-0 NPK ratio; bat guano, at 10-3-1; or cottonseed meal, at

6-2-1. Good sources of phosphorus include bonemeal, with a 1-11-0 NPK ratio; colloidal phosphate, at 0-2-2; and rock phosphate, at 0-3-0. For potassium, you could add greensand, with a 0-0-7 NPK ratio; Sul-Po-Mag, at 0-0-22; or wood ashes, at 0-1.5-8. These and other good nutrient sources are listed in "The Perennial Gardener's Guide to Organic Fertilizers" on page 194, along with their suggested application rates. Balanced, pre-mixed organic fertilizers are also readily available from garden centers and mail-order catalogs.

Secondary and Trace Elements

In addition to the primary nutrients, perennials need secondary nutrients (calcium, magnesium, and sulfur) as well as trace quantities of micronutrients (boron, chlorine, copper, iron, manganese, molybdenum, and zinc) to grow well. If your

ARE YOUR PERENNIALS MISSING SOMETHING?

If your plants have a nutrient deficiency, they may look stunted or diseased. Deficiency "diseases" are called disorders. Unless you see mold, rot, or another definite disease symptom on your plants, check this list for deficiency symptoms before concluding that your perennials are diseased.

If your plants' symptoms match one of the deficiencies in this table, turn to "The Perennial Gardener's Guide to Organic Fertilizers" on page 194 to find a source of the missing nutrient. But bear in mind that pH may be the real culprit: If your soil is alkaline, your plants may exhibit symptoms of iron, zinc, or phosphorus deficiency, while an acid soil can cause magnesium, potassium, and boron deficiencies. Even though these nutrients are present in adequate quantities in the soil, they're "locked up," unavailable to your perennials. So bringing your pH closer to neutral may solve your deficiency problems.

Symptoms	Deficiency
Leaves small; lower leaves turn pale green; chlorosis (yellowing) follows; older leaves drop. Eventually, all leaves may turn yellow. Undersides of leaves may turn bluish purple.	Nitrogen
Plant grows slowly and becomes spindly and stunted; individual branches may die.	Nitrogen
Leaves small but not chlorotic (yellowed). Undersides of leaves turn reddish purple in spots in the web of the leaf; color then spreads to entire leaf.	Phosphorus
Stems slender, fibrous, and hard; plants and roots may be stunted.	Phosphorus
Leaves small, turning dark purple to black while young. Leaf petioles (stems) and midribs become thickened, curled, and brittle. Terminal shoots curl inward, turn dark, and die.	Boron

plants aren't getting enough of any of these essential elements, they'll let you know by showing deficiency symptoms—the plant may be stunted, or the leaves may turn yellow along the veins or even display purple blotches. (For a rundown of deficiency symptoms, see "Are Your Perennials Missing Something?" below.) Fortunately, many fertilizers also supply these elements, and some, such as seaweed (kelp) and compost, supply all of the micronutrients.

If you've taken a soil test, the results will tell you how much nitrogen and so on to apply. If you don't have soil test recommendations to guide you, there are also general application guidelines for each fertilizer. (See the "The Perennial Gardener's Guide to Organic Fertilizers" on page 194 for descriptions and application rates.) Calcium, magnesium, and sulfur are often supplied by materials you'd use to balance soil pH, like dolomitic

Symptoms	Deficiency
Lateral buds grow, then die, creating a bushy witches'-broom effect.	Boron
Leaves normal size, but new leaves and terminal branches deformed. Upper leaves may be dark green, but they curl upward and leaf edges turn yellow, then leaves dry up and fall. Lower leaves normal.	Calcium
Stems fibrous and hard; roots short and brown.	Calcium
Plant wilts, becoming weak and flabby, even though it's adequately watered.	Calcium
Leaves small and/or mottled with yellow or necrotic (dead) areas.	Zinc
Internodes are shortened. Plant may form a rosette of leaves.	Zinc
Leaves normal size, but leaf margins of older leaves are tanned, scorched, or have black or brown necrotic (dead) spots. Leaf margins become brown and cup downward. Leaves are mottled with yellow and may turn ashen gray-green, bronze, or yellowish brown. Symptoms begin at the bottom of the plant and work up. Young leaves crinkle and curl.	Potassium
Roots poorly developed and brown. Stems slender, hard, and woody. Plants may be stunted.	Potassium
Leaves normal size, but veins of lower leaves remain dark green while the area between veins turns yellow and then dark brown. Leaves are brittle and curl upward. Tissue breaks down; leaves fall prematurely.	Magnesium
Leaves normal size. New leaves turn yellow, but chlorotic (yellowed) spots not usually followed by necrosis (dead tissue). Distinct yellow or white areas appear between veins; veins eventually become chlorotic. Symptoms are rare on mature leaves.	Iron

limestone (usually sold as dolomite) and elemental sulfur.

Applying Fertilizers

Commercial organic fertilizers are usually packaged as a dry powder, though some may be pelleted. Spread fertilizer around your plants before you mulch, then mulch over the fertilizer. If your beds are already mulched, pull the mulch back, fertilize, then replace the mulch. Don't dump fertilizer right on your plants—it's concentrated and could burn them. Some organic fertilizers, like fish emulsion and liquid seaweed, are sold in liquid form. Dilute them according to package directions and water them in, or use them as the base ingredient for foliar feeding.

Foliar Feeding

Foliar feeding is the best way to supply nutrients to your perennials quickly. Instead of becoming available in solution in the soil—a process that can take years for some rock fertilizers—and then being taken up by plant roots, the nutrients are absorbed directly through the leaves and can be used by the plant at once.

If your perennials are showing deficiency symptoms, use foliar feeding to provide a fast but temporary cure. First, identify the deficiency, then apply manure tea or fish emulsion directly to the leaves to correct major nutrient deficiencies, or apply liquid seaweed or compost tea for micronutrient deficiencies. You can also buy fish-emulsion/seaweed combinations. For a long-term solution, amend the soil; meanwhile, foliar-feed as often as necessary to keep your plants growing and healthy.

When and How to Foliar-Feed

Even if your perennials don't have obvious deficiencies, they may start looking a bit peaked as the season wears on. They'll also flower better with a gentle boost when they're setting buds. If they have a long bloom season, they'll appreciate additional nutrients every 2 weeks during flowering. Foliar feeding is perfect for these uses.

To foliar-feed, choose a cloudy day, if possible, and fertilize in the morning or evening, when absorption is highest. If you're using a commercial organic fertilizer, dilute it according to package directions. If you want to make your own compost or manure tea, see the directions in "Tea Time for Your Plants" on the opposite page. Use a clean plant sprayer turned to its finest setting, or a plant mister, and spray your perennials' leaves thoroughly, including the undersides.

WATERING WISELY AND WELL

There are two rules to keep in mind when it comes to watering perennials: When you need to water, water deeply; and put the water on the ground, not in the air or on the plants. If you break the rules, you'll end up with shallow-rooted, wilt-prone plants and mildewed foliage.

With a few exceptions, perennials like consistently (and preferably evenly) moist soil. In general, you need to water when the top inch or so of soil dries out and no rain is predicted. When you water, be sure to moisten the top 5 to 6 inches of soil to encourage deep root growth. Use a hose instead of a sprinkler so you can direct the water to the base of the plants without wetting the foliage. (An even better alternative is drip or trickle irrigation. For more on this method, see "Drip Irrigation" on page 197.) Don't water in the evening when the water will stay on your plants all night—this encourages fungal infections like powdery mildew.

There is actually a third rule of perennial irrigation, where conditions permit:

(continued on page 197)

TEA TIME FOR YOUR PLANTS

Your perennials will find a bucket of manure tea or compost tea as refreshing as you find your morning cup, and it's just as easy to make. Put a shovelful of fresh or dried manure (or finished compost) into a burlap or cheesecloth bag. Tie the top closed and sink the sack into a large bucket or barrel of water. Cover the container, and steep the "tea" for 1 to 7 days. (As with real tea, the longer it steeps, the stronger it is.)

Use compost tea full strength as a liquid fertilizer around your plants, or dilute either tea and use it to give plants a boost when you water. (Don't use manure tea full strength or it may burn your plants.) You can also use manure or compost tea with drip irrigation systems if you filter it through cheesecloth or old pantyhose first so it doesn't clog the tubes. Manure and compost tea are both great for foliar feeding; for more on this technique, see "Foliar Feeding" on the opposite page.

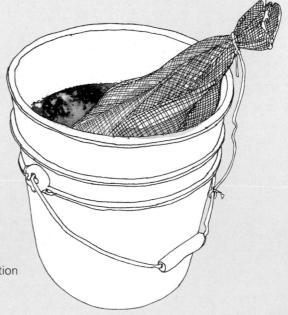

Making manure or compost tea. This illustration shows how easy it is to make "tea" for your plants—just like steeping a giant tea bag.

THE PERENNIAL GARDENER'S GUIDE TO ORGANIC FERTILIZERS

Organic fertilizers are gentle on the soil and good for your plants. Use bloodmeal, cottonseed meal, fish meal, guano, hoof and horn meal, leatherdust, or chicken manure for nitrogen. Bonemeal, fish meal, guano, colloidal phosphate, rock phosphate, and wood ashes are good sources of phosphorus. If your perennials need potassium, choose granite dust, greensand, langbeinite, seaweed, or wood ashes. Bonemeal, dolomite, gypsum, and wood ashes provide calcium; gypsum, langbeinite, and elemental sulfur are good sulfur sources. For trace minerals, choose granite dust, greensand, guano, colloidal or rock phosphate, seaweed, or wood ashes. Don't apply more than the recommended amount of any of these; more is definitely *not* better where fertilizers are concerned.

Organic Fertilizer	Nutrients Supplied	Application Rate	Comments
Bloodmeal, dried blood	Bloodmeal: 15% nitrogen, 1.3% phosphorus, 0.7% potassium Dried blood: 12% nitrogen, 3% phosphorus, 0% potassium	Up to 3 lb. per 100 sq. ft. (more will burn plants)	Source of readily available nitrogen. Add to compost pile to speed decomposition. Repels deer and rabbits. Lasts 3 to 4 months.
Bonemeal	3% nitrogen, 20% phosphorus, 0% potassium, 24% to 30% calcium	Up to 5 lb. per 100 sq. ft.	Excellent source of phosphorus. Raises pH. Lasts 6 to 12 months.
Cottonseed meal	6% nitrogen, 2% to 3% phosphorus, 2% potassium	2 to 5 lb. per 100 sq. ft.	Acidifies soil; it's best for plants that prefer low pH, or use it with bonemeal or wood ashes. Lasts 4 to 6 months.
Dolomite	90% to 100% MgCa (CO$_3$)$_2$ (51% calcium carbonate, 40% magnesium carbonate)	To raise pH 1 point, use 7 lb. per 100 sq. ft. on clay or sandy loam, 5½ lb. on sand, and 10 lb. on loam soil	Raises pH and adds magnesium, which is needed for chlorophyll production and photosynthesis. Repeated use may cause magnesium excess. Also sold as Hi-Mag or dolomitic limestone.
Fish meal, fish emulsion	Fish meal: 10% nitrogen, 4% to 6% phosphorus, 0% potassium Fish emulsion: 4% nitrogen, 4% phosphorus, 1% potassium	Fish meal: up to 5 lb. per 100 sq. ft. Fish emulsion: dilute 20:1 water to emulsion	Fish meal: Use in early spring, at transplanting, and any time plants need a boost. Lasts 6 to 8 months. Fish emulsion: Apply as a foliar spray in early morning or evening. Strong smell. Also sold as fish solubles.

Organic Fertilizer	Nutrients Supplied	Application Rate	Comments
Granite dust	0% nitrogen, 0% phosphorus, 3 to 5% potassium, 67% silica; 19 trace minerals	Up to 10 lb. per 100 sq. ft.	Very slowly available. Releases potash more slowly than greensand but lasts up to 10 years. Improves soil structure. Use mica-rich type only. Also sold as granite meal or crushed granite.
Greensand	0% nitrogen, 1% phosphorus, 5% to 7% potassium, 50% silica, 18% to 23% iron oxide; 22 trace minerals	Up to 10 lb. per 100 sq. ft.	Slowly available. Lasts up to 10 years. Loosens clay soils. Apply in fall for benefits next season. Also sold as glauconite or Jersey greensand.
Guano, bat	8% nitrogen, 4% phosphorus, 2% potassium average, but varies widely; 24 trace minerals	Up to 5 lb. per 100 sq. ft; 2 T. per pint of potting soil; 1 lb. per 5 gal. water for manure tea	Caves protect guano from leaching, so nutrients are conserved.
Guano, bird	13% nitrogen, 8% phosphorus, 2% potassium; 11 trace minerals	3 lb. per 100 sq. ft.	Also sold as Plantjoy.
Gypsum (calcium sulfate)	23% to 57% calcium, 17.7% sulfur	Up to 4 lb. per 100 sq. ft.	Use when both calcium and sulfur are needed and soil pH is already high. Sulfur will tie up excess magnesium. Helps loosen clay soils.
Hoof and horn meal	14% nitrogen, 2% phosphorus, 0% potassium	Up to 4 lb. per 100 sq. ft.	High nitrogen source but more slowly available than bloodmeal. Unpleasant smell. Takes 4 to 6 weeks to start releasing nitrogen; lasts 12 months.
Langbeinite	0% nitrogen, 0% phosphorus, 22% potassium, 22% sulfur, 11% magnesium	Up to 1 lb. per 100 sq. ft.	Will not alter pH. Use when there is abundant calcium but sulfur, magnesium, and potassium are needed. Also sold as Sul-Po-Mag or K-Mag.
Leatherdust	5.5% to 12% nitrogen, 0% phosphorus, 0% potassium	½ lb. per 100 sq. ft.	2% nitrogen is immediately available; remainder releases slowly over growing season. Does not burn or leach.

(continued)

The Perennial Gardener's Guide to Organic Fertilizers (cont.)

Organic Fertilizer	Nutrients Supplied	Application Rate	Comments
Manure, chicken	1.3% nitrogen, 2.7% phosphorus, 1.4% potassium	10 lb. per 100 sq. ft.	Good source of fast-release nitrogen. Use dry or compost; fresh chicken manure can burn plants.
Phosphate, colloidal	0% nitrogen, 18% to 22% phosphorus, 0% potassium, 27% calcium, 1.7% iron; silicas and 14 other trace minerals	Up to 10 lb. per 100 sq. ft.	More effective than rock phosphate on neutral soils. Phosphorus availability higher (2% available immediately) than rock phosphate because of small particle size of colloidal clay base. Half the pH-raising value of ground limestone. Lasts 2 to 3 years.
Phosphate, rock	0% nitrogen, 33% phosphorus, 0% potassium, 30% calcium, 2.8% iron, 10% silica; 10 other trace minerals	Up to 10 lb. per 100 sq. ft.	Releases phosphorus best in acid soils below pH 6.2. Slower release than colloidal phosphate. Will slowly raise pH 1 point or more. Also sold as phosphate rock.
Seaweed (kelp meal, liquid seaweed)	1% nitrogen, 0% phosphorus, 12% potassium; 33% trace minerals, including more than 1% of calcium, sodium, chlorine, and sulfur, and about 50 other minerals in trace amounts	Meal: up to 1 lb. per 100 sq. ft. Liquid: dilute 25:1 water to seaweed for transplanting and rooting cuttings; 40:1 as booster	Contains natural growth hormones. Best source of trace minerals. Lasts 6 to 12 months. Also sold as Thorvin Kelp, FoliaGro, Sea Life, Maxicrop, Norwegian SeaWeed, liquid kelp.
Sulfur	100% sulfur	1 lb. per 100 sq. ft. will lower pH 1 point	Lowers pH in alkaline soil. Ties up excess magnesium. Also sold as Dispersul.
Wood ashes	0% nitrogen, 0% to 7% phosphorus, 6% to 20% potassium, 20% to 53% calcium carbonate; trace minerals such as copper, zinc, manganese, iron, sodium, sulfur, and boron	1 to 2 lb. per 100 sq. ft.	Nutrient amounts highly variable. Minerals highest in young hardwoods. Will raise soil pH. Put on soil in spring and dig under. Do not use near young stems or roots. Protect ashes from leaching in winter. Lasts 12 or more months.

mulch. Mulch will slow down soil water evaporation, but it won't stop it completely. (For more on mulch, see "Much Ado about Mulch" on page 198.)

Drip Irrigation

Drip irrigation systems are ideal for perennial beds because you don't have to disturb the plants or beds to use them. Just lay the system down after you plant your bed, or snake it between plants in an established bed. Mulch on top of the hoses, and you have an invisible but very effective watering system. You won't waste water because very little will be lost to evaporation, and the water will go where it does the most good: into the soil of the root zone. (In fact, you'll use one-quarter to one-third less water if you choose drip irrigation, a huge consideration if you live in a drought-prone area or anywhere water use is restricted.) Another benefit: Because the water oozes out slowly but evenly, it saturates the soil rather than puddling or running off. You can also use drip systems in the evening or at night because they don't wet the foliage.

Drip irrigation benefits the gardener as well as the garden. You won't have to haul out a hose every time you need to water, then run back and forth moving it every 10 minutes, battering plants as you drag the hose over them. Instead, you just turn on the faucet and relax.

The first time you use drip irrigation, you'll need to fine-tune your watering time. Start when the soil is dry. Check the soil every hour—just stick a finger into it. When the soil is moist 5 to 6 inches deep at the far edge of the hose's range, turn off the faucet and record the amount of time it was on. This will be a good guideline for future watering. Since you'll be watering for only a few hours at a time, you can disconnect the system from the faucet when it's not in use, or disconnect the hose at the end of the bed so the connector hose isn't trailing across the lawn.

Soaker Hoses

The simplest and least expensive drip system is a soaker hose, a black rubber hose (usually made from recycled tires) with pinpoint holes all over it. The hose attaches to a regular garden hose and water oozes out of all the holes as long as the water is on, irrigating an area about 2 to 3 feet wide along the hose's length. A plug keeps the water from running out the other

How Much Is Enough?

The rule of thumb for watering is 1 inch of water (including rainwater) a week. But that's more than you'd think—especially if you're the one hauling the water! To give a 1,000-square-foot perennial bed an inch of water, you'll need 625 gallons.

end. You can buy soaker hoses through garden centers, hardware and home stores, and mail-order garden supply catalogs in 25- to 250-foot lengths. (For longer hoses, simply screw several together.) Suppliers also sell flow and pressure regulators for the longer hoses.

To use a soaker hose, attach it to a length of garden hose that runs between your faucet and your perennial bed. If your bed is 5 by 25 feet, you'll need at least 50 feet of soaker hose. Run the soaker hose up one side of the bed about 1½ feet from the edge, turn it about 1 foot from the end of the bed, and run it back down the other side, again about 1½ feet from the edge. When you've got the hose down the way you want it, cover it with mulch so it will "disappear" into the bed. You can leave the hose in place all season, then drain and store it over the winter.

A Drip System

A drip irrigation system is more complex—but more precise—than a soaker hose. Instead of soaking the ground around the hose, these plastic hoses deliver water directly to the base of each plant through a thin plastic pipe called a spaghetti tube. An emitter at the end of the tube delivers water or liquid fertilizer solution slowly and evenly.

Drip systems can have timers, pressure regulators, filters, and feeder tubes for fish emulsion or other liquid fertilizers. Better systems allow you to attach the spaghetti tubes precisely where they'll reach your plants. Unlike soaker hoses, drip systems can branch, eliminating multiple hose lines down the beds. A drawback of drip irrigation, besides the cost, is the tendency of emitters to clog from hard water or fertilizer buildup, but you can soak them in vinegar to clear them.

If you decide to invest in a drip system, explore the market carefully. There are many systems available through garden centers and specialty catalogs. Familiarize yourself with the types offered, and choose the system that suits your budget and garden best. Most drip systems can be installed underneath mulch so they're less visible. And like soaker hoses and garden hoses, drip systems are durable.

MUCH ADO ABOUT MULCH

Mulch has come into its own as a prime garden problem solver. After good soil, mulch does more for plants than any other additive or technique. Here are the major benefits of mulch.

- Mulch conserves water, so mulched soil stays more evenly moist, holds moisture longer, and requires less frequent watering.
- Mulch keeps down weeds whose seeds need light to germinate, so you save weeding time.
- Organic mulches add humus and some nutrients to the soil as they break down.
- Mulch keeps soil and nutrients from washing away during hard rains.
- Mulch keeps soil temperatures more even, protecting plant roots and benefi-

Soaker hoses and drip irrigation. For small beds, soaker hoses (*left*) are great, releasing water slowly and evenly to the whole bed. Cover the hoses with mulch to conserve moisture. For large beds, use a drip system (*right*), which delivers water through spaghetti tubes directly to the base of each plant.

cial soil organisms against violent swings in soil temperature. This is especially critical in winter, when unmulched soil is prone to freezing and thawing, causing frost-heaving and exposing sensitive roots to freezing air and drying out.

In addition, mulch protects plants from some soilborne diseases and nematodes that could splash up onto the foliage when it rains or when you water your plants. It keeps dirt off your plants, so they stay clean and attractive. Pale mulches like straw can reflect light back onto foliage. But the main benefit of mulch to many gardeners is aesthetic—it just looks good. To make sure it looks attractive but still provides the other benefits that have made it famous, use mulch with moderation. Don't bury your perennials in a mound of mulch; 2 to 3 inches is plenty. When the mulch begins to break down, turn it into the soil, or remove and compost it. Replace it with fresh mulch.

Types of Mulch

Actually, one of the best mulches you can use is simply a thick covering of plants over the soil. A thickly planted garden, where foliage shades the ground and there are no bare patches of soil, provides all the advantages of other types of mulch. The plant cover helps retain water, protects the soil, and keeps down weeds. When the garden dies down in fall, apply a winter mulch to protect the plants. By the time the winter mulch decomposes in late spring, the foliage will once again have taken over as a living mulch.

There are two categories of applied mulch: organic and inorganic. Organic mulches are made from plants: shredded leaves, bark or wood chips, straw and hay, newspapers, compost, and so on. Inorganic mulches include plastics, pebbles, and landscape fabrics (also called geotextiles).

Inorganic mulches are most useful in the landscape and the vegetable garden: Black plastic heats up the soil and suppresses weeds, clear plastic can be used to solarize the soil, and landscape fabrics prevent erosion on slopes and are used to keep weeds down around shrubs. Water can't soak through plastic mulch (many gardeners lay irrigation systems under the plastic), but landscape fabrics are water-permeable. Landscape fabric works best when it's set in place and not removed (as it would be when you're transplanting or dividing plants). Moving the fabric can cause it to tear and may also injure established roots.

Pebbles, bark, or wood chips can be used to disguise plastics and landscape fabrics, making them look more natural.

For the perennial garden, organic mulches are best. They hold in soil moisture, keep down weeds, and add organic matter to the soil as they decompose. Don't overlook local materials when you're choosing mulch. Nearly everyone has leaves they can shred, and they make ideal mulch. In areas where they are readily available, cocoa hulls or peanut shells make excellent, affordable, and attractive mulch. If you decide to use shredded wood chips or bark, such as those available free from tree trimmers, it's best to compost them for a year by just letting them sit in an out-of-the-way spot before using them. That way, they can begin to decompose and aren't so sharp and hard to work with when you apply them. For an overview of the use and advantages of other organic mulches, see "More on Mulch" on the opposite page.

Consider attractiveness when you're choosing a mulch: The perennial garden is, first and foremost, ornamental. Newspaper is a good mulch material because it's readily available, it holds water, and it biodegrades; if you use it, cover it with something more appealing, like a thick layer of shredded leaves, shredded wood, or bark chips.

There are also some organic mulches to avoid, like sawdust, peat moss, and what we'd like to call "trashy wood chips." Sawdust has several drawbacks: It's unattractive, it's often splintery and hard to work

MORE ON MULCH

These are the best mulches for perennial gardens. All of them will biodegrade over time, adding humus to the soil. They provide mulch's other benefits as well: retaining moisture and suppressing weeds. Shredded leaves, compost, and pine needles are the most attractive, while newspaper and straw are most readily available (of course, leaves are abundant in fall). Grass clippings will give your perennials a nitrogen boost, but they break down quickly and are best used to supplement more stable mulches in areas where appearance is not as important.

Material	Primary Benefits	When to Apply	How to Apply
Compost	Adds humus. Suppresses weeds. Fertilizes. Warms soil.	At planting time and as needed throughout the season	Spread 1 inch or more as a topdressing around plants.
Grass clippings	Add nitrogen and humus.	At planting time and as needed throughout the season	Apply a 1- to 4-inch layer around plants. May burn plants if placed too close to stems.
Leaves, shredded	Add humus. Suppress weeds well. Modulate soil temperature.	At planting time and as winter cove.	Apply in 3-inch layers; best if chopped and composted.
Newspaper	Suppresses weeds well. Retains moisture.	At planting time	Lay down whole sections of the paper and anchor with soil or stones, or shred paper and apply 4- to 6-inch layers. Use under more attractive mulches.
Pine needles	Attractive. Suppress weeds well. Some control of fungal diseases.	At planting time and as winter cover	Apply in 2- to 4-inch layers. Needles tend to acidify soil; don't use around non-acid-loving plants.
Straw	Adds humus. Suppresses weeds well. Cools soil.	At planting time and as winter cover	Lay down 8-inch layers around but not touching plants. May tie up nitrogen in soil; oat straw best.
Wood or bark chips, shredded	Attractive. Suppress weeds well. Cools soil and retains water.	At planting time and as needed throughout the season	Best to compost before using. Apply in 1- to 2-inch layer.

through, and it steals soil nitrogen from your perennials as it breaks down, causing poor plant growth. Peat forms a hard, dry crust on the soil, making it hard for water and nutrients to get through. It's also acidic, lowering soil pH as it leaches. If you'd like a lower pH in your perennial bed, incorporate the peat into the soil, don't use it on top. As for the "trashy wood chips"—you'll recognize these dyed mulches in bags and beds by the screaming orange and other appalling and unnatural colors; unless you want mulch to be the primary focus of your garden bed, just say no. Please.

Applying Mulch

The best time to put a winter mulch on your beds or to mulch fall transplants is when the soil cools and the plants have been killed back by a hard frost. Good materials for winter mulch are pine needles, shredded leaves, and weed- and seed-free straw. (Don't use unshredded leaves, which can pack down and encourage disease.) But the best material for winter mulch is snow, a natural insulator. Don't be afraid to pile it up on your beds for a uniform winter cover. Follow nature's example: Put down your leaves or other mulch, then add a snow blanket.

In spring, pull off winter mulch until the soil has warmed, then pull it back up to—but not over—the plants. This is important when setting out transplants as well. If you cover the crowns of the plants with mulch, you'll encourage crown rot, and mulching up to the stems of tender transplants creates an ideal environment for cutworms. So leave a mulch-free ring about 1 inch out from the crown.

As summer wears on, mulches may begin to break down as they compost under the surface layer. Watch organic mulches through summer and renew them when they start to look thin. This is especially important in the Deep South, where high heat and humidity combine to create rapid decomposition.

WEEDING WISELY

Weeding is a fact of life in the perennial garden. It will be easier and more effective if you start weeding as soon as you see a problem and then continue to monitor for any new weeds. Control is much more difficult if you let the weeds take over the garden and then try to bring the situation under control in one marathon weeding session.

Here are some surefire ways to minimize your weeding chores.

- Mulch your garden. Mulch not only suppresses weed germination and growth, it also makes those weeds that do turn up easier to pull because the soil stays soft and moist beneath the mulch.
- Get out the whole weed the first time. A lot of weeds can spread from a tiny piece of root or stem left in the ground, and taprooted weeds like dandelions

grow back if you don't take out the whole taproot.

- Don't let weeds set seed. Some perennials like coneflowers, alliums, and ornamental grasses self-sow so enthusiastically that they fall into the weed category here, too. If you don't plan to start your own nursery, cut their flower heads before the seed ripens and drops.
- Don't bring potential weed problems (like uncomposted manure, which may carry weed seeds, and seed-rich hay) into the garden with you. Always specify weed-free straw or hay if you use them in your garden.
- Don't compost mature weed seedheads. A really hot compost pile will kill weed seeds, but you can't guarantee that the seeds will be in the hottest part of the pile or that your pile will get hot enough. It's better to throw them out than to spread weeds along with your compost.

Even if you use these preventive tactics, you'll have weeds. There are weed seeds, roots, and crowns already in your soil. Birds, wind, and even pets can bring weed seeds to the garden. But only 5 to 10 minutes a day can keep even a fairly large mulched perennial garden under control. The key to effective weeding is persistence. A year-round weeding program saves time and labor in the long run. Weed in winter, when the soil tends to be damp and weed seedlings are vulnerable, as well as throughout the growing season.

Types of Weeds

Like flowers, there are annual, biennial, and perennial weeds. Each group poses its own control problems, so you can control weeds more effectively if you know which group they fall into.

Annual Weeds

Annual weeds, like lamb's-quarters, wild mustard, pigweed, purslane, crabgrass, and ragweed, live only a season, but they produce thousands of seeds, guaranteeing success through strength of numbers. Most garden weeds are annuals. Control them by pulling them before they flower and set seed.

Biennial Weeds

Biennial weeds, like mullein and Queen-Anne's-lace, form a rosette of leaves their first season. The following year, they flower, set seed, and die. Control them by looking for their rosettes and removing them the first season. If you miss some, pull them the second season before they set seed.

Perennial Weeds

Perennial weeds include dandelion, bindweed, dock, wild garlic, ground ivy, plantain, pokeweed, and wood sorrel. Some of the worst perennial weeds are grasses, including Johnsongrass and quackgrass. They live for years, set seed, have deep, persistent root systems, and often have creeping stems as well, so a single plant can send up offspring all over the perennial bed (think

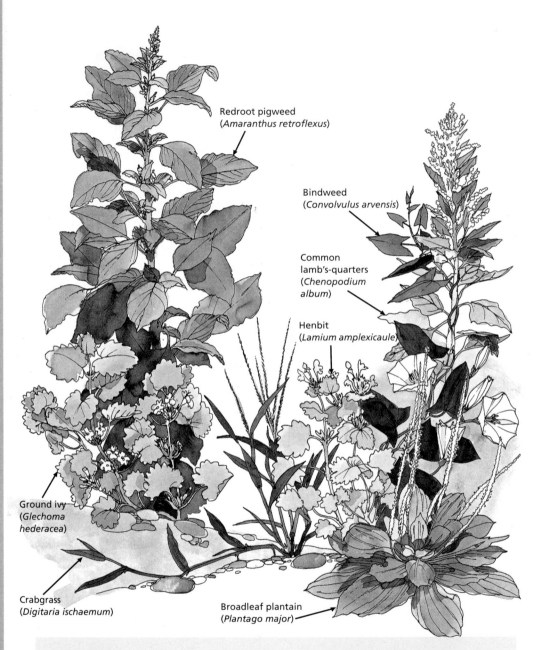

Redroot pigweed
(*Amaranthus retroflexus*)

Bindweed
(*Convolvulus arvensis*)

Common
lamb's-quarters
(*Chenopodium
album*)

Henbit
(*Lamium amplexicaule*)

Ground ivy
(*Glechoma
hederacea*)

Crabgrass
(*Digitaria ischaemum*)

Broadleaf plantain
(*Plantago major*)

Seven worst weeds. Don't let these weeds make your life miserable. Preventive tactics and a little diligence will rout the worst of them. Lamb's-quarters, crabgrass, and redroot pigweed are annuals, henbit is biennial, and bindweed, ground ivy, and broadleaf plantain are perennials.

thistles). The same is true for woody weeds like poison ivy and multiflora roses. To control these difficult weeds, dig carefully to try to remove as much of the root system as possible. Then pull up the plants that grow from the pieces you've missed. Don't give up; persistence will pay off.

Rooting Out Weeds

Hand weeders will help you get the better of really stubborn weeds. A dandelion weeder (also called an asparagus fork) has a blade like a snake's forked tongue that is great for rooting out deep taproots without disturbing nearby perennials. You can use a three-tined hand cultivator to shallowly disturb soil between perennials, uprooting weed seedlings. And bent-bladed pavement weeders will remove weeds in cracks between bricks or flagstones, which are notoriously hard to hand-pull.

If you'd rather spray your weeds than pull them, you have several safe, organic options. In addition to common table vinegar (acetic acid) and acetic acid-based products (see "Woe to Weeds!" below), there's an organic weed killer called AllDown that combines acetic and citric acids with garlic and yucca extracts to produce a potent weed-fighting brew. There's even a soap-based organic herbicide, SharpShooter. (Unlike the acetic acid-based weed killers, it's most effective on seedling weeds.) Sprays are great before you plant a new bed, but afterward they should be considered a last resort because they'll kill any perennials they get on. Excluding weeds with mulch and hand-pulling any that come up through the mulch are much better tactics—at least as far as your perennials are concerned!

SUBTLE STAKING

Gardening with perennials means gardening for beauty. Many plants are beautiful whether their stems are straight, curved, or trailing. But there's nothing

WOE TO WEEDS!

You've probably heard fans of the late Euell Gibbons urging people to eat their weeds. But new research shows that you can end their salad days for good—with common vinegar! Tests by the Cornell Cooperative Extension of Rensselaer County pitted common vinegar (5 percent acetic acid), a 20 percent acetic acid concentrate, and two commercial acetic-acid-based weed killers (Nature's Glory Weed and Grass Killer, and BurnOut Weed and Grass Killer, both with 25 percent acetic acid) against the herbicide RoundUp. When plots were sprayed with three applications, all the weed killers tested showed over 95 percent control—including the common table vinegar! It would appear from the results that reapplying every 5 weeks provides best control.

attractive about delphiniums or gladioli pitched flat on their faces after a high wind, or the peonies you've been waiting for bent facedown in the mud after a hard rain. An entire season can be ruined by a single violent storm. Some perennials—usually the ones with tall flower spikes or full, heavy flowers—are especially prone to toppling.

The solution to flopped flowers is staking. If this brings to your mind giant tomato stakes or cages, remember that you want to see the flowers, not the stakes. If you've chosen the right kind of staking for each plant and done a good job of setting them in place, the stakes should disappear in the bed's foliage. The only sign of good staking should be that the plants remain upright.

Staking Tall Flowers

Match the kind of staking you use to the plant's growth habit. For perennials with tall, slender bloom stalks like foxgloves (*Digitalis*) and delphiniums, use a tall, slender branch, a slender bamboo cane, or a dark green plastic "cane" for each stalk. Insert the stakes as soon as you see the bloom stalks emerging. Place the stake as close to the stalk as you can without damaging the plant's crown, and push it deep enough into the ground so a storm won't knock it over. (The final height of the stake should be about 6 inches shorter than the mature bloom stalk.)

The best way to tie the bloom stalk to the stake is with a loose loop (so you don't put pressure on the stem or even cut or snap it off as it grows). Put soft string, yarn, or a fabric strip around the stem, turn it to form a loop or circle, then tie it to the stake. As the stem grows taller, add more ties as needed.

Staking for success. Discreet staking, like the plant hoops shown here, keep plants neat and upright, even when storms and high winds come through.

Three standard methods of staking. Match your staking method to each plant's growth habit. Use a single stake per bloom stalk for perennials with heavy flower spikes, like this delphinium (*left*). Plants with airy habits, like coreopsis (*center*), do best staked with twiggy brush. Hold up bushy plants with heavy flowers, like peonies and mums (*right*), by growing them in a wire ring. The foliage will hide the stakes as the plants grow.

Plant Frames for Bushy Flowers

For perennials like peonies, chrysanthemums, and bleeding hearts (*Dicentra*) that have a bushy habit, circular plant frames are ideal. These are circles of wire with three or four wire legs that hold the entire plant upright. Again, set them out over the plant when growth begins, push them deeply into the ground, and avoid the crown. As the plant grows, gently pull stray stems back into the circle. As an alternative, put four stakes around the plant and connect them with string to make a frame.

Supporting Airy Flowers

Some perennials, like baby's-breath (*Gypsophila*), artemisias, and yarrows (*Achillea*), have an airy habit but still tend to fall over. Support them with slender, twiggy branches

PERENNIALS AT STAKE

The perennials listed here are especially prone to flopping and are therefore good candidates for staking. Stake each flower spike of hollyhocks, delphiniums, foxgloves, gladioli, lilies, and lupines. Grow yarrows, asters, baptisias, hardy mums, blanket flowers, heleniums, peonies, and salvias in a wire ring or cage. And use twiggy brush or a branch-and-string "web" to hold up coreopsis and baby's-breath.

Achillea spp. (yarrows)
Alcea spp. (hollyhocks)
Aster spp. (asters)
Baptisia australis (blue false indigo)
Chrysanthemum ×morifolium (garden mum)
Coreopsis spp. (coreopsis)
Delphinium spp. and hybrids (delphiniums)
Digitalis spp. (foxgloves)
Gaillardia ×grandiflora (blanket flower)

Gladiolus spp. (gladioli)
Gypsophila paniculata (baby's-breath)
Helenium spp. (sneezeweeds, Helen's flowers)
Lathyrus latifolius (perennial sweet pea)
Lilium spp. (lilies)
Lupinus hybrids (lupines)
Paeonia lactiflora hybrids (common garden peonies)
Salvia spp. (sages)

set into the ground around the plant's perimeter. Another effective staking system for these ferny or feathery plants is a network of slender branches or stakes with a netting of string woven between them. Again, place these supports when growth begins. Dark string will be less obtrusive than white.

A More Relaxed Look

If you don't want stakes in your garden, the keys to success are planning ahead and knowing your plants' habits. One way to avoid staking is by selecting lower-growing plants that don't fall over. You can also design your border with an English or cottage-garden feel, allowing plants like asters to sprawl and encouraging perennials like boltonia (*Boltonia asteroides*) and coreopsis

(*Coreopsis*) to weave their feathery branches over and through surrounding plants. Results can be surprising and delightful.

Planting perennials closer together can also provide natural staking—a peony is less likely to be bent to the ground by a storm if it has Siberian iris (*Iris sibirica*) on either side. Giving plants the right cultural conditions can also make them sturdier, requiring less staking. Yarrows will grow leggy and fall over in a shady site with rich soil, but they stay compact and upright in full sun and average to poor soil. False and wild indigos (*Baptisia*) will become spindly and need staking in shade but grow bushy in full sun and rich soil. Check your plants' cultural requirements in "The Perennial Encyclopedia," beginning on page 265, and give them what they need.

GROOMING

Some gardens look better than others, even when their gardeners are growing the same plants. If plant selection and cultural conditions are similar, plant grooming is usually the reason a garden looks better. Grooming is the finishing touch for perennials. And fortunately, grooming techniques—thinning, pinching, disbudding, and deadheading—are easy and fast. But grooming provides more than a tidy garden. It can change the shape of your plants, double your bloom, or produce huge, showy flowers.

Thinning

Thinning is removing some of the stems of dense, bushy plants to let in light and air circulation. This technique helps prevent mildew on susceptible plants like garden phlox (*Phlox paniculata*), bee balm (*Monarda didyma*), and delphiniums. Thin in spring by cutting or pinching out stems at soil level. Thin each plant to the four or five strongest shoots, leaving 2 to 4 inches between each stem.

Pinching

Pinching creates more compact, bushier plants, prevents flopping, and ensures more bloom. To pinch a plant, start in late spring or early summer. Use your forefinger and thumb to pinch out the tips of the stems. From each pinched stem, two branches will grow. You can pinch again a few weeks later for even bushier plants with still more flowers, but don't pinch after flower buds are set or you'll cut off flowers rather than encouraging them.

If you aren't sure when to pinch your perennials, keep these basic guidelines in

PINCH THESE PERENNIALS!

Curb the often-leggy habit of these perennials by pinching back the stems when growth takes off in spring. You'll be rewarded for your efforts with compact growth and heavier flowering.

Artemisia spp. (artemisias, wormwoods)

Aster spp. (asters)
Boltonia asteroides (boltonia)
Chrysanthemum spp. (chrysanthemums)
Helianthus spp. (sunflowers)
Lobelia spp. (lobelias)
Lychnis spp. (campions, catchflys)

Monarda didyma (bee balm)
Phlox paniculata (garden phlox, summer phlox)
Physostegia virginiana (obedient plant, dragon mint, false dragonhead)
Salvia spp. (sages)
Sedum spp. (stonecrops, sedums)

mind. For fall-blooming plants like mums, stop pinching around the first of July so that the plants can set flower buds for fall bloom. Pinch plants that bloom in late spring or summer once or twice in early spring so you don't risk removing the flower buds by pinching later. Experiment by pinching one or two stems on different plants, and note the results in your garden journal so that you'll know what to do the following year. Don't pinch an entire plant if you're not sure it's the right time! It's better to have a leggy plant that blooms than a compact one that doesn't.

Pinching produces more flowers, but the individual flowers will be slightly smaller than those from an unpinched plant. If you want extra-large, fair-prize-size flowers, the technique for you is disbudding.

Disbudding

Like pinching, disbudding is a simple technique: Where one bud is larger than the others in a cluster, pinch out the smaller buds and leave only the largest. Disbudding will give you showy results on plants like peonies and roses. Don't use this technique on spike-blooming perennials like delphiniums and lobelias (*Lobelia*) because a single large flower on the top of a denuded flower spike wouldn't be ornamental. However, you can pinch out smaller side spikes of perennials like delphiniums and monkshoods (*Aconitum*) for a larger central spike.

Deadheading

Deadheading is a gruesome name for a very useful technique—removing spent flowers. Some perennials deadhead themselves, dropping old flowers unobtrusively to the ground. But the brown, papery ruins of other flowers will spoil your pleasure in a perennial border unless you take them off regularly. (Daylilies and bearded irises are prime offenders.)

Deadheading provides your perennials with more than good looks, though. It's an important maintenance technique for several reasons.

- Flowers usually fade after pollination, so if you leave them on the plant, you're encouraging seed formation. This robs the plant of vigor because it takes a great deal of the plant's energy to mature seed. By deadheading, you'll allow the plant to channel that energy back into flower, leaf, and root production.
- Removing spent flowers (and potential seeds) keeps invasive perennials from self-sowing all over your garden— always an unwelcome surprise the following season.
- Deadheading often extends the bloom season: The plants will keep flowering rather than stopping after the first flush, as they would if they had set seed. In fact, if you shear back some plants after blooming, you'll often get a second flush of bloom later in the season.

Pinching, disbudding, and deadheading. Pinch out the growing tips of each stem of perennials like this chrysanthemum (*left*) for bushier plants with more flowers. To disbud perennials like this dahlia (*center*) for fewer but larger blooms, pinch out side buds, leaving only the central or highest bud in each cluster. Deadhead flowers like this daylily (*right*) by pinching or cutting off spent flowers.

Deadhead as you're weeding, throw the spent flowers into a bucket with the weeds, then take it all off to the compost pile. As with weeding, it pays to keep up with deadheading. Don't let it get away from you.

If there's more than one flower on a single stalk and the flowers open at different times, like daylilies, carefully snap off the faded blooms with your fingers or trim them off with garden shears. With plants like yarrows (*Achillea*) that bear one flower head on the end of each stalk, cut the stalks at or near the ground when the flowers fade.

Some spring-blooming plants get leggy by midsummer and benefit from harsher treatment. This is especially true of mat-forming plants such as wall rock cress (*Arabis caucasica*), perennial candytuft (*Iberis sempervirens*), and moss phlox (*Phlox subulata*). After bloom, shear these perennials back to half their former height. Besides keeping them from

Plan for protection. If you live in a cold-winter area or on a flat, exposed site that's windy, plan to place your borders in a protected spot. Plant them on the south side of a wall, hedge, or fence, or where a dip in the landscape will offer some shelter. (Remember, snow is good insulation.) If you grow perennials in a sheltered site (*top*), you can often gamble successfully on plants that are normally hardy a zone warmer than your garden. If you leave your plants exposed (*bottom*), you'll be lucky if perennials that are normally hardy in the next-coldest zone last the winter.

sprawling, cutting back hard sometimes results in a second flush of bloom later in the season.

Some plants, like ornamental grasses and coneflowers (*Rudbeckia* and *Echinacea*), have attractive seedheads that you may want to leave on the plants for winter interest. Deadhead these plants in early spring before growth resumes.

WINTER PROTECTION

In areas where the temperature drops below freezing, your plants need winterizing as much as your car. Begin in fall with a thorough cleanup. After frosts have killed back your plants, cut them back to the ground and compost the trimmings. (Throw out diseased trimmings rather than composting them.) When the ground is cold, give your plants a winter mulch. (For more on winter mulching, see "Applying Mulch" on page 202.) Water the garden thoroughly whenever the soil is dry but not frozen—drought is actually a bigger threat to most perennials than cold.

Plan for Protection

There are commonsense measures you can take all year to help your perennials face winter. First, site your garden in a protected place where winds won't roar over it, dropping temperatures and drying out the ground. (This is even more critical if you leave four-season perennials like ornamental grasses and coneflowers standing in winter to add landscape interest.) If the only place you can grow perennials is exposed, add extra protection like pine branches over your mulch, and consider investing in a fence or shrub border to block the wind and provide permanent protection.

Check Plant Hardiness

Next, make sure the perennials you grow are winter-hardy in your area. Check the USDA Plant Hardiness Zone Map on page 162 to find your zone. (Because climate varies so much regionally, it's wise to discuss your immediate area with gardening neighbors or your local garden club. They can tell you if your garden might be a zone warmer or colder than the base zone shown on the map.) Then look up the perennials you want to plant in "The Perennial Encyclopedia," beginning on page 265, or in mail-order plant catalogs to make sure they're hardy in your zone.

If you'd like to try growing perennials that are hardy in the next zone down but questionable in yours, site them in your warmest, most protected place (like in front of a south-facing wall), mulch heavily over winter, and hope for the best. In areas with consistent snow cover, plants can often survive farther north than in warmer zones with uneven winter conditions. If you want to grow tender perennials (those that definitely won't overwinter outdoors in your area, like coleus), either treat them like annuals or pot them up and bring them in for the winter.

Avoid These Mistakes

Finally, avoiding two common mistakes can give your perennials a better chance of survival. First, don't fertilize your plants after they stop active growth in late summer. Give them time to prepare for dormancy rather than pushing them to grow tender, leafy shoots into fall. Overfertilizing is one of the main reasons plants don't survive winter. Second, don't ignore drainage problems. Waterlogged soil causes rotten roots and crowns and is another reason plants often don't survive winter. Your goal, summer and winter, is moist but well-drained soil. Prepare your garden soil with lots of organic matter before you put in plants, and keep mulch pulled back from plant crowns. If you think you have a drainage problem, site your garden elsewhere or consider raised beds.

Welcoming Spring

Don't succumb to the need to see green and pull back your winter mulch on the first warm day. When days are reliably warm, carefully remove the mulch, watching for tender shoots that are easy to damage or snap off. Leave the mulch alongside the bed so you can pull the "blanket" back over it if freezing temperatures threaten. You may have to remove and replace the mulch several times before the weather evens out. Once the weather has moderated and growth has begun, take your winter mulch to the compost pile.

THE PERENNIAL GARDENER'S TOOLSHED

You can have a wonderful perennial garden with only three tools: a trowel, a garden fork, and a bucket. The trowel will take care of planting, transplanting, weeding, and other close work. The garden fork is for digging and double-digging beds, compost turning, lifting and dividing perennials, mulching, and other heavy chores. And the bucket does everything else: It carries water or soil amendments; holds cut flowers, trimmings, or weeds; and even provides a crude seat for the worn-out gardener.

Of course, a few more tools are helpful. A shovel is good for digging and soil lifting. You can carry a lot more in a wheelbarrow or garden cart than you can in a bucket. And a hose or irrigation system beats a bucket for watering any day. Hedge shears, scissors, and hand pruners are helpful for cutting flowers, shearing back plants, and pruning off dead or diseased stems. And stakes and string are great for propping and tying up floppy perennials.

Buy Well-Made Tools

Tools are like clothes: Cheap ones wear out fast, but good ones last. Whether

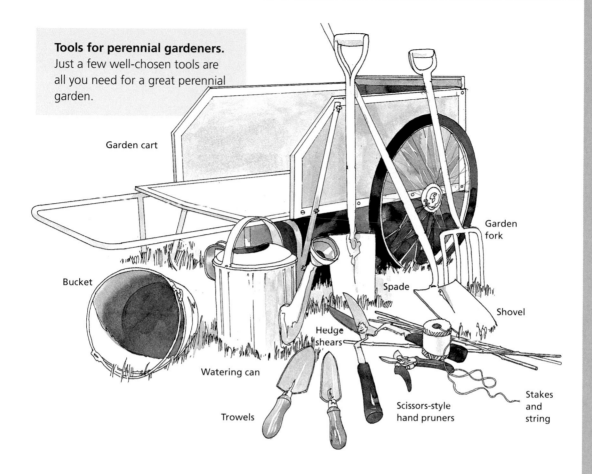

Tools for perennial gardeners. Just a few well-chosen tools are all you need for a great perennial garden.

Garden cart

Garden fork

Bucket

Spade

Shovel

Hedge shears

Watering can

Trowels

Scissors-style hand pruners

Stakes and string

your tool collection has outgrown your garage or you have only a trowel and spade by the back door, make sure your essential tools are well made and well maintained. Good tools make work easier and faster. Having a spade break off in the middle of planting is a high price to pay for choosing a shoddy tool. (For more on choosing good tools, see "How to Choose a Quality Tool" on page 216.)

Earth-Working Tools

When you're getting ready to dig or enlarge a perennial bed, carve out a path, or do some transplanting, you need earth-moving tools: forks, shovels, spades, and trowels.

Forks

Garden forks are wonderful for loosening soil, removing stones and other debris, and lifting and dividing perennials.

How to Choose a Quality Tool

Even in this age of instant breakdown, a tool can still last a lifetime—if it's a good tool, and if you use it for its intended purpose. (Levering out boulders can break even the best garden fork.) The best tool isn't necessarily the most expensive, but it certainly isn't the cheapest. Here are some things to look for—and things to avoid—when you're tool shopping.

Handle. The best wood for a tool handle is white ash, which is strong and light. Check the grain of the wood when you're looking at a handle. The lines should run up and down the length of the handle, not from side to side or in irregular patterns, which can cause breakage. Don't buy handles that have knots in the wood—they also weaken the handle. And pass up tools with painted handles, which can hide cheap wood or bad grain lines. If the tool has a short handle with a grip on top, make sure the grip is sturdy and you can see that it's securely fastened to the handle, not stuck on.

Socket. The socket is the metal "collar" that attaches the blade to the handle. Avoid tools that have jagged rivets or sharp edges on the socket. Choose solid-socket rather than open-socket construction. In solid-socket tools, the base of the handle is completely enclosed by a seamless, single-forged piece of steel. An open-socket tool, where the metal wraps around the handle, leaves an open strip of wood where the base of the handle is exposed to mud and water. This can cause rot and warping, as well as rusting on the inside of the socket. Open-socket construction is also weaker than solid-socket construction, making the blade more likely to snap off during use.

Blade. Make sure a tool's blade is smooth and strong. Don't buy tools with warped, jagged, or cracked blades. Most good carbon-steel blades are half-painted, so you can see the steel on the business end of the tool. Avoid tools

They have thick, square, fairly blunt-tipped tines. Manure forks, which have a scooped head with slender, rounded, sharp-tipped tines, are better for lifting compost, mulch, and manure, though a garden fork will do if you want to buy only one fork.

Shovels and Spades

Beginning gardeners may not know the difference between a spade and a shovel. A spade has a slender, straight, rectangular blade. It's ideal for creating straight sides in perennial beds, edging lawns and paths, and slicing under and removing sod from new beds. A shovel has a scooped blade with a rounded edge that comes to a point. As its shape suggests, a shovel is designed for scooping and lifting soil and soil amendments, for digging large holes, and for removing large perennials from their holes. Different blade widths are available for different purposes: For example, you might buy a small-bladed "poacher's spade" for working between perennials.

with completely painted blades; they're usually cheaply made. Stainless blades are unpainted so you can enjoy their sleek look. Spades that have a flattened tread on either side of the handle to hold your foot are a lot more comfortable to use than those without.

Metal. The most expensive tools have stainless steel blades, which don't rust, so they require minimal maintenance. However, they cost as much as three times the price of a good carbon-steel blade, and they don't hold a sharp edge as well as carbon-steel. If you want to go all out, stainless steel is great for spades, forks, and trowels, but well-maintained carbon-steel tools will give you more than your money's worth. (For more on tool maintenance, see "The 10 Commandments of Tool Maintenance" on page 218.)

Size. Bigger isn't always better when it comes to tools—a large, heavy tool may be harder and more exhausting to use than a lighter model. And when doing garden chores, you want your tools to work *with* you, not against you. Pick up the tools in the store and pretend you're hoeing, spading, or doing whatever you'd do with that tool in the garden. Make sure the handle length and the weight of the tool are comfortable for you. If the tool has a grip on the handle end, make sure your hand fits in it comfortably. If you garden in gloves, take the extra size into account.

Shape. If you have arthritis or are disabled—or if gardening's not as easy as it used to be—there are specially shaped tools to help you. Trowels and hand forks have special grips that take the pain out of gardening for arthritis sufferers. Others have longer handles for wheelchair gardening. And ergonomically shaped tools have handles that seem bent at odd angles, but they really work with your body to make gardening chores much easier. Buy the tool that's shaped for your needs.

Trowels

For close work, the best earth-moving tool is a trowel. A wide, sturdy trowel with a comfortable grip is indispensable for digging around established plants, digging up weeds and small plants, and transplanting small perennials. Hold a trowel handle as if you were shaking hands with it. Try a number of different trowels in your garden center, making digging motions with your wrist and hand. Buy the most comfortable trowel—it's the tool you'll use most often. You can also buy a narrow-bladed trowel for transplanting bulbs, volunteer seedlings, and other very small plants. It's the best trowel for digging in extremely tight quarters, and its slim, sharp sides are also excellent for hacking off divisions.

Weeding Tools

As with earth-moving tools, there are different types of weeding tools: hand weeders for close work, and hoes for larger areas. For more on hand weeders, see "Rooting Out Weeds" on page 205.

The 10 Commandments of Tool Maintenance

Tool maintenance makes sense. You wouldn't leave shop tools or sewing supplies lying around the yard or leave pots and pans unwashed for months after you use them. You've invested in good garden tools—you might as well spend a few minutes taking care of them. And a few minutes per use is all it takes!

1. **Buy the best tools you can afford.** You'll be surprised by how much less maintenance good tools need.

2. **Know where your tools are.** The most expensive tool is useless if you can't find it. If you have lots of tools, it might be worthwhile to rig up a hanging wall system to store them in the basement, garage, or toolshed. No matter how many you have, keep them all in the same place.

3. **Keep your tools indoors.** They'll last longer and stay in better shape if they're protected from the elements.

4. **Get the dirt off.** When you're through in the garden, clean and dry your tools. Knock off soil with a wooden scraper. A bucket of sand will remove stubborn particles if you plunge the blade in a few times.

5. **Get rid of rust.** Use a wire brush to remove rust regularly. If you disinfect your tools with alcohol or a bleach solution, dry and oil them afterward to prevent rust from forming.

6. **Heal your handles.** Smooth handles are essential—you're not going to use a tool that hurts your hands. Keep wooden handles oiled. If they start splintering, sand them smooth, then oil them with linseed oil.

7. **Keep sharp tools sharp.** If you've ever tried to use dulled pruners, you'll know why this is necessary—dull tools need more strength behind them, take longer to do the job, and do a poor job. Keep an eye (or a cautious finger) on your tools' edges: Sharpen them yourself if you know how, or take them to a hardware store for sharpening.

8. **Keep smooth edges smooth.** Nicks and burrs on a spade or shovel blade cause soil to stick and make more work for you. Use a ball-peen hammer to flatten burrs, and smooth out nicks with a fine-gauge metal-cutting file.

9. **Make your tools hard to lose.** It's amazing how easy it is to lose tools in the yard. Sometimes they just seem to disappear, turning up warped and rusted months later. You'll be able to spot them before they get away if you paint a bright stripe or circle on each handle—preferably in fluorescent orange.

10. **Give your tools a rest.** At the end of the season, polish tool blades with steel wool, oil them to prevent rust, and store them in a dry place.

Hoes

A straightforward garden hoe with a squared-off blade is all you really need for weeding the perennial garden. Use the hoe to skim off weeds just below the surface of the soil, pulling the blade lightly toward you with the blade's edge horizontal to the soil. Because you're planting perennials in mulched beds rather than as row crops, you shouldn't have to hoe among the perennials very often.

Pruners and Other Maintenance Tools

A sharp pair of scissors can cut many flowers in the perennial garden, but for plants with thick-stemmed blooms like peonies or woody stems like Russian sage (*Perovskia atriplicifolia*), hand pruners are indispensable. You also need them for surgically precise removal of damaged and diseased branches, as well as for cutting perennials back after bloom, also called deadheading. They're handy for taking cuttings and trimming stakes to size. Use scissors-style pruners, which cut the stems neatly, rather than anvil pruners, which mash the stems against their flat anvil blade, to achieve the healthiest cut.

Shears

Hedge shears are excellent for shearing plants back. They're also useful for cutting the flowering tops off self-sowing ornamental grasses before they can set seed, and shearing the grasses close to the ground in early spring before new growth begins.

That's all there is to basic perennial care: Prepare the soil, put in the plants, and maintain them sensibly. Two other aspects of growing perennials are dealt with in later chapters: In Chapter 9, we'll discuss the best ways to cope with the garden pests and diseases that plague your plants, and Chapter 10 gives you simple techniques for adding more plants to your garden.

9

PERENNIAL PEST AND DISEASE CONTROL

Effective pest and disease control is a three-step process for the perennial gardener: observe, refer, react. You'll apply the right preventives and controls at the right time *if* you watch your plants for signs of pests or diseases, check your references to identify pests or symptoms, and then use the recommended control for that particular problem.

In this chapter, you'll find out which pests and diseases attack perennials, what they look like, and what to do about them. But first, you'll learn how to prevent pests and diseases from becoming a major problem through wise plant selection and good cultural practices.

START WITH RESISTANT PLANTS

Some species and cultivars of perennials are resistant to certain pests and diseases that plague similar plants. Some of these plants are naturally resistant; others were bred for resistance. Using these plants is one of the easiest ways to solve pest and disease problems. Either look for and choose resistant plants when you're starting a new garden, or replace susceptible plants with resistant species or cultivars when problems arise.

Resistant plants are the best way to solve potential garden problems like powdery mildew. Garden phlox (*Phlox paniculata*) is notoriously susceptible to powdery mildew, which disfigures the foliage with a powdery white coating and reduces plant vigor. But phlox is a staple of many summer gardens, with its tall, showy panicles of red, white, pink, or salmon flowers.

If you feel that you simply *must* have phlox in your perennial bed or border, you have two choices: You can battle mildew with good cultural practices and preventive spraying, or you can plant mildew-resistant cultivars like 'Bright Eyes', a pink-flowered phlox with crimson centers, or 'David', a sparkling white-flowered form. Wild sweet William (*P. maculata*), which looks like garden phlox, is also mildew-resistant and an excellent substitute; there are pink, white, and rose-colored cultivars.

GROWING PLANTS RIGHT

Good gardening practices result in vigorous, healthy perennials. Careful site selection and soil preparation, adequate irrigation, and preventive mulching are some of the ways

you can make sure your plants are ready to resist pest and disease attacks. Just as we're less able to resist a cold when our bodies are already run down, stressed plants succumb more quickly to infection. Research has shown that weakened plants are the first to be attacked by pests.

Make sure your plants aren't water-stressed or waterlogged. Keep weeds, which are often alternate hosts for both pests and diseases, away from your garden. Add plenty of organic matter—especially compost—to your beds to enhance water and nutrient retention and fight nematodes. Space plants far enough apart for good air circulation. And grow a variety of species: Many pests and diseases are species-specific, or are confined to a few related species. Get your perennials off to a good start and keep them growing strongly by using these and other sound gardening practices outlined in Chapter 8, "Perennial Gardening Basics."

PESTS IN THE PERENNIALS

Pests build up most quickly when just one or two kinds of plants are grown. A bed of mixed perennials is less likely to be decimated than a bed of roses or petunias because the pests that prefer specific plants will have a harder time finding them when they're "hidden" among all those other perennials. That doesn't mean perennials are pest-free, though, as gardeners who've encountered borers in their bearded irises, Japanese beetles on

Aphids cluster under leaves and on growing tips, where they suck plant sap, causing leaf and bud distortion and blossom and leaf drop. As they feed, they excrete honeydew. Sooty mold grows on the honeydew, so you can also identify aphid damage by the presence of leaves with a black coating.

▼

Thrips feed on inner folds of leaves, causing stunted growth and russet or sooty areas on leaves. Tops of plants eventually turn brown and die. Flowers may be discolored, flecked with white, or deformed.

▶

Tarnished plant bugs pierce plant tissue to drink sap, injecting toxins that deform plant tissues. Their feeding also causes sunken, rounded, tan to dark brown spots on foliage. As leaves grow, the dead areas tear into holes.

Beetle damage can range from small holes in leaves to skeletonized foliage. Beetles will also eat holes in flowers.

▼

Weevils make characteristic "ticket punches" around leaf margins.

▲

Leafminers disfigure foliage, leaving slender, whitish, snaking tunnels behind them as they feed.

Slugs and snails chew large holes in foliage and stems; they also leave telltale shiny trails of mucus behind.

▼

▲

Spider mites cause leaves to yellow, dry up, and die. Heavy feeding turns foliage almost white. Fine webs cover leaves and growing tips.

Perennial pests: an overview. You can often identify pests by the type of damage they cause.

their hollyhocks, or slugs on their hostas can attest.

One cause of pests in perennial beds is the nature of perennials themselves: The plants are in place a long time, giving pest populations a chance to establish themselves over many growing seasons. Fortunately, there are five ways to keep pests at an acceptable level in your garden.

1. Grow resistant species and cultivars when available.
2. Use good cultural practices.
3. Apply biological controls, which are alive and often self-perpetuating.
4. Use manual controls, including barriers and traps.
5. Use insecticidal sprays and dusts when required.

These five tactics should keep perennial pests at the "few and far between" state so your plants can bloom and thrive unmolested.

We've discussed resistant plants and cultural controls earlier in the chapter; here's an overview of biological controls, manual controls, and sprays and dusts. But first, there are two techniques that are more important than any control: monitoring and using common sense.

Looking for Trouble

The best and easiest way to keep pests under control is to find them when they've just arrived and there still aren't many of them, so monitor your plants. If you can start control early, your perennials will suffer minimal damage, and you can usually use a simple control. Handpicking a few Japanese beetles is far better than coping with bug sprays and stripped plants. Become a garden detective: When you're weeding, watering, or just out strolling in your garden, check your plants for pests and signs of feeding injury. Make sure you're in the garden every day—pest populations can build up fast. Try to familiarize yourself with the major perennial pests so you'll know what you're looking for, then apply appropriate controls.

Using Common Sense

Don't panic at the first sight of a slug or a ragged leaf. Unless you're growing perennials for the florist industry or a flower show, a little damage is as acceptable as it is inevitable. The techniques we recommend will ensure that you have lush, healthy plants and plenty of perfect flowers. Your garden is a natural system, so be prepared for the occasional flaw. Use good sense; don't overreact.

The second time to let common sense come to your rescue is at the other end of the control spectrum. If, in spite of your best efforts, certain perennials are decimated every year, give up the fight. No matter how much you love columbines, if leafminers make them unsightly every season, it's time to throw in the trowel. There are plenty of other lovely perennials to choose from. Give it your best shot, but then let reason be your guide. Don't let pest-pocked perennials ruin the looks of your perennial garden.

If you can't live without them, remember this: You can always hide favorite but pest-plagued perennials in the cutting garden, where the colorful chaos will make pest damage less noticeable.

For a rogues' gallery of the worst perennial pests with descriptions, damage, and controls listed for each pest, see "Perennial Pests at a Glance" on page 226.

Using Biological Controls

Biological controls are microscopic living organisms that infest or attack pests. They are usually pest-specific, attacking only one kind of insect, and are thought to be harmless to the environment and nontargeted species. To be effective, biological

controls must be applied early because the infection takes several days to kill the pest. All are available from garden suppliers; apply according to directions.

Japanese beetles. These ½-inch-long, metallic blue-green beetles consume the leaves, stalks, and flowers of many perennials. The ¾-inch-long, C-shaped grub larvae feed on the roots of lawn grasses. Handpick adults into a can of soapy water. Traps will attract these pests to your yard unless your neighbors set up traps, too. Use milky disease or parasitic nematodes on lawn areas to control beetle larvae.

Grub

Adult

BT. *Bacillus thuringiensis*, known as BT, is a bacterial disease that infects insect larvae. Different strains of BT have been isolated for different pests: One infects caterpillars, a second attacks the grubs of Colorado potato beetles, and a third infects mosquito and blackfly larvae. (However, the strain of BT that kills pest caterpillars will kill *all* caterpillars, and so on, so please don't apply a biological control unless you're sure you have or will have a problem based on past years' infestations.) Make sure you buy the strain of BT that targets your pest problem.

Milky disease. *Bacillus popilliae*, milky disease, attacks Japanese beetle grubs. Apply this bacterial disease, often sold as milky spore, to the lawn where these grubs live. Milky disease is most effective in providing grub control if everyone in your neighborhood applies it to their lawns; one application will be effective for years.

Parasitic nematodes. These microscopic roundworms parasitize and kill insect larvae, including ground-dwelling caterpillars (like cutworms) and grubs. The nematodes feed on a dead insect; about 10 to 20 days after the first infection, huge numbers of nematodes leave the carcass in search of new victims. Because nematodes perish in sunlight or dry places, they are most useful against pests in soil or hidden locations. Although the larval stage can survive for long periods in the soil, for the greatest effect you need to release more nematodes each year.

Using Manual Controls

Manual controls are simple, low-tech methods like handpicking pests or putting barriers around plants. Some manual controls are preventive, like cutworm collars; their aim is to keep pests from reaching your plants. Others, like handpicking, come into play once pests attack. When you notice a pest problem, try these controls first; they're often all you'll need. If pest populations are too great for effective manual control, move on to dusts and sprays.

Handpicking. This is a simple technique that merely involves plucking a pest off a plant and squashing it or drowning it in a can of soapy water. (Soap breaks the surface tension of the water so the pests can't climb out.) It's not for the squeamish, but it is highly effective when used early when populations are light.

Copper barriers. Slugs and snails get an electric shock when their slimy bodies touch copper, so these copper strips keep them out of your beds. They're easiest to use if you have wood-sided raised beds and can nail the strip around the outside of the bed. This works on a barrel garden, too. Copper strips are available from garden supply companies and are sold as Snail-Barr.

Cutworm collars. Make your own "collars" to keep cutworms from attacking your seedlings and transplants. Use cardboard cylinders like toilet paper or paper

(continued on page 229)

PERENNIAL PESTS AT A GLANCE

This table lists the 13 top perennial pests. If pests are plaguing your plants and you can see them, check the description column and match your pest; if you can't find a pest, check the damage column for a match. Once you've found the culprit, a glance across the page will show you the most effective controls and which other perennials are likely to be attacked.

Pest Name and Description	Damage	Controls	Plants Attacked
Aphids *Adults:* $\frac{1}{12}$ to $\frac{1}{5}$ inch long; green, reddish, or blue-black; pear-shaped, with two tubes projecting back from abdomen; some winged, some wingless. *Larvae:* smaller version of adults.	Leaves, stems, and buds distorted, sticky; look for clusters of small insects.	Wash pests from plants with a strong spray of water; use insecticidal soap, neem, or pyrethrum sprays for serious infestations.	Many
Beetle, Asiatic Garden *Adults:* $\frac{1}{3}$-inch-long, brown, velvety beetles. *Larvae:* $\frac{3}{4}$-inch-long white grubs with light brown heads.	Leaves with irregular holes in edges.	Handpick adults at night into can of soapy water; spray heavily infested plantings with pyrethrum or neem.	Many
Beetle, Fuller Rose *Adults:* $\frac{1}{3}$-inch-long, gray, long-nosed weevils. *Larvae:* white or yellowish grubs with brown heads.	"Ticket-punch" holes around leaf margins.	Handpick adults at night into can of soapy water; shake plants over dropcloth or sheet in early morning and collect weevils.	*Chrysanthemum, Hibiscus, Penstemon, Plumbago, Primula, Rudbeckia, Scabiosa*
Beetle, Japanese *Adults:* $\frac{1}{2}$-inch-long, metallic blue or green beetles with coppery wing covers. *Larvae:* $\frac{3}{4}$-inch-long, plump, grayish white grubs.	Leaves and flowers with holes; may be skeletonized.	Handpick adults into can of soapy water; apply milky disease spores or parasitic nematodes to lawn to control grubs; set up traps away from beds; spray heavily infested plants with neem.	*Alcea, Aster, Astilbe, Digitalis, Gaillardia, Hemerocallis, Hibiscus, Paeonia*

Pest Name and Description	Damage	Controls	Plants Attacked
Borers *Adults:* moths or beetles. *Larvae:* caterpillars or grubs.	Stems break; leaves wilt; iris borers cause irregular tunnels in leaves and damaged or rotted rhizomes.	Apply *Bacillus thuringiensis* (BT) or parasitic nematodes at first sign of borers. Destroy weeds where borers overwinter. Crush borers in iris leaves.	Many
Bugs, True *Adults:* 1/16 to 1/2 inch long, usually shield-shaped; may be brown, black, green, or brilliantly colored and patterned. *Larvae:* oval to rounded nymphs with long snouts; may be yellow, red, bluish gray, or yellow-green; often patterned.	Buds and leaves deformed or dwarfed.	Handpick into can of soapy water. Spray with insecticidal soap; treat severe infestations with neem. Destroy weeds where bugs overwinter.	Many
Cutworms *Adults:* gray or brownish moths. *Larvae:* 1- to 2-inch-long grayish or brown caterpillars that curl up when disturbed.	Seedlings or young plants cut off at soil level.	Place plant collars in soil around seedlings or transplants.	Many
Leafminers *Adults:* 1/10 inch long; wasp-like, with yellow-striped black bodies and clear wings. *Larvae:* yellowish, stout, wormlike maggots.	Leaves with tan or brown blotches or serpentine tunnels.	Prune off and destroy infested leaves. Spray leaves weekly with insecticidal soap at the first sign of leafminers. Remove garden debris in fall.	*Aconitum, Aquilegia, Chrysanthemum, Delphinium, Dianthus, Eupatorium, Gypsophila, Heuchera, Lobelia, Primula, Salvia, Verbena*
Scales *Adults:* 1/12 to 1/5 inch long, with grayish, brownish orange, reddish brown, or cottony white shells; males are winged, females wingless. *Larvae:* tiny yellow, brown, or red nymphs.	Leaves turn yellow, drop; plants may die.	Prune off infested stems and leaves. Remove scales with a cotton swab dipped in rubbing alcohol; spray severe infestations with pyrethrum or neem.	*Helianthus, Iberis, Monarda, Opuntia, Paeonia, Phlox, Verbena*

(continued)

PERENNIAL PESTS AT A GLANCE (CONT.)

Pest Name and Description	Damage	Controls	Plants Attacked
Slugs and Snails *Adults:* 1/8 to 8 inches long; gray, tan, green, black, yellow, or spotted, with eyes at the tips of small tentacles; snails have single spiral shell; slugs are shell-less. *Young:* smaller, paler versions of adults.	Leaves with large, ragged holes.	Place copper strips around beds; sprinkle sawdust, ashes, or diatomaceous earth around plants. Set beer traps in garden. Handpick at night into can of soapy water.	*Alcea, Asarum, Begonia, Bergenia, Campanula, Delphinium, Hemerocallis, Hosta, Iris, Ligularia, Primula, Sedum, Viola*
Spider Mites *Adults:* 1/50-inch-long, reddish brown or pale spider-like mites with 8 legs; wingless. *Larvae:* smaller version of adults.	Leaves stippled, reddish to yellow, with fine webbing.	Spray plants daily with a strong stream of water. Keep soil moist. Use insecticidal soap sprays for serious infestations.	Many
Thrips *Adults:* 1/50 to 1/25 inch long, with yellow, brown, or blackish bodies and two pairs of fringed wings. *Larvae:* white or yellow with red eyes; wingless.	Flower buds die; petals distorted; growth stunted.	Remove and destroy infested plant parts. Destroy weeds where thrips overwinter. Use insecticidal soap for serious infestations.	Many
Whiteflies *Adults:* 1/12-inch-long, white, mothlike insects. *Larvae:* green, translucent, flat nymphs.	Leaves yellow; plant weakened.	Spray leaves with insecticidal soap. Destroy weeds to reduce whitefly populations.	*Chrysanthemum, Hibiscus, Lupinus, Primula, Rudbeckia, Salvia, Verbena*

towel rolls, or roll your own. Make each collar 2 to 3 inches tall and 1½ to 2 inches wide; push them into the soil so that about half the collar is below the soil surface. Remove the collars once plants are past the seedling stage.

Diatomaceous earth. This mineral dust is composed of fossilized diatom shells. The microscopic fossil shells have razor-sharp edges that pierce the skin of soft-bodied pests like caterpillars, slugs, and snails. The pests dehydrate and die. Diatomaceous earth also works as a repellent: Use it as a barrier on the soil around plants or around the outside of beds.

Traps. Shallow pans of beer will lure slugs and snails to a watery death. (Alcohol-free beer is even more effective, and you can use a brew of yeast and water, too.) Set the pans into the soil, placing the lip flush with the soil surface, and fill with stale beer; empty the traps daily. Snail traps are also commercially available. Other traps, like Japanese beetle traps, are available commercially but are less relevant to perennial gardeners; in fact, studies have shown that Japanese beetle traps often act as a lure, drawing pests into your garden.

Using Sprays and Dusts

The best control for a severe pest outbreak is sometimes a spray or dust. A number of sprays and dusts are harmless (like water); some are relatively harmless (like insecticidal soap); and others may be highly toxic for a short time (pyrethrins are toxic for about a day, rotenone for about a week). Don't underestimate the potential toxicity of organically acceptable insecticides like pyrethrins. If you choose to use them, wear protective clothing, a face mask, and gloves when handling or applying them. Whichever spray or dust you use, make sure you coat the undersides of the leaves; many pests congregate there, out of sight of potential predators.

Water. A forceful spray of water is often enough to control aphids and spider mites. It knocks them off the plants, and these slow-moving pests can't find their way back.

Insecticidal soap. Soap sprays are contact poisons that are effective against outbreaks of soft-bodied pests like aphids and whiteflies. You can buy insecticidal soap commercially (Safer is a commonly available brand) and dilute it according to directions, or make your own by mixing 1 to 3 teaspoons of liquid dish soap (not laundry or dishwasher detergent) in 1 gallon of water. For best control, spray plants every 2 or 3 days for 2 weeks.

Pyrethrum. Pyrethrum is made from the pulverized dried flowers of pyrethrum daisies (*Chrysanthemum cinerariifolium* and *C. coccineum*). Pyrethrum can be applied as a dust or used as a spray and is effective against a wide range of insects. For best control, apply pyrethrum in early evening; two applications 2 hours apart may be most effective. Because pyrethrum is not pest-specific, don't use it near water (it's extremely toxic to fish) or pets. Make sure you buy plant-derived pyrethrum, not synthetic pyrethrins or pyrethroids, which are more toxic and break down more slowly.

Adult

Larva

A PLAGUE OF PERENNIAL DISEASES

Perennials are more likely to be disease-free than annuals or vegetables because perennial beds usually contain a mixture of plants rather than a single species or cultivar (a monoculture). Monocultures draw diseases—and the pests that often spread them—like a magnet. Good cultural practices, like adding plenty of compost and other organic matter to the soil, mulching, and cleaning up plant debris in fall, also reduce the likelihood of diseases getting a foothold in your garden.

No matter how careful you are, though, you'll probably encounter diseases in your perennials from time to time. An especially hot, wet summer might provoke an outbreak of powdery mildew, a friend might inadvertently give you a peony division with botrytis blight, or an

Iris borers. In spring, borer larvae enter a fan of iris leaves at the top and burrow down to the rhizome. Pale, irregular tunnels in the leaves mark their travels. Borers also spread soft rot bacteria as they feed. To control borers, pinch and crush them in the leaves, or inject BT or parasitic nematodes into their holes. Also, remove dead leaves in fall and destroy infested fans in spring. If you've had serious borer problems, grow Siberian iris (*Iris sibirica*), which is usually borer-free, rather than bearded iris.

Bring On the Beneficials!

Beneficial insects prey on or parasitize pest insects, controlling your problems for you. In addition, they help fight disease by eating disease-spreading pests like thrips, leafhoppers, and whiteflies. Encourage beneficial insects like ladybugs (more correctly called lady beetles), lacewings, syrphid and tachinid flies, and parasitic wasps to take up residence in your garden by planting nectar- and pollen-producing perennials like goldenrod and achillea and composites like coneflowers and daisies.

Mulch your beds so these little guys will have a safe place to hide out. And make a "bug bath" by setting a shallow dish at ground level, putting stones in it to give the good bugs sure footing, and making sure that it has water in it at all times (leave the tops of the stones dry). Need we add that putting an ornamental birdbath in your perennial garden will attract yet another pest-eating ally?

One final note: Do *not* use insecticides: You'll kill off the beneficials along with the pests.

Lady beetle

Syrphid fly

Green lacewing

The good guys. Attracting beneficial insects to your perennial garden is an easy and effective way to fight pests and diseases.

unusually high leafhopper population might spread aster yellows to your chrysanthemums. Familiarize yourself with disease symptoms so when your plants show signs of infection, you can take prompt action to save them.

There are three types of diseases that infect perennials—bacteria, fungi, and viruses—as well as a related category of pests and problems that cause diseaselike symptoms in plants. These include microscopic nematodes, nutrient deficiencies, and other disorders like herbicide drift. Check the table "Are Your Perennials Missing Something?" on page 190 to make sure your plants don't have a simple deficiency before treating them for disease. For descriptions of perennial disease symptoms

Slug eggs in soil

Slug

Snail

Slugs and snails. These pests thrive in the cool, moist soil preferred by many perennials like hostas. Mulches and plants with low-growing leaves provide shady hiding places from which slugs and snails emerge to feed at night. They rasp large holes in leaves and stems and leave a characteristic shiny slime trail. To control these pests, drown them in beer traps or sprinkle bands of coarse, dry, scratchy materials such as wood ashes or diatomaceous earth around plants or beds.

What's New in Perennial Pest Control?

Neem seed extract is one of the latest and safest organic pest control sprays. Now that the toxicity of such natural controls as nicotine, rotenone, ryania, and sabadilla have taken them off most organic gardeners' lists, there aren't a lot of spray choices left. But neem's quick breakdown and relatively low toxicity have won the approval of organic gardeners, and it's a very effective pest control. Just remember, though, don't use neem as a preventive measure because it will kill beneficial insects as well as pests. If you have an out-of-control pest population, spray infested plants only.

and controls, see "Perennial Diseases at a Glance" on page 236.

Preventing Diseases

Prevention is the best—and often the only—cure for plant diseases. There is no cure for viral diseases, and once your garden soil becomes infested with nematodes, you may have to remove all the plants in your perennial bed and solarize the soil before trying again with new plants. Even fungi like *Verticillium* can survive for 20 years in the soil. So good gardening practices and commonsense precautions can be critical in keeping diseases out or minimizing their damage.

You can start with resistant species and cultivars, especially if a disease has been a problem in the past. For example, if powdery mildew has been a plague on your bee balm (*Monarda*), try 'Marshall's Delight', which is mildew-resistant. You might have to search for disease-resistant cultivars; breeding for resistance in perennials is a fairly new phenomenon. Resistant species and cultivars are mentioned in encyclopedia entries when a disease is a particular problem for a perennial.

Site selection is also important. If you're planning a new perennial bed, site it in well-drained soil in full sun and where it will get good air circulation. Don't overcrowd plants; space them far enough apart so air can circulate between them. If you have an established bed that has become overcrowded, thin plants to improve circulation. (You can find more on this technique in "Thinning" on page 209.)

Fungal and bacterial diseases and nematodes can all spread by water. You can avoid encouraging infections by careful watering. Water your perennials in the morning so they'll dry before night; water the ground around the plants, not the foliage; and don't work in your perennial beds when the foliage is still wet from a rain.

Another time-honored preventive tactic is to practice good garden hygiene: Wash

SOURCES OF ORGANIC PEST AND DISEASE CONTROLS

Many garden centers, nurseries, and hardware stores now carry a wide range of organic pest and disease controls. If you can't find a source near you, these mail-order suppliers offer an excellent selection.

Gardener's Supply Company
128 Intervale Road
Burlington, VT 05401

Gardens Alive!
5100 Schenley Place NE
Lawrenceburg, IN 47035

Harmony Farm Supply
P.O. Box 460
Graton, CA 95444

The Natural Gardening
 Company
217 San Anselmo Avenue
San Anselmo, CA 94960

Necessary Trading Company
703 Salem Avenue
New Castle, VA 24127

North Country Organics
R.R. 1 Box 2232
Bradford, VT 05033

Peaceful Valley Farm Supply
 Company
P.O. Box 2209
Grass Valley, CA 95945

Ringer Corporation
9959 Valley View Road
Eden Prairie, MN 55344

Smith & Hawken
25 Corte Madera
Mill Valley, CA 94941

your hands and tools after working with diseased plants. Keep the garden clean of potentially diseased plant debris, and weed religiously to remove alternate hosts of diseases and their carriers. Cut plants to the ground at the end of the growing season. Compost healthy trimmings, but destroy any that look diseased.

Curing or Controlling Disease

If disease strikes in spite of your attempts to prevent it, take prompt action to curtail its development and spread. In the following sections, specific controls are discussed with each disease category: For example, you'll find organic fungicides under "Fighting Fungal Diseases" on page 239. However, there are two techniques that are effective for a range of diseases.

The simplest but most painful control is to promptly remove and destroy infected foliage, flowers, or entire plants, if necessary. It's heartrending to pull out prized perennials, but sometimes that's the only alternative, especially if they have viral diseases or foliar nematodes; better to lose a plant or two than an entire bed. This technique will help control fungal and bacterial diseases as well. A more specialized technique that can be quite effective is called *soil solarization.*

Soil Solarization

If soilborne problems like wilts and nematodes have plagued your perennials in

(continued on page 239)

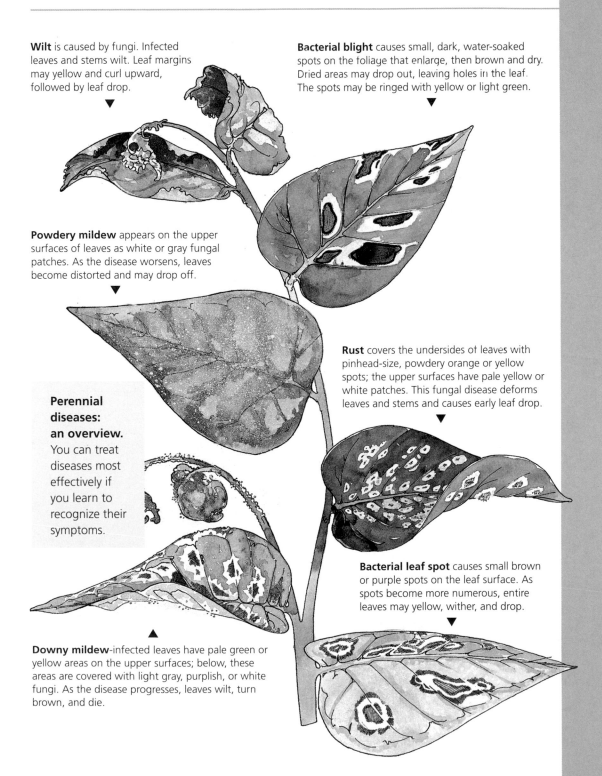

Wilt is caused by fungi. Infected leaves and stems wilt. Leaf margins may yellow and curl upward, followed by leaf drop.

Bacterial blight causes small, dark, water-soaked spots on the foliage that enlarge, then brown and dry. Dried areas may drop out, leaving holes in the leaf. The spots may be ringed with yellow or light green.

Powdery mildew appears on the upper surfaces of leaves as white or gray fungal patches. As the disease worsens, leaves become distorted and may drop off.

Rust covers the undersides of leaves with pinhead-size, powdery orange or yellow spots; the upper surfaces have pale yellow or white patches. This fungal disease deforms leaves and stems and causes early leaf drop.

Perennial diseases: an overview. You can treat diseases most effectively if you learn to recognize their symptoms.

Bacterial leaf spot causes small brown or purple spots on the leaf surface. As spots become more numerous, entire leaves may yellow, wither, and drop.

Downy mildew-infected leaves have pale green or yellow areas on the upper surfaces; below, these areas are covered with light gray, purplish, or white fungi. As the disease progresses, leaves wilt, turn brown, and die.

PERENNIAL DISEASES AT A GLANCE

This chart gives you an overview of the major diseases that infect perennials. If your plants have contracted a disease, they may display classic symptoms like spotted leaves, wilting, mold, or stunting. Look at the symptoms column of this table and match the symptoms described with those on your plant. Then you can look in the other columns to find out the name of the disease, how to control it, and what other perennials it's most likely to strike.

Disease Name	Symptoms	Controls	Plants Affected
Anthracnose	Stems with sunken lesions and pink blisters; plants may die.	Thin stems to improve air circulation; clean up garden in fall, destroying infected plant material. Treat severe infections with weekly sulfur sprays.	*Alcea, Hemerocallis, Hosta, Paeonia, Tulipa, Viola*
Aster yellows	Leaves yellow, flowers small and green; witches'-brooms at base of plant.	Remove and destroy infected plants. Control leafhoppers, which spread the disease; remove weeds, which may carry the disease.	*Campanula, Chrysanthemum, Coreopsis, Delphinium, Gaillardia, Rudbeckia, Salvia*
Botrytis blight	Shoots wilt suddenly and fall over, stem bases blacken and rot; gray mold may appear on crowns; buds wither and blacken; flowers and leaves turn brown.	Remove and destroy infected plant parts. Clear mulch from crowns in spring to let soil dry; site plants in well-drained soil.	*Gladiolus, Lilium, Paeonia, Tulipa*
Leaf spot, bacterial	Leaves with many small brown or purple spots; heavily spotted leaves may yellow and drop.	Remove and destroy infected plants. Wash hands and tools after handling diseased plants. Avoid injuring healthy plants and splashing water on plant foliage. Clean up garden debris.	*Aconitum, Delphinium, Geranium, Iris, Papaver*
Leaf spot, fungal	Leaves with yellow, brown, or black spots; leaves may wither.	Remove and destroy infected foliage; thin stems or space plants to encourage air circulation; avoid wetting foliage when watering. Apply preventive sulfur sprays if leaf spot was severe last season.	Many

Disease Name	Symptoms	Controls	Plants Affected
Mildew, downy	Cottony gray or white spots on undersides of leaves; angular yellow spots form on upper leaf surfaces.	Grow resistant species and cultivars. Space plants and thin stems to encourage air circulation. Mulch plants and avoid wetting foliage when watering. Remove and destroy infected leaves.	*Artemisia, Aster, Centaurea, Geranium, Geum, Lupinus, Rudbeckia, Veronica*
Mildew, powdery	Leaves covered with white powder.	Grow resistant species and cultivars. Spray with compost tea or soap sprays weekly, or with sulfur every 10 days during warm, wet weather. Water in the morning, and avoid wetting the foliage.	*Achillea, Aster, Coreopsis, Delphinium, Monarda, Phlox, Rudbeckia*
Nematodes, foliar	Leaves with brown blotches between veins; leaves die and turn brittle; symptoms move up the plant.	Remove and destroy infested plants and soil surrounding them. Clean up garden debris in fall. Mulch in spring to keep nematodes from leaves. Avoid wetting foliage when watering.	*Bergenia, Chrysanthemum, Heuchera, Phlox*
Nematodes, root knot	Plants stunted; leaves yellow, spotted; roots have tiny galls.	Increase soil organic matter; apply chitin or parasitic nematodes to soil.	*Clematis, Geranium, Gladiolus, Hemerocallis, Iris, Paeonia, Viola*
Rot, bacterial soft	Leaves with water-soaked spots; rhizomes rotted and soft.	Control iris borers; remove and destroy rotting rhizomes. Wash tools. Plant iris in well-drained soil in full sun.	*Iris*
Rot, crown	Stems blacken and rot at base; foliage turns yellow, wilts; crowns may mold.	Plant perennials in well-drained soil; avoid damaging crowns when digging around plants. Keep winter mulch away from crowns. Wash tools. Remove and destroy infected plants.	*Ajuga, Delphinium, Eremurus, Iris, Kniphofia, Platycodon*

(continued)

PERENNIAL DISEASES AT A GLANCE (CONT.)

Disease Name	Symptoms	Controls	Plants Affected
Rot, root	Leaves yellow; plant growth slows; roots rot off.	Plant perennials in well-drained soil; avoid damaging roots when digging around plants. Keep mulch away from base of plants. Wash tools. Remove and destroy infected plants.	Many
Rust	Leaf surfaces pale, powdery orange spots beneath.	Grow resistant cultivars; keep leaves dry; thin stems to encourage air circulation. Remove and destroy infected plant parts. Apply sprays of compost tea or soap sprays weekly, or wettable sulfur every 10 days.	*Achillea, Aconitum, Alcea, Anemone, Aquilegia, Campanula, Clematis, Delphinium, Dianthus, Iris, Liatris, Monarda*
Viruses	Leaves and flowers greenish yellow, distorted; leaves mottled or streaked; new growth spindly; plants stunted.	There is no cure for viral plant diseases; remove and destroy plants showing viral symptoms. Viruses are spread by sucking insects like aphids and leafhoppers; control them to limit the spread of viruses.	*Aquilegia, Aster, Chrysanthemum, Delphinium, Epimedium, Gaillardia, Iris, Lilium, Paeonia*
Wilt, fusarium	Leaves wilt, yellow, and die; stems droop; symptoms may first appear on a single branch.	Dig and destroy infected plants. Clean up garden debris thoroughly in fall. Plant resistant species and cultivars.	*Chrysanthemum, Dianthus*
Wilt, verticillium	Leaves, stems wilt; leaf margins may curl upward; leaves yellow and drop off; plants may die.	Dig and destroy infected plants. Clean up garden debris thoroughly in fall. Plant resistant species and cultivars.	*Aconitum, Aster, Chrysanthemum, Coreopsis, Delphinium, Paeonia, Papaver, Phlox*

the past few seasons, try soil solarization. This is an easy technique, but it does require planning because it takes several months to be effective. If you're starting a new bed, prepare the bed a season before you plan to use it if you live in the North; in the South and Southwest, you can dig the bed, solarize it, and be ready to plant the same growing season.

In spring in the South and midsummer in the North, rake the new bed smooth and water it well. Dig a trench several inches deep around the outside of the bed. Spread a thin (1 to 4 mils) clear plastic sheet over the bed and press it down against the soil surface. Press the edges of the sheet into the trench, and seal the plastic by filling the trench with soil. Leave the sheet in place for 1 to 2 months.

The technique works because heat builds up under the plastic sheet, essentially cooking the top 6 to 12 inches of soil in the bed. In addition to killing nematodes and diseases, solarization will also kill weeds, weed seeds, and insect pests. The drawback is that you need bare soil; if you have a serious nematode infestation in an existing bed, you may have to dig out and discard all the perennials, solarize the soil, and replant in fall.

Battling Bacterial Diseases

Bacteria are microscopic organisms. Most are beneficial decomposers—vital to the decay cycle and to composting—and some are major pest controls, like *Bacillus thuringiensis*. A few bacteria cause diseases in perennials. Bacterial infections can be spread by wind, water, and contact with contaminated tools or carrier pests. Once contracted, these diseases are difficult to control. Use preventive tactics and treat signs of disease promptly.

Controlling Bad Bacteria

To control bacterial diseases, remove and discard infected plant parts. Thin plants and avoid crowding future plantings. Wash your tools and hands after handling infected plants. Avoid overhead watering. Clean up plant debris to remove overwintering sites. The most common bacterial diseases of perennials are bacterial soft rot of iris, and leaf spot, which infects a number of plants. If you live in the South, your perennials may also be infected by pseudomonas wilt, which causes leaves and stems to wilt and may kill infected plants. Keep pseudomonas wilt from spreading by digging and destroying infected plants. (See also "New Developments in Disease Control" on page 241.)

Fighting Fungal Diseases

Most perennial diseases are fungal. Fungi are organisms like mushrooms that reproduce by spores, lack chlorophyll, and live on organic matter. Most fungi are beneficial, but parasitic fungi cause diseases, sapping the strength of host plants by growing and feeding on them. These fungi are microscopic, but they produce visible spores that are often easy to identify, like the white, cottony spores of powdery mildew or the orange spores of rust.

Botrytis blight. Peony shoots afflicted with this fungal disease wilt and fall over. Stem bases blacken and rot, and buds may wither and blacken. Flowers and leaves may turn brown and moldy. Remove and destroy infected plant parts. Avoid overwatering and wet, poorly drained soil. Clear mulch from crowns in spring to let the soil dry.

Controlling Fatal Fungi

Fortunately, because they're the diseases you're most likely to encounter in your garden, fungal diseases are the easiest to control. Besides growing resistant species and cultivars and using cultural practices to reduce the likelihood of infection, you can choose from a number of organic fungicides to treat stricken plants. These fungicides won't cure disease on infected plant parts, but they will keep the disease from spreading to healthy parts of the plant once you've removed the infected portions. Always follow label directions. Remember that some of these sprays may leave an unattractive coating on foliage, but this is a temporary effect—and it certainly looks no worse than fungus-covered leaves. (See also "New Developments in Disease Control" on the opposite page.) Here are some of the most effective fungicide sprays.

- **Antitranspirants.** Sprays like Wilt-Pruf that are intended to keep leaves from dehydrating have also been proven effective in preventing powdery mildew. Use one-third of the recommended summer rate and reapply to cover new growth and after rain.
- **Baking soda.** One homemade spray that tests have shown to be effective in controlling a wide range of fungal diseases, including leaf spot, anthracnose, and powdery mildew, is a 0.5 percent solution of baking soda and water. Mix 1 teaspoon of baking soda in 1 quart of water, add a few drops of liquid dish soap or cooking oil to help the mixture

New Developments in Disease Control

As in pest control, neem has emerged as a rising—or, more accurately, shooting—star in disease control. There are neem oil products to control fungal diseases (brands include Triact and Rose Defense for ornamentals). Make a spray with 2½ tablespoons per gallon of water, and apply it every week or two.

There's also a disease that fights diseases: a spray of streptomycin sulfate, sold as Agrimycin, that controls bacterial diseases like rots, wilts, and fireblight. Both neem oil products and Agrimycin are available at garden centers and by mail order.

Crown rot. Overcrowded plants and wet, poorly drained soil are the main causes of crown rot. The leaves and stems of afflicted plants turn brown or black at the base, and black spores may appear on stems. Plants may wilt suddenly or yellow and wilt slowly. Prevention is the best control: Avoid sites with poorly drained, wet soil; divide plants regularly; don't damage crowns when digging near plants; and keep winter mulch away from the base of the plant. Remove and destroy infected plants.

adhere to the leaves, and spray on infected plants.

- **Copper.** Copper is also a powerful broad-spectrum fungicide. Use copper fungicides sparingly: Repeated applications may stunt or damage plants.

- **Fungicidal soap.** Safer Garden Fungicide, which contains sulfur in a soap emulsion, controls fungi—including powdery mildew, leaf spot, and rust—on perennials. You can buy it in ready-to-spray or concentrate form.

Viral diseases. Perennials may be attacked by several viral diseases that cause symptoms such as spindly new growth and distorted, greenish yellow flowers and leaves. Viruses are spread by sucking insects such as aphids and leafhoppers; control these pests to limit virus problems. There's no cure for infected plants: Remove and destroy them; do *not* compost them. Viruses overwinter in perennials and perennial weeds, so clean up the garden thoroughly in fall if you've had problems with them. Wash any tools that come in contact with infected plants.

- **Sulfur.** Milder than copper, sulfur still prevents fungi from growing on perennials. You can apply elemental sulfur as a dust, or spray wettable or liquid sulfur onto your plants. Apply sulfur only when temperatures will stay below 85°F; higher temperatures make sulfur toxic to plants.

Viruses and Viruslike Diseases

Even though viral diseases aren't as common in perennials as fungal and bacterial infections and nematodes, it's still important to recognize the symptoms of viral infection and eliminate infected plants before they can spread disease. There is no cure for viral infection. Symptoms can vary from plant to plant, but infected plants tend to show certain characteristic traits like greenish flowers, ring spotting (concentric rings on the foliage), and rosetting (a deformed, tight clump of leaves that resembles a rosebud). Mosaic virus and aster yellows are common.

Viruses are spread from plant to plant by direct contact rather than by wind or water. The virus must be either rubbed against or injected by pests into a susceptible plant for it to contract the disease. You can spread viral diseases to your perennials by brushing against infected plants and then healthy plants, especially when plants are wet. Smokers can transmit tobacco mosaic virus from touching cigarettes or other tobacco products and not washing up before heading out to the garden. If you inadvertently propagate infected plants, you may also be spreading viral diseases.

Controlling Vile Viruses

Because there is no cure for plants that are infected by viruses, try to keep your garden virus-free. Plant resistant species and cultivars when possible. Viruses are carried by sucking insects such as aphids, whiteflies, and leafhoppers, which spread the diseases as they feed. Control these pests by spraying plants with a mixture of insecticidal soap and 70 percent isopropyl alcohol (1 tablespoon alcohol to 1 pint soap solution) to reduce the risk of infection. Wash tools used around infected plants. Viruses overwinter in perennials and weeds such as daisies and plantains; a good fall cleanup will reduce the chances of reinfection.

Viruses infect entire plants; you can't control their spread by removing infected leaves or stems. Once perennials show viral symptoms, remove and destroy them. Do not compost infected plants.

Nematodes: Microscopic Menace

Nematodes are microscopic roundworms, but when they attack plants, they produce disease-like symptoms rather than the damage typical of other insects. Three types of nematodes—root knot, foliar, and stem-and-bulb—attack a wide range of perennials. Nematodes are more likely to be a problem in the South or in perennial beds that were previously used for growing susceptible vegetables.

Controlling Nasty Nematodes

Nematodes travel over wet plants on a film of water, or on garden tools and gardeners moving among plants. Promote natural nematode controls by increasing soil organic matter. You can control root knot nematodes by applying chitin (ground seafood shell wastes) or parasitic nematodes to the soil; both are available from garden-supply companies. In severe cases, remove plants, solarize the soil, and replant with nematode-free stock.

There is no cure for either stem-and-bulb or foliar nematodes. Remove and destroy infested plants and the surrounding soil; do not compost the debris. Clean up debris in fall to destroy overwintering nematodes. Mulch in spring to keep nematodes from climbing up plants; avoid wetting leaves when watering.

10

PROPAGATING PERENNIALS

Perennials aren't cheap. In fact, if you've ever tried to order a row of peonies or a bed's worth of mixed perennials from catalogs—or filled a shopping cart on impulse one fine spring day at the garden center—you were probably shocked by the total cost. The tally can quickly rise from hundreds of dollars into the 1,000-plus range. Yikes! If you need more than a few plants, or if you'd like a large number of a choice cultivar, it pays to propagate your own perennials.

There are two basic ways to propagate perennials: sexually, and vegetatively (or asexually). To propagate perennials sexually, you simply grow them from seed. There are four methods of vegetative propagation used for perennials: division, stem cuttings, root cuttings, and tissue culture. Tissue culture is a specialized technique used by professional propagators who have access to a lab, but the other three methods require nothing but a little straightforward know-how.

In this chapter, we'll discuss each type of propagation (except tissue culture), how to do it, its advantages and drawbacks, and which perennials respond best to each technique.

Then you can choose the method or combination that suits your needs. Whichever you choose, the end result is the same—more perennials!

For more details on propagation, see the individual plant entries in "The Perennial Encyclopedia," beginning on page 265. There, you'll find special seed treatments required, if any, and any other details you need to propagate perennials successfully.

STARTING FROM SEED

Growing perennials from seed has definite advantages: It's the cheapest and easiest way to produce a large number of plants. However, it's usually also the slowest way because a plant that takes a season or less to reach blooming size from a division or cutting may take 3 years from a seedling. The other drawback to starting from seed is that many cultivars won't come true— you'll get seedlings of the same species, but most likely they won't carry the traits that made their parents outstanding. (For a list of cultivars that *do* come true from seed, see "Cultivars from Seed" on page 249.) If you're not in a hurry for plants, if money is a factor, or if you're trying to propagate species rather than cultivars, growing your plants from seed is the way to go.

When you order perennial seed, check the catalogs for planting depth, germination time, and other useful information. Seed packets feature this information, too.

Keep germination data handy where you plan to sow the seed so you can refer to it easily during planting. Once you've decided which seeds to order, it makes sense to copy the germination information for your seeds onto a sheet of paper, which you can post near your propagating area.

While you wait for the seed to arrive, prepare your propagating area. This can be anything from a greenhouse bench, cold-frame, or plant stand with lights to a card table in front of a bright window. Just make sure it's clean, sturdy, and in bright but indirect light.

You have several options for seed-starting containers. If you're not starting a lot of perennials, one of the best containers is the kind that comes in a tomato-growing kit (available at garden centers and from catalogs). These come with bottom-watering trays, and bottom watering is ideal for seedlings: It provides even moisture without getting the plants wet, which is an invitation to fungi.

If you're growing lots of perennials or don't want to invest in tomato kits, you'll want nursery flats—plastic trays shaped like oblong cake pans—to sow the seeds in. Flats are available from seed and garden-supply catalogs, garden centers, and nurseries. Make sure your flats have drainage holes. (Set them on cookie sheets with sides or other shallow trays if draining water is a problem.) The long, shallow flat is ideal for seedlings: It's easy to keep the soil moist but not soggy, and no space is wasted between pots. Of course, if you want to grow only a few seedlings, 4-inch plastic pots on the windowsill or recycled plastic cell packs (like the ones annuals are sold in) are fine.

Sterile conditions are vital to seed-starting success because fungal diseases (especially damping-off) are the bane of seedlings. Start with new flats or pots, or sterilize them in a 5 percent bleach solution (1 part bleach to 20 parts water). This also discourages algae, which can take over an uncleaned flat. Use a sterile soil mix—some are sold especially for seedlings. You can also make your own soil mix from equal portions of peat and perlite. Moisten the soil mix thoroughly before planting.

Remember that timing is important when you're sowing seed—you'll have to transplant all those seedlings. To avoid a monster transplant job, stagger sowing of perennials that germinate in the same amount of time so your transplanting chores will be manageable.

Special Seed Treatments

Many perennial seeds are ready for sowing straight from the packet; others need special treatments that mimic the conditions they'd get outdoors before they'll come up. They may need to have their thick seed coats scratched—a process called scarification—or soaked so the seedling can break through. Or they may need a period of moist chilling— stratification—to mimic winter conditions in order to germinate.

Scarifying Seed

Perennials with hard seed coats like false and wild indigos (*Baptisia*) and lupines (*Lupinus*) often need more help germinating than a moist soil medium provides. Fortunately, scarification is an easy technique. If you have only a few seeds to treat, you can scrape the seed coats with a nail file. Otherwise, scarify seeds by putting a sheet of medium-grade sandpaper inside a cookie sheet or rectangular metal cake pan (one you don't mind getting scraped up), putting a layer of seeds on top of the sandpaper, and rubbing over them with a sander block to wear down the seed coats.

An equally effective and even easier method is soaking the seeds, as you do before cooking dried beans. Just boil water, take it off the burner, wait until the water stops boiling, and put in the seeds. Leave the seeds in the water overnight, and they will swell and then germinate faster.

Stratifying Seed

Perennial seeds that need moist chilling, or stratifying, have inhibitors that prevent them from sprouting until they've been through 6 to 8 weeks of winterlike conditions. This is especially true for perennial woodland wildflowers like trout lilies (*Erythronium*) that bloom in spring and ripen seed in summer, and for fall bloomers like asters (*Aster*). If the seeds germinated in fall, they'd be killed by the harsh winter that followed. Instead, they lie dormant through winter and sprout the following spring. Then they'll have a whole season to grow before winter comes again.

If you've purchased or collected seeds that need stratifying, it's important to sow them outdoors while they are fresh. (Check the encyclopedia entries for seeds that should be stratified.) If you do not sow them soon after you collect or receive them, germination rates can drop drastically. Seeds sown outdoors will receive moist chilling naturally during winter. If you must start the seeds indoors, provide winter conditions by stratifying them. To stratify seeds, sow them in a container of moist sand and store for 6 to 8 weeks in the refrigerator, or sow them in flats or pots and set them outdoors in a coldframe for the same time period. The seeds will actually respond better to the natural cycle of winter freezing and thawing.

Seed-Sowing Secrets

Sow your perennial seed in rows rather than randomly over the soil surface. Rows

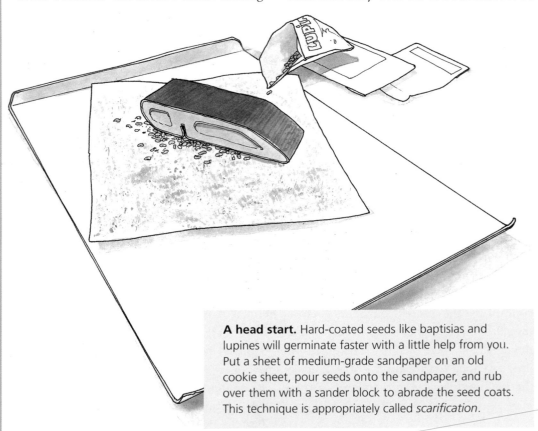

A head start. Hard-coated seeds like baptisias and lupines will germinate faster with a little help from you. Put a sheet of medium-grade sandpaper on an old cookie sheet, pour seeds onto the sandpaper, and rub over them with a sander block to abrade the seed coats. This technique is appropriately called *scarification*.

of plants are easier to transplant, and you can water the soil between rows, cutting the risk of fungal attack. To get neat rows, pour some seed from your pack onto a 3-by-5-inch card with a fold in the middle. The card lets you see what you're sowing and sow evenly. Shake the seed from the card onto the soil. Sow one cultivar or species in each row to avoid confusion, rather than mixing them up in the rows. If you're sowing in pots, stick to one cultivar or species per pot.

Small seeds are hard to handle, even with the card trick. Mix them first with a small quantity of sterilized play sand (the pure-white sand sold for sandboxes, not

CULTIVARS FROM SEED

If you want named cultivars without paying for individual plants, look for seed packets of the perennials in this list. Unlike many perennials—like hosta, peony, or iris cultivars, which must be propagated vegetatively by division to preserve their special characteristics—these strains come relatively true from seed.

Achillea ptarmica 'The Pearl'
Achillea taygetea 'Debutante'
Aquilegia ×*hybrida* 'McKana' hybrids, 'Biedermeier', and 'Nora Barlow'
Armeria hybrida 'Ornament'
Asclepias 'Gay Butterflies'
Aurinia saxatilis 'Gold Dust'
Bergenia cordifolia 'Redstart'
Campanula carpatica 'Blue Clips' and 'White Clips'
Chrysanthemum 'Autumn Glory'

Chrysanthemum coccineum 'James Kelway' and 'Robinson's Mix'
Chrysanthemum ×*superbum* 'Alaska' and 'Snow Lady'
Coreopsis grandiflora 'Early Sunrise' and 'Sunburst'
Delphinium ×*elatum* 'Pacific Giant' (or 'Round Table') Series
Dianthus deltoides 'Zing Rose'
Digitalis purpurea 'Excelsior Hybrids' and 'Foxy'
Echinacea purpurea 'Bravado' and 'White Swan'
Erigeron karvinskianus 'Profusion'
Gaillardia ×*grandiflora* 'Torch Light'
Geum 'Mrs. Bradshaw'
Heuchera micrantha var. *diversifolia* 'Palace Purple'
Heuchera sanguinea 'Bressingham Mix'
Liatris spicata 'Floristan Violet', 'Floristan White', 'Kobold'

Linum perenne 'Saphyr'
Lobelia cardinalis 'Queen Victoria'
Lobelia speciosa 'Compliment Scarlet'
Lupinus Russell hybrids and 'Minarette'
Lychnis ×*arkwrightii* 'Vesuvius'
Lychnis coronaria 'Angel Blush'
Monarda didyma 'Panorama Mix'
Papaver orientale 'Brilliant' and 'Dwarf Allegro'
Physostegia virginiana 'Crown of Snow'
Platycodon grandiflorus 'Fugi' Series and 'Shell Pink'
Potentilla nepalensis 'Miss Wilmott'
Rudbeckia fulgida var. *sullivantii* 'Goldsturm'
Scabiosa caucasica 'Fama'
Solidago canadensis 'Golden Baby'
Veronica spicata 'Sightseeing'

coarse builder's sand), so you'll be able to see what you're sowing and won't scatter the fine, dustlike seed all in one spot. Press the row of sand and seed into the soil surface, but don't cover it with soil.

Tamp down larger seeds after sowing to achieve good contact between the soil and the seeds. Cover seeds that don't need light to germinate to the depth recommended on the packet—a safe general rule is to cover them with a layer of soil one to three times their width. Then tamp the soil down. For a light, even cover, you can use a flour sieve or colander to scatter soil over the seeds. Once you've covered the seeds, moisten the soil gently and evenly.

There aren't many perennials that need light to germinate, but if you're starting seed of one that does, treat it as you would fine seed—just press it into the soil surface. (The encyclopedia entries and the seed packets will tell you if your perennials need light to germinate.)

As you sow the seed, label each row in the flat or each pot clearly so you'll know what you have and can monitor each perennial's progress. Write the name of the perennial and the date you sowed the seed clearly on the label. (Make sure the labels are waterproof or they'll disintegrate in the humid environment seedlings require.) Cover the flat or pots with plastic wrap, a sheet of plastic, a pane of glass, or a rigid plastic cover (available from catalogs). To maintain humidity for the pots, set them in an empty aquarium covered with glass or a sheet of plastic, or sit each pot in a plastic bag and close the top with a twist tie.

Set the flats or pots in a bright place that's out of direct sunlight. Make sure the top $\frac{1}{8}$ to $\frac{1}{2}$ inch of soil stays evenly moist (not soaked) until the seeds germinate. With covered flats or pots, you shouldn't have to water again until the seeds germinate, but it won't hurt to check soil moisture every day or two.

Dos and Don'ts When Seeds Come Up

Once the seeds have germinated and become seedlings, they need different conditions. Here's what to do—and what *not* to do—to get healthy seedlings.

- **Do** remove plastic or glass covers to bring the humidity down and give the seedlings as much light as possible.
- **Do** cut down on water—let the top $\frac{1}{4}$ inch of soil dry between waterings—and resist the urge to feed the emerging plants. Both overwatering and fertilizing result in soft, tangled growth and rot.
- **Do** water carefully—remember that damping-off threatens seedlings. If you are watering from above, water next to the row of seedlings rather than on top of them. Water as gently as possible—you can use a nozzle to break the force of the water. If possible, water seedlings from below by pouring water into the tray or saucer in which the flats or pots are sitting and letting it soak up into the soil. Water in the morning, not in the evening.
- **Do** transplant before the roots of adjacent seedlings get tangled together. The best

time is when the seedlings have developed their first set of true leaves. When seedlings sprout, they first send up seed leaves, called cotyledons, which are shaped like the seed coat. The next set of leaves, the true leaves, often look very different from the seed leaves. All the rest of the leaves will be true leaves.

- **Don't** handle seedling stems—they're very fragile and easy to crush. Instead, dig up the seedling with a houseplant trowel or Popsicle stick, then hold it by the leaves to move it.

- **Do** plant each seedling in a clean cell pack, Styrofoam cup (with drainage holes added), or plastic pot of its own. Replant the seedling at the depth at which it grew in the flat, and firm the soil to make sure there's good root-to-soil contact.

- **Do** handle seedlings as little and as quickly as possible, and **don't** leave them lying out. Have your pots set up and ready before you start to transplant, and transplant one seedling at a time. The roots can dry out in a matter of minutes.

- **Do** protect newly transplanted seedlings until they've reestablished themselves. Keep them in bright but indirect light.

- **Don't** fertilize the plants until they're established or you'll shock them. Once they're growing again, you can give them a boost with one-third- to one-half-strength liquid seaweed.

- **Don't** let your seedlings overheat. Seedlings prefer cooler temperatures than you might think—around 60°F is fine for most species. When in doubt, keep them cool.

- **Do** start hardening off the plants when frost danger is over and the soil has

TIPS FOR SEED-STARTING SUCCESS

Perennial gardeners have developed many secrets for successful seed-starting. Here are some favorites.

- Mix clean, nonclumping clay cat-box litter into your potting mix to loosen up a heavy mix; it also retains moisture and nutrients.
- Try soaking seeds in black tea to scarify tough seed coats—

the tannin in the tea does the trick.
- If your seed flats are in a greenhouse or coldframe, watch out for mice—they love freshly sown seed.
- When sowing fine seed, mix it with unflavored powdered gelatin. Its orange color is easy to see, and it will actually nourish the seedlings by releasing a little nitrogen as it breaks down.

- Use those discarded plastic cell packs (the kind bedding plants are sold in) to save steps in seed starting. Sow one seed in each cell, then just pop the seedlings out when it's time to transplant. If you're not sowing a lot of seeds and have room, this will really reduce transplant shock.
- Store seeds in plastic zip-top bags in the refrigerator—they take up less space than jars.

warmed: Set them outside during the day, and bring them in again at night. Select a protected location, such as a spot against a north-facing wall. If possible, mist them in the heat of the day, and put them in the shade or cover them with moist newspaper or a spunbonded row cover like Reemay. After a week of this, you can put them in a coldframe or nursery bed until they're big enough to hold their own in the perennial bed. (To learn more about setting up a nursery bed for your perennials, see "Make Your Own Nursery Bed" on page 262.)

Storing Seed

Whether you collect seed from your perennials, have some left over from the packets you ordered, or aren't ready to plant your seeds when they arrive, how you store them can make a big difference as to how well they'll come up when you plant them. The best place to store them is in the refrigerator, where the seed ages more slowly and stays fresher. Make sure you put the seed on the bottom shelf of the refrigerator, far from the freezer.

If you have a lot of one kind of seed, put it in a small jar with a label in the jar. If you have packets of several types of seed, store them all in a mayonnaise jar, pint canning jar, or other medium-size jar.

Seeds will live longer and germinate better if they're kept dry. To keep moisture away from your seeds, wrap 2 heaping tablespoonfuls of powdered milk in four layers of facial tissue, and secure the packet with a rubber band. Put the packet in the bottom of the jar to absorb moisture, and be sure to replace it every 6 months. You can also use 1 tablespoon of silica gel—available at drugstores, camera shops, hardware stores, or craft suppliers—instead of the powdered milk.

When you're ready to plant, take the seeds out of the refrigerator. Keep them in the closed jars and let them warm up to room temperature before planting. Otherwise, moisture will condense on the seeds and they'll clump together.

Don't get carried away and store seeds in the freezer or they'll die from shock. It's true that seeds overwinter in the freezing ground, but in the ground, they freeze gradually in a high-humidity environment, not instantly in a low-humidity freezer.

DIVIDE AND MULTIPLY

Division is the perennial propagation method of choice for the backyard gardener—it's low-tech, reliable, and easy. Basically, you just dig up established plants and cut or pull them apart. In addition to making more plants, division is an excellent way to rejuvenate an old, overgrown perennial that's no longer flowering well and is crowding its neighbors.

The time to divide your perennials is when they're growing vegetatively, not when they're blooming. As a general rule, divide midsummer- to fall-blooming perennials like coneflowers (*Rudbeckia*) in early spring, and spring and early-summer bloomers like false spireas (*Astilbe*) and daylilies (*Hemerocallis*) in late summer or early fall.

There are two ways to divide perennials once you've dug them up. You can divide them into either a few large pieces or many smaller pieces, depending on your needs.

Division for a Few Big Plants

If you want each parent plant to yield a few large plants that will get established and bloom in a short time, quarter the original plant. Use a tool that's the right size for the job: A trowel is fine for a loose-knit plant like a coneflower, while a sharp knife is better for perennials like astilbes and peonies that have a more solid crown. A heavy-crowned plant like a daylily may need a very sharp spade or two garden forks set back to back. (Remember that big old clumps of perennials are heavy. Try to get someone to help you lever them out of the ground.) Leave the daughter plants' healthy roots as intact as possible.

Division for Many Small Plants

If, instead of a few large divisions that will reestablish themselves quickly and bloom the following season, you want the largest possible number of divisions, here's what to do: Dig up the parent plant and cut off the lower roots—up to two-thirds of their total length. Then, with a propagating knife or other sharp knife, cut the parent plant into 1- or 2-inch plugs (in the case of plants with multiple crowns like asters, boltonias, and coneflowers) or individual fans (in the case of plants like daylilies and irises).

You'll get lots of new plants, but they'll take longer to reach blooming size than larger divisions, and the smaller plants will require more care. In fact, you'll have the best luck with this technique if you pot up the divisions and grow them under your watchful eye until they're well established, then transplant them to their new location.

Division Dos and Don'ts

No matter which method of division you use, there are some basics that apply. Remember that division shocks your plants—treat them like the postoperative patients they are.

- **Do** prepare the site for your new divisions before you divide your perennials.
- **Do** take plants out of the ground before you divide them.
- **Do** make sure your tools are sharp. Sharp knives, trowels, or other tools cause fewer open wounds. Since they damage the roots less, plants are less susceptible to disease.
- **Do** discard or compost the dead, woody centers of old plants. Cut the remaining

DIVISION STEP BY STEP

Division is a great way to propagate your perennials. Here are the basic steps to follow.

1. To start dividing a clump, cut around the mother plant with a trowel or spade (depending on the size of the plant), or loosen the soil with a garden fork. Lift the plant from the ground, shaking enough soil from the roots so you can see what you're doing when you divide the plant. If there's still too much soil clinging to the roots, hose them off.

2. Plunge two garden forks back to back into the clump, then press the handles together until the clump separates into two parts. Divide each part into halves to quarter the perennial, or pull off sections for smaller divisions.

Step 1

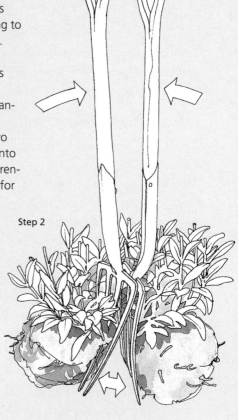

Step 2

section of healthy plant into smaller pieces and replant.

- **Do** remove one-half to two-thirds of the foliage on your divisions so it won't wick water away from the plant, but **don't** cut off more than that or you'll slow growth and invite rot.

- **Do** replant divisions as soon as possible. Divisions are vulnerable—**don't** leave them lying in the sun.

- **Do** plant divisions ½ inch higher than they were planted originally; they'll sink a little as the soil settles. The goal is for them to end up at the same level

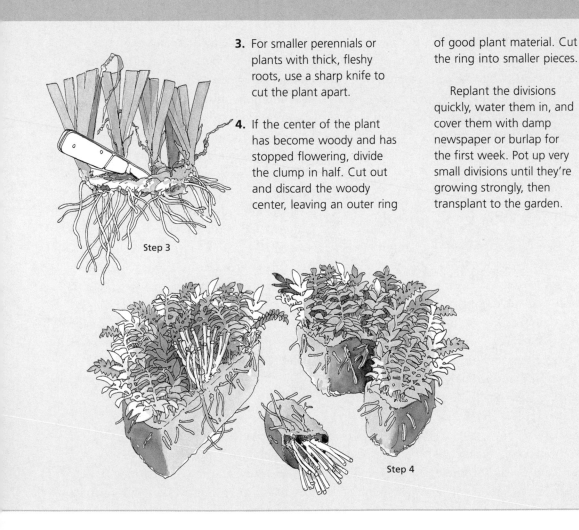

3. For smaller perennials or plants with thick, fleshy roots, use a sharp knife to cut the plant apart.

4. If the center of the plant has become woody and has stopped flowering, divide the clump in half. Cut out and discard the woody center, leaving an outer ring of good plant material. Cut the ring into smaller pieces.

Replant the divisions quickly, water them in, and cover them with damp newspaper or burlap for the first week. Pot up very small divisions until they're growing strongly, then transplant to the garden.

Step 3

Step 4

as the original plants were growing.

- **Do** water your divisions well. Give them a good soaking as soon as you plant them, and continue to water them regularly until they're established.
- **Do** shade newly planted divisions to protect them. Cover the plants with moist newspaper or burlap held down with rocks or soil for the first week after planting.
- **Do** give divided perennials and ornamental grasses a foliar feed of liquid seaweed or fish emulsion to provide trace elements and speed establishment.

- **Do** heavily mulch plants divided in fall when the soil cools to prevent shallow freezing and frost-heaving.
- **Don't** divide perennials after early October so the roots have time to establish themselves while the soil is warm.
- **Don't** divide taprooted perennials—start them from stem cuttings or seed. These include plants such as butterfly weed (*Asclepias tuberosa*), gas plant (*Dictamnus albus*), and rues (*Ruta*).

A CLEAR VIEW OF CUTTINGS

Cuttings are a mixed blessing for the perennial gardener. They're easy to make, but it's hard to get them to take. There are three big advantages to cuttings. First, they come true to type: No matter how many cuttings you take of *Veronica* 'Sunny Border Blue', they'll all be the same, not variations of 'Sunny Border Blue', as they would be from seed. But this is also true of divisions, which are a lot less trouble than cuttings. This brings us to the second advantage of cuttings: You can take a lot of them, usually many more pieces than you'd get from dividing. Third, cuttings are the way to go if you want to propagate a plant that is not yet large enough to divide or is one of the species that resents the disturbance associated with dividing.

This means that, on the plus side, cuttings provide some of the advantages of seed *and* division. The down side is that cuttings are tricky—you have to take them from growth that's in the right stage; then grow them in warm, humid conditions in a sterile medium; and you have to protect them from rot and other fungal problems, which are encouraged by the heat and high humidity. The upshot is that if you're prepared to coddle your cuttings and you want a lot of plants that are true to type, this is a good technique for you. Otherwise, stick with division and seed-starting.

There are two kinds of cuttings you can make with perennials: stem cuttings, and root cuttings. *Stem cuttings* are pieces of a stem, usually with leaves attached (stem cuttings taken from the growing tip of a stem are called *tip cuttings*), while *root cuttings* are, as their name implies, pieces of roots. Stem cuttings are easier, so let's start with them.

Stem Cuttings

The best time to take stem cuttings is when plants are putting out shoots and leaves, not when they're blooming or getting ready to bloom. Make your cuttings from the first flush of growth, in April through June or July in most of the country. If you want to take cuttings from an early-spring bloomer like woodland phlox (*Phlox divaricata*), wait for the first flush of foliage after bloom. You can also take perennial cuttings when vegetative growth resumes in fall.

When you're ready to take cuttings, choose the parent plant carefully. Don't take cuttings from wilted plants or from plants that are undernourished and stunted. On the other hand, don't take cuttings from an overfed plant with elongated, straggly stems, either. The ideal is soft but vigorous growth: soft enough so you can bend it, but strong enough to stand upright on its own.

Knowing about nodes is an essential part of taking cuttings. Nodes are the little

Taking stem cuttings. Make tip and stem cuttings from first-flush growth that's firm but not hard. Cut 1½- to 2-inch-long pieces with a sharp, sterile knife. Remove the lower leaves, and stick the cuttings in a pot or flat in moist, sterile potting medium so the bottom inch of the stem is in the medium and at least one node is at or below the soil surface. When all the cuttings are in the flat or pot, cover it with clear plastic draped over wire hoops so the plastic doesn't touch the plants.

bumps on the stem where leaves will or have come out, and where the roots will emerge from the buried part of the cutting. When taking cuttings, make each cut slightly below a node, as shown in the illustration on page 257.

Success with Stem Cuttings

Smaller cuttings tend to root better and faster—you'll root close to 100 percent of 1½-inch-long rosemary cuttings, while only about 10 percent of 4-inch cuttings will root. The only drawback is that smaller cuttings are also more prone to wilt, so they need more immediate attention. Take only as many cuttings at one time as you can stick into the soil in a half-hour. Keep the cuttings out of the sun. Even though you're going to plant them up almost immediately, be sure to wrap them in a damp paper towel to keep them moist.

For rooting cuttings, you'll want a pot or flat filled with sterile, fluffy potting soil. (A half-and-half mixture of peat and perlite works well.) Premoisten the mix before you start so that you aren't sticking cuttings into dry soil. Unless your cuttings are taken from the tip of a stem, make a straight cut at the top of the cutting and a slanted cut at the bottom or root end. When you are ready to plant the cuttings, this will help you remember which end goes up and which end you should stick into the potting soil.

Remove the bottom leaves from your cuttings so that you're sticking bare stems into the soil. If it's summertime and the plant is big and leafy, take off an extra set or two of the bottom leaves on each cutting before you stick it into the potting mix. Don't remove more than half of the leaves from a cutting, though—the goal is to take off enough foliage to cut down on water loss, while leaving enough greenery for photosynthesis to feed the plant. If the remaining leaves are extremely large, you may need to cut them in half to keep them from wilting unless you have a mist bed.

Stick in the cuttings so about 1 inch of stem—with at least one node—is below the soil surface. Be sure to put only cuttings from the same species or cultivar in each pot, and label them clearly with the plant name and the date you took the cuttings. You can root different cuttings in rows in a flat—just label each row. (Again, be sure to use moisture-proof labels and indelible ink.)

If you have to transport the cuttings any distance and can't plant them immediately, take slightly bigger cuttings than you plan to use. Label them, wrap them in moist newspaper, and put the moist paper in a plastic bag. Don't seal the bag; the cuttings will rot. Keep the cuttings cool—Styrofoam coolers are ideal for cool transport. When you get the cuttings home, cut them to the right size and stick them in the flat or pot.

Giving Your Cuttings a Good Home

Once you've potted up the cuttings, your goal is to give them an environment with close to 100 percent humidity and good air movement. The first step is to water the cuttings in thoroughly so the soil is moist to the bottom of the pot or flat. Then put clear plastic over wire hoops on top of the flat or pot, put a rigid plastic hood over them, or put them in an empty aquarium with a sheet of glass or plastic over the top. You can also sit each pot in a plastic bag and tie the top with a twist tie. Whichever method you choose, make sure the plastic or glass doesn't touch the cuttings, or leaf diseases may develop.

The cuttings also need warm soil to root and not rot. If you're not propagating in summer, give them bottom heat by putting a rubber mat with heating cables (available from garden centers and garden-supply catalogs) under your flat or pot. The soil should be at least 60°F—the higher the better, up to about 75°F.

If you are taking cuttings in summer, make sure they're kept moist and cool and out of the sun, or they'll cook inside the plastic like a microwave dinner. Provide

TIPS FOR SUCCESSFUL CUTTINGS

Perennial gardeners have developed their own tricks for getting good cuttings. Here are some of the best.

- Plastic soda bottles make great propagating tents for rooting cuttings. Cut off the bottoms, fill them with potting mix, stick in the cuttings, water, and replace the top part, sealing the sides with tape. Leave the bottle top off for ventilation.
- The clear plastic "clamshell" packs you get at salad bars are also great for rooting cuttings. Punch a few holes in the top for ventilation.
- If you're taking cuttings of virus-prone perennials, sterilize your knife between

plants by dipping it into skim milk. Research has shown that the milk prevents the spread of viruses.
- Use willow water to encourage your cuttings to root. Put willow branches in a 5-gallon pail of water to soak for 3 days, then soak the ends of the cuttings in this water for up to 24 hours before sticking them in the potting mix. The willow extract seems to make rooting hormones more effective. This is especially helpful with woodier perennials like rosemary, false and wild indigos (*Baptisia*), and thermopsis (*Thermopsis*).
- If you need cuttings but have missed your plants' first flush

of growth, trick plants like yarrows into creating a second flush by cutting the plants back almost to the ground. Take cuttings from the new growth.
- Home water softeners use salts that are harmful to plants. Make sure you're using unsoftened water or rainwater.
- One way to keep cuttings fresh if you're bringing them back from a friend's garden is to stick them in a raw potato. Slice the potato in half lengthwise, lay the cuttings along one half with the cut ends inside the potato, put the other half over them like a sandwich, and hold the halves together with rubber bands.

shading like burlap or a newspaper tent over the plastic for extra protection.

Many cuttings will root in 7 to 10 days. Check rooting after the first week by gently tugging on the plants—if you feel resistance, give them more ventilation, and start to remove the shading if you're using it.

Keep the soil in your flats or pots moist. Don't feed cuttings until they're rooted and growing. Once they are, give them a foliar feed with liquid seaweed or fish emulsion for a gentle boost.

Because of the high-humidity environment needed to root stem cuttings, you can't use this technique with every perennial. Succulents like sedums will rot in such high humidity. Root them in moist sand or a half-and-half mix of sand and perlite, and don't cover the pots or flats with plastic so that the humidity stays low. Silver-leaved plants like artemisias and lavender also tend to rot. You may find it easier to divide these plants or grow them from seed rather than from cuttings.

Dos and Don'ts for Stem Cuttings

Fungal problems are the major threat to cuttings. Here are some dos and don'ts for avoiding rots and other fungal disasters.

- **Do** sterilize your knife with alcohol between cuts.
- **Do** treat each cutting with a 5 percent bleach solution (1 part bleach to 20 parts water) if you want an extra guard against fungi. If you plan to put the cuttings in a plastic propagating tent or enclosure, use chamomile tea instead of bleach solution. Dip the entire cutting for a few seconds to a minute.
- **Don't** stick cuttings deeper than 1 inch or they may rot, and **don't** let leaves come in contact with the soil surface.
- **Do** stick cuttings far enough apart so the leaves of adjacent plants don't touch.
- **Don't** let the plastic you use to enclose the flat or pot touch the cuttings.
- **Do** open the plastic on your propagating containers at least once a day—good circulation prevents fungal problems, while stagnant air encourages them.
- **Do** check your cuttings daily for mildewed or dropped leaves. Remove dropped leaves and diseased cuttings as soon as you see them to keep fungi from spreading to healthy cuttings.

Root Cuttings Done Right

If you have a coldframe, unheated room, or greenhouse, you can also propagate perennials from root cuttings. The best perennials for root cuttings have fleshy roots, like Japanese anemone (*Anemone ×hybrida*), grapeleaf anemone (*A. vitifolia*), snowdrop anemone (*A. sylvestris*), giant coneflower (*Rudbeckia maxima*), Siberian bugloss (*Brunnera macrophylla*), poppies (*Papaver*), ligularias (*Ligularia*), bleeding hearts (*Dicentra*), cranesbills

(*Geranium*), and garden phlox (*Phlox paniculata*).

Take root cuttings in fall or winter when plants are dormant, grow them on in the greenhouse or coldframe, and plant them out in a nursery bed when they are growing strongly. (See "Make Your Own Nursery Bed" on page 262.)

Making Root Cuttings

Taking root cuttings isn't hard if you pay attention to what you're doing. To begin, hose off the roots of your freshly dug perennial so you can find fleshy, mature roots. They're usually tan rather than the white color of immature roots. Use a sterile propagating knife or other sharp knife to make

Making root cuttings. Choose fleshy, mature tan roots for root cuttings. Use a sterile propagating knife to cut 1½-inch-long segments of root. Start at the bottom of the root and cut up. Make a slanted cut at the bottom of the root cutting and a straight cut across the top so that you'll be able to plant it right side up.

the cuttings. Never use scissors, which will mash the cut surface. Sterilize your knife with alcohol between cuts—root cuttings are very vulnerable to fungal problems.

Bear in mind that perennial roots that grow down into the soil (as opposed to spreading sideways) won't grow if you plant them upside down. For this reason, it's important to plant them in the same direction they were growing in the ground. To remember which end is up, make a slanting cut on the bottom of the root section and a straight cut across the top. (If you forget, plant the root on its side.)

Make your root cuttings about 1½ inches long; you can make many cuttings from each root. Dip cut roots in a 5 percent bleach solution (1 part bleach to 20 parts water) for about a minute to sterilize them.

Pot up your root cuttings in pots or flats filled with a fluffy, sterile potting medium. A seedling mix is a good choice, mixed half-and-half with perlite to make a very porous medium to prevent rotting. When you plant your cuttings, leave about ⅛ inch of the top of each cutting exposed to the light to encourage it to green up and produce topgrowth.

Perennials with thin, wiry, mat-forming roots aren't as picky when it comes to directional planting. You can scatter root segments of plants like phlox, mulleins (*Verbascum*), drumstick primrose (*Primula denticulata*), buglosses (*Anchusa*), or hardy ageratum (*Eupatorium coelestinum*) horizontally on the soil surface of your pot or flat, then cover them lightly with one to two times their thickness of soil.

Some perennials produce their own root cuttings when you divide them: The roots that are cut, exposed, and left in the ground when you lift out the mother plant will produce plantlets in the old planting hole, which you can then dig, separate, and replant. Stokes' aster (*Stokesia laevis*), poppies (*Papaver*), blanket flower (*Gaillardia* ×*grandiflora*), sea hollies (*Eryngium*), and coneflowers (*Rudbeckia*) are especially prone to this.

Dos and Don'ts for Root Cuttings

Here are the critical dos and don'ts for successful root cuttings.

- **Do** keep root cuttings barely moist; they'll rot in wet soil.
- **Don't** add fertilizer until the plant is sending up leaves or you'll promote rot.
- **Do** give root cuttings bottom heat: Use a heating pad or heating cable (available from garden-supply catalogs) in a coldframe or unheated room, or set them on a greenhouse bench that has heat running underneath it.

MAKE YOUR OWN NURSERY BED

Once you have seedlings, divisions, and cuttings, where do you put them while they grow big enough for the perennial border? Some perennials may take several years to size up from cuttings or seedlings, and many take a growing season. The ideal is to make a special nursery bed just for growing plants on.

Prepare this bed as you would a standard perennial bed, making sure the soil is rich and smooth and drainage is good. (For more on making beds, see Chapter 8, "Perennial Gardening Basics.") Site it in partial shade, where the vulnerable plants are protected from heatstroke, where you have easy access to water, and where you'll pass it often so you can keep an eye on it. The ideal site is close to the house or your garden shed so you have easy access to both the bed and your tools and watering equipment, but discreetly out of the public view, since to any eye but yours—the proud parent's—there won't be much to see.

Once you've chosen the site, mulch the bed, make sure your nursery plants are well watered, and watch out for rabbits, slugs, and other invaders. One more critical thing: Label plants clearly, and make sure they *stay* labeled! (See "Those %$#@!! Labels" on page 130 for help with disappearing labels—or suddenly invisible ink.)

PART III

The Perennial
Encyclopedia

ACANTHUS

ah-KAN-thus • Acanthaceae, Acanthus Family

Bear's-breeches are robust plants valued equally for their architectural foliage and erect summer flower spikes. The huge, deeply lobed leaves with spiny margins reach 1 to 2 feet long. Flowers with purple hoods and three white lower petals are borne in tall dense spikes in spring and summer. Plants spread by thick, creeping rootstocks to form extensive colonies.

ACANTHUS

Common Name:
Bear's-breech

Bloom Time:
Late spring and summer bloom

Planting Requirements:
Full sun

Acanthus hungaricus (hun-GAH-ri-kus) (*balcanicus*), Hungarian bear's-breech. Size: 3 to 4 feet tall, 3 feet wide. The deeply lobed leaves of this hardy species are longer than wide and taper attractively at the base. Plants are free-flowering, making this one of the best species. USDA Plant Hardiness Zones 5 to 9.

A. mollis (MOLL-iss), bear's-breech. Size: 2½ to 4 feet tall, 3 to 4 feet wide. The bold broad leaves are dark green and lustrous with deep lobes and sparse teeth. 'Hollard's Gold' has gorgeous yellow leaves that fade to chartreuse. 'Aureum' and 'Fielding Gold' emerge golden and fade to green. Zones 7 to 10.

A. spinosus (spine-OH-sus), spiny bear's-breech. Size: 3 to 4 feet tall, 2 to 3 feet wide. Large erect leaves are narrower and more deeply lobed than those of *A. mollis* and are clothed with stiff, menacing spines that are more scary than dangerous. Plants quickly spread by underground

Bold and brassy best describe spiny bear's-breech (*Acanthus spinosus*), which adds a touch of drama to the garden with its tall spires and luscious leaves.

stems to form dense clumps. Spinosissimus Group applies to a variety of forms, most with narrow leaves densely clothed in spines. 'Summer Beauty' is a striking hybrid with *A. mollis* sporting lustrous leaves that add a tropical flair to the garden. Zones 7 to 10.

How to Grow

Plant bear's-breeches in moist, well-drained soil in full sun or partial shade. Space plants 3 to 4 feet apart. Clumps flower more freely in full sun. Cold winter weather may damage flower buds of less hardy species, but foliage will usually reappear. Foliage remains evergreen in mild climates but is damaged by hard freezes. Remove brown leaves in spring before new growth emerges. Spiny bear's-breech is hardier and more heat-tolerant. Bear's-breeches spread quickly from creeping roots and may need control. Propagate in spring by division or from root cuttings taken in spring or late fall.

Landscape Uses

Bear's-breeches are bold plants best used as accents or as focal points in a formal garden or foundation planting. Plant them against a background of flowering shrubs at the edge of a woodland or in a sunny border. Use containerized plants to add drama to a sagging spot in a summer border. The stately foliage is excellent in the partially shaded garden with groundcovers such as wild gingers (*Asarum*), bugleweeds (*Ajuga*), bergenias, phlox, and windflowers (*Anemone*).

ACHILLEA

ah-KILL-ee-ah • Asteraceae, Daisy Family

A well-grown yarrow is a stunning vision. Yarrows are prized for drought tolerance and free flowering under adverse conditions. Showy flattened flower heads composed of many tightly packed flowers in varying colors—white, yellow, pink, rose, or red—are carried above aromatic, often ferny green or gray foliage. Plants grow from fibrous-rooted crowns.

ACHILLEA

Common Name:
Yarrow

Bloom Time:
Late spring and summer bloom

Planting Requirements:
Full sun

Achillea filipendulina (fill-ih-pen-dew-LEE-nah), fernleaf yarrow. Size: 3 to 4 feet tall, 2 to 3 feet wide. A stately yarrow with deeply cut, olive-green leaves. Like all yarrows, fernleaf yarrow has aromatic foliage. The tall, leafy stems are topped by 4- to 5-inch-wide flattened flower heads of golden yellow flowers. Plants may need staking when they are in full flower. The cultivar 'Gold Plate' is taller, to 5 feet, with deep yellow flower heads up to 6 inches across. 'Parker's Variety' grows 3 to 4 feet tall, with golden yellow flowers borne on stronger stems than the species. The similar hybrid 'Coronation Gold' arose from a cross between *A. filipendulina* and *A. clypeolata*.

The earthy brick red color of *Achillea* 'Terra Cotta' combines beautifully with blue or purple flowers to create a stunning color contrast, or with creamy yellows to forge a mellow mood. Yarrows make long-lasting fresh cuts as well as valuable dried cuts. The seedheads are attractive left standing in the garden.

The plants are shorter (3 feet), more robust, and seldom need staking. The mustard yellow flowers are set off beautifully by the gray-green foliage. This is one of the best yarrows for use in the garden and for cutting. It blooms throughout the summer months and is tolerant of a wide range of conditions. It is the best yellow yarrow for areas with hot, humid summers. 'Schwellenburg' is another excellent selection with dense flower spikes and silvery foliage. USDA Plant Hardiness Zones 3 to 9.

A. grandiflora (gran-dih-FLOOR-ah), white yarrow. Size: 3 to 5 feet tall, 2 to 3 feet wide. A tall, stout plant with tropical-looking, deeply cut leaves and huge heads of dusty white flowers in early to mid-summer. Zones 5 to 8.

A. millefolium (mill-eh-FO-lee-um), common yarrow. Size: 1 to 2½ feet tall, 2 to 3 feet wide. Common yarrow is a popular old-fashioned perennial with delicate, fine-textured foliage. This Eurasian yarrow has escaped from cultivation and become established in the wild. Most garden selections have pink or red flowers. They bloom throughout the summer months on stems 1½ to 3 feet tall. The dense clumps spread rapidly and need dividing every 3 years to control their roaming. The cultivar 'Cerise Queen' is a strong grower, to 18 inches tall. 'Feuerland' ('Fireland') has deep red flowers that fade to rose-red flowers on 3-foot stems. 'Oertel's Rose' is an improved, heat-tolerant rose-pink selection with stout stems. 'Snowtaler' ('Snow Sport') has excellent pure white flowers. Zones 3 to 9.

Hybrids

The German Galaxy Series of *A. mille-folium* ×*A. taygetea* hybrids expanded the color choice and rekindled interest in these hardy but underused plants. The Galaxy hybrids have larger flower heads on sturdy stems. Flower color ranges from brick red 'Fanal' to pink 'Heidi' and 'Apfelblute', salmon 'Lachsschonheit', and pale yellow 'Hoffnung'. The flowers have a tendency to fade as they age and give the plants an interesting multicolored effect. A number of new introductions of mixed parentage are revolutionizing the color palette, especially 'Mascarade' with red-flecked yellow flowers, 'Royal Tapestry' with purple flowers, 'Summerwine' with plum-red flowers, and 'Terra Cotta' with burnt orange and yellow flowers. Zones 3 to 9.

A. 'Moonshine', 'Moonshine' yarrow. Size: 1 to 2 feet tall and wide. The 3-inch sulfur yellow flower heads are produced all summer on sturdy stems, which seldom need staking. The pale yellow flowers are easier to blend into the flower border than the harsh yellows of other yarrows. Its smaller stature also contributes to this plant's popularity because it takes up less room in the garden. The ferny foliage is soft blue-gray and forms dense, wide clumps. The plants prefer a well-drained situation and do not tolerate extreme heat and high humidity. 'Anthea' is a new reblooming selection with sulfur yellow flowers that fade as they age. 'Credo' grows 3 to 4 feet tall with chiffon yellow flowers that fade to creamy white. Zones 3 to 8.

A. ***ptarmica*** (TAR-mih-kah), sneezewort. Size: 1½ to 2 feet tall, 1 to 2 feet wide. This sprawling yarrow was called sneezewort because the dried root was used as a substitute for snuff. This species bears little resemblance to other yarrows, having lance-shaped leaves without the characteristic ferny appearance. The species is somewhat weedy, but the popular cultivars 'Ballerina' and 'The Pearl' bear a profusion of double, creamy white flowers in early summer. 'Stephanie Cohen' is a dwarf, single pink selection. Plants may easily escape cultivation and become invasive. Zones 2 to 9.

A. ***tomentosa*** (toe-men-TOE-sah), woolly yarrow. Size: 8 to 12 inches tall, 1 to 2 feet wide. This hairy plant does best in northern gardens, as it is intolerant of extreme heat and humidity. The plant's compact form makes it excellent for rock gardens or the front of the border. The soft yellow flowers resemble those of *A.* 'Moonshine'. This European native flowers throughout the summer. *A. lewisii* 'King Edward VIII', King Edward yarrow, is similar but hardy only to Zone 4. Both are adversely affected by extreme heat and humidity. Zones 3 to 7.

How to Grow

Yarrows are low-maintenance plants that thrive on neglect. Don't pamper them. Plant them in full sun in light, average to poor, well-drained soil. Rich soils encourage luxuriant growth that may require staking. Plant container-grown or bareroot stock in well-worked soil. Yarrows are quick to establish and spread to form dense clumps. Space plants 2 to 3 feet apart to accommodate their spread. Some species, especially common yarrow, can be invasive. Plants need dividing every 3 to 5 years. Lift the clumps in early spring or fall and remove any dead stems from the center of the clump. Replant divisions in well-worked soil. Propagate yarrows from tip cuttings in spring or early summer. In areas with warm nights and high humidity, plants may develop powdery mildew or rust that disfigures leaves. Stem rot can also be a problem, especially in soggy soil. Remove affected parts or treat with an organic fungicide. Plant species suitable for your growing conditions to avoid problems.

Landscape Uses

Versatile yarrows have innumerable uses in the garden. They are at home in the formal border or in informal situations. They are good for the front or middle of the border as well as for softening bold textures. The taller fernleaf yarrow combines well with globe thistle (*Echinops ritro*), purple coneflower (*Echinacea purpurea*), and summer phlox (*Phlox paniculata*). Use the rounded shape of common yarrow to complement vertical plants such as irises, gayfeathers (*Liatris*), and ornamental grasses. The smaller yarrows are good weavers—plants used to unify plantings and fill voids. They grow and bloom well on dry, sunny banks; in rock gardens; or when naturalized in meadow gardens. These long-blooming plants are excellent for cutting or drying.

ACONITUM

ah-coe-NY-tum • Ranunculaceae, Buttercup Family

Gorgeous spires of deep purple, blue, or yellow monkshoods add drama to the late-season border. The flower clusters of these highly desirable border beauties are carried above deeply lobed foliage on erect to arching stems. Richly colored flowers have curious, protruding helmetlike hoods above three lower petals. Though monkshoods are poisonous if ingested, plants can be safely handled. They grow from stout crowns with brittle, fleshy roots.

ACONITUM

Common Name:
Monkshood

Bloom Time:
Summer and fall bloom

Planting Requirements:
Partial shade

Aconitum ×***cammarum*** (kam-MAR-um), bicolor monkshood. Size: 3 to 4 feet tall, 2 feet wide. A tall, showy perennial with blue, purple, or bicolor flowers borne in tall spikes in late summer. The leaves have five to seven lobes. The cultivar 'Bicolor' has two-tone flowers. The hood is pale blue with white streaks; the lower petals are intense blue. 'Bressingham Spire' is shorter, with rigid 2½- to 3-foot stems that seldom need staking. 'Eleanor' is a new summer-blooming compact grower, white with a picotee blue edge. 'Newry Blue' sports rich blue flowers in sun or light shade on 5-foot stems in early summer. The flowers are blue-violet. USDA Plant Hardiness Zones 3 to 7.

A. carmichaelii (kar-mih-KELL-ee-ee), azure monkshood. Size: 2 to 3 feet tall, 2 to 3 feet wide. A sturdy, tough plant with thick, three-lobed leaves and deep blue hooded flowers borne in elongated spikes from late summer through fall. Also sold as *A. fischeri*. Cultivars are taller than the species. 'Arendsii' has 3- to 4-foot stems that don't need staking. 'Barker's Variety' has deep blue flowers and 6-foot stems that need staking. Zones 2 (with protection) or 3 to 7.

A. hemslyanum (hems-lee-AYE-num), climbing monkshood. Size: 3 to 5 feet tall, 1 foot wide; leaves 6 inches long. Climbing stems of this underutilized species twine loosely through shrubs and reward you with pendant masses of rich purple-blue flowers in late autumn. The deeply lobed leaves are rich green with pale edges. Zones 6 to 8.

A. lycoctonum (lie-kok-TOE-num) ssp. *lycoctonum* (*septentrionale*), wolfsbane. Size: 1 to 3 feet tall, 1 to 2 feet wide. We

Autumn-flowering azure monkshood (*Aconitum carmichaelii*) sports tall spikes of indigo flowers in a sunny garden with rich soil.

prize this white-flowered species for its early summer bloom and decorative foliage, which looks like ragged shields. Basal rosettes of nearly round leaves are deeply lobed with sharp teeth. Stem leaves are smaller and sparsely cover the lax stems. This species is mostly offered as the selection named 'Ivorine'. The subspecies *neapolitanum* (*lamarckii*) opens its soft yellow flowers on lax stems in mid- to late summer. Zones 3 to 7.

A. napellus (nah-PELL-us), common monkshood. Size: 3 to 4 feet tall, 1 to 2 feet wide. This old-fashioned flower is no longer as popular as its sturdier cousins but still deserves a place in the garden. Its lovely dark blue-violet hooded flowers open on tall spikes in late summer. 'Rubellum' has pale pink flowers; 'Snow White' is pure white. Zones 3 to 8.

How to Grow

Monkshoods have thick, fleshy roots that are reputed to dislike disturbance. Plant them in spring or fall in rich, moist soil in full sun. Wolfsbane tolerates partial shade. Space the plants 2 to 3 feet apart, and place the crowns just below the surface. The roots are brittle and easily damaged. They prefer cool night temperatures. At the southern limit of their range, site them where they'll get afternoon shade. Propagate by division of the brittle roots in fall or early spring. Plants recover more quickly than their reputation would suggest.

Landscape Uses

Monkshoods are best for the middle or back of the border. Don't crowd them; empty space around the tall spikes shows them off to best advantage. Plant them with late-blooming perennials such as Joe-Pye weeds (*Eupatorium*), Russian sage (*Perovskia atriplicifolia*), and asters. They provide strong vertical form and cool blue or purple flowers in a garden dominated by flat daisies in shades of yellow and orange. Create bright combinations of purple and yellow with common sneezeweed (*Helenium autumnale*), oxeyes (*Heliopsis helianthoides*), canna 'Bengal Tiger', and sunflowers (*Helianthus* 'Lemon Queen'). For a softer combination, grow monkshoods with obedient plants (*Physostegia virginiana*) or pink turtleheads (*Chelone lyonii*). Wolfbane looks stunning at the edge of a woodland or in a lightly shaded border with ferns and bugbanes (*Cimicifuga*).

ADIANTUM

a-dee-AN-tum • Pteridaceae, Brake Fern Family

Maidenhairs are airy, deciduous or semievergreen ferns with delicate fronds divided into small, diamond- to fan-shaped leaflets carried on wiry black stipes. Their delicate, lacy appearance has endeared them to gardeners worldwide. The genus is largely tropical, and many tender species are grown indoors. The temperate species are hardy and popular garden plants. They grow from creeping rhizomes with dense, fibrous roots.

ADIANTUM

Common Name:
Maidenhair fern

Bloom Time:
Foliage plant

Planting Requirements:
Light to full shade

Adiantum aleuticum (a-LEW-ti-kum), five finger maidenhair, western maidenhair. Size: 2 to 3 feet tall and wide. This species was recently separated from its eastern counterpart. The stiff fronds sport elongated central pinnae resembling extended fingers. 'Subpumilum' is a handsome dwarf only 6 inches tall. USDA Plant Hardiness Zones 4 to 9.

A. capillus-veneris (ca-PIL-lus VEN-er-is), southern maidenhair. Size: 1 to 2 feet tall and wide. Cascading, triangular fronds bear bright green, wedge-shaped pinnules. Plants require moist, limy soils and often grow on wet rocks. A. ×*mairisii* is a vigorous hybrid hardy to Zone 5. Zones 6 to 9.

A. pedatum (pe-DAH-tum), northern maidenhair fern. Size: 1 to 3 feet tall, 2 to 3 feet wide. A unique, airy fern with delicate, pale green horseshoe-shaped fronds bearing linear branches covered with overlapping shell-shaped pinnae. Fronds emerge in early spring like pink fists and turn deep blue-green as they mature. Zones 3 to 8.

A. venustum (ven-OOS-tum), Himalayan maidenhair. Size: 4 to 8 inches tall, 12 inches wide. A diminutive fern with overlapping, triangular fronds with tiny, teardrop-shape gray-green pinnae. Slow growing. Zones 4 to 8.

How to Grow

Maidenhair ferns prefer moist, humus-rich soil in partial to full shade. Plants tolerate some drought but will go dormant under extremely dry conditions. Divide clumps when they become so congested that you cannot see the individual form of the fronds.

Landscape Uses

Plant maidenhair ferns in groups or drifts in woodland gardens, under shrubs and flowering trees, or with other ferns as a foundation planting. Combine the delicate pink fiddleheads with bulbs and spring wildflowers.

Delicate triangular fronds of Himalayan maidenhair (*Adiantum venustum*) overlap like water ebbing over rocks. The fronds remain crisp and green after frosts that crumple most ferns.

ADONIS

ah-DON-iss • Ranunculaceae, Buttercup Family

Adonis are true harbingers of spring, emerging while the snow is still present to spread their exquisite yellow chalices in the spring sunshine. The genus is named for the handsome Greek youth Adonis, who was killed by jealous Aries. His lover, Aphrodite, turned Adonis into a flower that blooms and fades rapidly to symbolize the fleeting quality of youth. Plants are slow to establish and increase, but they are worth the wait.

ADONIS

Common Name:
 Adonis

Bloom Time:
 Early spring bloom

Planting Requirements:
 Sun or summer shade

The cheery yellow chalices of amur adonis (*Adonis amurensis*) greet the first warm days of spring when few other perennials are stirring. After flowering, the ferny leaves expand and flourish for several weeks before going dormant in early summer.

Adonis amurensis (am-er-EN-sis), amur adonis. Size: 4 to 10 inches tall and wide. Globular buds poke through the chilly soil to open their bright yellow, multipetaled flowers when the first warm spring sun shines. Flowers close in evening, prolonging flowering for several weeks, though the entire show can be quite ephemeral if the days are warm. After flowering, intricately cut three-lobed leaves emerge for a few weeks before slipping into summer dormancy. 'Flore-plena' is a showy though small-flowered double. 'Fukuju Kai' is a lovely selection with flowers to 2 inches across. USDA Plant Hardiness Zones 4 to 8.

A. vernalis (ver-NAY-lis), pheasant's eye. Size: 8 to 12 inches tall and wide. Sunny yellow flowers top unbranched stems with stalkless leaves that seem to clasp the stems. The bright green leaves have three lobes with ragged, threadlike segments. Plants bloom in mid- to late spring and go dormant by midsummer. Zones 3 to 8.

How to Grow

Plant adonis in well-drained but rich soil in sun. After dormancy, the spot may be shaded. Take care not to dig into dormant crowns. Wet soil will cause rot, especially if it freezes after stems emerge. Surround crowns with gravel for extra protection. Slugs may devour foliage. Propagate by division as plants are going dormant. It takes a year or two for plants to recover.

Landscape Uses

Adonis are early bloomers, so place them with early birds such as Lenten roses (*Helleborus* ×*hybridus*), winter cyclamen (*Cyclamen coum*), snowdrops, and other minor bulbs.

AGAPANTHUS

ag-ah-PAN-thus • Alliaceae (Amaryllidaceae), Onion Family

African lilies are de rigueur in Florida and California bedding schemes, but take a second look at these bodacious beauties. Far hardier than originally thought, the huge heads of royal blue, open funnelform flowers add a tropical flair to temperate gardens. Use them in the ground as accents or en masse, or in containers for an elegant splash of summer color.

AGAPANTHUS

Common Names:
 Lily of the Nile,
 African lily

Bloom Time:
 Summer bloom

Planting Requirements:
 Full sun or light shade

Agapanthus africanus (af-ree-KAN-us), African lily. Size: 3 to 5 feet tall and wide. This is the largest and most attractive species, with huge heads of blue, lilac, or white flowers on a 4-foot stalk above thick, straplike evergreen leaves. USDA Plant Hardiness Zones 8 to 11.

A. campanulatus (kam-pan-you-LAY-tus), lily of the Nile. Size: 2 to 4 feet tall, 2 to 3 feet wide. A delicate, deciduous species with tennis ball-size heads of outward-facing blue or white flowers that open in early to late summer over narrow, strappy basal leaves. Zones 7 (with protection) to 11.

Hybrids

Many of the best selections are hybrids of mixed parentage. 'Bressingham Blue' has deep indigo flowers on slender 3-foot stems. 'Cayle's Lilac' is a small plant to 1½ feet tall with open clusters of pale lilac-blue flowers. 'Headbourne Hybrids' are some of the hardiest (to Zone 5 with protection), varying from blue to violet in flower color. 'Kingston Blue' has deep royal blue flowers on 2-foot stems. 'Loch Hope' is one of the loveliest selections, with rich blue-violet flowers on 4- to 5-foot stems in late summer and autumn. 'Peter Pan' is a popular dwarf selection to 1 foot with sky blue flowers. 'Storm Cloud' is an upright selection to 3 feet with deep indigo flowers. 'Tinkerbell' is a diminutive selection with white-edged leaves and 1-foot stalks of medium blue flowers.

Lily of the Nile (*Agapanthus campanulatus*) is a common sight in California, but this surprisingly hardy South African native is a novelty for gardeners in warm eastern zones. North of Zone 7, plants thrive in containers if allowed to become potbound.

How to Grow

Plant African lilies in full sun or light shade in rich, well-drained soil. Plants are heavy feeders and deplete the soil in a few years, so top-dress the dense clumps annually with rich compost or well-rotted manure. Plants seem to thrive in spite of crowding, especially in pots. Divide them any time they are not in flower.

Landscape Uses

African lilies work well as bedding plants for seasonal color in warm climates, but their true worth lies in their use as accents in borders or containers. Plants are spectacular in bloom, and the globular heads add drama to any mixed border.

AGASTACHE

ag-a-STASH-e • Lamiaceae, Mint Family

Fiesta colors, a long season of bloom, and easy care make anise hyssops ideal for gardeners on the go. This underutilized genus of drought-tolerant perennials hails from the Desert Southwest, so you know the plants are tough. The brightly colored tubular flowers are edible, and the thick leaves emit the scent of licorice when crushed. Try them in beds and borders and in containers, too.

AGASTACHE

Common Name:
  Anise hyssop

Bloom Time:
  Summer and autumn bloom

Planting Requirements:
  Sun or light shade

Agastache foeniculum (fwa-NIC-u-lum), fragrant anise hyssop. Size: 1 to 3 feet tall, 1 to 2 feet wide. Crushed leaves of this native prairie wildflower emit the pungent smell of anise. Tall, stiff stems sport paired, wedge-shaped leaves and are crowned with dense spikes of blue to blue-violet flowers in mid- to late summer. 'Licorice Blue' has lavender-blue flowers, and 'Licorice White' has slender, off-white spikes. 'Blue Fortune' is a robust hybrid with *A. rugosum* prized for dense candelabra spikes of soft blue flowers on stout 2- to 3-foot stems. USDA Plant Hardiness Zones 3 to 8.

A. rugosum (rew-GO-sum), rough anise hyssop. Size: 2 to 4 feet tall, 1 to 2 feet wide. This stout, rather coarse species with rosy violet or cream flowers on branched stems is uncommon in gardens but should be more widely grown. Zones 5 to 8.

A. rupestris (rew-PES-tris), rock anise hyssop. Size: 2 to 4 feet tall and wide. Rosy and orange bicolor flowers crowd dense spikes atop the willowy stems of this High Plains native. People can't seem to keep their hands off the fragrant gray-green linear leaves, which lend a soft texture to this shrubby beauty. Zones 5 to 8.

Hybrids

Some of the most beautiful anise hyssop selections are hybrids. A few of our favorites for a spot of warm color are 'Apricot Sunrise', with pale orange flowers borne all summer on 18- to 20-inch stems; and 'Firebird', a must with orange-raspberry flowers on upright plants 3 feet tall and 2 feet wide. If you prefer glowing pink, try 'Big Bazooka', aptly named for its shocking pink flowers on stems 3 or more feet tall; or rose-pink 'Pink Panther' and 'Tutti Frutti', with bright pink flowers topping upright stalks that tower above the others at 4 to 6 feet.

How to Grow

Anise hyssops hail from arid regions of the country, so give them a well-drained spot in full sun or very light shade. Plants prefer alkaline soils but are widely tolerant. Heavy clay is sure death to all but fragrant anise

Bees and butterflies love the beautiful blue-violet spires of anise hyssop (*Agastache foeniculum*). The scented leaves make a fragrant, pleasing tea.

hyssop. Propagate by stem cuttings taken in early summer or seed sown indoors in winter or outdoors in spring.

Landscape Uses

The tall, spiky wands of anise hyssops add exclamation points to the sunny summer garden. Use them to break up the rounded forms of catmints (*Nepeta*), yarrows (*Achillea*), phlox, and sedums. Accent the bold foliage of cannas and eye-catching dahlia flowers with their tall spires. In meadow and prairie gardens, plant them with sunflowers (*Helianthus*), milkweeds (*Asclepias*), and asters.

AJUGA

ah-JOO-ga • Lamiaceae, Mint Family

Bugleweeds are easy-care deciduous groundcovers with excellent summer foliage and showy spring flowers. The dense spikes of purple, pink, or white flowers are carried just above the creeping mats of glossy, purple-stained leaves. Some selections are valued more for their luscious foliage than for their flowers. Plants spread quickly to form a dense, weed-free carpet.

AJUGA

Common Name:
Bugleweed

Bloom Time:
Foliage groundcover with late spring and early summer bloom

Planting Requirements:
Sun or shade

Ajuga genevensis (gen-e-VEN-sis), Geneva bugleweed. Size: 6 to 12 inches tall, 12 to 24 inches wide. A dense, upright bugleweed with broad, deep green foliage and blue or pink flowers in whorled clusters on open spikes. USDA Plant Hardiness Zones 4 to 9.

A. pyramidalis (peer-a-mid-AH-lis), upright bugleweed. Size: 6 to 9 inches tall, 12 to 24 inches wide. A bushy, slow-creeping plant with glossy puckered foliage and bright blue flowers. 'Green Crispa' has crinkled leaves like spinach. 'Metallica Crispa' has very shiny foliage with crinkled margins. Zones 3 to 9.

A. reptans (REP-tanz), common bugleweed. Size: 4 to 10 inches tall, 12 to 36 inches wide. A prostrate, fast-spreading groundcover with dark green or bronze foliage and blue flowers (var. *alba* has white flowers and green leaves). 'Burgundy Glow' has multicolored white, pink, and green foliage. 'Catlin's Giant' has bronze foliage and 8-inch-tall flower spikes.

'Cristata' is a small-leaved, tightly crinkled plant. 'Jungle Beauty' has large, upright wine-red leaves and deep blue flowers. 'Pink Beauty' has deep pink flowers and green leaves. 'Silver Beauty' has gray-green leaves edged in white, while leaves of 'Silver Carpet' are gray edged with green. *A.* 'Chocolate Chip' is a departure from the norm, with deep purple-brown, elongated, spatula-shaped leaves and blue flowers. Zones 3 to 9.

How to Grow

Bugleweeds grow in average to rich, well-drained garden soil in sun or shade. Plant plugs or divisions in spring or fall. The plants establish and spread quickly. Common bugleweed can be invasive. Propagate by cuttings in spring or summer and division throughout the growing season. Crown rot may cause entire clumps of bugleweed to wither and die. Provide good drainage and air circulation to help prevent problems. Remove diseased portions and treat with an organic fungicide or a solution of 1 part bleach to 10 parts water.

Landscape Uses

Need a solid, weedproof groundcover? You've got it. Bugleweed's dense mats of foliage exclude all but the most persistent weeds. Use bugleweeds in the dry shade of lawn trees where no grass will grow. They are perfect for edging beds or under downspouts and gutters where intermittent

Common bugleweed (*Ajuga reptans*) is an easy-care groundcover for sun or shade. Plants spread quickly to form a weedproof barrier that is both functional and attractive. The short spires of blue or white flowers open in early summer.

water beats down. Try clumps of Geneva bugleweed in a rock garden. Use upright bugleweed where you need a slower-growing groundcover. Plant fancy-leaved varieties at the front of perennial gardens or in combination with other foliage plants in a shade garden. 'Silver Beauty' bugleweed brightens up a planting of wildflowers and ferns. The lovely flowers are an added bonus: They transform a mass planting into a showy spectacle in spring and early summer. Spent flower spikes will wither away or can be removed where necessary to tidy up smaller plantings.

ALCEA

AL-kee-a • Malvaceae, Mallow Family

Hollyhocks are old-fashioned flowers, beloved by generations for their prolific flowering and easy care. These erect, showy biennials or short-lived perennials have coarse foliage that is rounded or lobed and showy hibiscus-like flowers.

ALCEA

Common Name:
 Hollyhock

Bloom Time:
 Summer and early fall bloom

Planting Requirements:
 Full sun

Deep chocolate-colored flowers line the tall spires of black hollyhock (*Alcea rosea* 'Nigra') in summer. Hollyhocks do best in regions with cool nights and low humidity, though they can be grown as annuals in warm regions.

Alcea ficifolia (feye-ke-FO-lee-ah), Antwerp hollyhock. Size: 5 to 6 feet tall, 1 to 3 feet wide. This cold-hardy species has deeply lobed leaves and erect spires of yellow to copper flowers. USDA Plant Hardiness Zones 2 to 8.

A. rosea (RO-zee-a), hollyhock. Size: 2 to 8 feet tall, 2 to 4 feet wide. Single or double flowers come in a range of colors from yellow and white through pink and deep red. They open over a long period, starting at the base of the wandlike spike, to 6 feet tall. 'Charter's Double' hybrids have double flowers in mixed or individual colors. 'Old Barnyard Mix' sports single flowers in a variety of colors. 'Nigra' has gorgeous chocolate-red single flowers. 'Powder Puffs' hybrids are fully double in mixed colors. Zones 2 to 8.

A. rugosa (rue-GO-sah), yellow hollyhock. Size: 4 to 6 feet tall, 2 to 3 feet wide. A stunning perennial hollyhock with rust-resistant foliage and tall spires of soft yellow flowers in late spring and summer. Zones 4 to 8.

How to Grow

Hollyhocks thrive in average to rich, well-drained soils in full sun or light shade. Set out young plants in spring for summer bloom or in fall for bloom the following year. Propagate by seed sown in winter for summer bloom or outdoors for bloom the second year. Rust, anthracnose, and spider mites can be serious problems. Although infected plants usually flower well, the foliage is extremely unattractive. Good culture is the best preventive. Keep plants well fertilized and keep soil evenly moist but not too wet or dry. Spray rust- or anthracnose-infected plants with an organic fungicide. Control mites with a soap spray or organic insecticide.

Landscape Uses

Plant hollyhocks at the back of a perennial border or along fences and walls. Create a cottage garden by combining the showy flower spikes with shrubs such as lilacs, roses, and other old-fashioned perennials, such as irises, phlox, peonies, and pincushion flowers (*Scabiosa*). A stately clump in full flower makes an excellent accent beside a gate or by the door of a garden shed. Hollyhocks also combine well with tropicals such as cannas and coleus, and they add early color while the tropicals are rising to full glory.

ALCHEMILLA

al-keh-MILL-ah • Rosaceae, Rose Family

Water beads like jewels spangled over the soft, hairy foliage of these attractive clump-forming perennials. In early summer, they are festooned with mounded clusters of frothy green or chartreuse flowers. A quintessential border plant in England, the billowing flowers soften hard walkways and line rock or brick walls in every garden. American gardeners in the northern tiers have the best luck with these plants.

ALCHEMILLA

Common Name:
Lady's-mantle

Bloom Time:
Spring and early summer bloom

Planting Requirements:
Sun or partial shade

Alchemilla alpina (al-PEEN-a), mountain mantle. Size: 6 to 8 inches tall, 10 to 12 inches wide. A low, delicate plant with deeply lobed leaves edged with silver hairs. Extremely cold-hardy and intolerant of excessive heat. *A. conjuncta*

Lady's-mantle (*Alchemilla mollis*) excels in foliage and flower. The frothy chartreuse flowers billow over scalloped gray-green leaves that catch the dew in pearl-like beads.

(kon-JUNK-ta) is similar but grows to 12 or more inches. USDA Plant Hardiness Zones 3 to 7.

A. erythropoda (eh-ryth-ro-POH-da), red-stemmed lady's-mantle. Size: 6 to 8 inches tall, 10 to 12 inches wide. Neat, mounding plant with small gray-green scalloped leaves on red petioles and frothy narrow flower clusters. Zones 3 to 7.

A. glaucescens (glaw-KES-sens), hairy lady's-mantle. Size: 1 foot tall, 1 to 1½ feet wide. Soft-hairy, scalloped sea green leaves and densely clustered chartreuse flowers. Zones 3 to 7.

A. mollis (MOL-lis), lady's-mantle. Size: 12 inches tall, 12 to 24 inches wide. Ro-bust, mounding plant grows into an impressive clump from a slow-creeping rootstock. The pale green, soft, hairy foliage is round and deeply pleated and makes a lovely contrast to the yellow-green flowers. Zones 4 to 8.

How to Grow

Grow lady's-mantles in rich, evenly moist soil in sun or shade. Place plants 2 to 2½ feet apart. Plants prefer cool conditions. Where summer temperatures are high, grow in partial to full shade. Cut plants to the ground after flowering or when foliage becomes tattered. They will quickly produce a new set of fresh, attractive leaves. Divide overgrown clumps in spring or fall, or propagate by seed. Plants are mostly pest-free. In hot summers, fungal rot may be a problem on foliage. Keep excess water off foliage or treat with an organic fungicide.

Landscape Uses

Enjoy the elegant foliage and flowers of lady's-mantles at the front of the perennial border, along a wall, edging a walk, or in a shaded rockery. Plant them in a low spot with other moisture-loving plants. Use the velvety foliage in combination with phlox, bellflowers (*Campanula*), cranesbills (*Geranium*), false spireas (*Astilbe*), and Siberian iris (*Iris sibirica*). The smaller species are perfect for rock gardens, troughs, and containers.

ALLIUM

a-LEE-um • Alliaceae (Amaryllidaceae), Onion Family

Spherical *Allium* heads in a rainbow of colors, including yellow, white, pink, lavender, purple, and blue, make dramatic statements in beds and borders. Plants vary in height from 3 inches to 4 feet. Try them in the cutting garden, or mix them with herbs. Plant the tallest species as exclamation points in low groundcover plantings or among annuals. Ornamental onions produce fleshy, straplike leaves from pungent bulbs.

> **ALLIUM**
>
> **Common Name:**
> Ornamental onion
>
> **Bloom Time:**
> Spring, summer, and fall bloom
>
> **Planting Requirements:**
> Full sun

Allium acuminatum (a-kew-min-AY-tum), pink wild onion. Size: 6 to 12 inches tall, 2 to 6 inches wide. A delicate onion with erect starry flowers ranging in color from pink to dark rose in summer. USDA Plant Hardiness Zones 4 to 7.

A. aflatunense (a-fla-tun-EN-see) (*hollandicum*), Persian onion. Size: 2 to 3 feet tall, 6 to 12 inches wide. Showy onion with 4½-inch rounded clusters of red-violet flowers borne in spring or early summer. The basal, straplike leaves disappear soon after flowering. 'Purple Sensation' is noted for its deep violet flowers. Hybrids include 'Firmament' with silvery purple flowers, while those of 'Gladiator' are light violet on 3- to 4-foot stems. 'Lucy Ball' has huge heads of medium purple flowers. Zones 4 to 8.

A. caeruleum (kie-RU-lee-um), blue globe onion. Size: 1 to 2 feet tall, 6 to 12 inches wide. Tightly packed clusters of deep sky blue flowers are borne in summer atop thin stems. Zones 2 to 7.

The purple spheres of Persian onion (*Allium aflatunense*) add a touch of class to beds and borders. The rich color combines well with silvery pink to create a soothing garden picture.

A. cernuum (KER-new-um), nodding onion. Size: 1½ to 2 feet tall, 6 to 8 inches wide. Nodding, tear-shaped buds open into loose clusters of pink flowers in summer. Zones 4 to 9.

A. christophii (kris-TOF-ee-ee) (*albopilosum*), star of Persia. Size: 1 to 2 feet tall, 12 to 18 inches wide. Spectacular 10-inch rounded clusters of metallic violet flowers are carried on stout stems above the coarse foliage. The summer flowers give way to showy dried seedheads. Zones 4 to 8.

A. cyaneum (see-AH-nee-um). Size: 1 to 1½ feet tall, 6 to 10 inches wide. Clusters of

The flowers and foliage of garlic chives (*Allium tuberosum*) are mildly flavored and add zest to soups and salads. Outdoors they add a spot of late color to an herb garden or border.

small nodding yellow flowers sit on a pair of leafy bracts in summer. Zones 5 to 10.

A. flavum (FLAH-vum), yellow onion. Size: 10 to 12 inches tall, 4 to 6 inches wide. Butter yellow flowers explode like fireworks from the papery buds of this attractive onion. *A. pulchellum* has a similar form, with rose-violet flowers. Zones 4 to 8.

A. giganteum (gi-GAN-tee-um), giant onion. Size: 3 to 5 feet tall, 1 to 2 feet wide. Huge round heads of purple flowers are carried high above a basal rosette of broad leaves in spring or early summer. Zones 4 to 8.

A. karataviense (ka-ra-tah-vee-EN-see), Turkestan onion. Size: 6 to 12 inches tall, 6 to 12 inches wide. Two to four broad gray-green leaves curve outward from a short, stout stem bearing a large, rounded cluster of pale pink flowers. Zones 4 to 9.

A. moly (MO-lee), lily leek. Size: 12 to 15 inches tall, 6 to 8 inches wide. The golden yellow flowers of this attractive late-spring bulb are held in open clusters between a pair of narrow, flat leaves. Zones 3 to 9.

A. neapolitanum (nee-ah-pol-i-TAH-num), Naples onion. Size: 8 to 12 inches tall, 6 to 8 inches wide. A deliciously fragrant spring-blooming onion with white flowers borne in open, flat-topped clusters. Zones 7 to 9.

A. oreophilum (o-ray-O-fil-um), ornamental onion. Size: 6 to 8 inches tall, 4 to 6 inches wide. A bright rose-red onion with 2-inch clusters of open, star-shaped flowers in late spring. Zones 4 to 9.

A. rosenbachianum (ro-sen-BACH-ee-a-num), ornamental onion. Size: 3 to 4 feet tall, 6 to 12 inches wide. Lilac to violet flowers borne on tall stalks in late spring and early summer. Zones 4 to 8.

A. roseum (RO-see-um). Size: 12 to 16 inches tall, 6 to 10 inches wide. Mauve to rose flowers borne in mounded clusters on stiff stems in early summer. Zones 7 to 9.

A. schoenoprasum (skoyn-o-PRAH-sum), common chives. Size: 10 to 20 inches tall, 6 to 12 inches wide. Pungent hollow leaves in thick clumps with numerous pink to mauve flower clusters throughout summer. Zones 3 to 9.

A. senescens (sen-ES-sens). Size: 10 to 12 inches tall, 6 to 12 inches wide. Rounded clusters of mauve flowers borne above dull green leaves in midsummer. 'Glaucum' is shorter (8 to 10 inches), with blue-gray foliage growing in a whorl. Zones 3 to 9.

A. sphaerocephalum (sphay-row-SEPH-a-lum), drumstick chives. Size: 1½ to 3 feet tall, 6 to 10 inches wide. Small red-violet flowers are tightly packed into diamond-shaped clusters that teeter on thin stems in early summer. Zones 4 to 9.

A. stellatum (stel-LATE-um), prairie onion. Size: 6 to 12 inches tall, 4 to 6 inches wide. Pale pink to rose flowers borne in open clusters throughout summer. Zones 3 to 8.

A. thunbergii (thun-BERG-ee-ee), Japanese onion. Size: 18 to 24 inches tall, 8 to 10 inches wide. This cutie has the distinction of blooming at the end of the season. Oversize violet flowers crowd the squat stems in autumn. 'Ozawa' has rich violet flowers. Zones 4 to 8.

A. triquetrum (tri-KWEE-trum), three-cornered onion. Size: 8 to 12 inches tall and wide. Distinctive one-sided clusters of showy nodding white flowers top the bright green foliage of this shade-tolerant species. Bulbs from dealers are sold moist and must be planted immediately or they rot. Zones 4 to 9.

A. tuberosum (tew-be-ROW-sum), garlic chives. Size: 1½ to 2 feet tall, 6 to 12 inches wide. Floriferous plant with erect stems bearing starry white flowers in late summer. Zones 4 to 8.

How to Grow

Ornamental onions thrive in average to rich, well-drained soils in full sun. Some need excellent drainage and dry soil following flowering, especially *A. acuminatum, A. caeruleum, A. flavum, A. moly,* and *A. pulchellum.* Plant dormant bulbs in fall. Divide crowded clumps as they go dormant. Plant spring- and early summer-blooming species with bushy plants that will hide the yellowing foliage. Later-blooming species generally remain attractive throughout the growing season. Most are easily grown from seed sown outdoors when ripe.

Landscape Uses

Ornamental onions come in a wealth of shapes, sizes, and colors. Plant the taller varieties in large masses or drifts in the middle of a perennial border. They combine beautifully with mounded plants such as cranesbills (*Geranium*), bee balms (*Monarda*), yarrows (*Achillea*), and ornamental grasses. A rock garden is a good place for those needing excellent drainage.

Amsonia

am-SON-ee-a • Apocynaceae, Indian Hemp Family

Blue stars are elegant perennials with quiet charms and subtle flowers that are best appreciated on close inspection. These easy-care plants hold their starry, steel blue flowers in terminal clusters above the foliage. Their bright green leaves remain attractive all season, giving the dense clumps a shrublike appearance. The willowlike leaves turn yellow to fiery orange in the fall.

AMSONIA

Common Names:
  Blue star, amsonia

Bloom Time:
  Spring and early summer bloom

Planting Requirements:
  Full sun to light shade

Amsonia ciliata (sil-e-ATE-a), downy blue star. Size: 1 to 3 feet tall, 1 to 2 feet wide. A fine-textured, bushy plant with very narrow, downy leaves that cluster toward the end of the stems and pale blue flowers. USDA Plant Hardiness Zones 6 to 10.

A. hubrichtii (hew-BRICK-tee-ee), Arkansas blue star, Hubricht's blue star. Size: 2 to 3 feet tall and wide. The meteoric rise in popularity of this stunning plant attests to its garden worth. Fine, needle-like leaves to 3 inches long ring the stems like bottle brushes. Pale metallic blue flowers quickly fade, leaving the plant to shine in foliage until it turns bronze and gold in the autumn. Zones 4 to 9.

A. illustris (il-LUS-tris), Ozark blue star. Size: 3 feet tall, 3 to 4 feet wide. A large, showy, wide-spreading plant with glossy leaves and light to medium blue flowers in large clusters. Zones 4 to 9.

A. ludoviciana (lew-do-vich-ee-AH-na), Louisiana blue star. Size: 2 to 3 feet tall and wide. This distinctive species has broad leaves with rusty felted undersides and medium blue flowers. Zones 4 to 9.

A. tabernaemontana (ta-ber-nie-mon-TAN-uh), willow blue star. Size: 1 to 3 feet tall and wide. A robust shrublike perennial with steel blue flowers and lance-shaped leaves densely covering the stems. Var. *montana* is a dwarf, 18 to 24 inches tall with a dense, rounded form and full-size medium blue flowers, creating a stunning clump in full flower. 'Blue Ice' is a selection with rich, medium blue flowers with staying power. 'Short Stack' is a squat 10 inches tall by 18 inches wide with medium blue flowers. Var. *salicifolia* has narrower, glossy willowlike leaves. Zones 3 to 9.

How to Grow

Plant blue stars in average to rich, evenly moist soil in full sun or partial shade. Give these large plants plenty of room. Space clumps at least 30 inches apart. Once established, they are tolerant of adverse conditions. Prune plants growing in shade back to 10- to 12-inch stems after flowers fade to avoid flopping. The new growth will be compact, and the plants may reflower. Divide overgrown clumps in fall. Propagate from tip cuttings taken in early summer, or by seed. Collect seeds and store, refrigerated, for 4 to 6 weeks; soak overnight in water before sowing. Sow ripe seed outdoors for germination the following spring.

Landscape Uses

Blue stars add structure to the perennial garden. Use their broad rounded form to contrast with tall plants such as meadow rues (*Thalictrum*), Joe-Pye weeds (*Eupatorium*), and boltonia (*Boltonia asteroides*). A mass planting makes a good hedge or low screen. Combine the flowers with foliage plants such as lady's-mantle (*Alchemilla mollis*), lamb's ears (*Stachys byzantina*), and bergenias, or with colorful cranesbills (*Geranium*), evening primroses (*Oenothera*), Siberian iris (*Iris sibirica*), and sages (*Salvia*).

The steely blue flowers of willow blue star (*Amsonia tabernaemontana* var. *salicifolia*) make a nice show in late spring, but it's the foliage that secures this plant's place in the border. The shrublike clumps remain flawless through summer and the foliage takes on orange tones in fall.

ANAPHALIS

a-NAH-fa-lis • Asteraceae, Aster Family

Pearly everlastings look and feel like velvet. The airy plants have downy gray-green, lance-shaped foliage with deeply impressed veins. The sturdy stems are topped with clusters of white, papery flowers. The yellow centers of the open flowers give a pleasing two-tone effect. Plants spread by creeping stems to form broad, dense clumps.

ANAPHALIS

Common Name:
Pearly everlasting

Bloom Time:
Late summer bloom

Planting Requirements:
Full sun

The soft, felted leaves and silvery straw flowers of three-veined everlasting (*Anaphalis triplinervis*) are reserved for northern and high-altitude gardens where nights are cool and humidity is low.

Anaphalis margaritacea (mar-ga-ri-TAH-kee-a), pearly everlasting. Size: 1 to 3 feet tall, 1 to 2 feet wide. The narrow downy leaves appear to be in whorls beneath the silvery, button-like flower clusters. Plants form dense clumps. Both flowers and stems dry well for use in arrangements. Var. *cinnamomea* has white felted leaves with rusty undersides. USDA Plant Hardiness Zones 3 to 8.

A. triplinervis (tri-plee-NER-vis), three-veined everlasting. Size: 12 to 18 inches tall, 1 to 2 feet wide. A shorter plant than pearly everlasting, with broader, woolly leaves and a slightly irregular form. Zones 3 to 8.

How to Grow

Pearly everlastings thrive in average to rich, evenly moist soil in full sun or light shade. In dry soil, the plants lose their lower foliage. Being northerners, they sulk in the heat and humidity of southern gardens. The plants spread by underground stems to form tight clumps with many stems. Regular rejuvenation is necessary to keep the plants vigorous. Divide every 3 or 4 years in early spring or after they go dormant in late fall. Propagate by cuttings taken in early summer or by seed sown indoors or outside.

Landscape Uses

Pearly everlastings are beautiful additions to the late-summer garden. Their straw flower heads are pretty when fresh or dried. They are the best choice for adding gray foliage to a moist site. They are lovely with pink and purple flowers such as asters, chrysanthemums, sages (*Salvia*), and monkshoods (*Aconitum*). Soft yellows pick up the center of the flowers. Try a combination of garden phlox (*Phlox paniculata*), 'Moonbeam' coreopsis, Japanese anemones (*Anemone ×hybrida*), and yellow chrysanthemums. Ornamental grasses are also excellent companions.

ANCHUSA

an-KEW-sa • Boraginaceae, Borage Family

The dazzling blue color of bugloss is a magnet for gardeners. This ephemeral beauty graces the early-summer garden with its electric blue flowers but fades in the heat of summer. Plants live just a few seasons before dying out, but their beauty makes planting them worthwhile. They grow from fibrous-rooted crowns.

ANCHUSA

Common Name:
Bugloss

Bloom Time:
Late spring bloom

Planting Requirements:
Full sun

Anchusa azurea (a-ZEWR-ee-a), Italian bugloss. Size: 2 to 5 feet tall, 1 to 2 feet wide. An erect plant with large, oblong leaves covered with stiff hairs. Bright blue flowers are carried above foliage in elongated, multibranched clusters. Plants are short-lived and have a tendency to self-sow too freely. 'Dropmore' is 4 feet tall and has deep blue flowers. 'Little John' is short, growing only 1½ feet tall. 'London Royalist' is 3 feet tall with gentian blue flowers. USDA Plant Hardiness Zones 3 to 8.

How to Grow

Plant buglosses in rich, well-drained soil in full sun or light shade. Choose one of the named cultivars for better form and longevity. Cut plants back after flowering to encourage reblooming. Divide clumps at the same time on a 2- or 3-year schedule. Propagate by root cuttings taken in early spring, or move self-sown plants into desired locations.

Landscape Uses

Gardeners welcome buglosses in spring, when bright blue flowers are at a premium. Combine the plants with other bright colors,

Like sapphires in the summer sun, the spikes of gentian blue *Anchusa azurea* 'Koda' glow when planted against light yellow and chartreuse flowers. Plants demand good drainage and cool conditions.

such as orange oriental poppies (*Papaver orientale*), yellow yarrows (*Achillea*), Siberian iris (*Iris siberica*), and peonies (*Paeonia lactiflora*). Electrify subtle combinations of soft yellow 'Moonshine' yarrow (*Achillea* 'Moonshine') and pale pink cranesbills (*Geranium*) with silver-gray lamb's ears (*Stachys byzantina*) and mugworts (*Artemisia*). The blue flower color shows off nicely against a hedge or in a shrub border with early bloomers such as white lilacs, deutzias, and single-flowered kerria (*Kerria japonica*).

ANEMONE

a-NEM-o-nee • Ranunculaceae, Buttercup Family

Windflowers are aptly named; the blooms tremble in the slightest breeze. Fragile, five-petaled flowers with fuzzy, bright yellow stamens and white, pink, red, purple, or blue petal-like sepals. Double flowers may have 6 to 14 sepals. Leaves are usually deeply lobed and borne paired or whorled below the flower clusters as well as in loose rosettes from the crown. Some species are tuberous-rooted, while most spread from creeping rhizomes.

ANEMONE

Common Name:
Windflower

Bloom Time:
Spring, summer, or fall bloom

Planting Requirements:
Sun to shade

Anemone apennina (a-pen-NEE-na), Apennine anemone. Size: 6 to 8 inches tall, 8 to 12 inches wide. A low, spring-blooming woodland plant with narrow-sepaled, semi-double, sky blue flowers borne with deeply lobed foliage. Plants go dormant after flowering. 'Alba' has snow white flowers. USDA Plant Hardiness Zones 4 to 8.

A. blanda (BLAN-da), Grecian windflower. Size: 6 to 8 inches tall, 8 to 12 inches wide. Similar to *A. apennina* but the dark blue flowers are larger, to 2 inches across. Plants go dormant after flowering. 'Blue Star' has 2½-inch dark blue flowers. 'Pink Star' has light pink flowers of similar size. 'Radar' has deep rosy violet flowers. 'White Splendor', the best-selling spring anemone, is a good pure white. Zones 4 to 8.

A. canadensis (kan-a-DEN-sis), meadow anemone. Size: 1 to 2 feet tall, 2 to 3 feet wide. An exuberant grower with bright white flowers held on slender stems above a whorl of three deeply cut leaves. Zones 3 to 7.

A. coronaria (ko-ro-NAH-ree-a), poppy anemone. Size: 8 to 12 inches tall and wide. Showy spring-flowering plant with 2-inch pink, red, purple, or blue saucer-shaped flowers and finely divided leaves. 'Admiral' is a semi-double violet-flowered selection. 'De Caen' hybrids have single flowers in single or mixed colors. 'Mona Lisa' series is similar to 'De Caen' with larger flowers. 'Governor' has semi-double scarlet flowers. 'St. Brigid' Series boasts semi-double flowers in a range of single or mixed colors. Zones 6 to 9.

A. ×*fulgens* (FUL-gens), St. Baro anemone. Size: 8 to 12 inches tall and wide. A stunning species, similar to poppy anemone but with narrower sepals of deep scarlet and a blue-black eye. *A. pavonina* has larger flowers in red, creamy salmon, or yellow. Zones 7 to 9.

A. *hupehensis* (hew-pee-HEN-sis), Chinese anemone. Size: 2 to 3 feet tall and wide. Slender stalks support fragile, five-petaled rose-pink flowers above mostly basal three-parted lobed leaves. Plants bloom in late summer and fall; they grow from thick, tuberous roots. 'September Charm' has rose-colored flowers that fade toward the center. Zones 5 to 8.

A. ×*hybrida* (HIB-ri-da), Japanese anemone. Size: 3 to 5 feet tall, 2 to 3 feet wide. Similar to Chinese anemone but taller. Single and semidouble flowers range in color from white to pink and rose. 'Hadspen Abundance' is a strong-growing deep pink single with a darker reverse. 'Honorine Jobert' is perfection: pure white single flowers with bright yellow stamens on 3- to 4-foot stems. 'Lady Gilmore' is a sturdy rose-pink semidouble. 'Margarete' has semidouble deep pink flowers on 3-foot stems. 'Max Vogel' has lovely single 4-inch pink flowers on 4-foot stems. 'Prinz Heinrich' is a tidy semidouble with rich rose-pink flowers. 'Queen Charlotte' has 3-inch, semidouble pink flowers. 'Whirlwind' is 4 to 5 feet tall with 4-inch semidouble flowers. Zones 4 (with protection) or 5 to 8.

Toward the end of the season when most garden flowers are fading, the bright pink flowers of Chinese anemone (*Anemone hupehensis* 'Hadspen Abundance') open in profusion. Bloom continues well into fall, even after light frost has quieted more-delicate flowers.

A. ×*lesseri* (LESS-ser-ee). Size: 12 to 16 inches tall and wide. This hybrid has rose-red flowers held high above deeply lobed, soft hairy foliage in early summer. *A. multifida*, a parent, has creamy white flowers and is lovely in rock gardens. Zones 3 to 8.

A. *nemorosa* (nem-o-RO-sa), wood anemone. Size: 4 to 10 inches tall, 10 to 12 inches wide. Like stars that fell to earth, this low, spreading woodland plant has three deeply lobed leaves below 5- to 7-petaled flowers. Plants go dormant after spring flowering. 'Allenii' has large, pale lavender-blue flowers. 'Bowles' Purple' has deep blue-violet flowers. 'Bracteata' has a white-and-green ruffle around the white double flowers. 'Lychette' has huge white flowers. 'Monstrosa' and 'Green Fingers' are oddities with spidery double green flowers. 'Robinsoniana' has small but profuse medium blue flowers, while those of 'Royal Blue' are deep blue. 'Vestal' has a double white pompon center. Var. *rosea* has single, pale rose flowers. Zones 4 to 8.

A. ranunculoides (rah-nun-kew-LOI-dees), buttercup anemone. Size: 4 to 6 inches tall, 6 to 10 inches wide. A yellow-flowered species similar to *A. nemorosa*. There are two forms: large and small. 'Pleniflora' has semidouble flowers. *A. ×lipsiensis* is a beautiful hybrid, sporting soft yellow flowers. Zones 4 to 8.

A. rivularis (riv-u-LAR-is), brook anemone. Size: 1 to 3 feet tall, 1 to 2 feet wide. An attractive anemone for moist soil, with white flowers stained blue above three-lobed leaves. Zones 4 to 7.

A. sylvestris (sil-VES-tris), snowdrop anemone. Size: 12 to 18 inches tall and wide. A lovely, snow white, single-flowered anemone for the spring garden. The erect stems each bear one flower above the deep green divided foliage. Quickly spreads by creeping rhizomes. 'Elsie Fellmann' has stylish double flowers with a hint of green. Zones 4 to 8.

A. tomentosa 'Robustissima' (to-men-TO-sa), Japanese anemone. Also sold as *A. vitifolia*. Size: 2 to 3 feet tall and wide. Similar to other Japanese anemones but hardier, with metallic pink flowers and attractive dark green foliage. Zones 3 to 8.

How to Grow

Anemones can be placed into three groups based on their cultural requirements. The first group contains the spring-flowering woodland species. Plant *A. apennina, A. blanda, A. nemorosa, A. ranunculoides,* and *A. sylvestris* in moist, humus-rich soil in sun or partial shade. All but *A. sylvestris* will go completely dormant after flowering. Plant the tuberous roots in early spring or fall. Divide the clumps after flowering or when dormant. *A. coronaria* and *A. ×fulgens* may be short-lived and can be grown as annuals. Soak the dried tubers for at least 12 hours before planting. Fall planting is recommended for best flowering. The last group contains *A. canadensis, A. hupehensis, A. ×lesseri, A. hybrida, A. rivularis,* and *A. tomentosa.* Give these beauties a rich, evenly moist soil in sun or light shade. They spread by creeping underground stems to form showy clumps. Canada anemone may become invasive and is best used in the wild garden. Divide clumps in spring or after flowering. Propagate from root cuttings taken after the plants are dormant or by sowing fresh seed outdoors.

Landscape Uses

The garden uses of anemones are as varied as their shapes and sizes. Grow the woodland species in mass plantings under the shade of trees or in combination with spring bulbs, wildflowers, and ferns. Take care not to dig into dormant clumps when doing summer or fall planting. Plant exuberant Canada anemones in a meadow or the moist soil of a bog garden. They are excellent groundcovers and are perfect for underplanting shrubs. Snowdrop anemone is also an excellent groundcover. The snow white flowers add grace to spring combinations of bulbs, ferns, phlox, old-fashioned bleeding heart (*Dicentra spectabilis*), and bellflowers (*Campanula*). Choose poppy anemones for any garden spot where you need a colorful spring show. Combine them with bulbs and early perennials such as bleeding hearts (*Dicentra*), Virginia bluebells (*Mertensia virginica*), primroses (*Primula*), and columbines (*Aquilegia*). Use the stunning fall-flowering anemones in mass plantings to enliven the late border. Their airy, swaying heads are perfect compliments to asters, goldenrods (*Solidago*), sunflowers (*Helianthus*), ornamental grasses, monkshoods (*Aconitum*), sages (*Salvia*), and Kamchatka bugbane (*Cimicifuga simplex*). Plant the taller varieties in front of flowering shrubs or with the yellowing fronds of large ferns such as ostrich fern (*Matteuccia struthiopteris*) or cinnamon fern (*Osmunda cinnamomea*).

ANEMONELLA

ah-nem-o-NEL-ah • Ranunculaceae, Buttercup Family

The quivering flowers of rue anemone will seduce even the most jaded gardener. The wiry stems dance in the breeze but always spring back into position as the wind fades. This combination of fragility and hardiness embodies the tenacity of our native woodland denizens. Plants bloom throughout the spring, making them valuable companions for more-fleeting beauties.

ANEMONELLA

Common Names:
Rue anemone, windflower

Bloom Time:
Spring bloom

Planting Requirements:
Light to full shade

Anemonella thalictroides (thal-ick-TROY-dees), rue anemone. Size: 4 to 8 inches tall and wide. Many botanists place this lovely wildflower in the genus *Thalictrum*. The divided, lobed foliage of this delicate wildflower resembles a meadow rue, hence the name rue. The exquisite white to pink flowers have five to eight petal-like sepals in a loose umbel at the crown of the stem. Plants form compact clumps of flowering stems from clusters of fleshy tubers. 'Betty Blake' ('Green Dragon') sports soft, lime green, starry double flowers with narrow petals. 'Cameo' bears lovely, soft pink double flowers and is very vigorous. Some of the outer petals are elongated, giving a mild starburst look. 'Jade Feather' is green with a flattened pinwheel of stamens at the center. 'Schoaf's Double Pink' has deep rose-pink pompons that last for a week or more. USDA Plant Hardiness Zones 3 to 8.

The charming rue anemone (*Anemonella thalictroides*) is a favorite of wildflower enthusiasts. The cheery flowers open for a month or more on delicate stems that tremble in the breeze before the plant quietly slips into dormancy.

Plants in sunny situations flower more freely and remain in active growth longer. If the soil becomes dry, plants will go dormant but will not be harmed. Avoid unnecessary competition from larger plants; they will surely win and the rue anemone will disappear. Double species need division every 2 or 3 years or the congested tubers will rot. Propagate by dividing the tubers as the plants go dormant. Sow fresh seeds outdoors. Seedlings take several years to flower.

How to Grow

Plant rue anemones in rich, moist but well-drained soil in light to full shade.

Landscape Uses

Rue anemones require a special place in the garden. Combine them with slow-growing groundcovers such as wild gingers (*Asarum*), fairy wings (*Epimedium*), and Allegheny spurge (*Pachysandra procumbens*), as well as delicate ferns that will not swamp them but will fill the void left when they go dormant. Spring bulbs make good partners.

ANGELICA

an-GEL-i-ka • Apiaceae, Parsley Family

Angelica's dramatic form and long medicinal history have ensured a preeminent place in horticulture. Huge, intricately divided leaves and plate-size inflorescences provide unique architecture to borders and herb gardens alike. Plants are monocarpic—they bloom once and die after flowering.

ANGELICA

Common Names:
Angelica, archangel

Bloom Time:
Summer bloom

Planting Requirements:
Full sun to partial shade

The deep red flower heads of Korean angelica (*Angelica gigas*) are unique in both color and structure. The flattened umbels open from knobby buds in mid- to late summer. Place them against a bright background so the dark flowers will show up.

Angelica archangelica (ARC-an-gel-i-ka), wild parsnip. Size: 5 to 6 feet tall, 2 to 3 feet wide. This architectural beauty offers tiered layers of exquisite foliage on stout, purple-stained stems topped with domed, dinner-plate-size clusters of creamy flowers in early summer. As flowers fade, the clusters of rounded seedheads make a show more dramatic than the flowers. Unlike many angelicas, this one is edible. The stems are candied, and it is often added to spring's rhubarb recipes. USDA Plant Hardiness Zones 4 to 7.

A. gigas (GEE-gahs), Korean angelica, purple parsnip. Size: 3 to 5 feet tall, 2 to 3 feet wide. For drama, you can't beat the towering stems of this Asian beauty, with huge compound leaves arrayed up the stems and multiple clusters of deep Cabernet red flowers in late summer. Zones 4 to 8.

A. stricta var. *purpurea* (STRIC-ta var. pur-pew-REE-ah), stiff angelica. Size: 3 to 5 feet tall, 1 to 3 feet wide. A relative newcomer, this attractive plant has glossy, deep purple compound leaves that fade to bronzy green with purple veining by summer. Pinkish white to rosy flower clusters stained with purple open in early summer. 'Vicar's Mead' has purple leaves and large pink flower clusters. Zones 5 to 8.

A. venenosa (ven-en-OH-sa), hairy angelica. Size: 2 to 6 feet tall, 1 to 2 feet wide. This charming native perennial angelica has deep, glossy green leaves and creamy white flowers in summer. Zones 5 to 8.

How to Grow

Plant angelica in rich, evenly moist soil in sun or partial shade. Hairy angelica tolerates dry soil. Like all biennials, angelicas produce a foliage rosette the first year, overwinter, and flower the second year before they die. The abundant seeds guarantee new plants for future blooms. To assure bloom every season, set out first-year plants for two successive years, so there will always be new and blooming plants in the garden.

Landscape Uses

Place this highly architectural beauty where it can be admired in foliage and flower. Combine this angelica with the rich purple leaves of fringed loosestrife (*Lysimachia ciliata* 'Purpurea'). Illuminate the combination with pale yellow *Tulipa* 'Yellow Present', the starry white clusters of Bowman's root (*Porteranthus trifoliatus*), meadow rue (*Thalictrum*) and the purple catkinlike flowers of burnet (*Sanguisorba tenuifolia*). Place plants against a light background such as golden elderberry (*Sambucus racemosa* 'Sutherland Gold') or the deep flowers will be lost in the shadows.

ANTHEMIS

AN-them-is • Asteraceae, Aster Family

Marguerites are luminescent daisies for the early summer garden. The orange to bright yellow flowers with large buttonlike centers smother the clumps for a month or more. The plants have a lax, open habit, and the wiry stems are clothed with pungent, finely divided foliage. Plants are best in areas with low humidity and cool nights.

ANTHEMIS

Common Name:
  Marguerite

Bloom Time:
  Summer bloom

Planting Requirements:
  Full sun

Anthemis carpatica (car-PAH-tea-ka), mountain dog daisy. Size: 6 to 12 inches tall and 1 to 3 feet wide. This low, spreading species has gray-green leaves and white daisies in spring. 'Snow Carpet' forms compact, 6-inch cushions. USDA Plant Hardiness Zones 3 to 7.

A. sancti-johannis (sank-te yo-HAN-is), marguerite. Size: 2 to 3 feet tall and wide. An erect, branching, shrublike plant with white-tipped foliage and deep orange flowers. Plants often flop. Zones 4 to 8.

A. tinctoria (tink-TO-ree-a), golden marguerite. Size: 1 to 3 feet tall and wide. Erect to sprawling plant with soft, hairy stems and bright yellow flowers borne in profusion throughout the summer. 'E. C. Buxton' has lemon yellow flowers on 2½-foot-tall stems. 'Kelwayi' has bright yellow flowers and broad rays. 'Moonlight' is light yellow in flower. 'Wargrave' has creamy flowers topping 3-foot stems. Zones 3 to 8.

How to Grow

Marguerites prefer lean soil and are quite drought-tolerant once established. Plant them in a well-drained spot in full sun. In light shade, they will bloom but flop laxly in all directions. Deadhead plants regularly to promote bloom. Cut them back by at least half as flower production wanes to encourage new growth. In warmer zones, prune plants to the ground after flowering. Divide plants every 2 or 3 years in spring or fall. Propagate by stem cuttings in spring or early summer. Sow seeds indoors or outside.

Landscape Uses

Combine these cheery yellow daisies with perennials, herbs, or vegetables. The mounds of summer flowers complement larger white daisies, blue sages (*Salvia*), cranesbills (*Geranium*), and bee balms (*Monarda*). Use them in dry sites with yarrows (*Achillea*), butterfly weed (*Asclepias tuberosa*), spurges (*Euphorbia*), and stonecrops (*Sedum*). The plants grow well in rockeries and are perfect for container culture.

The milky yellow daisies of golden marguerite (*Anthemis tinctoria* 'E. C. Buxton') combined with a white-flowered selection brighten up the dry garden in summer.

AQUILEGIA

a-kwi-LEE-gee-a • Ranunculaceae, Buttercup Family

The curious flowers of columbines never fail to attract the attention of gardeners and hummingbirds alike. Five long-spurred petals and five petal-like sepals surround a central column of projecting yellow stamens (male reproductive structures). The flowers may nod on slender stems or stand upright. Blue, purple, red, pink, white, yellow, golden, and bicolor flowers are common. Lush mounds of compound foliage with fan-shaped leaflets arise from a thick taproot.

AQUILEGIA

Common Name:
Columbine

Bloom Time:
Spring and early summer bloom

Planting Requirements:
Sun to partial shade

Aquilegia alpina (al-PEEN-a), alpine columbine. Size: 1 to 2 feet tall and wide. A blue-flowered species of exceptional garden merit. The abundant, short-spurred flowers nod over dense clumps of blue-green foliage. 'Hensol Harebell', a hybrid between *A. alpina* and *A. vulgaris*, bears deep blue flowers through midsummer. The plants are longer-lived than other hybrids. USDA Plant Hardiness Zones 3 to 8.

A. caerulea (kie-RU-lee-a), Rocky Mountain columbine. Size: 1 to 2 feet tall and wide. This lovely columbine has 2-inch-wide bicolor flowers with white petals and pale to deep blue sepals. Rocky Mountain columbine is prized for breeding because of its upward-facing flowers and long spurs. 'Blue Star' resembles the species with deep blue-and-white flowers. It is heat- and drought-resistant. 'McKana' strain is a series of large-flowered hybrids in white, red, yellow, and blue. 'Maxistar' is bright yellow. Zones 3 to 8.

A. canadensis (kan-a-DEN-sis), wild columbine. Size: 1 to 3 feet tall, 1 foot wide. A beloved eastern wildflower with nodding red-and-yellow flowers produced in profusion for 4 to 6 weeks. The graceful plants often grow from cracks in rocky ledges, although they are equally at home in garden soil. 'Canyon Vista' is compact and floriferous. 'Corbet' has pure primrose-yellow flowers. Zones 3 to 8.

A. chrysantha (kris-ANTH-a), golden columbine. Size: 2 to 3 feet tall, 1 to 2 feet wide. A wide-spreading, open plant with long-spurred golden yellow flowers. This plant is an important parent of the spurred hybrids. 'Silver Queen' has white flowers. 'Yellow Queen' has lemon yellow flowers. 'Blazing Star' is a hybrid with long, spurred yellow-and-crimson flowers. Zones 3 to 9.

For a bright accent in the spring shade garden, plant generous drifts of free-flowering wild columbine (*Aquilegia canadensis*). Although individual plants may live but a few years, self-sown seedlings will perpetuate the plants.

A. flabellata (fla-bel-LAH-ta), fan columbine. Size: 6 to 16 inches tall, 6 to 12 inches wide. Short-spurred blue or white flowers are held just above the thick blue-green foliage. This compact columbine is long-lived and comes true to parental color and form from seed. 'Alba' has white flowers. 'Blue Angel' is a deep blue dwarf selection. 'Cameo Series' comes in a mix of white, blue, and pinks. 'Mini-star' is a dwarf blue-and-white bicolor. 'Nana Alba' is 8 to 10 inches tall with white flowers. Zones 3 to 9.

A. formosa (for-MOS-a), crimson columbine. Size: 2 to 4 feet tall, 1 to 2 feet wide. A tall, openly branching columbine with spreading deep red-and-yellow flowers. Zones 3 to 7.

A. ×hybrida (HI-brid-a), hybrid columbine. Size: 2 to 3 feet tall, 1 to 2 feet wide. A mixed group of hybrids originating from A. *canadensis*, A. *chrysantha*, A. *caerulea*, A. *formosa*, and A. *vulgaris*. Dozens of cultivars are variously colored and have short, medium, or long spurs. 'Biedermeier' hybrids are compact 12-inch bicolors in a variety of colors. 'Black Barlow' has purple-black truncated flowers like sea anemones. 'Crimson Star' is 2½ feet tall with crimson-and-white flowers. 'Dragonfly' hybrids are under 2 feet tall in mixed colors. 'Nora Barlow' has double flowers in red, pink, and green. 'Spring Song' hybrids are 3 feet tall in mixed colors. Zones 3 to 9.

A. longissima (long-GIS-si-ma), long-spur columbine. Size: 2 to 3 feet tall, 1 to

The huge, long-spurred flowers of *Aquilegia caerulea* 'Maxistar' open throughout early summer, followed by curious upright capsules that bear copious seeds. After seed is cast, cut the stems back and enjoy the delicate ferny foliage until hard frost.

2 feet wide. The yellow flowers with 6-inch spurs are showstoppers. Plants may be short-lived in cultivation. Zones 4 to 9.

A. rockii (ROCK-ee-ee), Chinese columbine. Size: 3 feet tall, 1 to 2 feet wide. This graceful, stately columbine has deep lilac flowers edged with white. Zones 4 to 8.

A. viridiflora (ve-rid-e-FLOOR-ah), green columbine. Size: 8 to 12 inches tall and wide. This curiosity has chocolate brown-and-green flowers on delicate stems. Zones 4 to 8.

A. vulgaris (vul-GAH-ris), European columbine. Size: 1½ to 3 feet tall, 1 to 2 feet wide. A short-spurred blue to violet species most noted as a parent for popular hybrids. Var. *nivea* has white flowers on vigorous, 3-foot plants. Zones 3 to 9.

How to Grow

Columbines, though often short-lived, are of the easiest culture. They reward the gardener with a month or more of brightly colored flowers that sway with every breeze. Plant columbines in light, average to rich, moist but well-drained soil. Heavy or soggy soils will hasten their demise. They grow well in full sun or partial shade. Plants self-sow freely, but only the true species produce attractive seedlings. Hybrid seedlings are often pale or grotesquely misshapen. They are easily uprooted and discarded. Propagate from purchased, named seed or collect from species grown in isolation from other columbines. Sow fresh seed outdoors. It germinates easily in fall or the following spring. Sow seed indoors after 4 weeks of cold storage. The foliage of columbines is sometimes plagued with leaf miners, which create pale tan tunnels or blotches in the blades of the leaves. Remove and destroy infected leaves immediately and continually. If the problem is severe, spray weekly with insecticidal soap. Borers can also be a problem. They cause the whole plant to collapse dramatically. Remove and destroy portions of infected plants above and below ground. BT (*Bacillus thuringiensis*) is also effective if applied in early spring.

Landscape Uses

Columbines are aristocrats of the spring garden. Plant them in groups of three or five—or in large sweeps—to complement spring perennials and late bulbs. They start blooming with the late tulips and continue through the early summer with cranesbills (*Geranium*), evening primroses (*Oenothera*), irises, peonies, and lupines. Use columbines around the base of tall, shrubby perennials such as blue stars (*Amsonia*), wild indigos (*Baptisia*), monkshoods (*Aconitum*), delphiniums, and others. Wild columbine is lovely in drifts in the rockery or woodland garden with Virginia bluebells (*Mertensia virginica*), trilliums, wild blue phlox (*Phlox divaricata*), and ferns. Use Rocky Mountain and fan columbines in the rock garden or in the border. Accent a shrub planting with drifts of mixed hybrids or a single species.

ARABIS

AR-a-bis • Brassicaceae, Mustard Family

Early flowers smother this diminutive groundcover like cheese on a pizza. Plants bloom for weeks in late winter and early spring, then quietly offer a summer green carpet. An old-fashioned favorite, this perennial is best in a well-drained rockery or wall garden where its delicate clumps will not be suffocated by tall border perennials.

ARABIS

Common Name:
Rock cress

Bloom Time:
Early spring bloom

Planting Requirements:
Full sun

Arabis caucasica (kaw-KAS-i-ka), wall rock cress. Size: 6 to 10 inches tall, 12 to 14 inches wide. A low mat-forming perennial with toothed gray woolly leaves and upright clusters of four-petaled white flowers. 'Flore Plena' has double flowers. 'Rosabella', a pink-flowered cultivar of the hybrid A. ×arendsii, is often sold as A. caucasica. 'Snowball' is compact and floriferous. 'Variegata' has the added bonus of yellow-striped leaves. USDA Plant Hardiness Zones 3 to 7.

A. procurrens (pro-KER-rens), rock cress. Size: 6 to 12 inches tall, 12 to 24 inches wide. A creeping groundcover plant with broad, lance-shaped evergreen leaves and sprays of white flowers. Zones 4 to 7.

How to Grow

Plant rock cresses in average to good, well-drained soil in full sun or light shade. These mountain or seaside plants require cool temperatures and low humidity for best growth. Select a position with afternoon shade when growing them in warm regions. Cut plants back after flowering to keep them neat, as they go into a dramatic flop when temperatures rise. Divide clumps every 2 to 4 years after flowering, depending on their vigor. Propagate by taking cuttings in spring.

For the well-drained rock garden, be sure to include a generous planting of early-blooming wall rock cress (*Arabis caucasica*). The evergreen foliage is all but smothered by scads of white flowers that are produced for a month or more.

Landscape Uses

Place rock cresses in the company of spring bulbs such as crocuses, species tulips, daffodils, and glory-of-the-snows (*Chionodoxa*). In a rock wall, they form a colorful drapery in the company of rock ferns such as common polypody (*Polypodium virginianum*), hart's-tongue ferns (*Asplenium*), and southern maidenhair (*Adiantum capillus-veneris*). Add wildflowers such as rue anemone (*Anemonella thalictroides*), wild columbine (*Aquilegia canadensis*), and coral bells (*Heuchera*) to complete the spring picture.

ARACHNOIDES

ar-ak-NOY-deez • Dryopteridaceae, Shield Fern Family

Stunning foliage is the hallmark of this genus of hardy ferns. The plants have triangular fronds with many delicate dissections that create a lacy effect. Plants grow from slow-creeping rhizomes.

ARACHNOIDES

Common Name:
Upside-down fern

Bloom Time:
Foliage plant

Planting Requirements:
Light to full shade

Variegated ferns are rare, which makes the yellow-striped fronds of *Arachnoides simplicior* var. *variegata* valuable for adding luminescent spots in the dark shade of summer.

Arachnoides simplicior (sim-PLICK-e-or), holly fern. Size: 1 to 3 feet tall and wide. Lustrous, leathery fronds form elongated triangles with coarse, toothed pinnae. The variety *variegata* has attractive yellow stripes along the veins. *A. aristata* is similar, but the waxy, deep green fronds have narrow segments. USDA Plant Hardiness Zones 6 to 9.

A. standishii (stan-DIS-ee-ee), upside-down fern. Size: 2 to 3 feet tall, 3 to 4 feet wide. An arching, vase-shaped fern with intricately cut fronds. The veins are deeply impressed on the upper surface of the frond, giving the impression that it is up-side down. Zones 4 to 9.

How to Grow

Plant in rich, evenly moist soil in light to full shade. Plants are late to emerge in spring. They grow slowly from spreading rhizomes and in time form impressive, showy clumps of unique beauty. Divide them in early spring or after foliage hardens in summer.

Landscape Uses

Upside-down ferns are commanding plants best used as accents or focal points. Surround them with short plants that set off the beautiful form and foliage such as fairy wings (*Epimedium*), wild gingers (*Asarum*), dwarf hostas, and sedges.

ARENARIA

a-ray-NAH-ree-a • Caryophyllaceae, Pink Family

Lush, mossy clumps spread ever-outward as this diminutive groundcover eagerly creeps over the ground. The tiny flower buds, scarcely larger than a moss spore capsule, make moss sandwort a perfect moss substitute for sunny or dry sites. Fill the space between stepping stones with these low, cushion forming plants with small narrow leaves and white 5-petaled flowers. The stems root as they creep.

ARENARIA

Common Name:
Sandwort

Bloom Time:
Spring and early summer bloom

Planting Requirements:
Full sun or partial shade

Arenaria montana (mon-TAH-na), mountain sandwort. Size: 2 to 4 inches tall, 4 to 8 inches wide. A mounding, soft hairy plant with disproportionately large, flat ½-inch flowers on 12-inch stalks. USDA Plant Hardiness Zones 4 to 8.

A. verna (VER-na), also listed as *Minuartia verna*, moss sandwort. Size: 2 inches tall, 2 to 4 inches wide. A cushion-forming plant with small white flowers. 'Aurea' has yellow-green leaves. Zones 5 to 8.

How to Grow

Plant sandworts in average, sandy or loamy, well-drained soil in full sun. They prefer neutral to slightly acid soil. Add ground limestone according to label directions if you have strongly acid soil. They spread slowly to form undulating mounds of dense foliage. Plants are shallow-rooted and must be watered during dry spells. Propagate by division in spring or fall or by seed sown indoors.

Diminutive, mat-forming mountain sandwort (*Arenaria montana*) is an excellent groundcover for the sunny rock garden or the front of a border. The small leaves form dense carpets that clamber over rocks and between pavers.

Landscape Uses

Sandworts make excellent low groundcovers for rock gardens and walls or for use between pavers in a walk or patio. Combine them with smaller spring bulbs, dwarf irises, sedges (*Carex*), fan columbine (*Aquilegia flabellata*), and sun-loving ferns such as brakes (*Pellaea*) and lip ferns (*Cheilanthes*). For summer interest, underplant foliage plants such as mountain mantle (*Alchemilla alpina*), black mondo grass (*Ophiopogon planiscapus* 'Nigrescens') and long-leaved lungwort (*Pulmonaria longifolia*). In fall, set off the delicate pink flowers and variegated, heart-shaped leaves of cyclamen against this low green backdrop. Sandworts also grow well in trough gardens with alpine plants and succulents or around the bases of bonsai.

ARISAEMA

a-ris-EE-ma • Araceae, Arum Family

People are instinctively drawn to these curious woodland treasures. Unusual, fleshy flowers resembling green calla lilies sport hoods (spathes) surrounding thick central columns (spadix). Pulpy red berries form in late summer. The divided leaves with 3 to 12 leaflets are borne singly or in pairs. Dozens of species have become available. The following are some distinctive, easy-to-grow choices.

ARISAEMA

Common Name:
Jack-in-the-pulpit

Bloom Time:
Spring or early summer bloom

Planting Requirements:
Full to partial shade

Arisaema candidissimum (can-di-DIS-se-mum), ghost jack, white jack. Size: 1 to 2 feet tall, 1 foot wide. The luscious white-and-pink spathe of ghost jack emerges naked from the ground before the dramatic, three-lobed leaves arise. USDA Plant Hardiness Zones 7 to 9.

A. consanguineum (con-san-GUIN-ee-um), purple jack. Size: 1 to 3 feet tall, 1 to 2 feet wide. This is one of several dramatic species with circular leaves, each sporting a whorl of 12 to 18 long, slender leaflets and

Sensational inflated green-and-black flowers of the aptly named cobra jack (*Arisaema ringens*) open as a pair of bold, three-lobed leaves begins to unfold. In fall, red-orange berries brighten up shaded recesses and open woods.

striped green spathes. *A. concinnum* and *A. ciliatum* are similar in leaf. Zones 6 to 8.

A. dracontium (dra-KON-tee-um), green dragon. Size: 1 to 3½ feet tall, 1 foot wide. A single horseshoe-shaped leaf with seven to nine leaflets towers above the green spathe with a long, tongue-like spadix. Zones 4 to 9.

A. heterophyllum (he-ter-o-FILE-um), dancing crane jack. Size: 2 to 3 feet tall, 1 foot wide. A stately species with single, horseshoe-shaped leaves with a dozen leaflets that sit below the green spathe with its 12-inch, erect tongue. Zones 5 to 9.

A. ringens (RIN-gens), cobra jack. Size: 1 to 2 feet tall and wide. Inflated spathes like a hissing cobra are carried between pairs of glossy, three-lobed leaves in spring. The inside of the spathe is shiny purple-black and contrasts dramatically with the pale green striped exterior. Zones 5 to 9.

A. robustum (ro-BUS-tum), often incorrectly sold as *A. ringens*, jack-in-the-pulpit. Size: 1 to 1½ feet tall, 1 foot wide. Single or paired, five-parted leaves appear above a squat white-and-green-striped spathe with a purple interior. Zones 6 to 9.

A. sikokianum (see-ko-kee-A-num), gaudy jack. Size: 1 to 1½ feet tall, 1 foot wide. Aristocrat of the genus, the five-part leaves stand guard above the showy purple-and-white flower, exposing the creamy insides. Zones 4 to 8.

A. triphyllum (tri-FILE-um), jack-in-the-pulpit. Size: 1 to 3 feet tall, 1 foot wide. Single or paired three-lobed leaves frame the showy green-and-purple spathe, which droops at the tip to hide the short spadix. Zones 3 to 9.

How to Grow

Plant these woodland treasures in humus-rich, evenly moist but well-drained soil in full to partial shade. Green dragon prefers full to partial sun. Jacks tolerate very deep shade and poorly drained soils. Plant in spring or fall. Propagate by sowing cleaned seed outdoors when ripe. It takes several years for the plants to grow to flowering size. At first, the seedlings will have only one leaf. As they mature, a second leaf will appear. Their unique flowers and showy foliage are beloved by all who know wildflowers.

Landscape Uses

Use jacks as specimens in the shade garden in company with fairy wings (*Epimediums*), foamflowers (*Tiarella*), wild gingers (*Asarum*), and ferns. Punctuate a low carpet of wild ginger or foamflower with their upright forms. Complement the creamy variegation of Japanese Solomon's seal (*Polygonatum odoratum* var. *thunbergii* 'Variegatum') with the white flowers of *A. candidissimum*. The commanding foliage of green dragon, dancing crane jack, and purple jack makes a wonderful accent in front of shrubs or in foundation plantings.

ARMERIA

ar-ME-ree-a • Plumbaginaceae, Leadwort Family

The tidy cushions of thrifts sport cheery, vibrant pink to white flowers borne abundantly in dense, rounded heads atop naked stems. In nature, thrifts grow along rocky coasts, in mountain meadows, or on alpine slopes. In the garden, they are easy-care perennials for rock and wall gardens, between pavers, or in troughs.

ARMERIA

Common Name:
Thrift

Bloom Time:
Late spring and summer bloom

Planting Requirements:
Full sun

Armeria juniperifolia (joo-ni-pe-ri-FO-lee-a), juniper-leaved thrift (also sold as *A. caespitosa*). Size: 2 to 3 inches tall, 3 to 5 inches wide. The soft pink or white flowers of this diminutive species are carried just above tight cushion-shaped clumps of stiff needle-like foliage. 'Alba' has pure white flowers. 'Bevan's Variety' is a rock garden favorite with globular pink heads. USDA Plant Hardiness Zones 4 to 8.

A. maritima (ma-RI-ti-ma), sea pink. Size: 10 to 14 inches tall, 6 to 12 inches wide. A variable species with gray-green, linear foliage and pink to rose flowers.

'Alba' has pure white flowers on 6-inch stalks. 'Bee's Ruby' is a hybrid with large flowers on 18-inch erect stems suitable for cutting. 'Dusseldorf Pride' has bright pink flowers and is 6 to 8 inches tall. 'Laucheana' is an old cultivar with large, deep pink flowers. 'Rubrifolia' is an exciting departure with wine red leaves and vivid pink flowers. 'Vindictive' is compact, to 6 inches, with abundant, rosy red flowers. Zones 4 to 8.

How to Grow

Plant thrifts in average, well-drained, loamy or sandy soil in full sun. Juniper-leaved thrift requires excellent drainage, especially in winter; wet soil for extended periods encourages root rot. Thrifts prefer cool temperatures and low humidity. Provide afternoon shade where summers are hot. Sea pink is tolerant of seaside conditions; it thrives despite both airborne and soilborne salt. Propagate by division in spring or fall or by seed sown on a warm (70°F) seedbed.

The pink cushions of sea pink (*Armeria maritima* 'Vindictive') cling to rock faces along windswept shores in the wild. In the garden, place them in a rockery with bellflowers (*Campanula*), rock cresses (*Arabis*), and dwarf bulbs.

Landscape Uses

Use thrift in combination with low rock-loving plants such as sandworts (*Arenaria*), rock cresses (*Arabis*), stonecrops (*Sedum*), candytuft (*Iberis sempervirens*), and sun-loving ferns.

ARTEMISIA

ar-tay-MIS-ee-a • Asteraceae, Aster Family

Wormwoods are shrubby, aromatic plants with showy green or gray foliage and terminal clusters of insignificant late-season flowers. Foliage varies from deeply lobed or divided to broadly lance-shaped. Most species originate in arid regions or prairies. This diverse genus contains ornamental, culinary, and medicinal plants. Plants grow from crowns or creeping rhizomes with fibrous roots.

ARTEMISIA
Common Names:
  Artemisia, wormwood
Bloom Time:
  Foliage plant with summer and fall bloom
Planting Requirements:
  Full sun

Artemisia absinthium (ab-SIN-thee-um), common wormwood. Size: 2 to 3 feet tall and wide. A robust sub-shrub, wormwood becomes somewhat woody with age. The deeply lobed aromatic foliage is covered in silky hairs. Inconspicuous yellow flowers are borne in late summer. This plant was once the source of commercial absinthe. 'Lambrook Silver' has lovely silver-gray foliage. USDA Plant Hardiness Zones 3 to 9.

A. canescens (ka-NESS-sens), silver sage. Size: 12 to 18 inches tall and wide. An open, mounding plant with finely divided, silver-gray foliage. Zones 4 to 8.

A. dracunculus (dra-KUN-kew-lus), tarragon. Size: 2 to 5 feet tall, 2 to 3 feet wide. An aromatic culinary herb and garden ornamental, tarragon has an open habit and green lance-shaped foliage. Zones 3 to 8.

A. lactiflora (lak-ti-FLO-ra), white mugwort. Size: 4 to 6 feet tall, 2 to 4 feet wide. White mugwort is the only artemisia grown for its fragrant flowers rather than its foliage. Plumes of small, creamy flowers are held high atop erect, leafy stalks in late summer. The broad, deeply divided leaves are bright green. Plants prefer moist soil. 'Guizho' has purple-stained leaves and flowers on deep mahogany stems. Zones 4 to 9.

A. ludoviciana (loo-do-vik-ee-AH-na), white sage. Size: 2 to 4 feet tall, 2 to 3 feet wide. A slightly aromatic plant with creeping roots and slender stems covered in white, woolly, lance-shaped leaves. 'Silver King' is erect and compact. 'Silver Queen' has rounded leaves and tends to flop. 'Valerie Finnis' is a lovely cultivar with broadly lance-shaped leaves and dense, upright stems. Zones 3 to 9.

A. 'Powis Castle', Powis Castle wormwood. Size: 2 to 3 feet tall, 3 to 4 feet wide. This is a shrubby hybrid having common wormwood as a parent. The silvery white foliage is deeply cut. Plants retain a compact form throughout the growing season. Where winters are mild, plants form a woody base and stems, which may get open and leggy without regular pruning. 'Beth Chatto' is more compact, to 18 inches. 'Huntington' is elegant and compact but may reach 3 to 4 feet in mild zones. Zones 5 to 8; trial in Zone 4.

A. schmidtiana (shmit-ee-AH-na), silvermound artemisia. Size: 1 to 2 feet tall and

'Silver Brocade' beach wormwood (*Artemisia stelleriana* 'Silver Brocade') is a dense, shiny silver selection of this tough, salt-tolerant perennial. Use plants in a well-drained spot in full sun where the silver foliage accents blue, pink, and soft yellow flowers to create dreamy combinations.

wide. A dense, mounded plant with finely divided silver-gray foliage. In warm regions, plants may flop, leaving an open center, spoiling the mounded appearance. 'Nana' is more common in cultivation than the species. Also sold as 'Silver Mound', this cultivar is similar to the species but shorter and more compact. Zones 3 to 7.

A. stelleriana (stel-la-ree-AH-na), beach wormwood. Size: 10 to 12 inches tall, 12 to 24 inches wide. A low, spreading plant with lobed, silvery foliage. Tolerant of seaside conditions. Zones 3 to 8.

How to Grow

Plant most species of wormwoods in average, well-drained soil in full sun. They are easy-care species that thrive on neglect. Once established, they are extremely drought-tolerant. Give white mugwort moist, well-drained soil for best growth. In warm, humid regions, the mounding species, especially silvermound artemisia, tend to fall open from the center. Plant the upright and shrubby species instead of the mounding species if heat is a problem. Prune all species back hard if they start to lose their form. Proper siting and good culture seems to eliminate any pest or disease problems. Propagate shrubby types such as *A. absinthium* and *A.* 'Powis Castle' by taking cuttings from new shoots with a piece of old wood attached. A side branch works well for this technique. Such cuttings are called mallet cuttings and are best taken in late summer. The older wood allows root

Drought-tolerant prairie sage (*Artemisia ludoviciana* `Valerie Finnis') is a good weaver, used to tie clumps of plants together. A large clump makes a lovely specimen in the dry garden in foliage or in flower. The tawny spikes of tiny flowers top erect stems in mid- to late summer.

production without rotting. A rooting hormone will speed root production. Fast-spreading species such as white mugwort and prairie sage need dividing every 2 or 3 years to restrain their exuberant growth and to rejuvenate old clumps. Lift clumps in spring or fall and replant divisions into well-prepared soil. Take softwood cuttings in early summer or semi-hardwood cuttings as above. They root quickly in a half-and-half peat-and-perlite mix.

Landscape Uses

The showy, soft silver-gray or white leaves of artemisias are a valuable asset in the garden. It is often said that silver foliage calms clashing color combinations, but to our eyes it heightens or aggravates them. Use the foliage to brighten colors, especially hot pinks, reds, and oranges, or to create cool pictures with pastel pinks, purples, and blues. Combine the shrubby species with yuccas, ornamental grasses, groundcovers, and flowering shrubs. Use the herbaceous species with annuals and perennials in beds, borders, and containers. The low-growing species are suitable for edging or in rock gardens. Most species, especially beach wormwood, are good plants for seaside gardens and other areas where salt is a problem. The showy plumes of white mugwort are perfect for adding grace and motion to heavy-headed daisies and mums or as a background for other plants. They are especially beautiful with Japanese anemones (*Anemone* ×*hybrida*) and monkshoods (*Aconitum*). Mix tarragon with other herbs or with perennials in the border or in pots.

ARUM

A-rum • Araceae, Arum Family

Arums are suddenly popular, and deservedly so. Their evergreen, tropical-looking arrowhead foliage and colorful autumn berries add impact when the garden needs it most. Plants grow from buttonlike tubers. Foliage is produced in fall, persists through winter, and disappears after flowering. Plants thrive with little care and go dormant in summer when conditions are hot and dry. They grow from fleshy tubers.

ARUM

Common Name:
Arum

Bloom Time:
Foliage plant with spring bloom

Planting Requirements:
Partial to full shade

Arum dioscoridis (dye-o-SCORE-e-dis). Size: 1 foot tall, 1 to 3 feet wide. This variable species has large green, purple-spotted, or pure purple spathes and elongated, spearlike leaves. USDA Plant Hardiness Zones 7 to 9.

A. elongatum (e-lon-GAY-tum). Size: 1 foot tall, 1 to 2 feet wide. A dramatic arum in flower, this species holds its dark spathes with purple-and-white interiors above the green, arrow-shaped foliage. Red berries follow in late summer. Zones 6 to 9.

A. italicum (ee-TA-li-cum), Italian arum. Size: 1 to 1½ feet tall, 1 to 3 feet wide. Italian arum is the most widely available species and the most attractive in leaf. The cream to pale yellow flowers are less dramatic than many other species. The fleshy, wide arrowhead-shape leaves are deep green, often veined with yellow. Showy orange-red berries are borne in dense clusters in late summer before the new leaves emerge. 'Marmoratum' ('Pictum'), the best cultivar, has large leaves that are lightly mottled with yellow, and the flowers are tinged with purple at their bases. Many plants of variable merit are sold under this name. Many excellent unnamed seedlings are available with fabulous foliage. Zones 6 to 9.

How to Grow

Arums are woodland and meadow plants. Give them moist, humus-rich soil in sun or light shade. You can allow the soil to become dry without ill effect in summer when plants are leafless. Propagate by dividing clumps in summer as leaves wither. If severe winter weather damages foliage, new leaves will appear in spring. Sow ripe seed outside after the pulp is removed. Plants may self-sow around the garden and are invasive in some regions. Check before you plant.

Landscape Uses

Superb in foliage and in fruit, arums provide year-round interest in the garden. Use the handsome mottled foliage to echo yellow colors of the winter garden such as yellow-

Winter gardens are short on foliage, but the marbled arrow-shaped leaves of Italian arum (*Arum italicum* 'Pictum') emerge in autumn when most perennials are going dormant. The leaves fade away in spring before the flowers emerge. In late summer, scarlet berries add a hint of color.

twig dogwood (*Cornus sericea* 'Flaviramea') and Corsican hellebore (*Helleborus argutifolius*). The leaves withstand cold and snow. Combine them with other evergreens such as heart-leaved bergenia (*Bergenia cordifolia*), purple small-flowered alumroot (*Heuchera micrantha* 'Palace Purple'), and golden sedges (*Carex*). Spring bulbs and wildflowers are natural companions, followed by lush foliage colors and textures in summer. The flowers are usually borne under the leaves. Set the berries against a background of mottled foliage and ferns.

ARUNCUS

a-RUN-kus • Rosaceae, Rose Family

If you're tired of small plants with subtle flowers, try goat's beard. These showy perennials have exuberant open plumes of fuzzy white flowers that resemble huge *Astilbe*. Male and female flowers are borne on separate plants (dioecious). Male flowers are showier due to the many fuzzy stamens (male reproductive structures). The female flowers are also attractive. Nurseries do not identify the sexes for you. Large, thrice-divided leaves have many broad, quilted leaflets that lend elegance throughout the growing season. The species vary from tall, broad, shrubby plants to low clumpers barely 8 inches tall. All grow from a stout, fibrous rootstock.

ARUNCUS

Common Name:
Goat's beard

Bloom Time:
Late spring and early summer bloom

Planting Requirements:
Sun to partial shade

Aruncus aethusifolius (aye-THOOS-i-fo-lee-us), dwarf goat's beard. Size: 8 to 12 inches tall, 1 to 1½ feet wide. This dwarf clumping plant gives the impression of a lacy fern. In late spring, branched cylindrical clusters of creamy white flowers dance above the shiny, deep green compound leaves. 'Hillside Gem' is selected for its finely divided leaves. USDA Plant Hardiness Zones 4 to 7.

A. dioicus (dee-o-EE-kus), goat's beard. Size: 3 to 6 feet tall, 2 to 4 feet wide. A stately perennial of shrublike proportions, goat's beard has 2-foot open plumes of creamy white flowers on stout stems with huge divided leaves. 'Child of Two Worlds' is more compact, reaching 3 to 4 feet in height. 'Glasnevin' is a compact selection from the Scottish botanic garden that bears its name. 'Kneiffi' is 3 feet tall with deeply cut, ferny foliage with narrow leaflets. Zones 3 to 7.

How to Grow

Goat's beards are plants of open woodlands and woods edges. Plant them in moist, humus-rich soil in light to partial shade. In cooler areas, they will stand full sun if kept constantly moist. In deep shade, plants will bloom sparsely and lack the character of open-grown plants. Place them at least 4 feet apart when planting in groups. Once established, the stout rootstocks do not move easily. If division is necessary, lift clumps in spring and cut the rootstock with a sharp knife. Leave at least one eye per division. Dwarf goat's beard is easily divided in the same manner. Sow fresh seed on the surface of a warm (70°F) seedbed. Seedlings will appear in 2 to 3 weeks.

Landscape Uses

Goat's beards are bold accent plants. Use them singly or in small groups at the edge of a woodland path or in front of flowering shrubs. Combine them with ferns, Solomon's seals (*Polygonatum*), irises, and groundcovers. In the perennial or mixed border, treat them like herbaceous shrubs. Give them plenty of room to spread. Each plant may reach 4 feet across. Where space is limited, plant one of the smaller cultivars; their compact form makes them suitable for smaller gardens and they combine more easily with perennials. Choose dwarf goat's beard for shaded rock gardens in combination with small-leaved hostas and delicate wildflowers. They are also suitable for the front of the border or for edging paths.

The creamy plumes of stately goat's beard (*Aruncus dioicus*) open above divided foliage that remains attractive long after the early-summer flowers have faded. Mature plants reach shrublike proportions in a sunny to lightly shaded garden.

ASARUM

a-SAH-rum • Aristolochiaceae, Birthwort Family

Wild gingers are lovely foliage plants of low stature with creeping aromatic rhizomes that smell like commercial ginger (*Zingiber officinalis*), from which they borrow their common name. The unusual jug-shaped brown or red flowers rest on the soil. Each flower is borne between two evergreen or (rarely) deciduous leaves. Evergreen species often have mottled foliage. The inflated flowers are fleshy, with three flaring lobes. Evergreen species are often placed in the genus *Hexastylis*.

ASARUM

Common Name:
 Wild ginger

Bloom Time:
 Foliage plant with spring bloom

Planting Requirements:
 Partial to full shade

Asarum arifolium (are-i-FOL-ee-um), arrow-leaf wild ginger. Size: 6 to 12 inches tall, 12 to 18 inches wide. A showy evergreen species with arrow-shaped gray-green leaves mottled with silver and inconspicuous light brown flowers. USDA Plant Hardiness Zones 5 to 9; Zone 4, with protection.

A. canadense (kan-a-DEN-see), Canada wild ginger. Size: 6 to 12 inches tall, 12 to 24 inches wide. A fast-spreading native groundcover with satiny, broad heart-shaped deciduous leaves and reddish brown flowers with long, pointed lobes. Zones 3 to 8.

A. caudatum (kaw-DAH-tum), long-tailed ginger. Size: 6 to 8 inches tall, 12 to 18 inches wide. A creeping plant similar to Canada wild ginger with deciduous to semi-evergreen, heart-shaped leaves and purple-brown flowers with long tails. Zones 4 to 7.

A. europaeum (yoo-RO-pay-um), European wild ginger. Size: 6 to 8 inches tall, 12 to 24 inches wide. A lovely groundcover with glossy, evergreen, kidney-shaped leaves, often with faint mottling. The flowers are insignificant. Zones 4 to 8.

A. maximum (MAX-e-mum), panda ginger. Size: 6 to 8 inches tall, 12 to 24 inches wide. Gorgeous satiny white flowers edged in deep purple-brown. The fat, heart-shaped leaves are evergreen and may be mottled with creamy white. 'Green Panda'

The glossy, heart-shaped evergreen leaves of Virginia wild ginger (*Asarum virginicum*) form a luminescent groundcover that brightens up the shaded garden. The foliage patterns vary from scalloped mottling to nearly pure silver.

has glossy green leaves, while those of 'Ling Ling' are splashed with chartreuse on either side of the midvein. Zones 7 to 9.

A. shuttleworthii (shuttle-WORTH-ee-ee), mottled wild ginger. Size: 4 to 6 inches tall, 12 to 24 inches wide. An open groundcover with dark, mottled evergreen leaves and attractive broad-lipped flowers. 'Callaway' is a fast-spreading, small-leaved selection that makes an excellent groundcover. Zones 5 to 9.

A. speciosum (spee-see-O-sum), Harper's heartleaf. Size: 8 to 12 inches tall, 12 to 18 inches wide. Large, heart-shaped leaves with subtle mottling stand above showy maroon flowers striped with creamy white. 'Buxom Beauty' has large flowers ringed in deep purple and striped on the inside. 'Woodlander's Select' has silvery mottled leaves and flowers with stripes on the dark, wavy petals. Zones 5 to 9.

A. splendens (SPLEN-denz), showy wild ginger. Size: 4 to 8 inches tall, 12 to 16 inches wide. This beautiful groundcover is now widely available from tissue culture. The glossy, heart-shaped evergreen leaves are generously splotched with silver on both sides of the midvein. Plants creep to form beautiful clumps. Cold winter wind may burn the foliage. Zones 7 to 9; colder with protection.

A. takaoi (TAK-ah-oy), Japanese ginger. Size: 2 to 4 inches tall, 6 to 12 inches wide. This cute ginger creeps slowly outward, making dense clumps of nearly round gray-green hearts attractively mottled with silvery gray. 'Galaxy' has star-studded leaves. Zones 6 to 9.

How to Grow

Wild gingers are easy-care woodland denizens. Plant them in continually moist, humus-rich soil in partial to full shade. Canada wild ginger tolerates lime, but the other species prefer acid soils. Long-tailed ginger from the Pacific Northwest is not tolerant of excessive heat. Best results are achieved north of Zone 7. Canada, European, and long-tailed gingers spread rapidly to form dense, neat groundcovers of exceptional beauty. Divide overgrown clumps in spring or fall. Other species spread slowly from branching rhizomes to form tight clumps. Division is seldom necessary, except for propagation; lift plants in fall. Propagate all wild gingers by mallet cuttings in late spring or early summer: Remove a 1- to 1½-inch tip section of the rhizome with a pair of leaves attached. Stick the cuttings in a half-and-half mix of peat moss and perlite or sand. Cuttings will root in 4 to 6 weeks.

Sow fresh seed inside or outside when ripe in midsummer. Seedlings germinate quickly but plants develop slowly, especially the evergreen species. Canada and long-tailed gingers will freely self-sow in the garden. Although once thought to be pollinated by slugs or ants, research has shown that the flowers are visited by gnats that perform their mating dance inside the flowers and accomplish pollination in the process.

Landscape Uses

Wild gingers are unparalleled groundcovers. Combine them with hostas, ferns, and wildflowers in the shade garden or rockery. Plant miniature bulbs among clumps of the evergreen species for early spring show. Larger bulbs, especially daffodils, are also excellent companions. The flowers show off best when clumps are planted on a slope or at the edge of rock walls where the foliage does not obscure them.

ASCLEPIAS

a-SKLAY-pee-as • Asclepiadaceae, Milkweed Family

Milkweeds are magnets for butterflies. These tough, showy, summer-blooming plants are found in fields and prairies. They are aptly named for the milky sap produced when plants are picked or damaged. The unusual waxy flowers have five reflexed petals with forward-protruding lobes. They are borne profusely in rounded clusters in the axils of the leaves or in flat-topped terminal clusters. Color varies among species from green to

ASCLEPIAS

Common Name:
Milkweed

Bloom Time:
Summer bloom

Planting Requirements:
Full sun to light shade

orange, yellow, pink, and purple. Stems may be single or in dense clumps. In fall, inflated seedpods split to release the seeds that are carried away by the breeze on silken parachutes. Milkweed leaves are the sole food source for the caterpillars of the monarch butterfly. The flowers are important nectar plants for a wide variety of adult butterflies.

Asclepias currassavica (ku-ra-SAH-vi-ka), bloodflower. Size: 3 to 4 feet tall, 1 to 2 feet wide. A tall milkweed with opposite, lance-shaped leaves and terminal clusters of bicolor orange-and-red flowers. Stems are produced in a sparse clump from a creeping rhizome. USDA Plant Hardiness Zones 7 to 10.

A. exaltata (ex-al-TA-ta), poke milkweed. Size: 3 to 5 feet tall, 1 to 3 feet wide. A handsome plant with opposite, oval leaves and rounded axillary clusters of bicolor green-and-rose flowers. Zones 4 to 7.

A. incarnata (in-car-NAH-ta), swamp milkweed. Size: 3 to 5 feet tall, 1 to 3 feet wide. A stately denizen of moist to wet soils, with flat, terminal clusters of rose-pink flowers. Stems covered in opposite, lance-shaped leaves arise in loose clumps to form a creeping rhizome. 'Ice Ballet' has ghostly white flowers. 'Soul Mate' is deep rosy purple. Zones 3 to 8.

A. speciosa (spee-see-OH-sa), showy milkweed. Size: 1 to 3 feet tall, 1 to 2 feet wide. Compact plant with opposite pale green leaves and axillary clusters of starry rose-purple flowers. The petals of this species are not fully reflexed so they surround the lobes to form the ½-inch starry flowers. Zones 3 to 8.

A. tuberosa (tew-be-RO-sa), butterfly weed. Size: 1 to 3 feet tall, 1 to 2 feet wide. Dense clumps of leafy stems are topped with broad, flat clusters of fiery orange, red, or (rarely) yellow flowers. The plant grows from a brittle, fleshy taproot. 'Gay Butterflies' is a seed-grown strain of mixed yellow, red, and orange flowering plants. 'Hello Yellow' is yellow flowered. Zones 3 to 9.

A. verticillata (ver-ti-kil-LAY-ta), whorled milkweed. Size: 1 to 2 feet tall and wide. Bottlebrush best describes the willowy stems densely covered with needle-like leaves. In summer, the stems are topped with open clusters of creamy white flowers. Zones 3 to 8.

How to Grow

Milkweeds grow along roadsides, in meadows, and on prairies. Give them average, loamy, or sandy soil in full sun. Swamp milkweed will succeed in dry soil but prefers moist to wet humus-rich soil. Plant poke milkweed in partial shade or full sun and give it evenly moist soil for best growth. Most species of milkweeds spread by rhizomes and have the potential to be rampant, especially in rich soils. Remove unwanted shoots as they appear. Butterfly weed grows from a thick taproot. Do not disturb plants once they are established. Take tip cuttings in May or

June. They root in 4 to 6 weeks. Produce milkweeds from root cuttings or pieces of rhizome removed in fall and placed in a sandy rooting mix. All milkweeds are easily grown from seed sown outdoors when fresh. Indoors sow fresh seed in flats, water them well, and place them in a warm (70°F), sunny spot. Germination will occur in 3 to 5 weeks. Indoors or out, transplant seedlings of butterfly weed as soon as the second set of true leaves is formed. Delaying transplanting may cause damage to the taproot. The other species are rhizomatous, and early transplanting is not critical.

Bees as well as butterflies find the brilliant orange clusters of butterfly weed (*Asclepias tuberosa*) irresistible. The huge domed clusters make a perfect landing pad and smorgasbord for the hungry adult butterflies, and the larvae of monarchs feed on the foliage.

Landscape Uses

Milkweeds are equally at home in informal or formal landscapes. Use a generous planting in a meadow with native grasses and sun-loving wildflowers. Butterfly weed and showy milkweed are native to prairies as well as meadows. Use them in restored grasslands or stylized prairie gardens. Plant poke milkweed at a woodland's edge with ferns, shrubs, and other roadside flowers such as goat's beard (*Aruncus dioicus*), false indigos (*Baptisia*), and blue stars (*Amsonia*). Use swamp milkweed in a bog or water garden. Place containerized plants in shallow pools and garden ponds. In formal perennial borders, choose butterfly weed for the front or middle of the border in combination with yarrows (*Achillea*), blanket flower (*Gaillardia aristata*), garden sage (*Salvia nemorosa* 'Caradonna'), and silver-leaved artemisias. Plant other milkweeds toward the back of the border with ornamental grasses, asters, Joe-Pye weeds (*Eupatorium*), and bee balms (*Monarda*).

ASPLENIUM (PHYLLITIS)

a-SPLEE-nee-um • Aspleniaceae, Spleenwort Family

The undivided fronds of hart's-tongue look more like a tropical than a temperate fern. In North America, this fern is rare, but it is widespread and common in Europe. The distinctive look is common in the tropics, where familiar species like the bird's nest fern thrive.

ASPLENIUM

Common Name:
Hart's-tongue fern

Bloom Time:
Foliage plant

Planting Requirements:
Sun or shade

The elongated, strap-shaped leaves of hart's-tongue fern (*Asplenium scolopendrium*) are decidedly different from most temperate ferns, which are usually lacy.

Asplenium scolopendrium (sko-lo-PEN-dree-um), hart's-tongue fern. Size: 1 to 2 feet tall and wide. Hart's-tongue is unique among hardy ferns because it has undivided, leathery, straplike evergreen fronds that arise like a vase from a thick rhizome. Linear fruit dots are borne in pairs along the veins of fertile fronds. 'Cristatum' is a variable selection with 6- to 12-inch fronds with crests and tassels. 'Kaye's Lacerate' is a 6-inch dwarf selection with jagged, crested fronds. 'Marginatum Irregulare' is an 8- to 12-inch selection with narrow wavy margins and occasional crested tips. 'Undulatum' has 12-inch ruffled fronds. USDA Plant Hardiness Zones 6 to 8.

How to Grow

The American hart's-tongue (var. *americanum*) is rare in the wild and difficult to grow. Plant European hart's-tongue (var. *scolopendrium*) in moist, neutral, or alkaline humus-rich soil in sun or shade. Plants often grow in wall crevices and among rocks. Add concrete rubble or oyster shells to sweeten acid soils. Slugs and snails may devour the fronds.

Landscape Uses

Use hart's-tongue as an accent among woodland plants or in stone walls and steps. They grow well in containers and troughs. Plants will self-sow under ideal conditions.

ASTER

A-ster • Asteraceae, Aster Family

Asters dominate autumn meadows and roadsides from coast to coast in a rainbow of rich colors. This large genus of showy, floriferous perennials produces mounds of flowers so familiar and characteristic in composition that similar flowers are often referred to as asterlike. They consist of overlapping rows of thin petal-like rays surrounding a round, yellow disk of many tightly packed, petal-less flowers. The rays come in a rainbow of colors including purple, lavender, rose, pink, red, and white. Plants vary in size from 1 to 8 feet tall. The stems may be densely clothed in clasping leaves or have sparsely arranged heart-shaped leaves on short stalks. Many species have basal leaf clusters in addition to the stem leaves. All species grow from creeping rhizomes with fibrous roots.

ASTER

Common Name:
  Aster

Bloom Time:
  Summer and fall bloom

Planting Requirements:
  Full sun to partial shade

Aster ×alpellus 'Triumph.' Size: 12 to 15 inches tall, 12 to 24 inches wide. A hybrid between *A. amellus* and *A. alpinus*. Violet-blue flowers with orange disks borne on dense, 1½-foot stalks. Zones 4 to 8.

A. alpinus (all-PEE-nus), alpine aster. Size: 6 to 12 inches tall, 12 to 18 inches wide. A low, mounding plant with many single-flowered stems. The early summer flowers are purple with yellow centers. The slender, oblong leaves are mostly basal. Stem leaves reduce in size toward the flower head. 'Albus' has pure white flowers. 'Dark Beauty' has deep blue-violet flowers. 'Happy End' is rose-pink. USDA Plant Hardiness Zones 3 to 7.

A. amellus (a-MEL-lus), Italian aster. Size: 2 to 2½ feet tall, 1 to 2 feet wide. Large-flowered plant with purple rays and a yellow center. Flowers appear in dense clusters atop leafy stems arising from clumps of rough, hairy foliage. 'Blue King' has 2-inch sky blue flowers atop 2-foot stems. 'Pink Zenith' has deep pink flowers on compact, 2-foot plants. 'Rudolph Goethe' has violet flowers on 2- to 3-foot stems. 'Veilchen-konigin' ('Violet Queen') has royal purple flowers on 1½-foot stems. Zones 5 to 8.

A. cordifolius (kord-i-FO-lee-us), heart-leaf aster. Size: 1 to 3 feet tall, 1 to 2 feet wide. This shade-tolerant woodland aster performs equally well in sun. Sprays of white to blue flowers top stems in early to late autumn. 'Little Carlow' has lavender-blue flowers on 2-foot stems. 'Photograph' is a 3-foot selection with near-purple flowers. Zones 4 to 8.

A. divaricatus (dee-var-i-CAT-us), white wood aster. Size: 1 to 1½ feet tall, 1 to 2 feet wide. A shade-tolerant aster with large clusters of starry white flowers on wiry stems.

'Eastern Star' has dense flower heads on jet black stems. 'Fiesta' has leaves variegated with white confetti. Zones 4 to 8.

A. ericoides (e-ri-KOI-deez), heath aster. Size: 1 to 3 feet tall and wide. A leafy, densely flowered aster with hundreds of white or pale blue flowers borne on stiff terminal and side branches. 'Blue Star' has sky blue flowers on 2- to 3-foot stems. 'Cinderella' has white flowers with reddish centers. 'Enchantress' and 'Esther' have pale pink flowers densely packed on 16-inch stems. 'Pink Star' is a rosy pink selection to 2 feet tall. 'Snowflurry' is a creeping selection only 2 to 4 inches tall smothered in small, white flowers. Zones 3 to 8.

A. ×frikartii (fri-KART-ee-ee), Frikart's aster. Size: 2 to 3 feet tall and wide. A

'Woods Pink' aster (*Aster novi-belgii* 'Woods Pink') is one of a series of compact, profusely blooming selections that provide an alternative to mums in the fall garden. Plants are mildew-resistant, and unlike many selections, they hold their lower leaves through the season.

group of hybrids between *A. amellus* and *A. thomsonii*, the fuzzy-leafed plants are of loose habit. The 2½-inch lavender-blue flowers are borne from midsummer through fall. 'Monch' has erect stems and deeper blue flowers than the similar 'Wunder von Stafa' ('Wonder of Stafa'). Zones 6 to 8; colder with snow protection.

A. laevis (LIE-vis), smooth aster. Size: 2 to 5 feet tall, 1 to 2 feet wide. A pale lavender-blue aster with attractive blue-green foliage. The basal leaves are narrowly heart-shaped. The stem leaves are greatly reduced. 'Bluebird' has lavender-blue flowers on 4-foot stems. 'Calliope' is taller with jet black stems to 6 feet. Zones 2 to 7.

A. lateriflorus (la-ter-i-FLOOR-us), calico aster. Size: 2 to 4 feet tall, 1 to 3 feet wide. A bushy aster with hundreds of small white flowers on branching, leafy stems. 'Horizontalis' is a compact grower to 2½ feet, with burgundy red foliage and white flowers with reddish disks. 'Prince' has darker purple foliage, and 'Lady in Black' is darker still on spreading clumps. Zones 4 to 8.

A. macrophyllus (mack-ro-FILE-lus), bigleaf aster. Size: 1 to 2½ feet tall and wide. A woodland aster with large, heart-shaped leaves and leafy stems bearing broad, flat clusters of white to pale blue flowers. 'Twilight' has deep blue flowers. Zones 3 to 7.

A. novae-angliae (NO-vie ANG-lee-ie), New England aster. Size: 3 to 6 feet tall. A tall, leafy-stemmed aster with clusters of showy 2-inch purple flowers with bright yellow centers. Many selections have been made for large flower size, flower color, and compact growth. 'Alma Potschke' has deep salmon-pink or cerise flowers on dense 3-foot plants. Blooms in late summer. 'Barr's Pink' has semidouble rose-pink flowers on 4-foot plants. 'Harrington's Pink' is an older cultivar with late-blooming, pale salmon-pink flowers on 3- to 5-foot stems. 'Hella Lacy' has royal purple flowers on dense 3- to 4-foot plants. 'Mt. Everest' has white flowers on 3-foot plants. 'Purple Dome' is a rounded, compact plant to 2 feet with late-season royal purple flowers. 'September Ruby' has deep ruby-red flowers on floppy 3- to 5-foot plants. 'Treasure' has lavender-blue flowers on 4-foot stems. Zones 3 to 8.

A. novi-belgii (NO-vee-BEL-gee-ee), New York aster, Michaelmas daisy. Size: 1 to 6 feet tall, 1 to 3 feet wide. A variable, fall-blooming species with smooth, lance-shaped leaves and 1- to 1½-inch-wide flowers with wide, densely packed, blue to white rays and yellow centers. This is an important species, long selected by British and, more recently, German nurseries for compact growth, rich flower color, and floriferous habit. Shorter selections are sometimes listed as *A. dumosus*. Scores of cultivars are listed by nurseries; a few of the best are included here. 'Ada Ballard' has double lavender-blue flowers on 3-foot stems. 'Alert' is a good compact red, only 12 to 15 inches high. 'Audrey' has lilac flowers on 1-foot plants. 'Bonningdale White' has semidouble white flowers on 4-foot plants. 'Eventide' has 2-inch, semidouble lavender-blue flowers on 3- to 4-foot stems. 'Heinz Richard' has pink flowers on 18-inch stems. 'Jenny' has red flowers on 1-foot stems. 'Lady in Blue' has lavender-blue flowers on compact, 16-inch stems. 'Marie Ballard' is an old cultivar with double, powder blue flowers on 4-foot stems. 'Professor Anton Kippenburg' is a tried-and-true selection, with semidouble lavender-blue flowers on compact, 1-foot plants. 'Royal Opal' has opalescent blue flowers on domed 10-inch plants. 'Woods Light Blue, Pink, and Purple' are mildew-resistant selections 12 to 18 inches tall. Zones 3 to 8.

A. oblongifolius (ob-long-i-FOL-ee-us), aromatic aster, shale aster. Size: 1 to 3 feet tall and wide. This late aster is tough as nails. Native to difficult sites, it thrives in the comfort of a sunny garden. Lax stems covered in elongated, fragrant foliage are smothered in mounds of lavender-blue flowers. 'Fanny' is a large selection to 3 feet. 'October Skies' is a superb selection with nearly true-blue flowers on compact stems to 18 inches. 'Raydon's Favorite' has deep lavender-blue flowers on lax stems. Zones 3 to 8.

A. spectabilis (spek-TAH-bi-lis), showy aster, seaside aster. Size: 1 to 2 feet tall and wide. A compact, leafy aster with 1-inch violet flowers in summer. Grows best in sandy, well-drained soil. Zones 4 to 8.

A. tataricus (ta-TAH-ri-cus), Tatarian aster. Size: 5 to 8 feet tall, 2 to 4 feet wide. A late-blooming aster with tall, leafy stems and rounded clusters of pale blue to lavender flowers. 'Jindai' is a compact selection to 4 feet. Zones 3 to 8.

A. thomsonii (tom-SON-ee-ee), Thomson's aster. Size: 1 to 3 feet tall, 1 to 2 feet wide. A long-blooming aster with lilac-blue flowers on bushy plants. 'Nanus' is compact, less than 2 feet tall. Zones 5 to 9.

A. tongolensis (ton-go-LEN-sis), East Indies aster. Size: 1 to 2 feet tall and wide. A handsome, clumping groundcover with leafless stems bearing a single pale violet to lavender flower with drooping rays and a bright orange center. Plants bloom in late spring and summer. 'Berggarten' has 2- to 3-inch violet-blue flowers. 'Napsburg' has blue flowers. 'Wartburg Star' is violet-blue. Zones 5 to 8.

A. umbellatus (um-bel-LAY-tus), flat-topped aster. Size: 3 to 6 feet tall, 1 to 3 feet wide. A tall, leafy aster with neat foliage and broad, flat clusters of small white flowers borne in mid- to late summer. Zones 3 to 8.

How to Grow

Asters are a diverse group of plants with varying cultural requirements. They can be divided into three broad groups. The first group contains plants of mountains and seasides that require average to rich soil with excellent drainage in full sun. Excess moisture or wet soil is sure death for these species. Most also prefer cool night temperatures. *A.* ×*alpellus, A. alpinus, A. amellus, A.* ×*frikartii, A. spectabilis,* and *A. tongolensis* belong in this group. These plants form clumps and spread by slow-creeping stems. Divide plants in spring or fall as necessary or for propagation. They may be short-lived in cultivation.

The second group contains meadow, prairie, marsh, and roadside species. They thrive in average to rich, evenly moist soil. Some are more tolerant of dry soil than others. *A. ericoides, A. laevis, A. lateriflorus, A. oblongifolius, A. tartaricus,* and *A. thomsonii* tolerate the widest range of conditions. *A. novae-angliae, A. novi-belgii,* and *A. umbellatus* require even moisture for best growth. Many of these plants spread rapidly and need frequent division to keep them attractive. Divide clumps in spring. Discard old, woody portions and replant clumps into amended soil. Propagate by stem cuttings taken in May and June.

The third group contains woodland species that tolerate deep shade but bloom best in light to partial shade. They prefer moist, humus-rich soil but tolerate dry soil. *A. cordifolius, A. divaricatus,* and *A. macrophyllus* are in this group. These plants spread to form attractive groundcovers. Divide overgrown clumps as needed.

All asters are easily grown from seed, but germination can be uneven. Sow ripe seed outdoors or indoors in flats. Place watered flats in the refrigerator for 4 to 6 weeks and then return them to a sunny position. Seedlings germinate and develop quickly. Many asters are susceptible to aster wilt, a fungus that attacks the roots. Good drainage is the best preventative. Treat badly infected clumps with an organic fungicide, or take cuttings and discard the old plants. Powdery mildew may be a problem on some species, especially New England and New York asters. Promote good air circulation and keep water off the leaves. Treat with an organic fungicide if the problem persists.

Landscape Uses

There is an aster for every garden situation. Use the low-growing species that prefer dry soil in rock gardens, dry-soil gardens, and containers. Plant the woodland species in combination with ferns and wildflowers. The foliage is good for covering the bare spots left by early wildflowers, such as spring beauty (*Claytonia virginica*) and trout lilies (*Erythronium*), and spring-flowering bulbs. Use them as groundcover around tree roots or under flowering shrubs. In a more formal setting, plant white woodland aster with hostas or heart-leaved bergenia (*Bergenia cordifolia*). Plants in the second group are the most versatile garden plants. These species are low, mounding plants for the front or middle of the border and tall plants for the background. Use them with a variety

The latest of the native asters to bloom is the tough and adaptable aromatic aster (*Aster oblongifolius* 'October Skies'). The flowers tolerate light frost and smother the clumps in October and November.

of perennials, fall bulbs, and ornamental grasses. Match the plants carefully to their soil moisture requirements for the most effective display. Stressed plants often lose their lower foliage or do not flower well.

ASTILBE

a-STIL-bee • Saxifragaceae, Saxifrage Family

Astilbes are aristocrats reserved for gardens with consistently moist soil. Their airy plumes of densely packed, tiny flowers are showstoppers in the summer garden. Flower clusters vary in size from 6 inches to 2 feet. Some are stiff and upright; others are open and plumelike. Still others cascade outward like fireworks. Flower color varies from red through all shades of magenta, rose, and pink to lavender, lilac, cream, and white. The foliage is twice to thrice divided, with many small, toothed leaflets. Some

ASTILBE

Common Name:
False spirea

Bloom Time:
Late spring and summer bloom

Planting Requirements:
Full sun to full shade

leaves are hairy while others are glossy. Some, especially the red-flowered selections, have leaves and stems tinged with bronze or red. The smallest species are less than 1 foot tall, while the tallest may top 5 feet. All grow from thick, often woody rootstocks to form clumps or slow-spreading patches.

Astilbe ×*arendsii* (ah-RENDZ-ee-ee), astilbe. Size: 2 to 4 feet tall and wide. This hybrid species was created by famed German nurseryman George Arends by crossing *A. chinensis* var. *davidii* with *A. astilboides*, *A. japonica*, and *A. thunbergii*. These and other crosses have been repeated by other hybridizers and many selections exist. Some of the best are listed here. Plants are grouped by flowering time.

Early (May in the South to June in the North)

'Amethyst' has lilac-purple flowers on 1½- to 2-foot stems. 'Bridal Veil' has nodding, snow white flowers on 2-foot plants. 'Fanal' has deep cherry red flowers and red foliage on 2-foot plants. 'Gloria' has dark pink flowers on 2½-foot stems. 'Spinel' is a bushy species with carmine red flowers on 2½-foot stems. USDA Plant Hardiness Zones 3 to 8.

Midseason (June in the South to July or early August in the North)

'Anita Pfeifer' has salmon-pink flowers on 2- to 2½-foot stems. 'Avalanche' has white flowers on 2½- to 3-foot stems. 'Cattleya' is lilac-pink and reaches 3 feet in height. 'Ellie' has huge plumes of pristine white flowers. 'Hyazinth' has lilac-rose flowers on 2-foot stems. 'Irrlicht' is white-tinged pink on 2-foot stems. 'Radius' has glowing red flowers on 2-foot stalks above deep red spring foliage. Zones 3 to 8.

Late Season (July in the South to August in the North)

'Feur' has fire red flowers on 2½-foot stems. 'Flamingo' is shocking pink. 'Glut' has light red flowers on 1½-foot stems. Zones 3 to 8.

A. biternata (bi-ter-NAY-ta), false goat's beard. Size: 3 to 5 feet tall, 2 to 3 feet wide. An American woodland plant with glossy leaves and off-white flowers in open clusters held well above the foliage. Zones 3 to 8.

A. chinensis (chin-EN-sis), Chinese astilbe. Size: 1 to 3 feet tall, 1 to 2 feet wide. A floriferous creeping plant with bright green leaves and abundant rose-pink flowers in late summer and early fall. Var. *pumila* is a low groundcover plant with vibrant rose-pink flowers on 8- to 24-inch stems. Several cultivars of this variety have been reclassified from *A. ×arendsii*. 'Finale' has pale rose-pink flowers on 1- to 1½-foot stalks. 'Intermezzo' is salmon-pink and less than 1 foot tall. 'Serenade' is rose-red and 1 foot tall. Var. *taquetii* is similar to the species but is quite tall, to 4 feet, and more tolerant of dry conditions. The inflorescence is upright and tightly packed. The cultivar 'Intermezzo' has narrow plumes of salmon-pink flowers. 'Purpurkerze' ('Purple

Candle') has red-violet flowers. 'Superba' is a tall, slender midseason bloomer with lavender-pink flowers. 'Veronica Klose' bears 16-inch rose-purple spikes. The Visions Series offers flowers in various shades of rose and pink. Zones 3 to 8.

A. japonica (ja-PON-i-ka), Japanese astilbe. Size: 1 to 2 feet tall, 2 to 2½ feet wide. An early bloomer with dense, pyramidal flower clusters and glossy leaves often tinged with red. Hybrid cultivars include 'Deutschland', with spikes of white flowers on 1½-foot stems. 'Europa' has light pink flowers on stems 2½ feet tall. 'Koblenz' has carmine red flowers on 2-foot stems. 'Red Sentinal' has bright red flowers on 2-foot stems. Zones 4 to 8.

A. rivularis (riv-u-LAH-ris), tall astilbe. Size: 2 to 5 feet tall, 2 to 4 feet wide. A showy plant of monstrous proportions when grown in rich soil, with large clusters of creamy white flowers over deep green, quilted leaves of exceptional merit. Zones 4 to 8.

A. ×rosea (ROS-ee-a), astilbe. Size: 2 to 3 feet tall, 1 to 2 feet wide. Hybrids between *A. chinensis* and *A. japonica* with rose-pink flowers in midsummer. 'Peach Blossom' has salmon-pink flowers in large clusters. 'Queen Alexandra' is deep salmon-pink. Zones 4 to 8.

A. simplicifolia (sim-pli-ki-FO-lee-a), astilbe. Size: 8 to 12 inches tall, 12 to 24 inches wide. The glossy leaves of this dwarf species are lobed but not divided. The flowers are borne in open, often nodding clusters. Hybrids include 'Aphrodite', which has bronze foliage and rosy red

The erect pink spires of Chinese astilbe (*Astilbe chinensis*) open later than other species, extending the season into late summer. Plants tolerate drier soils than the familiar Arends hybrids, but they still require even moisture.

flowers on 18-inch stalks. 'Bronze Elegans' and 'Rosea' have pink flowers. 'Hennie Graafland' and 'Jacqueline' have the attractive combination of pink plumes over bronze foliage. 'Sprite' has pale creamy pink flowers. Zones 5 to 8 for the species; most hybrids to Zone 4.

A. thunbergii (thun-BERG-ee-ee), Thunberg's astilbe. Size: 2 to 3 feet tall, 2 to 3 feet wide. A showy plant with open, nodding flower clusters on tall stems above hairy foliage. Plants bloom in July and August. 'Straussenfeder' ('Ostrich Plume') has coral-pink flowers. 'Professor van der Wielen' is creamy white. Zones 4 to 8.

How to Grow

Astilbes are long-lived, easy-care perennials. They have one overriding requirement: moisture. Do not attempt to grow them unless you have an ample supply in summer. Plant them in consistently moist, slightly acid, humus-rich soil in light shade to filtered sun. Dry soil is sure death to astilbes, especially when they are in sunny situations. Wet or soggy soil can also be detrimental, causing rot. Astilbes are tolerant of a wide range of light levels. In northern gardens, full sun in tandem with moist soil is acceptable. Provide shade from hot afternoon sun to prolong the attractive foliage display after flowering. In warmer regions, light to partial shade is mandatory. Plants will grow in deep shade but won't produce flowers as prolifically. Astilbes spread steadily from thick woody crowns to form broad clumps. Crowns often rise above the surrounding soil as they grow. Top-dress with rich humusy soil or lift and replant the clumps. Divide them every 3 or 4 years in spring or fall. Replant into well-

prepared soil. They benefit from a balanced organic fertilizer applied annually in spring. Removal of the flower heads does not promote continued flowering. The seedheads are attractive in their own right. Leave them standing for late-season interest. Propagation of cultivars must be by division as seeds do not come true to their parents. Seeds of true species are short-lived and difficult to germinate. Sow them

Arends hybrid astilbes (*Astilbe ×arendsii*) come in a wide range of colors. They thrive in wet to moist, humus-rich soil and open their showy plumes in early summer. Flower clusters vary in shape from conical and wandlike to full-bodied plumes.

immediately when ripe. Give them a warm (70°F) moist treatment for 2 weeks, followed by a cool (40°F) moist treatment for 4 weeks.

Landscape Uses

The regal astilbes have a place in every garden where their moisture requirements can be satisfied. Plant them along a stream or at the edge of a pond where their graceful plumes are reflected in the water. Combine them with ferns, irises, hostas, and other moisture-loving plants.

They are suitable to borders where moist soil is assured. Create attractive combinations with lady's-mantle (*Alchemilla mollis*), lungworts (*Pulmonaria*), and Siberian iris (*Iris siberica*). In warmer areas, their crisping foliage can be a liability. Dwarf astilbes are suitable for edging along walks or under planting shrubs. Chinese astilbes tolerate dryer soils. Plant the dwarf varieties in rock gardens or as groundcover around the roots of trees. Mix taller varieties with Solomon's seals (*Polygonatum*) and ferns in partial shade.

ASTRANTIA

a-STRAN-tee-ah • Apiaceae, Parsley Family

Masterwort is a curious name, bestowed on this attractive and serviceable plant in the Middle Ages. Though the common name conjures up images of bane rather than beauty, this underused perennial is spectacular in bloom. The inflorescence consists of a starry collar of pointed bracts surrounding a button-shaped umbel of small white or pink flowers. The showy bracts vary in color from green and white to deep rose. Multiple heads are carried in branched clusters. The palmately lobed foliage is mostly basal, and the rosettes are attractive in early spring when they emerge, and after the flowers fade.

ASTRANTIA

Common Name:
  Masterwort

Bloom Time:
  Early summer bloom

Planting Requirements:
  Full sun to partial shade

Astrantia major (MAY-jor), masterwort. Size: 2 to 3 feet tall and 1 to 2 feet wide. Like bold Elizabethan buttons, intricately appointed and fit for a queen, the showy heads of this species are eye-catching in the early-summer garden. 'Hadspen Blood' has the darkest red flowers. 'Lars' is one of the darkest pinks, but it never

The rich ruby red pincushions of 'Hadspen Blood' masterwort (*Astrantia major* 'Hadspen Blood') make a dramatic show at the edge of a stream or in any humus-rich soil that stays consistently moist in summer. The inflorescence consists of a starry collar of pointed bracts surrounding a button-shaped umbel of small flowers.

reaches the red described in catalogs. 'Rose Symphony' has rosy pink heads. 'Shaggy' is gorgeous, with huge green-tipped white bracts. 'Sunningdale Variegated' starts the season with creamy yellow variegation, but turns green by summer. USDA Plant Hardiness Zones 3 to 8.

A. maxima (MAX-e-ma), large masterwort. Size: 1 to 2 feet tall and wide. The broad flower heads of this species have a wide collar of sharp pink teeth. The foliage is simpler, with three broad, toothed lobes. Zones 4 to 8.

How to Grow

Masterworts demand very rich soil that stays consistently moist throughout the growing season. Though plants flower best with some sun, protection from hot afternoon sun is advisable. Plants will languish under less than optimum conditions, and the foliage will brown and shrivel if the soil dries out. Hot summer nights are sure death to this northern European native, so it is not recommended for the Southeast. After flowering, cut the spent flowerstalks to the ground. The foliage stays attractive all season, and if the weather is cool, plants may flower again.

Landscape Uses

Masterworts look their ravishing best when accented with bold foliage that sets off the flower color. Place the rose-flowered selections with purple-leaved bigleaf ligularia (*Ligularia dentata* 'Othello'), bloody dock (*Rumex sanguineus* 'Sanguineus'), fringed loosestrife (*Lysimachia ciliata* 'Purpurea'), and purple wood spurge (*Euphorbia amygdaloides* 'Purpurea'). Pair the white-flowered selections with white or blue Siberian iris (*Iris siberica*) and white-edged hostas. Ferns are lovely with any color.

ATHYRIUM

a-THEE-re-um • Dryopteridaceae, Shield Fern Family

The lacy, intricately cut fronds of lady ferns set the standard for fernyness. This familiar plant is found in woodlands and swamps throughout the northern hemisphere. Deciduous fronds emerge early and add elegance to the spring and summer garden. Lady ferns send up their clustered, fertile fronds in early summer along their fast-creeping rhizomes.

ATHYRIUM

Common Name:
Lady fern

Bloom Time:
Foliage plant

Planting Requirements:
Light to full shade

Athyrium filix-femina (FIL-ix FAY-mi-na), lady fern. Size: 1 to 3 feet tall and wide. Billowing clusters of lacy fronds arise from the creeping rhizome. Many regional varieties exist in North America and Eurasia. The western American variety may grow to 4 feet. 'Axminster' has deeply dissected fronds that resemble soft shield fern. 'Fancy Frond's Strain' is a dwarf selection with congested, fringed pinnae and an apical crest. 'Frizelliae' has linear fronds with small, round pinnae. 'Victoriae' is a beautiful selection with tall, narrow fronds of paired pinnae that form crosses. USDA Plant Hardiness Zones 3 to 8.

A. niponicum (ni-PON-e-kum), Japanese lady fern. Size: 1 to 2½ feet tall and wide. This fern resembles lady fern and is most often grown as one of the showy silvery gray forms. Plants need sun for best color. 'Branford Beauty' and 'Ghost' are hybrids with pale silver-green fronds. 'Pictum' (Japanese painted fern) has silvery fronds. 'Silver Falls' has uniform pale silver fronds. 'Ursula's Red' has silver fronds with red staining along the veins. Zones 4 to 8.

A. otophorum (o-to-FOR-um), eared lady fern. Size: 1 to 2 feet tall and wide. This attractive fern is new to cultivation. Leathery, triangular fronds emerge chartreuse and mature to deep blue-green with red veins. Zones 4 to 8.

Silver foliage is common in plants adapted to dry soils and sunny sites. The beautiful variegated fronds of Japanese painted fern (*Athyrium niponicum* 'Pictum') bring this luminescent color to shaded spots with moist soil.

Deparia acrostichoides (de-PAR-e-a a-krow-st-KOY-deez) (formerly classified as *A. thelypteroides*), silvery glade fern, silvery spleenwort. Size: 2 to 3 feet tall and wide. This attractive fern is often overlooked because it resembles other common ferns. Plants form robust, leafy deciduous clumps that remain attractive all season. Fronds turn straw-colored in fall. Zones 4 to 8.

Diplazium pycnocarpon (di-PLAZE-e-um pick-no-KAR-pon) (formerly listed under *Athyrium*), glade fern, narrow-leaf spleenwort. Size: 2 to 3 feet tall and wide. Glade fern is an architectural gem. Deep green, arching, deciduous fronds have undivided lance-shaped pinnae that resemble sword ferns. The fronds are clustered along the creeping rhizome. Zones 4 to 8.

How to Grow

Plant lady ferns in moist to wet, neutral to acid, humus-rich soil in partial to full shade. Ferns in constantly moist soil tolerate sun. Fronds turn brown quickly if soil gets too dry. All *Athyrium* spread rapidly. Divide overgrown clumps in spring or fall to control their spread.

Landscape Uses

Lady ferns form dense leafy clumps that combine well with bold perennials such as hostas and ligularias, and vertical plants such as irises and cohoshes (*Cimicifuga*). Plant them in drifts or as a groundcover in moist sites. Clumps spread rapidly and may overrun delicate plants. Use glade ferns in drifts with wildflowers and bold-leaved plants such as hostas. They combine well with the strap-like leaves of Siberian iris and the spiky inflorescences of foxgloves and astilbes. The russet autumn fronds are a nice accent with evergreens.

AUBRIETA

o-bree-AY-ta • Brassicaceae, Mustard Family

Rock cresses are floriferous, low, mat- or cushion-forming plants that spread by thin rhizomes. The evergreen leaves are covered with fine hairs and have coarse teeth along the edges of the central part of the leaf. In spring, the cushions are buried in mounds of four-petaled white, rose, or purple flowers from ¾ to 1 inch across.

AUBRIETA

Common Name:
Rock cress

Bloom Time:
Spring bloom

Planting Requirements:
Sun to light shade

Aubrieta deltoidea (del-TOI-dee-a), rock cress. Size: 6 to 8 inches tall, 12 to 18 inches wide. This species and its hybrids make up the bulk of commonly available rock cresses. Many garden cultivars are available in the trade. Some authorities ascribe them to the hybrid species *Aubrieta ×hybridum*. 'Argenteovariegata' has white-edged leaves and blue flowers. 'Borsch's White' has white flowers. 'Dr. Mules' is a free-flowering purple form. 'Noralis Blue' has 1-inch, nearly true-blue flowers. 'Royal Blue' has deep blue flowers. 'Royal Red' has magenta flowers. 'Whitewell Gem' has rich violet-blue flowers. USDA Plant Hardiness Zones 3 to 8.

The rosy purple flowers of rock cress (*Aubrieta deltoidea*) smother the foliage in early spring. After flowering, plants are dull, so choose some attractive, late-blooming companions to carry the show.

How to Grow

Plant rock cresses in average, well-drained soil in full sun or light shade. In acid soil areas, add lime to bring the pH close to neutral. Plants thrive in the limey soils of the Midwest. They revel in areas with warm sunshine, cool nights, and low humidity. Give plants a hard shearing after flowering to encourage rebloom. In midsummer cut plants back again to promote compact growth, especially in areas with warm, humid nights. Divide plants in fall to rejuvenate clumps. Propagate by cuttings taken after flowering. Transplant in fall with a ball of soil.

Landscape Uses

Rock cresses are free-flowering spring perennials for rock and wall gardens. They are natural companions for rocks because of their need for well-drained soil. Plant them in the crevices of unmortared walls or between pavers at the edge of walks. Combine them with species bulbs such as tulips, crocuses, daffodils, and snowdrops. In the front of the border blend them with cranesbills (*Geranium*), hellebores (*Helleborus*), crested iris (*Iris cristata*), and basket-of-gold (*Aurinia saxatilis*).

AURINIA

ow-RIN-ee-a • Brassicaceae, Mustard Family

Golden waves wash over rock walls, cascade down slopes, and lap along pathways, drawing you through the spring garden. The frothy flowers open early and continue blooming for a month. Out of bloom, the silvery leaves complement summer flowers. Plants grow from fibrous-rooted crowns.

AURINIA

Common Name:
 Basket-of-gold

Bloom Time:
 Spring bloom

Planting Requirements:
 Full sun

For bright spring color that captures the glow of the sun, you can't beat basket-of-gold (*Aurinia saxatilis*). Plant it among rocks or at the base of a wall to soften the hard lines.

Aurinia saxatilis (saks-AH-ti-lis), also sold as *Alyssum saxatile,* basket-of-gold. Size: 10 to 12 inches tall, 12 to 24 inches wide. The glowing yellow four-petaled flowers of basket-of-gold light up the early spring border. The individual flowers are small, but they are borne in dense, branching clusters above rosettes of fuzzy, oblong gray-green foliage. The leaves grow from a somewhat woody basal stem that branches frequently to form broad, tufted clumps. 'Citrinum' has pale, lemon yellow flowers. 'Compactum' is more compact and rounded than the species. 'Dudley Neville Variegated' has variegated foliage. 'Plena' has fully double flowers. 'Sunny Border Apricot' has apricot flowers. 'Tom Thumb' is a true dwarf, only 3 to 6 inches tall. USDA Plant Hardiness Zones 3 to 7.

How to Grow

Basket-of-gold demands a well-drained position with average soil in full sun. In rich and overly moist soils, the clumps flop and may rot. High temperatures and excessive humidity have a similar effect. Cut the flowering stems back by two-thirds after flowering to encourage compact growth. Treat plants as annuals or biennials in hot areas. Plant them in fall and remove them after flowering the next spring when they begin to look shabby. Propagate by dividing clumps in fall or by cuttings taken in spring or fall.

Landscape Uses

Basket-of-gold is an invaluable addition to the spring garden. The cheerful yellow flowers are perfect for rock and wall gardens. Plant generous drifts at the edge of ledges or in crevices between rocks where they can tumble exuberantly over the edge to soften harsh lines. Position them along steps or walks, or at the front of borders with spring bulbs, perennial candytuft (*Iberis sempervirens*), and stonecrops (*Sedum*).

BAPTISIA

bap-TIS-ee-a • Fabaceae, Pea Family

False indigos are handsome perennials with colorful spikes of pea-like flowers in blue, yellow, cream and white. The flowers look like those of lupines, but the habit is quite different, as the plants attain shrublike proportions. They branch profusely to form rounded mounds. The 1- to 3-inch leaves have three rounded leaflets, usually gray-green or bluish in color. The gray or brown seedheads are like thickened pea pods. They persist throughout the fall and are quite showy. They are attractive when dried. Cut pods after they color and hang them upside down until they dry.

BAPTISIA

Common Names:
 False indigo, wild indigo

Bloom Time:
 Late spring and early summer bloom

Planting Requirements:
 Full sun or light shade

Baptisia alba (AL-ba), white wild indigo. Size: 2 to 5 feet tall, 2 to 3 feet wide. The white indigos are spectacular plants with erect spikes of white flowers held well above the foliage. Botanists have placed all the white-flowered species here, so size and bloom time is quite variable. Var. *alba* (*B. pendula*), nodding wild indigo. Size: 3 to 4 feet tall, 2 to 3 feet wide. A showy species with erect flower spikes and nodding seedpods. USDA Plant Hardiness Zones 5 to 8. Var. *macrophylla* (*B. leucantha*), prairie wild indigo. Size: 3 to 5 feet tall, 2 to 3 feet wide. A tall plant with erect, pointed spikes of white flowers held well above the horizontal clump of foliage. Zones 4 to 9.

B. australis (ow-STRAH-lis), blue false indigo. Size: 2 to 4 feet tall and wide. One of the most popular species, the indigo-blue flowers are carried on open spikes up to a foot long, held just above the soft blue-green foliage. Each clump produces many stems from a tough, gnarled, deep taproot. Var. *minor* is a compact plant to 2 feet tall and wide with small leaves and dense royal blue flower spikes followed by oversized inflated pods for winter interest. 'Purple Smoke' is a stunning hybrid with *B. alba*, producing milky purple flowers on tall spikes with black stems. Zones 3 to 9.

B. bracteata (brac-tee-AY-ta) (*leucophaea*), plains wild indigo, buffalo-pea. Size: 1 to 2 feet tall, 2 to 3 feet wide. A low, compact, spreading plant with tightly packed, drooping clusters of creamy yellow flowers and fuzzy, gray-green leaves. Blooms in early spring before other species. Zones 3 to 9.

B. perfoliata (per-FO-lee-a-ta), Georgia wild indigo. Size: 1 to 2 feet tall. A unique baptisia with disklike leaves pierced in the center by the stem. The plant resembles a sprawling eucalyptus and is grown more for its foliage than its flowers. A single yellow flower is produced in early summer above each point where the stem emerges from the leaf (node). Zones 7 to 9; trial in northern zones.

B. sphaerocarpa (spheer-o-CAR-pa) (*viridis*), yellow wild indigo. Size: 1 to 3 feet tall and wide. The intense yellow flowers of this rounded species are carried in short clusters above the leaves. The spherical seedheads make an autumn show. 'Screamin' Yeller' has glowing canary yellow flowers. 'Carolina Moonlight' is a fabulous hybrid with *B. alba,* producing tall spikes of lemon-chiffon–colored flowers. Zones 5 to 9.

B. tinctoria (tink-TORE-ee-a), wild indigo, horsefly weed. Size: 1 to 3 feet tall and wide. A charming species overshadowed by its more flamboyant cousins, this species has small clusters of yellow flowers that spangle the rounded clumps in midsummer. This plant, used as a source of dye, bestows the name of wild indigo to the genus. Zones 5 to 9.

How to Grow

Wild indigos are tough, long-lived, low-maintenance perennials. Plant them in average to rich, moist but well-drained soil in full sun or light shade. All species are drought-tolerant once established. Plants will bloom well in light shade, but they may need staking. Place rounded peony hoops over clumps as they emerge in early spring. Wild indigos grow slowly at first but eventually spread to form huge clumps. The tough taproots are massive on established plants. Start with young plants for best results. Space individual plants at least 3 feet apart. Leave them in place once they are established unless they overgrow their position. Divide in fall if necessary. You will need a sharp knife or shears to cut through the tough clumps. Leave at least one bud, or "eye," per division. Propagation is best accomplished by seed. The seeds have an extremely hard seed coat. Soak them overnight in hot water. Germi-

Tough, drought-tolerant yellow wild indigo (*Baptisia sphaerocarpa*) does triple duty in the garden. In early summer it produces spikes of screaming yellow flowers. In summer, the rounded, shrublike mound of three-parted leaves gives structure to the garden; the spherical gray-black seedpods are interesting in winter.

nation will occur over a 2- to 4-week period. Keep seedlings on the dry side to prevent damping-off, a disease caused by fungi that attacks seedlings at the soil line, causing them to topple over.

Landscape Uses

Wild indigos are prepossessing border plants. Use them toward the middle or back of the border in the company of bold flowers such as irises, peonies, oriental poppies (*Papaver orientale*), border phlox (*Phlox maculata*), sages (*Salvia*), sunflowers (*Helianthus*), and asters. Plant airy plants such as columbines (*Aquilegia*), bleeding hearts (*Dicentra*), and cranesbills (*Geranium*) around the bases of the clumps to hide the ugly "ankles" of the tall stalks. After flowering, the shrubby plants make an excellent background for late-blooming perennials. Contrast the blue-green foliage with fine-textured ornamental grasses. The showy seedpods add interest in the late-summer and fall garden. Add a splash of color to meadow and prairie plantings with clumps and sweeps of these beautiful perennials.

BEGONIA

bay-GON-ee-a • Begoniaceae, Begonia Family

Begonias are beloved the world over for their spectacular, colorful foliage; cheerful flowers; and easy cultivation. Most species are bedded as annuals or grown indoors, but a few species, including some new introductions from China, are expanding the perennial choices for garden use. They thrive in shaded spots and form broad, dramatic clumps that add an exotic flair to humdrum groundcover plantings.

BEGONIA

Common Name:
Begonia

Bloom Time:
Late summer and fall bloom

Planting Requirements:
Partial to full shade

Begonia grandis (GRAN-dis), hardy begonia. Size: 1 to 2 feet tall, 2 to 3 feet wide. Hardy begonia grows from succulent, jointed stems with large, angel-wing leaves. Open clusters of four-petaled pink flowers are borne in the axils of the upper leaves. After the flowers fade, the three-lobed seedpods retain their pink color, extending the display until frost. The plants grow from a small, shallow tuber. 'Alba' has white flowers. 'Heron's Pirouette' is noted for its deep rose pink flowers in huge, 12-inch clusters. 'Wildwood Premier' has light pink flowers and deep green leaves with red veins and a dark red reverse. USDA Plant Hardiness Zones 5 (with protection) or 6 to 10.

B. pedatifida (pe-dah-TIF-e-dah), hardy begonia. Size: 1 foot tall and wide. The dramatic, deeply lobed leaves resemble hands with the fingers spread wide. Plants form dense clumps accented by slender spikes of pink flowers in late summer. Zones 7 to 10; trial in colder zones.

B. sinensis (sih-NEN-sis), Chinese begonia. Size: 6 to 12 inches tall and wide. A diminutive version of hardy begonia, with pale pink flowers in summer. Plants spread rapidly and may need occasional weeding out. They go dormant in late summer. 'Wolong Rose' has deep rose flowers borne well into autumn. Zones 5 to 9.

B. sutherlandii (suth-er-LAND-ee-ee), Sutherland's begonia. Size: 8 to 12 inches tall, 12 to 18 inches wide. Dreamsicle orange flowers drip from the tips of the succulent, spreading stems of this species. The leaves resemble small angel wings. Zones 8 to 10; colder with protection.

How to Grow

Plant hardy begonias in evenly moist, humus-rich soil in light to partial shade. In cooler climates, plants tolerate considerable sun. *B. grandis* tolerates full shade. Plants will spread to form open masses that never seem crowded—and seldom need division. Propagate by division or by the bulbils found in the leaf axils of *B. grandis* and *B. sinensis*.

Landscape Uses

Hardy begonias are excellent for underplanting flowering shrubs. Use them in the shaded border or as a foundation plant. Their coarse, open texture combines well with ferns, Japanese anemones (*Anemone ×hybrida*), and hostas. Scatter clumps among low groundcovers to add late season interest. The nodding flower clusters are attractive when reflected in the water of a shaded pool. Sutherland's begonia is more delicate and resents crowding.

If you crave an exotic touch, you will love hardy begonia (*Begonia grandis*). This easy-care plant thrives in any moist, shaded spot and rewards the gardener with lush, tropical-looking foliage and open sprays of pink flowers.

BELAMCANDA

bel-am-KAN-da • Iridaceae, Iris Family

Blackberry lilies are grown for their flowers and their showy seedpods. Blossoms in shades of orange and yellow open throughout summer in branching clusters. Each flower has three petals and three petal-like sepals. They are often speckled with deeper shades of the same petal color. The inflated seed capsules split to reveal rows of jet black seeds, for which the plant is named. Like most plants in the iris family, blackberry lilies have fans of lance-shaped leaves that grow from a creeping rhizome.

BELAMCANDA

Common Name:
Blackberry lily

Bloom Time:
Summer bloom

Planting Requirements:
Full sun to light shade

Belamcanda chinensis (CHIN-en-sis), blackberry lily. Size: 2 to 4 feet tall, 1 to 2 feet wide. Plants have bright orange flowers with darker speckles. 'Freckle Face' has yellow flowers with brown speckles. USDA Plant Hardiness Zones 4 to 10. The closely related *Pardanthopsis dichotoma* has been crossed with *B. chinensis* to produce the hybrid genus ×*Pardancanda norrisii*. It is similar in form to blackberry lily but flowers in an array of colors including reds, pinks, purples, and stunning bicolors. Hardiness north of Zone 5 is not established.

B. flabellata (fla-bel-LA-ta), blackberry lily. Size: 1 to 2 feet tall and wide. This species is similar to *B. chinensis* but is shorter with yellow flowers spotted with orange. 'Hello Yellow' has unspotted flowers. Zones 4 to 10.

Tough and beautiful, the speckled orange blackberry lily (*Belamcanda chinensis*) flowers are attractive in their own right, but the clustered black berries that pop out of papery capsules are the real charm of this easy-care perennial.

How to Grow

Blackberry lilies are easy-care perennials. They are often found persisting in abandoned gardens or growing along roadsides. Plant them in average to rich, well-drained soil in full sun. In hot regions, shading from afternoon sun prolongs bloom. Divide overgrown clumps in late summer or spring as necessary. Self-sown seedlings will appear regularly. Sow fresh seed outdoors. Germination will occur in 3 to 4 weeks.

Landscape Uses

The small flowers of blackberry lily show up best when planted against fine-textured plants such as yarrows (*Achillea*), baby's-breath (*Gypsophila paniculata*), and asters (*Aster*), or in contrast to larger flowers such as balloon flower (*Platycodon grandiflorus*) and daylilies (*Hemerocallis*). They will bloom for 4 to 6 weeks. The showy capsules hold up well indoors when cut as they split open.

BERGENIA

ber-GEEN-ee-a • Saxifragaceae, Saxifrage Family

Bergenias are handsome, clump-forming or groundcover foliage perennials with bold, leathery, usually evergreen leaves that turn red or bronze in winter. Dense clusters of fleshy rose, pink, or white flowers rise from the center of the foliage rosette in late winter or early spring. They grow from thick, creeping rootstocks that branch frequently.

BERGENIA

Common Names:
Bergenia, winter begonia

Bloom Time:
Foliage plant with early spring bloom

Planting Requirements:
Full sun to partial shade

Bergenia ciliata (kil-e-A-ta), winter begonia, fringed bergenia. Size: 1½ to 2 feet tall, 2 to 3 feet wide. A robust perennial with hairy oval or rounded leaves that, unlike other species, die back in fall. The white or clear pink flowers are borne in early spring. USDA Plant Hardiness Zones 5 to 9.

B. cordifolia (kor-di-FO-lee-a), heart-leaved bergenia. Size: 12 to 14 inches tall, 12 to 24 inches wide. The bold, rounded, or heart-shaped foliage is borne in dense rosettes that turn bronze or purple with the onset of cold weather. The rose or pink flowers are usually produced in spring, but occasional flower spikes may develop at any

The bold oval leaves of bergenia (*Bergenia purpurascens*) turn rich burgundy-red in fall. Clusters of deep magenta flowers rise on fleshy stalks in early spring.

glossy green leaves set off the 1-foot spikes of white to pale pink flowers borne in early spring. Plants are heat-tolerant and good for the South. 'Appleblossom' is one of the best hybrids, hardier than the species with excellent foliage and red-flowering stems topped with pale pink flowers. 'Britten' has white flowers that fade to rich pink. Zones 5 to 8.

B. purpurascens (pur-pur-AS-sens), bergenia. Size: 12 to 15 inches tall, 12 to 24 inches wide. Despite many new hybrids, this species is still one of the best bergenias. Elliptic to oval leaves are blushed on the underside with deep red. The purple or magenta flowers are produced on stout stalks in spring. Zones 4 to 9.

B. stracheyi (STRAY-kee-ee). Size: 6 to 10 inches tall, 12 inches wide. This diminutive species is a charmer, with elongated leaves and short clusters of deep pink flowers. 'Alba' has white flowers. Zones 4 to 8.

Hybrids

'Abendglut' ('Evening Glow') has broad oval leaves that turn bronze in fall. The flowers are dark red. 'Bressingham Bountiful' is a compact hybrid with rose-pink flowers. 'Bressingham White' has clean white flowers. 'Morgenrote' ('Morning Red') has smaller round leaves and produces carmine-red flowers throughout the growing season. 'Rosi Klose' is a fabulous new selection with good foliage tinted deep bronze-red in winter and medium pink flowers in dense clusters. 'Silberlicht'

time throughout the growing season. 'Perfecta' has exceptional form and deep rose-red flowers. 'Purpurea' has large round foliage and magenta flowers. 'Rotblum' ('Redbloom') is red-flowered. Zones 3 to 9.

B. crassifolia (crass-e-FOL-ee-a), leather bergenia. Size 1 to 1½ feet tall, 2 feet wide. A new introduction with exceptional foliage and dark rose-red flowers. 'Autumn Red' and 'Red Star' are two dark-flowered selections. Zones 4 to 8.

B. emeiensis (ee-my-e-EN-sis), Chinese bergenia. Size: 1 foot tall, 1 to 2 feet wide. Heartbeats accelerated when this new species was introduced from China. Broad,

('Silver Light') is a strong grower whose white flowers blush to pink. 'Sonningdale' has bright rose-red leaves in winter and exceptional cold tolerance.

How to Grow

Plant bergenias in moist, humus-rich soil with sun or light shade. They are widely adaptable and are tolerant of limey soils and droughty conditions. Grow them in full sun in the North, but in warm southern gardens, protect them from hot afternoon sun to avoid leaf scald. The cabbage-like clumps are very tough, but in cold areas without consistent snow cover, the leaves may brown and the growing point may be damaged. Mulch with coarse leaves or marsh hay for winter protection. Remove mulch when temperatures moderate to allow early flowerstalks to emerge unhampered. In summer, slugs may be a problem. Exclude them from contact with plants by using a barrier of dry sand or ash. If this is not feasible, use beer traps or hand-pick them. Divide plants when they become open in the center. Lift clumps in spring and sever the thick stems with a sharp knife. Replant divisions at a depth sufficient to support the large rosettes. Sow ripe seed immediately and leave it uncovered. Seedlings develop quickly when kept at 68° to 70°F. Reduce temperature slightly after germination. Transplant to the garden after 2 or 3 years.

Landscape Uses

Bergenias were made for drama. Place them at the front of the border, or use them as an accent along a walk, spilling over a wall, or in a rockery. Underplant shrubs with a glossy, deep green groundcover planting. Bergenias even perform well in containers.

BLETILLA

bleh-TIL-la • Orchidaceae, Orchid Family

Orchids as easy to grow as hostas may seem too good to be true, but here they are! Chinese ground orchids are elegant in foliage and flower. Two to six long, pleated, palm-like leaves look good all season. In late spring, the delicate magenta flowers, each like a miniature corsage orchid, open in loose clusters atop wiry stems. Plants grow from bulblike tubers with fleshy roots.

BLETILLA

Common Name:
  Chinese ground orchid

Bloom Time:
  Late spring bloom

Planting Requirements:
  Light to partial shade

Bletilla formosana (for-mo-SAY-na), Formosan ground orchid. Size: 1 to 2 feet tall and wide. A lovely, delicate species with shell pink flowers accented by a red-spotted, yellow lip. 'Alba' is white-flowered. USDA Plant Hardiness Zones 5 to 9 or 10.

B. ochracea (o-CRAY-see-a), yellow ground orchid. Size: 1 to 2 feet tall and wide. The creamy yellow flowers of this stunning species wave above a triad of long, slender leaves in early summer. Zones 6 to 10.

B. striata (stree-AH-ta), Chinese ground orchid. Size: 2 to 3 feet tall and wide. This attractive species forms wide clumps of exotic foliage, accented in spring by spikes of 6 to 10 magenta flowers. 'Alba' has white flowers. 'Albostriata' has white-edged leaves and purple flowers. Zones 5 to 10.

How to Grow

Plant in moist, well-drained, humus-rich soil in light to partial shade. Top-dress annually with compost or rotted manure to enrich the soil. Plants spread steadily to form dense, dramatic clumps with dozens of flowers. Plants emerge early and may be damaged by a late frost. The leaf tips and flower buds are most often affected. Frosted plants will not rebloom until the next season. Protect plants if frost threatens. Propagate by dividing fleshy tubers in fall.

Landscape Uses

The luscious leaves of bletilla add class to a shaded spot with ferns, sedges (*Carex*), hellebores, and other shade perennials. Contrast the bold leaves with fine textures. Shrubs are excellent companions. Plants are stunning in containers placed in the garden or on a patio.

Hardy Chinese ground orchid (*Bletilla striata*) emerges early and can be damaged by frost. Flower buds open to perfectly formed magenta orchids that dance in open spikes above bold, pleated leaves.

BOLTONIA

bol-TOE-ni-a • Asteraceae, Aster Family

The sheer exuberance of frothy white boltonia wins it a place in every garden. Perky white daises with delicate rays form billowing clouds reminiscent of asters, but the flowers are larger. The effect looks like a mound of summer snow. This versatile and adaptable perennial is native to marshes and low meadows, so it thrives in moist or soggy soils.

BOLTONIA

Common Name:
Boltonia

Bloom Time:
Late summer and fall bloom

Planting Requirements:
Sun or light shade

Boltonia asteroides (as-ter-OI-des), boltonia. Size: 4 to 6 feet tall and wide. A tall, rounded plant with blue-green willow-like foliage and a profusion of dainty, 1-inch white asterlike flowers with yellow centers. Plants grow from a stout crown with long fibrous roots and thick upright stems. The cultivars are superior to the species in form and flower. 'Madiva' is a compact plant smothered in white flowers. 'Nana' is a compact pink selection just over 2 feet tall. 'Pink Beauty' is a lovely cultivar with pale pink flowers in August and September and an open habit. 'Snowbank' grows 3 to 4 feet tall with upright, stout stems that seldom need staking. The bright white flowers are borne in dense clusters in September and October. USDA Plant Hardiness Zones 3 to 9.

How to Grow

Plant easy-care boltonias in moist, humus-rich soil in full sun or light shade. Estab-lished plants are drought-tolerant. In consistently dry soil, plants will grow but will be smaller in stature. Divide oversize clumps in spring. In rich soils, this may be

White boltonia (*Boltonia asteroides* 'Snowbank') opens its pristine white daisies in late summer atop erect stems that seldom flop. Flowering continues well into fall, complemented by ornamental grasses and late-blooming asters.

necessary every 3 to 5 years. Plants do not come true from seed. Tip cuttings root easily when taken in May or June.

Landscape Uses

Boltonia looks great with grasses. Create a charming combination with switchgrass (*Panicum virgatum*), Japanese anemone (*Anemone* ×*hybrida*), asters, and golden-rods (*Solidago*). Use pink selections with obedient plants (*Physostegia*), sweet Joe-Pye weed (*Eupatorium purpureum*), and one of the white variegated Japanese silver grasses (*Miscanthus sinensis* 'Cabaret'). Other late-blooming perennials that are suitable companions for boltonias include sunflowers (*Helianthus*), 'Autumn Joy' sedum, common sneezeweed (*Helenium autumnale*), and monkshoods (*Aconitum*).

BRUNNERA

BRUNN-er-a • Boraginaceae, Borage Family

Siberian bugloss is an old-fashioned favorite of gardeners. The sky blue flowers are carried in early spring above the emerging leaves. Blooms continue opening for a month or more as the luscious heart-shaped leaves expand to make a weedproof groundcover for a moist shady spot. Plants grow from stout crowns with fleshy, fibrous black roots.

BRUNNERA

Common Name:
Siberian bugloss

Bloom Time:
Spring bloom and bold summer foliage

Planting Requirements:
Partial to full shade

Brunnera macrophylla (mak-ro-FILE-a), Siberian bugloss, forget-me-not. Size: 1 to 1½ feet tall and wide. A showy plant in flower and foliage, small forget-me-not blue flowers emerge with heart-shaped leaves in early spring. After flowering, foliage expands to provide a showy display that lasts all summer. 'Hadspen Cream' has leaves with a creamy white border. 'Jack Frost' takes the cake, with silver netted foliage that really sets off the flowers. 'Langtrees' sports an even row of silver spots around the foliage. 'Marley's White' is white-flowered with green leaves. 'Dawson's White' ('Variegata') has a large, irregular white border and requires constantly moist soil. USDA Plant Hardiness Zones 3 to 8.

How to Grow

Give Siberian bugloss continually moist, humus-rich soil and light to full shade for best growth. Plants do well in drier soils, but foliage will be smaller. If drought persists, plants will go dormant to conserve energy. Division is seldom necessary. To propagate, lift plants in early spring or fall and tease or cut clumps apart. Take 3- to 4-inch root cuttings in fall or early winter and place them into moist sand in a coldframe. They will form shoots the following spring. Self-sown seedlings will appear around the parent plants and are easily transplanted.

Landscape Uses

Plant Siberian bugloss as a groundcover under trees or shrubs with spring bulbs, wildflowers, and ferns. Use a generous planting with daffodils, bleeding hearts (*Dicentra*), and leopard's banes (*Doronicum*). The dramatic, heart-shaped leaves also combine well with foliage plants such as barrenworts (*Epimedium*), lungworts (*Pulmonaria*), hostas, and ferns.

'Langtrees' Siberian bugloss (*Brunnera macrophylla* 'Langtrees') combines good foliage with attractive flowers, making it an invaluable mainstay for the lightly shaded garden. As the deep blue spring flowers fade, large heart-shaped leaves ringed with silvery spots expand to claim prominence for the remainder of summer.

CALAMAGROSTIS

kal-a-ma-GROS-tis • Poaceae, Grass Family

The airy blooms of reed grass wave above dense basal foliage clumps. Most species spread slowly, but a few are runners that form broad clumps. Reed grasses, referred to as cool-season grasses, green up early in the season and bloom in early summer while later-blooming, warm-season grasses are just starting growth. The stout crowns have dense, fibrous roots.

CALAMAGROSTIS

Common Name:
Reed grass

Bloom Time:
Summer bloom

Planting Requirements:
Sun or light shade

Calamagrostis* ×*acutiflora (ah-que-te-FLOOR-a), feather reed grass. Size: 2 to 6 feet tall, 1 to 3 feet wide. Feather reed grass is aptly named for its airy plumes that become strongly upright after flowering. The stems sway gracefully with the slightest breeze, adding motion to the garden. This hybrid species is sterile, so it will not self-sow. 'Karl Foerster' ('Stricta') has large, pink-tinted plumes that meld with the deep green, glossy foliage. 'Overdam' has attractive white variegation along the margins of leaves and grows to 4 feet tall. 'Avalanche' is noted for a broad band of white down the center of each leaf. USDA Plant Hardiness Zones 4 to 8.

C. brachytricha (brak-e-TRICK-a), Korean feather reed grass. Size: 3 to 4 feet tall, 1 to 2 feet wide. The strictly upright clumps of this attractive species are accented in early summer by pink plumes like clouds of cotton candy. The basal foliage is deep green. Zones 4 to 8.

C. canadensis (kan-a-DEN-sis), Canada bluejoint. Size: 2 to 3 feet tall and wide. This airy grass spreads by runners to form wide clumps. The drooping plumes are held above thin, blue-green foliage in early summer. Plants are best in naturalistic settings. Zones 3 to 8.

How to Grow

Plant reed grasses in evenly moist, rich soil in full sun or light shade. Leaf blades will curl if conditions become dry. Under persistent drought, plants will go dormant. They are native to northern zones and do not perform where nights are hot and humid. Canada bluejoint tolerates wet soil and considerable shade. Plants form tight clumps that can remain in place for years. If vigor declines, lift the entire clump and separate beefy portions for replanting. Division is the only means of propagation.

Landscape Uses

Reed grasses are perfect accent or specimen plants. Place them against an evergreen backdrop or site them to complement an urn or garden sculpture. In beds and borders, plant in drifts with bulbs between clumps for early color. Sages (*Salvia*), anise hyssops (*Agastache*), evening primroses (*Oenothera*), and asters are good companions. Use masses along walls, fences, and driveways.

Few grasses are as lithe and graceful as feather reed grass (*Calamagrostis ×acutiflora* 'Karl Foerster'). Erect pink plumes open in June and sway with the breeze like waves on the sea. The flowers dry to tawny gold by late summer.

CALAMINTHA

kal·a-MIN-tha • Lamiaceae, Mint Family

Clouds of pale lilac to white flowers festoon the full, rounded clumps of calamints from midsummer though autumn. Few perennials bloom as long with so little care. These blooming machines do not need staking or deadheading. The fragrant oval leaves smell of pennyroyal. Bees and other insects love the nectar in the tiny flowers. Plants form woody crowns with deep, thick roots that bestow exceptional drought tolerance.

> **CALAMINTHA**
>
> **Common Name:**
> Calamint
>
> **Bloom Time:**
> Summer bloom
>
> **Planting Requirements:**
> Sun or partial shade

Calamintha grandiflora (gran-di-FLO-ra), large-flowered calamint. Size: 1 to 1½ feet tall and wide. A compact plant with rounded leaves on sturdy stems crowned with elongated clusters of small pink flowers that mingle with the leaves. 'Variegata' has foliage flecked with creamy white. USDA Plant Hardiness Zones 4 to 7.

C. nepeta (NEP-e-ta) (*nepetoides*), calamint. Size: 1 to 2 feet tall and wide. A powerhouse of bloom with airy clusters of small white to pale lavender flowers on wiry stems covered in small, dark green leaves. Summer flowers are white; in cool fall air

Large-flowered calamint (*Calamintha grandiflora*) forms a tight mound of attractive, mint-scented foliage accented throughout summer by tubular pink flowers. Plants thrive in dry, sandy soils.

How to Grow

Give calamints a site with average to rich, well-drained soil in full sun to partial shade. Established plants are drought-tolerant. Flowering begins in midsummer and continues until frost. Flowering is heavier and more sustained in sunny sites, but plants perform admirably in shade, giving months of color. Propagate by stem cuttings taken in early summer or by division in spring or fall.

Landscape Uses

Contrast is the key to successful use of calamint. Surround the bold purple flowers of coneflowers (*Echinacea*), daylilies (*Hemerocallis*), and phlox with the airy flower cluster. For fall drama, use asters, Japanese anemones (*Anemone* ×*hybrida*), and sedums. Spiky iris foliage and the vertical forms of torch lilies (*Kniphofia*), gayfeathers (*Liatris*), and sages (*Salvia*) add height and drama.

they open to lavender. Plants bloom non-stop from midsummer through frost. 'Blue Cloud' has lavender-blue flowers. 'Gottlieb Friedkund' has larger foliage and dark lavender flowers. 'White Cloud' is compact and very free-flowering. Zones 4 to 8.

CALLIRHOE

kal-le-ROW-ee • Malvaceae, Mallow Family

Winecups are floriferous blooming machines from the arid West with five squared-off petals that together form a flower that resembles a teacup. Plants have weakly upright to trailing stems; some species form broad colonies. They grow from thick, branched taproots.

CALLIRHOE

Common Name:
  Winecups, poppy mallow

Bloom Time:
  Season-long bloom

Planting Requirements:
  Sun or light shade

Callirhoe digitata (dij-e-TAH-ta), staning winecups. Size: 1 to 4 feet tall, 1 foot wide. Lax stems are sparsely covered with deeply dissected decorative leaves bearing five to seven narrow, linear lobes that resemble slender fingers. The 1- to 2-inch flowers are carried singly or in few flowered clusters above the foliage. Color varies from white to light rose and wine red. Plants will grow up through large perennials or shrubs for support. USDA Plant Hardiness Zones 4 to 9.

C. involucrata (in-vol-ew-KRAY-tah), purple poppy mallow, winecups. Size: 1 foot high, 1 to 3 feet wide. A sprawling to creeping plant with attractive, deeply dissected leaves with five to seven toothed lobes. The 2½-inch-deep wine-red flowers are carried singly above the foliage. Plants begin blooming in mid- to late spring and flower for several months on new growth. 'Logan Calhoun' is pure white. Var. *tenuissima* has pale lavender flowers. Zones 4 to 9.

C. triangulata (tri-ang-ew-LAY-tah), poppy mallow. Size: 1 to 2 feet tall and wide. Similar in habit to purple poppy mallow, but undivided leaves are broadly triangular to heart-shaped. Deep purple-red flowers are carried in open clusters in the leaf axils at the ends of the 1- to 2-foot stems. Zones 4 to 8.

How to Grow

Plant in average, well-drained, loamy or sandy soil in full sun or light shade. Set out young plants in their final position; they do not move well due to their taproots.

Plants may form wide clumps by midsummer. If bloom wanes, cut stems back by half to encourage branching and more flowers. Seeds need cold, moist stratification to germinate. Sow in winter and place covered flats in the refrigerator for 4 to 6 weeks. Transplants will be ready by fall or the following spring.

Landscape Uses

Poppy mallows are excellent weavers, best used to knit plantings together. The trailing stems creep between or over clumps of plants, and flowers pop up here and there.

Winecups is an apt name for *Callirhoe involucrata*. The creeping mats are smothered with rich rosy purple chalices throughout spring and early summer, with scattered blooms until frost.

In rich soils, plants form more dense clumps best used at the edge of a bed or along a path. In formal garden situations, combine them with sedums, lamb's ears (*Stachys byzantina*), ornamental onions, yarrows (*Achillea*), and asters. In prairie gardens, plant them with milkweeds (*Asclepias*), asters, blanket flowers (*Gaillardia*), spiderworts (*Tradescantia*), and ornamental grasses. Choose them for a long-flowering carpet in rock walls and rock gardens. The tall stems of standing winecups are excellent see-through plants for the front of the border.

CALTHA

KAL-tha • Ranunculaceae, Buttercup Family

Marsh marigolds are wetland plants that bloom as soon as snow melts. Their early emerging leaves were prized by Native Americans and settlers after a long winter with no fresh greens. The bright flowers open for a month or more before plants go summer dormant. Plants grow from thick crowns with succulent roots.

CALTHA

Common Name:
  Marsh marigold

Bloom Time:
  Spring bloom

Planting Requirements:
  Sun or partial shade

Caltha leptosepala (lep-to-SEE-pa-la) (*biflora*), western marsh marigold. Size: 6 to 12 inches tall and wide. A lovely white-flowered species with deep green, heart- to kidney-shaped leaves. Native to alpine marshes, this plant needs rich, moist soil and cool nights for best growth. USDA Plant Hardiness Zones 3 to 7.

C. palustris (pa-LUS-tris), marsh marigold, cowslip. Size: 1 to 2 feet tall, 2 to 3 feet wide. An early spring wildflower with open clusters of butter yellow flowers borne with round leaves. Flowering begins as soon as shoots emerge from the ground and persists until the plant reaches full

If you have a sunny wet spot, you are lucky enough to be able to grow marsh marigold (*Caltha palustris*). This harbinger of spring adds a touch of glowing yellow to a spot that most gardeners consider a liability.

size. After flowering, the entire plant goes dormant. The crowns produce thick, cord-like roots that persist through the dormant period. 'Alba' is a small, white-flowered selection. 'Flore Pleno' ('Multiplex') has fully double flowers that persist for several weeks. Var. *polypetala*, king's cups, is a Eurasian native of monstrous proportions compared with *C. palustris*, which is similar in every detail but size and hardiness (Zones 4 to 7). Zones 2 to 8.

How to Grow

Marsh marigolds are plants of open marshes, wet meadows, and low woods. They demand constantly moist or wet soil and will even grow in standing water. Give them humus-rich or loamy soils and full sun to light shade when flowering and growing actively. After flowering (as plants go dormant), water content of the soil is less critical, but it must not become dry for extended periods. Divide clumps in summer and replant into moist soil. Sow fresh seeds outdoors in constantly moist soil. They will germinate the following spring. Double-flowered selections do not come true from seed.

Landscape Uses

Choose marsh marigolds for stream or pondside plantings where flowers are reflected in the water. Plant with primroses (*Primula*), irises, false spireas (*Astilbe*), lobelias, and ferns in a moist low spot or bog garden.

CAMASSIA

ka-MAS-see-a • Hyacinthaceae (Liliaceae), Hyacinth Family

Tall racemes of starry, five-petaled pale to deep blue flowers come just after the spring bulb rush is subsiding, when they are most appreciated to extend the season. Whorls of glossy green leaves, folded upward in the middle to form a V-shape, grow from true bulbs, which were eaten by native people and early settlers.

CAMASSIA

Common Names:
Wild hyacinth, quamash, camas

Bloom Time:
Late spring and early summer bloom

Planting Requirements:
Full sun to light shade

Camassia cusickii (que-SICK-ee-ee), Cusick's camas. Size: 2 to 3 feet tall, 1 foot wide. This hardy northern species has dozens of pale blue flowers on stout stems. 'Zwanenberg' has large, deep blue flowers. USDA Plant Hardiness Zones 3 to 8.

C. leichtlinii (licked-LIN-ee-ee), Leichtlin's quamash. Size: 1 to 4 feet tall, 1 to 2 feet wide. The most robust and showy species with sturdy, dense spikes of pale to deep blue flowers. 'Alba' has creamy white flowers that glow when planted with blues. 'Blue Danube' is stunning with deep indigo flowers on 3-foot stems. 'Semi-Plena' has double, creamy white flowers like a delicate tuberose. Zones 4 to 9.

C. quamash (KWAH-mahsh), quamash. Size: 1 to 2 feet tall, 1 foot wide. A more delicate species, with slender inflorescences of deep purple-blue flowers. 'Blue Melody' is coveted for its yellow-margined leaves contrasting with the richly colored flowers. 'Orion' is deep blue. Zones 3 to 8.

C. scilloides (skill-OY-deez), wild hyacinth, Atlantic camas. Size: 1 to 2 feet tall, 1 foot wide. Wild hyacinth is the only eastern species, with icy to medium blue flowers above sparse basal foliage. Some wild plants are white-flowered but unnamed. Zones 4 to 8.

Though the bulbs of Leichtlin's quamash (*Camassia leichtlinii* 'Blue Danube') are edible, the deep blue flowers give more joy in the garden than the bulbs do in the kitchen. Give plants a moist spot in full sun for best performance.

How to Grow

Plant in rich, evenly moist soil in full sun or light shade. In the wild, meadows where this plant grows are quite dry in summer, so moderate summer drought is no problem, but bone-dry soil for extended periods will compromise next year's flowers. Place the large bulbs 4 to 6 inches deep. Plants will not rebloom if planted in too much shade. After flowers fade, remove old bloom stalks.

Landscape Uses

Tall spikes protruding from a planting of cranesbills (*Geranium*), sedges (*Carex*), ferns, and emerging leaves of meadow rues (*Thalictrum*) are stunning in the spring garden. Group at least a dozen bulbs together, and plant several drifts for maximum impact. In more-formal settings, combine them with Siberian irises (*Iris* *siberica*), masterwort (*Astrantia major*), and other moisture-loving perennials. Contrast the spiky inflorescences with the spherical heads of ornamental onions (*Allium*) and the blowsy elegance of catmints (*Nepeta*).

CAMPANULA

kam-PAN-yew-la • Campanulaceae, Bellflower Family

Known as bluebells in mountain meadows of northern Europe, this variable genus of showy plants is valued for its true blue flowers. Plants range in form from low-profile creepers to tall, upright specimens for the back of the border. Flowers are bell-shaped or starry with five petals fused for varying portions of their length. Some flowers are borne singly, others in clusters. Most are upfacing while others are nodding. The taller species have larger basal leaves while stem leaves reduce in size as they ascend toward the flowers.

> **CAMPANULA**
>
> **Common Names:**
>   Bellflower, harebell
>
> **Bloom Time:**
>   Spring and summer bloom
>
> **Planting Requirements:**
>   Sun or partial shade

Campanula carpatica (car-PA-ti-ca), Carpathian harebell. Size: 8 to 18 inches tall, 1 to 2 feet wide. Mounding, floriferous species with 2-inch, cup-shaped, blue or white flowers from spring through summer. The triangular leaves form a tight clump against which flowers are set off to excellent advantage. 'Blue Clips' has 3-inch medium blue flowers on compact plants and comes true from seed. 'China Doll' has azure blue flowers. 'Wedgewood Blue' bears 2½-inch violet-blue flowers on 6-inch stems. 'White Clips' has 2½- to 3-inch flowers on compact plants. USDA Plant Hardiness Zones 3 to 8.

C. cochlearifolia (kok-lee-ah-ree-FO-lee-a), spiral bellflower. Size: 4 to 6 inches tall, 1 foot wide. Low, mat-forming plant with small, nearly round leaves and profuse ¾-inch blue-lilac, bell-shaped flowers in summer. Plants spread outward from underground runners. Var. *alba* is a vigorous grower with clear white flowers. 'Bavaria Blue' and 'Bavaria White' are two compact selections to 5 inches tall. 'Miranda' has pale sky blue flowers. Zones 4 (with protection) or 5 to 8.

C. garganica (gar-GAH-ni-ca), Gargano bellflower. Size: 5 to 6 inches tall, 1 to 1½ feet wide. A fast-spreading groundcover with fuzzy, heart- to kidney-shaped leaves and starry blue flowers with white centers. 'Blue Diamond' has clear pale blue flowers. 'Dickson's Gold' has lime green foliage and lavender-blue flowers. Zones 4 to 8.

C. glomerata (glo-me-RAH-ta), clustered bellflower. Size: 1 to 3 feet tall, 1 to 2 feet wide. A stout, upright, summer-blooming plant bearing purple or violet flowers clustered at the nodes and at the apex of the hairy stems. The clumps spread by creeping underground stems to form open clumps. Var. *acaulis* is a dwarf plant to 5 inches tall with violet-blue flowers in early summer. 'Alba' has white flowers. 'Caroline'

Carpathian harebell (*Campanula carpatica* 'Blue Clips') produces tight, spreading clumps of bright blue flowers that enliven a rock garden or the front of a perennial bed. After flowering, the tidy foliage mounds should be kept free from flopping neighbors.

has mauve flowers on 12- to 18-inch stems. 'Crown of Snow' has white flowers on 2-foot stems. 'Joan Elliot' has deep blue-violet flowers on multiple 1½- to 2-foot stems. 'Superba' is a vigorous grower with deep violet flowers on 2½-foot stems. Zones 3 to 8.

C. lactiflora (lak-ti-FLOR-a), milky bellflower. Size: 3 to 4 feet tall, 1 to 3 feet wide. A large, showy, summer-blooming bellflower with tight clusters of 1-inch blue or white starry bells. Var. *alba* has white flowers. 'Loddon Anna' has stout stems with pale pink flowers. 'Prichard's Variety' has deep blue flowers on 3- to 4-foot stalks. 'Pouffe' is a diminutive selection with pale, sky blue flowers on 12- to 18-inch stems. Zones 4 to 7.

C. latifolia (lat-i-FO-lee-a), great bellflower. Size: 2 to 5 feet tall, 1 to 3 feet wide. A tall, coarse bellflower producing a brief but glorious show of spiky clusters of 2- to 3-inch purple-blue, upright, bell-shaped flowers in early summer. 'Alba' is white-flowered. 'Brantwood' is a robust, multi-stemmed selection with violet flowers. 'Gloaming' is a nice pale blue. Zones 3 to 7.

C. latiloba (lat-e-LOBE-a), delphinium bellflower. Size: 2 to 4 feet tall, 2 to 3 feet wide. Closely allied to peach-leaved bellflower, the large open flowers are stalkless and intermingle with the narrow stem foliage. Basal leaves are deep green and elongated. Thanks to Allan Armitage for the common name. 'Alba' is a snow white selection. 'Hidcote Amethyst' has gorgeous, translucent soft purple flowers. 'Highcliffe Variety' has deep purple flowers. Zones 3 to 7.

C. persicifolia (per-sik-i-FO-lee-a), peach-leaved bellflower. Size: 1 to 3 feet tall, 1 to 2 feet wide. A lovely, graceful species with narrow leaves and 1- to 1½-inch open, bell-shaped, blue-violet flowers in summer. 'Alba' has white flowers. 'Chettle Charm' is a stunning white picotee with a blue edge. 'Telham Beauty' is 3 to 4 feet tall with pale lavender-blue flowers. Zones 3 to 7.

C. portenschlagiana (por-ten-schlag-ee-AH-na), dalmatian bellflower. Size: 4 to 6 inches tall, 1 to 2 feet wide. A low, creeping plant with tight rosettes of small triangular leaves and a profusion of 1-inch blue-purple starry bell-shaped flowers in late spring and early summer. 'Lisolette' has lavender-purple flowers. 'Resholdt's Variety' has indigo blue flowers. Zones 4 to 8.

C. poscharskyana (pos-shar-skee-AH-na), Serbian bellflower. Size: 6 to 12 inches tall, 1 to 2 feet wide. A trailing, fast-spreading species with open, starry blue flowers in spring and early summer. 'Birch Hybrid' is a compact, slower-spreading hybrid with medium blue flowers. 'Blue Gown' has large, showy blue flowers. 'E. H. Frost' is white-flowered. Zones 3 to 7.

C. punctata (punk-TAY-ta), spotted bellflower. Size: 1 foot tall, 1 to 2 feet wide. A long-distance runner in a former life, this robust, fast-creeping plant has coarse, heart-shaped leaves and huge pink bells faintly edged in white. Zones 4 to 8.

C. rotundifolia (ro-tun-di-FO-lee-a), harebell. Size: 4 to 14 inches tall, 6 to 12 inches wide. A delicate, clump-forming plant with nodding, sky blue bell-shaped flowers borne on slender stems. 'Olympica'

The tall blue spires of peach-leaved bell-flower (*Campanula persicifolia* 'Telham Beauty') add lift to a combination of rich orange oriental poppies (*Papaver orientale*) and soft pink lupines in a sunny border.

is a long-flowering selection with 1-inch deep blue bells. Zones 2 to 7.

How to Grow

Bellflowers are easy-care perennials for borders and rockeries. Cultural requirements vary between species. In general, the low-spreading species such as *C. carpatica*, *C. cochlearifolia*, *C. garganica*, *C. portenschlagiana*, *C. poscharskyana*, and *C. rotundifolia* require average to rich, well-drained soil in full sun or light shade. *C. portenschlagiana* tolerates more shade than the others. Divide plants as necessary in early spring or fall. *C. garganica* and *C. poscharskyana* are particularly rapid spreaders and may need division every 2 or 3 years. Propagate by tip cuttings in early summer. Sow ripe seed indoors on a moist medium and cover slightly or not at all. In warm (70°F) conditions, seedlings germinate in 3 to 6 weeks. Several species, especially *C. carpatica,* may self-sow.

Plant the larger bellflowers in moist, well-drained, humus-rich soil in full sun or light shade. Most species are sensitive to high temperatures. Provide afternoon shade in warmer regions to prolong the life of the plants. *C. glomerata* prefers evenly moist, limey soil and tolerates partial shade. Divide overgrown clumps in early spring or fall. Take tip cuttings in early summer or propagate from seed as above. Slugs are the only serious pest. Exclude them with a barrier strip of ash or sand or use a dish of beer as bait to drown them. (The drawback to this method is the disgusting task of discarding the corpses.)

Landscape Uses

Choose the low-growing and creeping bellflowers for rock gardens and for crevices in rock walls. The blue and purple flowers are lovely against the lush foliage, and they contrast well with rough, neutral surfaces of rocks. They will clamber and creep through every crevice and soften even the harshest rock face. Try these low gems at the front of a border or spilling over the edges of walkways. Plant medium-size clustered bellflower in a moist site with Siberian iris (*Iris siberica),* leopard's banes (*Doronicum*), Bowles' golden sedge (*Carex elata* 'Aurea'), and ferns. Use the tall bellflowers in beds and borders and along walls, hedges, or fences. They are lovely in large drifts as accents or combined with goat's beard (*Aruncus dioicus*), Bowman's root (*Porteranthus trifoliatus*), yarrows (*Achillea*), and cranesbills (*Geranium*).

Icy white stars decorate the creeping mats of Serbian bellflower (*Campanula poscharskyana* 'E. H. Frost') for a month in early summer. Plants creep gracefully over rock walls and weave attractively through taller plants.

CAREX

KAH-rex • Cyperaceae, Sedge Family

The selection of garden-worthy sedges is vast indeed. The only criteria we have applied to this selection is personal preference. All sedges are beautiful and add grace in many difficult sites, including dense shade, the driest soils, and the wettest soils. The thin, long leaves resemble grasses, but sedges differ botanically in the structure of the stems and foliage (sedges have edges), as well as the flowers. They grow from tufted, fibrous-rooted crowns.

> **CAREX**
>
> **Common Name:**
>   Sedge
>
> **Bloom Time:**
>   Spring and summer bloom
>
> **Planting Requirements:**
>   Full sun to full shade

Carex buchananii (bew-can-AN-ee-ee), leatherleaf sedge. Size: 1 to 2 feet tall, 1 foot wide. Popular brown- or bronze-leaf sedge affectionately referred to by enthusiasts as a "dead sedge." Plants are upright and vase-shaped, quite distinct from other species. USDA Plant Hardiness Zones 7 to 9.

C. comans (CO-manz), New Zealand hairy sedge. Size: 1 foot tall, 2 feet wide. Another "dead sedge" forming a low, spreading mound. 'Bronce' is richly red-brown colored. Zones 7 to 9.

C. dolichostachya (dol-i-ko-STAY-ke-a) 'Kaga Nishiki', Kaga brocade sedge. Size: 8 to 12 inches tall, 12 to 18 inches wide. This relatively new introduction was an instant favorite. The gold variegated foliage is fine-textured and soft and is carried in dense, graceful clumps. Zones 5 to 8.

C. elata (e-LAY-ta) 'Aurea', Bowles' golden sedge. Size: 2 to 4 feet tall and wide. This beauty produces a rounded, fine-textured clump of glowing yellow leaves. It grows best in standing water in rich soil with full sun or light shade. 'Kightshays' is stunning with entirely yellow foliage. Zones 5 to 8.

C. flacca (FLAK-a) (*glauca*), carnation grass. Size: 6 to 8 inches tall, 12 inches wide. Confused in the trade with *C. nigra*, this running species for sun or shade has bright gray-blue, narrow foliage. Zones 4 to 8.

C. flagellifera (fla-gel-LIF-er-a), thread-leaf sedge. Size: 2 to 3 feet tall and wide. This "dead sedge" forms broad, nestlike clumps of red-brown leaves. It is longer-lived than others and has a rich ruddy bronze color with a hint of green. Plants grow in moist soil in full sun and form mop-headed clumps of hairlike leaves. Zones 7 to 9.

C. fraseriana (fra-zer-e-AYE-na), Fraser's sedge, flowering sedge. Size: 1 foot tall, 1 to 2 feet wide. Wide, leathery, black-green leaves in an open mound form a perfect

The descriptively named New Zealand hairy sedge (*Carex comans* 'Bronce') forms beautiful flowing clumps of burnished bronze leaves as fine as a horse's mane.

accompaniment to the fuzzy white flowers that make this the most handsome of the woodland sedges when in bloom. Zones 5 to 8.

C. morrowii (mo-ROW-ee-ee), morrow sedge. Size: 1 to 1½ feet tall and wide. Bold, stiff, wide leaves form an open, vase-like clump. Variegated selections are more common than the species. 'Goldband' has a creamy white edge. 'Ice Dance' is a Zone 4 hardy new selection. White-edged, stiff, upright to arching green leaves and a running groundcover habit. 'Silver Scepter' is a compact selection 1 foot tall and wide. 'Variegata' has shorter leaves with light margins. Zones 6 to 9.

C. nigra (NYE-gra), black sedge. Size: 6 to 10 inches tall, 10 to 12 inches wide. This silken groundcover is like a bed of eel grass when the tide is high. The long, slender blades all seem to lie in the same direction, and the clump sways in the breeze as if responding to the flux of incoming tides. The black inflorescences are responsible for the common name. 'Variegata' has long, soft yellow-edged leaves. Zones 4 to 8.

C. oshimensis (o-shi-MEN-sis) 'Evergold', evergold sedge. Size: 1 foot tall, 1 to 2 feet wide. Crisp, precise, and beautifully variegated describes the foliage of evergold sedge. The long, narrow blades sport a central yellow stripe hemmed in by green margins in neat, decidedly aristocratic clumps. Zones 6 to 8.

C. pendula (PEN-dew-la), drooping sedge. Size: 2 to 3 feet tall and wide. The crisp, leathery, high arching leaves form a fountainlike clump worthy of the fountains of Trevi. Each leaf tapers gradually to a long sharp point. In late spring, tall stalks rise above the leaves and dangle their green inflorescences like worms on a hook, or perhaps ear-bobs in an elegant Victorian ear. Fringed sedge (*C. crinita*) is a native sedge with a similar look. Light green leaves form a mounding, fine-textured clump that is a bit more refined than drooping sedge, with which it is sometimes confused. The only drawback to this beauty is that it is deciduous and flops pitifully with the first frost. Zones 5 to 9.

C. pensylvanica (pen-sil-VAN-e-ka), Pennsylvania sedge. Size: 6 to 12 inches tall, 18 to 24 inches wide. A delicate, creeping sedge with thin, hairlike leaves that forms dense mats. A good lawn substitute in shade. Zones 3 to 8.

C. phyllocephala (phy-lo-se-FAL-a), Tenjiki sedge. Size: 1 to 2 feet tall and wide. This stunning plant has palmlike stems topped with whirligigs of glossy green blades. 'Sparkler', a stunning variegated selection with white-edged leaves, belongs in every garden. Zones 7 (with protection) to 10.

C. platyphylla (platee-FILE-a), seersucker sedge. Size: 6 to 12 inches tall, 12 to 18 inches wide. Broad, bright evergreen, puckered leaves like straps radiate from the dense crowns of this drought-tolerant woodland species. The yellow-green flowers smother the clump in early spring. Plants form a bold, attractive groundcover. Zones 4 to 9.

C. siderosticha (sid-er-o-STEE-ka), Japanese woodland sedge. Size: 4 to 6 inches tall, 1 foot wide. Woodland sedge has bright green strappy leaves that burst from the soil in early spring. Plants quickly form tight clumps from short creeping rhizomes. Despite their eager spread, the plants are never invasive. The plain green form is seldom seen in American gardens. 'Variegata' is widely available and is preferable to the species. The leaves are striped with creamy white. Two new variegated cultivars have recently been introduced. The leaves of 'Island Brocade' are edged in golden yellow. 'Spring Snow' has a wide white stripe down the center of the leaf but does not hold its variegation. Zones 4 to 8.

How to Grow

No doubt about it, sedges are tough. Despite heat and drought, they always look crisp and tidy. Sedges are diverse in their requirements; many thrive under adverse conditions where grasses quickly fail. Woodland species prefer rich, well-drained soil in light to full shade. Wetland natives such as drooping, fringed, and Bowles' golden sedge will grow in standing water or evenly moist soil. Once established, they will tolerate periodic drought. The "dead sedges" need full sun to light shade in moist soil. Remove dead leaves to keep the clumps vigorous. Cut water-damaged foliage only in spring. Divide plants in early spring. Sow fresh seed on a moist, well-drained medium. Self-sown seedlings may be abundant with some species, absent from others.

Southern gardeners can enjoy the dramatically striated whorls of *Carex phyllocephala* 'Sparkler' in a moist, sunny spot in the garden. Farther north, grow them in containers kept through winter in a cool, sunny spot.

Landscape Uses

Sedges suffer from relative anonymity; they are really just being discovered by gardeners. A well-turned *Carex* provides a garden with season-long texture and distinctive form. From linear and threadlike to boldly strap-shaped, sedge foliage comes in a remarkable array of colors from chartreuse to nearly black, as well as stripes and bands of white and brilliant yellow. Sedges are ideal as a lawn substitute. They take light foot traffic and can even be mowed. Most sedges are shade-tolerant, so they are great for woodland gardens. We like to use variegated selections to brighten shadows. Employ sedges with small, fine-textured leaves between pavers or on the edge of a patio to soften edges. Use upright, vase-shaped or widely arching selections to add height and variety to dull groundcover plantings. Sedge leaves catch light and seem to glow from within when properly placed with the sun behind them. The increased popularity of water and bog gardening provides a huge unpainted canvas to be painted with colorful sedges such as Bowles' golden and drooping sedges. Contrast them with bold leaves such as hostas, bergenias, rodgersias, and ligularias.

CATANANCHE

kat-a-NAN-che • Asteraceae, Aster Family

The blue straw flowers of Cupid's dart open from buds like globular hat pins. The plants are smothered with flowers in early summer but offer little to the garden once flowering has past. When grown well, the plants are stunning, but in heavy soil or wet conditions, the plants sulk and quickly die. They grow from fibrous-rooted crowns.

CATANANCHE

Common Name:
Cupid's dart

Bloom Time:
Summer bloom

Planting Requirements:
Full sun or light shade

Catananche caerulea (kie-RU-lee-a), Cupid's dart. Size: 18 to 24 inches tall, 1 foot wide. A plant of dry meadows with tight clumps of hairy, linear foliage. The 2-inch lilac-blue flowers resemble small cornflowers and are borne singly on wiry stems. 'Blue Giant' has deep blue flowers on 2-foot stems. 'Major' stands 3 feet tall with lilac blue flowers. USDA Plant Hardiness Zones 4 to 9.

How to Grow

Grow Cupid's darts in humus-rich, sandy, well-drained soils in full sun or light shade.

They tolerate limey soils. Plants may be short-lived, especially in heavy soils. Annual division of clumps helps maintain vigor. Propagate by root cuttings taken in fall or winter. Sow seeds indoors in late winter. Cover sparsely if at all. They germinate quickly and will bloom the first summer.

Landscape Uses

Plant Cupid's darts in masses to increase their visual power. Place them toward the front of the border, in rock gardens, or in containers and troughs To dry the flowers, cut them as soon as the rays (petals) expand.

For a sunny garden with dry sandy soil, try the blue-flowered Cupid's dart (*Catananche caerulea*). The strawlike flowers are excellent for cutting and drying.

CENTAUREA

sen-TOR-ee-a • Asteraceae, Aster Family

Cornflowers are informal, often somewhat weedy plants with fringed flowers in shades of blue or rarely yellow. The flowers have rounded, scaly receptacles below the rays (petal-like flower parts). Many species are extremely invasive; a few are on noxious weed lists. Choose carefully. Cornflowers have tough fibrous rootstocks that bestow drought tolerance.

CENTAUREA

Common Names:
Cornflower, knapweed

Bloom Time:
Late spring and early summer bloom

Planting Requirements:
Full sun to light shade

Centaurea hypoleuca (hi-po-LOO-ca), also sold as *C. dealbata*, knapweed. Size: 1½ to 2½ feet tall, 2 to 3 feet wide. A bushy, fast-spreading perennial with pinnately divided leaves and showy 1½-inch rose-pink flowers held singly above the foliage. 'John Coutts' is superior to the species, with 2-inch flowers on sturdy,

Cornflower blue flowers make mountain bluet (*Centaurea montana*) a valuable addition to the summer garden with gray-leaved lamb's ear (*Stachys lanata*) and pastel flowers like phlox and catmint (*Nepeta*).

compact plants. USDA Plant Hardiness Zones 3 to 7.

C. macrocephala (mak-ro-CEPH-a-la), Armenian basket flower. Size: 3 to 4 feet tall, 4 to 5 feet wide. A coarse plant with 3-inch yellow thistle-like flowers on 4-foot stems. Zones 2 to 8.

C. montana (mon-TAN-a), mountain bluet. Size: 1½ to 2 feet tall, 2 to 3 feet wide. A lovely, weedy perennial with 2½-inch cobalt blue flowers on un-branched stems. Spreads by rapidly creeping rootstocks to form colonies. 'Alba' has white flowers. Zones 3 to 8.

C. scabiosa (scab-e-OH-sa), tall knapweed. Size: 2 to 3 feet tall, 1 to 2 feet wide. An upright species with deep purple flowers in late summer and autumn. Zones 3 to 9.

How to Grow

Plant carefree cornflowers in average to rich, moist but well-drained soil in full sun or light shade. Divide overgrown clumps in spring or fall as necessary, usually every 2 or 3 years. Sow fresh seed outdoors in fall or indoors in late winter. Plants develop quickly after germination.

Landscape Uses

Cornflowers are well suited to informal gardens. The flowers are excellent for cutting fresh or for drying. Fresh cuts may last several weeks. Harvest flowers for drying as soon as they are fully expanded. Combine them with grasses and meadow flowers like black-eyed Susan (*Rudbeckia*) and coneflowers (*Echinacea*).

CENTRANTHUS

ken-TRAN-thus • Valerianaceae, Valerian Family

Visitors to British gardens are besotted by walls dripping with Jupiter's beard. Stateside, plants are difficult to grow in warm zones and in areas with acid soil. Where happy (in cool northern zones and where the soil is on the sweet side), plants are lush and smothered with flowers throughout the summer. Beware this plant's exuberance; where it is happy it self-sows freely. This beauty is outlawed in some western states because of its invasive nature in that region. Plants grow from fibrous-rooted crowns.

CENTRANTHUS
Common Names:
  Jupiter's beard, red valerian
Bloom Time:
  Spring and early summer bloom
Planting Requirements:
  Full sun

Centranthus ruber (ROO-ber), red valerian. Size: 1 to 3 feet tall, 2 to 4 feet wide. An attractive perennial with domed terminal and axillary clusters of small, pink, rose, coral-red, or white flowers on erect branching stems. The smooth leaves are blue-green and quite attractive during and after flowering. Var. *coccineus* ('Coccineus') has deep scarlet flowers. Var. *roseus* ('Roseus') has rose-red flowers. USDA Plant Hardiness Zones 4 to 8.

How to Grow

Red valerian is easily grown in average to sandy, neutral or limey soils in full sun. Plants thrive in rockeries and stone walls, seemingly in no soil at all. They will grow in moist, well-drained soils in cooler regions. Shear clumps after flowering if they become floppy. Plants may self-sow freely under favorable conditions and are invasive in some western regions.

Landscape Uses

This adaptable plant is ideal for rock gardens and stone walls. The coral-red flowers can be difficult to use in combination with other plants but are perfect with neutral rock surfaces. In the border, plant the softer colors with yarrows (*Achillea*), asters, speedwells (*Veronica*), and coreopsis.

Frothy cerise clouds make red valerian (*Centranthus ruber*) a standout in rock walls or borders, where it thrives in well-drained soil and cool temperatures.

CERASTIUM

ser-ASS-ti-um • Caryophyllaceae, Pink Family

Well named for the dense white carpet of flowers that blanket the ground in early summer. Low, mounding sub-alpine plants with small, white woolly foliage and clusters of ½- to 1-inch white flowers with five deeply notched petals give the illusion of double the true number. The main clump has thick fibrous roots, and the lax stems may root at the nodes.

CERASTIUM

Common Names:
  Snow-in-summer,
  mouse-ear chickweed

Bloom Time:
  Late spring and early
  summer bloom

Planting Requirements:
  Full sun

Cerastium biebersteinii (bee-ber-STINE-ee-ee), snow-in-summer. Size: 6 to 12 inches tall, 12 to 18 inches wide. White woolly mounding or mat-forming perennials with spreading stems and ¾-inch flowers in sparse clusters. USDA Plant Hardiness Zones 3 to 7.

C. tomentosum (toe-men-TOE-sum), snow-in-summer. Size: 6 to 10 inches tall, 12 to 24 inches wide. Woolly, mat-forming perennial with 1-inch white flowers in many flowered clusters. 'YoYo' is more compact than the species. Zones 2 to 7.

How to Grow

Give the carefree *Cerastium* average, well-drained soil and full sun. Divide plants if they spread too aggressively. Poorly drained soils will encourage fungal rots that blacken foliage; avoid problems by providing good drainage. High heat and summer humidity can cause similar problems in the South. Propagate by tip cuttings taken in summer or by division.

Copious white flowers above fine-textured gray foliage are the charm of snow-in-summer (*Cerastium tomentosum*). Plants seed freely to form low, spreading mounds similar to snowdrifts.

Landscape Uses

Mouse-ear chickweed is well adapted to growing among rocks. Plant in walls, along gravel walkways, or in rock gardens with spring bulbs, saxifrages (*Saxifraga*), moss phlox (*Phlox subulata*), primroses (*Primula*), and bellflowers (*Campanula*). The creeping mats are also attractive on dry and sandy banks. Mouse-ear chickweed will also grow in containers.

CERATOSTIGMA

ser-at-o-STIG-ma • Plumaginaceae, Plumbago Family

Electric blue flowers open late in summer, breathing new life into the garden as many flowers are fading. Underplanted with bulbs like meadow saffrons (*Colchicum*) and spider lilies (*Lycoris*), the elegant groundcover carries the garden into winter, when the leaves turn rich orange and burgundy. Plants grow from creeping stems with tough, fibrous roots.

> **CERATOSTIGMA**
>
> **Common Names:**
> Plumbago, leadwort
>
> **Bloom Time:**
> Summer and fall bloom
>
> **Planting Requirements:**
> Full sun to partial shade

Ceratostigma plumbaginoides (plumba-gin-OI-deez), plumbago. Size: 6 to 12 inches tall, 12 to 36 inches wide. A creeping semiwoody perennial with deep green, diamond-shaped leaves and terminal clusters of five-petaled gentian blue flowers nearly an inch across. Established colonies form a dense tangle of wiry stems. USDA Plant Hardiness Zones 5 to 9.

Clumps spread rapidly to form an attractive groundcover. New shoots appear in late spring. Prune out winter-killed stems before new growth expands. Flowering starts in early to midsummer and often continues until fall. Leaves turn fiery red or orange after frost. Divide clumps in spring. Propagate by tip cuttings in summer or by layering stems anytime during the growing season.

How to Grow

Plant plumbago in average to rich, moist but well-drained soil in sun or partial shade.

Landscape Uses

Choose plumbago when you need a tough, fast-growing groundcover. Plants will succeed on dry sunny banks or between rocks in a wall. They tolerate partial shade but will not compete well in the dry shade of mature trees. Try overplanting small spring bulbs and early wildflowers with plumbago. As the bulb foliage begins to fade, the new reddish green shoots of the plumbago cover them over, keeping things looking tidy.

Plumbago (*Ceratostigma plumbaginoides*) is a tough and beautiful groundcover that does well in sun or light shade. The bright green foliage and deep blue flowers are suitable for walls, rock gardens, and borders.

CHELONE

key-LOW-nee • Scrophulariaceae, Figwort Family

This robust perennial with coarse lanceolate leaves along upright or arching stems produces unusual inflated tubular flowers borne in terminal and axillary clusters. They resemble the head of a turtle with the mouth agape. The dried seedheads are also attractive. Turtleheads produce large clumps from stout, fibrous-rooted crowns.

CHELONE

Common Name:
Turtlehead

Bloom Time:
Late summer and fall bloom

Planting Requirements:
Full sun to partial shade

Chelone glabra (GLA-bra), white turtlehead. Size: 3 to 5 feet tall and wide. A lovely, upright to slightly vase-shaped plant with white flowers blushed with violet. The dark green leaves are narrow and lance-shaped. USDA Plant Hardiness Zones 3 to 8.

C. lyonii (lye-ON-ee-ee), pink turtlehead. Size: 1 to 3 feet tall, 3 to 4 feet wide. Bright rose-pink flowers are borne on compact plants against wide, lush foliage. 'Hot Lips' is a compact selection with lush foliage and hot pink flowers. Zones 3 to 8.

C. obliqua (o-BLEE-qua), red turtlehead. Size: 2 to 3 feet tall, 2 to 4 feet wide. A floriferous species with rose or red-violet flowers on upright stems. Leaves narrower and shorter-stalked than the similar pink turtlehead. 'Alba' has white flowers. Zones 4 to 9.

How to Grow

Turtleheads are plants of wet meadows, low ditches, and other moist soils. They are quite adaptable to garden conditions. Give them rich, evenly moist soil in full sun or partial shade. In warmer zones, plants in full sun must have constant moisture. Early pinching will decrease height but may compromise the plant's form. Divide the fleshy-rooted crowns in spring or late fall after flowering. Propagate by stem cuttings taken in early summer. Sow seeds outdoors when ripe. Indoors, sow seeds in winter and place in the refrigerator for 4 to 6 weeks. Then remove the flat to the light and maintain a temperature of 60°F. Plants germinate in 2 to 3 weeks and can be transplanted in summer.

Landscape Uses

Turtleheads are regal accent plants for the late-summer and fall garden or in the symphony of the late-season border. Combine them with Joe-Pye weeds (*Eupatorium*), asters, pearly everlastings (*Anaphalis*), and Japanese anemones (*Anemone* ×*hybrida*). In the informal garden or meadow, plant drifts of turtleheads with goldenrods (*Solidago*), sunflowers (*Helianthus*), asters, and grasses. At pond's edge, where the flowers are reflected in the still water, plant turtleheads with water irises, great blue lobelia (*Lobelia siphilitica*), and ferns.

Plant drifts of hot pink turtlehead (*Chelone lyonii* 'Hot Lips') in moist spots with full sun or partial shade. It is perfect for bog gardens or the edge of a pond with ferns and iris.

CHRYSANTHEMUM

kris-AN-the-mum • Asteraceae, Aster Family

Chrysanthemum is a large, variable genus of colorful daisy-flowered perennials. Garden mums (*Chrysanthemum ×morifolium*) have been in cultivation in China for over 500 years. These timeless plants are extremely popular and many hybrids have been developed. Recently, botanists have expended tireless energy reevaluating the proper classification in this genus. As a result, most species have been reassigned to new genera. Look for favorites like Shasta daisies (*Leucanthemum*), and painted daisies, and feverfew (*Tanacetum*) under their new names.

CHRYSANTHEMUM

Common Name:
Chrysanthemum

Bloom Time:
Summer or fall bloom

Planting Requirements:
Full sun

C. frutescens (fru-TES-senz) (*Anthemis frutescens*), marguerite. Size: 2 to 3 feet tall, 1 to 2 feet wide. A bushy, erect plant with stiff, dissected foliage and 2-inch white or sulfur yellow flowers on sturdy

The popular garden mum (*Chrysanthemum ×morifolium* 'Emperor of China') opens its double pink flowers in early fall. Be sure to pinch back the stems in early summer to assure dense, heavily flowered clumps.

stalks. USDA Plant Hardiness Zones 9 to 11; grown as an annual in other zones.

C. ×morifolium (mo-ri-FO-lee-um) (*Dendranthema ×grandiflorum*), garden chrysanthemum, florist's chrysanthemum, mum. Size: 1½ to 5 feet tall, 2 to 5 feet wide. Garden mums have maintained unparalleled popularity for nearly 2,500 years. The Chinese first "domesticated" garden mums through extensive hybridization of several species native to China and Japan. Judicious selection was made based on size, form, and color to get the best plants. Hybridization continues today, especially to create new flower forms and for increased cold-hardiness. The first mums reached Europe in the 17th century, where they were an instant sensation. Today over 5,000 cultivars are named. Many are suitable only for cultivation under glass for cut flowers or show. Others are quite hardy. The newer selections from the University of Minnesota; Morden Arboretum in Manitoba, Canada;

and the USDA in Cheyenne, Wyoming, are excellent plants for northern gardeners. Flowers run the gamut of color from white through pink, rose, red, burgundy, bronze, gold, yellow, and cream. Heads may be daisylike, pompon (with double, ball-like flowers), cushions (with flat double flowers), decoratives (with large semidouble or double flowers), buttons (with small tightly packed double flowers), or novelty types such as spiders, spoon-petaled, thistle, and brush varieties. Flower size varies from under 1 inch to 6 inches across. Enjoy the flowers in the garden with other plants or as long-lasting cut flowers. *Chrysanthemum* ×*morifolium* hybrids are short-day plants. This means that bud set and flowering are triggered by decreasing day length; hence their fall blooming period. Forced florist's mums make poor garden plants because they are selected to bloom very late in the season. Buy varieties developed for outdoor culture. Mums have deep green, often hairy lobed leaves that are attractive as the plant grows throughout spring and summer prior to blooming. Cultivars are too numerous to list and vary in hardiness. Check with your local garden center or nursery to obtain the best selections for your area. USDA Plant Hardiness Zones 4 to 9.

C. zawadskii var. latilobum (za-WAD-ski-ee lat-i-LOB-um) (also sold as C. ×*rubellum*) (*Dendranthema zawadskii*), hardy garden chrysanthemum. Size: 1 to 3 feet tall, 2 to 4 feet wide. An extremely hardy, early-blooming mum with deeply lobed leaves, often edged in red, with 2- to 3-inch pink flowers. 'Clara Curtis' is 2 to

Single apricot daisies of 'Mary Stoker' mum (*Chrysanthemum zawadskii* var. *latilobum* 'Mary Stoker') are among the last flowers to open in the fall garden. The flowers are appreciated by tiny native pollinators called halictid, or flower bees, as well as by gardeners reluctant to let the season end.

2½ feet tall with deep pink flowers. 'Mary Stoker' has pale straw yellow flowers. Zones 4 to 9.

How to Grow

Chrysanthemums are easy to grow. Plant them in average to rich, moist but well-drained soil in full sun. Garden mums thrive in neutral or limey soils. Waterlogging is sure death, especially in winter. Many chrysanthemums spread quickly by creeping stems to form broad clumps. Because they grow so quickly, they often die out in the center. Division is necessary every 1 or 2 years to keep them healthy and attractive. Lift clumps in spring and discard older portions. Replant into improved soil. Chrysanthemums are easily grown from cuttings taken in late spring or early summer. Most will bloom the first year. Aphids and occasionally spider mites can be problems. Spray with an organic insecticide such as soap or a botanical such as nicotine or pyrethrins. Mites are difficult to control. Remove badly infested portions and discard. Do not compost insect-ridden herbage.

Garden and hardy mums require pinching to control their height and to make them bushy. Start pinching when the plants have six to eight well-formed leaves. Remove the growing point, taking care to make a clean break. After side shoots have started to develop, pinch them again to two to four leaves. Additional pinching may be required for some selections. Stop pinching altogether before July 1. Later pinching may compromise your flower display.

Increase the size of individual mum flowers by removing all but one flower bud on each stem. This process is known as disbudding. Florists use this technique to create the huge pompon flowers carried by homecoming queen hopefuls the country over. Potted mums also benefit from disbudding to produce large, well-spaced flowers. To disbud, first determine which is the dominant bud on each stem, usually the top and largest bud. Simply pinch off the other buds clustered below the dominant one. Do this when the buds are still in the button stage, before they show any color. Take care not to damage the main stem. When the flower opens, it will be larger and more full because it isn't competing with the others.

Landscape Uses

Free-flowering mums are so varied in bloom time, color, size, and adaptability that they have a place in almost every garden. Hardy garden mums are the most familiar. Use their brilliant fall flowers in mixed color plantings or combined with asters, sedums, ornamental grasses, and shrubs.

CHRYSOPSIS

kri-SOP-sis • Asteraceae, Aster Family

Golden asters light up roadsides and open woods in late summer where they grow wild. In the garden, they produce dozens of cheery yellow asterlike flowers on bushy plants with small, leathery, oval leaves. Their tawny seedheads resemble miniature dandelions. Plants grow from fibrous-rooted crowns and are extremely drought-tolerant when established.

CHRYSOPSIS

Common Name:
Golden aster

Bloom Time:
Summer and fall bloom

Planting Requirements:
Full sun

Chrysopsis graminifolia (gram-in-if-FO-lee-a) (*Pityopsis graminifolia*), silk grass. Size: 1 to 3 feet tall, 1 to 2 feet wide. An attractive fall-blooming plant with stiff, silvery, grasslike leaves in a loose rosette and clusters of ½-inch yellow flowers. USDA Plant Hardiness Zones 6 to 9.

C. mariana (mar-ee-AH-na) (*Heterotheca mariana*), Maryland golden aster. Size: 1 to 3 feet tall, 1 to 2 feet wide. A floriferous, mounding plant with deep green, lance-shaped leaves covered in gray hairs. In late summer, ½-inch bright yellow flowers cover the plant, often persisting well into fall. Zones 4 to 9.

C. villosa (vill-O-sa) (*Heterotheca villosa*), hairy golden aster. Size: 1 to 5 feet tall, 1 to 3 feet wide. A variable species ranging in height and size of flowers, owing to natural geographic variation. The widely available cultivar 'Golden Sunshine' is 4 to 5 feet tall with broadly lance-shaped foliage covered in long soft hairs. The 1½- to 2-inch golden yellow flowers are held in broad flat clusters from late summer through fall. Zones 4 to 9.

How to Grow

Golden asters are tough heat- and drought-tolerant plants. Give them average or sandy, well-drained soil and full sun. They will not thrive in rich or overly moist soils. Clumps are easily divided in spring. Propagate by cuttings taken in early summer, or by seed. Sow seed outdoors when ripe or indoors with 4 to 6 weeks of cold stratification at 35° to 40°F. Fungal root rot

Bright yellow late-summer flowers open on the decumbent stems of Maryland golden aster (*Chrysopsis mariana*) in spite of drought and heat. Plants demand a well-drained site in full sun to light shade.

may be a problem under moist conditions. Plant in well-drained sandy soil to avoid this disease.

Landscape Uses

Golden asters are well suited to dry-soil gardens with thymes (*Thymus*), yarrows (*Achillea*), wormwoods (*Artemisia*), lavenders (*Lavandula*), beardtongues (*Penstemon*), and pinks (*Dianthus*). They perform well in rockeries, on dry sunny banks, and in other tough sites.

CIMICIFUGA

sim-me-sif-YOU-ga • Ranunculaceae, Buttercup Family

Stately plants of open woodlands and glades. Dozens of creamy white, fuzzy, petalless flowers crowd together on tall stalks that branch like enormous candelabras. The compound foliage resembling *Astilbe* emerges in early spring and remains attractive through frost. Plants grow from thick, slow-spreading rootstocks. Botanists have re-assigned *Cimicifuga* to the genus *Actaea* (baneberry), but we have maintained the genus for easy reference.

CIMICIFUGA

Common Names:
  Bugbane, cohosh, snakeroot

Bloom Time:
  Summer and fall bloom

Planting Requirements:
  Full sun to open shade

Cimicifuga americana (a-mer-i-KA-na), summer cohosh, mountain bugbane. Size: 3 to 5 feet tall, 2 to 3 feet wide. A late-summer-blooming cohosh with single or sparsely branching inflorescenses of sweetly fragrant, clear white flowers. USDA Plant Hardiness Zones 4 to 8.

C. japonica (ja-PON-i-ka), bugbane. Size: 2 to 3 feet tall, 1 to 2 feet wide. Up-right flower spikes with pure white flowers are held over the thrice-divided leaves with huge, shiny toothed leaflets. Plants bloom in late summer or early fall. Zones 3 to 8.

C. racemosa (ra-see-MO-sa), black co-hosh, black snakeroot. Size: 4 to 7 feet tall, 2 to 3 feet wide. A regal plant with tall, branching spikes of creamy white ill-scented flowers in early summer. 'White Lightning' is a compact plant with black stems to 4 feet that creep to form broad clumps. Zones 3 to 8.

C. rubifolia (rue-be-FO-le-a) (*cordifolia*), Kearney's bugbane, Appalachian bugbane. Size: 1 to 4 feet tall, 2 to 3 feet wide. The gorgeous foliage of this Appalachian native is reason enough to grow it. Broad, shiny green leaflets create a unique look below bloom stalks of creamy, late-summer flowers. This mountain species does not tolerate high night temperatures. Zones 4 to 8.

C. simplex (SIM-plex), Kamchatka bugbane. Size: 3 to 6 feet tall, 2 to 3 feet wide. A variable species with several varieties of different sizes. They bloom in autumn on branched stalks. The white flowers are deliciously sweet-scented. Var. *simplex* (*ramosa*) has 5- to 6-foot narrow, sparsely branching spikes. 'Atropurpurea' has deep reddish purple foliage and flower stalks. 'Brunette' has deep bronze foliage and is 3 to 4 feet tall. 'Hillside Black Beauty' and 'Black Neglige' have deep purple leaves that hold their color in summer. Var. *matsumarae* is shorter, to 3 feet. 'Elstead' is a dark-stemmed selection with purple-tinged buds. 'White Pearl' has gracefully drooping, openly branched spikes. Many plants sold incorrectly under the name 'White Pearl' get taller. Plants do not tolerate heat and humidity, and may partially defoliate by the time they bloom. Zones 3 to 8.

How to Grow

Plant these long-lived woodland plants in moist, humus-rich soil in sun or shade. In warmer regions, consistent moisture and shade from hot afternoon sun will extend the life of the foliage, which scalds in hot sun. All species will bloom even in full but open shade. They are fairly drought-tolerant once established but retain attractive foliage in consistently moist soil. Plants grow slowly and can remain in position for many years. Divide the tough rootstocks in fall with a sharp knife, leaving at least one eye per division. Sow fresh seeds outdoors. They have a complex dormancy and may not germinate for 2 years. Seedlings develop slowly.

The soaring white spikes of black cohosh (*Cimicifuga racemosa*) open in June woods long after other wildflowers have flowered. The plants are equally at home in a sunny to lightly shaded perennial garden.

Landscape Uses

Bugbanes are beautiful on the edge of a woodland with a backdrop of lush green shrubs or accented by tall tree trunks. In woodland gardens, plant them with hostas, Solomon's seals (*Polygonatum*), wild geranium (*Geranium maculatum*) and ferns. In borders, contrast their vertical forms with rounded plants such as phlox, catmints (*Nepeta*), and monkshood (*Aconitum*).

CLEMATIS

KLEM-a-tis • Ranunculaceae, Buttercup Family

A large genus of woody vines, subshrubs, and herbaceous plants that bloom on new growth. The subshrubs and herbaceous species are not as showy as some of the huge-flowered hybrids but they have a subtle, restrained beauty. The flowers have showy sepals that resemble petals, usually four per flower. They can be carried singly or in clusters, and may be star- or bell-shaped. The seeds have long fuzzy tails that are tangled in a tight mass.

CLEMATIS

Common Name:
Clematis

Bloom Time:
Late spring, summer, or fall bloom

Planting Requirements:
Full sun or light shade

The rambling stems of solitary clematis (*Clematis integrifolia*) are perfect for filling bare spots left by early-blooming perennials. The nodding flowers open in succession for more than a month in summer.

Clematis alpina (al-PEEN-a), alpine clematis. Size: 8 to 10 feet long. A lovely clematis with nodding, four-sepaled violet-blue flowers on old wood in spring. An important parent of many fine selections and hybrids. USDA Plant Hardiness Zones 3 to 9.

C. crispa (KRIS-pa), blue jasmine. Size: 3 to 6 feet long. Herbaceous climber with pinnately compound leaves with five to nine leaflets. The weakly bell-shaped, wide-flaring solitary blue flowers are 1 to 2 inches across. The margins of the sepals are wavy and paler in color than the flower. Zones 6 to 9; may be hardy farther north.

C. heracleifolia (her-ak-lee-i-FO-lee-a), tube clematis. Size: 1 to 3 feet tall and wide. A subshrub with weakly upright stems and compound leaves with three broad leaflets. The 1-inch starry blue flowers are clustered in the axils of the upper leaves. Var. *davidiana* is more erect and showy with fragrant indigo-blue flowers. Zones 3 to 8.

C. integrifolia (in-teg-ri-FO-lee-a), solitary clematis. Size: 1½ to 3 feet tall, 3 to 4 feet wide. A weakly upright to sprawling plant with paired ovate leaves and solitary, wide-flaring indigo bells with recurved sepals. Var. *caerulea* has light blue flowers. Zones 4 to 9.

C. recta (REK-ta), ground clematis. Size: 2 to 4 feet tall and wide. A weakly upright to open shrublike plant with compound leaves having five to nine small leaflets. The starry, fragrant white flowers are borne in dense terminal clusters in summer and fall. 'Purpurea' has red-violet foliage that sets off the flowers to good advantage. Zones 3 to 7.

C. texensis (tex-EN-sis), scarlet clematis. Size: 3 to 6 feet long. Herbaceous climbing vine with leaves 2 to 3 inches long. A rambling vine with pinnately compound blue-green leaves and solitary, nodding scarlet bells with pale yellow insides. Zones 4 (with protection) or 5 to 9.

C. virginiana (vir-gin-ee-AH-na), virgin's bower. Size: 6 to 12 feet long. Herbaceous climbing vine with leaves 2 to 3 inches long. A fragrant autumn-blooming clematis with masses of starry white flowers that swamp the three-lobed leaves. Zones 4 to 9.

Hybrids

Hundreds of gorgeous hybrids are available in a variety of double and single forms. They are classed according to their parentage. Below are a few of the most popular. 'Betty Corning' (Viticella Group) is a deciduous climber with nodding flowers of four lavender-pink tepals. 'Blue Bird' (Atragene Group) has nodding, semidouble lavender-blue flowers in early spring. 'Carmencita' (Vitacella Group) has outfacing, four-tepaled wine-red flowers. 'Durandii' (Integrifolia Group) is a shrubby species with 4-inch outfacing purple-blue flowers with six tepals. 'Etoile Violette' (Vitacella Group) has outfacing violet flowers with six tepals. 'Helsingborg' (Atragene Group) has nodding royal purple bells with four tepals. 'Huldine' is a lovely white with upfacing, slightly cupped flowers. 'Jackmanii' has dark outfacing violet flowers with four tepals. 'Sieboldii' has six white tepals accented by a purple anemone-flowered central boss.

How to Grow

Plant clematis in moist, humus-rich soil in full sun. Most species resent hot weather. The old saying goes "put their heads in the sun and their feet in the cool shade." A cool, evenly moist and fertile root run is as important as sun for good growth and bloom. Propagate by stem cuttings before flowering in spring or early summer. Sow fresh seeds outdoors.

Landscape Uses

Clematis were made to partner with shrubs and small trees. Train the climbing species and hybrids up through their woody supports for multiple seasons of bloom. Shrubby forms are best used with some support like a peony hoop in mixed borders or perennial beds with phlox, yarrows (*Achillea*), cranesbills (*Geranium*), and a wealth of other summer-blooming plants.

COLCHICUM

KOL-kee-kum • Colchicaceae (Liliaceae), Colchicum Family

The elegant pink or white chalices of colchicums appear like magic in late summer and fall. The lush, glossy leaves appear in early spring and die down in summer. All parts of the plant are poisonous, so they are deer- and vole-proof. They grow from true bulbs. One of the common names—autumn crocus—is a misnomer, as the plants are not true crocuses.

COLCHICUM

Common Names:
Colchicum, meadow saffron

Bloom Time:
Late summer and fall bloom

Planting Requirements:
Sun or partial shade

Colchicum autumnale (awe-tum-NAH-le), autumn crocus. Size: 10 to 12 inches tall and wide, flowers 4 to 6 inches tall. A popular species with elongated, rose-pink goblets and coarse, vase-shaped foliage. 'Alboplenum' has double white flowers. 'Album' is a single white. 'Pleniflorum' has double rose-pink flowers. USDA Plant Hardiness Zones 4 to 8.

C. byzantinum (by-zan-TEE-num), Byzantine colchicum. Size: 6 to 8 inches tall and wide, flowers 3 to 5 inches tall. A diminutive species with light rose-pink flowers checkered in darker rose and low, spreading foliage rosettes. Zones 5 to 8.

C. cilicium (ke-LI-kee-um), colchicum. Size: 6 to 8 inches tall and wide, flowers 4 to 6 inches tall. A delicate species with checkered rose-pink flowers and spreading vases of lush foliage. Zones 5 to 8.

C. speciosum (spe-see-O-sum), meadow saffron. Size: 10 to 12 inches tall and wide, flowers 8 to 10 inches tall. The showiest species with sturdy, rounded, rose-pink flowers with white eyes and upright vases of lush, elegant foliage. 'Album' is an elegant snow white selection. Zones 4 to 8.

Hybrids

A number of exceptional hybrids also grace the garden. 'Giant' has huge lilac-rose flowers with white eyes. 'Lilac Wonder' has upright, rose-violet flowers with narrow segments. 'Violet Queen' has deep rose-violet flowers of excellent substance. 'Waterlily' is a fully double rose-pink with large flowers. Zones 4 to 8.

How to Grow

Plant colchicums in rich, well-drained soil in full sun or light shade. Do not remove the large, floppy leaves until they are completely yellow or you may sacrifice bloom.

Though the foliage ripens early, plants in deep shade do not bloom as freely. Also, flowers flop in shade as they try to reach the light. Planting in a dense groundcover helps hold the flowers erect. Bulbs are sold in summer and fall, along with spring-flowering species such as *Narcissus*. Order early as supplies are usually limited and early planting is preferred.

Landscape Uses

Colchicums add rich color to the late-season landscape. Place them among low plants and groundcovers to avoid large blank spots when the foliage goes dormant. Low-growing asters, phlox, sedums, thymes (*Thymus*), and creeping speedwells (*Veronica*) are good companions. In light shade, combine them with sedges (*Carex*), ferns, and foamflowers (*Tiarella*).

Meadow saffron (*Colchicum speciosum*) opens its pink chalices in late summer. The flowers emerge from the bare ground, making a dramatic display when planted among ground-hugging plants like stonecrops (*Sedum*). The foliage emerges in early spring and dies away in summer.

CONVALLARIA

kon-val-LAIR-ee-a • Convallariacea (Liliaceae), Lily-of-the-Valley Family

The fragrant, nodding flowers lined on a curved stalk have been celebrated in poetry and song. A lovely ground-cover in flower and foliage, plants can spread rapidly to form dense, broad mats. The flowers are appreciated in a vase, where you don't have to kneel to see them. Plants grow from creeping underground rhizomes, which root at the nodes.

CONVALLARIA

Common Name:
Lily-of-the-valley

Bloom Time:
Spring bloom

Planting Requirements:
Sun or shade

The delightfully fragrant bells of lily-of-the-valley (*Convallaria majalis* 'Striata') are beloved by all who know them. Add handsome yellow stripes and lush foliage to form a distinctive groundcover in partial to full shade.

Convallaria majalis (ma-JA-lis), lily-of-the-valley. Size: 6 to 8 inches tall, 12 to 24 inches wide. A dense, fast-spreading groundcover with two or three broad leaves arising from each bud, or "pip," along the tough, slender rhizome. In spring, erect stems carry fragrant nodding white bells that are beloved by gardeners of all ages. Glossy red berries are produced in summer, often obscured by the lush foliage. 'Flore Pleno' is fully double. 'Fortin's Giant' is 12 to 15 inches tall with large ¾-inch bells. 'Haldon Grange' is a robust plant with leaves edged in gold. 'Rosea' has dusty pink flowers. 'Striata' ('Aureo-variegata') is sensational, with bright gold stripes down the leaves. USDA Plant Hardiness Zones 2 to 8.

How to Grow

Lily-of-the-valley thrives in a wide range of soil and moisture conditions in sun or shade. The ideal spot has moist, rich soil in partial or filtered shade, but since it thrives elsewhere, lily-of-the-valley is often relegated to less hospitable sites. In warm regions, moisture and shade are mandatory. Divide overgrown plants in summer or fall. You will soon have enough lily-of-the-valley to beautify the entire neighborhood.

Landscape Uses

Choose lily-of-the-valley for a fast-spreading groundcover under flowering shrubs or trees. In the shade garden, use it sparingly with ferns, wild gingers (*Asarum*), geraniums, and creeping phlox (*Phlox stolonifera*). Plant the variegated selection with black mondo grass (*Ophiopogon planiscapus nigrescens*) for dramatic impact. Frequent control is necessary when planted in proximity to other perennials.

COREOPSIS

kor-ee-OP-sis • Asteraceae, Aster Family

Coreopsis lights up the meadows and roadsides where it grows wild, with glowing color throughout much of the summer. This large genus is made up of summer- and autumn-blooming perennials that produce profuse, cheerful yellow daisy-like flowers. Plants range in height from under a foot to 6-foot giants. They are all easy-care plants worthy of the highest praise. Coreopsis grows from fibrous-rooted crowns, and some produce creeping rhizomes and form broad clumps.

COREOPSIS

Common Names:
 Tickseed, coreopsis

Bloom Time:
 Late spring and summer bloom

Planting Requirements:
 Full sun

Coreopsis auriculata (a-rik-u-LA-ta), mouse-ear coreopsis. Size: 1 to 2 feet tall and wide. A low, spreading groundcover with fuzzy, triangular-eared leaves and 2-inch yellow-orange flowers held well above the foliage in spring. Creeping stems advance the clumps steadily outward, but it is seldom invasive. 'Nana' is a compact cultivar. USDA Plant Hardiness Zones 4 to 9.

C. grandiflora (gran-di-FLO-ra), large-flowered tickseed. Size: 1 to 2 feet tall and wide. A popular, old-fashioned perennial with clumps of lance-shaped, entire, or three- to five-lobed leaves on leafy stems with 2½-inch, deep yellow flowers. An excellent flower for cutting. 'Early Sunrise' is compact with double flowers. This handsome plant won the 1989 All-America Award. 'Goldfink' is compact (9 inches) with single flowers. This cultivar is often listed under the closely related *C. lanceolata*. Zones 4 to 9.

C. helianthoides (hee-lee-an-THOY-deez), swamp tickseed. Size: 2 to 2½ feet tall

and wide. A broad, leafy species with mounds of showy, bright yellow flowers from summer through fall. *C. integrifolia* is similar, but the flowers have dark eyes and are held 2 to 3 feet above the leaves on decumbent stems. Zones 7 to 10.

The starry, red-eyed flowers of pink tickseed (*Coreopsis rosea* 'Sweet Dreams') seem to smother the plants in midsummer.

C. lanceolata (lan-see-o-LA-ta), lance-leaf coreopsis. Size: 1 to 2 feet tall and wide. Similar to *C. grandiflora,* not as floriferous but perhaps longer-lived. Listed cultivars may belong here or may be of hybrid origin from these two species. 'Brown Eyes' has single yellow flowers with a maroon eye. 'Sunburst' has semidouble flowers on 2-foot stems. 'Sunray' is a popular, long-flowering cultivar with 2-inch double flowers on 2-foot plants. 'Tequila Sunrise' has variegated cream and yellow foliage that emerges pinkish. Zones 4 to 9.

C. rosea (RO-zee-a), pink tickseed. Size: 1 to 2 feet tall and wide. A low, mounding plant with three-lobed needle-like leaves and dozens of 1-inch pink flowers with bright yellow centers. 'Limerock Ruby' is a new hybrid with ruby red flowers. 'Sweet Dreams' has large flowers like a bull's eye, light pink on the outside, cherry red at the center. Zones 4 to 8.

C. tripteris (TRIP-ter-is), tall tickseed. Size: 3 to 9 feet tall, 3 to 4 feet wide. A stately, stiff plant with stout stems clothed in three-lobed, lance-shaped leaves and topped with wide clusters of 2-inch starry yellow flowers. Zones 3 to 8.

C. verticillata (ver-ti-kil-LA-ta), threadleaf coreopsis. Size: 1 to 3 feet tall and wide. An airy, mounding plant with three-lobed, needle-like leaves and dozens of 1- to 2-inch yellow flowers borne throughout summer. 'Golden Gain' is a compact selection with deep yellow flowers. 'Golden Showers' is a 2-foot selection with 2½-inch golden yellow flowers. 'Moonbeam' is 1 to 2 feet tall with 1-inch sulfur yellow flowers from early summer through frost. 'Zagreb' is a compact version of 'Golden Showers,' only 8 to 18 inches tall. Zones 3 to 8.

How to Grow

Coreopsis are tough, easy-care perennials. Plant them in average to rich, moist soil in full sun. They are quite drought-tolerant once established and thrive even under stress. Overly rich soils promote flopping. To prolong flowering, remove spent flowers regularly, especially on the *C. grandiflora/lanceolata* types. Mouse-ear tickseed grows well in partial or open shade and retains its attractive foliage all season if the soil remains moist. Divide overgrown or declining plants in spring or

Rich yellow, late-season flowers make Chipola River tickseed (*Coreopsis integrifolia*) a valuable addition to a sunny or lightly shaded bed.

fall. Sow ripe seeds indoors under warm (70°F), moist conditions. They germinate in 2 to 4 weeks. Take stem cuttings in early summer. They root quickly and can be planted out in the same season.

Landscape Uses

Coreopsis are excellent border plants. Combine the golden-yellow flowers with white, blue, red, and purple for lively viewing. The soft yellow flowers of *C. verticillata* 'Moonbeam' are nice with more restful colors, such as pink and lavender. Asters, iris, blanket flowers (*Gaillardia pulchella*), coneflowers (*Echinacea*), and phlox are comfortable companions. Use mouse-ear coreopsis along walks or in an informal setting with groundcovers and ferns. Plant tall coreopsis at the back of the border or in meadow and prairie plantings with native grasses, coneflowers, asters, Joe-Pye weeds (*Eupatorium*), gayfeathers (*Liatris*), and other yellow daisies.

CORYDALIS

ko-RI-day-lis • Fumariaceae, Fumitory Family

Bright flowers and lacy foliage make corydalis indispensable weavers in the garden tapestry. The curious flowers are irregularly shaped, with a slightly gaping lip or spur at the rear of the flower where it attaches to the stalk. Corydalis are called fumeroots because of the pungent fragrance emitted when their roots are crushed. The genus contains both bulbous and rhizomatous members.

CORYDALIS

Common Name:
Corydalis, fumeroot

Bloom Time:
Spring and summer bloom

Planting Requirements:
Sun to shade

Corydalis 'Blackberry Wine', blackberry wine corydalis. Size: 1 foot tall, 1 to 2 feet wide. This handsome new introduction has violet flowers over bright green leaves on wide clumps. Plants begin blooming in late spring and flower sporadically through autumn. USDA Plant Hardiness Zones 5 to 9.

C. cheilanthifolia (kay-lanth-i-FO-lee-a), fern-leaf fumeroot. Size: 1 foot tall and wide. This spring-blooming species looks more like its fern namesake than a corydalis. Butter yellow flower clusters complement the tufted clumps of tapering, finely dissected leaves that emerge bronze in spring. Zones 4 to 9.

C. flexuosa (flex-ewe-OH-sa), blue fumeroot. Size: 10 to 15 inches tall and wide. The mystique and allure of this species lie in its unique azure blue color, which is shared by few flowers. The deeply lobed leaves with fan-shaped leaflets are produced in fall and spring. Plants rest in hot summer weather (the smaller-flowered *Corydalis elata* is a more heat-tolerant species that performs better in most gardens). This plant requires mild winters and cool summer weather and is not for every garden. 'China Blue' has bronze leaves spotted with red, and sky blue flowers; 'Golden Panda' has gorgeous golden leaves; 'Pere David' has red, blotched leaves and blue-violet flowers. 'Purple Leaf' is named for purple-tinted foliage and blue-violet flowers. Another blue species, *C. curviflora* ssp. *rosthornii,* has large blue cornucopia flowers carried tight above the blue-green foliage. Zones 5 to 7.

C. lutea (lew-TEE-a), golden fumeroot. Size: 6 to 12 inches tall and wide. An exuberant, everblooming groundcover that opens the first of its many intense canary

Blue fumeroot (*Corydalis flexuosa* 'China Blue') sports ferny foliage and abundant bright blue flowers that easily weave a garden into a seamless whole.

yellow flowers in midspring above bright gray-green filigreed foliage. Plants bloom throughout summer. Zones 4 to 8.

C. ochroleuca (o-crow-LEW-ka), white fumeroot. Size: 6 to 12 inches tall and wide. Creamy white flowers with a dark flair are held above lacy, gray-green foliage. Plants self-sow freely. Zones 4 to 8.

C. scouleri (SKOOL-er-ee), Scouler's fumeroot. Size: 2 to 3 feet tall, 3 to 4 feet wide. A native of moist woods throughout the Pacific Northwest, this tall species spreads by fleshy runners to form broad clumps. Terminal spikes of rosy pink flowers seem to float above elegant tiers of large, lacy foliage. Zones 4 to 8.

C. solida (SO-lee-da) (*C. bulbosa*), spring fumeroot. Size: 4 to 6 inches tall, 8 to 12 inches wide. Gray-green foliage and short, dense spikes of pink to lavender flowers emerge in late winter from tubers that resemble oversized yellow corn kernels. Plants are summer-dormant. 'George Baker', sometimes listed as *C. transylvanica,* has stunning brick red flowers. 'Beth Evans' is soft pink. The similar *C. cava* has tall clusters of white to soft yellow flowers. Zones 3 to 9.

How to Grow

With a few exceptions, corydalis are easy to grow and pest-free. Most species grow best in cool, moist conditions. Early flowering tuberous species are the least fussy. They thrive in any good, moist soil with sun when they are in active growth. Plants are summer-dormant. In time, they form broad clumps of densely packed tubers. Occasional division keeps plants vigorous and free-flowering. Lift them as the foliage is going down, separate tubers, and replant in enriched soil. Self-sown seedlings will contribute to the carpets that form in time.

Rhizomatous-rooted species are a bit more exacting in their requirements; give them rich, humusy soil that stays evenly moist. Plants require light shade, especially where summers are hot. In northern zones, they can take a good deal of sun. Most perennial species rest in summer but seldom go dormant unless it is hot and dry, and they keep their foliage through mild winters. If voles reside in your garden, plant the tubers in wire cages.

Landscape Uses

The true charm of any corydalis lies in its ability to weave together plantings with diverse foliar attributes. Contrast the delicate foliage as a foil for bold hostas, coral bells (*Heuchera*), epimediums, and hellebores. Combine early deciduous species with season-long foliage plants like peonies and hostas that will fill the void left when they go dormant. Most corydalis eventually retreat underground as the sun and the mercury climb. Try corydalis along paths and atop rock walls. Seedlings will find a foothold in even the smallest crevice and transform a plain wall into a colorful garden with enchanting results.

CRAMBE

KRAM-be • Brassicaceae, Mustard Family

Crambes are succulent plants with blowsy leaves like edible kale or collards. The leaves and young stems are eaten in Europe, where they are often blanched like endive. Branched clusters of small, honey-scented white to cream flowers are carried well above the leaves in summer. They grow from thick, succulent taproots and are extremely drought-tolerant.

CRAMBE

Common Names:
Crambe, kale

Bloom Time:
Summer bloom

Planting Requirements:
Sun or light shade

Crambe cordifolia (kord-i-FOE-lee-a), giant kale. Size: 4 to 7 feet tall, 3 to 5 feet wide. In bloom, this plant resembles baby's-breath on steroids. Huge domed clusters of white flowers float above the large, heart-shaped leaves that look like giant cab-

bages. USDA Plant Hardiness Zones 5 to 8.

C. maritima (ma-RI-tea-ma), sea kale. Size: 2 to 3 feet tall and wide. A demure relation of giant kale with thick, wavy blue leaves and dense clusters of creamy white flowers in summer. These beach-dwelling plants are extremely salt-tolerant. Zones 4 to 8.

How to Grow

Crambes require full sun and fast-draining sandy or loamy soil. Established plants are deep-rooted and difficult to move. After flowering, the foliage may become tattered and worn. Remove the worst leaves, but do not cut the plants back completely. Propagate by root cuttings in early spring.

Landscape Uses

Plant giant kale at the middle or back of a dryland border for a dramatic show. Place full-crowned plants like phlox, yarrows (*Achillea*), and nepetas in front of the basal rosettes to hide the summer foliage. Use sea kale in rock gardens, at the front of borders, or in containers.

The thick, deep penetrating taproot of giant kale (*Crambe cordifolia*) bestows astounding drought tolerance and enables mature plants to grow to gigantic proportions. Use plants in borders and informal plantings with grasses and drought-tolerant perennials.

CROCOSMIA

kro-kos-ME-a • Iridaceae, Iris Family

Crocosmias set the summer and fall garden ablaze with their fiery hues in sunset colors. Their funnelform flowers are carried on arching, zigzag stems that are good for cutting. Lush green swordlike foliage emerges from papery buttonlike corms similar to those of gladioli, which spread to form tight clumps. Use them in borders or containers. Crocosmias are a common sight in the Pacific Northwest, where they are naturalized on roadsides.

CROCOSMIA

Common Names:
  Crocosmia, montbretia

Bloom Time:
  Summer and fall bloom

Planting Requirements:
  Full sun

Croscosmia ×***crocosmiiflora*** (kro-kos-mee-i-FLO-ra), crocosmia. Size: 2 to 3 feet high, 3 to 5 feet wide. A hybrid species from various free-flowering parents. First bred by French hybridizer Lemoine in 1880, most modern cultivars are of English origin. The flowers are slightly nodding. 'Citronella' has 1-inch orange-yellow flowers. 'Morning Light' is clear yellow. 'Norwich Canary' sports yellow-orange buds that open to bright yellow. 'Solfatare' has yellow flowers and bronze foliage. USDA Plant Hardiness Zones 6 to 9.

C. masoniorum (may-son-ee-OR-um), crocosmia. Size: 2½ to 3 feet tall, 3 to 5 feet wide. A tall plant with upfacing flowers of fiery orange. 'Firebird' has red-orange flowers with a yellow throat. 'Jenny Bloom' has warm orange buds that open intense orange. 'Kathleen' is scarlet. Zones 5 to 9.

Hybrids

Many showy new cultivars have been created through crosses between related genera as well as among different species. They vary in size and hardiness from Zones 5 to 9. C. 'Constance' has yellow-and-red flowers. 'Emberglow' has burnt orange flowers on 2- to 3-foot plants. 'Emily McKenzie' has 2½-inch orange flowers with a crimson throat. 'Lucifer' has deep scarlet flowers and is an extremely popular selection. 'Spitfire' has large orange-red flowers with a yellow throat.

How to Grow

Plant crocosmias in spring in moist, humus-rich soil in full sun. They spread enthusiastically to form tight clumps of beautiful foliage. In Zones 5 and colder, lift bulbs in fall and store indoors in a cool, dry spot. In warmer areas, divide clumps in fall. Leaves may be attacked by thrips or spider mites. Spray with insecticidal soap as necessary or with a botanical insecticide. Remove badly infested foliage to the

The striking sword leaves and gaping bi-color flowers of crocosmia (*Crocosmia masonorum* 'Emily McKenzie') grow from corms similar to those of gladiolus. In cold zones, lift the corms in fall and store them over winter in a cool place.

ground and destroy or discard it. Voles love the corms.

Landscape Uses

Crocosmias add fire to the summer garden. Choose cultivars by size to fit the particular spot in your garden. The richly colored flowers complement a wide range of companions. The spiky leaves add lift and contrast to plantings dominated by rounded forms. Combine the reds and oranges with blue and purple flowers such as sages, asters, and stokes aster (Stokesia). Use the mellow yellows with pink, lavender, and blue of catmint, geraniums, and phlox.

CROCUS

KRO-cus • Iridaceae, Iris Family

Colorful crocuses are among the best-loved spring bulbs. To many gardeners, their delightful flowers signal the end of winter and the start of a new gardening season. However, many species bloom in fall; in milder climates, winter bloom is common. Crocuses grow from squat, buttonlike corms that are wrapped in dry, papery leaves. Flowers emerge just ahead of or with foliage. Each flower has three petals and three petal-like sepals ranging in color from white, cream, and yellow to lilac and purple. The outside of the flowers is often blushed or striped with a contrasting darker color. The grasslike leaves are keeled along the central vein, which is usually white, making the leaves striped. As summer approaches, plants go dormant and disappear.

CROCUS

Common Name:
Crocus

Bloom Time:
Winter, spring, or fall bloom

Planting Requirements:
Full sun or partial shade

Crocus ancyrensis (an-see-REN-sis), golden bunch crocus. Size: 4 to 6 inches tall and wide. An early crocus with bright yellow flowers borne with the leaves. 'Golden Bunch' is a floriferous cultivar. USDA Plant Hardiness Zones 3 to 9.

C. biflorus (bi-FLO-rus), Scotch crocus. Size: 4 to 6 inches tall, 8 inches wide. An early white, yellow-throated crocus striped with purple on the outside of the petals. 'Adamii' has lilac flowers striped outside with brown. Var. *alexandri* ('Alexandri') has white flowers blushed with purple on the outside. 'Fairy' ('Waldenii Fairy') is silver-white with a blue-gray outer blush. 'Miss Vain' is white with a pale blue base. Zones 5 to 9.

C. chrysanthus (kris-AN-thus), golden crocus. Size: 4 to 6 inches tall, 6 inches wide. An early yellow crocus with honey-scented flowers. Many hybrids are available. 'Advance' is lemon yellow with a blue-violet outer blush. 'Ard Schenk' is pure white. 'Bluebird' is violet-blue outside and creamy white inside. 'Cream Beauty' is creamy yellow. 'E. P. Bowles' has butter-yellow flowers blushed with brown. 'Lady Killer' is pale purple, darker on the outside. 'Princess Beatrix' is soft violet-blue infused with white. 'Snowbunting' is pure white with dark lilac feathering. Zones 4 to 9.

C. goulimyi (goo-LIM-ee-ee), crocus. Size: 4 to 6 inches tall and wide. A fall crocus with starry lavender flowers held above the foliage. Zones 7 to 9.

C. kotschyanus (kots-shee-AH-nus), Kotschy's crocus. Size: 4 to 6 inches tall and wide. A fall bloomer with lilac to rose-lilac flowers borne before leaves appear. Zones 5 to 9.

C. minimus (MIN-i-mus). Size: 3 to 4 inches tall and wide. An early crocus with bowl-shaped lilac flowers. Zones 6 to 9.

C. pulchellus (pul-KEL-lus). Size: 4 to 6 inches tall and wide. A fall crocus with lilac-blue flowers. 'Zephyr' is white with outer gray blush. Zones 5 to 9.

C. sativus (sa-TI-vus), saffron crocus. Size: 4 to 6 inches tall, 8 to 10 inches wide. An autumn crocus with deep lilac flowers veined in purple. The dried stigmas (female reproductive structures) are the source of the pungent spice saffron. Zones 5 to 9.

C. sieberi (SEE-ber-ee). Size: 4 to 6 inches tall and wide. A late-winter crocus with lilac-blue flowers with purple veins.

'Bowles White' is white with a gold heart. 'Firefly' is lilac-pink. 'Hubert Edelsten' is white inside and violet outside. 'Violet Queen' is deep violet. Zones 5 to 9.

C. speciosus (spee-see-O-sus), showy crocus. Size: 4 to 6 inches tall and wide. Early fall crocus with large lavender-blue flowers. Var. *albus* ('Albus') has white flowers. 'Artabir' has light blue flowers with darker veins. 'Cassiope' has violet-blue flowers. 'Conqueror' has large, deep sky blue flowers. Zones 5 to 9.

C. tomasinianus (tom-ma-sin-ee-AH-nus), Tomasini's crocus. Size: 4 to 6 inches tall, 6 to 10 inches wide. Spring crocus with lilac flowers, paler on the outside, borne with the leaves. A good self-sower. 'Albus' is creamy white. 'Barr's Purple' has large deep purple flowers. 'Ruby Giant' has

Species crocus reseed themselves freely so they are perfect for naturalizing in lawns and among open groundcovers. Although the early-spring blooms of *Crocus tomasinianus* 'Barr's Purple' are often dusted with late-winter snows, they are seldom damaged.

large red-violet flowers. 'Whitewell Purple' has violet flowers. Zones 5 to 9.

C. vernus (VER-nus), spring crocus, Dutch crocus. Size: 4 to 6 inches tall, 8 to 10 inches wide. Large-flowered spring crocus with white to pale violet flowers with purple streaks. This is a popular species, often in the parentage of the huge flowered Dutch hybrid crocuses. 'Haarlem Gem' has lilac flowers with gray outsides. 'Remembrance' has silvery violet flowers. 'Vanguard' has violet flowers. Zones 3 to 9.

How to Grow

The garden centers are flooded with "bulbs" in late summer. This is planting time for crocuses, especially the fall-blooming species. Get them into the ground early. If you order by mail, specify an early shipping date, especially if you live in the North. Spring-blooming species and hybrids can be planted later (September and October are ideal months). Once established, crocuses need little care and the species often spread by self-sown seeds. The corms also multiply, forming great clumps. Divide when flowering begins to wane or when clumps appear too crowded. Rodents can be a problem, so use a repellent, or better yet plant corms in wire boxes or baskets to protect them.

Landscape Uses

Few experiences are more memorable than finding the first crocus in bloom as the snow of a long winter is receding. Plant crocuses anywhere a bit of early color is desired. Use them in rock gardens, massed in borders, or naturalized in the lawn. Combine early-spring species and hybrids with hellebores (*Helleborus*), early-blooming cushion spurge (*Euphorbia polychroma*), bergenias, wildflowers, and other bulbs like snowdrops (*Galanthus*). Plant fall-blooming varieties among foliage plants like wild gingers (*Asarum*), foamflowers (*Tiarella*), and ferns for late color.

CYATHEA

sigh-A-the-a • Cyatheaceae, Lacy Tree Fern Family

Tree ferns add a lush, tropical elegance to gardens in the ground or in containers. Stout, rough stalks elevate the huge, lacy fronds that form a circle high above your head when they are fully mature. The shadows cast by the fronds turn dull pavement into a dazzling light show. Plants demand high humidity or the fronds will get crispy around the edges.

CYATHEA

Common Name:
Lacy tree fern

Bloom Time:
Foliage plant

Planting Requirements:
Sun to partial shade

Cyathea cooperi (COO-per-ee), lacy tree fern. Size: 8 to 16 feet tall, 4 to 5 feet wide. This popular tree fern has huge, lacy pale green fronds radiating from a central crown atop a slender trunk. Each 10-foot frond is supported by a stout stipe and rachis. USDA Plant Hardiness Zones 9 to 11.

Dicksonia antarctica (DIK-so-knee-a ant-ARC-te-ka), soft tree fern. Size: 8 to 25 feet tall, 4 to 10 feet wide. This impressive tree fern is widely grown wherever it is hardy. The broad, spreading crown is composed of many 6- to 8-foot, stiff, deep green fronds supported by a stout trunk. Zones 9 to 11.

Tree ferns (*Dicksonia antarctica*) are elegant in any setting, both indoors and out. In areas where they are not hardy, containerized plants can summer outdoors and spend the cold months in a cool, high-humidity location indoors.

from strong winds, which may desiccate the fronds or topple the plants.

How to Grow

Plant tree ferns in constantly moist, well-drained, humus-rich soil in light to full shade. They are easily transplanted, even when mature. They require lots of fertilizer and respond well to an annual topdressing with composted manure. Protect plants

Landscape Uses

Lacy tree ferns are popular as accents in subtropical gardens. They lend an exotic flavor to courtyards, entryways, and large gardens. Combine them with flowering and evergreen shrubs and other ferns. They also grow well in containers.

CYCLAMEN

SIK-la-men • Primulaceae, Primrose Family

Though the comparison of cyclamen flowers to butterflies has become a cliché, it is so apt that it bears repeating. Few flowers are as whimsical and charming as these, with five perky white, pink, or magenta wings swept back as though poised for flight. Add their light perfume, and the winter garden offers few equals. Plants grow from flattened tubers.

CYCLAMEN

Common Name:
 Hardy cyclamen

Bloom Time:
 Winter, spring, or fall bloom

Planting Requirements:
 Full sun or partial shade

The distinctive pink flowers of winter cyclamen (*Cyclamen coum*) have rounded petals marked at their bases by deep maroon flairs. Even the white-flowered form *pallidum* sports the rich markings. Only the rare form *albissimum* is pure white.

Cyclamen cilicium (ke-LI-kee-um), hardy cyclamen. Size: 2 to 4 inches tall, 6 to 10 inches wide. The fragrant pink nodding flowers with pointed, reflexed petals of this fall-blooming species are sweetly fragrant. The rounded leaves are delicately mottled with silver or gray. USDA Plant Hardiness Zones 6 to 8.

C. coum (KOO-um), winter cyclamen. Size: 2 to 4 inches tall, 6 to 10 inches wide. Magenta to white dark-eyed flowers with rounded petals open in winter and early spring. Kidney- to heart-shaped, glossy, plain green, silver-variegated, or entirely silver-gray leaves emerge in fall and disappear as summer temperatures heat up. 'Album' is white with a dark eye. Zones 6 to 8; colder with protection.

C. hederifolium (hed-er-e-FO-lee-um) (*neapolitanum*), ivy-leaf cyclamen. Size: 4

to 6 inches tall, 8 to 12 inches wide. The flowers of this charming species begin appearing in late summer after a soaking thunderstorm and continue well into fall as new leaves emerge. Each flower has elongated petals in shades of rose and pink, as well as pure white. The wedge-shaped leaves are often sea green, mottled with lighter green and silver. As flowers fade, their stalks begin to spiral, which pulls seedpods close to the soil before they split open. Self-sown cyclamen are common. Zones 5 to 8.

C. purpurascens (pur-pur-AS-sens), cyclamen. Size: 4 to 6 inches tall, 6 to 10 inches wide. Evergreen rounded leaves with sparse mottling set off deep magenta to pink flowers borne in summer. Zones 4 (with protection) to 8.

C. repandum (re-PAN-dum), cyclamen. Size: 4 to 6 inches tall, 6 to 12 inches wide. Deep magenta flowers with narrow, pointed petals nod above triangular- to heart-shaped dark green mottled leaves in spring. Zones 7 to 9.

How to Grow

Dormant plants are most often sold in summer and fall, though potted cyclamen may be available from retail nurseries in spring or fall when in active growth or flower. Set plants with rounded tubers just below soil surface. Plant seedlings with special care so they do not get covered too deeply. Light, well-drained soil with humus and small gravel is best. They thrive around the bases of mature trees, where greedy tree roots ensure essential summer dryness. If planting dormant tubers, soak them for 24 hours in warm water to help break dormancy and initiate root growth. Temptation may lead you to cover the foliage against winter's cold. Resist! Leaves need sunshine to produce food for next year's bloom. When heat and drought of summer threaten, you retreat indoors to your air-conditioning, and cyclamen retreat underground for the season.

Landscape Uses

We combine cyclamen with a host of early bloomers in our winter gardens, placed outside a window for easy enjoyment. Companions include snowdrops (*Galanthus*), spring snowflake (*Leucojum vernum*), crocuses, winter daphne (*Daphne odora*), early daffodils, and several species of hellebores. Plant generous drifts on slopes and rocky hillsides with ferns, trilliums, Dutchman's breeches (*Dicentra cucullaria*), epimediums, and more hellebores.

CYRTOMIUM

KERR-tow-me-um • Dryopteridaceae, Shield Fern Family

The coarse, leathery evergreen fronds of holly fern make it a favorite for gardens, especially in hot climates where other ferns do not thrive. The stiff, arching fronds have wide scythe-shaped pinnae that arise in an open-vase shape from a stout scaly rhizome.

CYRTOMIUM

Common Name:
  Holly fern

Bloom Time:
  Foliage plant

Planting Requirements:
  Light to full shade

The lustrous fronds of holly fern (*Cyrtomium falcatum*) are often used as foundation plantings in the South. Try a mass planting either alone or combined with evergreen and deciduous shrubs as well as groundcover such as strawberry begonia (*Saxifraga stolonifera*).

Cyrtomium caryotideum (kar-e-o-TID-e-um), holly fern. Size: 1 to 2½ feet tall and wide. A broad vase-shaped fern with few, large pale green pinnae on squat fronds. USDA Plant Hardiness Zones 6 to 10.

C. falcatum (fal-KAY-tum), holly fern. Size: 2 to 2½ feet tall and wide. Deep black-green fronds have thick, hollylike pinnae on stiff, arching fronds. Zones 7 to 11.

C. fortunei (for-TUN-ee-ee), Fortune's holly fern. Size: 1 to 2½ feet tall and wide. This fern has narrower, more erect sea green fronds. Zones 6 (with protection) to 11.

How to Grow

Plant holly ferns in moist, acid, humus-rich soil in sun or shade. In colder zones, fronds may be damaged by dry winter winds. Cut damaged fronds to the ground in spring.

Landscape Uses

Plant holly ferns singly as accents among groundcovers or in drifts with perennials, shrubs, and trees. They are excellent as foundation plants alone or combined with flowering shrubs such as azaleas and rhododendrons. The glossy foliage catches light to brighten up shaded spots.

DELPHINIUM

del-FIN-ee-um • Ranunculaceae, Buttercup Family

Delphiniums are the holy grail for many perennial gardeners. Out of reach in hot climates, these jewels are reserved for regions where summer nights are cool and humidity is low. The showy flowers are densely packed on open-branching spikes. Each flower has five petal-like sepals in shades of blue or purple, the top one bearing a long, recurved spur. At the center of the flower are two or four fuzzy, true petals that give the flower a beard, or *bee*. Tall sturdy stalks clothed in deeply lobed or divided maple-like leaves grow from thick, fleshy roots. Although many wild species are attractive garden plants, the majority of the cultivated delphiniums are hybrids.

DELPHINIUM

Common Name:
Delphinium

Bloom Time:
Late spring and summer bloom, fall rebloom

Planting Requirements:
Full sun

Delphinium elatum (e-LAY-tum), bee delphinium. Size: 4½ to 6 feet tall, 2 to 4 feet wide. Stately perennial having deeply cut leaves with five to seven lobes and 1-inch blue-violet flowers. USDA Plant Hardiness Zones 4 to 7.

D. exaltatum (ex-al-TA-tum), tall larkspur. Size: 2 to 6 feet tall, 1 to 2 feet wide. An erect, sparsely branching plant with deeply divided leaves and ¾-inch spurred blue flowers. Zones 5 to 7.

D. grandiflorum (gran-di-FLO-rum), Chinese delphinium. Size: 1 to 2½ feet tall, 1 foot wide. Popular for its heat tolerance and easy care, this floriferous, compact species with deeply divided leaves with threadlike segments sports 1- to 1½-inch gentian blue flowers. 'Album' has white flowers. 'Blue Dwarf' ('Blue Elf') is only 1 foot tall. 'Blue Mirror' has marine blue flowers on 2-foot stems. Zones 4 to 8.

D. nudicaule (nu-di-KAW-le), canon delphinium. Size: 1½ to 2 feet tall and wide. Gorgeous orange-flowered delphinium with spurred, somewhat tubular flowers in open spiky clusters. The sparsely branching stem bears leaves with three or four broad lobes. Plants go dormant after flowering. Zones 5 to 7.

D. semibarbatum (sem-i-bar-BA-tum), delphinium. Size: 1 to 2 feet tall, 1 foot wide. An erect plant with deeply lobed leaves and funnelform, spurred yellow flowers. Plants go dormant after flowering. Zones 6 to 7.

D. tricorne (TRI-korn), dwarf larkspur. Size: 1 to 3 feet tall, 1 foot wide. A succulent, spring-blooming delphinium with 1- to 1½-inch deep blue spurred flowers and three to five lobed leaves. Heat-tolerant plants go dormant after flowering. Zones 4 to 7.

Hybrids

D. ×belladonna (bel-a-DON-a), belladonna delphinium. Size: 3 to 4 feet tall, 3 to 5 feet wide. A group of hybrids produced from crosses between *D. elatum* and *D. grandiflorum.* They are shorter than *D. elatum* hybrids because of the shorter *D. grandiflorum* parent. The summer and fall flowers are carried on branching stems above deeply lobed leaves. 'Bellamosum' has deep blue flowers on 4-foot plants. 'Casablanca' is pure white. 'Clivedon Beauty' has large, sky blue flowers on 3-foot plants. Zones 3 to 7.

D. elatum hybrids were produced from crosses utilizing *D. elatum, D. exaltatum,* and *D. formosum.* All have showy, dense spikes of large flowers in white, pink, blue, and purple on 4- to 6-foot stems that usually need staking against wind and rain.

Blackmore and Lingdon hybrids are a seed-grown series of mixed colors.

The Connecticut Yankee Series is similar to *D. ×belladonna* hybrids. 'Blue Fountains' has flowers in the medium to pale blue range and performs well in the heat of Zone 8.

Mid-Century hybrids are tall (4 to 5 feet), sturdy, and mildew-resistant.

'Ivory Towers' is white. 'Moody Blues' has light blue flowers. 'Rose Future' has pink flowers. 'Ultra Violet' is dark blue.

Pacific hybrids have huge, single to semidouble flowers on 4- to 5-foot stems. 'Astolat' has lavender flowers with a dark center. 'Black Knight' has dark purple flowers. 'Blue Bird' is clear blue with a

The towering spikes of hybrid delphiniums (*Delphinium elatum* hybrids) are quite top-heavy. Plant them where they are protected from strong winds, and stake each stem separately to keep them erect.

white bee. 'Galahad' is a late-summer bloomer with white flowers. 'Guinevere' is a blue bicolor, darkest on the outside. 'King Arthur' has dark blue flowers on 5-foot stems. 'Summer Skies' is light blue with a darker center.

How to Grow

Delphiniums are lovely old-fashioned perennials that are popular but often disappointing garden plants. They are extremely cold-hardy but do not tolerate hot summer nights or extended warm growing seasons. Plant delphiniums in deep, moist, humus-rich soil in full sun. The soil should be alkaline or only slightly acid. Feed them regularly with a balanced organic fertilizer or top-dress annually with rich compost or manure. It is next to impossible to overfeed delphiniums. In warmer areas, light shade and good air circulation are a must.

Plant containerized or bareroot plants in spring or fall. Take care not to damage brittle roots. As plants emerge in spring, thin stems to promote vigor and reduce chance of disease. Three to five stems per mature clump is recommended. Delphiniums are often short-lived and are treated by some as annuals, especially in hot climates. Stems are often succulent and susceptible to wind damage. Staking is recommended for all hybrids over 2 feet tall.

To promote reblooming, cut plants back to a point above foliage but below flower spikes. After new basal shoots have developed, remove spent shoots. New shoots will flower as cool weather returns.

The species forms of delphiniums are often longer-lived than the hybrids. Plant them in sun or light shade in rich, moist soil. Dwarf larkspur is a plant of sunny spring woodlands that become shaded in summer.

Divide overgrown clumps in spring and replant into amended soil. Delphiniums are easily propagated by fresh seed sown immediately upon collection. Take stem cuttings in early spring from newly emerging shoots. Slugs are the most insidious pest of delphiniums, but powdery mildew can be a problem, especially in warmer zones.

Landscape Uses

Place hybrid delphiniums at the rear of the border where their towering spikes will show off against a wall or hedge. Combine them with lilies, peonies, irises, poppies, and roses to create a charming cottage garden effect. Use them for vertical accent with summer perennials such as yarrows (*Achillea*), cranesbills (*Geranium*), catmints (*Nepeta*), baby's-breath (*Gypsophila paniculata*), and garden phlox (*Phlox paniculata*). Plant them in bold masses of mixed color as an accent along a wall or fence. Choose species delphiniums for borders or informal or woodland gardens in the company of wildflowers, ferns, hostas, and grasses.

DIANTHUS

di-AN-thus • Caryophyllaceae, Pink Family

Fragrance and elegance come to mind when one thinks of pinks. The showy five-petaled flowers are borne singly or in loose clusters on wiry stems. The flowers are produced in such profusion as to cover the foliage. The petals are often fringed or deeply cut, giving an attractive, ragged look to the tight clumps. Low carpet- or mound-forming perennials have awl-shaped foliage or bushy rosettes of lance-shaped leaves.

DIANTHUS

Common Names:
Pinks, carnation

Bloom Time:
Spring and summer bloom

Planting Requirements:
Full sun to light shade

Dianthus ×allwoodii (all-WOOD-ee-ee), Allwood pinks. Size: 1 to 1½ feet tall and wide. A tufted plant with blue-green lance-shaped leaves and white, pink, or purple fringed flowers often borne in pairs. The plants bloom tirelessly for up to 8 weeks. 'Alpinus' has single flowers in mixed colors. 'Aqua' has double white flowers on 12-inch stems. 'Doris' has fragrant salmon-pink flowers with a dark eye. 'Essex Witch' has pink flowers and is less than 6 inches tall. 'First Love' opens white and fades to lavender with a pink intermediate color. 'Frosty Fire' has double, bright red flowers. 'Mars' has double pink flowers on 3- to 6-inch stems. 'Pike's Pink' is excellent with bright pink flowers. 'Robin' has bright coral-red flowers. USDA Plant Hardiness Zones 4 to 8.

D. alpinus (al-PEEN-us), alpine pinks. Size: 3 to 6 inches tall, 6 to 12 inches wide. Clump-forming plant with bright green, rounded linear leaves and 1½-inch single,

flat-faced pink flowers in spring. Var. *albus* has white flowers. 'Joan's Blood' has semi-double crimson flowers. The Star Series contains hybrids of exceptional merit with semi- to fully double flowers in a variety of colors. 'Brilliant Star' is a favorite with its white flowers with deep wine-red centers. Zones 3 to 7.

D. barbatus (bar-BA-tus), sweet William. Size: 10 to 18 inches tall, 18 to 24 inches wide. A biennial or short-lived perennial with tufts of deep green lanceolate leaves and leaf stalks crowned by dense, rounded heads of bicolored or "eyed" flowers. 'Blood Red' is aptly named for its deep red flowers. 'Indian Carpet' is a seed strain in various colors on 10-inch stems. 'Newport Pink' has deep pink flowers and is 10 to 12 inches tall. 'Pink Beauty' has salmon-pink flowers on 15-inch stems. 'Scarlet Beauty' is deep scarlet. Zones 3 to 9.

D. deltoides (del-TOY-deez), maiden pinks. Size: 6 to 12 inches tall, 12 to 24 inches wide. Mat-forming plant with a profusion of single, ¾-inch pink or rose flowers borne one to a stem. 'Albus' has white flowers. 'Arctic Fire' has white flowers with magenta eyes. 'Brilliant' has scarlet-red flowers. 'Flashing Light' has ruby red flowers. 'Nellie' has dark red flowers with a darker halo over tight, dense rosettes. 'Zing Rose' has deep red flowers. Zones 3 to 9.

D. gratianopolitanus (grah-tee-ah-na-po-li-TAH-nus), cheddar pinks. Size: 9 to 12 inches tall and wide. A spring-blooming pink with 1-inch fragrant rose-pink flowers carried singly or in pairs. This is a popular species with many choice cultivars. Var. *grandiflorus* has 1½-inch rose-pink flowers. 'Albus' is pure white. 'Bewitched' is a heat-tolerant selection with pink flowers sporting bicolor red-and-white eyes. 'Feuerhexe' ('Firewitch') is heat-tolerant with brilliant magenta flowers. 'Karlicks' is deep rose. 'Petite' is a true dwarf with 4-inch cushions of foliage and small pink flowers. 'Splendens' has deep red flowers. 'Tiny Rubies' has cushion foliage and deep rose-pink flowers. Zones 3 to 9.

D. knappii (NAP-ee-ee), hairy garden pinks. Size: 12 to 18 inches tall and wide. This yellow-flowered species is a departure in flower color and form. The flowers are carried well above the hairy foliage on wiry stems in spring and summer. For the collector. Zones 3 to 7.

D. plumarius (ploo-MAH-ree-us), cottage pinks. Size: 1½ to 2 feet tall, 1 to 1½ feet wide. A cushion-forming plant with

Choose the open-flowered clusters of Allwood pinks (*Dianthus ×allwoodii*) for a sunny, well-drained spot along a stone walkway where the fragrant flowers can be enjoyed at close range.

grasslike basal leaves and fragrant white or pink flowers borne two to five per stem. Cultivars sold under *D. plumarius* are often hybrids with *D. gratianopolitanus*. 'Mrs. Sinkins' has fragrant double white flowers. 'Spring Beauty' is a seed strain of clove-scented semidouble to double flowers in white, pink, rose, and red. Zones 3 to 9.

D. superbus (su-PER-bus), lilac pinks. Size: 1 to 2 feet tall and wide. Open mounds of grasslike leaves and fragrant, deeply cut, ragged flowers in lilac, pink, or white. Zones 4 to 8.

How to Grow

Give pinks a sunny position with moist to dry, well-drained, alkaline to slightly acid soil. They spread quickly and are often short-lived, so divide the clumps every 2 or 3 years to keep them vigorous. Judicious deadheading will keep most species and cultivars in bloom for 6 weeks or more. Propagate pinks from stem cuttings in summer. Take a 2- to 3-inch portion of stem with a whorl of foliage and strip the leaves from the lower third. Cuttings from dwarf varieties may be an inch or less long. Place in a humid environment in a medium with excellent drainage. Roots will appear in 2 to 3 weeks. Sow seeds outdoors in spring or indoors in winter. Germination takes 15 to 20 days. Self-sown seedlings often appear around the garden. The most serious pest of pinks is rust, a fungus that forms yellow-green spots on the leaf surface. A preventive program of sulfur treatments is recommended if you have had problems. Good air circulation and drainage are the best precautions against problems.

Plant drought-tolerant maiden pinks (*Dianthus deltoides* 'Microchip') in the sunny rock garden where their small, bright flowers and mat-forming foliage show off to best advantage.

Landscape Uses

Pinks are beloved for their old-fashioned charm and delightful fragrance. They call to mind the eclectic cottage gardens of another generation. Plant them at the front of beds and borders where their mat-forming foliage makes a neat, attractive groundcover. Combine them with the broad gray foliage of lamb's ears (*Stachys byzantina*) and with threadleaf coreopsis (*Coreopsis verticillata*), dwarf bearded iris (*Iris pumila*), catmints (*Nepeta*), wormwoods (*Artemisia*), and columbines (*Aquilegia*). Use dwarf and cushion-forming species such as *D. alpinus* and *D. deltoides* in rock gardens or stone walls in the company of harebells (*Campanula*), thymes (*Thymus*), stonecrops (*Sedum*), and dwarf yarrows (*Achillea*). Combine the larger species and hybrids with creeping baby's-breath (*Gypsophila repens*), cinquefoils (*Potentilla*), creeping varieties of phlox (*Phlox bifida* and *subulata*), and low ornamental grasses such as fescues (*Festuca*).

DIASCIA

di-ASH-kee-a • Scrophulariaceae, Snapdragon Family

Oodles of small, eyed flowers in rosy hues and warm earth tones smother these beautiful workhorse plants throughout the growing season. The succulent stems bear sparse oval foliage and grow in open to trailing mounds from dense, fibrous-rooted crowns. Plants grow best where nights are cool and comfortable. Try them in the garden or in containers.

DIASCIA

Common Names:
  Twinspur, diascia

Bloom Time:
  Spring and summer bloom

Planting Requirements:
  Full sun to light shade

Diascia vigilis (vig-ILL-is), twinspur, and hybrids. Size: 1 foot tall, 1 to 2 feet wide. Wild species are seldom grown, but there are many exciting hybrids available that are more heat-tolerant and longer-flowering than older varieties. 'Andrew' has large watermelon pink flowers. 'Blackthorn Apricot' has ruffled apricot-orange flowers. 'Blue Bonnet' is pale apricot with a bluish blush. 'Emma' is raspberry and floriferous. 'Jack Elliot' is pink. 'Lucy' is deep coral. 'Twinkle' is lavender-pink. USDA Plant Hardiness Zones 7 to 9.

How to Grow

Plant in rich, moist but well-drained soil in full sun or light shade. Plants demand good drainage as well as good air circulation. Many new heat-tolerant selections have been developed, expanding the usefulness and bloom period of these floriferous perennials. Afternoon shade is appreciated where summers are hot and humid. Shear plants heavily when blooming wanes to encourage a new round

Scads of pinkish apricot twinspur flowers (*Diascia* 'Little Flamingo') completely smother the rambling stems throughout summer. In northern zones, use them as container annuals for a full season of continuous bloom.

of flowers. Propagate by stem cuttings taken anytime during the growing season.

Landscape Uses

Traditionally a container plant, twinspur performs well in the ground in rock gardens or in wall crevices. In borders, place them to the front where they will not be smothered by enthusiastic neighbors. Combine them with sages (*Salvia*), daylilies (*Hemerocallis*), dwarf bearded iris (*Iris pumila*), *Osteospermum*, and grasses.

DICENTRA

dy-SEN-tra • Fumariaceae, Fumitory Family

Bleeding hearts are heirloom woodland perennials that have been popular in gardens for centuries. The apt name of bleeding hearts typifies the unique flowers, which resemble pink hearts with drops of blood dangling from their tips. The flowers have paired, inflated lobes that may be rounded (as in bleeding hearts) or extended into a pointed hollow tube, as in Dutchman's breeches. The compound foliage is deeply dissected and often fernlike. Dicentras grow from thick, brittle roots or tuberous rhizomes.

DICENTRA

Common Name:
  Bleeding heart

Bloom Time:
  Spring and summer bloom

Planting Requirements:
  Sun or shade

Dicentra canadensis (kan-a-DEN-sis), squirrel corn. Size: 8 to 12 inches tall and wide. A delicate woodland plant with hyacinth-scented white hearts crowded at the end of a weak stalk. The ferny foliage disappears as soon as seeds ripen in early summer. USDA Plant Hardiness Zones 4 to 7.

D. cucullaria (kew-kew-LAR-ee-a), Dutchman's breeches. Size: 10 to 12 inches tall and wide. A dainty woodland plant with ferny leaves and flowers resembling strings of inverted pantaloons hung out to dry in the spring breeze. The plant disappears soon after flowering. Zones 3 to 8.

D. eximia (ex-EE-me-a), wild bleeding heart. Size: 10 to 18 inches tall, 12 to 24 inches wide. A bushy, floriferous plant with mounds of clustered pink hearts borne throughout spring and summer. The ferny blue-green foliage sets off the flowers to good advantage. 'Alba' has greenish white flowers. 'Boothman's Variety' has soft pink flowers and blue-gray foliage. 'Langtrees', possibly a hybrid, has white flowers with a dark spot of blood. 'Snowdrift' has pure white flowers. Zones 3 to 9.

D. formosa (for-MO-sa), Pacific bleeding heart. Size: 8 to 18 inches tall, 12 to 24 inches wide. Similar to *D. eximia,* but the pink to rose flowers are more squat and heart-shaped, the foliage is more blue-gray, and the plants spread by creeping rhizomes. 'Adrian Bloom' has raspberry-red flowers and blue-gray foliage. 'Bacchanal' has deep cherry-red flowers. 'Bountiful' has rose-pink flowers. 'Ruby Mar' has deep ruby-red flowers on compact plants. 'Zestful' has large rose-red flowers. 'Luxuriant', a floriferous selection with rose-red flowers, is thought to be a hybrid with *D. eximia.* 'King of Hearts', a hybrid with *D. perigrina, D. eximia,* and *D. formosa,* has full-figured hearts of rich rose-pink over finely divided blue-gray foliage that resembles a fern. Zones 3 to 8.

D. scandens (SCAN-denz), climbing bleeding heart. Size: 8 feet long. Pendant clusters of yellow hearts complement the green lobed leaves of this attractive but vigorous herbaceous vine. Plants grow best with a stout shrub or trellis for support. Zones 6 to 8.

D. spectabilis (spek-TAH-bil-is), old-fashioned bleeding heart. Size: 1 to 2½ feet tall, 2 to 4 feet wide. A beloved spring perennial with strings of 1-inch bright pink hearts on tall, arching stems. The leaves have wider leaflets than other species and persist through summer in more northern zones. 'Alba' has pure white flowers. 'Gold Heart' has golden spring foliage that fades to chartreuse, making a dramatic contrast with the deep pink flowers. 'Pantaloons' is a more robust, pure white selection. Zones 2 to 9.

How to Grow

Plant bleeding hearts (and other *Dicentra*) in evenly moist, humus-rich soil in full sun to partial shade. In cooler climates, bleeding hearts can grow in full sun as long as the soil is consistently moist. In fact, *D. formosa* and *D. eximia* will bloom all summer if given full sun to light shade. Shading from hot afternoon sun is important in warmer zones to avoid leaf scorch. Plant Dutchman's breeches and squirrel corn in the shade of deciduous trees. They need the

The beloved old-fashioned bleeding heart (*Dicentra spectabilis*) blooms with the tulips and daffodils.

spring sun and moist soil to bloom well; once dormant, shade and dry soil are incidental. Old-fashioned bleeding heart will bloom for 4 to 6 weeks if the temperature is moderate and the soil is constantly moist. The foliage remains attractive through most of the season. In warm climates or in dry soil, they go dormant by midsummer. Divide overgrown clumps in fall or as they go dormant. Take care not to damage brittle roots or rhizomes. Propagate by sowing fresh seed outdoors as soon as it is ripe.

Landscape Uses

Combine old-fashioned bleeding heart with daffodils, ferns, wild bleeding heart, and hostas in the light shade of an informal woodland garden. The foliage and flowers of the two species grown together creates a wonderful contrast of size and shape. In a border, plant old-fashioned bleeding heart with tulips, peonies, irises, primroses (*Primula*), early phlox such as *Phlox divaricata,* columbines (*Aquilegia*) and hardy geraniums. Use wild bleeding heart in formal and informal plantings with garden perennials, ferns, wildflowers, and hostas. Plant Dutchman's breeches and squirrel corn with plants that expand to fill the blank spots left when they go dormant, such as lungworts (*Pulmonaria*), Siberian bugloss (*Brunnera macrophylla*), wildflowers, and ferns.

DICTAMNUS

dik-TAM-nus • Rutaceae, Rue Family

Northern gardeners are lucky to count the dramatic gas plant among the beautiful, long-lived perennials for their borders. The spikes of rose or white flowers stand well above the rich green, divided leaves in early summer. The spiny, buttonlike seedpods extend the seasonal interest. Patience is required as the plants get established, but even young plants will reward you with a few flowers. Plants grow from stout crowns with thick, fleshy roots.

DICTAMNUS

Common Names:
   Gas plant, dittany

Bloom Time:
   Late spring and early summer bloom

Planting Requirements:
   Full sun to light shade

Dictamnus albus (AL-bus), gas plant. Size: 1 to 4 feet tall and wide. A stout, long-lived perennial growing from thick, almost woody rootstocks. The erect stems are clothed in pinnately compound leaves with bright green, rounded leaflets. The white flowers, borne in spiky terminal clusters, have five showy petals and 10 long curled stamens (male reproductive structures) that give the flowers a frivolous look. The plant is so named because the flowers emit an inflammable oil. All parts of the plant are strongly lemon-scented when bruised. 'Purpureus' has violet-purple flowers with dark veins. 'Ruber' has pale red-violet flowers with darker veins. USDA Plant Hardiness Zones 3 to 8.

How to Grow

Plant gas plant in a well-drained site with average to rich soil in full sun or light shade. Plants are slow to reach maturity and resent disturbance, so site them carefully. Take care not to disturb roots when planting containerized stock in spring. They bloom tirelessly for many years with little or no care. Dividing the tough roots often compromises plants, so propagate from seed. Sow seed outdoors as soon as it is ripe. Seedlings will appear the following spring but will take 3 or 4 years to bloom. Root rot may be a problem in soggy soil and hot weather. Good drainage is the best preventive. Longer, deep-penetrating waterings are preferable to frequent light waterings.

The hardy and long-lived gas plant (*Dictamnus albus* 'Purpureus') takes several years to achieve its full stature. Established plants reach shrublike proportions and bloom profusely in early summer.

Landscape Uses

Combine gas plant with other perennials that demand good drainage. Oriental poppies (*Papaver orientale*), yarrows (*Achillea*), sages (*Salvia*), catmints (*Nepeta*), blue stars (*Amsonia*), and asters are excellent companions. The flowers are short-lived but the foliage and starry seed capsules remain attractive all season. The purple-flowered varieties look lovely with a basal planting of color-coordinated hardy geraniums spread about their feet. Small or fine-textured flowers such as baby's-breath (*Gypsophila paniculata*), columbine meadow rue (*Thalictrum aquilegifolium*), and ground clematis (*Clematis recta*) set the flowers off to nice advantage.

DIGITALIS

dij-i-TAH-lis • Scrophulariaceae, Figwort Family

Foxgloves are heirloom classics for cottage gardens and borders. Erect, leafy stems and tall spikes of funnel-form flowers add lift to the garden's profile. Flower color varies from pink and rose to white, yellow, and brown. The insides of flowers are often spotted with dark purple. Plants form dense, tufted basal rosettes of broadly lance-shaped leaves each fall from which the flowering stalk appears the next year. Many are biennial or short-lived perennials. All portions of the plants are poisonous. Digitalis species are invasive in certain regions of the country.

DIGITALIS

Common Name:
 Foxglove

Bloom Time:
 Summer bloom

Planting Requirements:
 Sun to partial shade

The large flowers of hybrid foxglove (*Digitalis* ×*mertonensis*) are carried in dense, upright spikes. Plants are longer-lived than the invasive biennial *D. purpurea* and come in a wider range of colors.

Digitalis ferruginea (fer-roo-GIN-ee-a), rusty foxglove. Size: 4 to 5 feet tall, 1 to 2 feet wide. A stately plant with rusty brown flowers spotted in dark red. Each fat flower is tubular with a flared, flat lower lip. USDA Plant Hardiness Zones 4 to 7.

D. grandiflora (gran-di-FLO-ra) (also listed as *D. ambigua*), yellow foxglove. Size: 2 to 3½ feet tall, 1 to 2 feet wide. A handsome, long-lived plant with graceful spikes of soft yellow flowers and densely tufted persistent rosettes of rich green foliage. Zones 3 to 8.

D. lanata (la-NA-ta), Grecian foxglove. Size: 2 to 3 feet tall, 1 to 2 feet wide. A coarse plant with dense spikes of creamy white flowers with dark netted veins. This plant is the source of the commercial drug digitalis. Zones 7 to 9.

D. lutea (lew-TEE-a), straw foxglove. Size: 2 to 3 feet tall, 1 to 2 feet wide. Creamy yellow flowers are borne in one-sided spiky clusters above glossy leaves.

'Temple Bells' is a compact selection. Zones 3 to 8.

D. ×mertonensis (mer-toe-NEN-sis), strawberry foxglove. Size: 3 to 4 feet tall, 1 to 2 feet wide. A hybrid foxglove with the biennial *D. purpurea* crossed with perennial *D. grandiflora*. The hybrid selections vary in longevity; most persist a minimum of 3 years. The blowsy, spotted flowers come in shades of rose, pink, and white. Zones 3 to 8.

D. purpurea (pur-pew-REE-a), common foxglove. Size: 4 to 5 feet tall, 1 to 2 feet wide. This stately species with dense spikes of large-spotted flowers in a range of colors from white and pink to deep rose is a biennial. Plants form basal rosettes the first winter and bloom the following summer. Zones 4 to 8.

How to Grow

Plant foxgloves in moist, humus-rich soil in full sun or partial shade. The perennial species need little attention; the biennial and hybrid types must be prevented from setting seed to keep them growing. Lift plants after flowering and remove new rosettes from old flowering stems. If this is not practical, cut flowerstalks back to the ground as the last flowers fade. Leave at least one stalk so self-sown seedlings will appear. Young plants are generally more vigorous. Propagate by sowing seeds indoors or out. Plants bloom the second year.

Landscape Uses

Foxgloves are lovely when combined with perennials or used in mass plantings with flowering shrubs and evergreens. Combine the lovely yellow species with clustered bellflower (*Campanula glomerata*), bleeding hearts (*Dicentra*), irises, cranesbills (*Geranium*), daylilies (*Hemerocallis*), hostas, and ferns. Plant the taller species with goat's beard (*Aruncus dioicus*), early phlox (*Phlox maculata*), bugbanes (*Cimicifuga*), yuccas, and snowdrop anemone (*Anemone sylvestris*).

DISPORUM

di-SPO-rum • Convallariaceae (Liliaceae), Lily-of-the-Valley Family

Fairy-bells are delicate woodland plants with nodding, bell-shaped flowers paired at the tips of the stems. The broad oval-pleated leaves alternate up the erect stems. Plants are as showy in leaf as in flower. They have been compared to bamboos in their grace and elegance. Spidery roots spread out from a thickened creeping rhizome.

DISPORUM

Common Names:
Fairy-bells, mandarin

Bloom Time:
Spring bloom

Planting Requirements:
Partial to full shade

Disporum bodinieri (bo-din-e-AIR-ee), Chinese fairy bells. Size: 4 to 6 feet tall, 2 to 4 feet wide. This huge plant grows the size of a shrub and is evergreen in mild climates. Bamboo-like stems bear deep green leaves and nodding greenish white flowers. *D. cantoniense* is similar but variable in the wild. Cultivated selections are generally smaller in size, and the flowers are red or green. Variegated selections are available. Berries of both species are blue-black. USDA Plant Hardiness Zones 6 to 9.

D. sessile (SES-il-ee), nodding mandarin. Size: 1 to 2 feet tall and wide. A rhizomatous perennial forming open clumps of leafy stems with nodding white flowers. 'Variegatum' is the cultivar commonly grown for its white-variegated leaves. Two forms are available. "Narrow-leaf form" is shorter, 8 to 12 inches. "Wide-leaf form" is larger, with broad showy leaves. The species is seldom seen in cultivation. Zones 4 to 8.

D. smilacinum (smile-a-SEE-num), dwarf fairy-bells. Size: 4 to 6 inches tall, 6 to 12 inches wide. A demure, elegant species with wide-spreading rhizomes forming open clumps of arched stems clothed in wide leaves. Paired creamy bells dangle from stem tips in spring. Variegated forms such as yellow edged 'Aureovariegata' are more attractive than the species. Zones 5 to 9.

D. smithii (SMITH-ee-ee), white fairy-bells. Size: 1 to 2 feet tall and wide. A charming species with deeply pleated green leaves and showy white bells followed by red berries. *D. hookeri* is similar, but the greenish white flowers are flared open. Zones 4 to 9.

D. uniflorum (u-knee-FLOOR-um), (*flavum*), yellow fairy-bells. Size: 2 to 3 feet tall and wide. A sturdy, clump-forming plant with oval, satiny leaves and lemon-yellow flowers that begin opening as the plants emerge from the ground and continue for several weeks as the stems elongate. Black berries follow the flowers. Zones 4 (possibly 3) to 8.

The closely related genus *Disporopsis* contains several evergreen species with arching stems covered with alternating black-green leaves and small green flowers in axillary clusters. Zones 6 to 9.

How to Grow

Plant fairy-bells in moist, humus-rich soil in partial to full shade. They are easy-care plants that spread to form showy clumps. After flowers fade, the foliage remains neat throughout the season. Divide clumps after

Yellow fairy-bells (*Disporum uniflorum*) are stately plants for a moist, shaded spot. Plant them in drifts with ferns and wildflowers for best display. The lush foliage remains attractive all summer.

foliage hardens in spring if they become crowded or spread beyond their assigned borders. Replant into enriched soil. Sow fresh seed outdoors. Germination may take 1 or 2 years. Plants develop slowly.

Landscape Uses

Combine graceful fairy-bells with woodland wildflowers, hostas, astilbes, and ferns. Wild blue phlox (*Phlox divaricata*), creeping Jacob's ladder (*Polemonium reptans*), bloodroot (*Sanguinaria canadensis*), Allegheny foamflower (*Tiarella cordifolia*), and trilliums are possible companions. Plant them in the dry shade of mature trees with Solomon's seals (*Polygonatum*) and barrenworts (*Epimedium*) or as a groundcover under shrubs where they perform admirably. They also grow well in pots.

DODECATHEON

doe-de-CATH-ee-on • Primulaceae, Primrose Family

Shooting-stars are delicate plants of woods, alpine slopes, and low meadows. They produce basal rosettes of broadly lanceolate foliage that usually disappear after flowering. The naked flowerstalks are crowned with circles of gracefully arching flowers that resemble cyclamen but have dart-like points that protrude forward. Flower color varies from white to pink, rose, and violet.

DODECATHEON

Common Name:
  Shooting-star

Bloom Time:
  Spring bloom

Planting Requirements:
  Sun or shade

Dodecatheon clevelandii (kleve-LAND-ee-ee), Padres shooting star. Size: 8 to 16 inches tall, 10 to 12 inches wide. Slender plant with spatulate leaves and tightly packed clusters of magenta to white flowers. USDA Plant Hardiness Zones 6 to 7.

D. dentatum (den-TATE-um), toothed shooting-star. Size: 6 to 12 inches tall and wide. An attractive and adaptable species with toothed basal leaves and soft pink flowers. Zones 4 to 8.

D. jeffreyi (JEF-ree-ee), Sierra shooting-star. Size: 8 to 24 inches tall, 10 to 12 inches wide. A plant of wet meadows and bogs with magenta to pink flowers. Zones 4 to 7.

D. meadia (ME-dee-a), shooting-star. Size: 1 to 2 feet tall, 12 to 16 inches wide. A stout woodland and prairie perennial with white or pale pink flowers. 'Queen Victoria' has deep rose flowers. Zones 4 to 8.

How to Grow

Plant shooting-stars in moist, humus-rich soil in sun or shade. Once plants are dor-

After flowering, the delicate shooting-stars (*Dodecatheon meadia*) quickly disappear, leaving only a cluster of seedheads on a slender stalk. Take care not to disturb the crowns when planting or dividing other plants.

mant, the soil can be allowed to dry and the site can become quite shady. Most species prefer a neutral or slightly acid soil. Sierra shooting-star grows in moist acid soil. Divide clumps in summer or fall and replant crowns with roots spread in a circle. Take root cuttings in summer or fall. Sow fresh seed outdoors. Plants develop slowly and take several years to bloom.

Landscape Uses

Interplant shooting-stars among leafy plants that will hide the spaces left during dormancy, but don't crowd them when they are in bloom. In the shade garden, choose bloodroot (*Sanguinaria canadensis*), creeping Jacob's ladder (*Polemonium reptans*), wild gingers (*Asarum*), and ferns. In a rock garden, plant them with primroses (*Primula*), columbines (*Aquilegia*), barrenworts (*Epimedium*), and mounding or carpet-forming plants.

DORONICUM

do-RON-i-cum • Asteraceae, Aster Family

Leopard's banes are cheery spring daisies with a profusion of butter yellow flowers borne singly on slender stems. They bloom in the company of daffodils, tulips, and wildflowers. The bright green foliage is triangular or heart-shaped with distinctive teeth along the margins. The plants disappear altogether by midsummer. The shallow fleshy roots are sensitive to high soil temperatures.

DORONICUM

Common Name:
Leopard's bane

Bloom Time:
Spring and early summer bloom

Planting Requirements:
Full sun or partial shade

Doronicum austriacum (awe-stri-A-cum), hairy leopard's bane. Size: 2 to 4 feet tall, 1 to 2 feet wide. A tall, fuzzy species with branching flowers stems and 2-inch flowers. USDA Plant Hardiness Zones 5 to 8.

D. orientale (or-i-en-TA-le) (also listed as *D. caucasicum* or *D. cordatum*), leopard's bane. Size: 1 to 2 feet tall and wide. Showy 1- to 2-inch daisies are borne throughout the spring. 'Magnificum' has 2-inch flowers of great beauty. *D. grandiflorum* is similar and contains the popular cultivars 'Little Leo', with semidouble flowers on 12- to 15-inch stems, and 'Miss Mason', with large flowers. Hybrids include 'Finesse', a semidouble suitable for cutting, and 'Fruhlingspracht' ('Spring Beauty'), which is double-flowered. Zones 3 to 8.

D. pardalianches (par-dal-e-AN-keys), tall leopard's bane. Size: 3 to 4 feet tall, 2 to 3 feet wide. A vigorous species with tall stems crowned by open clusters of 1-inch daisies in early summer after other species have faded. Plants form broad clumps by runners and may need frequent control. Self-sown seedlings are common. Zones 4 to 8.

How to Grow

Plant leopard's banes in consistently moist, humus-rich soil in sun or shade. Mulch soil to keep its temperature cool during the growing season. Divide plants every 2 or 3 years to keep them vigorous. Replant into amended soil. Soil moisture is important even when the plants are dormant, especially in warmer zones.

Leopard's bane (*Doronicum orientale*) is prized for its summertime, bright yellow daisies with spaghetti-strap petals that radiate from the yellow buttonlike center.

Landscape Uses

Combine the bright flowers of leopard's bane with wildflowers such as Virginia bluebell (*Mertensia virginica*), trilliums, and woodland phlox (*Phlox divaricata*). Bulbs such as tulips and daffodils are excellent companions. Add some foliage plants such as lungworts (*Pulmonaria*) or lady's-mantle (*Alchemilla mollis*) to fill in when plants go dormant. For late spring, try bellflowers (*Campanula*), hostas, and irises. Plant tall leopard's bane with large plants such as shield ferns (*Dryopteris goldiana* and *D. wallichiana*), Solomon's seals (*Polygonatum*), and bugbanes (*Cimicifuga*).

DRYOPTERIS

dry-OP-ter-is • Dryopteridaceae, Shield Fern Family

Shield ferns produce exquisite vase-shaped clumps of fronds from stout rhizomes with dense, fibrous roots. The fronds arise in a circle around the upright growing point. Sizable crowns develop with time. Shield ferns are named for the shield-shaped cover over their spore-producing fruit dots.

DRYOPTERIS

Common Names:
Shield fern, wood fern

Bloom Time:
Foliage plant

Planting Requirements:
Light to full shade

The leathery, semievergreen fronds of male fern (*Dryopteris filix-mas*) emerge crisp and green in midspring, along with early wild-flowers and bulbs. In summer, the graceful vases of fronds add interest to groundcover plantings in a shaded woodland.

Dryopteris affinis (AFF-in-is), golden scaled male fern. Size: 3 to 4 feet tall and wide. This semievergreen species is similar to male fern, but the fronds are more upright and the pinnae are layered up the frond like rungs on a ladder. Plants form bold 3- to 4-foot clumps in moist, humus-rich, acid soil. Many crested selections are available. 'Crispa Gracilis' is a dwarf selection with lance-shaped fronds with curve-tipped, dull green pinnae. 'Cristata Angustata' has narrow 2-foot fronds with rounded, densely crested pinna. 'Cristata The King' is a popular cultivar with fan-shaped, crested pinnae and frond tips. 'Revolvens' has backward-rolled pinnae. USDA Plant Hardiness Zones 4 to 9.

D. ×australis (au-STRAL-is), Dixie wood fern. Size: 3 to 5 feet tall, 2 to 4 feet wide. This stunning giant resembles its parent, Goldie's fern, but the erect, stiff fronds are glossy green and taper at both ends. *D. celsa*, log fern, another parent, is smaller in stature and has narrower fronds. Zones 6 to 10.

D. cycadina (sigh-ka-DEE-na), shaggy shield fern. Size: 2 to 3 feet tall and wide. This bold fern has bright evergreen, lance-shaped fronds with simple, coarsely toothed pinnae. The stiff fronds radiate in an open vase shape from a central crown. The fiddleheads and young fronds are clothed in dense black scales. Zones 4 to 9.

D. erythrosora (e-ryth-row-SORE-a), autumn fern. Size: 1 to 2 feet tall and wide. Autumn fern is rapidly becoming one of the most popular garden ferns. Broad triangular evergreen fronds emerge copper-colored in spring and unfurl to a pinkish green. Mature fronds are deep shiny green. Zones 5 to 9.

D. filix-mas (FIL-ix MAS), male fern. Size: 2 to 3 feet tall and wide. Male fern has stiff, lustrous dark green fronds that form a flattened vase from a crown-forming rhizome. The leathery, lance-shaped fronds taper at both ends. Plants are native to North America and Europe. Many crested and tasseled forms of European origin are available. 'Barnesii' has narrow, upright ruffled fronds. 'Cristata Martindaleis' is a frilled selection with crested tips. 'Grandiceps' has a tasseled crest and pinnae tips on 3-foot fronds. 'Linearis Polydactylla' has fine-textured, crested linear pinnules on 3- to 4-foot fronds. Zones 3 to 9.

D. goldiana (gold-ee-AH-na), Goldie's fern. Size: 3 to 4½ feet tall, 2 to 3 feet wide. The upright, arching, oval to triangular fronds of this giant deciduous fern arise from a stout rhizome with an elevated crown. The flattened pinnae are pale green along the margins, giving young fronds a two-tone effect. Zones 4 to 8.

D. marginalis (mar-gin-AL-is), leather wood fern. Size: 1 to 2 feet tall and wide. This tough, adaptable fern has a place in every garden. The stiff arching evergreen fronds are dull olive-green in color and arise in a vase shape from a central crown. Zones 4 to 8.

D. wallichiana (wal-lick-e-AY-na), Wallich's wood fern. Size: 2 to 4 feet tall and wide. A gorgeous fern with tropical-looking semievergreen fronds with glossy, tightly arranged pinnae on gracefully arching fronds. *D. crassirhizoma* is another excellent species with large, 2- to 2½-foot glossy fronds in a voluptuous vase. Zones 5 to 8.

How to Grow

Plant wood ferns in moist, well-drained, acid, humus-rich soil in sun or shade. Shade is mandatory in warmer zones. Plants get large when mature; leave ample room when setting them out. Offsets from the main crown can be removed in spring for propagation.

Landscape Uses

Wood ferns are striking accent plants for moist, shaded gardens. Position them next to stumps, logs, or tree trunks for dramatic effect. Use them in mass plantings with flowering shrubs or along a foundation. The fancy-leaved selections are curious additions to wildflower gardens.

The upright, pinked fronds of golden scaled male fern (*Dryopteris affinis* 'Crispa Barnes') form dense clumps in a lightly shaded spot.

E

ECHINACEA

ek-in-A-cee-a • Asteraceae, Aster Family

Coneflowers are beloved by cottage gardeners and butterfly enthusiasts. The large daisylike flowers with mounded heads and showy rose or pink rays (petals) are usually borne singly on stout stems, well above the foliage. Coneflowers are erect perennials with coarse lanceolate to ovate, often toothed leaves. Plants grow from thick taproots that are quite deep on mature plants. Coneflowers are used as medicinal plants for alleviating skin rashes and internally for stimulating the immune system.

ECHINACEA

Common Name:
Purple coneflower

Bloom Time:
Summer bloom

Planting Requirements:
Full sun to light shade

Echinacea angustifolia (an-gus-ti-FO-lee-a), narrow-leaved coneflower. Size: 1 to 2 feet tall and wide. A compact coneflower with spare, lance-shaped basal leaves with stiff hairs and mostly leafless stems topped by 2-inch heads with short (1-inch) drooping rose-pink rays. USDA Plant Hardiness Zones 3 (possibly 2) to 8.

E. pallida (PAL-i-da), pale purple coneflower. Size: 3 to 4 feet tall, 1 to 2 feet wide. A sparsely branching plant with stout, nearly leafless stems topped with large heads of drooping pale rose rays. The basal leaves are lance-shaped and covered in stiff hairs. *E. laevigata,* smooth coneflower, is similar but has smooth leaves. Zones 4 to 8.

E. paradoxa (par-a-DOX-a), yellow coneflower. Size: 2½ to 3 feet tall, 1 to 2 feet wide. This is an unusual coneflower in that its rays are bright yellow. The plants grow in tight, multistemmed clumps with mostly basal leaves. The

leaves are broadly lance-shaped. An important plant in current breeding programs. Zones 4 to 8.

E. purpurea (pur-pew-REE-a), purple coneflower. Size: 2 to 4 feet tall (rarely to 6 feet), 2 to 3 feet wide. A shrubby, well-branched plant with leafy stems and dozens of flowers with flat or drooping rose-pink to red-violet rays. 'Bright Star' is a graceful selection with mostly flat rose-pink flower heads. 'Kim's Knee High' is an excellent compact selection to 2½ feet with large heads of gracefully drooping rays. 'Kim's Mop Head' is white. 'Magnus' has huge, flat flower heads. 'Springbrook's Crimson Star' has delicate, deep crimson flowers on sturdy 3-foot stems. One of the best. 'White Lustre' has larger, brighter white flowers than 'Alba' and 'White Swan'. Zones 3 to 8.

E. tennesseensis (ten-e-see-EN-sis), Tennessee coneflower. Size: 1 to 3 feet tall, 1 to 2 feet wide. The upswept rays of this species make it unique among coneflowers; the overall impression is of a rose-purple cup. This species has contributed its unique form to many new hybrids that will be released in the future. Zones 4 to 8.

How to Grow

Coneflowers are plants of prairies and open woods. Give them average, loamy soil in full sun or light shade. Plants grow best with adequate moisture but are quite tolerant of extended drought. These tough plants have deep taproots that enable them to store some water for lean times. Plants increase to form broad clumps. They flower throughout summer, and the rayless seedheads are attractive throughout fall and winter. Division is seldom necessary and not recommended. Once divided, plants tend to become bushy with compromised flower production. Propagate by root cuttings in fall. Sow seed outdoors in fall or indoors in winter. Give seeds 4 to 6 weeks of cold, moist stratification to promote uniform germination.

Showy purple coneflowers (*Echinacea purpurea* 'Alba') are extremely heat- and drought-tolerant. They have thick, deep taproots that store moisture for lean times.

Landscape Uses

Coneflowers are comfortable additions to formal and informal landscapes alike. Plant them in borders with catmints (*Nepeta*), garden phlox (*Phlox paniculata*), blazing-stars (*Liatris*), yarrows (*Achillea*), and Shasta daisies (*Leucanthemum maximum*). Create a pastel combination with lamb's ears (*Stachys byzantina*), verbenas, pink bee balms (*Monarda*), calamints (*Calamintha*), and cranesbills (*Geranium*) backed with ornamental grasses. In meadow and prairie gardens, plant coneflowers with native grasses, gray-headed coneflower (*Ratibida pinnata*), goldenrods (*Solidago*), butterfly weed (*Asclepias tuberosa*), and black-eyed Susans (*Rudbeckia*). They respond well to pot culture if planted in a deep container.

ECHINOPS

EK-in-ops • Asteraceae, Aster Family

The blue spheres of globe thistle garner praises from gardeners and flower arrangers. These erect perennials have lobed, spiny leaves and spherical heads of tightly packed, steel blue or white flowers. These stately, long-lived plants produce several stout stems from a thick, branching taproot.

ECHINOPS

Common Name:
Globe thistle

Bloom Time:
Summer bloom

Planting Requirements:
Full sun

Echinops exaltatus (ex-al-TATE-us), Russian globe thistle. Size: 5 to 8 feet tall, 3 to 4 feet wide. A huge plant for big borders. Erect stems are covered in spiny leaves and crowned with dramatic clusters of silvery spheres in mid- to late summer. USDA Plant Hardiness Zones 3 to 8.

E. ritro (RIT-ro), globe thistle. Size: 2 to 4 feet tall, 2 to 3 feet wide. A coarse, tall species with rich blue flowers above gray-green, spiny leaves. 'Veitch's Blue', best for small gardens, has dark blue heads on sturdy 3-foot stems. The similar *E. bannaticus* is more coarse, with blue flowers. 'Blue Globe' is floriferous with deep blue globes all summer on 3½ foot stems. 'Taplow Blue' has 2-inch, steel blue heads on 4- to 5-foot stems. Zones 3 to 8.

E. sphaerocephalus (sphere-o-ceph-AL-us) 'Arctic Glow', 'Arctic Glow' globe thistle. Size: 2½ to 3 feet tall, 1 to 2 feet wide. Noted for its silvery white globes atop mahogany stems covered in silvery green leaves. Zones 3 to 8.

Globe thistles (*Echinops ritro* 'Veitch's Blue') thrive on neglect. Plant them in lean, well-drained soil for best growth.

How to Grow

Plant globe thistles in average to rich, sandy or loamy soil in full sun. Once established, plants are quite drought-tolerant. Heavy wet soils are sure death to these tough plants, as good drainage is essential, especially in winter. Division is seldom necessary but is best accomplished in fall. Lift huge roots carefully, or remove an auxiliary rosette from plants without disturbing the entire clump. Take root cuttings in spring or fall.

Landscape Uses

Plant globe thistles in the company of other drought-tolerant perennials, such as catmints (*Nepeta*), yarrows (*Achillea*), inulas, oriental poppies (*Papaver orientale*), and ornamental grasses. Position them near the middle or back of the border with fine-textured plants that act as a foil to their bold foliage. Baby's-breath (*Gypsophila paniculata*), garden phlox (*Phlox paniculata*), 'Autumn Joy' sedum (*Sedum* 'Autumn Joy'), and Russian sage (*Perovskia atriplicifolia*) are good companions.

EPIMEDIUM

ep-i-MEE-dee-um • Berberidaceae, Barberry Family

Fairy wings are finally popular! Dozens of new species recently discovered in China, and many excellent garden hybrids have revolutionized the choices in this fascinating genus. They form attractive, easy-care mats of evergreen foliage from wiry rootstocks. The leaves are divided into small, glossy, heart-shaped or triangular leaflets on wiry petioles. The unusual flowers are carried in open clusters in early spring before the new leaves emerge. Each flower has eight petal-like sepals and four often spurlike petals. Color ranges from white to yellow, bronze, purple, red, and pink.

EPIMEDIUM

Common Name:
Fairy wings, barrenwort

Bloom Time:
Foliage plant with spring bloom

Planting Requirements:
Partial to full shade

Epimedium acuminatum (a-kew-min-A-tum), long-spurred fairy wings. Size: 6 to 12 inches tall, 12 to 24 inches wide. A Chinese species scarce in cultivation until recently. White flowers with purple spurs are held above beautiful spear-shaped evergreen leaves. USDA Plant Hardiness Zones 4 (with protection) to 8.

E. alpinum (al-PEEN-um), alpine barrenwort. Size: 1 foot tall, 1 to 2 feet wide. A compact plant with triangular, pointed leaves and small crimson-red flowers. The foliage is deciduous and dies back in fall.

Good for dry shade. 'Shrimp Girl' has coral flowers. Zones 3 to 8.

E. brachyrrhizum (brackee-RHIZ-um), fairy wings. Size: 6 to 8 inches tall, 8 to 12 inches wide. Fabulous 2-inch pink, spider-shaped flowers open in early spring before the purple-mottled, evergreen leaves expand. *E. leptorrhizum* is similar, but the plants spread by creeping rhizomes to form broad clumps. Zones 5 to 8.

E. franchetii (fran-CHET-ee-ee), barrenwort. Size: 1 to 1½ feet tall, 1 to 2 feet wide. This is one of the showiest of the new, spurred, yellow-flowered Chinese species. The large rich yellow flowers are held above the evergreen, spear-shaped foliage that emerges tinged bronze. *E. chlorandrum, E. davidii, E. lishihchenii* (USDA

The pert violet flowers with white tipped spurs of *Epimedium grandiflorum* 'Lilafee' are held in showy clusters above the foliage in spring. After flowering, the dense foliage clumps make a beautiful groundcover in shade.

Plant Hardiness Zone 4), *E. membranaceum* and *E. rhizomatosum* are other spurred yellow species of exceptional beauty and garden merit. Zones 5 to 8.

E. grandiflorum (grand-i-FLO-rum), Japanese fairy wings. Size: 8 to 15 inches tall, 1 to 2 feet wide. A large plant with broad, arrow-shaped leaflets and showy, long-spurred flowers. There are dozens of selections from several subspecies now available. A few of the best are 'Bandit' with brown-edged leaflets and copious white flowers; 'Harold Epstein' with huge butter yellow flowers and creeping rhizomes that form large, open clumps; 'Lilofee' with purple flowers and white-tipped spurs; 'Orion' with tall stems and deep red-violet flowers; 'Purple Prince' with deep purple flowers and rosy bronze spring foliage; 'White Queen' with large, bright white flowers; and 'Yubae' with rose-pink flowers. The similar *E. sempervirens* has evergreen leaves and many excellent cultivars. Zones 4 to 8.

E. ×omeiense (oh-my-e-EN-see), barrenwort. Size: 1 to 2 feet tall and wide. This robust natural hybrid takes many forms, all dramatic. Large spear- to shield-shaped foliage is overtopped with 2- to 3-foot branched sprays of purple, brown, or terracotta flowers in spring and summer. 'Storm Cloud' has purple-bronze flowers and large, decorative leaves. Zones 5 to 8.

E. ×perralchicum (per-ral-CHEE-cum), barrenwort. Size: 10 to 12 inches tall, 12 to 30 inches wide. Spikes of bright yellow flowers are carried on leafless stalks above emerging mounds of bronze, heart-shaped leaves. The dense mats of evergreen foliage are drought-tolerant. 'Frohnleiten' is a widely available selection with black-green mature leaves. 'Wisley' has pale veins that contrast with the deep green, wavy leaves. Zones 4 to 8.

E. pinnatum (pin-NAY-tum), barrenwort. Size: 8 to 12 inches tall, 1 to 2 feet wide. A leafy, drought-tolerant evergreen plant with bright yellow flowers. Zones 4 to 8.

E. ×rubrum (ROO-brum), red barrenwort. Size: 8 to 12 inches tall, 2 to 3 feet wide. A hybrid of *E. alpinum* with ¾-inch bright rosy red and yellow flowers. Zones 4 to 8.

E. sagittatum (sag-et-TATE-um), barrenwort. Size: 1 to 1½ feet tall, 1 to 2 feet wide. A large, handsome species grown more for its dramatic, shield-shaped leaflets that emerge copper-colored in spring than for its sprays of small white flowers. *E. myrianthum* is similar, with spear-shaped glossy leaflets and slightly larger flowers. Zones 5 to 8.

E. ×versicolor (VER-see-kol-or), bicolor barrenwort. Size: 10 to 12 inches tall, 2 to 3 feet wide. A popular, drought-tolerant hybrid with yellow flowers held above the foliage. 'Cherry Tart' is a fabulous new introduction with pink flowers. 'Neosulphureum' has pale yellow flowers. 'Sulphureum' is medium yellow. Zones 4 to 8.

E. ×warleyense (war-ley-EN-se), orange barrenwort. Size: 8 to 12 inches tall, 12 to 24 inches wide. A deciduous species with brick red flowers borne before new leaves emerge. 'Orangekonigin' is paler orange. Zones 4 to 8.

E. ×youngianum (young-ee-A-num), Young's barrenwort. Size: 6 to 8 inches tall,

Buttery yellow flowers with spurs like the clenched claws of an eagle open along with the expanding leaves of *Epimedium grandiflorum* var. *koreanum* 'Harold Epstein'.

1 foot wide. A compact, delicate plant with flowers held above foliage that emerges purple in spring. 'Be My Valentine' is diminutive with deep rose-pink and white flowers. 'Merlin' is a favorite with cherry red and white flowers. 'Milky Way' is pure white with long spurs. 'Purple Heart' has deep purple spring leaves and bicolor pink-and-white flowers. Zones 4 to 8.

Hybrids

'Amonogawa' has purple and white flowers over mottled spring foliage. 'Enchantress' has silvery pink flowers over spear-shaped foliage. Zones 4 to 8.

How to Grow

Barrenworts thrive on benign neglect. Plant them in moist, average to humus-rich soil in partial to full shade and they will thrive for years with little attention. Not even dry shade can discourage most of these versatile plants. They perform admirably under mature trees where little else will grow. Avoid waterlogged soils, especially during winter months. This situation is sure death to plants at the northern edge of their hardiness zone. In spring, cut old foliage to the ground unless it has survived the winter undamaged. New leaves emerge with or just after flowers to fill the gap. Divide plants as necessary to control their spread or for propagation. Just after foliage hardens and late summer are the best times, but these tough plants tolerate disturbance at any time.

Landscape Uses

Plant the adaptable fairy wings in the shade garden with early bloomers like daffodils, tulips, windflowers (*Anemone*), Pacific bleeding heart (*Dicentra formosa*), primroses (*Primula*), Virginia bluebells (*Mertensia virginica*), trilliums, and ferns. The emerging foliage is often tinged with russet and gives an added dimension to the spring garden. In the shade of large trees, plant barrenworts with Solomon's seals (*Polygonatum*), spotted dead nettle (*Lamium maculatum*), and bergenias. Use extensive clumps along the garden path or at the edge of the bed alone or combined with medium-size hostas. These plants are excellent groundcovers for the dense shade and root competition of shrubs and trees.

ERANTHIS

er-AN-this • Ranunculaceae, Buttercup Family

The cheery, upfacing buttercup yellow flowers of winter aconite add a splash of sunshine to the early spring garden. Each single flower is surrounded by a collar of dissected leaves with narrow segments on succulent stems 1 to 4 inches tall. Plants grow from small tuberous roots.

ERANTHIS
Common Name:
   Winter aconite
Bloom Time:
   Winter and early
   spring bloom
Planting Requirements:
   Sun

Eranthis cilicia (ki-LI-kee-a), winter aconite. Size: 2 to 4 inches tall, 4 to 6 inches wide. A delicate species with large flowers in proportion to the collars of leaves, which have very thin, spidery segments that emerge tinged with bronze, creating a showy effect. USDA Plant Hardiness Zones 4 to 8.

E. hyemalis (hy-e-MAH-lis), winter aconite. Size: 4 to 8 inches tall and wide. Robust plants with broad collars bearing fatter leaf segments that dwarf the showy yellow flowers. Zones 4 to 8.

E. stellata (stel-LAY-ta), white aconite. Size: 2 to 3 inches tall and wide. This rare species is finally becoming more available. Handsome white flowers with blue stamens open atop a ring of deeply dissected leaves. Zones 4 to 8.

How to Grow

Plant in rich humusy or loamy soil in a spot with plenty of spring sun. Soak dormant tubers overnight in warm water before planting, and set them 1 to 2 inches below the soil. Plants will self-sow to form large, showy colonies that become quite congested in time. Transplant "in the green" after flowering, or just as leaves are yellowing off.

Landscape Uses

Snowdrops (*Galanthus*), cyclamens, and other early bloomers are good companions, intermingled with hellebores, primroses (*Primula*), and ferns. Use a generous planting under winter-blooming shrubs such as white forsythia (*Abeliophyllum distichum*), daphne, *Viburnum bodnantense* 'Dawn', and witch hazels (*Hamamelis*).

Like perky buttercups blooming out of season, the up-facing cups of winter aconite (*Eranthis hyemalis*) announce the onset of spring. They scatter lots of seed before going dormant for the summer, so large sweeps develop after a few seasons.

EREMURUS

er-ee-MU-rus • Asphodelaceae (Liliaceae), Asphodel Family

Tall, stout wands of yellow, pink, or white flowers are held high above clumps of pointed, straplike leaves in this breathtaking perennial. The starry flowers are densely packed into spikes that open from the bottom up. A difficult beauty to keep happy, foxtail lily is worth the effort in fast-draining soil. It can be easily grown as an annual if planted in autumn for a single summer of glorious bloom. The plants grow from a hard crown with brittle, horizontally spreading roots.

EREMURUS

Common Names:
Foxtail lily, desert-candle

Bloom Time:
Spring and summer bloom

Planting Requirements:
Full sun to light shade

The stately hybrid foxtail lily (*Eremurus stenophyllus* 'Cleopatra') produces straplike foliage and towering wands of small starry flowers from a stout crown with thick, fleshy roots. This drought-tolerant perennial demands a sunny, well-drained site.

Eremurus himalaicus (him-a-LAY-e-kus), Himalayan foxtail lily. Size: 6 to 7 feet tall, 2 to 3 feet wide. A huge species with commanding white spires. USDA Plant Hardiness Zones 5 to 9.

E. robustus (ro-BUS-tus), foxtail lily. Size: 4 to 6 feet tall, 2 to 3 feet wide. This showy species is a late-spring bloomer with dense spikes of pink flowers. Zones 5 to 9.

E. stenophyllus (sten-o-FILE-lus), foxtail lily. Size: 2 to 3 feet tall, 1 to 2 feet wide. This spring-blooming species has yellow flowers on short stalks. 'Cleopatra' is a hybrid with stunning burnt orange flowers. 'Moneymaker' has yellow flowers with orange stamens. 'Shelford Hybrids' are a hybrid group with white, yellow, or pink flowers. Zones 5 to 9.

How to Grow

Give foxtail lilies moist but well-drained humus-rich soil in full sun or light shade. Wet soil, especially in winter, is fatal, causing freezing and root rot, especially in northern zones. Plant them out in summer or fall, taking care to spread roots horizontally and not to bury them more than 4 to 6 inches deep. A mound of gravel over crowns helps to shed water. Divide old, crowded clumps in fall. Sow fresh seed indoors or out as soon as it is ripe. Germination may take 6 months. Seedlings develop slowly.

Landscape Uses

Stately foxtail lilies are beautiful in the early-summer garden. Combine them with small-flowered plants such as catmints (*Nepeta*), sages (*Salvia*), and baby's-breath (*Gypsophila paniculata*), or with bold flowers such as oriental poppies (*Papaver orientale*) and peonies (*Paeonia* hybrids). Use them as specimen plants in front of walls and hedges or in the company of flowering shrubs.

ERIGERON

e-RIJ-er-on • Asteraceae, Aster Family

Fleabanes are a diverse group of floriferous summer-blooming, asterlike plants. The clusters of white, orange, pink, rose, or purple flowers are held on leafy stems above basal rosettes of fuzzy lance-shaped or oval leaves. The dense broad clumps are often buried in mounds of flowers. Plants grow from fibrous-rooted crowns.

ERIGERON

Common Name:
   Fleabane

Bloom Time:
   Summer bloom

Planting Requirements:
   Full sun

Erigeron aurantiacus (awe-ran-TEE-ah-cus), orange fleabane. Size: 9 to 12 inches tall and wide. A low-spreading plant with orange flowers borne singly in early summer. USDA Plant Hardiness Zones 4 to 8.

E. compositus (kom-POZ-i-tus), cut-leaf daisy. Size: 3 to 4 inches tall, 6 to 10 inches wide. A dwarf plant with deeply incised leaves and white to pale lavender flowers borne one to a stem. Zones 3 to 7.

E. glaucus (GLOW-kus), beach flea-bane. Size: 6 to 12 inches tall, 12 to 18 inches wide. Floriferous summer-blooming species with blue-violet flowers. 'Albus' is white. 'Sea Breeze' is a robust, compact selection with pink flowers, placed in this species though it grows to 2 feet or more tall. Zones 5 to 8.

E. karvinskianus (kar-vin-skee-AH-nus), rock fleabane. Size: 4 to 6 inches tall, 6 to 12 inches wide. A delicate plant at home in rock crevices and mortared walls. Plants have small leaves dwarfed by ¼-inch white flowers with bright yellow centers.

Plants lack hardiness but self-sow freely. Zones 8 to 10.

E. pulchellus (pul-KEL-us), robin's plantain. Size: 10 to 18 inches tall, 12 to 24 inches wide. A creeping groundcover plant with 1-inch lilac to pale blue flowers

On a dry sunny bank or at the front of a border, try daisy fleabane (*Erigeron speciosus*). Plants flower in late spring and summer. As an added bonus, the foliage is attractive after the flowers fade.

held singly above the matlike foliage. Zones 4 to 8.

E. speciosus (spee-see-O-sus), daisy fleabane. Size: 1½ to 2½ feet tall and wide. A showy, floriferous species blooming throughout summer. Plants form broad clumps from a central crown. Leafy stems bear a profusion of flowers for 4 to 6 weeks. Many hybrids of this species are available. 'Dunkelste Aller' ('Darkest of All') has violet-blue flowers. 'Foerster's Darling' has pink double flowers. 'Pink Jewel' ('Rose Jewel') is a popular pink selection. 'Prosperity' is an excellent older cultivar with lavender-blue flowers. 'Sincerity' has clear pink flowers. Zones 2 to 7.

How to Grow

Plant fleabanes in moist but well-drained rich soil in full sun or light shade. Cut-leaf daisy prefers sandy soil or rock crevices. Robin's plantain also tolerates impoverished conditions. Good drainage is a must for all species. They are long-lived but benefit from division every 2 or 3 years to keep them flourishing. Take tip cuttings in early summer or propagate from seed sown indoors or out. Seedlings will germinate indoors within 2 weeks of sowing. Seedlings appear the spring after sowing.

Landscape Uses

Plant fleabanes in borders and beds with spiky forms such as catmints (*Nepeta*) and sages (*Salvia*) for contrast. Other good companions include larger daisies like black-eyed Susans (*Rudbeckia*), as well as phlox (*Phlox*), evening primroses (*Oenothera*), and ornamental grasses. Use robin's plantain in meadows and other informal places. Cut-leaf and rock daisies are well-suited to rock garden culture. All species are good for cutting.

ERYNGIUM

e-RINJ-ee-um • Apiaceae, Parsley Family

Dramatic, globose heads of small, tightly packed flowers surrounded by showy stiff bracts add pizzazz to summer borders. It is the bracts that command attention in most species, not the small flower clusters. They are silvery gray, blue, or purple and are often elaborately incised or lobed. The glossy heart-shaped or pinnately divided leaves form tufted rosettes at the base of the stiff flowerstalks. A variable genus of taprooted biennial and perennial species.

ERYNGIUM

Common Names:
Sea holly, eryngo

Bloom Time:
Summer and fall bloom

Planting Requirements:
Full sun

Eryngium agavifolium (ah-gav-e-FO-lee-um), agave-leaved sea holly. Size: 4 to 5 feet tall, 3 to 4 feet wide. Dramatic in stature, the deep green spiny leaves command attention, as do the tall spires of green cone-shaped flower heads. USDA Plant Hardiness Zones 6 to 9.

E. alpinum (al-PEEN-um), alpine sea holly. Size: 1 to 2 feet tall, 2 feet wide. The three to five steel blue flower heads are surrounded by leafy rings of upturned purple-blue bracts. The basal leaves are heart-shaped; the stem leaves are lobed and often tinged with blue. 'Amethyst' grows to 3 feet tall. 'Blue Star' has good form and deep blue color. 'Opal' is similar but only 2 feet tall. 'Superbum' has large deep blue flowers. Zones 4 to 8.

E. amethystinum (am-ee-thist-EYE-num), amethyst sea holly. Size: 1 to 1½ feet tall, 2 to 3 feet wide. A floriferous species with small steel blue heads surrounded by sparse, narrow blue bracts. The stems are also blue. The basal leaves are pinnately divided. 'Blue Sapphire', a sterile hybrid, has deep steel blue bracts. Zones 2 to 8.

E. bourgatii (bour-GAT-ee-ee), Mediterranean sea holly. Size: 1 to 2 feet tall, 2 feet wide. A compact plant with pinnately divided leaves with prominent white veins. The silvery blue flowers are surrounded by long spiny bracts. Zones 5 to 8.

E. giganteum (ji-GAN-tee-um), giant sea holly, Miss Wilmot's ghost. Size: 4 to 6 feet tall, 3 to 4 feet wide. A coarse plant with green flower heads and broad, spiny, gray-blue bracts. The basal leaves are heart-shaped. This species is a biennial or short-lived perennial. Zones 4 to 8.

E. planum (PLAN-um), flat sea holly. Size: 2 to 3 feet tall and wide. This species is similar to *E. alpinum* and although not as showy, it is better for hot regions. The bracts are fewer and form a flattened ring around the mostly green flower head. Zones 5 to 9.

E. yuccifolium (yuck-ki-FO-lee-um), rattlesnake master. Size: 2 to 3 feet tall, 1 to 2 feet wide. A unique species with leafy rosettes of lance-shaped, gray-green leaves and tall stout stalks crowned by open clusters of pale green heads with inconspicuous bracts. Zones 4 to 9.

Mediterranean sea holly (*Eryngium bourgatii*) is the showiest of the blue-flowered species and a must for combinations of yellow and orange flowers. Compact stems to 2 feet tall sport silvery blue flowers surrounded by long spiny bracts.

E ×*zabelii* (za-BEL-ee-ee), Zabel sea holly. Size: 1 to 1½ feet tall, 1 to 2 feet wide. A showy plant with bright blue flower heads and bracts carried in a mound atop branching stems. 'Donard Variety' is a stout selection developed for the cut-flower market. Zones 4 to 8.

How to Grow

Plant sea hollies in average, well-drained soil in full sun. They tolerate all manner of adversity, thriving in gravel and sand in full summer sun. Plants seldom need division. Sow fresh seed outdoors or indoors with 4 to 6 weeks of cold, moist stratification. Seedlings will often appear in the garden spontaneously. Move "volunteers" to their desired position while they are young as they resent disturbance.

Landscape Uses

Sea hollies are bold architectural gems that command attention and add interest to the garden. Plant them in the company of floriferous perennials such as catmints (*Nepeta*), evening primroses (*Oenothera*), goldenrods (*Solidago*), Helen's flowers (*Helenium*), asters (*Aster*), pearly everlastings (*Anaphalis*), and ornamental grasses. Float the bold heads of larger species above a fluffy cloud of baby's-breath (*Gypsophila paniculata*), sea lavender (*Limonium latifolium*), or flowering spurge (*Euphorbia corollata*). Use rattlesnake master in the border with purple coneflower (*Echinacea purpurea*), culver's root (*Veronicastrum virginicum*), and blazing-stars (*Liatris*), or in prairie and meadow gardens with other native wildflowers and grasses.

ERYSIMUM

e-RE-see-mum • Brassicaceae, Mustard Family

The heady fragrance of wallflowers perfumes the late winter and spring air. No wonder these plants are so popular. The four-petaled flowers open from winter through midsummer. The linear, needle-like foliage creates a bottle-brush effect on the stems of these subshrubs grown as perennials. Plants have persistent stems in mild climates and dense, fibrous roots.

ERYSIMUM

Common Name:
Wallflower

Bloom Time:
Spring and summer bloom

Planting Requirements:
Sun or light shade

Erysimum **×*allionii*** (al-lee-OWN-ee-ee), Siberian wallflower. Size: 12 to 24 inches tall and wide. Brilliant orange flowers top the stems of this spicy fragrant species. Plants are short-lived and best grown as biennials, especially in warm climates. Many cultivars in a range of yellows, oranges, reds, and warm pinks exist if you can find them. *E.* (*Cheiranthus*) *cheiri,* common wallflower, is the parent of the English wallflowers grown as annuals. USDA Plant Hardiness Zones 4 to 7.

E. kotschyanum (kot-shee-AH-num), Kotschy wallflower. Size: 3 to 6 inches tall, 6 to 12 inches wide. A low groundcover for the rock garden, with bright yellow flowers over tight tufts of carpet-forming foliage. 'Orange Flame' has orange-yellow flowers. Zones 6 to 8.

E. linifolium (line-i-FO-lee-um), flax wallflower. Size: 1 to 2 feet tall and wide. A shrubby species with tall, woody stems crowned with sweet-scented purple flowers. 'Bowles' Mauve' is well known, with elongated heads of deep lavender flowers. 'Variegatum' combines lavender flowers and white-edged foliage to excellent effect. Zones 5 to 8.

How to Grow

Plant wallflowers in rich, well-drained soil in full sun or light shade. Plants grow quickly and will often bloom the first season from seed sown indoors in winter. Unfortunately, few species survive long in the swelter of the South. Do not crowd them—they need good air circulation. Set out flowering-size plants in fall or early spring and enjoy the blooms as long as they last. Take cuttings in summer to overwinter plants for propagation.

Landscape Uses

Use tall species to edge walks or in containers to add scent to the garden, patio, or conservatory. Rock garden species look great in wall crevices or in rockeries with phlox, rock cresses (*Arabis*), blue fescue (*Festuca ovina*), and other diminutive companions.

Flax wallflower (*Erysimum linifolium* 'Bowles' Mauve') has a delicious fragrance that delights the senses all the more because it is carried on the early spring air. Cut the woody stems back after flowering to shape the crown and to encourage fresh, free-blooming growth.

ERYTHRONIUM

er-i-THROW-nee-um • Liliaceae, Lily Family

Delicate spring wildflowers with paired green or mottled leaves and single to triple nodding flowers with colorful reflexed petals and sepals and protruding stamens (male reproductive structures). The woodland wildflowers with mottled leaves are called trout lilies because their leaves resemble a spotted trout. They also bear the name fawn lily, as they also resemble a speckled fawn. They spread by slender stolons that form bulbs at their ends. The plants go dormant immediately after flowering.

ERYTHRONIUM

Common Name:
  Trout lily, avalanche lily, adder's tongue

Bloom Time:
  Spring bloom

Planting Requirements:
  Sun or shade

Erythronium albidum (AL-bid-um), white trout lily. Size: 4 to 8 inches tall and wide. This species has white flowers with a purple or blue blush on the outside of the sepals and mottled leaves. USDA Plant Hardiness Zones 4 to 8.

E. americanum (a-mer-i-CAN-um), yellow trout lily. Size: 6 to 10 inches tall and wide. A yellow-flowered species with mottled foliage. Zones 3 to 8.

E. dens-canis (denz-CAN-is), dogtooth violet. Size: 4 to 6 inches tall and wide. A short, floriferous plant with rose-pink to deep lilac flowers and mottled leaves. Zones 2 to 7.

E. grandiflorum (grand-i-FLO-rum), avalanche lily. Size: 6 to 18 inches tall and wide. The tall flowering stems bear one to three bright yellow flowers above green leaves. *E. tuolumnense* is another tall, yellow-flowered western species with plain green leaves. Zones 3 to 7.

E. revolutum (rev-o-LEWT-um), coast fawn lily. Size: 4 to 12 inches tall and wide. A showy species with pink flowers and mottled leaves. Zones 5 to 8.

Combine delicate fawn lilies (*Erythronium* 'White Beauty') with leafy plants that will fill the gap left when they go dormant. These early-spring bulbs disappear soon after flowering.

Named Selections

A number of selections are available: 'Kondo' has three to five yellow flowers with a brown basal ring above weakly mottled leaves that fade to green. 'Pagoda' has one to three clear yellow flowers and mottled leaves. 'Pink Beauty' has clear pink flowers. 'White Beauty' has creamy white flowers with a brown ring at the throat on compact stems to 6 inches tall. 'Pagoda', of hybrid origin, has one to three clear yellow flowers and mottled leaves. Zones 4 to 8.

How to Grow

Plant trout lily bulbs in summer or fall in moist, humus-rich soil. Spring sun is essential, but once the plants are dormant the site can become quite shady. Take care not to dig into clumps during the dormant season. Divide plants in summer as leaves are yellowing. Sow fresh seed outdoors as soon as it is ripe. Seedlings develop slowly and may take 3 to 5 years to bloom. Voles love trout lilies, so plant in baskets.

Landscape Uses

Combine graceful trout lilies with spring bulbs, wildflowers, and early perennials. Wood anemone (*Anemone nemorosa*), trilliums, Jacob's ladders (*Polemonium*), fairy wings (*Epimedium*), and primroses (*Primula*) are good companions. Plant them in proximity to ferns and foliage plants such as lungworts (*Pulmonaria*), wild bleeding hearts, (*Dicentra eximia* or *formosa*), and hostas to cover the gaps left in summer.

EUPATORIUM

ewe-pa-TOR-ee-um • Asteraceae, Aster Family

Bold perennials of shrublike proportions with voluptuous heads of fuzzy, dusty rose or white flowers and opposite or whorled leaves. The plants form strong multistemmed clumps from a stout crown with tough fibrous roots. Joe Pye was a medicine man who believed in the special powers of these plants. The common name, boneset, comes from the early use of this plant to aid in the mending of broken bones. Plants grow from huge, fibrous-rooted crowns.

EUPATORIUM

Common Names:
Joe-Pye weed, boneset

Bloom Time:
Summer and fall bloom

Planting Requirements:
Full sun

Purple flower clusters seem to float like cumulus clouds atop the tall, straight purple stems of sweet Joe-Pye weed (*Eupatorium purpureum* 'Atropurpureum').

Eupatorium cannabinum (can-a-BYEN-um), hemp-leaf boneset. Size: 4 to 5 feet tall, 2 to 4 feet wide. An attractive species with flat clusters of rosy pink flowers in late summer and deeply cut leaves. 'Flore Pleno' is a sterile, double-flowered selection that is quite showy. USDA Plant Hardiness Zones 4 to 8.

E. coelestinum (co-les-TIE-num), hardy ageratum. Size: 2 to 3 feet tall and wide. An open, bushy plant resembling the popular annual ageratum, with small clusters of powder blue flowers in late summer and fall. 'Album' has grayish white flowers. 'Cori' is a less-invasive upright selection with clear, sky blue flowers. Zones 6 to 10.

E. fistulosum (fist-yoo-LO-sum), Joe-Pye weed. Size: 5 to 14 feet tall, 3 to 5 feet wide. A stately giant with four or five whorled leaves and elongated domes of dusty rose flowers in summer. Plants vary considerably in height according to soil fertility and moisture. Zones 4 to 9.

E. maculatum (mak-yoo-LA-tum), spotted Joe-Pye weed. Size: 4 to 6 feet tall, 3 to 4 feet wide. Similar to Joe-Pye weed but shorter, with compact, flattened clusters of cherry-red to rose-purple flowers. 'Big Umbrella' has huge, oversize flower heads and red stems. 'Carin' is a departure with silvery pink flowers. 'Purple Bush' is compact with deep raspberry flowers and dark stems only 4 feet tall. Zones 2 to 8.

E. perfoliatum (per-fo-lee-A-tum), boneset. Size: 3 to 5 feet tall, 2 to 3 feet wide. A more delicate species with opposite, lance-shaped foliage joined in the middle and pierced by the sturdy stem. The airy clusters of white flowers are produced in mid- to late summer. Zones 3 to 8.

E. purpureum (pur-pew-REE-um), sweet Joe-Pye weed. Size: 3 to 6 feet tall, 2 to 4 feet wide. Similar to *E. maculatum* but with only four leaves per whorl and mounded or domed clusters of pale rose or light purple sweet-scented flowers. 'Atropurpureum' has wine red stems and darker purple, fragrant flowers. *E.* 'Gateway' is likely a hybrid between the two species. Zones 3 to 8.

E. rugosum (rew-GO-sum), white snakeroot. Size: 3 to 4 feet tall, 1 to 2 feet wide. An attractive late-summer bloomer with opposite triangular leaves and white flowers in small clusters. The silver seedheads of this prolific spreader are also very showy. 'Chocolate' has deep purple-brown leaves that fade to deep green with dark accents in summer. Zones 3 to 7.

How to Grow

Plant Joe-Pye weeds in moist, average to rich soil in full sun or light shade. They are of easy culture and need little care once established. It takes at least two seasons for new plants to reach full size. They spread steadily outward to form dense bushy clumps of unparalleled beauty and stature. Divide oversize clumps in spring or fall. Separate the tough crown into sections using a sharp knife or shears. Replant into well-prepared soil. Hardy ageratum and white snakeroot need lifting every 3 or 4 years. The other species need division only when they outgrow their position. Propagate by tip cuttings taken in early summer. Sow seed outdoors in fall. Many species will self-sow freely in the garden. White snakeroot is very prolific.

Remove the majority of the heads before seeds form.

Landscape Uses

Joe-Pye weeds are equally at home in formal and informal landscapes. Use them in borders for their full-bodied form and soft cottony flowers. Combine them with common rose mallow (*Hibiscus moscheutos*), coneflowers (*Echinacea*), garden phlox (*Phlox paniculata*), bush clover (*Lespedeza thunbergii*), sunflowers (*Helianthus*), and all manner of daisies, asters, daylilies, irises, and ornamental grasses. In meadows and other informal sites plant them with asters, goldenrods (*Solidago*), and grasses. White snakeroot thrives in the dry shade of woodlands and enlivens dark recesses with its late-season white flowers. Hardy ageratum is a bit aggressive for the border but is perfect for informal sites or along roadside ditches and driveways.

EUPHORBIA

yoo-FOR-bee-a • Euphorbiaceae, Spurge Family

The yellow flower heads of spurges light up the garden both day and night. These succulent perennials have leafy stems and milky sap that flows freely when the leaves or stems are picked or damaged. They are grown for their smooth, often blue-green foliage and their colorful bracts (modified leaves) that surround the inconspicuous yellow flowers. Most species spread by creeping underground stems.

EUPHORBIA

Common Names:
Spurge, euphorbia

Bloom Time:
Spring and summer bloom

Planting Requirements:
Full sun to partial shade

Euphorbia amygdaloides (a-mig-da-LOI-dez), wood spurge. Size: 1 to 2 feet tall, 2 to 6 feet wide. A creeping spurge with thick stems covered in dark evergreen leaves and topped with open clusters of rounded light green bracts. 'Purpurea' ('Rubra') has deep ruby-red leaves that contrast beautifully with the chartreuse flowers. It is a less aggressive spreader. Var. *robbiae* has broad, spatulate, black-green leaves aggregated at the tip of the stems below the chartreuse flowers. USDA Plant Hardiness Zones 7 to 8; trial in Zone 6.

E. characias (kar-AH-kee-as), Mediterranean spurge. Size: 3 to 4 feet tall and wide. A stout, bushy perennial with stems densely covered in long, narrow, gray-blue leaves and huge elongated clusters of chartreuse flowers. The subspecies *characias* has flowers with black eyes. 'Blue Hills' has powder blue foliage. 'Portugese Velvet' has velvety blue-green leaves and compact clusters of bronzy yellow flowers. Ssp. *wulfenii*—thought by some to be a separate species—is similar but has larger, eyeless, yellow flowers. 'John Tomlinson' is compact with huge flower clusters that taper at the base like a light bulb. 'Lambrook Gold' is an excellent selection with gray-green leaves and dense flower heads on purple stems. Variegated forms like 'Burrow Silver' lack vigor and heat tolerance. The hybrid ×*martinii* with wood spurge is compact with red-tinted winter leaves and fat heads of chartreuse flowers. Zones 7 to 9.

E. corollata (kor-o-LAY-ta), flowering spurge. Size: 1 to 3 feet tall, 1 to 2 feet wide. A creeping plant with slender stems sparsely covered by pale green leaves and topped with broad clusters of flowers with white petal-like bracts. The plant resembles a stout baby's-breath. Zones 3 to 8.

E. griffithii (gri-FITH-ee-ee), Griffith's spurge. Size: 2 to 3 feet tall, 3 to 4 feet wide. A shrublike spurge with pale green pointed leaves tinged pink in spring and turning red in fall. The fiery orange-red flowers are borne in summer. 'Firecharm' is a compact selection to 2 feet tall. 'Fireglow' has bright

The chartreuse bracts of Mediterranean spurge (*Euphorbia characias* ssp. *characias*) reflect light and appear illuminated from within. Plant them near a window or around a terrace where you can enjoy their ghostly beauty in the evening.

orange bracts and red-veined leaves. 'Dixter' has darker orange flowers. Zones 4 to 8.

E. myrsinites (mur-sin-EYE-teez), myrtle spurge. Size: 6 to 10 inches tall, 12 to 24 inches wide. A prostrate plant with thick stems covered in scaly blue-gray leaves. The yellow flowers are carried at the end of the stems in spring. *E. rigida* is more upright with awl-shaped foliage and is hardy only to Zone 7. Zones 5 to 9.

E. polychroma (poly-KRO-ma) (*epithymoides*), cushion spurge. Size: 12 to 18 inches tall, 12 to 24 inches wide. This compact plant forms a mound of bright yellow flowers in early spring. The fall foliage turns red and orange. 'First Blush' has leaves dramatically edged in white. Zones 4 to 8.

How to Grow

Euphorbias are easy-care, long-lived perennials. *E. characias* can be short-lived but self-sows. It is invasive in some regions. Plant spurges in well-drained, average to rich soil in full sun or partial shade. Most species are quite drought-tolerant. The exception is *E. griffithii,* which prefers continually moist soil. *E. amygdaloides* tolerates full shade. Winter protection is necessary to prevent leaf burn and stem damage where cold temperatures persist for long periods without snow cover. Divide spreading clumps as necessary to control their advance or for propagation. *E. amygdaloides* is a particularly fast spreader. Propagate by tip cuttings taken in summer and stuck in a well-drained soil.

The brilliant chrome yellow bracts of cushion spurge (*Euphorbia polychroma*) open with the early daffodils and continue adding color to the spring garden all the way through tulip season. The foliage color is apricot to orange in fall.

Landscape Uses

Combine euphorbias with perennials or flowering shrubs. Plant the early-blooming species such as cushion spurge and *E. characias* with spring bulbs, forget-me-nots (*Myosotis*), and silver-leaved plants such as lamb's ears (*Stachys byzantina*), catmints (*Nepeta*), and artemisias. Use wood spurge around shrubs or in the dry shade of large trees with other tough groundcovers and shade perennials such as Solomon's seals (*Polygonatum*), bergenias, and barrenworts (*Epimedium*). Myrtle euphorbia is perfect for the front of the border, along walks, or in a rockery with dwarf conifers and bright perennials. Choose Griffith's spurge for a moist site with irises, astilbes, hostas, and other lush foliage plants.

FILIPENDULA

fil-i-PEN-dew-la • Rosaceae, Rose Family

Meadowsweets are elegant perennials with frothy heads of tiny five-petaled flowers with protruding stamens (male reproductive parts). Flower color ranges from white through pink to rose. The plants spread by creeping stems to form broad clumps of deep green, pinnately divided leaves with maple-like terminal leaflets. The bloom stalks are sparsely covered with the attractive, deeply lobed, divided leaves.

FILIPENDULA

Common Names:
Meadowsweet,
queen-of-the-meadow

Bloom Time:
Late spring and
summer bloom

Planting Requirements:
Full sun to partial
shade

Filipendula glaberrima (glab-e-REEM-a), smooth meadowsweet. Size: 3 to 4 feet tall, 2 to 3 feet wide. A little-known species that excels in foliage and flower. Compact stems hold white flowers above leaves with

Big, bold, and bright queen-of-the-prairie (*Filipendula rubra* 'Venusta') can reach 6 feet tall, with plucky foliage and large clusters of foamy pink flowers. Many plants offered under this name are seed-grown and variable in flower color.

broad, rounded terminal leaflets. USDA Plant Hardiness Zones 3 to 8.

F. kamtschatica (kamp-CHAT-i-ca), Kamtschatica meadowsweet. Size: 4 to 6 feet tall, 3 to 4 feet wide. An erect shrub-like plant with huge 6- to 8-inch clusters of fragrant white flowers atop leafy stems and lush mounds of deep green, quilted, basal foliage. Zones 4 to 8.

F. palmata (pal-MA-ta), Siberian meadowsweet. Size: 3 to 4 feet tall and wide. A compact plant with open, 4- to 5-inch clusters of pink flowers and leaves with a distinctive, broad, terminal leaflet. 'Elegans' is more compact with white flowers. 'Nana' (*F. multijuga*) is very short, to 10 inches tall, with pale pink flowers. Zones 4 to 8.

F. purpurea (pur-pew-REE-a), Japanese meadowsweet. Size: 2 to 4 feet tall and wide. An elegant species with broad, palmate leaves and deep rose-pink to magenta flowers held above the mostly basal leaves. The best, as well as least well-known, species. Zones 4 to 8.

F. rubra (ROO-bra), queen-of-the-prairie. Size: 4 to 6 feet tall, 2 to 4 feet wide. A tall, stately plant with bold foliage and large (to 9 inches) clusters of pink or rose flowers. 'Venusta' ('Venusta Magnifica') has deep rose flowers. Zones 3 to 9.

F. ulmaria (ul-MAH-ree-a), queen-of-the-meadow. Size: 3 to 6 feet tall, 2 to 3 feet wide. A medium-size plant with bold foliage and creamy white flowers in 6-inch clusters. 'Aurea' has leaves mottled with golden yellow. Its flowers are insignificant. 'Flore-plena' has showy double flowers. 'Variegata' has a central yellow stripe against a deep green background. Stunning. Zones 3 to 9.

F. vulgaris (vul GAH-ris), dropwort. Size: 2 to 3 feet tall and wide. A short plant with mostly basal, deeply dissected foliage and weakly upright stalks bearing flattened clusters of creamy white flowers. 'Flore Pleno' is shorter, to 2 feet tall, with showy double flowers. 'Rosea' is pale pink. Zones 3 to 8.

How to Grow

Plant frivolous filipendulas in evenly moist, humus-rich soil in full sun or light shade. All but dropwort thrive in highly moist soils, some even growing creek- or pondside. If leaves become tattered or crispy, remove them to the ground and fresh foliage will emerge. Clumps spread rapidly by creeping stems and need frequent division to keep them from crowding other plants. Lift clumps in fall and replant into amended soil. Division is the best means of propagation.

Japanese meadowsweet (*Filipendula purpurea* forma *albiflora* 'Alba') possesses a quiet charm compared to its rose-pink relations. Flower clusters are held erect above moderate-size, palmately lobed leaves that form a dense, attractive rosette.

Landscape Uses

Use meadowsweets in formal borders, with shrubs, or in meadow and pondside plantings. Combine their cotton-candy flowers with roses, irises, daylilies (*Hemerocallis*), phlox, and daisies of all types. Although the plants have a fairly short bloom time, by planting several species you can have plants in bloom for 4 to 6 weeks in summer. In untamed spots, plant them with ferns, bee balms (*Monarda*), bellflowers (*Campanula*), purple coneflower (*Echinacea purpurea*), and grasses. Use dropwort to edge beds or to soften the harsh lines of walkways and paths.

FRITILLARIA

fri-ti-LAH-ree-a • Liliaceae, Lily Family

Fritillarias are spring-blooming bulbs with nodding, bell-shaped flowers borne in open clusters or in erect spikes. The foliage is often blue-green and dies back after the flowering season. All parts of the plants have a curious, pungent odor. There are many species, only a few of which are readily available as nursery-propagated plants. Bulbs are often collected from the wild. Do not buy them unless they are labeled "nursery-propagated."

FRITILLARIA

Common Names
  Fritillary, checkered lily

Bloom Time:
  Spring bloom

Planting Requirements:
  Full sun or partial shade

Fritillaria imperialis (im-pe-ree-AL-is), crown imperial. Size: 2½ to 3 feet tall, 1 foot wide. A stout plant with leafy stems crowned by a tight cluster of nodding red, orange, or yellow flowers with a curious topknot of leaves. 'Aurora' has orange-red flowers. 'Lutea Maxima' is a hardy yellow-flowered form. 'Prolifica' has double orange flowers. 'Rubra Maxima' has large fiery orange flowers. USDA Plant Hardiness Zones 5 to 8.

F. lanceolata (lan-see-o-LAY-ta), mission bells. Size: 1 to 3 feet tall, 6 to 12 inches wide. A slender, wiry plant with three to five brown-and-yellow mottled bells and narrow linear leaves. Zones 5 to 8; trial in Zone 4.

F. meleagris (mel-ee-A-gris), checkered leaves. Size: 10 to 15 inches tall, 6 to 10 inches wide. A delicate plant with oversize, inflated bells on slender stems with narrow blue-green leaves. Flower color varies from white to brown and purple; plants are usually sold as mixed colors. 'Alba' has creamy white flowers. Zones 4 to 8.

F. michailovskyi (mi-kale-OV-ske-ee), Michailovskyi's fritillary. Size: 4 to 10 inches tall and wide. Thin stems with sparse gray-green leaves sport up to four yellow-edged purple bells. Zones 4 to 8.

F. persica (PER-see-ka), bells of Persia. Size: 2½ to 3 feet tall, 1 foot wide. Leaf stems are topped with elongated spiky clusters of nodding purple-brown bells. 'Adiyaman' is a vigorous cultivar with plum-colored flowers. Zones 5 to 7.

How to Grow

Plant fritillary bulbs in fall, 4 to 6 inches deep, in light but rich, well-drained soil in full sun or partial shade. Once established, they are long-lived, with the exception of crown imperial, which is

treated as an annual in most of the
eastern United States. Checkered lily will
grow in quite moist soils in warmer regions; in areas with severe winters, good
drainage is essential to survival. Divide
established clumps after flowering if they
become overcrowded.

Landscape Uses

Plant drifts of crown imperial in combination with flowering shrubs and foliage
perennials. Use bells of Persia as an accent
among early perennials and other bulbs.
Choose the smaller species for rock gardens, troughs, or pot culture either alone or
in combination with early-blooming plants
such as moss phlox (*Phlox subulata*), rock
cresses (*Arabis, Aubrieta*), and chickweeds
(*Cerastium*).

The imposing crown imperial (*Fritillaria imperialis* 'Aurora') is worthy of praise despite its foul-scented foliage and flowers.
These popular bulbs are often short-lived
in gardens and are therefore treated as
annuals.

GAILLARDIA

gay-LARD-ee-a • Asteraceae, Aster Family

Blanket flowers are showy summer perennials with single or double rows of ragged petal-like rays surrounding a broad buttonlike disk. These cheery daisies are grown for their fiery orange, yellow, and brown 4-inch flowers. The wiry flower stalks arise from a tight clump of lobed, hairy foliage. The spherical seedheads are covered in stiff, tawny bristles. Plants grow from fibrous-rooted crowns.

GAILLARDIA

Common Name:
  Blanket flower

Bloom Time:
  Summer bloom

Planting Requirements:
  Full sun

Gaillardia aristata (air-i-STAT-a), blanket flower. Size: 2 to 2½ feet tall, 1 to 2 feet wide. A plant of dry prairies with yellow rays often blazed with brown, and a purple-brown disk. USDA Plant Hardiness Zones 2 to 10.

G. ×grandiflora (grand-i-FLO-ra), blanket flower. Size: 2 to 3 feet tall and wide. A showy hybrid between *G. aristata* and the annual *G. pulchella,* this popular plant is floriferous and hardy, but may be short-lived because of its annual parentage. The flowers are orange and yellow, often with brick red bands or eyes. 'Baby Cole' is a floriferous, long-lived dwarf selection only 8 inches tall. 'Bremen' has copper-red flowers tipped in yellow on 2- to 3-foot stems. 'Burgundy' is a lovely deep wine red. 'Dazzler' has yellow-centered flowers with red tips. 'Goblin' is a 12-inch dwarf with red-and-yellow flowers. 'Golden Goblin' is of similar size to 'Goblin' with all-yellow flowers. 'Yellow Queen' is a tall yellow selection. Zones 4 to 9.

How to Grow

Plant blanket flowers in average, well-drained soil in full sun. They seem to thrive on neglect and heat. They are perfect for seaside gardens because they are salt- and drought-tolerant.

Add a spot of bright color to the sunny seaside garden with blanket flowers (*Gaillardia ×grandiflora* 'Goblin'). They thrive in sandy, well-drained soil and full sun.

The only place they don't seem to thrive is in rich, moist soil, which makes them floppy and shortens their life expectancy. Old plants tend to die out from the center. Divide blanket flower every 2 to 3 years in early spring to keep the clumps thriving. Propagate by stem cuttings in early summer. Sow seeds outdoors in fall or indoors after 4 weeks of cold, moist stratification. Seedlings develop quickly and may bloom the first year.

Landscape Uses

Blanket flowers produce mounds of brilliant flowers from early summer through fall. Plant them with other warm-colored perennials such as tickseeds (*Coreopsis*), butterfly weed (*Asclepias tuberosa*), and yarrows (*Achillea*). Add interest and excitement with the spiky yellow leaves of Spanish bayonet (*Yucca filamentosa* 'Golden Sword'), catmints (*Nepeta*), and purple flowers such as sage (*Salvia* ×*superba* 'East Friesland'). They are perfect for borders, rock gardens, and containers. In seaside gardens combine them with stonecrops (*Sedum*), Nippon daisy (*Chrysanthemum nipponicum*), beachgrass (*Amophila breviligulata*), and wax myrtles (*Myrica*).

GALANTHUS

ga-LANTH-us • Amaryllidaceae, Amaryllis Family

Snowdrops are one of the most popular bulbs, beloved more for their early flowering than for arresting color or large flower size. The diminutive plants have two or three strap-shaped leaves around a slender stalk bearing a single, nodding fragrant flower with three floppy outer sepals and three overlapping inner segments stained with green. Plants grow from true bulbs. Hundreds of selections of species as well as hybrids are available. Collectors will pay outrageous prices for new introductions.

GALANTHUS

Common Name:
Snowdrop

Bloom Time:
Winter or spring bloom

Planting Requirements:
Sun

Galanthus elwesii (el-WES-ee-ee), giant snowdrop. Size: 6 to 10 inches tall, 10 to 12 inches wide. A stout species with wide, upright gray-green leaves and large flowers with rounded sepals around inner segments with green at both the tip and the base. USDA Plant Hardiness Zones 4 to 8.

G. nivalis (ni-VAL-is), common snowdrop. Size: 4 to 8 inches tall, 10 to 12 inches wide. By far the most common and prolific species, with narrow, paired gray-green leaves and delicate flowers held one to a stem in late winter. 'Atkinsii', possibly a hybrid, has erect flowerstalks and flowers nearly an inch long. 'Flore-Pleno' has fully double flowers with frilly centers surrounded by three sepals. 'Magnet' has large flowers borne on slender, arching pedicels. 'S. Arnott' ('Sam Arnott') is a robust selection 6 to 8 inches tall with large, showy flowers held on erect stalks above the leaves. 'Viridapices' sports a green signal on each of the outer sepals. Zones 3 to 8.

G. plicatus (ply-CATE-us), snowdrop. Size: 6 to 12 inches tall and wide. A robust species with the unique feature of the edges of the gray-green leaves folded backward. Showy white flowers have long sepals. Var.

Few can resist the charm of diminutive common snowdrops (*Galanthus nivalis*). Perhaps the early flowering makes the pristine white flowers all the more alluring, as few other plants are stirring in the chilly winter air.

byzantinus has greener leaves and apical as well as basal flairs on the inner flower. Zones 3 to 8.

G. woronowii (war-ren-OWE-ee-ee) (*ikariae*), snowdrop. Size: 4 to 6 inches tall, 6 to 12 inches wide. This species has wide green leaves and smallish flowers with green-edged inner segments. Zones 4 to 8.

How to Grow

Plant snowdrops in humus-rich, evenly moist soil with plenty of winter and early-spring sun. Soak dormant bulbs overnight in warm water to increase their chances of success. Often, bulbs stored dry over summer are desiccated and slow to recover. For this reason, the practice of digging snowdrops while still actively growing (called "in the green") was started. This method can be effective, but bulbs must be replanted immediately. Digging as leaves are fading ensures success with less stress to bulbs.

Landscape Uses

Plant drifts of snowdrops among early bloomers such as hellebores, or combined with other bulbs like cyclamens, crocuses, winter aconites (*Eranthis*), and fumeroots (*Corydalis*). Ferns, phlox, blue-eyed Marys (*Omphalodes*), and barrenworts (*Epimedium*) are excellent companions. Plant drifts under early-blooming shrubs such as witch hazel (*Hamamelis*), daphne, and spike hazel (*Corylopsis*).

GALEGA

gal-EE-ga • Fabaceae, Pea Family

The colorful spires of goat's rue are often seen in European gardens but are conspicuously absent from the American gardening scene. These are tall pea relatives, with succulent stems bearing pinnately divided leaves and crowned in early summer with showy clusters of white, pink, blue, or bicolor flowers. After flowering, they offer little to the garden show, so pair them with later-blooming plants such as sunflowers, bush clovers, and asters.

> **GALEGA**
> **Common Name:**
> Goat's rue
> **Bloom Time:**
> Summer bloom
> **Planting Requirements:**
> Full sun to light shade

Galega officinalis (of-fic-i-NAY-lis), common goat's rue. Size: 3 to 4 feet tall, 2 to 3 feet wide. Blue, pink, or white flowers in upright spikes crown stems clothed with 1- to 2-foot leaves with narrow leaflets. 'Alba' is pure white. 'Her Majesty' is a bicolor mauve and pink. 'Lady Wilson' is widely available, with lilac-blue flowers. USDA Plant Hardiness Zones 3 to 7.

G. orientalis (o-ree-en-TAY-lis), oriental goat's rue. Size: 3 to 4 feet tall, 2 to 3 feet wide. Erect spikes of intense violet-blue flowers held above lush foliage make this a commanding species. Zones 3 to 7.

How to Grow

Plant in rich but light soil in full sun or light shade. Plants grow best where summers are not too hot. After flowering, plants may look messy. Cut them back to encourage fresh growth. Plants self-sow freely in some areas and may be considered invasive in some regions.

Landscape Uses

Good for the middle or back of the border where partners can obscure the lower stems, which may be a bit gangly. The husky clumps are covered with flowers and make quite a show. Plant with goat's beards (*Aruncus*), sages (*Salvia*), torch lilies (*Kniphofia*), catmints (*Nepeta*), Carolina phlox (*Phlox carolina*), and other early-summer bloomers.

The tall stems of common goat's rue (*Galega officinalis*) need staking or the support of sturdy companions to look their best.

GALIUM

Gay-lee-um • Rubiaceae, Madder Family

The scent of sweet woodruff, reminiscent of newly mown hay, has endeared it to generations of gardeners. Mattresses were once stuffed with the fragrant thatch, and woodruff also lends its uniquely pungent scent to May wine. All species are creeping or sprawling plants with whorled foliage and starry, four-petaled white flowers. Plants grow from creeping stems with thin, fibrous roots.

GALIUM

Common Names:
   Sweet woodruff, bedstraw

Bloom Time:
   Spring bloom

Planting Requirements:
   Sun or shade

Galium boreale (bor-e-A-lee), northern bedstraw. Size: 1½ to 2 feet tall, 2 to 3 feet wide. A floriferous, airy plant with open clusters of flowers atop branching stems. USDA Plant Hardiness Zones 2 to 7.

G. odoratum (o-dor-AY-tum), sweet woodruff. Size: 4 to 10 inches tall, 12 to 24 inches wide (or more). A showy groundcover with whorls of broadly lance-shaped leaves and tight flower clusters on erect stems. Zones 4 to 8.

How to Grow

Plant northern bedstraw in moist, rich soil in full sun or light shade. This tough prairie species is tolerant of drought. Sweet woodruff requires even moisture and is more shade-tolerant. Both spread steadily outward to form broad clumps. Divide them in spring or fall to control their spread. Propagate by stem cuttings in early summer. Remove any flowers or seedheads from cuttings.

If you need to cover ground quickly, choose sweet woodruff (*Galium odoratum*). Delicate white flowers and whorls of fragrant foliage make this creeping plant a favorite for a shady spot.

Landscape Uses

Use sweet woodruff in large patches in the shade of trees and shrubs. Plant spring bulbs and wildflowers such as Virginia bluebell (*Mertensia virginica*), trilliums, and Solomon's seals (*Polygonatum*) among the creeping stems. When spring bloomers go dormant in early summer, the woodruff foliage will cover the bare spots. Choose northern bedstraw for weaving among bold perennials such as coneflowers (*Echinacea*), black-eyed Susans (*Rudbeckia*), and phlox. Prairie plants and grasses are good companions in both formal and informal gardens.

GAURA

GAW-ra • Onagraceae, Evening Primrose Family

Elegant, delicate, and tough as nails are the contradictions of gaura. This hardy native of dry plains and prairies demands good drainage and rewards you with a summer-long display of white butterflies fluttering on wiry stems above the diminutive foliage. Many colorful pink selections are now available. Plants grow from thick deep taproots and are quite drought-tolerant.

GAURA

Common Name:
Gaura

Bloom Time:
Summer bloom

Planting Requirements:
Full sun

Gaura lindheimeri (lind-HI-mer-ee), white gaura. Size: 3 to 4 feet tall, 1 to 2 feet wide. An exuberant, shrubby perennial with erect stems carrying spikes of 1-inch white flowers well above deep green foliage. Each flower consists of four petals that surround the protruding stamens (male reproductive structures), which resemble the antennae of a pure white butterfly. As the flowers age, they blush to pale rose. In warm regions, the plant blooms from June through at least September. In northern areas, the bulk of the bloom comes in late summer and fall. The clumps grow from a thick, deep taproot. 'Blushing Butterflies' is compact with blush pink flowers. 'Corries Gold' has striking gold-edged leaves and white flowers. 'Crimson Butterflies' is just 18 inches tall with deep rosy red flowers and rosy foliage. 'Siskiyou Pink' is compact with reddish foliage and deep rose flowers. 'Whirling Butterflies' is tall and graceful with white flowers held well above the leaves. USDA Plant Hardiness Zones 5 to 9.

White gaura (*Gaura lindheimeri*) blooms from June until frost if the spent bloom spikes are removed regularly. This arid-region native thrives equally well in moist or dry soil in a spot with full sun.

How to Grow

Plant gaura in any moist, well-drained soil in full sun. Once established, the plants are drought-tolerant, but they perform best with even moisture. Gauras are valued by gardeners in warm regions because they tolerate heat and humidity and still bloom well. Plants seldom need division. Sow seed outside in fall. Self-sown seedlings will likely appear.

Landscape Uses

Choose gauras for borders, informal gardens, or as specimen plants. Combine the airy spikes with ornamental grasses and small-flowered plants such as verbenas, sedums, red valerian (*Centranthus ruber*), sea lavender (*Limonium latifolium*), and pink baby's breath (*Gypsophila paniculata*). Use as a weaver to tie together bold plants such as daylilies (*Hemerocallis*) and coneflowers (*Echinacea*). In the fall garden, plant gauras with a profusion of asters to add a spiky form to the floriferous mounds. Plants perform well in containers.

GENTIANA

jen-shee-A-na • Gentianaceae, Gentian Family

The lovely fall-flowering gentians have funnel- or bottle-shaped flowers of an intense indigo or ultramarine blue that has come to be called gentian blue. The plants vary in size and shape from low and sprawling to stiffly upright. The flowers may be completely closed or open at their tips with five often-spotted lobes. The clumps grow from tough cordlike roots.

GENTIANA

Common Name:
Gentian

Bloom Time:
Fall bloom

Planting Requirements:
Sun or partial shade

Gentiana andrewsii (an-DREWS-ee-ee), bottle gentian. Size: 1½ to 2 feet tall, 1 to 2 feet wide. The erect stems with glossy, oval to broadly lance-shaped leaves are crowned by tight clusters of 1-inch inflated but closed flowers. The plant blooms from late summer through fall. USDA Plant Hardiness Zones 3 to 8.

G. asclepiadea (as-klep-e-a-DE-a), willow gentian. Size: 1½ to 2 feet tall, 2 to 3 feet wide. A leafy gentian with weakly upright stems covered in stiff, lance-shaped leaves. The axillary clusters of late summer flowers cover the upper half of the stems. Each flower is an inflated tube with tips reflexed to form a wide starry rim. Zones 5 to 7.

G. clausa (CLOW-sa), closed gentian. Size: 1 to 2 feet tall and wide. This lovely fall-flowering gentian has intense indigo bottle-shaped flowers on low clumps that form a wide, ascending vase. Watching a bumblebee maneuver into the tight opening to pollinate the flower is a true spectacle. After pollination, the flowers fade to pink before withering. Zones 4 to 8.

Lovely, late-flowering soapwort gentian (*Gentiana saponaria*) has intense indigo bottle-shaped flowers tightly packed into the axils of the leaves, as well as at the apex of the stem. Plants are low and sprawling, forming a wide, ascending vase loaded with flowers.

How to Grow

Plant gentians in evenly moist, humus-rich soil in full sun or partial shade. Protection from afternoon sun, especially in warmer zones, is recommended to avoid scorching foliage. Plants dislike disturbance and seldom need dividing. Propagate by lifting clumps in spring and carefully splitting crowns. Sow fresh seed outside or indoors with 4 to 6 weeks of cold, moist stratification. Plants bloom in 3 years.

Landscape Uses

Combine gentians with ferns and woodland asters in the fall garden. Their rich blue color is a lovely antidote to the ubiquitous yellow of the season. Good companions include small-leaved hostas, variegated sedges (*Carex*), toadlilies (*Tricyrtis*), and other lush foliage plants. In the border, plant gentians with virgin's bower (*Clematis virginiana*), ornamental grasses, patrinias, and asters.

GERANIUM

jer-A-nee-um • Geraniaceae, Geranium Family

Hardy geraniums are at the top of the list for long-blooming, colorful summer perennials. A large genus of mounding or bushy long-lived plants, it is not to be confused with tender bedding "geraniums" of the genus *Pelargonium*. Most species have rounded, palmately lobed leaves, some quite elaborately incised. The showy five-petaled flowers are somewhat saucer-shaped, or occasionally cupped. Flower colors range from white to blue, purple, rose, and pink, often with deeper-colored veining. Geraniums are called cranesbills because the seeds are held on a rigid, tapered "beak" that serves as a launching pad to project seeds outward from the plants. Plants grow from thickened rhizomes with wiry roots.

GERANIUM
Common Names: Geranium, cranesbill
Bloom Time: Spring and early summer bloom
Planting Requirements: Full sun or partial shade

Geranium cantabrigiense (kan-tab-rig-EE-en-see), Cambridge geranium. Size: 6 to 8 inches tall, 8 to 12 inches wide. Scalloped leaves cover trailing stems to form a tight groundcover smothered in rosy flowers in spring and early summer. 'Biokobo' has white to pale pink flowers with dark calyses. 'Cambridge' has rosy purple flowers. 'Karmina' has raspberry red flowers. 'St. Ola' is a dwarf white-flowered selection. USDA Plant Hardiness Zones 4 to 8.

G. cinereum (sin-e-REE-um), grayleaf cranesbill. Size: 6 to 12 inches tall, 12 inches wide. A low, spreading plant with deeply incised leaves and 1-inch saucer-shaped pink flowers lined with purple veining. 'Alba' has white flowers. 'Ballerina' is a hybrid between two subspecies of *G. cinereum*, with large lilac-pink flowers boldly veined and eyed with deep purple borne throughout the summer. 'Guiseppii' is deep red-violet with a dark eye. 'Laurence Flatman' is compact with soft pink leaves with magenta veining. 'Splendens' has bright pink flowers with dark eyes. Zones 4 (with protection) or 5 to 7.

G. clarkei (klar-KEY-ce), Clark's geranium. Size: 15 to 20 inches tall, 1 to 2 feet wide. A floriferous species with ¾-inch purple or white flowers above deeply incised foliage. 'Kashmir Purple' has deep purple-blue flowers. 'Kashmir White' has white flowers with pale pink veins. Zones 4 to 8.

G. dalmaticum (dal-MAT-i-cum), dalmatian cranesbill. Size: 4 to 6 inches tall, 12 to 14 inches wide. A low, mounding plant that spreads rapidly by creeping rhizomes but is never invasive. The 1-inch soft mauve flowers cover the tight, rounded foliage in late spring and early summer. Var. *album* ('Album') has white flowers. 'Biokoro' is a hybrid with *G. macrorrhizum*, having pink flowers held high above the foliage. 'Karmina' is raspberry red. Zones 4 to 8.

G. ×oxonianum (ox-o-knee-AY-num). Size: 15 to 18 inches tall, 12 to 24 inches wide. A mounding to sprawling hybrid between *G. endressi* and *G. versicolor*, with starry leaves and dozens of 1-inch soft pink flowers. 'A. T. Johnson' has silvery pink flowers. 'Claridge Druce' is a vigorous grower and has lilac-pink flowers with darker veins. 'Wargrave Pink' has rich pink flowers. Zones 4 to 8.

G. himalayense (him-a-lay-EN-se), lilac geranium. Size: 12 to 15 inches tall, 24 to 30 inches wide. A sprawling plant with deeply cut palmate leaves and

The free-seeding *Geranium* ×*oxonianum* 'A. T. Johnson' appears in gaps in the garden as though its placement had been planned. Plants bloom throughout summer, adding a touch of silvery pink to a sunny or lightly shaded spot.

1½- to 2-inch violet-blue flowers borne throughout summer. 'Birch Double' ('Plenum') has small double lavender flowers. 'Gravetye' is more compact than the species, with 2-inch bright blue flowers. Zones 4 to 8.

G. ibericum (i-BEER-i-cum), Caucasus geranium. Size: 1½ to 2 feet tall, 2 feet wide. A robust, dense mounding plant with round, broad-lobed, soft hairy leaves with elongated petioles (leaf stalks) and violet flowers. Zones 3 to 8.

G. macrorrhizum (mak-ro-RISE-um), bigroot geranium. Size: 15 to 18 inches tall, 24 to 36 inches wide. Clusters of bright pink flowers are carried above aromatic, palmately lobed leaves. Clumps spread easily by underground stems. 'Album' has white flowers surrounded by pink sepals. 'Breven's Variety' has magenta flowers and deep red sepals. 'Ingwersen's Variety' has light pink flowers and glossy leaves. 'Spessart' has white flowers and pale pink sepals. 'Variegatum' has leaves irregularly edged in cream and sea green below pink flowers. Zones 3 to 8.

G. maculatum (mak-u-LAY-tum), wild geranium. Size: 1 to 2 feet tall, 1 foot wide. A tall plant with loose clusters of clear pink or white flowers above open clumps of starry rounded leaves. 'Elizabeth Ann' has deep chocolate brown leaves, darker than those of 'Espresso', and pink flowers. 'Hazel Gallagher' and 'Album' are white-flowered. Zones 4 to 8.

G. ×magnificum (mag-NIF-i-cum), showy geranium. Size: 1½ to 2 feet tall, 2 to 3 feet wide. This robust, bushy hybrid between G. ibericum and G. platypetalum has large, rounded velvety leaves with broad lobes and clusters of 1½-inch blue-violet flowers held above the foliage. Zones 3 to 8.

G. phaeum (FIE-um), mourning widows. Size: 1 to 2½ feet tall and wide. Attractive foliage, often marked with maroon, and brooding cabernet red flowers make this an attractive if somber species. 'Album' has white flowers. 'Lily Lovell' is pale lavender. 'Samobor' has broad leaves with deep maroon blotches. Zones 4 to 7.

G. platypetalum (plat-ee-PET-a-lum), broad-petaled geranium. Size: 1½ to 2 feet tall and wide. A rounded, mounding plant with deep purple flowers and round, lobed, hairy leaves with long petioles (leaf stalks). Zones 3 to 8.

G. pratense (pray-TEN-se), meadow cranesbill. Size: 2 to 3 feet tall and wide. A vigorous plant with deeply incised starry leaves and 1½-inch purple flowers veined in red. 'Glactic' is white-flowered. 'Mrs. Kendall Clarke' has pale blue flowers with rose stripes. 'Midnight Reiter' has deep purple spring foliage. 'Plenum Violaceum' is an attractive purple double. 'Splish Splash' has white petals splashed with blue à la abstract impressionist Jackson Pollock. Zones 5 to 8.

G. psilostemon (sye-LO-ste-mon), Armenian geranium. Size: 2 to 4 feet tall, 3 to 4 feet wide. A magnificent perennial with large starry evergreen leaves and 2-inch deep magenta flowers with black eyes.

'Bressingham Flair' grows only 2 feet tall. Zones 5 to 8.

G. renardii (re-NARD-ee-ee), Renard's cranesbill. Size: 10 to 12 inches tall, 12 to 16 inches wide. An endearing species with velvety, lobed leaves and white flowers streaked with violet. 'Phillippe Vapelle' is a hybrid with blue flowers. Zones 3 to 8.

G. ×riversleaianum (rivers-lee-A-num), hardy cranesbill. Size: 1 to 1½ feet tall, 2 to 3 feet wide. An attractive hybrid ground-cover with small gray-green leaves and deep pink to magenta flowers. 'Mavis Simpson' has powdery deep pink flowers. 'Russell Pritchard' is deep magenta. Zones 6 to 8.

G. sanguineum (sang-GWIN-ee-um), bloody cranesbill. Size: 8 to 12 inches tall, 12 to 24 inches wide. A low, wide-spreading geranium with mounds of deeply incised spidery leaves and flat, 1-inch bright pink flowers held just above the foliage. 'Album' grows to 18 inches and is more open. The white flowers are saucer-shaped. 'Alpenglow' is a compact mounding plant with brilliant rose-red flowers. 'Holden' has pink flowers. 'New Hampshire Purple' is rosy magenta. 'Purple Flame' is the closest to violet of any selection. 'Shepherd's Warning' is only 6 inches tall and has deep rose-pink flowers. Var. *striatum* (*lancastriense*) has pale pink flowers with deep rose veins. Zones 3 to 8.

G. sylvaticum (sil-VAT-i-cum), wood cranesbill. Size: 2½ to 3 feet tall, 1 to 2 feet wide. An early-blooming geranium with 1-inch violet-blue flowers on open bushy plants. The leaves are rounded with deep lobes. 'Immaculate' is white. 'Lilac Time' is lavender blue. 'Mayflower' is a more compact cultivar. Zones 5 to 8.

Hybrids

'Alaska' has blue flowers on 18- to 24-inch stems. 'Ann Folkard' has trailing stems to 3 feet wide with chartreuse leaves and black-eyed magenta flowers. 'Brookside' is a compact improvement over the true blue-flowered 'Johnson's Blue'. 'Dilys' is a rambler with deep rosy red flowers. 'Rozanne' is spectacular with 1-inch deep blue-violet flowers with pale eyes. 'Spinners' is a large sprawler to 3 feet with deep blue-violet flowers.

How to Grow

Plant geraniums in moist but well-drained humus-rich soil in sun or partial shade. In warmer zones, shading from hot afternoon sun is essential. Some species, especially bigroot geranium, bloody cranesbill, and Endress's geranium, are drought-tolerant. Dalmatian and bloody cranesbills and bigroot and wild geraniums are quite shade-tolerant. Most species are slow-spreading and can grow for many years in the same spot without division. Others grow quickly to form broad clumps. Divide the most vigorous spreaders every 2 or 3 years. To increase your supply, lift plants in early spring or fall and pull clumps apart. Remove divisions for propagation without disturbing the clump by using a trowel or by hand-pulling. Many geraniums will self-sow. If you catch the seeds before they are catapulted toward the neighbor's yard, sow them outdoors or inside on a warm seedbed. Seedlings develop in 3 to 5 weeks.

Landscape Uses

Geraniums are versatile plants for the summer border. Combine them with bold flowers and spiky forms, or use them as weavers to tie together different combinations. Siberian iris (*Iris siberica*), sages (*Salvia*), garden phlox (*Phlox paniculata*), bellflowers (*Campanula*), evening primroses (*Oenothera*), and ornamental grasses are good companions. In the shaded garden plant them with lady's-mantle (*Alchemilla mollis*), woodland phlox (*Phlox divaricata*), and showy foliage plants such as lungworts (*Pulmonaria*) and ferns. Grayleaf cranesbill and other dwarf selections are good for the rock garden. Use the shade- and drought-tolerant species such as bigroot geranium as groundcovers with flowering shrubs or under open-canopied trees. Most species have lovely burgundy red, scarlet, or orange fall foliage color.

GEUM

GEE-um • Rosaceae, Rose Family

Fiery colors typify this genus of showy, tough perennials for climates with cool summers. Basal rosettes of fuzzy evergreen, pinnately divided leaves are crowned by slender stalks bearing fiery orange, red, or yellow flowers in spring and early summer. A few species have fuzzy seedheads resembling those of clematis. They grow from stout, slow-creeping rootstocks.

GEUM

Common Name:
Avens

Bloom Time:
Spring and early summer bloom

Planting Requirements:
Full sun to light shade

Geum chiloense (chil-o-EN-se) (*quel-lyon*), Chilean avens. Size: 1½ to 2 feet tall and wide. A leafy geum with rosettes of pinnately divided leaves with broad, lobed terminal leaflets. The scarlet flowers are borne in early to midsummer in loose clusters atop wiry stalks. 'Fire Opal' is a floriferous, deep red semidouble selection. 'Georgenberg', a hybrid with *G. montanum*, has bright yellow-orange flowers. 'Lady Stratheden' has semidouble bright yellow flowers. 'Mrs. Bradshaw' is an old cultivar with semidouble scarlet flowers. 'Princess Juliana' has yellow-orange, semidouble flowers. USDA Plant Hardiness Zones 4 to 7.

G. coccineum (kock-SIN-ee-um) (*G. ×borisii*), scarlet avens. Size: 9 to 12 inches tall and wide. The showy brick red flowers of this avens are 1½ to 2 inches across. They are held well above the basal, thrice-divided leaves with broad, rounded terminal leaflets. 'Borisii' has dark orange-red flowers on 10-inch stems. 'Red Wings' has orange-red, semidouble flowers. 'Werner Arends' is brilliant orange. Zones 4 to 7.

G. reptans (REP-tanz), creeping avens. Size: 6 to 8 inches tall, 8 to 12 inches wide. A low, creeping plant with dense mats of pinnately divided leaves and yellow flowers borne singly on slender stalks. Zones 4 to 7.

G. rivale (ree-VAH-lee), purple avens. Size: 1 to 2½ feet tall, 1 to 2 feet wide. A plant of wet meadows and bogs with pinnately divided leaves and tall stalks bearing a triad of nodding dusty purple bell-like flowers and tufted plumes of seeds. 'Leonard's Variety' is a hybrid with wine-red flowers. Zones 3 to 7.

G. triflorum (tri-FLOOR-um), prairie smoke. Size: 4 to 12 inches tall, 12 to 24 inches wide. A slow-creeping plant with stout rootstocks bearing rosettes of ferny, pinnately divided foliage. Early-spring flowers are carried in a triad. Each flower has dusty rose sepals and creamy white petals. Each flower is capped by long, pointed purple bracts. The seeds have long, fuzzy tails that collectively form plumes that look like puffs of smoke. Zones 3 to 8.

The odd dusty rose flowers of prairie smoke (*Geum triflorum*) are borne in triads and resemble medieval maces. The seed-heads turn soft smoky pink and resemble a smoldering fire when viewed from afar.

How to Grow

Plant avens in evenly moist but well-drained, humus-rich soil in full sun or light shade. Purple avens will grow quite happily in wet soils and prairie smoke fares well in drier soils. Most species are sensitive to high temperatures and should be protected from hot afternoon sun when grown in warm zones. Hot, dry conditions scorch foliage and increase their susceptibility to spider mites. Scarlet and Chilean avens can be short-lived in many zones. Frequent division in spring or fall helps prolong their lives. Other species seldom need dividing. Sow ripe seed outdoors. Germination occurs the following spring.

Landscape Uses

Plant fiery-colored avens near the front of the border with other brightly colored flowers. Black-eyed Susan (*Rudbeckia hirta*), tickseeds (*Coreopsis*), green-and-gold (*Chrysogonum virginianum*), and swordleaf inula (*Inula ensifolia*) are good companions. Add blue 'Rozanne' geraniums, catmints (*Nepeta*), and sages (*Salvia*) for contrast. Choose creeping avens and prairie smoke for the rock garden, or plant prairie smoke along the edge of a walk with white moss phlox (*Phlox subulata*), sedges (*Carex*), and bloody cranesbill (*Geranium sanguineum*). Plant purple avens in the border or in a moist soil garden with ferns.

GLADIOLUS

glad-EE-o-lus • Iridaceae, Iris Family

Gladioli are well known as cut flowers that are boldly displayed with abandon in funeral parlors across the country. These stalwart harbingers of summer are grown for their tall spikes of brightly colored flowers. The irislike foliage emerges from a large buttonlike corm in early summer. The one-sided spikes follow, clothed in spreading, funnelform flowers.

GLADIOLUS

Common Names:
Gladiolus, sword lily

Bloom Time:
Summer bloom

Planting Requirements:
Full sun

Gladiolus cardinalis (car-din-AH-lis), red gladiolus. Size: 1 to 1½ feet tall, ½ to 1 foot wide. Stunning red flowers with white throats adorn this dramatic but tender species. USDA Plant Hardiness Zones 8 to 10.

G. communis (kom-MEW-nis), common gladiolus. Size: 2 to 3 feet tall, 1 foot wide. Two-foot-long swordlike leaves and uneven spikes of pink flowers. Ssp. *byzantinus* (*G. byzantinus*) has deep reddish purple flowers. 'Albus' has pure white flowers. Zones 6 to 10.

G. tristis (TRIS-tis), gladiolus. Size: 1½ to 2½ feet tall, ½ to 1 foot wide. A lovely species with nodding, creamy yellow flowers with a delicious fragrance most notable in evening. Zones 7 to 10.

G. ×hortulans (hort-U-lanz), garden gladiolus. Size: 2 to 4 feet tall, 1 to 2 feet wide. Countless hybrids in a riot of colors with large, tightly packed flowers are available. They are treated as annuals in colder climates. Most are hardy to Zone 7 with protection. *G. ×gandavensis* has been passed around the South for generations. 'Boone' is butterscotch yellow with a hint of rose. Zone 7.

How to Grow

Plant gladiolus corms in spring 4 to 8 inches deep, into moist but well-drained, light, humus-rich soil. Full sun is necessary to promote bloom the following year, especially for the hybrids. Approximately 90 days are necessary for the plants to root, grow, bloom, and store enough energy for the next year. Remove flowerstalks as soon as the flowers fade. Staking is usually necessary, especially for large-flowered hybrids. Pests and diseases are often numerous. Thrips are a serious problem; they produce pale blotches or lines between the veins of the leaf. In serious cases, they may deform flowers. Early detection is critical. Spray with insecticidal soap at 3-day intervals for 2 weeks. Remove and destroy badly infested foliage. Aphids may also be a problem but are easily controlled with insecticidal soap. Voles love the corms.

The magenta spikes of Byzantine glad (*Gladiolus communis* ssp. *byzantinus*) look great in the garden or in a vase. The flowers are smaller than familiar florists' glads, so plant them in drifts for greatest impact. Some plants sold under this name are inferior in flower size and color.

Landscape Uses

The unusual, often top-heavy gladiolus plant is difficult to work into garden situations. They are often relegated to the cutting garden or planted among annuals. Species often fit better into borders than hybrids do. Combine them with bushy perennials and ornamental grasses. Baby's-breath (*Gypsophila*) and other airy, floriferous plants are also good companions. For indoor use, cut flowers as the lowest buds are showing color. Pinch out the tip of the spike to encourage all the flowers to open.

GYPSOPHILA

jyp-SOFF-ill-a • Caryophyllaceae, Pink Family

Baby's-breaths are beloved perennials both in the garden and as cut flowers. Clouds of tiny white or pink flowers appear in broad round clusters above the mostly basal leaves. The plants grow from thick, deep taproots. Plants are invasive in many areas of the Midwest and West, especially in alkaline soils.

GYPSOPHILA

Common Name:
Baby's-breath

Bloom Time:
Summer bloom

Planting Requirements:
Full sun or light shade

Gypsophila paniculata (pan-ik-u-LAY-ta), baby's-breath. Size: 3 to 4 feet tall, 2 to 3 feet wide. This airy plant attains shrublike proportions when in full bloom. The flowers smother rosettes of narrow blue-green leaves. 'Bristol Fairy' is a compact, 2-foot grower with double flowers. 'Compact Plena' is 18 inches tall with double flowers. 'Perfecta' is robust with large double flowers. 'Pink Fairy' is a pink version of 'Bristol Fairy'. 'Pink Star' has bright pink flowers. 'Red Sea' has double rose-pink flowers on 4-foot stems. 'Viette's Dwarf" is compact, 15 inches, and white. USDA Plant Hardiness Zones 3 to 9.

G. repens (REE-penz), creeping baby's-breath. Size: 4 to 8 inches tall, 8 to 12 inches wide. This low, creeping plant is a miniature version of baby's-breath. Clumps spread to form leafy mats of gray-blue foliage. The flowers are carried in broad, flat clusters. 'Alba' has clear white flowers. 'Rosea' has pale pink flowers. Zones 3 to 8.

Plant airy baby's-breath (*Gypsophila paniculata* 'Bristol Fairy') where its broad crowns will fill gaps left by dormant perennials such as bulbs or poppies. Before planting this old-fashioned favorite, make sure it is not invasive in your region.

How to Grow

Gypsophila means "lime-loving," and both species thrive in rich, moist, neutral to slightly alkaline soils in full sun or light shade. Creeping baby's-breath is tolerant of acid soils. Plant them out in spring and do not disturb clumps once they are established. Some cultivars tend to be short-lived. Good drainage is essential for longevity. Taller cultivars over 18 inches need staking. Slip a wire hoop over clumps in spring. As they begin to expand, raise the hoop to contain expanding flower stalks. Encourage reblooming by cutting old stalks to the ground as the last flowers fade. Many double selections are grafted onto seed-grown single forms. Plant them deeply to encourage rooting of the stems. Plants are longer-lived when they produce their own roots. Today, many selections are grown on their own roots through tissue culture. Propagation by cuttings in spring is possible but not easy at home without a greenhouse.

Landscape Uses

Baby's-breaths are indispensable fillers for perennial gardens. Use them to hide the yellowing foliage of bulbs and other plants with summer dormancy. The airy mounds of flowers are lovely in combination with spikes of gayfeathers (*Liatris*), sages (*Salvia*), daylilies (*Hemerocallis*), irises, and speedwells (*Veronica*), and with large flowers such as purple coneflower (*Echinacea purpurea*), daisies (*Leucanthemum* ×*superbum*), and asters. Use the diminutive creeping baby's-breath as an edger for beds, along walks, or in rock and wall gardens. The flowers are long-lasting when cut and hung upside down to dry.

H

HEDYCHIUM

he-DEE-kee-um • Zingiberaceae, Ginger Family

The gardenia-scented flowers with rounded petals open a few at a time, so each cluster sweetens the garden for weeks on end. Stiff, linear leaves to 2 feet long alternate up the stalk like climbing spikes on a telephone pole. Plants grow from thick, fibrous rhizomes nearly identical to culinary ginger you find at the grocery store.

HEDYCHIUM

Common Names:
Ginger lily, garland lily

Bloom Time:
Summer and fall bloom

Planting Requirements:
Sun to partial shade

Hedychium coccineum (kok-SIN-ee-um), scarlet ginger. Size: 5 to 7 feet tall, 4 to 5 feet wide. This stately species produces flaming torches of fragrant orange to red flowers that open simultaneously for a dazzling show. 'Disney' has peachy red flowers. 'Flaming Torch' lives up to its name, with slender spikes of burnt orange-red flowers from late summer through frost. A hardy Himalayan native. USDA Plant Hardiness Zones 7 to 11.

H. coronarium (kor-o-NAH-re-um), butterfly ginger. The scent of butterfly ginger instantaneously transports you to gardens of the Deep South, where moist air is perfumed with their gardenia-like scent in summer. The foot-long terminal flower clusters sport 2-inch, snow white flowers with the texture of powdered snow. Zones 7 to 11.

H. gardnerianum (gard-ner-ee-A-num), Kahili ginger. Size: 4 to 6 feet tall, 4 to 5 feet wide. This huge species has smaller flowers in dense 2-foot spikes atop stems towering more than 6 feet. A wealth of hybrids claim this species as one parent. Colors of the mildly fragrant flowers range from soft yellow 'Moy Giant' and orange-eyed 'Daniel

The fiery orange torches and lush foliage of scarlet ginger (*Hedychium coccineum*) add a tropical touch to any garden. In cold zones, plants are easily grown in a container and dropped into an empty spot in a bed for the summer.

Weeks' to deep orange-red 'Elizabeth'. Zones 7 (with protection) or 8 to 11.

How to Grow

Gingers are big plants with big appetites. Give these gluttons rich, consistently moist soil and a spot in full sun to partial shade. Work a generous supply of rotted manure or compost into the planting hole along with a balanced fertilizer, and top-dress annually with manure to keep plants healthy. Lift the huge rootstocks in fall and store them in bushel baskets of dry peat in a frost-free place. Plants are easy to grow in containers.

Landscape Uses

Gingers fit comfortably into almost any garden setting, from formal borders to lavish woodlands. They add tropical elegance among traditional perennials like garden phlox (*Phlox paniculata*) and lobelias. Create a lush oasis with crinums, spider lilies (*Hymenocallis*), bamboos, and elephant's ears (*Alocasia*). Contrast the architectural foliage with fine-textured meadow rues (*Thalictrum*), bugbanes (*Cimicifuga*), and irises, as well as ferns, sedges, and grasses. For simple drama, try a pot full of ginger as a focal point or accent in a garden bed.

HELENIUM

hel-EE-ne-um • Asteraceae, Aster Family

Abundant yellow or orange daisylike flowers with spherical centers top the erect, winged stalks of these showy late-season perennials. Sneezeweed gets its name from the old-time use of the dried, powdered root for snuff. The flowers are insect-pollinated and nonallergenic. The sparsely branching stems arise from stout, fibrous-rooted crowns.

HELENIUM

Common Names:
Sneezeweed, Helen's flower

Bloom Time:
Late summer and fall bloom

Planting Requirements:
Full sun

Helenium autumnale (awe-tum-NAH-lee), common sneezeweed. Size: 3 to 5 feet tall, 2 to 3 feet wide. A tall plant with leafy stems topped by broad clusters of 2-inch yellow or orange, yellow-centered flowers.

The bright green leaves are broadly lance-shaped with toothed margins. 'Brilliant' has orange-bronze, dark-centered flowers on sturdy 3-foot plants. 'Butterpat' has bright yellow flowers on 3- to 4-foot plants.

'Crimson Beauty' has mahogany flowers. 'Riverton Beauty' has golden yellow flowers with bronze-red centers. USDA Plant Hardiness Zones 3 to 8.

H. flexuosum (flex-u-O-sum), sneezeweed. Size: 2 to 3 feet tall, 1 to 2 feet wide. A compact grower with leafy stems and broad clusters of flowers with drooping yellow rays (petals) and brownish purple spherical centers. Zones 5 to 9.

H. hoopesii (hoop-ESS-ee-ee), orange sneezeweed. Size: 2 to 4 feet tall, 1 to 2 feet wide. An open plant with basal rosettes of large oval leaves and stems covered in small leaves and topped with sparse clusters of flowers with narrow, drooping, 3-inch golden yellow rays. Zones 3 to 7.

Hybrids

The American perennial market is seeing an influx of German and Dutch hybrids of mixed parentage that are extremely floriferous and quite hardy. 'Baudirektor Linne' is a late-blooming selection bearing mahogany flowers with brown centers. 'Kugelsonne' has bright yellow flowers on erect, usually self-supporting 4- to 5-foot stems. 'Mornheim Beauty' is the best red, with stems to 3 feet. 'Rotgold' has brick red and golden yellow flowers. 'Waldtraut' is golden brown. 'Zimbel-

stern' is an early-flowering selection with gold rays and brown centers.

How to Grow

Sneezeweeds are native to the edges of woods, low meadows, and moist prairies. They thrive in evenly moist, humus-rich soil in full sun. Orange sneezeweed is more tolerant of dry soil than are the other species and hybrids. Choose common sneezeweed for a moist or wet spot. The leafy stems are attractive during early summer as plants grow toward flowering. Pinch stem tips once or twice in spring to promote sturdy, compact growth. Some cultivars are naturally compact and self-supporting. In warmer zones, plants tend to stretch and may require staking. Divide clumps every 3 or 4 years to

A mixed planting of hybrid sneezeweeds (*Helenium autumnale* hybrids) adds a touch of bright butter yellow and rich terra-cotta to the fall garden. Plants thrive in moist soil or ordinary garden loam.

keep them vigorous. Propagate by stem cuttings in early summer. The species can be grown from seed sown outside in fall, but cultivars will not come true from seed.

Landscape Uses

Sneezeweeds are invaluable additions to late-season borders and informal meadow plantings. Contrary to their name, they do not make you sneeze: Their pollen is carried by insects, not wind. Plant them in the company of Siberian iris (*Iris siberica*), garden phlox (*Phlox paniculata*), bee balm (*Monarda didyma*), asters, coreopsis, goldenrods (*Solidago*), and ornamental grasses. Use common sneezeweed in informal plantings at the edge of a pond with ferns, grasses, New England aster (*Aster novae-angliae*), Joe-Pye weeds (*Eupatorium*), and ironweeds (*Veronica*). Plant orange sneezeweed in a dry spot with calamints (*Calamintha*), yarrows (*Achillea*), sages (*Salvia*), and stonecrops (*Sedum*).

HELIANTHEMUM

hee-le-AN-the-mum • Cistaceae, Rock Rose Family

Party colors and drought tolerance make rock roses perfect for adding excitement to a summer rockery, a wall garden, or a decorative trough. This subshrub thrives with little care and blooms all summer where nights are cool. The dense trailing stems arise from fibrous-rooted crowns.

> **HELIANTHEMUM**
>
> **Common Name:**
> Sun rose, rock rose
>
> **Bloom Time:**
> Summer and fall bloom
>
> **Planting Requirements:**
> Sun to light shade

Helianthemum nummularium (num-ew-LAH-ree-um), common sun rose. Size: 1 to 2 feet tall, 2 feet wide. Festive, five-petaled flowers like single roses in party colors cover the creeping to sprawling stems of this little-known treasure for the summer garden. The 1- to 2-inch flowers may be pink, white, yellow, or orange. Soft, hairy, oval gray-green leaves are carried opposite on the stems of this subshrub. Many selections commonly grown are hybrids with the closely related *H. appeninum*. 'Apricot' is deep apricot. 'Ben Nevis' is brilliant orange. 'Fireball' has double red flowers. 'Raspberry ripple' has raspberry-striped pink flowers. 'Wisley Primrose' has soft yellow flowers. USDA Plant Hardiness Zones 4 (with protection) to 8.

The burnt orange flowers of common sun rose (*Helianthemum nummularium* 'Ben Heckla') open throughout summer on spreading plants that cascade artfully over rocks and down the faces of walls.

How to Grow

Plant sun roses in rich, well-drained, sandy to gritty soil in full sun or light shade. Plants detest heavy soil and grow best where nights are cool and humidity is low. Propagate from stem cuttings taken as new growth hardens off.

Landscape Uses

Sun roses are best used in rock gardens or atop walls where the sprawling stems produce carpets of color for much of summer. Plants also grow well in containers. Grasses, phlox, lavenders (*Lavandula*), and sages (*Salvia*) are good companions.

HELIANTHUS

hee-lee-AN-thus • Asteraceae, Aster Family

Bold beauty is defined by the flowers of hybrid sunflowers. Their engaging, flat faces follow the light and resemble a child's illustration of the sun. A large genus of robust summer- or fall-blooming plants with stout leafy stems from thick, tough rootstocks. The starry yellow daisylike flowers are carried in flat or elongated clusters. Individual single flowers have a prominent round center. Semidoubles and doubles are also found. The common sunflower, *Helianthus annus*, an annual, is a commercial oil and seed plant with limited border potential.

HELIANTHUS

Common Name:
Sunflower

Bloom Time:
Summer and fall bloom

Planting Requirements:
Full sun

Helianthus angustifolius (an-gus-ti-FO-lee-us), swamp sunflower. Size: 4 to 8 feet tall, 3 to 4 feet wide. A commanding plant with thick stems clothed in deep green lance-shaped leaves and crowned with elongated, branching clusters of 3-inch bright yellow flowers with purple centers in September and October. 'First

Light' is compact and floriferous, to 4 feet. *H. simulans* is a giant version of this species (to 12 feet tall), with wider leaves. USDA Plant Hardiness Zones 6 to 9.

H. decapetalus (dek-a-PET-a-lus), thin-leaved sunflower. Size: 4 to 5 feet tall, 3 to 4 feet wide. A clump-forming sunflower with mounded, open clusters of 2- to 3-inch yellow flowers with yellow centers. 'Capenoch Star' has clear yellow flowers and is quite floriferous. 'Loddon Gold' is a popular double hybrid. 'Meteor' has semi-double flowers on 5-foot stems. 'Lemon Queen' is an excellent hybrid with sturdy stems and 2-inch lemon yellow flowers. Zones 4 to 8.

H. divaricatus (die-var-e-KATE-us), woodland sunflower. Size: 2 to 4 feet tall and wide. A shade-tolerant sunflower with starry, rich yellow flowers in late summer and fall. *H. strumosus* is similar but has rough, hairy leaves and stems. Zones 4 to 8.

H. maximilianii (max-i-mill-ee-A-nee), Maximilian sunflower. Size: 4 to 10 feet tall, 3 to 5 feet wide. A stately sunflower with drooping, lanceolate gray-green leaves and elongated clusters of 2- to 3-inch flowers in late summer and fall. Similar to swamp sunflower (though less floriferous) but hardy in the North. Zones 3 to 8.

H. mollis (MOL-lis), ashy sunflower. Size: 3 to 4 feet tall and wide. The dense clumps of this hairy gray-leaved sunflower are topped with 2½-inch clear yellow flowers in summer. Zones 4 to 8.

H. ×multiflorus (mul-tee-FLO-rus), many-flowered sunflower. Size: 3 to 5 feet tall, 2 to 3 feet wide. A coarse summer sunflower of hybrid origin from a cross between *H. decapetalus* and *H. annuus*. Several popular cultivars originated in gardens. 'Flore-Plena' has double, bright yellow flowers on 5-foot stems. 'Loddon Gold' has huge 5- to 6-inch double golden yellow flowers on 5- to 6-foot plants. Zones 4 to 8.

H. salicifolius (sal-is-i-FO-lee-us), willow leaf sunflower. Size: 3 to 4 feet tall, 2 to 3 feet wide. A delicate sunflower with narrow, drooping gray-green leaves and slender upright clusters of 2-inch flowers in fall. Zones 4 to 8.

Soft lemon yellow sunflowers (*Helianthus* 'Lemon Queen') thrive in average to poor soils and produce dozens of flowers in mid-summer. Goldfinches love the seeds, so leave the stems standing, along with those of its garden companion, black-eyed Susan (*Rudbeckia fulgida* 'Goldsturm').

How to Grow

Sunflowers are tough, hardy plants. Give them moist, average to rich soil in full sun. They are all quite drought-tolerant once established. Swamp, thin-leaved, and Maximilian sunflowers tolerate wet soil. They are of easy culture but require sufficient room to spread. Stems seldom need staking except in windy areas. *H. mollis* is a romper; give it room to spread. Divide overgrown clumps every 3 or 4 years in fall. Propagate by stem cuttings in early summer or by seed sown outdoors when ripe.

Landscape Uses

Sunflowers are indispensable additions to the summer and fall garden. Plant them with airy and small-flowered plants such as garden phlox (*Phlox paniculata*), baby's-breath (*Gypsophila paniculata*), Michelmas daisies and other asters (*Aster*), ironweeds (*Vernonia*), boltonias, and ornamental grasses. They combine well with tropicals such as dahlias and cannas. Plant them in informal meadow and prairie plantings with yarrows (*Achillea*), blazing-stars (*Liatris*), purple coneflowers (*Echinacea*), bergamot (*Monarda fistulosa*), and all manner of grasses.

HELICTOTRICHON

he-lick-to-TRY-kon • Poaceae, Grass Family

Blue fountains of this tough, drought-tolerant ornamental grass add elegance to the front of a bed throughout the season. The flattened blades spring from a tight clump to form a nearly perfect sphere. Early summer provides tall delicate plumes that dry to straw color. Plants produce dense tufts from fibrous-rooted crowns.

> **HELICTOTRICHON**
>
> **Common Name:**
>   Blue oat grass
>
> **Bloom Time:**
>   Early summer bloom
>
> **Planting Requirements:**
>   Sun

Helictotrichon sempervirens (sem-per-VIR-enz), blue oat grass. Size: 2 to 3 feet tall and wide. Dense, spiky mounds of powder blue lances create an enchanting effect in the evening garden among pale-flowered perennials. This handsome grass has decorative 1-foot evergreen leaves as well as tall, airy beige plumes atop wiry stems that wave above the rosettes. This cool-season grass begins growth in early spring and flowers in late spring and early summer. 'Pendula' is noted for its large, nodding plumes. 'Saphisprudel' ('Sapphire Fountain') is a superb rust-resistant selection with steel blue leaves. USDA Plant Hardiness Zones 4 to 8.

How to Grow

Plant blue oat grass in sandy to loamy, moist to dry, well-drained soil in full sun or light shade. Excessive soil moisture, especially in winter, promotes root rot and plants quickly decline. Where summers are humid, plants may develop rust, which produces orange growth on leaves and may disfigure the plant. Good air circulation helps keep plants healthy. Remove flowers as they fade or they will collapse haphazardly and ruin the plant's beauty. Shear clumps into smooth mounds in late winter to allow fresh growth to emerge.

Landscape Uses

Blue oat grass is a dramatic plant best used as a single accent or in a small grouping. Give the clumps plenty of room to develop their full, nearly spherical form. Combine them with low carpet-forming thymes (*Thymus*), verbenas, winecups (*Callirhoe*),

The fine-textured mounds of blue oat grass (*Helictotrichon sempervirens*) make an elegant addition to both formal and informal settings. They thrive in any well-drained spot in full sun or light shade.

and other plants that will not hide the foliage. For a colorful background, choose catmints (*Nepeta*), ornamental onions (*Alliums*), asters, and shrubs with berries.

HELIOPSIS

hee-lee-OP-sis • Asteraceae, Aster Family

Native perennials are often ignored, but this bright yellow daisy has long been a favorite of perennial gardeners and wildflower enthusiasts alike. A denizen of prairies and roadsides, this exuberant plant provides scads of flowers for months on end with little care. Plants produce stout, woody but deciduous stems from fibrous-rooted crowns.

HELIOPSIS

Common Name:
Oxeye

Bloom Time:
Summer bloom

Planting Requirements:
Full sun or partial shade

Heliopsis helianthoides (hee-lee-an-THOY-deez), oxeye. Size: 3 to 6 feet tall, 2 to 3 feet wide. Oxeyes are bushy plants that resemble well-branched sunflowers. They have 2- to 3-inch bright yellow flowers with yellow centers. The triangular leaves are borne in pairs on slender, branching stems. Var. *scabra* is a stout, floriferous variety with large, rough foliage. Many garden selections with single or double flowers have been made. 'Gold Greenheart' has double yellow-green flowers with green centers. 'Golden Plume' is a floriferous, double-flowered compact selection growing 3 to 3½ feet tall. 'Incomparabilis' has yellow-orange, 3-inch semidouble flowers. 'Karat' has 3-inch, bright yellow single flowers. 'Loraine's Sunshine' is curiously variegated, with all the veins green against a creamy background. 'Prairie Sunset' is deep yellow with an orange eye. 'Summer Sun' is a heat-tolerant, compact grower to 3 feet, with 4-inch single flowers. Zones 3 to 8.

How to Grow

Oxeyes are tough, drought-tolerant plants. Grow them in moist or dry, average to rich soil in full sun or partial shade. Border performance is best in full sun. Most named cultivars have self-supporting stems. The wild forms may need staking. Clumps will bloom for 4 to 6 weeks in summer. Divide plants growing in rich soils every 2 or 3 years to promote longevity. Cultivars are more reliable. Divide them when necessary to control their spread or rejuvenate clumps. Propagate by stem cuttings taken in late spring. Self-sown seedlings may be abundant.

Landscape Uses

Combine oxeyes with summer perennials and grasses in borders, meadows, and prairies. Garden phlox (*Phlox paniculata*), hardy mums (*Chrysanthemum*), speedwells (*Veronica*), and asters are excellent companions. In wild gardens, plant them with wild phlox (*Phlox pilosa* and others), butterfly weed (*Asclepias tuberosa*), blazing-stars (*Liatris*), and rose mallows (*Hibiscus*).

Oxeye (*Heliopsis helianthoides*) is the first of summer's yellow daisies to bloom. Flowering begins in early June and continues into August. With so many flowers, self-sown seedlings are plentiful.

HELLEBORUS

hell-e-BOR-us • Ranunculaceae, Buttercup Family

Hellebores are aristocrats of the winter and early-spring garden. Beautiful nodding bells grace their stems when few plants brave the elements. Their leathery foliage is attractive throughout summer and, in mild regions, during winter as well. All parts of the plant are poisonous. Two groups of species are divided on the basis of persistent aboveground stems versus creeping underground rhizomes with ephemeral flowering stems. Those with persistent stems produce flower buds at the top of the stems in fall. The buds of the rhizomatous species emerge as temperatures moderate in early spring. The flowers consist of five showy petal-like sepals surrounded by leafy bracts. Flowers may be flat with many fuzzy stamens, or tube-like with the stamens concealed. The leathery sepals persist for over a month, well after seed capsules begin to form.

HELLEBORUS

Common Names:
Hellebore, Christmas rose, Lenten rose

Bloom Time:
Winter and spring bloom

Planting Requirements:
Light to partial shade

Helleborus argutifolius (ar-goot-i-FO-lee-us) (*corsicus*), Corsican hellebore. Size: 1 to 2 feet tall, 2 to 3 feet wide. A coarse plant of shrublike proportions with thick, erect stems and glossy, toothed, three-lobed evergreen leaves. The buds form in fall at the apex of the stem and open to nodding, bowl-shaped green flowers in early spring. The sepals persist well after seed capsules begin to develop. 'Janet Starnes' and 'Pacific Frost' are two variegated selections that lack the vigor of the species, especially where summers are humid. A lovely hybrid with the Christmas rose, *H. ×nigercors* is coveted for its stout stems crowned with up to 30 outfacing, creamy white to soft green flowers. 'Alabaster' and 'Blackthorn Strain' are two outstanding selections. *H. ×sternii*

excels in its stiff, mottled to fully silver foliage and its spreading trusses of soft green to creamy rose flowers. 'Boughton Beauty', 'Blackthorn' and 'Pine Knot' are a few good strains. USDA Plant Hardiness Zones 6 (with protection) or 7 to 9.

H. foetidus (FOET-i-dus), stinking hellebore. Size: 1½ to 2 feet tall and wide. A stemmed hellebore with deep green spidery leaves, each with seven to nine narrow, toothed leaflets. The nodding, tube-like green flowers with a red-brown edge on each sepal are carried above the foliage in erect, branching clusters. Named selections of particular interest include 'Wester Flisk', with red stems and red-tinged petioles set off by gray-green leaves. Plant Delights nursery owner Tony Avent lists several named clones, including the huge 'Green Giant', as well as 'Sienna,' with nearly black leaves. Zones 5 (with protection) or 6 to 9.

H. niger (NYE-ger), Christmas rose. Size: 1 foot tall, 1 to 2 feet wide. A rhizomatous hellebore with long petioled, deep green leaves with five to seven irregular pedate lobes. The 2- to 3-inch white flowers rise singly on succulent stalks from the center of the clump in winter or earliest spring. They fade to pink and are often quite persistent. 'Potter's Wheel' strain has 3-inch flowers. 'Blackthorn Strain' has pink buds opening to white flowers on tall, dark stems; and 'Sunrise' has 3½-inch flowers flushed with pink. 'Wilder' and 'Nell Lewis' strains are heat-tolerant and good for the South. Zones 3 to 8.

H. odorus (o-DOOR-us), sweet hellebore. Size: 1 to 2 feet tall and wide. Beauty and fragrance go a long way in creating a flawless plant. Add chartreuse flowers and perfection is attained. This plant is a must for collectors and enthusiastic gardeners. The 1½- to 2-inch luminescent flowers vary in fragrance from sweet to slightly musty. This species is easily confused with *H. cyclophyllus*, which is similar in many respects. Zones 4 to 8.

H. orientalis (or-i-en-TA-lis), Lenten rose. Size: 1 to 1½ feet tall, 1 to 2½ feet wide. The showiest hellebore, with clusters of white, pink, or purple, often spotted nodding flowers borne on succulent stems from a creeping rhizome. The evergreen compound leaves have five to seven broad, irregular leaflets excellent for winter color. *H. ×hybridus* is the correct name for most Lenten roses, as they are of mixed parentage. Most of the best hybrids available in America today are seed strains developed from named varieties. A seed strain is a lineage of plants, in this case of hybrid origin, that come true to type from seed. No need to buy named selections. Seed strains now offer excellent flower color and form. A few good strains are 'Lady', 'Picadilly', and 'Royal Heritage', as well as doubles like 'Party Dress' and the 'Eliza-

The new color selections of the Lenten rose (*Helleborus ×hybridus*) 'Pine Knot' strain far surpass those grown in old-fashioned gardens. Rich colors, picotee edges, and rounded flowers are just a few of the characteristics favored by breeders and enthusiasts.

bethtown' and 'Pine Knot' strains of singles and doubles. Zones 4 to 9.

H. purpurascens (pur-pur-AS-cens). Size: 12 to 16 inches tall and wide. The deeply divided palmate circular leaves cap stiff petioles up to 2 feet tall. They are deciduous and are completely gone by late winter. The 1½ to 2-inch saucer-shaped flowers vary from rich plum purple to sea green and may open as early as December in mild climates. Zones 4 to 8.

H. thibetanus (thib-e-TAY-nus), Chinese hellebore. Size: 1 to 2 feet tall and wide. This blowsy species with pink to rose, nodding to outfacing flowers with pointed petals is reminiscent of *Glaucidium palmatum* rather than of a hellebore. Plants go dormant in summer after flowering. Plants are at last becoming available. Zones 6 to 8.

H. viridis (VEER-i-dis), green hellebore. Size: 10 to 16 inches tall and wide. A dainty hellebore with clustered nodding green flowers carried on leafy stems and deciduous deeply lobed leaves with 7 to 11 narrow leaflets. Zones 5 to 8.

How to Grow

Hellebores are long-lived, easy-care perennials for flower and foliage interest. Plant them in evenly moist but well-drained, sandy, humus-rich soil in light to partial shade. Most species will tolerate deep summer shade if given sun in winter and spring before tree leaves emerge. Plants thrive in limey or slightly acid soils. Cor-

The pewter-gray foliage of 'Wester Flisk' stinking hellebore (*Helleborus foetidus* 'Wester Flisk') adds a bright spot to the shade garden even after the chartreuse flowers have faded.

sican hellebore is quite drought-tolerant once it is established and prefers a sunny situation. This and *H. foetidus* may be short-lived but self-sow freely. In early spring, remove any leaves damaged by winter cold. If the stemmed species lose vigor, cut them to the ground to encourage new stems. Plants take 1 or 2 years to become established and dislike disturbance. Divide only for purposes of propagation. Lenten rose is an exception. It is easily divided but seldom needs to be. Self-sown seedlings may appear around the parent plants, as Lenten rose is particularly prolific. Sow seed outdoors as soon as it is ripe. Transplant seedlings to their permanent location as soon as they are large enough to move easily. They will flower in 2 to 5 years.

Landscape Uses

Hellebores bloom throughout winter and spring, depending on the climate. Flowering shrubs, especially those with attractive bark and early flowers, are often combined with hellebores. Red- and yellow-stemmed dogwoods (*Cornus*), witch hazels (*Hamamelis*), daphnes, spiked hazels (*Corylopsis*), silvery shadbushes (*Amelanchier*), and purple-leaved shrubs such as hazels (*Corylus*) are good choices. The smaller bulbs, such as snowdrops, winter aconites, early crocuses, *Iris reticulata,* and species forms of daffodils and tulips are good companions. Spring- or fall-blooming cyclamen are lovely in flower and their mottled, heart-shaped foliage combines nicely with the dark green of the hellebore leaves. Take care not to plant large floppy perennials near hellebores. Smothering by exuberant neighbors promotes fungal rot and blocks the sun from the foliage.

HEMEROCALLIS

hem-er-o-KAL-lis • Hemerocallidaceae (Liliaceae), Daylily Family

Daylilies are popular garden perennials with their origins in antiquity. The handsome daylily has been cultivated in China for food, medicine, and ornament for over 2,500 years. The roots and leaves were used as a pain reliever and for other medicinal purpose and the flowers, flower buds, and young leaves are still eaten as vegetables. Daylilies first came to Europe in the mid-16th century. The yellow daylily, or lemon lily (*H. lilioasphodelus*), presumably arrived first in Hungary via Mongolia, and the familiar tawny daylily (*H. fulva*) was brought to Venice by Arabs and to Lisbon by Portuguese merchants. Both species took well to their

HEMEROCALLIS

Common Name:
  Daylily

Bloom Time:
  Spring and summer bloom

Planting Requirements:
  Full sun to partial shade

adopted homes and quickly naturalized. By the 19th century, new species and hybrids were exported to the United States and Europe from China and Japan.

In America, the tawny daylily is a common site along roadsides, in meadows, and around abandoned homesteads. The plant's persistence and durability has made it an instant sensation for tough spots. It earned the name "outhouse lily" because of its frequent use with phlox and hollyhocks around outhouse foundations. It is also called "ditch lily" because it is so often seen naturalized along roadsides.

Today, daylilies are among the most popular and varied perennials. Their colorful flowers are composed of three broad petals and three narrow, petal-like sepals that overlap for a portion of their length, creating a tubular appearance. Each flower lasts only a day, but a profusion of new buds keeps the plants in bloom for 2 to 4 weeks. Some new varieties are rebloomers that produce new stalks throughout the season. Flower buds are still eaten today as a vegetable or in soups. Daylily foliage is long and straplike, with a central vein running the entire length, producing a keel in cross-section. The plants grow from stout crowns with thick tuberous roots radiating outward in a circle. Established clumps have multiple crowns and produce a plethora of flowering stalks in a season.

Modern hybrids exploit every color in the rainbow except blue. Pure white has also eluded hybridizers, but many pale yellow or pink selections are very close. Bicolor and even tricolor forms boast bold stripes, eyes, and bands. Flower form is also variable, including tubular, saucer, and spider shapes with thick or thin petals and smooth, wavy, or frilly margins. Some hybrids have flowers fully 6 inches across; others have miniature 2-inch flowers. Height ranges from dwarf cultivars under 1 foot tall to well over 6 feet, although most cultivars are 2 to 3 feet tall.

Hemerocallis altissima (al-TIS-si-ma), tall daylily. Size: 5 to 6 feet tall, 2 to 4 feet wide. This lofty species has fragrant pale yellow flowers throughout summer and early fall and is an important plant for hybridizing. The species form is regrettably scarce in gardens. USDA Plant Hardiness Zones 4 to 9.

H. aurantiaca (a-ran-ti-A-ka) daylily. Size: 2½ to 3 feet tall and wide. A fast-spreading daylily with coarse, persistent foliage and tubular orange flowers blushed with purple on the outside. Zones 7 to 9.

H. citrina (si-TRI-na) night-blooming daylily. Size: 3½ to 4 feet tall, 2 to 3 feet wide. A coarse-leaved species with nocturnal, fragrant lemon-yellow flowers. Zones 5 to 9.

H. dumortieri (dew-mor-tee-AY-ree), early daylily. Size: 1½ to 2 feet tall and wide. Early daylily is an early-blooming species with fragrant, funnelform, brown-tinged yellow flowers held just above or with the foliage. Zones 2 to 9.

H. fulva (FUL-va), tawny daylily. Size: 3 to 4 feet tall (rarely 5 feet), 3 to 4 feet wide. Can be invasive. This familiar species has rusty orange flowers carried well above the foliage in many-flowered clusters. 'Europa' is a sterile, triploid selection with bright orange flowers. 'Kwanso' has fully double flowers and occasionally variegated foliage. Zones 2 to 9.

H. lilioasphodelis (lil-ee-o-ass-fo-DEL-us), lemon lily. Size: 2½ to 3 feet tall and wide. A sturdy plant with fragrant, lemon yellow flowers held well above the foliage. Zones 3 to 9.

H. middendorfii (mid-den-DORF-ee-ee), Middendorf's daylily. Size: 2 to 2½ feet tall and wide. This short species has fragrant yellow-orange flowers held with or just above the leaves and reblooms throughout summer. Zones 3 to 9.

H. minor (MY-nor). Size: 1 to 1½ feet tall and wide. This floriferous dwarf species has fragrant yellow flowers held above dense clumps of grassy foliage. Zones 4 to 9.

H. thunbergii (thun-BERG-ee-ee) Thunberg's daylily. Size: 2 to 3 feet tall and wide. The fragrant lemon yellow flowers of this species are carried above the foliage on flattened stems. Zones 4 to 9.

Hybrids

Modern daylily cultivars are of hybrid origin, arising from crosses between species forms and earlier cultivars. Today's hybrids fall into two main groups: diploids (having a single complement of chromosomes) and tetraploids (with an artificially doubled

One of the last daylilies to bloom is 'Autumn Minaret', a selection of the graceful tall daylily *Hemerocallis altissima*. With careful planning, you can have daylilies in bloom all season.

chromosome complement). In addition to color, form, and season of bloom, tetraploid daylilies offer larger flowers with exceptionally thick petals that help them hold through the heat of the day and keep their color. In the frenzy to create new cultivars with broad petals, bicolor bands and blazes, extra frills, and extended bloom, some of the grace of the species and older cultivars has been compromised. In fact, many of these older plants are seldom available from nurseries and risk being displaced from American gardens altogether. The hybrids are far too numerous to list. To select plants for your garden, consult local nurseries or your state chapter of the American Hemerocallis Society. To choose the correct colors, it is best to see the plant before you buy to ensure you get what you want. Catalog descriptions and photographs are often inadequate or misleading.

How to Grow

Plant tough and adaptable daylilies in average to rich, well-drained soil in full sun or light shade. Plants tolerate wet soil as well as extended drought. Some older cultivars and species can grow in partial shade but today's hybrids need considerable sun for optimum flowering. Buy containerized or bareroot plants in spring or fall and set them out with the crown just below soil level. Spread the thick, tuberous roots out radially and cover them with soil. Once established, they spread quickly to form dense, broad clumps. Some tetraploids spread more slowly than others. The older selections are "self-cleaning," but the newer cultivars need daily deadheading to keep them looking their best. Though most have excellent foliage that stays tidy all season, some cultivars may have yellowing leaves, even during blooming season. Remove these as they appear by grasping them firmly and tugging quickly to snap them off at the base. Remove the entire flowerstalk after the last blossom is spent. Plants can remain in place for many years, but some hybrids produce so many stalks that the flowers get too crowded to be appreciated if the clumps are not divided every 3 years or so. Lift the entire clump in late summer and pull or cut the thick tangled roots apart. Thick clumps of older selections can be chopped apart with a sharp spade or popped apart by inserting two garden forks back to back and then clapping the handles together. Take care with choice cultivars to divide crowns without damaging roots.

Daylilies are fairly pest- and disease-free, but aphids and thrips may be a problem on bloom stalks and flower buds. The soft-bodied aphids are readily detected, but thrips often go unnoticed until the flowers are deformed. Spray with insecticidal soap according to label instructions.

Landscape Uses

Daylilies have infinite uses in both public and private landscapes. They are favored for large-scale and mass plantings because of their adaptability, rapid spread, and extended bloom period. Repeat bloomers are

Hemerocallis 'Red Thrill' is a beautiful example of the long-petaled flower form known as a spider. These expressive flowers have a wild beauty that contrasts markedly with the frilly, overlapping daylily flowers popular with many hybridizers and gardeners.

gaining popularity in these large-scale applications. In the home landscape, species and older, fast-growing selections are good for mass plantings in tough spots such as banks and swales, or in combination with shrubs and trees. Accent plantings around foundations or in concert with groundcovers are also popular. The slower-spreading selections are excellent border plants. Combine them with favorites such as garden phlox (*Phlox paniculata*), yarrows (*Achillea*), veronicas, sages (*Salvia*), and Siberian iris (*Iris sibirica*). Small flowers set off bold daylilies to good advantage. Try a planting with baby's-breath (*Gypsophila paniculata*), early-blooming asters, and hardy geraniums. Use miniatures with early perennials and ornamental grasses; choose dwarf varieties for rock gardens.

HEPATICA

he-PAT-e-ka • Ranunculaceae, Buttercup Family

Hepaticas herald the promise of spring with delicate multipetaled flowers wrapped in warm down. These early wildflowers have three-lobed evergreen leaves that resemble the lobes of the liver. Under the "Doctrine of Signatures" (a spiritual philosophy popularized in the 1600s that states that one can determine a plant's purpose by observing the shape of the leaves, flower color, or other signatures), this plant was used to treat ailments of the organ it resembled. The rosette of basal leaves radiates from a fibrous-rooted crown.

HEPATICA

Common Names:
  Hepatica, liverleaf, harbinger of spring

Bloom Time:
  Spring bloom

Planting Requirements:
  Light to full shade

The flowers of liverleaf (*Hepatica americana*) emerge in earliest spring wrapped in down for protection. They nod shyly on cold, overcast days but open fully when the warm sun shines.

Hepatica acutiloba (a-kew-ti-LOW-ba), sharp-lobed hepatica. Size: 6 to 8 inches tall, 8 to 12 inches wide. This plant has large leaves, up to 5 inches, with sharp, pointed lobes. The flowers vary in color from white through pink and blue to lavender and purple. Plant in humus-rich, moist limey soil in light to full shade. Multipetaled and double-flowered forms are available. 'Eco White Fluff' is a shaggy double with large flowers. 'Eco White Giant' has sparkling white flowers 1¾ inches across and extra lobes on the leaves. 'Louise' is a double blue. USDA Plant Hardiness Zones 3 to 8.

H. americana (a-mer-i-KAN-ah) *nobilis* var. *americana*), round-lobed hepatica, liverleaf. Size: 3 to 6 inches tall, 6 to 8 inches wide. The rounded lobes of the leaves separate this hepatica from its close relative. The furry, ¾- to 1-inch flowers have 5 to 12 petal-like sepals in shades of blue, white, or (rarely) pink. The foliage turns bronzy in fall. 'Eco Indigo' has the deepest blue flowers available. Zones 3 to 8.

How to Grow

Plant in humus-rich, moist, acid soil in light to full shade. Sharp-lobed hepatica prefers limey soil but is adaptable. Hepaticas tolerate deep shade because of their evergreen leaves. Plant on a slope or where leaves will not smother the rosettes. Plants are slow to establish but in time form multicrowned clumps. Lift plants after the new leaves are fully formed or in fall, and gently pull crowns apart. Sow fresh seed outdoors uncovered. Seedlings take 2 or 3 years to bloom.

Landscape Uses

Plant hepaticas on a mound or against a rock where early flowers are sure to be noticed. Combine them with evergreen wild gingers (*Asarum*), bloodroot (*Sanguinaria canadensis*), trilliums, rue anemone (*Anemonella thalictroides*), and other woodland wildflowers. Dwarf ferns such as Himalayan maidenhair (*Adiantum venustum*) and fragile fern (*Cystopteris fragilis*) are good companions.

HEUCHERA

HOY-ka-ra or *HUE-ker-a* • Saxifragaceae, Saxifrage Family

Coral bells foliage rivals that of hosta for beauty and versatility, and soon there may be as many varieties. A large genus of lovely foliage plants, many of which also have showy flowers. The evergreen leaves are rounded, heart-shaped, or triangular and usually have lobes and toothed margins. Some resemble maple leaves. The leaves have long, slender petioles (leaf stalks) and arise directly from a stout woody crown with thin, fibrous roots. They may be hairy or smooth, green, mottled with gray and silver, or in some cases purple. The flowers are borne on narrow, upright stalks. They are carried singly or in open, branched clusters. Many have green or brown mostly insignificant flowers, but those of several species are showy bells of white, red, or pink.

> **HEUCHERA**
> **Common Names:**
>   Alumroot, coral bells
> **Bloom Time:**
>   Foliage plant with spring and summer bloom
> **Planting Requirements:**
>   Full sun to full shade

Heuchera americana (a-mer-i-KAN-ah), alumroot, rock geranium. Size: 1½ to 3 feet tall and wide. An open, mounding plant with long-petioled, mottled, silvery green heart-shaped leaves and insignificant green flowers. The foliage turns ruby red or purplish in fall. 'Garnet' turns burgundy in winter, green in summer. 'Dale's Strain' has

The old-fashioned coral bells (*Heuchera sanguinea* hybrids) lack the colorful foliage of new introductions, but their prolific, colorful flowers ensure their place in the garden. Some of the new hybrids are combining showy flowers such as these with colorful leaves.

gray-green leaves with silver mottling. USDA Plant Hardiness Zones 4 to 9.

H. cylindrica (si-LIN-dri-ka), poker alumroot. Size: 1 to 2½ feet tall and wide. Poker alumroot has slender spikes of single flowers surrounded by creamy white inflated tubular petal-like bracts. The hairy, rich green, rounded leaves are arrayed in tight clusters. 'Green Ivory' has showy creamy white flowers with green bases. Zones 3 to 8.

H. micrantha (mi-KRAN-tha), small-flowered alumroot. Size: 1 to 2 feet tall and wide. The shiny maple-like leaves of this alumroot are covered with soft hairs. The small greenish white flowers are carried in airy clusters. 'Palace Purple' is a superior selection of *H. micrantha* var. *diversifolia*, with deep purple-brown foliage that sets

off the flowers to good advantage. This seed-grown strain comes fairly true to seed but is somewhat variable. In warm zones, leaves fade to bronze by midsummer. Shade from hot afternoon sun is recommended wherever it is grown. Zones 4 to 8.

H. richardsonii (richard-SON-ee-ee), prairie alumroot. Size: 2 to 3 feet tall, 1 to 2 feet wide. A tufted plant with bright green, hairy rounded leaves and slender stalks bearing small flowers surrounded by inflated, greenish white bracts. Zones 3 to 8.

H. sanguinea (san-GUIN-ee-a), coral bells. Size: 1 to 1½ feet tall and wide. The showiest species of the genus, coral bells have bright crimson flowers above gray-green heart-shaped leaves. Plants have been selected for flower color and many cultivars have been named. 'Alba' has white flowers. 'Bressingham Blaze' has scarlet flowers. 'Splendens' has carmine red flowers. Zones 3 to 8.

H. villosa (vil-LOW-sa), hairy alumnroot. Size: 1 to 3 feet tall and wide. An attractive species for shade and dry soil with angular, lobed leaves and airy greenish white flowers. Var. *macrorrhiza* has large, fuzzy maple-like leaves of exceptional size and beauty. Zones 4 to 8.

H. ×brizoides (briz-OI-deez), hybrid coral bells. Size: 1 to 2½ feet tall and wide. This group of hybrids is a result of crosses between *H. sanguinea*, *H. micrantha*, and *H. americana*. They vary in size and flower color and are more heat-tolerant than *H. sanguinea* cultivars. 'Chatterbox' has large pink flowers. 'Coral Cloud' is a floriferous, coral-pink selection. 'Fire Sprite' has broad, compact clusters of rose-red flowers. 'June Bride' is a large-flowered white selection. 'Mt. St. Helens' has brick red flowers. 'Pluie de Feu' ('Rain of Fire') has bright cherry red flowers. 'White Cloud' is an excellent white with hundreds of flowers on multiple stalks. Zones 3 to 8.

Hybrids

Several breeders have concentrated on developing colorful foliage. A few good selections include 'Amber Waves' with gold and pink leaves, 'Frosted Violet' with sil-

Silver overlay on purple leaves is one of the many combinations of colors that new introductions such as *Heuchera* 'Pewter Veil' offer eager gardeners. The airy flower spikes form a translucent cloud high above the foliage in summer.

very purple leaves darker at the centers, 'Mint Frost' with silver and mint green leaves, 'Pewter Veil' with smoky gray and purple leaves, 'Silver Scrolls' with silver leaves bearing purple veins that emerge purple, and 'Velvet Knight' with deep purple leaves. Zones 4 to 9.

How to Grow

Plant alumroots and coral bells in moist but well-drained, humus-rich soil in full sun or partial shade. In warm regions, shade from hot afternoon sun is imperative to keep foliage from bleaching. In heavy shade plants produce leggy mounds of foliage and seldom flowers. As clumps grow, they rise above the ground on woody rootstocks. Lift clumps every 3 years, remove the oldest woody portions of the rootstocks, and replant the rosettes into reworked soil. Encourage *H.* ×*brizoides* to rebloom by removing spent flowerstalks. The cooler the summer temperatures, the greater the likelihood of continued bloom. Grow species from seed sown inside or outside. Cover the small seeds lightly and keep them warm (70°F). Borers may pierce the crown and feed on the stem, killing the foliage rosette. Cut out affected portions and replant.

Landscape Uses

Alumroots offer impeccable foliage and airy, often subtle flowers. Coral bells have similar foliage and showy colorful flowers. Use these versatile plants in rockeries with dwarf iris (*Iris cristata* or *I. pumila*), primroses (*Primula*), bellflowers (*Campanula*), and ferns. Plant coral bells at the front of beds and borders with low to medium-size plants such as dwarf baby's-breath (*Gypsophila repens*), geraniums, pinks (*Dianthus*), catmint (*Nepeta mussinii* 'Blue Wonder'), irises, and asters. Combine purple-leaved selections with bleeding hearts (*Dicentra*), phlox, bronze sedges such as *Carex flagellifera,* and hostas.

×HEUCHERELLA

HOY-ka-rell-a or *HUE-ker-rell-a* • Saxifragaceae, Saxifrage Family

×*Heucherella* is a hybrid genus produced from a cross between *Heuchera* (coral bells) and *Tiarella* (foamflower). (Bigeneric hybrid genera are preceded by an "×" to indicate their hybrid origin.) Plants excel in both foliage and flowers. The basal leaves emerge from a thick, woody crown with fibrous roots.

> **×HEUCHERELLA**
>
> **Common Name:**
> Foamy bells
>
> **Bloom Time:**
> Spring and summer bloom
>
> **Planting Requirements:**
> Light to full shade

×*Heucherella tiarelloides* (tee-a-rel-LOI-deez), foamy bells. Size: 1 to 2 feet tall and wide. This lovely plant combines the pink color of *Heuchera sanguinea* with the triangular evergreen foliage and foamy flowers of *Tiarella*. The plants grow in tight clumps from stout rootstocks. A flush of flowers is produced in spring, with scattered flowers throughout summer and fall. 'Bridget Bloom' is the most celebrated cultivar of the genus, with shell pink flowers. 'Heart of Darkness' has deep maroon veins and white flowers. 'Kimono' has deeply cut, lacquered leaves with near-black centers and creamy white flowers. 'Sunspot' has chartreuse leaves with maroon veins and pink flowers. Wow. USDA Plant Hardiness Zones 3 to 8.

How to Grow

Plant foamy bells in moist, humus-rich soil in sun to light shade. In all but northern zones, foamy bells requires some afternoon shade to keep foliage from burning, but plants will not flower well in deep season-long shade. Divide clumps every 3 years and replant into enriched soil. The flowers are sterile and do not set seed.

Landscape Uses

Combine foamy bells with flowering shrubs or with spring bulbs, woodland wild-flowers, and ferns. Plant drifts of several plants in the filtered shade of serviceberries (*Amelanchier*), silverbells (*Halesia*), yellow-wood (*Cladrastis lutea*), and other flowering trees alone or in combination with groundcovers such as lungworts (*Pulmonaria*), Siberian bugloss (*Brunnera macrophylla*), and hostas. In northern gardens, plants tolerate more sun, and the pink flowers combine beautifully with the purple foliage of 'Vera Jameson' sedum and ornamental grasses such as white-and-green bulbous oat grass (*Arrhenatherum elatius bulbosum* 'Variegatum').

The delicate flower spires of the hybrid genus ✕*Heucherella* 'Bridget Bloom' combine the foamy flowers of foamflower (*Tiarella*) with the bright pink of its other parent, coral bells (*Heuchera*).

HIBISCUS

hi-BIS-kus • Malvaceae, Mallow Family

Names like disco bell and fireball give you a clue to the drama of these exotic flowers. Hibiscus are perennials of shrublike structure and proportions. Thick, erect stalks arise from a woody crown with deep, spreading roots. The leaves, arrayed alternately on the stems, are palmately lobed. Some species have deeply cut spidery leaves; others resemble maples. The stems are crowned with open clusters of huge flowers, each with five petals that seem to be made of crepe paper with a long central bottlebrush that bears the male and female reproductive structures. Individual flowers last only 1 day, but flowers open in succession for 3 to 6 weeks. The woody seed capsules are quite attractive in fall and winter.

HIBISCUS

Common Names:
 Rose mallow, hibiscus

Bloom Time:
 Summer bloom

Planting Requirements:
 Full sun to light shade

Hibiscus coccineus (kok-SIN-ee-us), scarlet rose mallow. Size: 5 to 10 feet tall, 3 to 6 feet wide (larger possible). This stately plant has broad, deeply incised palmately lobed or divided leaves, often with red-tinged margins. The 6-inch saucer-shaped flowers are bright red. USDA Plant Hardiness Zones 6 to 10.

H. grandiflorus (gran-di-FLO-rus), great rose mallow. Size: 5 to 6 feet tall, 2 to 4 feet wide. This species is noteworthy for its size alone. Huge, 12-inch gray-green leaves and 6-inch pink or rose-purple flowers ornament the stalk. Zones 6 to 10.

H. militaris (mil-i-TAR-is), soldier rose mallow. Size: 4 to 7 feet tall, 3 to 4 feet wide. This plant has beautiful triangular or narrow heart-shaped leaves with two shallow side lobes and a long central lobe. The 5- to 6-inch flowers are white to pale pink with a crimson eye. Zones 4 to 9.

H. moscheutos (mos-SHOO-tos or mos-KA-tos), common rose mallow. Size: 4 to 8 feet tall, 3 to 5 feet wide. This popular perennial has broadly oval leaves with three to five shallow lobes and 6- to 8-inch white flowers with red centers. Subsp. *palustris* (marsh mallow) has three-lobed leaves and white, pink, or rose flowers without an eye. Many hybrids have been made combining the compact growth of this species with the red flowers of *H. coccineus*. The hybrids have huge 8- to 10-inch flowers in pure white, white with a crimson eye, pink, rose, and bright red. 'Fantasia' has huge rosy violet flowers.

'Fireball' is a fantastic scarlet. Zones 4 (with protection) or 5 to 10.

How to Grow

Plant rose mallows in evenly moist, humus-rich soil in full sun or light shade. Plant young plants in spring or fall, leaving 3 to 4 feet between each to allow for their eventual spread. Propagate by tip cuttings taken in July. Remove flower buds and reduce leaf size by half unless you have a mist bed. Sow seeds outdoors in fall or inside in late

The huge, saucer-shaped flowers of scarlet rose mallow (*Hibiscus coccineus*) last only a day, but new buds keep the plants in flower all summer.

winter. Seedlings germinate in 1 to 2 weeks and may flower the same season.

Landscape Uses

The bold hybrid hibiscus are best used alone as accent plants against walls or hedges or as eye-catching focal points in large perennial gardens. Plant them as shrubs in combination with fine-textured flowers and grasses. In meadow or waterside gardens, combine them with irises, ferns, astilbes, and ornamental grasses.

HOSTA

HOS-ta • Agavaceae (Liliaceae), Agave Family

Hostas are the most popular shade plants. Valued for their bold, dramatic foliage, the leafy clumps vary greatly in size from 6 inches to over 3 feet in height. The leaves arise directly from a stout crown with thick spidery white roots. Each leaf has a long, furrowed or cupped petiole (leaf stalk) and a broad heart- or lance-shaped blade with deep, distinctive venation. Leaf surfaces may be puckered between the veins and the entire blade may cup upward or droop outward toward the tip. Leaf margins vary from smooth to wavy. Leaf color is an outstanding attribute, ranging from deep green through chartreuse, yellow, and gold to blue. Many have leaves variously edged, striped, or irregularly

HOSTA

Common Names:
Hosta, plantain lily, funkia

Bloom Time:
Foliage plant with summer and fall bloom

Planting Requirements:
Light to full shade

patterned with white, cream, yellow, or sea green. The spike-like bloom stalks may be up to 3 feet tall. The white, lilac, or purple flowers are bell-shaped or funnelform with six or more spreading lobes. Some are delightfully scented.

Hostas are native to Japan, China, and Korea, where they grow in moist woodlands, open grasslands, and along stream banks and rivers. Many species, especially *H. plantaginea* and *H. ventricosa*, have been in cultivation for hundreds of years. Other species, which may actually be hybrids, are known only from gardens and are not found in the wild. Because of this long history of cultivation in Asia—and more recently in Europe and North America—the nomenclature is confused, with some cultivars ascribed to two or more species, and many of so uncertain a parentage as to be listed without a species name at all. The following species listings are the most widely accepted up-to-date listings available. Cultivars are ascribed to species only when their origin is reasonably certain.

Hosta crispula (KRISP-ew-la), curled leaf hosta. Size: 2 to 3 feet tall, 1 to 2 feet wide. A slow-growing species having dense clumps of leaves with short petioles and elongated, white-edged, heart-shaped leaves with drooping tips and wavy margins. The flowers are deep lilac, somewhat pendulous and are borne in midsummer on open spikes. USDA Plant Hardiness Zones 3 to 8.

H. decorata (dek-or-AH-ta), blunt hosta. Size: 1½ to 2 feet tall and wide. This rhizomatous hosta spreads rapidly to form wide clumps of broadly heart-shaped leaves with creamy white edges and slightly wavy margins. The 2-foot flower spikes bear violet flowers in mid- to late summer. Zones 3 to 8.

H. elata (e-LAY-ta), tall hosta. Size: 2½ to 3 feet tall, 1 to 2 feet wide. Long petioles support the elongated, heart-shaped leaves of this species. The leaf margins are quite wavy and the surface is shiny, deep green. The flower spike bears blue-violet, funnelform flowers with reflexed lobes in early summer. Zones 3 to 8.

H. fortunei (for-TEWN-ee-ee), Fortune's hosta. Size: 1 to 2 feet tall and wide. The elongated, heart-shaped leaves are green to gray-green with long, deeply furrowed and winged petioles. The pale lilac flowers are gathered toward the top of the stout scapes. Below each flower is a shovel-shaped, deep violet leafy bract. Many excellent cultivars are available. 'Albopicta' ('Aureomaculata') has yellow blades with green margins. The leaves turn green as the season progresses. 'Aurea' ('Albopicta Aurea') has bright yellow leaves that fade to yellow green in summer. 'Albo-marginata' ('Marginata-alba') has large leaves with broad, irregular white margins. 'Aoki' has gray-green foliage similar to the species. 'Aureomarginata' has large glaucus green leaves with yellow margins. 'Gold Standard' has light gold leaves edged with green. 'Obscura' has large gray-green leaves. 'Hyacinthina' has large gray-green leaves. Zones 3 to 8.

H. lancifolia (lan-si-FO-lee-a), lance-leaf hosta. Size: 1½ to 2 feet tall and wide. A venerable hosta with glossy green, broadly lance-shaped leaves and floriferous spikes of deep lilac flowers in late summer. 'Kabitan' has

Bold, sun-tolerant *Hosta* 'Sum and Substance' produces short spikes of lavender flowers in late summer above the huge, chartreuse leaves that are among the largest in the genus.

bright yellow leaves with narrow green edges. The plants seldom flower. Zones 3 to 8.

H. montana (mon-TAH-na), mountain hosta. Size: 1½ to 2 feet tall and wide. Similar to *H. elata,* plants have broadly oval to heart-shaped leaves with puckered surfaces. 'Aurea-marginata' is a popular cultivar with wide green leaves with wavy gold margins. Zones 3 to 8.

H. plantaginea (plan-TAGE-i-nee-a), fragrant hosta. Size: 2 to 2½ feet tall and wide. The large, broad, heart-shaped leaves are bright, glossy green. They act as a lovely backdrop to the sparkling white, fragrant flowers that crowd toward the tips of the stout leafy flowerstalks. Var. *grandiflora* has flowers bunched at the top on the bloom stalk. 'Aphrodite' has exquisite double flowers. 'Honeybells' has trumpetlike, pale lavender flowers with spreading, twisted lobes. 'Royal Standard' is similar to the species with white flowers. Zones 3 to 8.

H. sieboldiana (see-bold-ee-AH-na), Siebold hosta. Size: 2½ to 3 feet tall and wide. A large hosta with stiff, heart-shaped, blue-green leaves and pale lilac flowers held in leafy clusters just above the foliage. 'Elegans' has broad, heart-shaped, blue-green leaves with a puckered surface. The flowers vary in color from light violet to white. 'Frances Williams' ('Aureomarginata') is the darling of hosta enthusiasts and neophytes as well. The huge gray-green leaves have wide, dark yellow margins. The plants are slow to reach their mature size. Zones 3 to 8.

H. sieboldii (see-BOLD-ee-ee), seersucker hosta. Size: 2 to 2½ feet tall, 1 to 2 feet wide. This species has long, pointed green leaves edged in white. The late-summer lilac-colored flowers are evenly spaced along the bloom stalk. 'Louisa' is a slow-growing cultivar with a broader white edge. Zones 3 to 8.

H. ×tardiana (tar-dee-A-na). Size: 1 to 2½ feet tall and wide. This hybrid species was produced from crosses between *H. sieboldiana* 'Elegans' and *H. tardiflora.* Most cultivars have narrow, heart-shaped or oval, waxy blue-green leaves and lilac flowers crowded into dense clusters and held above the foliage. 'Halcyon' has deep blue-gray, waxy spear-shaped leaves. 'Blue Wedgewood' has wedge-shaped, deep blue-

The crisp, creamy yellow–edged leaves of medium-size *Hosta* 'So Sweet' light up a shaded spot along a path in summer. The lavender flowers are a bonus.

gray foliage. 'Hadspen Heron' is a small plant with narrow blue foliage. Zones 3 to 8.

H. tardiflora (tar-di-FLOR-a), late hosta. Size: 10 to 12 inches tall, 1 to 1½ feet wide. A small hosta with lance-shaped dark green leaves and pale purple flowers in fall. Zones 3 to 8.

H. undulata (un-dew-LAH-ta), wavy hosta. Size: 12 to 18 inches tall and wide. A variable species known only in cultivation, this group of plants is probably of hybrid origin. The leaves are narrowly oval to lance-shaped, with wavy margins. The light purple flowers are held high above the foliage on leafy stalks. 'Albo-marginata' has leaves with a narrow, creamy white band around them. 'Erromena' has shiny green leaves. 'Variegata' has white-and-cream leaves with green margins. 'Univittala' is a vigorous grower with green leaves striped down the center with white. Zones 3 to 8.

H. ventricosa (ven-tri-KO-sa), blue hosta. Size: 2 to 3 feet tall, 1 to 2 feet wide. Blue hosta is a popular species with broad, heart-shaped dark green leaves and blue-violet, funnelform flowers with wide-flaring lobes. 'Aureo-maculata' has creamy yellow stripes and speckles on the leaves that fade to green in summer. 'Aureo-marginata' has leaves with a creamy white border. Zones 3 to 9.

Hybrids

Myriad hostas of mixed or uncertain parentage are available from garden centers and mail-order nurseries. Cultivars vary in size from miniatures with leaves the size of a fingernail to those with leaves fully 2 feet long. They vary in the puckering of the leaf surface, waving of the leaf margin, leaf shape, and color. All are extremely hardy, usually rated for Zones 3 to 8.

How to Grow

Plant hostas in evenly moist, humus-rich soil in light to full shade. Hostas are tough, versatile, and adaptable. Filtered sun is best for the colorful varieties to reach their full potential, especially gold and blue forms. The green-leaved varieties are the most shade-tolerant. Most species need protection from too much direct sunshine, especially hot afternoon sun. This is most critical where temperatures are high. Variegated varieties, especially those with a lot of white in the leaves, burn very easily. Blue-leaved varieties will bleach to green with too much direct sun. Plants with thick and waxy leaves are better adapted to dry soil conditions than thin-leaved ones, but none is able to thrive or even survive with dry or thin soil.

Hostas emerge late in the season but quickly unfurl to fill their allotted space. They grow slowly and may take 2 to 4 years to attain their full size, longer for the largest species and cultivars. Allow plenty of room when you plant to accommodate for their mature size. Small varieties spread three times as wide as they are tall. Medium-size varieties spread twice their height, and the larger varieties are at least as wide as they are tall. Hostas are disease-resistant, but their succulent leaves are no match for slugs and snails. Keep a watchful eye on the emerging leaves and pick off the assailants as you find them. In moist, humid climates, use exclusion techniques such as rings of ash around the plants, or use saucers of beer as bait.

Landscape Uses

Hostas are the mainstays of the shade garden. Their luscious foliage is unparalleled for accent and groundcover effect. Plant hostas with ferns, wildflowers, and shade perennials on the north side of a house or under the canopy of large trees. Use them as specimens or accents on the shaded side of a shrub border or under flowering trees. In the darkest recesses between buildings, under carports, or in narrow passages, hostas will grow and thrive if the soil is rich and moist. Take advantage of the fact that hostas emerge late and plant the large open expanses with spring-flowering bulbs and ephemeral wildflowers such as toothworts (*Dentaria*), spring beauties (*Claytonia*), and trout lilies (*Erythronium*). As the early bloomers are dying away and looking shabby, the newly emerging hosta leaves will hide them from sight. Snowdrops (*Galanthus*), miniature daffodils, and winter aconites (*Eranthis*) are good bulb companions. Combine the lovely foliage with sedges (*Carex*); ferns such as ostrich fern (*Matteuccia struthiopteris*), and lady fern (*Athyrium filix-femina*); and foliage perennials such as lungworts (*Pulmonaria*), Siberian bugloss (*Brunnera macrophylla*), and wild gingers (*Asarum*). In cooler areas, combine white-flowered *H. plantaginea* with variegated Japanese silver grass (*Miscanthus sinensis* 'Caberet'), garden phlox (*Phlox paniculata*), and other perennials in borders protected from the hottest afternoon sun. Use the medium-size varieties as groundcovers in front of flowering shrubs or in mass plantings of mixed leaf colors and shapes under shade trees. Plant the small-leaved selections in rock gardens or in containers and trough gardens.

HOUTTUYNIA

hoo-TIE-nee-a • Sauraceae, Lizard's Tail Family

Vivid red and yellow leaves with the scent of citrus make 'Chamaeleon' a treasured plant for water gardens and moist spots. The plain green wild form has little to recommend it. All forms of this plant are aggressive spreaders and are best used in containers so they cannot consume the garden. They creep by underground runners with dense, fibrous roots. Beware.

HOUTTUYNIA

Common Name:
Houttuynia

Bloom Time:
Foliage plant with late spring bloom

Planting Requirements:
Sun to partial shade

Houttuynia cordata (kor-DAY-ta), houttuynia. Size: 1½ to 2 feet tall, 2 to 3 feet wide. This fast-spreading rhizomatous perennial forms broad clumps of erect stems covered in heart-shaped, bright green leaves. The unusual flowers consist of a thick, dense spike of petalless flowers with fuzzy yellow stamens (male reproductive structures) that rise from the center of four white, petal-like bracts. The crushed foliage has a strong citrus scent. The species is seldom seen in cultivation, but several showy cultivars are available. 'Chameleon' ('Cameleon') has attractive leaves irregularly banded with white, pink, and red. The white flowers are ½ inch long and are borne as the leaves unfold. USDA Plant Hardiness Zones 3 to 8.

How to Grow

Plant houttuynia in constantly moist or wet, humus-rich soil in full sun or light shade. The plants will grow in standing water or moist garden soil with equal vigor. The clumps spread rapidly by creeping rhizomes and can easily become a nuisance. Yearly roguing is necessary to avert a full-scale takeover. Containerized plants placed in 18 inches of water with crowns just below the water surface often remain contained. Thin pots every year or two and replenish the soil. Propagate by division or stem cuttings taken in early summer.

Fast-spreading chameleon plant (*Houttynia cordata* 'Chameleon') romps wildly in moist or wet soils. To control its spread, sink containers in a pool or pond so the roots are confined.

Landscape Uses

Choose houttuynia for moist soil or pondside gardens. Combine it with other vigorous plants such as ostrich fern (*Matteuccia struthiopteris*), water iris (*Iris laevigatus* and others), large-leaved hostas, astilbes, hibiscus, and sedges (*Carex*). In shallow water, it thrives with arrowhead (*Sagittaria*), lotus (*Nelumbo*), and water lilies (Nymphaea).

HYACINTHOIDES

hy-a-sinth-OY-deez • Hyacinthaceae (Liliaceae), Hyacinth Family

Bluebells are beloved spring bulbs in Europe. They carpet British woodlands with their delicate, intense blue flowers. They have been popular in North America since colonial times. Basal, straplike glossy leaves emerge along with buds that open to blue, pink, or white flowers. Plants keep their leaves longer than other species, so they need light to ripen their foliage. Plants grow from true bulbs and go dormant after flowering. (They self-sow freely and can be a nuisance.)

HYACINTHOIDES

Common Name:
Bluebells

Bloom Time:
Spring bloom

Planting Requirements:
Sun

Spanish bluebells (*Hyacinthoides hispanica*) are one of the last bulbs to bloom as spring slips into summer. The flowers can be classic bluebell blue, as well as pink or white.

Hyacinthoides hispanica (his-PAH-ni-ka), Spanish bluebell. Size: 6 to 14 inches tall and wide. A stout bluebell with ½-inch bells that open in late spring. USDA Plant Hardiness Zones 4 to 7.

H. non-scripta (non-SKRIP-ta), English bluebell. Size: 6 to 12 inches tall and wide. Sheets of blue carpet woodlands, where this species happily self-sows. Plants are more delicate and bloom earlier than their continental cousin. 'Alba' is white-flowered. 'Rosea' is pink. Zones 5 to 8.

How to Grow

Plant in rich, moist soil in full sun or light shade. Divide overgrown clumps as they are going dormant.

Landscape Uses

Bluebells look good en masse in open woods and meadows along with shrubs and flowering trees. In beds, combine them with late-spring bloomers such as irises, phlox, and fairy wings (*Epimedium*), as well as ferns.

IBERIS

Candytufts brighten the early spring garden with their pristine white flowers. Plants bloom for weeks on end atop mounds of deep green, needlelike leaves. The four-petaled flowers open in spirals in dense, flat clusters. The semi-woody stems of this subshrub grow from a stout, fibrous-rooted crown.

IBERIS

Common Name:
Candytuft

Bloom Time:
Early spring bloom

Planting Requirements:
Full sun to light shade

Iberis saxatilis (saks-AH-ti-lis), rock candytuft. Size: 3 to 6 inches tall, 12 to 18 inches wide. A low plant that forms broad, round clumps with brittle stems clothed in needlelike leaves. The ½-inch late-winter to early-spring flowers often fade to purple. USDA Plant Hardiness Zones 2 to 7.

I. sempervirens (sem-per-VY-renz), perennial candytuft. Size: 6 to 12 inches tall, 12 to 24 inches wide. In early spring, mounded clumps are shrouded in a profusion of ¼-inch white flowers in tight rounded clusters. The persistent stems bear deep green leaves. 'Autumn Snow' is 8 to 10 inches tall with clear white flowers in spring and again in fall. 'Little Gem' is a floriferous, compact grower only 5 to 8 inches tall. 'Pygmaea' is a low spreader with 4- to 5-inch stems. 'Snowflake' is compact and floriferous with flat, 2- to 3-inch inflorescences. Zones 3 to 9.

Early-blooming perennial candytuft (*Iberis sempervirens* 'Alexander's White') is perfect for planting in a rock garden with spring bulbs or as an edging along walks or walls.

How to Grow

Plant candytufts in average, well-drained soil in full sun or light shade. Space plants 1 to 1½ feet apart in informal plantings to accommodate their eventual spread. Place them 6 to 12 inches apart if you are using them to edge a bed or as a groundcover. Compact cultivars are best for this purpose. Shear plants back by one-third after flowering to encourage compact growth and fresh foliage. Prune them hard, at least two-thirds back, every few years to keep them fresh and vigorous and to promote flower production. Plants seldom need division. The prostrate stems may root as they spread and are easy to transplant. Take tip cuttings in early summer; they will root in 2 to 3 weeks. Sow seed outdoors in spring or fall.

Landscape Uses

Candytufts are consummate edging plants. Their low compact growth, early flowers, and evergreen foliage make them perfect for planting along stairs or walls, or at the front of beds and borders. They perform well in soil pockets between rocks in a wall or planted just behind a wall where they will spill over and soften its edge. In rock gardens, combine them with spring bulbs, bleeding hearts (*Dicentra*), basket-of-golds (*Aurinia*), rock cresses (*Arabis*), and purple rock cresses (*Aubrieta*). In the border, plant candytuft with tulips, columbines (*Aquilegia*), forget-me-nots (*Myosotis*), and other spring perennials.

INULA

IN-u-la • Asteraceae, Aster Family

Inulas are magnificent giants for large gardens with expressively ragged daisy flowers in early to midsummer. Huge, dramatic oval to broadly heart-shaped leaves cover sturdy stems that grow from stout, fibrous-rooted crowns.

INULA

Common Names:
  Elecampane, inula

Bloom Time:
  Summer bloom

Planting Requirements:
  Sun to light shade

Inula ensifolia (en-see-FO-lee-a), swordleaf inula. Size: 1 to 2 feet tall and wide. A small, compact species unlike its gargantuan relatives, with short stems densely covered in stiff linear leaves and topped with 2½-inch, yellow-orange daisies. USDA Plant Hardiness Zones 3 to 7.

The needle-like foliage of swordleaf inula (*Inula ensifolia*) makes a tidy clump against which the showy yellow flowers stand out in summer. Give plants full sun and well-drained soil for optimum performance.

I. helenium (he-LEE-ne-um), elecampane. Size: 4 to 6 feet tall, 3 to 4 feet wide. Ragged, 3-inch daisies are carried in open clusters atop tall stems covered in huge leaves that decrease in size as they ascend the stem. Zones 3 to 8.

I. magnifica (mag-NIF-e-ka), giant inula. Size: 5 to 6 feet tall, 4 to 5 feet wide. A giant with huge leaves and terminal clusters of 6-inch daisies with thin, drooping rays. Stunning if you have the room. Zones 3 to 7.

I. royleana (royl-e-AH-na), Himalayan elecampane. Size: 2 to 3 feet tall and wide. This compact species with yellow-orange flowers should be more widely grown. Leafy green bracts around heads extend the ornamental season. The 10-inch elongated oval leaves emerge from a basal rosette. Plants prefer cool nights. Zones 3 to 7.

How to Grow

Inulas offer drama to sunny spots with rich, constantly moist soil. Set out young plants where they will remain permanently, as large plants are difficult to move. Swordleaf inula prefers well-drained soil. Propagate by seed, division, or root cuttings taken in late summer.

Landscape Uses

Use smaller species in borders toward the front or middle. Large inulas are best kept to the rear of amply sized beds or placed in open meadows, along streams, or at the edge of a pond. Irises, cranesbills (*Geranium*), phlox, false indigos (*Baptisia*), and asters are good companions.

IPHEION

IF-ee-on • Alliaceae (Amaryllidaceae), Onion Family

Starry, sweet-scented blue flowers open en masse on sunny days, all pointing toward the light and thus presenting an enthusiastic show. Plants produce straplike sea-green leaves from true bulbs that increase rapidly to form dense, floriferous clumps. This onion relative reveals its kinship when the foliage or the bulb is damaged: It smells like an onion.

IPHEION
Common Name:
Star flower
Bloom Time:
Late winter and early spring bloom
Planting Requirements:
Sun

Ipheion uniflorum (yew-nee-FLO-rum), star flower. Size: 3 to 6 inches tall, 6 to 12 inches wide. The only species commonly in cultivation, though bulb specialists grow several others. The 1-inch, starry sky blue flowers open over several weeks after the earliest bulbs like snowdrops have passed. 'Album' is white. 'Charlotte Bishop' has rose-pink flowers. 'Froyle Mill' has royal purple flowers. 'Rolf Fiedler' is deep blue. 'Wisley' is soft sky blue. USDA Plant Hardiness Zones 4 to 9.

How to Grow

Plant in average to rich, humusy or loamy soil in full sun to partial shade. New leaves are produced in late fall; plants begin flowering in late winter, with the show gaining momentum in spring. After a month or more of bloom, plants go dormant in summer and can tolerate very dry conditions. Self-sown seedlings are plentiful. Color varies in the offspring of any named selection.

Landscape Uses

Star flowers really shine when planted en masse as a groundcover under shrubs and flowering trees or in drifts among late-emerging plants like peonies and hostas. Place them in a rockery or atop a rock wall, and plants may seed into the crevices between rocks to produce an enchanting effect.

The clear blue stars of *Ipheion uniflorum* 'Wisley Blue' brighten the spring garden en masse.

IRIS

EYE-ris • Iridicaeae, Iris Family

Irises are among the most beautiful and popular perennials available to gardeners. The genus takes its name from Iris, who in Greek mythology was the messenger to Juno, the goddess of marriage. Legend holds that Iris traveled over the rainbow to reach Earth, and that from her footsteps sprang flowers arrayed in the colors of the rainbow. The iris has been revered since the sixth century and became an icon for nobility in the 1100s, when King Louis VII of France adopted the iris as his Fleur-de-Louis, now known as fleur-de-lis.

IRIS

Common Name:
  Iris

Bloom Time:
  Spring and summer bloom

Planting Requirements:
  Full sun to open shade

The iris flower has an unusual construction. Six segments comprise the corolla (collective compliment of petals). Three segments, called the falls, ring the outside of the flower. The falls are held flat or are reflexed downward. Each one has a white or yellow blaze at its base. Some species sport a fuzzy beard in place of the blaze. The inner ring of three segments, called the standards, stands erect or is slightly elevated above the falls. Most species have very showy, colorful standards and falls, but in some, the standards are reduced in size or absent, leaving the falls to carry the show. The final component of the complex flower is a triad of columns containing the male and female reproductive structures. The columns curve out of the center of the flower and lie directly above the falls, forming a tunnel through which bees must travel in order to fertilize the flowers. Color varies from white to pink, red, purple, blue, yellow, and brown. Different species flower from winter through summer. Many are excellent for cutting.

Iris leaves are grassy, flat and straplike, or curled and cylindrical with parallel veins. They vary in size, according to species, from 3 inches to well over 3 feet long and may be deciduous or evergreen. Plants grow from thick creeping rhizomes, fibrous roots, or bulbs. An iris exists for every conceivable garden situation: sun or shade, moist soil or dry soil, early bloom or late bloom, and so on. Hundreds of hybrids and cultivars are available, developed from over 100 species.

Iris bucharica (bew-KAH-ree-ka), Bokhara iris. Size: 1 to 1½ feet tall, 1 foot wide. A bulbous iris with thick stalks and alternate, keeled leaves up the stem. Spring flowers are carried in the axils of the leaves. They have yellow falls and cream standards. The plants go completely dormant by midsummer. USDA Plant Hardiness Zones 4 to 9.

I. cristata (kris-TAH-ta), crested iris. Size: 4 to 8 inches tall, 1 to 2 feet wide. A creeping, rhizomatous iris with fans of short, broad leaves and flattened, sky blue spring flowers with a yellow-and-white blaze. 'Abbey's Violet' has deep blue-violet flowers. 'Alba' has pure white flowers. 'Navy Blue Giant' has 3-inch, deep blue flowers. 'Shenandoah Skies' has sky-blue flowers. Zones 3 to 9.

I. danfordiae (dan-FORD-ee-eye), Danford iris. Size: 4 to 6 inches tall and wide. A bulbous iris with curled, cylindrical leaves and yellow flowers in late winter. The leaves elongate immediately after flowering and disappear by summer. Plants may be short-lived. Zones 5 to 9.

I. douglasiana (doug-laz-ee-AH-na), Douglas' iris. Size: 2 to 2½ feet tall and wide. A strap-leaved plant with blue, pink, or white flowers resembling a Siberian iris. The Pacific hybrids were produced by crossing Douglas' iris with other western natives such as *I. tenax* and *I. innominata*. They are delicate, colored in soft shades of blue and purple, and perform best in well-drained soils in Zones 7 to 9. Zones 6 to 8.

I. ensata (en-SAH-ta) (includes plants listed as *I. kaempferi*), Japanese iris. Size: 2 to 2½ feet tall and wide. A variable species native through much of temperate Asia. The wild forms have strap-shaped leaves and flowers with small standards and broad floppy falls in blue or violet in summer. Exquisite hybrids have been produced through years of selection. They have round, flat flowers with broad, reflexed standards and wide falls in a rainbow of blues, purples,

The common blue or the unusual white-flowered form of dwarf crested iris (*Iris cristata* 'Alba') makes a dense, spring-blooming groundcover in sun or partial shade. Moist soil encourages the foliage to remain neat all season long.

pinks, reds, and white. Many bicolor forms are found, as well as doubles and peony-flowered selections. 'Variegata' is edged with cream that fades to white. Requires acid soil. Zones 4 to 9.

I. foetidissima (fet-i-DIS-i-ma), stinking iris. Size: 1½ to 2 feet tall and wide. This species has evergreen, strap-shaped leaves that emit a foul odor when crushed. Blue-gray flowers fade to large pods that split in fall to reveal showy scarlet seeds. 'Citrina' has yellow seeds. Zones 6 to 9.

I. fulva (FUL-va), copper iris. Size: 3 to 4 feet tall, 3 to 5 feet wide wide. A red-flowered early-summer iris with strap-shaped leaves. The red flowers bring a unique color to hybrids in a genus that consists of mostly blue and purple flowers. Louisiana hybrids are popular with southern gardeners who must contend with extreme heat. They were produced from hybrids with *I. brevicaulis* and come in a wide range of blues and reds. Zones 7 to 10.

I. histrioides (his-tree-OI-dez), harput iris. Size: 6 to 9 inches tall, 4 to 6 inches wide. An early spring bulbous iris with bright blue flowers similar to *I. reticulata*. 'Major' has deep blue flowers. Zones 5 to 9.

I. laevigata (lev-ee-GAY-ta), rabbit-ear iris. Size: 1½ to 2 feet tall and wide. A deep blue-violet iris with waxy foliage similar to *I. ensata*. 'Variegata' has creamy white edges. Zones 5 to 9.

I. missouriensis (mi-sur-ree-EN-sis), Missouri iris, Rocky Mountain iris. Size: 1 to 2 feet tall and wide. A delicate iris with strap-shaped leaves and white to blue flowers in summer with slender standards and falls. Zones 3 to 8.

I. pallida (PAL-li-da), sweet iris. Size: 2 to 3 feet tall, 1 to 2 feet wide. A bearded iris with stiff fans of gray-green foliage and tall stalks bearing fragrant, light violet flowers with broad standards and falls. 'Argentea Variegata' has white variegation. 'Variegata' ('Aurea-variegata' or 'Zebra') has yellow variegated foliage. Zones 4 to 8.

I. pseudacorus (sood-a-KOR-us), yellow flag iris. Size: 3 to 4 feet tall and wide. A stout, coarse iris with stiff, straplike leaves and bright yellow flowers in spring. 'Flore-Pleno' has unusual double flowers. 'Argentea 'Variegata' has leaves striped with yellow. Invasive in many areas. Zones 5 to 9.

I. pumila (PEW-mil-a), dwarf iris. Size: 4 to 8 inches tall, 8 to 12 inches wide. A small, creeping iris with 2-inch bearded flowers in shades of blue and purple. This species is an important parent of dwarf bearded hybrids. Zones 3 to 8.

I. reticulata (re-tik-ew-LAH-ta), reticulated iris. Size: 4 to 6 inches tall, 6 to 8 inches wide, flowers to 2 inches wide. This small bulbous iris blooms in late winter or early spring. After the fragrant blue to purple flowers fade, the cylindrical leaves elongate until the plant goes dormant in summer. 'Cantab' has pale blue flowers. 'Harmony' has royal blue flowers. 'Joyce' has sky-blue flowers. 'J. S. Dijt' has red-violet flowers. Zones 5 to 9.

Few perennials are as carefree and beautiful as Siberian iris (*Iris siberica*). Use them in borders, in containers, along a stream, or at the edge of a pond.

I. siberica (si-BEER-i-ka), Siberian iris. Size: 1 to 3 feet tall and wide. Siberian irises are popular garden plants for their foliage and flowers. Tidy clumps of narrow, sword-shaped foliage stay attractive all season. Flowers are borne in early summer. They have upright standards and broad flat or reflexed falls. Colors vary from blues and purples to yellow and white. Many bicolor forms are available. Hundreds of cultivars are available. 'Butter and Sugar' is a white-yellow bicolor. 'Ego' is an excellent blue bicolor with good foliage. 'Ewen' is a lovely wine red tetraploid. 'Flight of Butterflies' has small blue-and-white flowers on stems just over 1 foot tall. 'Fourfold White' is a good white with yellow at the bases of the falls. 'My Love' is a deep sky blue rebloomer. 'Summer Sky' has pale ice blue flowers. 'White Swirl' is a good pure white. Zones 3 to 9.

I. spuria (SPUR-e-a), spuria iris, seashore iris. Size: Variable, 1 to 4 feet tall, 1 to 2 feet wide. A species with a huge range from North America to Europe. Blue flowers are carried above crisp foliage. Hybrids such as 'Cambridge Blue' with lavender-and-yellow flowers and yellow-and-white 'Shelford Giant' are more commonly grown. Zones 3 to 7.

I. tectorum (tek-TOR-um), roof iris. Size: 1 to 1½ feet tall and wide. A rhizomatous iris with broad fans of wide, strap-shaped foliage. The somewhat flattened flowers are deep lavender-blue with dark blotches and are borne in late spring. 'Alba' has white flowers. Zones 4 to 9.

I. unguicularis (un-gwik-ew-LAH-ris), winter iris. Size: 10 to 12 inches tall and wide. This early-blooming iris has violet, blue, or white flowers and dense tufts of grassy, evergreen foliage. Zones 7 to 9.

I. verna (VER-na), vernal iris. Size: 6 to 12 inches tall and wide. A charming, diminutive species with narrow leaves that lengthen after early blue-violet flowers with orange blazes held just above ground have faded. 'Alba' is white-flowered. 'Brumback Blue' has medium blue flowers. Requires acid soil. Zones 5 to 9.

I. versicolor (VER-si-ko-lor), blue flag iris. Size: 1½ to 3 feet tall, 1 to 2 feet wide. Blue flags are stout, leafy irises with bold strap-shaped leaves and bright blue-violet flowers in early summer. This northern species is similar to southern blue flag (*I. virginica*), which is larger. 'Contraband Girl' is a giant to 4 feet. Zones 3 to 8.

I. xiphium (ZI-fee-um), Spanish iris. Size: 1 to 1½ feet tall, 1 foot wide. Spanish iris is a bulbous spring-bloomer that has been extensively hybridized with *I. xiphioides*, English iris, to produce the popular hybrids known as "Dutch iris," often sold under the name *I. ×hollandica*. Although the species are attractive in their own right, most American gardeners know only the colorful Dutch hybrids. Zones 6 to 9.

Hybrids

Bearded iris are a popular group of hybrids that have been cultivated in Europe for centuries. They are divided into six groups by the American Iris Society, based on height and species composition. If you grow only bearded irises, you can enjoy a remarkable range of fragrant flowers in a full range of colors over a long spring and early summer bloom period. Some bearded irises are rebloomers, or remontant, blooming in spring and again in summer or fall.

1. Miniature Dwarf Bearded (MDB) are the smallest, with stems from 2 to 8 inches tall. They are also the earliest to bloom. They are most effective in rock gardens or planted in drifts.

2. Standard Dwarf Bearded (SDB) are among the most useful species, ranging in height from 8 to 15 inches. They flower early and are look best in clumps.

3. Intermediate Bearded (IB) stand 16 to 28 inches tall, bloom in midspring, and are grown in clumps or as specimens.

4. Border Bearded (BB) stand 16 to 28 inches tall but bloom later than IB selections. They often have round, ruffled petals that complement their small size.

5. Miniature Tall Bearded (MTB) are small, 16 to 26 inches tall, and are distinguished by dainty flowers on thin, wiry stems. They are also called "Table Irises" because they are well suited for arrangements.

6. Tall Bearded (TB) have ruffled flowers on stalks over 27 inches and may be as tall as 40 inches. The stems branch and have multiple buds.

How to Grow

Irises are as varied in their requirements for growth as they are in their size and form. Most species perform well in full sun to light shade in evenly moist but well-drained, humus-rich soil. *I. douglasiana, I. pallida, I. pumila, I. spuria, I. tectorum,* Pacific coast, and bearded hybrids grow best under these conditions. Many irises are native to moist or wet soil environments but will grow well under the above conditions. *I. laevigata, I. missouriensis, I. pseudacorus, I. sibirica, I. versicolor,* and Louisiana hybrids fall into this group. All tolerate some shade but bloom best in full sun. *I. ensata* demands wet soil in spring and summer but needs drier soil in winter. They also need to be replanted every few years because they produce new roots above the old ones and eventually become too shallow-rooted to support themselves. Most of the above species are widely adaptable to neutral or

The diminutive reticulated iris (*Iris reticulata* 'Harmony') opens its richly colored flowers in earliest spring and disappears for another season by summer.

slightly acid soils. *I. ensata* and *I. versicolor* need acid soil. Woodland species such as *I. cristata, I. foetidissima,* and *I. verna* prefer rich, moist, slightly acid soil in light to partial shade. Bulbous species such as *I. bucharica, I. danfordiae, I. histrioides, I. reticulata, I. xiphium,* and Dutch hybrid irises prefer full sun for best bloom but are suitable for sites that get sun in spring or shade in summer after they have gone dormant. Give them moist, rich soil in spring, but let them dry out in summer, especially *I. danfordiae.* In many areas of the country, bulbous species are best grown as annuals or short-lived perennials because they do not rebloom well.

Irises are susceptible to a number of pests. Rhizome rot and bacterial soft rot are two bacterial diseases that destroy irises from the ground up. Good culture is the best preventative. Match species with their optimum soil moisture. Planting rhizomatous species such as bearded iris in overly moist soil or burying the rhizome below soil are sure ways to invite problems. Iris borer is another pest. Adult moths lay eggs on foliage, and larvae travel down leaves into the rhizome where they eat until nothing is left but a hollow shell. They also spread bacterial infections from plant to plant. Good culture is again the best prevention. Remove spent foliage in fall or early spring and watch for signs of infestation. Young borers tunnel through leaves, leaving dark streaks in their wake. Remove infested leaves and destroy them, or squash borers in their tunnels with your finger. Dig up infected plants and destroy the fat pink grubs by hand. Replant unaffected portions and keep a watchful eye.

Propagate irises by division after flowering in summer or early fall. Replant immediately in well-prepared soil. Bearded iris hybrids need frequent division to keep them vigorous. Remove and discard old portions of their thick rhizomes and replant with the top half of the rhizome above the soil line. Most other species need division only when they become crowded or when flowering wanes. Sow ripe seed outdoors. Germination will occur the following spring. Many hybrids will not produce viable seed.

Landscape Uses

Bearded iris, *Iris sibirica,* and other irises with similar cultural requirements are well-suited to beds and borders with spring and early-summer perennials. Combine their strap-shaped foliage with rounded forms and bold flowers. Choose moist-soil species for pondside with ferns, hostas, and other lush perennials. Plant smaller bulbous species, dwarf bearded, and *Iris cristata* in rock gardens or at the front of the border with spring bulbs and mounding or mat-forming plants for contrast. Plant larger bulbous species such as Dutch hybrids in the border with early perennials and other bulbs such as late tulips. In woodland gardens and rockeries, plant *I. cristata* and *I. verna* with phlox, cranesbills (*Geranium*), and ferns.

K

KALIMERIS

kal-e-MER-is • Asteraceae, Aster Family

Long cherished and passed around southern gardens, Mongolian aster, the most familiar plant of this group, is finally getting wider recognition for its summer-long bloom. This genus contains several botanically confused species that have finally found a collective home. All have prolific white to lavender daisylike flowers in open clusters. Plants slowly spread to form dense, fibrous-rooted clumps.

KALIMERIS

Common Names:
  Mongolian aster,
  Japanese aster

Bloom Time:
  Summer and fall
  bloom

Planting Requirements:
  Sun or partial shade

Kalimeris incisa (in-SIZE-a), cutleaf Japanese aster. Size: 1½ to 2 feet tall and wide. This single-flowered daisy has pale lavender flowers carried on open 2-foot clumps. Plants bloom throughout summer. 'Variegata' has leaves streaked with yellow and cream. *Gymnaster savatiera* is a late-season aster relative that keeps going until hard frost. Lobed leaves and ragged pale lavender flowers on 2- to 2½-foot stems adorn this undeservedly scarce plant. Clumps spread rapidly by creeping stems and may need to be thinned to control size. USDA Plant Hardiness Zones 4 to 8.

K. pinnatifida (pin-a-TIF-e-da) (*Asteromoea mongolica*), Mongolian aster. Size: 1 to 2½ feet tall and wide. Mongolian asters have been passed around southern gardens for generations. This workhorse perennial is valued for copious white, daisylike double flowers borne all summer and into fall. The stems are densely

covered in attractive, deeply incised leaves. Zones 4 to 8.

The perpetual flowering of Mongolian aster (*Kalimeris pinnatifida*) makes it an ideal filler plant among long-blooming perennials like daylilies, as well as one-shot wonders like poppies that open and fade in quick succession through the summer months.

How to Grow

Mongolian aster is easy to grow in average to rich, moist but well-drained soil in full sun or partial shade. If the profuse flower production wanes in late summer, shear plants back by half and a new flush of flowers will carry on through fall. If clumps begin to lose vigor, you can easily divide them in spring.

Landscape Uses

The delicate flowers of Mongolian aster are perfect for weaving around taller or bolder plants like daylilies (*Hemerocallis*), coneflowers (*Echinacea*), phlox, balloon flowers (*Platycodon*), cannas, gladioli, yuccas, and salvias. Mass plantings with shrubs are effective.

KIRENGESHOMA

ki-ring-e-SHOW-ma • Hydrangeaceae, Hydrangea Family

When the woodland garden has been stalled in shades of green all summer, yellow bells begin a wave of late-season color. The upright clusters of flared, waxen tubular bells light up shadows. Flowers are produced from terminal and side shoots, so clumps are in bloom for a month or more. Pale yellow foliage is another fall bonus. The stout crowns have thick fleshy roots.

KIRENGESHOMA

Common Names:
Yellow bells, waxbells

Bloom Time:
Late summer bloom

Planting Requirements:
Light to full shade

Kirengeshoma koreana (kor-e-AY-na) (*coreana*), Korean yellow bells. Size: 3 to 5 feet tall and wide. Paired leaves have shallowly lobed bright green leaves and flared yellow flowers that open in mid- to late summer. The two species of yellow bells are very closely related, and both are extremely variable. Some individuals may resemble one species in leaf and another in flower, and intergrades between the two are common. USDA Plant Hardiness Zones 4 to 8.

K. palmata (paul-MATE-a), Japanese yellow bells. Size: 3 to 4 feet tall and wide. Both species are closely related, but the leaves of Japanese yellow bells are more boldly lobed and the stems are attractively stained with deep purple. The inflated, soft yellow flowers nod on wiry stems and never fully open. They open several weeks after their Korean cousin. Plants are smaller and make a more rounded rather than upright clump. Zones 4 to 8.

How to Grow

Yellow bells needs evenly moist, rich soil in light to full shade. New growth emerges

In the late-summer woodland garden, few plants offer the color and drama of Japanese yellow bells (*Kirengeshoma palmata*). The tall stalks with dramatic foliage sport open clusters of flowers for nearly a month.

stemmed clump. Plants perform best where nights are cool. In warmer southern zones, or if the soil dries out, the margins of leaves turn brown. Divide plants in spring as the asparagus-like shoots emerge. Frost comes before seeds ripen in the North, but plants may self-sow in warmer areas.

Landscape Uses

Yellow bells open in late summer, in the company of asters, toad lilies (*Tricyrtis*), monkshoods (*Aconitum*), and Japanese anemones (*Anemone* ×*hybrida*). The stylish, shrublike clumps with their pairs of sculpted leaves add excitement to the summer foliage display in the company of graceful maiden-hair ferns (*Adiantum*), the spectacular vases of male ferns (*Dryopteris filix-femina*), and ornamental grasses. Early-spring compan-ions should carpet the ground around the newly emerging stems; good choices are sweet woodruffs (*Galium*), fairy wings (*Epi-medium*), dead nettles (*Lamium*), and wild gingers (*Asarum*).

late in spring, so care must be taken not to dig into clumps. As plants push from the ground, new sea green foliage resembles maple leaves. The purple-tinted stalks are laced with a chalky bloom. Plants may take a year or two to begin flowering and an-other year or two to form a stunning, multi-

KNAUTIA

NAUT-ee-a • Dipsacaceae, Teasel Family

The lacy, buttonlike heads of knautias resemble small pin-cushion flowers (*Scabiosa*), a close relative. The inflores-cences are composed of many small, flattened flowers, and each head is surrounded by leafy green bracts. The deeply cut foliage is mostly basal and decreases in size as it as-cends the multiple stems of each clump. Plants grow from fibrous-rooted crowns.

KNAUTIA

Common Name:
  Knautia

Bloom Time:
  Summer bloom

Planting Requirements:
  Full sun to light shade

Knautia arvensis (ar-VEN-sis), common knautia. Size: 1 to 2½ feet tall and wide. The lavender-rose flowers of this scarce species are lovely and quite unique in color. Plants bloom in early to mid-summer on open-crowned plants. USDA Plant Hardiness Zones 4 to 7.

K. macedonica (mak-e-DON-i-ca), knautia. Size: 1 to 2 feet tall and wide. A more compact and floriferous species with deep wine red flowers all summer. Zones 4 to 8.

How to Grow

Plant in moist, average to humus-rich soil in full sun or light shade. Plants are easy to grow and prolific bloomers. Do not crowd them, as stems may rot. As flowering wanes, cut out spent stems at the base to encourage more bloom. Plants may be short-lived, especially where nights are hot and humid.

Landscape Uses

Use knautias when you need a touch of red. The profuse flowers are always airy and combine well with bold flowers and foliage. Plant them en masse with irises, coneflowers (*Echinacea*), goldenrods (*Solidago*), asters, and sages (*Salvia*). Use fine-textured grasses for contrast.

The handsome red buttons of *Knautia macedonica* open in profusion throughout the summer. The rich flower color is beautiful combined with blue and purple flowers like catmints (*Nepeta*) and sages (*Salvia*).

KNIPHOFIA

nee-FOF-ee-a • Asphodelaceae (Liliaceae), Asphodel Family

Torch lilies are showy summer perennials with stout tufts of long, stiff linear leaves and tall, dense spikes of drooping tubular flowers. They provide bold and colorful vertical forms for the late-spring and summer garden. Flower color varies from pure scarlet, orange, yellow, and cream to bicolors. Plants grow from short creeping rhizomes with thick roots.

KNIPHOFIA

Common Names:
 Torch lily, red-hot poker

Bloom Time:
 Summer bloom

Planting Requirements:
 Full sun

Kniphofia citrina (ci-TRINE-a), yellow torch lily. Size: 1 to 2 feet tall and wide. The soft ivory to primrose yellow flowers are carried in slender spikes over fine-textured, grassy foliage. A popular parent for small and compact cultivars. USDA Plant Hardiness Zones 7 to 9.

K. galpinii (gal-PIN-ee-ee), torch lily. Size: 3 to 4 feet tall, 2 to 3 feet wide. Tall, intense tangerine spikes you can almost taste are the hallmark of this late-summer flower. The color begs to be combined with royal purple and burgundy asters, salvias, and yellow patrinias. Zones 5 to 9.

K. uvaria (oo-VAH-ree-a), common torch lily. Size: 3 to 5 feet tall, 2 to 3 feet wide. The gray-green leaves of common torch lily are grasslike and evergreen but decline after flowering. The lowest flowers are yellow; the upper ones are red. The spikes are 1 to 2 feet long. Zones 5 to 9.

Torch lilies (*Kniphofia* 'Shining Scepter') make an arresting late-summer show in light, well-drained soils in sunny perennial gardens.

Hybrids

Many hybrids have been produced from crosses between *K. macowanii, K. nelsonii, K. pauciflora,* and *K. uvaria.* They vary in size, flower color, and bloom time. 'Alcazar' has pure red flowers on 40-inch stalks. 'Apricot' has soft apricot spikes to 2 feet. 'Little Maid' is 2 feet tall with salmon-and-white flowers. 'Primrose Beauty' has light yellow flowers on 3-foot stalks. 'Royal Standard' is a classic, with red-and-yellow bicolor spikes. 'Springtime' has coral red-and-yellow bicolor flowers. 'Wayside Flame' has orange-red flowers in late summer.

How to Grow

Plant torch lilies in average to rich, well-drained soil in full sun. Good drainage is imperative. Excess water in soil or on crowns is sure death in winter. Plants spread by short rhizomes to form dense clumps. Space plants at least 2 feet apart to allow for spread. Once established, clumps are best left undisturbed. Propagate by removing one or more crowns from the edge of the clump in fall. Sow seed indoors in winter. Stratify at 40°F for 6 weeks. Germination takes 3 to 6 weeks.

Landscape Uses

Combine the fiery colors of torch lilies with yellow or orange daylilies (*Hemerocallis*), black-eyed Susans (*Rudbeckia*), oriental poppies (*Papaver orientale*), and ornamental grasses. Contrast the rich fiery colors with purple sages (*Salvia*), catmints (*Nepeta*), siberian irises (*Iris siberica*), and cranesbills (*Geranium*). Plant the softer corals and yellows with baby's-breath (*Gypsophila paniculata*), phlox, boltonia (*Boltonia asteroides*), and catmint (*Nepeta mussinii*).

KOSTELETZKYA

kos-te-LETS-key-ah • Malvaceae, Mallow Family

At the edge of the sea, bathed in salt spray, this elegant mallow thrives on diversity. The deep pink flowers add color in late summer to more hospitable environs such as garden beds and borders, as well as wet swales and meadow gardens. Plants form huge woody rootstocks with thick, fibrous roots.

KOSTELETZKYA

Common Name:
Seaside mallow

Bloom Time:
Late summer bloom

Planting Requirements:
Sun

K. virginica (vir-GIN-e-ka), seaside mallow. Size: 4 to 6 feet tall, 3 to 4 feet wide. A dainty hibiscus relative with stout stalks bearing soft triangular leaves with a long pointed central lobe. The 3-inch, deep clear pink flowers resemble miniature hibiscus and are carried in clusters at the tops of the stems. 'Immaculate' is white-flowered. USDA Plant Hardiness Zones 6 to 9.

How to Grow

Plant in rich, moist to wet soil in full sun. Plants are tolerant of windblown and soilborne salt. They thrive under ordinary garden conditions as long as the soil is not too dry. Plants emerge late, so take care not to dig into them. Propagate from seed, which ripens in late fall.

Landscape Uses

Height and dainty flowers make seaside mallow great for beds with grasses, sunflowers, boltonias, and goldenrods (*Solidago*).

Seaside mallow (*Kosteletzkya virginica*) is a dainty hibiscus relative with light-headed clusters of 3-inch, deep pink flowers in mid- to late summer. Tall, branched stalks bear soft triangular leaves with long, pointed central lobes.

LAMIASTRUM

lay-me-AY-strum • Lamiaceae, Mint Family

Archangel creeps through taller wildflowers in open woods, along roadsides, and in hedgerows across Britain and Western Europe where it is a familiar herb. The yellow flowers and silvery leaves add a bright spot to shaded areas of the garden. Use it as a groundcover in the dry shade under shrubs and flowering trees. Plants have trailing stems with thin, fibrous roots.

LAMIASTRUM

Common Name:
Yellow archangel

Bloom Time:
Foliage plant with spring bloom

Planting Requirements:
Partial to full shade

Lamiastrum galeobdolon (ga-lee-OB-do-lon), yellow archangel. Size: 8 to 14 inches tall, 14 to 24 inches wide. Yellow archangel is a fast-creeping stoloniferous groundcover with oval to triangular leaves mottled and spotted with silver. The yellow flowers are borne in spring in whorls around leaf axils. They resemble other plants in the mint family with their distinct upper and lower lips. 'Herman's Pride' has striking silver variegation and is a clumping plant and less-aggressive spreader. 'Petite Point' is a true dwarf to 10 inches tall. 'Variegata' has a silver ring through the middle of the leaf, and the edge and mid-vein are green. USDA Plant Hardiness Zones 4 to 9.

How to Grow

Yellow archangel is a tough, fast-spreading groundcover for difficult garden spots. Plant in average to rich, well-drained soil in partial to full shade. In northern zones, it tolerates some direct sun. Divide clumps as they spread out of bounds, or pull plants from places where they don't belong.

For a bright groundcover in dry shade, you can't beat yellow archangel (*Lamiastrum galeobdolon* 'Herman's Pride'). Plants thrive in this toughest of garden spots.

Propagate by tip cuttings taken in spring or summer.

Landscape Uses

Choose yellow archangel for dry shade where other plants don't grow well, or plant it where you need to cover a lot of ground in a short time. Spring bulbs and early wildflowers emerge easily through the delicate stems to make a lovely combination of bright flowers and variegated foliage. In moist sites, ferns are excellent for foliage contrast and low maintenance.

LAMIUM

LAY-mee-um • Lamiaceae, Mint Family

Curious flowers, attractive foliage, and easy care make dead nettles ideal garden plants. These European wildflowers, a common sight in meadows and gardens abroad, adapt well to cultivation and brighten shaded spots throughout the growing season. They are valued for their shade tolerance and easy culture. Plants grow from fibrous-rooted crowns.

> **LAMIUM**
>
> **Common Name:**
> Dead nettle
>
> **Bloom Time:**
> Foliage plant with spring and summer bloom
>
> **Planting Requirements:**
> Partial to full shade

Lamium maculatum (mak-ew-LAY-tum), spotted dead nettle. Size: 6 to 12 inches tall, 12 to 24 inches wide. Spotted dead nettle is a creeping, open groundcover with oval, silver-mottled, or striped leaves. The stems creep slowly, rooting and branching at the nodes. Rose-pink flowers are borne in the leaf axils in spring and are often partially obscured by the foliage. Most plants grown in the United States are named selections. Var. *aureum* ('Aureum') has soft yellow leaves with the characteristic silver midvein. 'Beacon Silver' has silver leaves with a thin green margin and bright rose-pink flowers.

'Chequers' grows 6 to 12 inches tall, with a broader green band on the leaves and violet-pink flowers. 'Dellam' has golden-edged foliage with green-and-silver midveins and pink flowers. 'Elizabeth deHaas' has pink flowers and gold-speckled foliage. 'Purple Dragon' has rose-purple flowers over silver-centered leaves. 'Shell Pink' has soft pink flowers. 'White Nancy' is a good spreader, similar to 'Beacon Silver' but with clear white flowers. USDA Plant Hardiness Zones 3 to 8.

L. orvala (or-VAL-a), tall dead nettle. Size: 1 to 1½ feet tall and wide. An attractive plant with pointed oval green leaves and tall stems that lift the red to dusty rose axillary flowers up where they can easily be appreciated. 'Album' is white-flowered. Zones 4 to 8.

How to Grow

Plant dead nettles in moist, well-drained, humus-rich soil in light to partial shade. Clumps spread steadily to form an excellent groundcover of bright foliage and colorful flowers. In warmer regions, plants need shearing after flowering to keep them compact. *L. orvala* forms a rounded, sturdy clump. Propagate by division in spring or fall or by tip cuttings in spring and summer.

Landscape Uses

Choose dead nettles for semishaded spots under flowering shrubs and evergreens or under high-canopied shade trees. Use the silver foliage to brighten up dark spots. Combine them with spring-flowering bulbs such as daffodils, crocuses, and Spanish bluebells (*Hyacinthoides hispanica*), and with foliage plants such as bergenias, lady's-mantle (*Alchemilla mollis*), bleeding hearts (*Dicentra*), and ferns.

Choose a groundcover planting of dead nettle (*Lamium maculatum* 'Beacon Silver') to brighten up a shaded spot under flowering shrubs or along a shaded path with hostas and ferns.

LAVANDULA

lav-AN-dew-lah • Lamiaceae, Mint Family

The scent of lavender carries you to romantic places. Lavender is an important herb for perfumes and potpourri as well as a lovely garden ornamental. The woody stems of this fibrous-rooted shrub are covered in aromatic, gray-green needlelike leaves that are evergreen in mild climates. In summer, spikes of lavender-blue flowers are held in profusion above the foliage.

LAVANDULA

Common Name:
Lavender

Bloom Time:
Summer bloom

Planting Requirements:
Full sun to light shade

Lavandula angustifolia (an-gust-i-FO-lee-a), common lavender. Size: 2 to 3 feet tall and wide. The best-known species with dense spikes held above the silver-gray to sea green foliage. Many selections are available. 'Coconut Ice' has white flowers over silver-gray foliage. 'Dwarf Blue' is a compact plant only 12 inches tall with dark blue flowers. 'Grey Lady' grows 18 inches tall and has lovely silver-gray foliage. 'Hidcote' grows 15 inches tall with very fragrant silver-gray foliage and deep blue-violet flowers. 'Jean Davis' is 18 inches tall with blue-green foliage and pink flowers. 'Munstead' is a long-blooming lavender-blue selection to 18 inches tall. 'Silver Edge' has silvery leaves with white edges and lavender-blue flowers. The hybrid *L. ×intermedia* is a compact group 24 inches or more tall with a long bloom season. 'Fred Boutin' is 18 to 24 inches tall with silver foliage and blue flowers. 'Grosso', commercially grown for its oil, has long, fat violet spikes all summer held above the foliage. It has gray foliage on 3-by-3-inch clumps and is heat- and humidity-tolerant. 'Provence' tolerates humidity well and has erect flower spikes. USDA Plant Hardiness Zones 5 (with protection) to 9.

L. stoechas (STOY-kas), Spanish lavender. Size: 2 feet tall and wide. An enchanting species with deeply cut green foliage and purple-blue flowers in tight clusters with purple ears (winglike bracts) at their tips held above the clumps. 'Avonview' is compact with pink flowers. 'Kew-Red' is a free-flowering purple with rosy pink bracts. 'Otto Quast' has rosy plum-purple flowers and rabbit-ear wings larger than the species. 'Willowbridge Calico' has silvery green ears and flowers. 'Wine Red' has red flowers. Ssp. *pedunculata* has large wings over deep blue-violet flower spikes. Pruning after flowering will promote reblooming. Zones 7 (with protection) or 8 to 9.

How to Grow

Plant lavender in average to rich well-drained soil in full sun. Good drainage is

Lavender (*Lavandula angustifolia* 'Munstead') thrives in dry, sandy, or loamy soil in full sun. The soft gray-green foliage is delightfully fragrant when crushed.

essential for survival, especially in regions with wet or severe winters. Established plants can endure extremely dry conditions. A neutral or slightly alkaline, sandy soil is recommended. In spring, prune off any shoots damaged by winter cold, and reshape the plants by cutting back by one-third. Every few years, give plants a hard shearing to encourage fresh growth and profuse flowering. For drying, cut flowers when the first hint of color shows at the base of the spike. Propagate by tip cuttings taken from new growth in fall.

Landscape Uses

The versatile lavender has many uses in ornamental and herb gardens. Use smaller, compact cultivars as edging for beds and borders or in knot gardens. Choose taller cultivars for a low, fragrant, colorful hedge. Plant them in rock gardens with dwarf yarrows (*Achillea ×taygetea*), rock cresses (*Arabis*), and other dry-soil plants. In the perennial border, combine lavender with eryngos (*Eryngium*), globe thistle (*Echinops ritro*), yarrows (*Achillea*), pinks (*Dianthus*), stonecrops (*Sedum*), and grasses.

LAVATERA

la-va-TE-ra • Malvaceae, Mallow Family

Tree mallows are underutilized plants that take the place of shrubs in mixed borders and beds. Their massive size relegates them to ample borders and in spots where you need a dramatic specimen plant or accent. The tall, leafy stems boast showy, 3-inch pink to rose flowers. The felted leaves have three to five lobes and resemble maple leaves. Plants grow from woody crowns with fibrous roots.

LAVATERA

Common Name:
Tree mallow

Bloom Time:
Summer and fall bloom

Planting Requirements:
Full sun

Lavatera thuringiaca (thur-in-GEE-a-ca), tree mallow. Size: 5 to 7 feet tall, 3 to 5 feet wide. A full-bodied plant with tall, leafy stems bearing pink flowers mingled with the foliage on the upper third. *L. olbia* is similar, but the flowers are carried above the leaves. Most selections are likely of hybrid origin. 'Aurea' has golden leaves and pink flowers. 'Barnsley' opens white and fades to pink with a contrasting red eye. Plants may reach 8 feet tall. 'Bredon Springs' has rich pink white-eyed flowers.

Though popular in Europe, tree mallows such as *Lavatera* 'Barnsley' are just gaining popularity in North America. The sturdy, shrublike stems are clothed with flowers throughout the summer months.

How to Grow

Plants are easy to grow in average to rich, well-drained soil in full sun. Choose your spot carefully, as mature plants are hard to move. Propagate by cuttings taken after growth hardens in summer. Japanese beetles may attack foliage and flowers. Pick off beetles and drop them in a pail of soapy water.

Landscape Uses

Lavatera needs room to spread. Don't crowd it. Place plants to the rear of ample borders with bodacious perennials like Joe-Pye weed (*Eupatorium purpureum*), rosinweeds (*Silphium*), sunflowers, bush clovers (*Lespedeza*), asters, and grasses. Choose tree mallows for accents in place of traditional shrubs.

'Burgundy Wine' is compact, to 5 feet, with burgundy flowers. 'Red Rum' is wine red. USDA Plant Hardiness Zones 6 to 9.

LESPEDEZA

les-pe-DEE-za • Fabaceae, Pea Family

The stems of these dense, attractive subshrubs droop lazily through surrounding plants to great effect. The three-lobed leaves alternate up the wiry stems. Plants flower on new wood, so any stems that displease you can be whacked back or, better yet, cut to the ground after flowering. In cold climates, plants are killed back to the woody fibrous-rooted crown each winter.

LESPEDEZA

Common Name:
Bush clover

Bloom Time:
Late summer and fall bloom

Planting Requirements:
Sun to light shade

Lespedeza bicolor (BYE-color), bicolor bush clover. Size: 2 to 4 feet tall and wide. This is a small, compact plant and is thus easy to accommodate in modest-size beds. The erect to slightly arching stems have larger leaves and are crowned in midsummer with frothy heads of rosy flowers. 'Alba' is prized for its midseason white flowers. USDA Plant Hardiness Zones 5 to 9.

L. thunbergii (thun-BERG-ee-ee), Thunberg bush clover. Size: 4 to 6 feet tall and wide. Colorful rosy fountains flow from the tall, arching stems of these attractive perennial-like shrubs. 'Edo Shidori' has rose-and-white bicolor flowers on 6-foot stems. 'Gempei' produces white and pink flowers simultaneously, so you get two for the price of one. The most popular and widely available selection is 'Gibraltar', which smothers itself in rose-violet flowers for several months in fall. Zones 4 to 8.

How to Grow

Plant bush clovers in average to rich, moist but well-drained soil in sun or light shade. Plants are slow to settle in but are ultimately deep-rooted. Established plants endure heat and prolonged drought with aplomb. Like all legumes, the roots fix atmospheric nitrogen and enrich the soil. Plants emerge late in the season (they hate getting up in spring).

Landscape Uses

Form, color, and grace are the attributes of this late-season beauty. The stems rise high, then elegantly droop at the tips. The flowers dangle naughtily through the erect stems of Joe-Pye weeds (*Eupatorium*), rosinweeds (*Silphium*), asters, hibiscus, patrinias, and other late-season perennials. Place one against a wall or in the center of a courtyard for a show-stopping accent.

Drooping clusters of rosy pink flowers turn the green mop of bush clover (*Lespedeza thunbergii* 'Pink Fountain') into a colorful fountain in late summer and fall, just when we need our spirits lifted.

LEUCANTHEMUM

lew-KAN-the-mum • Asteraceae, Aster Family

This genus of showy white summer daisies was recently split from the genus *Chrysanthemum*. Species vary in stature and bloom size, but the white rays around large yellow buttons are universal. Plants are adaptable, hardy, and bloom freely. They form broad clumps from short-creeping stems with dense, fibrous roots.

LEUCANTHEMUM

Common Name:
Shasta daisy

Bloom Time:
Summer bloom

Planting Requirements:
Sun to light shade

Leucanthemum maximum (MAX-e-mum) (*Chrysanthemum superbum*), Shasta daisy. Size: 1 to 2½ feet tall and wide. Shastas are cheerful summer flowers, looking like roadside oxeye daisies that went to finishing school. The 2- to 3-inch pure white rays with bright yellow centers are held on stout leafy stalks above oblong, deep green foliage. They are popular as cut flowers and in the garden. 'Alaska' is an older, extremely cold-hardy (to Zone 3) selection with 3-inch flowers. 'Becky' is one of the best with self-supporting stems and large single flowers. 'Little Miss Muffet' is only 8 to 12 inchs tall with 3-inch off-white flowers. 'Majestic' has 3- to 4-inch flowers. 'Mount Shasta' has fully double flowers on 2-foot stems. 'Polaris' is a giant with 5- to 6-inch somewhat floppy flowers on 3-foot stems. 'T. E. Killen' blooms in mid- to late summer on sturdy 3-foot stems and has shorter rays (petals) than the other selections. USDA Plant Hardiness Zones vary by cultivar—generally 4 to 8.

L. nipponicum (nip-PON-i-cum) (*Chrysanthemum nipponicum*), Nippon daisy. Size: 1 to 3 feet tall and wide. This mounding semiwoody subshrub with 3-inch white daisies on 1- to 3-foot stalks blooms in late summer and fall above glossy, oblong leaves. Plants tolerate seaside conditions, and are often called seaside or Montauk daisies. Zones 5 to 8.

L. vulgare (vul-GAR-e) (*Chrysanthemum leucanthemum*), oxeye daisy. Size: 1 to 2½ feet tall and wide. This summer daisy is a familiar sight along roadsides, where it has naturalized. White flowers with bright yellow centers wave above the deeply toothed, mostly basal foliage. 'May Queen' is an early and long-blooming plant of exceptional merit. Zones 2 to 10.

How to Grow

Plant these daisies in average to rich, moist but well-drained soil. Established plants are quite drought-tolerant. Deadhead to prolong flower production. Divide plants frequently to extend their short life span. Lift clumps in spring, discard older portions, and replant into improved soil. Self-sown seedlings may be prolific, especially those of oxeye daisy.

Landscape Uses

Plant a selection of white daisies in the border with summer-blooming perennials, such as cranesbills (*Geranium*), bowman's root (*Porteranthus trifoliatus*), catmints (*Nepeta*), sages (*Salvia*), irises, daylilies (*Hemerocallis*), yarrows (*Achillea*), and poppies (*Papaver*), as well as grasses.

The flop-proof stems of *Leucanthemum maximum* 'Becky' hold large, flat white daisies above rich green foliage in high summer. This exceptional cultivar performs equally well in the cool North and hot, humid South.

LEUCOJUM

lew-KO-jum • Amaryllidaceae, Amaryllis Family

The chunky fragrant bells of snowflakes look like white Victorian lamp shades decorated with drooping emerald tassels. Straplike foliage persists longer than many spring-flowering bulbs. These old-fashioned favorites are standouts in the spring garden. Plants grow from true bulbs.

LEUCOJUM

Common Name:
Snowflake

Bloom Time:
Spring bloom

Planting Requirements:
Sun to light shade

Leucojum aestivum (ESS-te-vum), summer snowflake. Size: 1 to 2 feet tall, 1 foot wide. Summer snowflake has been passed around southern gardens for gener-ations, where it blooms in early to mid-spring, not summer. Farther north, the four to six nodding white chalices with deep green flairs open in succession above the narrow leaves in late spring. Plants tolerate moist to wet soil and often grow in areas inundated by flood water. 'Garvetye Giant' is a particularly robust and floriferous selection. USDA Plant Hardiness Zones 4 to 9.

L. vernum (VERN-um), spring snowflake. Size: 4 to 6 inches tall and wide. The buds emerge just ahead of or with the glossy foliage, which expands to 6 inches as the flowers mature. The single or twin bell-shaped flowers have six fused tepals with pointed tips, each marked by a green flair. Var. *carpathicum* has yellow rather than green tips. Zones 4 to 8.

How to Grow

Plant in moist, humus-rich soil in full to partial sun. Soak the white bulbs overnight in warm water to rehydrate them before planting. Bulbs stored too long may be moldy or so desiccated that they do not grow. Order early and plant bulbs as soon as they arrive. This species can be moved "in the green," or as the leaves are yellowing.

The drooping bells of the misnamed summer snowflake (*Leucojum aestivum*) actually open in spring, often as early as March in the Deep South. Plants slowly increase to form dense clumps with dozens of flowerstalks.

Landscape Uses

Use drifts of this charming and showy bulb with ferns and hellebores, as well as other early bulbs. Because the flowers are an inch across, they show up better than the more delicate snowdrops, so they can be used under shrubs and trees at some distance from a path and still make a good show.

LIATRIS

LIE-a-tris • Asteraceae, Aster Family

Gayfeathers are native American perennials of outstanding beauty. Tall spikes bear dozens of small red-violet to purple flowers carried in buttonlike clusters or in narrow, dense, compact heads. The spikes open from the top down, a characteristic somewhat unique among perennials. The grasslike leaves and flowering stems grow from a fat corm or, in some species, a short rhizome. The basal leaves are longer and broader than the stem leaves. As the leaves ascend the stem, they reduce in size until they blend into the flowers. Gayfeathers are popular cut flowers. They were originally collected in the Midwest but were bred for the trade in the Middle East and in Holland. Many excellent species and cultivars are now available for garden and cut-flower use.

LIATRIS

Common Names:
 Gayfeather, blazing-star

Bloom Time:
 Summer bloom

Planting Requirements:
 Full sun

Liatris aspera (AS-per-a), button gayfeather, rough gayfeather. Size: 4 to 6 feet tall, 1 to 2 feet wide. This stout species has tall spikes with buttonlike clusters of flowers carried on short stalks, giving the inflorescence an open look. This species produces pale purple or pink flowers in mid- to late summer. USDA Plant Hardiness Zones 3 to 9.

L. cylindracea (sil-in-DRA-see-a), cylindric blazing-star. Size: 8 to 24 inches tall, 1 foot wide. This compact grower has large clusters of pale purple flowers in open spikes to 1 foot on leafy stems in late summer. Zones 3 to 9.

L. ligulistylis (lig-ew-li-STYLE-is), button liatris. Size: 3 to 5 feet tall, 1 to 2 feet wide. The bracts of the buttonlike flower heads are purple, and the dark violet heads have long stalks, so the spike is more open.

Plants are found in wet sites. Zones 3 to 8.

L. microcephala (micro-SEPH-a-la), small-headed blazing-star. Size: 1 to 2 feet tall, 1 foot wide. A slender plant with tiny heads of red-violet flowers in open spikes to 10 inches in midsummer. Zones 4 to 9.

L. punctata (punk-TAY-ta), dotted blazing-star. Size: 6 to 14 inches tall, 12 inches wide. A compact, densely clumping plant with small heads packed tightly into dense, short 6-inch spikes. Plants bloom in late summer. Zones 2 to 8.

L. pycnostachya (pik-no-STAK-ee-a), Kansas gayfeather, prairie blazing-star. Size: 3 to 5 feet tall, 1 to 2 feet wide. This stately plant has tall (1- to 2½-foot) spikes of densely packed, red-violet to mauve flower heads on stiff, leafy stems. Plants bloom in midsummer and are extremely showy when grown in clumps. Found in wet sites. Var. *alba* ('Alba') has creamy white flowers. Zones 3 to 9.

L. scariosa (skar-ee-O-sa), tall gayfeather. Size: 2½ to 3 feet tall, 1 to 2 feet wide. This species is similar to Kansas gayfeather but is smaller, is a bit less showy, and blooms a bit later. It is often compared to *L. aspera,* but the pale purple flowers are not borne in buttonlike clusters. 'September Glory' has purple flowers in July or August. 'White Spire' has off-white flowers. Zones 4 to 9.

L. spicata (spi-KAH-ta), spike gayfeather. Size: 2 to 3 feet tall, 1 to 2 feet wide. Spike gayfeather is the best garden plant in the genus. The compact (1- to 2½-foot) spikes are deep red-violet and the leafy stems are stiff and seldom need support. Excellent cultivars are available in a variety of colors and sizes. 'August Glory' has blue-violet flowers on 3- to 4-foot stems. 'Callilepis' is 4 feet tall with deep purple flowers. 'Floristan White' has creamy white flowers on 3-foot stems. 'Kobold' is the most popular cultivar. Dense spikes of mauve to violet flowers are held on stiff stems only 2 to 2½ feet tall. Zones 3 to 8.

How to Grow

Gayfeathers are tough, long-lived, easy-care perennials. Plant them in average to rich, moist but well-drained soil in full sun. *L. aspera* and *L. punctata* naturally occur in dry sandy soils and may overgrow and flop in rich, moist soil. *L. pycnostachya* and *L. ligulistylis* grow well in rich, moist soil but need support from other plants or staking to keep stems erect. Plants seldom need division but can be propagated by division of the corms in early fall. Protect corms from mice and voles. Sow ripe seed outdoors. Germination will occur the next spring. Indoors, stratify the seeds at 40°F for 4 to 6 weeks to encourage even germination. Plants bloom in 2 to 4 years.

Landscape Uses

Gayfeathers are lovely additions to formal gardens as well as informal meadow and prairie plantings. Combine them with yarrows (*Achillea*), coneflowers (*Echi-*

The easy-care spike gayfeather (*Liatris spicata* 'Kobold') is one of the best selections for cutting. The stiff spikes are borne profusely so you can remove a few without compromising the garden display.

nacea), wormwoods (*Artemisia*), Shasta daisies (*Leucanthemum maximum*), garden phlox (*Phlox paniculata*), and ornamental grasses. Choose *Liatris punctata* and *L. microcephala* for the rock garden with creeping baby's-breath (*Gypsophila repens*), asters, fleabanes (*Erigeron*), pinks (*Dianthus*), and sea lavenders (*Limonium*).

Plant the taller species in meadow and prairie gardens in the company of their native companions, such as coneflowers (*Echinacea*), bergamot (*Monarda fistulosa*), goldenrods (*Solidago*), penstemons, rosinweed (*Silphium integrifolium*), gray-headed coneflowers (*Ratibida pinnata*), and ornamental grasses.

LIGULARIA

lig-yew-LAIR-ee-a • Asteraceae, Aster Family

Bold, lush foliage is the hallmark of ligularias, which are variable in form and flower. The broad leaves have long petioles (stalks) and may be round or kidney-shaped to broadly triangular. Some have wavy margins while others are toothed, lobed, or deeply incised. In midday sun, the leaves go into a dramatic wilt that causes undue alarm. Evening sees the return of unwilted foliage and no obvious harm to the plant. The flowers are yellow or orange, with reflexed rays (petals) and fuzzy central disks. They may be arrayed in tall, slender spikes or grouped into domed or flat clusters. All grow from stout crowns with thick fleshy roots.

LIGULARIA
Common Names: Ligularia, groundsel
Bloom Time: Foliage plant with summer bloom
Planting Requirements: Light to partial shade

Ligularia dentata (den-TAH-ta), bigleaf ligularia. Size: 3 to 4 feet tall and wide. This bold species has broad, kidney-shaped leaves to 20 inches and in late summer produces bright orange flowers in flat, branched clusters. Each flower has 10 to 14 2½-inch rays. 'Desdemona' has red leaves in spring that fade to deep green on top but retain their reddish purple color on the underside. 'Othello' is similar to 'Desdemona' but has smaller foliage and flowers. 'Gregynog Gold' is a hybrid selection from crossing *L.* *dentata* with *L. veitchiana*. The plants are 4 to 6 feet tall with bright green leaves and bright orange flowers. USDA Plant Hardiness Zones 4 to 8.

L. ×palmatiloba (pal-mat-e-LOW-ba), ragged groundsel. Size: 3 to 5 feet tall, 2 to 3 feet wide. This hybrid has ragged, palmate leaves and tall stems crowned with orange daisies in wide, flat clusters. Zones 6 to 8.

L. przewalskii (sha-VAL-ske-ee), Shavalski's ligularia. Size: 4 to 6 feet tall,

3 to 4 feet wide. This handsome plant has deeply incised spidery leaves and tall 12- to 18-inch slender spikes of golden yellow flowers. The flowerstalks and petioles are deep purple to black. Zones 4 to 8.

L. stenocephala (sten-o-SEPH-a-la), narrow-spiked ligularia. Size: 3 to 4 feet tall and wide. This species is similar in flower to *L. przewalskii*, but the leaves are heart-shaped to triangular with tooth-like lobes. The popular cultivar 'The Rocket' is listed by most American nurseries under this species but by European nurseries under the former species. They are similar in landscape effect, except the incised foliage of *L. przewalskii* holds up better in sun and dry conditions. No matter what the name, they are both excellent plants; take your pick. 'Zepter' is a magnificent hybrid with large, arrow-shaped leaves and commanding yellow spires. Zones 4 to 8.

L. tussilaginea (tuss-sil-ag-in-EE-a) (*Farfugium japonicum*), leopard plant. Size: 1½ to 2 feet tall and wide. The evergreen, kidney-shaped leaves are the main prize of this somewhat tender species. 'Argentea' has uneven white and pale green variegation. 'Aureo-maculata' has leaves speckled with yellow. 'Crispata' has ruffled leaf margins. Zones 7 to 10.

L. veitchiana (vitch-e-AY-na), Veitch's groundsel. Size: 3 to 5 feet tall and wide. The broad, heart-shaped leaves of Veitch's groundsel demand to be noticed in the summer garden. The yellow flowers, arrayed in tall, narrow pyramidal spikes,

have reflexed rays (petals) and fuzzy central disks. *L. wilsoniana* is similar, but the leaves are kidney-shaped. Zones 4 to 8.

How to Grow

Plant ligularias in constantly moist, fertile, humus-rich soil in light to partial shade. Avoid direct afternoon sun, especially in warmer zones, or plants will spend most of their day in a collapsed state. Consistent

Choose the strikingly beautiful rocket groundsel (*Ligularia stenocephala* 'The Rocket') for a moist or wet spot to keep the large leaves from wilting. Under ordinary garden conditions, the plants flag during the day but recover in the evening with no ill effects.

soil moisture is essential for success. Plants languish in hot spots with dry soil and deteriorate beyond redemption. *L. tussilaginea* tolerates drier soil but is by no means drought-tolerant. Plants seldom need division but may be lifted for propagation in spring or fall. Replant into enriched soil. Slugs may be a problem. Remove them by hand or bait them with a saucer of beer.

Landscape Uses

The enormous foliage of ligularias makes a bold accent in the moist-soil garden. Plant them with ferns, sedges (*Carex*), irises, monkshoods (*Aconitum*), astilbes, hostas, meadowsweets (*Filipendula*), and primroses (*Primula*). Plant them at water's edge with irises, hostas, and ferns where they will be reflected in the water.

LILIUM

LIL-ee-um • Liliaceae, Lily Family

The genus *Lilium* is a large and varied one, prized by hobbyists and collectors alike for its diversity of size and color and its perfection of form. Few can resist the appeal of colorful lilies viewed in glossy catalogs during the depth of winter. Lilies are bulbous plants with overlapping naked bulb scales that lack the tunic (papery brown covering) of bulbs such as tulips and narcissus. The absence of a tunic makes the bulbs sensitive to drying out when not safely surrounded by soil, and the overlapping scales make a dish that can hold excess moisture in sodden soils. Both these properties are good tips for proper culture. A tall stalk rises from the center of the bulb, which is covered in leaves that may be narrow and grasslike or wider and more swordlike. The flowers are held in terminal clusters of 3 to 75, depending on the species. Color varies from white and cream through all shades of yellow, orange, and red to pinks and purples. Only black and blue are not represented. Each flower has three petals and three petal-like sepals that closely resemble the petals in shape and color. Many have dark spots or streaks. Seeds ripen in dry papery capsules that split when they ripen.

> **LILIUM**
>
> **Common Name:**
> Lily
>
> **Bloom Time:**
> Spring and summer bloom
>
> **Planting Requirements:**
> Full sun to partial shade

Lilium auratum (ow-RAH-tum), gold-banded lily. Size: 2 to 6 feet tall, 1 to 2 feet wide. Few can resist the scent of the flower named "queen of the lilies." This lovely plant is crowned with as many as 35 broad, bowl-shaped white flowers with bold yellow stripes down each petal and a generous sprinkling of crimson spots.

Var. *platyphyllum* is a robust variety with larger flowers on 6- to 8-foot stems. 'Casa Blanca' is a pure white selection. USDA Plant Hardiness Zones 4 to 9.

L. bulbiferum (bul-BIF-er-um), orange lily. Size: 3 to 4 feet tall, 1 to 2 feet wide. An important plant for hybridization; however, the species is seldom seen in gardens. Red-orange cup-shaped flowers face upward in open clusters up to 40 strong. Zones 2 to 8.

L. canadense (kan-a-DEN-see), Canada lily. Size: 4 to 5 feet tall, 1 to 2 feet wide. This tall, slender lily has whorls of leaves and terminal clusters of up to 20 nodding, bell-shaped yellow, red, or orange flowers. Plants grow from stoloniferous rootstocks that produce new bulbs each year. Zones 3 to 7.

L. candidum (KAN-di-dum), Madonna lily. Size: 2 to 4 feet tall, 1 to 2 feet wide. Ghostly white trumpet-shaped flowers are held in elongated clusters atop the leafy stems of this lovely species. Basal leaves are evergreen and overwinter alongside the old stem. Zones 4 to 9.

L. columbianum (ko-lum-bee-A-num), Columbia lily. Size: 3 to 5 feet tall, 1 foot wide. The tightly reflexed petals of this species resemble a small tiger lily. The clear orange flowers are spotted with maroon and are carried in open clusters above tiers of whorled foliage. Zones 4 to 7.

L. davidii (day-VID-ee-ee), David's lily. Size: 3 to 4 feet tall, 1 to 2 feet wide. Brilliant scarlet or orange black-spotted flowers with strongly reflexed petals hang in elongated clusters of up to 20 atop the leafy stems of this species. Zones 5 to 8.

L. formosanum (for-mo-SAY-num), Formosa lily. Size: 4 to 7 feet tall, 1 to 2 feet wide. This stately plant bears 3 to 10 white trumpets in late summer at the summit of stout stems thickly clothed in slender leaves. Zones 5 to 8.

L. henryi (HEN-ree-ee), Henry lily. Size: 4 to 6 feet tall, 1 to 2 feet wide. This tall lily has broad foliage along the stem and open clusters of up to 20 spotted orange flowers with reflexed petals. Zones 4 to 8.

L. lancifolium (lan-si-FO-li-um) (*tigrinum*), tiger lily. Size: 4 to 6 feet tall, 1 to 2 feet wide. The familiar tiger lily has leafy stems topped with spotted, bright orange flowers with strongly reflexed petals. Small purple-black bulbils form in the axils of leaves that drop to the ground and produce new plants. Zones 3 to 9.

L. longiflorum (lon-ji-FLO-rum), Easter lily. Size: 2½ to 3 feet tall, 1 foot wide. Everyone knows the fragrant pure white trumpets of the Easter lily. Three to five flowers crown stout leafy stems. Zones 7 (with protection) or 8 to 9.

L. martagon (MAR-ta-gon), martagon lily, Turk's cap. Size: 3 to 5 feet tall, 1 to 1½ feet wide. This lovely spring-blooming species has airy clusters of as many as 50 waxy flowers with reflexed petals crowning sturdy stalks with tiers of whorled foliage. Var. *album* has creamy white flowers. 'Claude Shride' has dark red flowers with ruffled petals on 5-foot stalks. 'Mrs. R. O. Backhouse', a hybrid, has orange flowers flushed with pink. 'Nepera' has rusty orange flowers on 3-foot stems. 'Pink Taurade' is a hybrid with dark-spotted orange and pink flowers on 4-foot stems. Zones 3 to 8.

L. philadelphicum (fil-a-DEL-fi-cum), wood lily. Size: 1 to 4 feet tall, 1 foot wide. An enchanting lily with one to five up-facing cup-shaped flowers on delicate stems with whorled foliage. Zones 3 to 8.

L. regale (re-GAH-lee), regal lily. Size: 4 to 6 feet tall and 1 to 2 feet wide. This exceptional lily has clusters of large trumpets with flaring throats atop tall leafy stems. The fragrant flowers are white on the inside and blushed with purple on the outside. Zones 3 to 8.

L. speciosum (spe-see-O-sum), showy lily. Size: 4 feet tall, 1 to 2 feet wide. A popular late-season, fragrant lily having flattened flowers with wavy, reflexed white petals with rose stripes. Coarse foliage loosely covers stems. Var. *album* ('Album') has white flowers with a green star in the throat. Var. *rubrum* ('Rubrum') has large, deep purple-pink flowers with white margins around the petals. 'Uchida' is a virus-resistant cultivar with deep pink flowers. Zones 4 to 8.

L. superbum (soo-PERB-um), Turk's-cap lily. Size: 4 to 7 feet tall, 1 to 2 feet wide. A tall, slender lily with tiered whorls of foliage and broad clusters of spotted, bright orange flowers with strongly reflexed petals. *L. michauxii* and *L. michiganense* are two similar orange-flowered native species with reflexed tepals. Zones 4 to 9.

The bold flowers of the auratum hybrid lily (*Lilium* 'Casa Blanca') are intoxicatingly fragrant. Plant the bulbs in well-drained, sandy soil for best success.

Hybrids

Lilies are divided into eight divisions by the American Lily Society, based on shape and position of the flowers and on hybrid origin.

Division I. Asiatic Hybrids. Asiatics are floriferous early-blooming lilies in bright yellows, oranges, and reds, as well as more subtle pinks, purples, creams, and white. Most have upfacing flowers, but a few have outfacing or nodding flowers. They are produced from complex hybrids among many species, including *L. amabile, L. bulbiferum, L. lancifolium, L. pumilum,* and many others. Hundreds of cultivars are available. 'Connecticut King' has rich yellow upfacing flowers. 'Connecticut Yankee' has salmon-orange upfacing flowers. 'Enchantment' has glowing orange upfacing flowers.

'Mont Blanc' has white outfacing flowers. 'Monte Negro' has deep red flowers. 'Montreux' is an excellent pink. 'Sorbet' is a white-and-pink bicolor.

Division II. Martagon (Turk's Cap) Hybrids. This hybrid group includes crosses of *L. martagon* with several similar species and is characterized by waxy Turk's cap flowers with strongly reflexed petals in yellows, oranges, reds, and whites. The Paisley hybrids and Marhan hybrids are typical of the group.

Division III. Candidum Hybrids. Crosses with the lovely trumpet-flowered Madonna lily (*L. candidum*) have produced large-flowered, fragrant hybrids.

Division IV. American Hybrids. Native American lilies, mostly from the West, have been hybridized to produce excellent plants for areas where summers are cool. Color choice ranges from yellow to orange and red. Most have nodding spotted flowers with strongly recurved petals. Bellingham cultivars in mixed colors are typical of this group. 'Shuksan' has yellow-orange flowers in summer.

Division V. Longiflorum Hybrids. This hybrid group is characterized by long, flaring trumpets produced from crosses of the Easter lily (*L. longiforum*) with *L. formosianum* and other species. The new *longifolium ×asiatica* hybrids are fantastic. The Royal Series has upright flowers on sturdy stems in a variety of colors.

Division VI. Trumpet Hybrids. This large and diverse group contains various hybrids divided into subgroups based on their parentage: *L. henryi, L. regale,* and others. The group is characterized by outfacing or nodding flared trumpets 6 to 8 inches long in pinks, reds, yellows, oranges, and white. The flowers are extremely fragrant. Many strains (seed-grown crosses that produce seedlings identical to their parents) and cultivars have been named. 'Black Dragon' strain has huge trumpets that are purple-brown outside and white inside. 'Golden Splender' strain has golden yellow flowers with reddish stripes on the outside. 'Pink Perfection' strain has bright rose-pink flowers.

Plant a generous grouping of long-lived native Canada lily (*Lilium canadense*) as an accent in perennial gardens or naturalized with flowering shrubs at the edge of a woodland.

Division VII. Oriental (Japanese) Hybrids. Some of the showiest late-summer lilies were produced from hybrids between *L. auratum, L. japonicum, L. speciosum,* and others. They are characterized by flattened or cupped flowers with broad, wavy, slightly reflexed petals. The various Imperial strains from Oregon are lovely plants in various shades of white, pink, rose, and red. 'Black Beauty' is a lovely deep crimson with a green star in the throat.

Division VIII. Other Hybrids. Flowers in this group may nod or be held upright and may be shaped like a trumpet, star, or bowl.

Division IX. Species. Covered in previous text.

How to Grow

Lilies are easy-care, long-lived bulbs if their simple requirements for growth are met. Soil, moisture, pH, and light requirements vary according to species and hybrid group. Most commonly grown lilies fall into one of three general sets of growing conditions. Most species and hybrids require deep, loamy, well-drained, neutral to slightly acid soil in full sun or light shade. Lime-tolerant species include *L. bulbiferum, L. candidum, L. longiflorum, L. martagon,* and *L. aurelian* hybrids. The American species and hybrids and most Japanese species, especially *L. auratum* and *L. speciosum,* need humus-rich, acid soils for success. Martagens, native American species, *L. henryi,* and *L. speciosum* tolerate partial shade as long as some direct sun is available. Good drainage is essential, especially in winter, to avoid rot.

Plant lily bulbs in fall (September to November) or in early spring (March to April). If you order through the mail, get your orders in early and specify a time of delivery that is best for your area. November shipments are no good to northern gardeners who already have frozen soil. Place the bulbs two to three times as deep as they are tall. Some species, such as *L. auratum, L. henryi, L. lancifolium, L. regale,* and *L. speciosum* root from the stem above the bulb as well as from the bulb, so plant them down three to four times their size. An important exception to this rule is *L. candidum,* which must be planted just below the soil surface. Arrange the bulbs in groups of three, five, or seven, with 12 to 18 inches between each bulb.

Protect the top-heavy plants from wind, which may cause the whole plant to topple over or break off near the base. Staking is recommended for any of the tall varieties.

Remove flowers as they fade unless you specifically want to save seeds. Seed production drains enormous amounts of energy from the bulb and may compromise the next year's bloom. In fall, cut the stalks back to, or just below, the soil line. Lilies are susceptible to a number of fungal and bacterial infections that damage or destroy the bulb. Good cultural conditions are the best control. Keep water off the bulb by planting in well-drained soil. If leaves develop yellow mottling, chances are you have a viral infection that is not curable. Dig and destroy all infected plants. Viral infections are spread by insects such as aphids. Apply insecticidal soap as directed on the label if aphids appear. Propagate by dividing bulbs in late summer as they go dormant. Replant bulbs immediately or store them in moist peat until you can replant. Opened stored bulbs will dry out quickly. Some species produce bulbils in the leaf axils. Remove these in late summer and plant them just under the soil surface. Sow seed outdoors as soon as it is ripe. Seeds need a combination of cool and warm treatments to germinate, so seedlings may not emerge for two seasons after sowing. Plants may take 5 to 7 years to bloom.

Landscape Uses

Lilies are beloved for the grace, beauty, and fragrance they add to the garden. Use generous groupings with perennials, ornamental grasses, and vines such as clematis. Use them as accents with shrubs and small flowering trees. Plant shade-tolerant species such as Martagons and natives in open shade with irises, ferns, hostas, and other foliage plants.

LIMONIUM

li-MON-ee-um • Plumbaginaceae, Plumbago Family

Fresh or cut, sea lavender has an airy elegance that few other flowers possess. Plants are tough as nails. They thrive in wind and salt-swept marshes and in dry, alkaline soils where few other plants survive. In well-drained garden soil, they make a dramatic show throughout the summer. The woody crowns have dense, fibrous roots.

LIMONIUM
Common Names:
  Sea lavender, statice
Bloom Time:
  Summer bloom
Planting Requirements:
  Full sun to light shade

Limonium latifolium (lah-tee-FO-lee-um), sea lavender. Size: 2 to 2½ feet tall and wide. Sea lavender produces broad, domed clusters of tiny pink to lavender flowers that form an airy haze above the basal rosettes of wide, spatula-shaped leaves. The flowers are produced in early to midsummer and the heads remain intact through fall. The wind often carries them off like tumbleweeds. Plants grow from stout woody crowns.

'Violetta' bears dark, blue-violet flowers. USDA Plant Hardiness Zones 3 to 9.

How to Grow

Plant sea lavenders in average to rich, well-drained soil in full sun or light shade. They prefer a slightly acid soil but tolerate lime and are extremely adaptable to seaside conditions and high salt levels. Plants take several years to settle in. Do not disturb established plants. Division is not recommended, although auxiliary crowns can be removed when young without disturbing the main clump. Sow seed outdoors in fall for spring germination. Seedlings are slow to reach blooming size.

Landscape Uses

Sea lavenders are grown mainly for their airy sprays of flowers, but don't overlook their broad, bright green leaves. Plant them toward the front of the border where the leaves are visible. Combine the flowers with bold textures and spiky forms. Irises, phlox, winecups (*Callirhoe*), calamints (*Calamintha*), yarrows (*Achillea*), evening primroses (*Oenothera*), sages (*Salvia*), and asters are good choices for garden combinations. Plant them in a seaside garden with blanket flowers (*Gaillardia*), goldenrods (*Solidago*), and Nippon daisies (*Leucanthemum nipponicum*).

Sea lavender (*Limonium latifolium*) is a hardy salt-, heat-, and drought-tolerant perennial that rewards gardeners with lush foliage and airy clusters of long-lasting flowers.

LINUM

LY-num • Linaceae, Flax Family

Flax has a long history of cultivation for fiber, oil, and ornament. High-quality flax fiber is used to make linen cloth and rope. The seed produces linseed oil, an important ingredient in paints. Several species are grown for their electric blue or yellow, five-petal flowers. Wiry stems covered in needlelike leaves grow from a stout rootstock.

LINUM

Common Name:
Flax

Bloom Time:
Summer bloom

Planting Requirements:
Full sun or light shade

Linum flavum (FLAY-vum), golden flax. Size: 1 to 1½ feet tall and wide. Golden flax produces mounds of cup-shaped flowers in open clusters atop branched wiry stems. The leaves are narrowly oval and cover the stems. 'Compactum' grows only 6 to 9 inches tall but produces a mound of flowers. USDA Plant Hardiness Zones 4 (with protection) or 5 to 8.

L. narbonense (nar-bon-EN-see), Narbonne flax. Size: 1½ to 2 feet tall and wide. The deep electric blue saucer-shaped flowers of Narbonne flax have white centers. They are held in open, branching clusters that droop at their tips. The blue-green foliage is small and needlelike. 'Heavenly Blue' is more compact with ultramarine flowers. Zones 4 (with protection) or 5 to 9.

L. perenne (per-EN-ee) (*lewisii*), blue flax. Size: 1 to 1½ feet tall and wide. Blue flax is similar to Narbonne flax with steel blue flowers. 'Alba' has white flowers. 'Blue Sapphire' is deep blue. 'White Diamond' has pure white flowers on 1-foot plants. The American species *L. lewisii* is similar and is hardier (Zone 3) than the European selections. Zones 4 to 9.

How to Grow

Flax is a tough, long-lived perennial. Plant it in average, sandy, or loamy well-drained soil in full sun or light shade. Once established, it needs little care and seldom requires division. The clumps increase to an impressive mound of soft foliage and bright flowers. Plants will die out if crowded or overfed. Propagate by stem cuttings taken in early summer. Sow seed outdoors when ripe.

Landscape Uses

The lovely, delicate flax is best displayed in groupings of three to five (or more) plants. Combine intense blue flax with yarrows (*Achillea*), Siberian iris (*Iris sibirica*),

For best effect, plant delicate but drought-tolerant perennial flax (*Linum perenne* 'Blue Sapphire') in groups of three or five plants.

garden phlox (*Phlox paniculata*), baby's-breath (*Gypsophila paniculata*), and cranesbills (*Geranium*). For a bold combination, underplant brilliant red or salmon-pink poppies with clouds of blue flax. White, yellow, and pink flowers are good choices to complement the blue-flowered species. Plant golden flax with deep blue or purple flowers such as sages (*Salvia*) and great blue lobelia (*Lobelia siphilitica*). In a rock or dry meadow garden plant flaxes with ornamental onions (*Allium*), dotted blazing-star (*Liatris punctata*), lupines (*Lupinus*), and geraniums (*Geranium*).

LIRIOPE

le-RYE-o-pee • Convallariaceae (Liliaceae), Lily-of-the-Valley Family

Lilyturf is a workhorse groundcover prized for its tufted mounds of tough, leathery, grasslike leaves from wiry creeping rootstocks, with spidery, fleshy roots. Tiny pale purple or white flowers are held in small clusters along spikelike flowerstalks in late summer. Flowers are followed by glossy black berries that persist into winter.

LIRIOPE

Common Name:
Lilyturf

Bloom Time:
Foliage plant with spring bloom

Planting Requirements:
Sun to full shade

Liriope muscari (mus-CAH-ree), blue lilyturf. Size: 12 to 18 inches tall, 18 to 24 inches wide. This lovely groundcover has straplike evergreen leaves 1 to 1½ inches wide. The erect flower spikes of pale blue-violet or white flowers are held above the foliage. 'Big Blue' has late-season violet flowers. 'Christmas Tree' has lilac flowers arrayed in tapering spikes that resemble Christmas trees. 'Gold Banded' bears broad leaves with narrow, golden yellow margins and lilac flowers. 'John Burch' has broad leaves with central chartreuse stripes and cockscomb-like flower heads held well above the foliage. 'Lilac Beauty' has deep lilac flowers held well above dark green foliage. 'Majestic' has deep lilac-purple flowers. 'Munroe's White' has showy elongated clusters of white flowers. 'Okina' has new foliage tipped in white. 'Pee Dee Gold Ingot' has gold spring foliage that fades to chartreuse. 'Royal Purple' has deep green leaves and purple flowers. 'Samantha' is pink-flowered. 'Silvery Sunproof' is a sun-tolerant variegated form with regular

A mainstay of southern gardens, tough evergreen lilyturf (*Liriope muscari* 'Majestic') makes a reliable if a bit overused groundcover under trees and shrubs or as an edging for a walkway.

creamy stripes on the leaves. Var. *variegata* ('Variegata') bears leaves with creamy white margins. USDA Plant Hardiness Zones 6 to 9.

L. spicata (spi-KAH-ta), creeping liriope. Size: 12 to 18 inches tall, 12 to 24 inches wide. Creeping liriope differs from lilyturf in having narrow leaves only ¼ inch wide, less showy flowers, fast creeping rootstocks, and good cold hardiness. 'Franklin Mint' has large showy flowers similar to lilyturf but maintains the narrow foliage and rapid growth. Zones 4 to 9.

How to Grow

Plant liriopes in average to rich, well-drained soil in full sun to full shade. They are tough, adaptable plants able to endure extreme heat, high humidity, and dry soil conditions. They hold their ground under the canopy of mature trees and endure root competition no worse for the wear. If foliage gets ratty in winter, mow, weed-whack, or cut plants to the ground. A new flush of growth will redeem the planting in spring. Divide clumps in spring or fall to control their spread or for propagation.

Landscape Uses

Liriopes are excellent for edging paths or planting at the front of beds and borders. Trail brightly colored verbenas through the variegated cultivars, or combine them with larger spiky plants such as blue oat grass (*Helictotrichon sempervirens*) or yuccas. Soften the planting with the nodding flowers of columbines (*Aquilegia*) in spring and airy plants such as sea lavender (*Limonium latifolium*) and baby's-breaths (*Gypsophila*) for summer interest. Plant them beneath flowering or shade trees for a uniform, low-maintenance groundcover or among flowering shrubs as a solid backdrop to accentuate the branching structure.

LOBELIA

lo-BEE-li-a • Campanulaceae, Bellflower Family

Colorful exclamation points are the hallmark of lobelias. They produce erect spikes of irregularly shaped tubular flowers with three lower lobes and two upper ones. The plants form rosettes in fall from a fibrous-rooted crown that remains green throughout winter except in the most rigorous climates. In spring, leafy flowerstalks begin to elongate. The brightly colored red or blue flowers open for 2 to 3 weeks in mid- to late summer. Button-shaped seed capsules each produce dozens of small brown seeds, enabling these short-lived plants to perpetuate their numbers.

LOBELIA

Common Name:
Lobelia

Bloom Time:
Summer and fall bloom

Planting Requirements:
Full sun to partial shade

Lobelia cardinalis (kar-di-NAH-lis), cardinal flower. Size: 2 to 4 feet tall, 1 foot wide. Dense spikes to 2 feet of flaming scarlet flowers crown the leafy stems of this streamside plant. Each flower looks like a bird rising in flight. Lower, spent flowers may have ripened seed while upper flowers are still opening. Several excellent hybrids of this species are available. 'Cotton Candy' is soft shell pink. 'Dark Crusader' has velvety red flowers. 'Monet Moment' has rich rose-violet flowers. 'Royal Robe' has ruby red flowers. 'Ruby Slippers' is rich ruby red. 'Sparkle DeVine' is magenta. USDA Plant Hardiness Zones 2 to 9.

L. ×*gerardii* (ger-ARD-ee-ee), purple lobelia. Size: 3 to 4 feet tall, 1 to 2 feet wide. This showy plant resulted from crosses between great blue lobelia and one of the red-flowering species. The flowers are royal purple and are intermediate in shape between the two species. 'Grape Knee High'

The myriad colors of hybrid lobelias are the result of crosses between two native species (*Lobelia cardinalis* ×*siphilitica*). 'Pink Spire' and 'Purple Zepter' are two welcome additions to late-summer gardens that are often dominated by golden yellow flowers.

is a dwarf purple only 2 feet tall. Zones 4 to 8.

L. siphilitica (si-fi-LI-ti-ka), great blue lobelia. Size: 2 to 3 feet tall, 1 foot wide. This species lacks the flaring "wings" of cardinal flower, but the blue, buck-toothed flowers are desirable for their midsummer color. This species is important in hybridization. 'Alba' has white flowers. 'Lilac Candles' is a soft smoky purple. 'White Candles' is a good pure white. Zones 4 to 8.

L. ×speciosa (spee-see-O-sa), hybrid cardinal flower. Size: 2 to 3 feet tall, 1 foot wide. This group of hybrids was developed in Canada from several species and selections of lobelia. 'Brightness' has cherry red flowers and bronze foliage. 'Hamilton Dwarf' has blood red flowers on 2-foot stems. 'Oakes Ames' has deep scarlet flowers and bronze leaves. The Compliment Series features blue, purple, and red selections. 'Wisley' has light red flowers and bronze leaves. Zones 3 (with protection) or 5 to 9.

L. splendens (SPLEN-denz) (*fulgens*), Mexican lobelia. Size: 2 to 3 feet tall, 1 foot wide. This species resembles cardinal flower but has bronze leaves and stems and is less hardy. 'Queen Victoria' has bright red flowers and maroon foliage and may be a hybrid. Zones 7 to 9.

How to Grow

Lobelias are plants of low woods, streamsides, and ditches. Plant them in rich, constantly moist soil in light to partial shade. Plants will tolerate full sun in mild regions.

The brilliant red tubular flowers of cardinal flower (*Lobelia cardinalis* 'Compliment Scarlet') are eagerly sought after by hungry hummingbirds. In fact, the plant and bird have almost the same distribution in central and eastern states.

Plants in warm zones with fluctuating winter temperatures often rot if mulched, but in cold zones, winter mulch or snow cover is mandatory. Remove mulch as soon as temperatures moderate to avoid killing the rosettes. Plants are often short-lived and respond to frequent division to keep them vigorous. Lift clumps in early fall and remove new rosettes from old rootstocks. Replant immediately in enriched soil. Plants self-sow prolifically where soil is bare of mulch. Sow seeds uncovered outdoors or indoors. They are quick to germinate and may bloom the first season.

Landscape Uses

Lobelias are best suited to moist-soil gardens. Plant them in the company of Siberian and Japanese irises (*Iris siberica* and *ensata*), astilbes, sedges (*Carex*), ferns, and bold foliage plants such as ligularias (*Ligularia dentata*), cannas, and hostas. They are good border plants if the soil does not dry out. Combine them with daylilies (*Hemerocallis*), spiderworts (*Tradescantia*), garden phlox (*Phlox paniculata*), sneezeweeds (*Helenium*), turtleheads (*Chelone*), and ornamental grasses.

LUPINUS

loo-PY-nus • Fabaceae, Pea Family

Many gardeners dream of growing lupines—few have unqualified success. The luscious lupines produce dense conical spikes of colorful pea-shaped flowers. Many species are blue-flowered, but hybrids may have white, pink, rose, carmine, violet, or bicolor flowers. The bloom spikes rise from clusters of fan-shaped, palmately divided leaves. Plants grow from sparse, thick rootstocks.

> **LUPINUS**
>
> **Common Name:**
> Lupine
>
> **Bloom Time:**
> Spring and summer bloom
>
> **Planting Requirements:**
> Full sun to light shade

L. perennis (per-EN-nis), wild blue lupine. Size: 1 to 2 feet tall and wide. Wild lupine is a delicate creeping plant with rounded leaflets arrayed in a circular fan on a 3- to 4-inch petiole (leaf stalk). The medium blue flowers are carried on an open 12-inch spike in late spring and early summer. USDA Plant Hardiness Zones 4 to 8.

L. polyphyllus (poly-PHYL-lus), garden lupine. Size: 3 to 5 feet tall, 2 feet wide. This stately lupine is a stouter version of wild lupine with dense flower spikes of white, pink, or blue flowers and long pointed leaflets on 6- to 8-inch petioles. Garden lupine is native to the West but naturalizes in cooler regions of the Midwest and East. Zones 3 to 7.

Hybrids

The popular Russell hybrids were produced in England from crosses between different colors of *L. polyphyllus*, *L. arborescens*, and other species to form a wealth of hardy hybrids. Although they tolerate Zone 3 winters with ease, they are not equally heat-tolerant and will not perform well in the eastern and central zones warmer than Zone 6. On the West Coast, they fare much better. Breeding of garden lupines continues today, and many fine cultivars are available. 'Chatelaine' is pink and white. Gallery Series is a dwarf line of named colors from white and yellow to red and blue. Minarette Series contains dwarf plants to 18 inches in mixed colors. 'My Castle' is 2 to 3 feet tall with brick red flowers. Russell hybrids come in mixed or individual colors. Plants are 2½ to 3½ feet tall and flower in late spring.

How to Grow

Plant garden and hybrid lupines in rich, acid, evenly moist but well-drained soil in full sun or light shade. An annual spring topdressing with a balanced fertilizer is rec-

The full-flowered spikes of hybrid lupines (*Lupinus* 'Russell Hybrids') reach their full potential in climates with warm sunny days, cool nights, and low humidity.

ommended. Hybrids will not tolerate dry or nutrient-poor soils and are best planted out of the path of warm, dry winds. Plants must have cool summer temperatures, especially at night, so are best grown by northern or West Coast gardeners. Plants may be short-lived, especially in warmer zones. Plants are best left undisturbed, but you can remove side shoots in fall without lifting the entire clump. Sow seeds outdoors when ripe or indoors in winter. Soak seeds overnight in warm water and cold-moist stratify them for 4 to 6 weeks. Seed is available as mixed or individual colors.

Wild lupine is more difficult to establish. Give plants well-drained, acid, sandy soil in sun or light shade. Plants are best started from seed. Inoculate seed with a bacterium specified for lupines (usually available with the seeds) and cold-moist stratify them for 4 to 6 weeks. The seedlings will bloom in 2 years.

Landscape Uses

Lupines are colorful aristocrats of the spring and summer garden. Plant them as an accent with flowering shrubs such as roses and lilacs, and vines such as clematis. In the border, combine them with cranesbills (*Geranium*), catmints (*Nepeta*), irises, peonies, bellflowers (*Campanula*), and annuals such as pansies (*Viola*), love-in-a-mist (*Nigella damascena*), and forget-me-nots (*Myosotis*). Plant wild lupines in wildflower meadows, in prairie gardens, on sandy banks, or along roadsides.

LYCHNIS

LIK-nis • Caryophyllaceae, Pink Family

Fiery colors add heat to the garden in spring and early summer. The rich hues are sure to seduce gardeners who are more accustomed to pastel schemes. A large genus, these are short-lived, showy plants with orange, red, rose, or white five-petaled flowers carried singly or in clusters. Plants form basal rosettes from which the flowerstalks rise in spring or summer. The roots are fibrous and thin.

> **LYCHNIS**
> **Common Names:**
>   Campion, catchfly
> **Bloom Time:**
>   Spring and summer bloom
> **Planting Requirements:**
>   Full sun to partial shade

Lychnis ×***arkwrightii*** (ark-RIGHT-ee-ee), Arkwright's campion. Size: 18 to 24 inches tall and wide. This showy garden hybrid between *L. chalcedonica* and *L.* ×*haageana* produces orange-red flowers with notched petals. Stems bear pairs of elongated, oval, dark bronze leaves. Plants bloom in early summer. 'Vesuvius' has scarlet-orange flowers. USDA Plant Hardiness Zones 6 to 8.

L. chalcedonica (chal-se-DON-i-ka), Maltese cross. Size: 24 to 36 inches tall, 12 to 24 inches wide. Maltese cross is an old-fashioned garden favorite with bright scarlet flowers with five deeply notched petals. The flowers are held in tight rounded clusters atop sturdy stems with opposite, oval leaves in midsummer. 'Alba' and 'Rauhreif' have white flowers. 'Morgenrot' bears pink flowers on 36- to 48-inch stems. Zones 3 to 9.

L. coronaria (ko-ro-NAH-ree-a), rose campion. Size: 24 to 36 inches tall, 12 to

Easy-care Maltese cross (*Lychnis chalcedonica*) provides a bright spot of color at the middle or rear of the garden with companions like oxeye (*Heliopsis helianthoides*) that thrive in moist, well-drained soil.

16 inches wide. Rose campion is the showiest of the campions. Brilliant deep rose-pink flowers are held in broad, open, branching clusters above rosettes of hairy, silver-gray leaves. Individual plants of this spring bloomer are short-lived. 'Abbotswood Rose' has magenta flowers. 'Alba' has white flowers. 'Angel's Blush' and Oculata Group have white flowers with cerise eyes. Zones 4 to 8.

L. ×haageana (hah-gee-AH-na), Haage campion. Size: 10 to 18 inches tall and wide. The showy flowers of Haage campion vary in color from deep red to crimson and are borne throughout summer. This hybrid was produced from a cross between *L. fulgens* and *L. coronata,* two little-known species. Zones 3 to 9.

L. viscaria (vis-CAH-ree-a), German catchfly. Size: 12 to 18 inches tall and wide. This showy spring-blooming plant produces basal rosettes of long, slender leaves and open, elongated clusters of magenta flowers. 'Alba' has white flowers on 1-foot stalks. 'Fire' has bright rose-red flowers. 'Zulu' has deep red flowers on maroon stems. Zones 3 to 8.

How to Grow

Campions vary in their requirements for growth. Give *L. ×arkwrightii, L. chalcedonica,* and *L. coronaria* light, average to rich, moist but well-drained soil in full sun or light shade. In warmer areas, afternoon shade is recommended to keep plants from frying. *L. ×haageana* needs consistent moisture for best growth. *L. viscaria* grows best in average, limey soil and is tolerant of dry conditions. Divide plants every 2 or 3 years in spring to keep them vigorous. *L. coronaria* is prone to dying out from the middle if soil is too wet, especially in winter. Plants self-sow readily and turn up in the oddest places.

Landscape Uses

The campions have strongly colored flowers that can be difficult to incorporate into the garden. All species look good when surrounded by green and combine well with shrubs. Plant the red- and orange-flowered species in combination with yellow and soft blue. Russian sage (*Perovskia atriplicifolia*), black-eyed Susans (*Rudbeckia*), yarrows (*Achillea*), golden marguerite (*Anthemis tinctoria*), and delphiniums are good companions. The white-flowered form of *L. coronaria* is a lovely and easy-to-use plant enhanced by its gray foliage. Combine it with lavender (*Lavandula angustifolia*), catmints (*Nepeta*), and white or pale pink lilies (*Lilium*). Plant the rose-colored selections with cranesbills (*Geranium*) and other pink- and blue-flowered plants. Choose *L. viscaria* for the front of the border or in a sunny rockery.

LYCORIS

ly-KOR-is • Amaryllidaceae, Amaryllis Family

Lycoris are showy summer- or fall-blooming bulbs with round clusters of six-petaled flowers with long, upturned stamens. The strap-shaped leaves rise from true bulbs in fall or spring and persist through midsummer. The flower-stalks emerge from the ground after foliage has disappeared, giving rise to the name "naked ladies."

LYCORIS

Common Names:
Spider lily, surprise lily

Bloom Time:
Summer and fall bloom

Planting Requirements:
Full sun to partial shade

Lycoris aurea (aw-RE-a), golden spider lily. Size: 1 to 2 feet tall, 1 foot wide. Golden spider lily has clusters of rich yellow flowers with narrow, recurved tepals and protruding stamens on naked stalks in early fall. Unlike naked ladies, the thin, straplike foliage is produced after flowering and persists through winter and into summer. USDA Plant Hardiness Zones 7 to 10.

L. radiata (raid-ec-AH-ta), spider lily. Size: 12 to 18 inches tall, 12 inches wide. This handsome species produces clusters of 2-inch deep red flowers with narrow, reflexed tepals and long stamens. New leaves emerge in late fall after flowers fade. *L. sanguinea* is similar, with red-orange flared flowers rather than reflexed tepals. Zones 7 to 10.

L. squamigera (skwa-MI-ge-ra), magic lily, naked ladies. Size 18 to 30 inches tall, 24 inches wide. Magic lily produces wide, straplike leaves in early spring that disappear by midsummer. In late July or August,

The naked stalks of spider lily (*Lycoris radiata*) explode into a mass of stunning color in early fall, long after the narrow, strappy foliage has disappeared for the summer.

the stout stalks rise to reveal as many as seven pink, funnelform flowers with wavy petals. *L. sprengeri* is similar, with narrow pink petals blushed with blue. Zones 4 to 9.

How to Grow

Plant new bulbs 6 inches deep in fall. Give them rich, moist but well-drained soil in full sun or light shade. Magic lily will bloom in partial shade. Plants take a while to establish and may not bloom until the second season. They are long-lived and increase steadily. Lift and divide bulbs after flowering if flower production wanes or for propagation.

Landscape Uses

Plant spider lilies in perennial gardens with late-summer bloomers such as asters, calamints (*Calamintha*), chrysanthemums, garden phlox (*Phlox paniculata*), goldenrods (*Solidago*), and ornamental grasses. Combine them with foliage plants for effective contrast, or underplant open-canopied trees with scattered drifts or clumps.

LYSIMACHIA

lis-i-MA-ki-a • Primulaceae, Primrose Family

Small but showy five- to seven-petaled yellow or white flowers may be arrayed in dense, elongated terminal clusters or in whorls above the foliage. A variable genus with creeping and upright species bearing opposite or whorled leaves. Plants spread from creeping stems with fibrous roots.

LYSIMACHIA

Common Name:
Loosestrife

Bloom Time:
Summer bloom

Planting Requirements:
Full sun to light shade

Lysimachia ciliata (kil-i-A-ta), fringed loosestrife. Size: 1 to 3 feet tall and wide. Fringed loosestrife is an open perennial with opposite oval leaves and pairs of five-petaled, fringed yellow flowers at each node (leaf joint). An attractive purple-leaf form is available. 'Purpurea' emerges deep purple-brown and fades a bit as the season progresses. USDA Plant Hardiness Zones 3 to 9.

L. clethroides (kleth-ROI-dez), gooseneck loosestrife. Size: 2 to 3 feet tall, 3 to 4 feet wide. This lovely, fast-spreading plant has opposite leaves and drooping, terminal 8- to 12-inch spikes of five- to six-petaled white flowers. In any one clump, all the flower spikes droop in the same direction, appearing like a flock of eager geese on the run. 'Geisha' has irregular yellow leaf margins to accent the white flowers. Zones 3 to 8.

L. ephemerum (e-FEM-er-um), loosestrife. Size 2 to 3 feet tall, 1 to 2 feet wide. This lovely perennial has erect, leafy stalks covered in lance-shaped gray-green leaves and crowned with long, erect, 1- to 1½-foot clusters of white flowers. Plants do not spread as rapidly as other species. Zones 6 to 8.

L. nummularia (num-ew-LAH-ree-a), creeping Jenny. Size: 2 to 4 inches tall, 12 to 24 inches wide. This fast-growing, often invasive groundcover spreads by creeping stems with opposite rounded leaves and five petaled yellow flowers. 'Aurea' has chartreuse leaves in spring that darken to lime green in summer. Zones 3 to 8.

L. punctata (punk-TAH-ta), yellow loosestrife. Size: 1 to 2½ feet tall, 2 to 3 feet wide. Yellow loosestrife bears wiry stems covered in tiered whorls of hairy foliage and 1-inch yellow flowers. 'Alexander' has foliage edged in creamy white. Zones 4 to 8.

How to Grow

Plant loosestrifes in evenly moist, humus-rich soil in full sun or partial shade. Periods of dryness will set plants back; extended drought is fatal. Plants spread rapidly in moist soil and may become pests if planted in proximity to delicate species. Divide clumps in spring or fall as necessary to control their spread or for propagation.

The exciting variegated form of yellow loosestrife (*Lysimachia punctata* 'Alexander'), with creamy-edged leaves, thrives in full sun and moist to wet soil. Plants spread quickly to form dense, elegant clumps.

Landscape Uses

The affinity loosestrifes have for moist soil makes them perfect for use along streams or at poolside. Plant them in combination with Siberian iris (*Iris sibirica*), ligularias (*Ligularia dentata, L. stenocephala*), meadowsweets (*Filipendula*), lady's-mantle (*Alchemilla mollis*), hostas, sedges (*Carex*), and ferns. Most species are adaptable to evenly moist borders with garden phlox (*Phlox paniculata*), daylilies (*Hemerocallis*), meadow rues (*Thalictrum*), Joe-Pye weeds (*Eupatorium*), and ornamental grasses. *L. ephemerum* provides an open but strong vertical accent for the middle or back of the border. Use *L. nummularia* as a groundcover between stepping-stones or under shrubs.

M

MACLEAYA

ma-KLAY-a • Papaveraceae, Poppy Family

If you have space, this towering perennial will fill it. Even if you don't, the fast spreading roots will press ever forward, gobbling up delicate plants in its wake. Choose this thug for the back of a large border or other spot where its rampant spread will not consume its companions. Pair it with large plants like cup plants (*Silphium*) and Joe-Pye weed, and the lacy pink spires will delight you.

MACLEAYA

Common Name:
Plume poppy

Bloom Time:
Summer bloom

Planting Requirements:
Sun to partial shade

Macleaya cordata (kor-DAY-ta), plume poppy. Size: 6 to 8 feet tall, 4 to 6 feet wide. A huge plant with towering stems covered in blue-green, oak-shaped lobed leaves. Huge, elongated terminal clusters of small cream flowers with fuzzy stamens open in summer. The seedheads are tinted pink and extend the ornamental season. 'Alba' has ivory flowers. 'Flamingo' is pink-flowered. USDA Plant Hardiness Zones 3 to 8.

How to Grow

Plant plume poppies in average to rich, moist but well-drained soil in sun or partial shade. Plants increase in size rapidly and romp through the garden with their stout underground stems. Unless you have unlimited space, you'll need to control their spread. Try planting in a huge bottomless container. Propagate by offsets.

If you have room to let it romp, the stately stems of plume poppy (*Macleaya cordata*), clothed in huge oaklike leaves and crowned with airy plumes, are knockouts. It is far too rampant for small gardens.

Landscape Uses

Plume poppies make a dramatic statement against a fence or wall or at the edge of a woodland. At the rear of a border, combine them with stout plants that won't be swamped, such as cannas, sunflowers (*Helianthus*), rosinweeds (*Silphium*), Joe-Pye weeds (*Eupatorium*), bush clovers (*Lespedeza*), and grasses.

MALVA

MAL-va • Malvaceae, Mallow Family

Mallows are closely related to hibiscus. Saucer-shaped flowers with five broad petals surround central columns that bear the male and female reproductive structures. Each flower lasts only a day, but successive flowers open up the stem as it elongates. Stout stems rise from woody crowns with thick, fibrous roots. Stems are loosely covered in alternate, puckered leaves with five deep lobes.

> **MALVA**
>
> **Common Name:**
> Mallow
>
> **Bloom Time:**
> Summer bloom
>
> **Planting Requirements:**
> Full sun or light shade

Malva alcea (AL-kee-a), hollyhock mallow. Size 2 to 3 feet tall, 1 to 2 feet wide. Rose, pink, or white flowers open in the axils of the leaves for over 6 weeks in early and midsummer. Var. *fastigiata* is an upright floriferous selection with rose-pink flowers. USDA Plant Hardiness Zones 4 to 8.

M. moschata (mos-KA-ta), musk mallow. Size: 2½ to 3 feet tall and wide. This species is similar to hollyhock mallow but has coarser-branching, deeply divided leaves and larger rose-pink flowers. 'Alba' has white flowers and comes true from seed. 'Rosea' has deep rose flowers. *M. sylvestris* is a similar coarse species with flowers intermingled with foliage. 'Zebrinus' has pink flowers striped with violet. Zones 3 to 7.

How to Grow

Plant mallows in average, neutral, well-drained soil in full sun or light shade. They grow best in cooler zones and are not suitable for warm, humid areas, where they are susceptible to foliar diseases. In dry air, plants may develop spider mites that cause leaves to look pale and speckled. To combat mites, spray with insecticidal soap at 3- to 5-day intervals for 2 weeks. Japanese beetles may also be in

Plant tall, shrublike clumps of hollyhock mallow (*Malva alcea* var. *fastigiata*) at the back of the border where the tall spires will add lift to the profile. These tough plants are easy to grow in well-drained soil in full sun in areas with cool nights.

evidence in summer. Pick them off individually and destroy them. Propagate by tip cuttings taken in early summer or by seed sown outdoors.

Landscape Uses

Use mallows for tall, bushy accents in the middle or back of the border. Their lovely rose flowers are borne over several weeks and combine well with catmints (*Nepeta*), garden phlox (*Phlox paniculata*), purple coneflower (*Echincea purpurea*), yarrows (*Achillea*), blazing-stars (*Liatris*), and wormwoods (*Artemisia*).

MATTEUCCIA

mat-TOOK-ke-a • Dryopteridaceae, Shield Fern Family

Ostrich fern surely ranks among the most familiar and popular garden ferns. The creeping rhizomes produce vast sweeps of lush green vases. Use this large fern, with huge, plume-like fronds carried in graceful clumps, at the edge of a woodland, along a ditch, or in a moist meadow where the plant has room to spread.

MATTEUCCIA

Common Name:
Ostrich fern

Bloom Time:
Foliage plant

Planting Requirements:
Sun or shade

Matteuccia struthiopteris (strew-the-OP-ter-is), ostrich fern. Size: 3 to 5 feet tall, 3 to 4 feet wide. Ostrich fern is a popular garden plant throughout its native range and beyond. The tall, plume-shaped deciduous fronds arise in a narrow vase from a creeping, crown-forming rhizome. Fronds taper gradually up from the base and are widest at the top. The tip of the frond is abruptly constricted. The fiddleheads are prized in spring for cooking. The persistent brown fertile fronds dry over

winter and release their spores in spring.
USDA Plant Hardiness Zones 2 to 8.

How to Grow

Plant ostrich ferns in moist, neutral,
humus-rich soil in light to full shade. Plants
in cool, wet locations tolerate full sun.
Clumps spread rapidly and may be invasive. Remove crowns that spread beyond
their position. Divide plants in fall.

Landscape Uses

Use ostrich ferns as foundation plants or in
drifts in the woodland garden. Combine
them with spring-flowering bulbs, wildflowers, and garden perennials. The fronds
emerge early and make vertical accents
among groundcovers such as sweet woodruffs (*Galium*), epimediums, foamflowers
(*Tiarella*), and trilliums.

The huge, arching vases of ostrich fern
(*Matteuccia struthiopteris*) are immediately recognizable because of their size
and elegant shape. Plants are valued
as ornamentals and for their edible
fiddleheads.

MERTENSIA

mer-TEN-see-a • Boraginaceae, Borage Family

Bluebells capture the color of the sky and bring it to earth.
These ephemeral spring wildflowers grace woodlands,
riverbanks, and meadows with their nodding clusters of
sky blue, bell-shaped flowers on delicate stems. They have
been prized in gardens on both sides of the Atlantic since
colonial times. Plants produce basal rosettes and stems
from stout, thickened roots.

MERTENSIA

Common Names:
   Bluebells, cowslips

Bloom Time:
   Spring bloom

Planting Requirements:
   Sun or shade

Mertensia asiatica (as-e-AT-i-ka), Asian bluebells. Size: 6 to 10 inches tall, 10 to 12 inches wide. Noted for its season-long show of blue-gray foliage, and accented in spring by nodding blue bells. USDA Plant Hardiness Zones 3 to 8.

M. paniculata (M. pan-ik-ew-LAH-ta), tall lungwort. Size: 2 to 3 feet tall, 1 to 1½ feet wide. Tall lungwort is an upright, succulent plant with thin blue-green leaves and ½-inch flowers. Zones 4 to 7.

M. virginica (vir-GIN-i-ka), Virginia bluebells. Size: 1 to 2 feet tall and wide. Virginia bluebells are lovely spring wild-flowers with pink buds that open to sky blue bells. The leaves are thin and deli-cate. The stems are thick and succulent and die down as soon as flowering is complete. 'Alba' has white flowers. Zones 3 to 9.

How to Grow

Plant bluebells in consistently moist but well-drained, humus-rich soil in sun or shade. Shoots emerge in early spring and quickly expand to reveal buds. Flowers begin opening as the stems elongate. Flow-ering lasts several weeks; soon after, the plants go completely dormant. Locate plants where you will not dig into dor-mant clumps accidentally. Divide large clumps after flowering for propaga-tion. Plants will self-sow readily on soil that is not heavily mulched. They bloom the third year from seed.

Plant fragrant Virginia bluebells (*Mertensia virginica*) with foliage plants such as ferns and hostas that will fill the bare spot left when this native wildflower goes dormant in early summer.

Landscape Uses

Bluebells are lovely nodding along-side a shaded garden path in the company of spring bulbs such as daf-fodils and species tulips, and wild-flowers such as columbines (*Aquilegia*), woodland phlox (*Phlox divaricata*), Canada wild ginger (*Asarum cana-dense*), and trilliums. Interplant the clumps with ferns, hostas, and other foliage perennials to fill in bare spots left when plants go dormant. Do not plant directly over clumps; allow a 1-foot area for bluebells to grow unimpeded.

MISCANTHUS

mis-KAN-thus • Poaceae, Grass Family

Japanese silver grass has been at the forefront of the ornamental grass craze for more than two decades. Prized for its elegant plumes and fine-textured foliage, this tough plant is now used in home gardens and municipal plantings. Unfortunately, plants are escaping cultivation and overtaking meadows and wetlands in much of North America. Please avoid this grass unless you grow a sterile cultivar.

MISCANTHUS

Common Name:
Japanese silver grass

Bloom Time:
Foliage plant with summer bloom

Planting Requirements:
Sun

Miscanthus sinensis (sigh-NEN-sis), Japanese silver grass. Size: 4 to 6 feet tall and wide. Japanese silver grass is by far the most popular and widely planted ornamental grass. To its credit, it forms luscious silvery plumes in summer that dry to tawny shades and persist well into winter. The foliage is widely variable, depending on the cultivar, from narrow and green to wide and beautifully streaked with white or yellow. Plants vary from 3 to 8 feet with an equal spread. On the darker side, *this* plant has become a serious pest in many areas of the country where it escapes cultivation and dominates natural areas. Some selections are seed-sterile, and they are to be preferred to the invasive fertile selections. 'Adagio' has narrow leaves and forms clumps 5 feet tall with plumes held above the leaves. 'Cabaret' and 'Cosmopolitan' belong to the variety *condensatus* and have dramatically white-striped leaves on plants to 7 feet tall. Both bloom late and seedlings are rare.

Japanese silver grass (*Miscanthus sinensis* 'Gracillimus') is a popular ornamental grass with exceptional beauty and grace. Its beauty is tempered by the fact that in many regions plants have become invasive and only sterile selections should be grown.

'Goldfeder' has leaves striped with yellow on 7-foot plants. 'Hinjo' is a compact selection with nonflopping stems to 6 feet and leaves banded, rather than striped, with yellow. 'Morning Light' is one of the best, with narrow white-striped leaves on tight clumps to 5 feet. USDA Plant Hardiness Zones 4 (with protection) to 9.

How to Grow

Plants are easy to grow in any average to rich, moist soil in full sun. They tolerate some shade but may flop when the flower spikes begin to elongate. Cultivars vary in bloom time and size of inflorescence. Late bloomers are less likely to set seed and become invasive. Established clumps are huge and difficult to divide, but eventually plants die out at the center and need rejuvenating. Dig plants in spring, and hack them apart with a maddox or saw.

Landscape Uses

All *Miscanthus* species blend beautifully with perennials and shrubs. Use them in the garden or as mass plantings on banks and other difficult spots. They are beautiful reflected in still water.

MOLINIA

mow-LIN-e-a • Poaceae, Grass Family

Elegant and well behaved, this grass should be used more often. Its lack of popularity is no doubt due to the inevitable comparisons made to the more dramatic Japanese silver grass. Choose this graceful beauty in place of invasive *Miscanthus* in areas where silver grass has become a weed. The weeping plumes are held well above dense clumps of soft foliage.

MOLINIA

Common Name:
  Moor grass

Bloom Time:
  Summer bloom

Planting Requirements:
  Sun or partial shade

Molinia caerulea (kie-REW-lee-a), purple moor grass. Size: 2 to 3 feet tall and wide. Purple moor grass is like a cool breeze on a sultry summer day. Airy plumes form an open, graceful vase over tight rosettes of gray-green leaves. Plants bloom in mid- to late summer. The foliage turns golden in fall. 'Moorhexe' forms an upright vase. 'Strahlenquelle' has a wide spread with flowers held well above the foliage. 'Variegata' has leaves attractively edged in yellow and a wide vase shape. Ssp. *arundinacea*, tall purple moor grass, is a giant subspecies with wider leaves that form gracefully disheveled mounds. The slender inflorescences grow to 8 feet tall and together form a giant airy vase in summer. 'Skyracer' is a huge selection with dazzling inflorescences.

The most graceful ornamental grass has to be purple moor grass (*Molinia caerulea* 'Variegata'). The arching foliage rosettes are mirrored by the tall, airy flower sprays that open in summer and maintain their structure well into winter.

'Windspiel' is slender and upright. USDA Plant Hardiness Zones 4 to 8.

How to Grow

Plant in evenly moist, average to rich soil in full sun or partial shade. In hot, dry areas, plants benefit from shade and require consistent moisture. This cool-season grass begins growth early in the season. Divide overgrown clumps in spring as new growth begins.

Landscape Uses

The airy inflorescences add motion to the garden as a specimen plant or in borders, surrounded by low plants that will not hide the flowers. Verbenas, calamints (*Calamintha*), creeping veronica (*Veronica peduncularis* 'Georgia Blue'), winecups (*Callirhoe*), and asters are a few good choices. Use them as architectural accents or as focal points to mark an entrance or end a vista.

MONARDA

mo-NAR-da • Lamiaceae, Mint Family

The aromatic foliage and colorful round heads of *Monarda* create a memorable impression in the summer garden. Tightly packed tubular red, violet, or lavender flowers are held above a circle of colored leafy bracts. The flowers have distinctive protruding upper lips that arch over the smaller lower ones. Like all mints, the stems are square and grow from fast-creeping runners with fibrous roots. Tea aficionados will recognize the pungent aroma of bergamot from Earl Gray tea, for which monarda is named.

MONARDA

Common Names:
  Bee balm, bergamot

Bloom Time:
  Summer bloom

Planting Requirements:
  Full sun to light shade

Monarda didyma (DID-i-ma), bee balm, Oswego tea. Size: 2 to 4 feet tall, 3 to 4 feet wide. Bee balm has brilliant scarlet flowers in round, 4-inch heads surrounded by deep red bracts. The stout, succulent stems have opposite, pointed leaves. Many garden selections have been named, some of which are hybrids with *M. fistulosa*. 'Adam' has ruby red flowers on compact 3-foot stems. 'Blue Stocking' has soft violet-blue flowers with bright violet bracts. 'Croftway Pink' has soft pink flowers. 'Gardenview Scarlet' has brilliant scarlet flowers. 'Jacob Cline' is an excellent mildew-resistant red. 'Marshall's Delight' has deep rose-pink flowers and good mildew resistance. 'Petite Delight' has lavender-rose flowers on 15-inch stems and

To attract hummingbirds, plant generous clumps of summer-blooming bee balm (*Monarda didyma*). The beautiful selection 'Jacob Cline' is compact and mildew-resistant. Plants thrive in moist soil in sun or light shade.

mildew-resistant foliage. 'Prairie Night' has red-violet flowers. 'Snow White' has creamy white flowers on 3-foot stems. 'Violet Queen' has reddish purple flowers. USDA Plant Hardiness Zones 4 to 8.

M. fistulosa (fist-ew-LOW-sa), bergamot. Size: 2 to 4 feet tall, 2 to 3 feet wide. Bergamot has soft lavender-pink to pale pink flowers and pink to white bracts. The flowers are carried in 3-inch heads atop wiry stems. The leaves are narrower, paler green, and hairier than those of *M. didyma*. Although named selections are not available, plants vary in color. If you desire a specific color intensity, select plants in bloom. 'Claire Grace' is a mildew-resistant selection. Zones 3 to 9.

M. punctata (punk-TA-ta), spotted horse mint. Size: 1 to 3 feet tall, 1 to 2 feet wide. This unusual plant is grown for its showy pink bracts rather than its flowers. Wiry stems with long, pointed leaves are crowned by tiered clusters of small, spotted green flowers above whorls of elongated pink bracts. Zones 3 to 9.

How to Grow

The native habitats of the different species give good clues to their growth requirements. *M. didyma* grows in moist, humusy soils in clearings and in roadside ditches. Plant it in evenly moist, humus-rich soil in full sun or partial shade. Plants must never be allowed to dry out. *M. fistulosa* and *M. punctata* grow in meadows, prairies, and on dry roadsides. Give plants average to rich soil in full sun to light shade. All spread rapidly from creeping stems, grow outward in a circle, and die out in the center. Lift and divide entire clumps every 2 or 3 years to keep them vigorous. Replant vigorous portions into enriched soil. *M. punctata* tolerates seaside conditions. All species show susceptibility to powdery mildew, which causes white blotches on leaves. *M. didyma* is the most susceptible and *M. punctata* is seldom affected. Keep plants well watered to prevent wilting, which open the leaves to infection.

Landscape Uses

These beautiful summer perennials attract attention from gardeners and humming-birds alike. Combine them with lilies (*Lilium*), garden phlox (*Phlox paniculata*), yarrows (*Achillea*), Shasta daisies (*Leucanthemum maximum*), cranesbills (*Geranium*), and goat's beards (*Aruncus*). In the moist wild garden, plant *M. didyma* with native lily species and hybrids or martagon lilies (*Lilium martagon*), Joe-Pye weeds (*Eupatorium*), queen-of-the-prairie (*Filipendula rubra*), astilbes, rose mallows (*Hibiscus*), and ferns. Plant *M. fistulosa* and *M. punctata* with meadow plants such as purple coneflowers (*Echinacea*), butterfly weed (*Asclepias tuberosa*), evening primroses (*Oenothera*), blazing-stars (*Liatris*), goldenrods (*Solidago*), black-eyed Susans (*Rudbeckia*), and ornamental grasses.

MUSCARI

mus-CAR-e • Hyacinthaceae (Liliaceae), Hyacinth Family

Grape hyacinths are aptly named for the conical clusters of plump bells in spring, like ripe Concord grapes. Long-lived and persistent, you often find them around old homesteads, in cemeteries, and marking gardens that have long been abandoned. The grassy, gray-green leaves are produced in autumn and persist through summer. They grow from true bulbs.

MUSCARI

Common Name:
Grape hyacinth

Bloom Time:
Spring bloom

Planting Requirements:
Sun

Muscari armeniacum (ar-meen-e-AK-um), Armenian grape hyacinth. Size: 4 to 6 inches tall and wide. A floriferous species with cobalt blue flowers and many named varieties. Plants may reseed prolifically. 'Blue Spike' is a sterile double. 'Cantab' is a bright blue, late-season bloomer. 'Saffier' is dark blue and sterile.

The clustered flowers of white grape hyacinth (*Muscari botryoides* 'Album') perk up an area under shrubs or lawn trees where few other plants thrive. Though summer dormant, they produce fresh leaves in fall and flowers in midspring.

The hybrid 'Valerie Finnis' is a beauty with intense but pale sky blue flowers, a unique color. USDA Plant Hardiness Zones 4 to 9.

M. botryoides (bot-re-OY-deez), common grape hyacinth. Size: 3 to 6 inches tall and wide. Heirloom bulb with medium to dark blue flowers, often found naturalized around old houses. 'Album' is white-flowered. *M. azureum* is another similar popular species with bright blue flowers. Zones 4 to 9.

M. comosum (ko-MO-sum), grape hyacinth. Size: 4 to 6 inches tall and wide. Best known in its double form 'Plumosum', with fantastic fuzzy, blue-violet flowers. Zones 4 to 9.

How to Grow

Plant grape hyacinths in almost any soil in a spot that is sunny in winter and spring. These bulbs are easy to grow and increase steadily to form full clumps. Divide them in early summer as the foliage is yellowing. Some species self-sow. Gardeners have long used grape hyacinths to mark spots occupied by other bulbs. The foliage emerges early in fall and will persist through winter, so even just a few bulbs will mark the spot where tulips and daffodils are located to keep you from inadvertently digging into them.

Landscape Uses

Plant grape hyacinths anywhere you need a little spring color. Use them under trees and shrubs, along paths, and even in the rose garden. Combine the purple-blue spikes with daffodils, tulips, anemones, and other early bloomers. Use ferns, sedges (*Carex*), and hostas to fill the gaps left by the dying foliage. They perform well in containers, too.

NARCISSUS

nar-SIS-us • Amaryllidaceae, Amaryllis Family

The beloved daffodils are true harbingers of spring. Along with crocuses and snowdrops (*Galanthus*), they signal the start of a new growing season that has been eagerly awaited by every gardener. First to emerge, often in January, are the tips of the gray-green foliage. As temperatures moderate, gardeners examine the elongating foliage tufts for the teardrop-shaped buds that will soon signal the end of winter. The characteristic flowers have a ring of three petals and three petal-like sepals, collectively called the *corolla,* or *perianth.* In the centers of the flowers are funnel-shaped cups of varying length called the *corona.* Together they form the cheery flowers that vary in size, shape, and color according to species or hybrid origin. Daffodils are classified by the Royal Horticultural Society and American Daffodil Society into 13 groups, based on the size and shape of the corona in relation to the size of the corolla, the color, and species origins of major hybrid groups. There are over 50 naturally occurring species, of which the following are readily available as nursery-propagated bulbs.

NARCISSUS

Common Name:
Daffodil

Bloom Time:
Winter and spring bloom

Planting Requirements:
Full sun to partial shade

Narcissus bulbocodium (bul-bow-KO-dee-um), hoop petticoat daffodil. Size: 6 to 12 inches tall and wide. Hoop petticoat daffodils have unique flowers, with short, narrow petals and wide, fat coronas that resemble a southern lady's undergarments. They bloom early in the season. The rush-like leaves are narrow, rounded, and deep green. Var. *conspicuus* ('Conspicuus') has deep yellow flowers in late spring. USDA Plant Hardiness Zones 5 to 9.

N. cantabricus (kan-TA-bre-cus), Cantabrian daffodils. Size: 6 to 10 inches tall and wide. This daffodil is an early-season bloomer with white petticoat flowers and rushlike leaves. Zones 6 to 9.

N. cyclamineus (SIK-la-min-ee-us). Size: 3 to 5 inches tall and wide. This whimsical daffodil has a long slender corona and narrow reflexed petals. This species is an important parent for many popular hybrids such as 'Peeping Tom'. Zones 6 to 9.

N. jonquilla (jon-QUILL-a), jonquil. Size: 6 to 12 inches tall and wide. This lovely, fragrant species has clusters of three to six flowers with wide petals and short coronas. The rushlike leaves are deep green and curled. Zones 4 to 9.

N. minor (MY-nor). Size: 5 to 6 inches tall and wide. A small yellow trumpet daffodil with a deep yellow corona. Var.

pumilus plenus ('Rip van Winkle') is a fully double form. Zones 5 to 9.

N. ×odorus (o-DOR-us), Campernelle jonquil. Size: 1 to 12 inches tall and wide. This delicate daffodil bears two to four fragrant flowers with wide petals and a short corona. Zones 4 to 9.

N. poeticus (po-ET-i-kus), poet's narcissus. Size: 1 to 1½ feet tall and wide. This late-blooming fragrant narcissus has wide, flat white petals and a short, soft-yellow corona rimmed in red. Flowers are borne singly. Var. *recurvus,* pheasant's eye, has recurved petals. 'Actaea' is a popular heirloom bulb with 2-inch bright white, red-eyed flowers. Zones 4 to 9.

N. rupicola (ru-PIK-o-la). Size: 5 to 7 inches tall and wide. This diminutive narcissus has bright yellow flowers with a starry corolla and short corona. The leaves are flattened and blue-green in color. Zones 5 to 9.

N. tazetta (ta-ZET-a), paper white narcissus. Size: 1 to 1½ feet tall, 1 foot wide. The fragrant creamy white flowers of this narcissus are carried in clusters of four to eight. The starry corolla surrounds the short pale yellow corona. Zones 6 to 10.

N. triandrus (tri-AN-drus), angel's-tears. Size: 5 to 10 inches long and wide. The nodding flowers of this lovely species have reflexed petals and an inflated, bell-like corona. One to five white, cream, or yellow flowers are carried above blue-green foliage. Zones 4 to 9.

Hybrids

Narcissus hybrids are divided by the American Daffodil Society into 13 groups based on shape and species origin.

Division I. Trumpet Narcissus. Trumpets bear one flower per stem with perianth segments as long or longer than the corona. Flowers may be yellow, white, or bicolor. 'Beersheba' has delicate white flowers. 'Cantatrice' has creamy white flowers. 'King

One of the first daffodils to bloom in spring is *Narcissus* 'Tête à Tête'. The nodding flower clusters open in early spring, when they are often covered by late snow.

Alfred' has large yellow flowers. 'Mount Hood' is an old-fashioned favorite that opens cream and fades to white. 'Rijnveld's Early Sensation' is the first of the daffodils to bloom in winter and has yellow flowers. 'Spellbinder' is pale yellow with a corona that fades to white. 'Unsurpassable' has huge bright yellow flowers with golden yellow coronas.

Division II. Large-Cupped Narcissus. Large-cupped daffodils have one flower per stem with the perianth segments more than two-thirds as long as the corona. Flowers are yellow, white, or bicolor. 'Ambergate' is yellow with an orange corona. 'Carlton' has bright yellow flowers. 'Flower Record' is white with a yellow corona. 'Ice Follies' has a white corolla and a yellow corona that fades to pale yellow. 'Precocious' is white with a wide-open, frilly coral cup. 'Salome' has a white corolla and an apricot corona. 'Sun Chariot' is yellow with a yellow-and-orange corona.

Division III. Small-Cupped Narcissus. Small-cupped daffodils have one flower per stem with the corona not more than one-third the length of the perianth segments. 'Barrett Browning' is white with an orange corona. 'Birma' has yellow flowers with an orange corona. 'Mint Julip' is white with a green corona. 'Pamona' is white with a bicolor yellow-and-red-orange corona.

Division IV. Double Narcissus. This group includes all double-flowered hybrids. 'Cheerfulness' is creamy white and yellow. 'Exotic Beauty' is unique with white petals and a double pink, trumpet-shaped corona. 'Flower Drift' has white flowers with white, yellow, and orange centers. 'Golden Ducat' has bright golden yellow flowers. 'Mary Copeland' is white with a white-and-red-orange center. 'White Lion' is white with a white-and-pale-yellow center.

Division V. Triandrus Narcissus. This hybrid group has the nodding clustered flowers of N. *triandrus* in white or yellow. 'April Tears' has 1-inch yellow flowers. 'Hawera' has small yellow flowers. 'Katie Heath' is white with a pink cup. 'Lemon Drop' has 2-inch, two-tone yellow flowers. 'Petrel' has dainty, pure white flowers. 'Thalia' has starry, 2-inch white flowers.

Division VI. Cyclamineus Narcissus. This hybrid group has slightly nodding flowers with medium to long coronas and reflexed perianth segments reminiscent of N. *cyclamineus*. 'February Gold' has golden yellow flowers. 'Foundling' is white with a coral corona. 'Jack Snipe' has a white corolla and a short yellow corona. 'Jetfire' is yellow with an orange corona. 'Peeping Tom' has bright yellow flowers with long coronas and reflexed perianth segments.

Division VII. Jonquilla Narcissus. The rushlike foliage and clustered, fragrant, flat flowers of N. *jonquilla* are evident in these hybrids. 'Baby Moon' has small yellow flowers. 'Kedron' is yellow with an orange corona. 'Pappy George' is golden yellow with an orange corona. 'Quail' is an excellent brassy yellow. 'Sundial' has pale yellow flowers. 'Trevithian' has lemon yellow flowers.

Division VIII. Tazetta Narcissus. These hybrids have clustered, fragrant flowers with characteristics of *N. tazetta*. 'Avalanche' is white with 15 to 20 flowers per cluster. 'Geranium' is white with an orange corona. 'Minnow' has small, lemon yellow flowers with golden yellow coronas. 'Scarlet Gem' is pale yellow with an orange corona. Cultivars sold as "paperwhites" are hardy in Zones 8 to 10 only.

Division IX. Poeticus Narcissus. The poets are fragrant hybrids with flat flowers and tiny coronas. 'Cantabile' has pale green flowers with a red-edged corona. 'Felindre' has large flowers with flared coronas with broad red rims.

Division X. Bulbocodium Narcissus. Reserved for hybrids of *N. bulbocodium*. 'Kenellis' is a cream-colored charmer with a starry corolla and a central megaphone corona.

Division XI. Split Corona Narcissus. These hybrids have coronas that are divided and petal-like, creating a semidouble effect. Unique and beautiful. 'Colblanc' is pure white with a green eye. 'Lemon Beauty' has a crisp white corolla and a yellow corona. 'Orangery' is white with a tangerine corona. 'Paradise Island' is cream and salmon.

Division XII. Other Narcissus. This group includes hybrids that do not fit elsewhere. 'Tête-à-Tête' is a miniature with one to three small yellow flowers per stem.

Division XIII. Distinguished solely by botanical name. Includes species and wild forms as listed above.

How to Grow

Plant daffodils in moist, well-drained, humus-rich soil in full sun or light shade. The foliage emerges early in the season and disappears by June. Sun is essential while the plants are actively growing to enable bulbs to store enough energy for next year's growth and flowers. As foliage yellows, sun is not important. Do not remove or mow over foliage until it is fully yellowed.

Plant daffodil bulbs from August through November into soil enriched with humus or a low-nitrogen, high-potassium fertilizer such as bonemeal. Excess nitrogen encourages lush foliage at the expense of flowers. Daffodils require a neutral to slightly acid soil for best growth. Add ground limestone according to label directions to raise the pH of acid soils. Place the top of the bulb 4 to 6 inches below the soil surface, depending on bulb size. Generally, plant them two to three times as deep as the bulbs are long. Space the larger hybrids 3 to 10 inches apart. The larger spacing is for bulbs that will stay down for many years. An annual topdressing of bonemeal or other bulb fertilizer can be made in spring.

Bulbs increase to form tight clumps that begin to lose vigor and cease flowering and that may exhaust nutrients in the soil. Lift bulbs as the foliage yellows. Cure bulbs in a dry, cool place for 3 months. Replant the largest bulbs in August or September into amended soil.

Some species daffodils need special treatment. *N. cyclamineus* needs moist, acid soil that bakes dry in summer. Other species must also be allowed to become dry in summer. Plant small bulbs only 1 to 4 inches deep, depending on size. Order species bulbs early and plant them immediately. They should not remain out of the ground for long. Many species bulbs are collected from the wild. Do not buy species unless the dealer can assure you beyond doubt that the bulbs are propagated. Many species are endangered because of overcollecting, especially *N. triandrus*.

Landscape Uses

Use generous groups of daffodils with flowering shrubs or in mixed plantings with shrubs and perennials. Naturalize them in rough grass in a meadow or lawn. Combine larger hybrids with spring perennials such as hellebores (*Helleborus*), bleeding hearts (*Dicentra*), Virginia bluebells (*Mertensia virginica*), wild blue phlox (*Phlox divaricata*), and perennial candytuft (*Iberis sempervirens*). Tulips, crocuses, and snowdrops also combine beautifully. Use species and smaller hybrids in rock gardens or with early

Rounded flowers with flattened faces make the miniature Jonquilla daffodil (*Narcissus* 'Sundial') a gem for the late- to midspring garden. The sweet-scented flowers are borne in pairs of triads.

bloomers such as wood anemone (*Anemone nemorosa*), spring beauty (*Claytonia virginica*), bloodroot (*Sanguinaria canadensis*), and Dutchman's breeches (*Dicentra cucullaria*).

NEPETA

NEP-e-ta • Lamiaceae, Mint Family

The billowing blue clouds of catmint create a quintessential early-summer garden scene. They are prized for their extended bloom season, floriferous nature, and easy culture. The soft gray-green opposite leaves clothe wiry stems crowned with tiered clusters of violet to lavender blue flowers. Each tubular flower has two upper and three lower lobes. The plants grow from a woody base with fibrous roots.

NEPETA

Common Names:
Catmint, nepeta

Bloom Time:
Spring and early summer bloom

Planting Requirements:
Full sun to light shade

The tall spikes of showy flowers set Siberian catmint (*Nepeta siberica*) heads above the rest. In full bloom the plants are simply stunning: a profusion of deep sky blue bloom. Lance-shaped, deep green leaves are paired up the thick, strong stems.

Nepeta clarkei (KLARK-ee-ee), Clark's catmint. Size: 2 to 3 feet tall and wide. This is a real showstopper, with full-flowered spikes of lovely bicolor flowers. Substantial, erect stems bear terminal clusters of large blue flowers with white lips that make a bigger show than more subtle trailing catmints. USDA Plant Hardiness Zones 5 to 9.

N. ×faassenii (fah-SEN-ee-ee), blue catmint. Size: 1½ to 2 feet tall and wide. Blue catmint has erect stems, the upper third of which are densely clothed with blue-violet flowers. This sterile hybrid is a cross between *N. mussinii* and *N. nepetella*. Listed cultivars may belong here, or may be complex hybrids involving additional species. 'Blue Wonder' is more compact with deeper blue flowers. 'Dropmore' has large lavender-blue flowers on 2-foot clumps. 'Joanna Reid' has sturdy upright stems with large blue-violet flowers. 'Six Hills Giant' grows to 3 feet, with 1-foot clusters of deep violet flowers. "White Wonder' is similar with white flowers. Zones 4 to 8.

N. govaniana (go-van-e-AH-na), yellow catmint. Size: 2 to 3 feet tall and wide. This species is an anomaly, with erect stems bearing loose, branched clusters of canary yellow flowers in midsummer. The broad, lance-shaped green foliage is only faintly scented, another departure from the usual catmint qualities. Zones 5 to 9.

N. racemosa (rac-e-MO-sa), Persian catmint. Size: 2 to 2½ feet tall and wide. Persian catmint is an upright, mounded plant with wiry stems and terminal clusters of soft lavender-blue flowers. 'Snowflake' is white-flowered. 'Walker's Low' is the best of the large selections, with erect stems that never flop and rich blue-violet flowers. *N. grandiflora* 'Dawn to Dusk' has pink flowers on 3-foot stems. Zones 3 to 8.

N. siberica (si-BEER-i-ka), Siberian catmint. Size: 3 to 4 feet tall, 2 to 3 feet wide. The tall spikes of showy blue flowers sit heads above the rest. In full bloom, the plants are simply stunning, a profusion of deep sky blue bloom. Lance-shaped, deep green leaves are paired up thick, strong stems. 'Souvenir d'Andre Chaudron' has large deep blue flowers on compact plants to 3 feet tall. Zones 3 to 8.

How to Grow

Plant catmints in average, sandy or loamy, well-drained soil in full sun or light shade. Plants bloom for 4 to 6 weeks in late spring and early summer. After flowering, shear plants back to half or two-thirds their size, depending on how sprawling they are. They will quickly produce attractive new foliage and will often rebloom in cooler zones. Propagate by 3-inch tip cuttings in early summer. Stems often root as they sprawl and are easily transplanted.

Landscape Uses

Catmints are lovely and versatile plants for edging beds or for planting along walks or stairs. Mix them with other plants that prefer lean soil, such as evening primroses (*Oenothera*), winecups (*Callirhoe*), yarrows (*Achillea*), sages (*Salvia*), and verbenas. In richer soil, plant them with cranesbills (*Geranium*), irises, garden phlox (*Phlox paniculata*), and peonies (*Paeonia*).

O

OENOTHERA

ee-no-THE-ra • Onagraceae, Evening Primrose Family

Evening primroses have lovely saucer-shaped flowers with four wide, overlapping petals and a prominent stigma (female pollen receptor) with divergent lobes. The weakly upright, often succulent stems are covered in lance-shaped foliage and crowned with elongated terminal clusters of flowers. Each flower lasts but a day, often fading in early afternoon. The plants grow from a thick taproot or fibrous roots.

OENOTHERA

Common Name:
Evening primrose

Bloom Time:
Spring and summer bloom

Planting Requirements:
Full sun

Oenothera caespitosa (say-spi-TOE-sa), tufted evening primrose. Size: 4 to 8 inches tall, 8 to 12 inches wide. This low, tufted plant has spreading stems with deep green lance-shaped leaves, and flowers that open white in afternoon and fade to pink. USDA Plant Hardiness Zones 4 to 7.

O. fruticosa (froo-ti-KO-sa), sundrops. Size: 1½ to 2 feet tall and wide. Sundrops are day-flowering plants with leafy, upright stems and bright yellow flowers that open from red-tinged buds. This species contains plants formerly classified as *O. tetragona*. 'Cold Crick' is the best of the sundrops, with small but profuse flowers set all season on clump-forming plants. 'Fireworks' grows 18 inches tall and has 2-inch flowers and reddish stems. 'Sonnenwende' is clear yellow and compact. 'Yellow River' grows to 2 feet tall and has 2-inch bright yellow flowers. Zones 4 to 8.

O. macrocarpa (mac-ro-CARP-a) (*missouriensis*), Ozark sundrops. Size: 6 to 12 inches tall, 12 to 24 inches wide. This showy species has large, lemon yellow flowers and thick, linear light green leaves. Ssp. *fremontii* and *incana* have gorgeous silvery leaves and paler yellow flowers. 'Greencourt Lemon' has 2- to 2½-inch soft sulfur yellow flowers. 'Lemon Silver' has large flowers and silver leaves. Zones 4 to 8.

O. speciosa (spe-see-O-sa), showy evening primrose. Size: 1 to 2 feet tall, 2 to 3 feet wide. This sprawling plant produces a profusion of fragrant, soft pink flowers on wiry stems. Plants spread by creeping roots and may be invasive. 'Alba' is white-flowered. 'Rosea' has rose-pink flowers. *O. berlandieri*, Mexican evening primrose, is similar, with rose-pink flowers. 'Siskiyou' is rich rose. 'Woodside White' opens white and fades to pink. Zones 5 to 8.

How to Grow

Evening primroses are plants of meadows, roadsides, and prairies. Plant them in average

Plant drought-tolerant sundrops (*Oenothera fruticosa* 'Fireworks') in a dry, sunny spot. The bright yellow flowers open from tear-shaped red buds.

to rich, well-drained soil in full sun or light shade. They spread by slow creeping root-stocks (except *O. speciosa*) to form dense clumps. They are tough, drought-tolerant plants of easy culture. Divide rosettes in early spring or after flowering in late summer. *O. speciosa* spreads rapidly in rich soil and may need to be rogued out each season.

Landscape Uses

In perennial gardens, combine tall sundrops with calamints (*Calamintha*), garden phlox (*Phlox paniculata*), cranesbills (*Geranium*), bellflowers (*Campanula*), and false indigos (*Baptisia*). Plant small spreading species such as *O. macrocarpa* and *O. speciosa* with catmints (*Nepeta*), baby's-breaths (*Gypsophila*), and irises. In the wild garden, plant them with yarrows (*Achillea*), black-eyed Susans (*Rudbeckia*), coneflowers (*Echinacea*), and ornamental grasses. Plant *O. caespitosa* in a sunny rock or alpine garden.

OMPHALODES

omf-a-LO-deez • Boraginaceae, Borage Family

The pure gentian blue flowers of this perennial add a touch of the twilight sky to the spring garden. Small, five-petaled flowers with rounded petals are held in open clusters above the broadly lance-shaped leaves. Navel seed grows best where summer nights are cool. Plants spread by creeping stems from fibrous-rooted crowns to form broad, floriferous clumps.

OMPHALODES
Common Names:
  Naval seed, blue-eyed Mary
Bloom Time:
  Spring bloom
Planting Requirements:
  Sun to partial shade

The true blue flowers of blue-eyed Mary (*Omphalodes verna*) are accented by quilted leaves that look tidy all summer in the shaded garden.

Omphalodes cappadocica (kap-pa-doe-SEE-ka), naval seed. Size: 8 to 12 inches tall, 2 to 3 feet wide. Broad leaves have prominent veins and flower spikes are held above the foliage. 'Cherry In-

gram' is a popular selection with medium blue flowers. 'Joy Skies' has sky blue flowers. 'Parisian Skies' is deep gentian blue. 'Starry Eyes' has indigo flowers outlined in white. USDA Plant Hardiness Zones 6 to 8.

O. verna (VER-na), blue-eyed Mary. Size: 4 to 8 inches tall, 12 inches wide. A delicate species with medium blue flowers over narrowly oval leaves. Hardier and easier to grow in hot regions. Zones 4 to 9.

How to Grow

Plant in rich, evenly moist soil in sun or partial shade. In warm zones, light shade is preferred. Plants dislike high summer temperatures and humidity. Clumps increase from creeping stems to form broad, dense clumps. Divide in early spring as growth starts or after flowering.

Landscape Uses

Choose naval seed as a groundcover under flowering shrubs or in shaded borders with bleeding hearts (*Dicentra*), Solomon's seals (*Polygonatum*), fairy wings (*Epimedium*), wood anemone (*Anemone nemorosa*), and ferns. Contrast the blue flowers with brilliant yellow hostas like 'Piedmont Gold'.

OPUNTIA

o-PUN-tee-a • Cactaceae, Cactus Family

Most cacti belong in the desert. Not Eastern prickly pear. This cactus grows in any well-drained site in sand or clay, and opens its gorgeous yellow flowers in early to mid-summer. Like all cacti, the spines can be painful, so wear gloves when making contact with the beaver-tail pads. Plants may shrivel in the winter, but they soon plump up when spring arrives.

OPUNTIA

Common Name:
Prickly pear

Bloom Time:
Early summer bloom

Planting Requirements:
Full sun

Opuntia humifusa (hew-mi-FEW-sa) (*compressa*), prickly pear. Size: 4 to 6 inches tall, 12 to 24 inches wide. This temperate-climate cactus has oval, flattened stems called pads that are armed with fierce, short spines. The lovely lemon yellow flowers are carried in rows along the tops of the pads. A green or purple fruit forms after flowering. Plants spread by rooting pads to form wide clumps. Roots are fibrous. USDA Plant Hardiness Zones 4 to 9.

How to Grow

Plant prickly pears in average, sandy or loamy soil in full sun. Take care to avoid sharp spines while setting out plants. Clumps spread steadily and require little or no care once established. Leaves and debris get caught within clumps and are the devil to remove. Propagate by removing pads and covering their bases with moist sand. They root quickly.

For sandy seaside gardens or dry sunny banks, you can't beat the bright yellow flowers of prickly pear cactus (*Opuntia humifusa*) alone or intermingled with creeping junipers.

Landscape Uses

Prickly pears grow in meadows, along rocky roadsides, and on dunes. Plant them with drought-tolerant perennials such as autumn sage (*Salvia greggii*), winecups (*Callirhoe*), butterfly weed (*Asclepias tuberosa*), yarrows (*Achillea*), stonecrops (*Sedum*), cushion spurge (*Euphorbia polychroma*), sundrops (*Oenothera*), and catmints (*Nepeta*). In the wild garden or seaside garden, plant them with ornamental grasses and other wildflowers such as blanket flowers (*Gaillardia*), asters, goldenrods (*Solidago*), and black-eyed Susans (*Rudbeckia*).

OSMUNDA

os-MUN-da • Osmundaceae, Flowering Fern Family

Flowering ferns are robust plants of unique beauty. They are dubbed *flowering fern* for their showy, spore-bearing pinnae that look like flower buds. The fertile pinnae are carried on the sterile fronds along with the nonfruiting pinnae in some species. The most dramatic is the cinnamon fern, which bears its spores on separate fertile fronds in the center of the clump. Plants grow from wiry, fibrous rhizomes that become huge with age.

OSMUNDA

Common Name:
Flowering fern

Bloom Time:
Foliage plant

Planting Requirements:
Sun or shade

Osmunda cinnamomea (sin-a-mo-MEE-a), cinnamon fern. Size: 3 to 5 feet tall and wide. Cinnamon fern is a statuesque plant with erect clusters of emerging fiddleheads clothed in tawny hairs. From the center of the clump arise congested, deep green fertile fronds that turn bright cinnamon-brown as they mature, hence the common name. Lustrous sterile fronds form a tall arching vase. USDA Plant Hardiness Zones 3 to 10.

O. claytoniana (clay-ton-ee-AH-na), interrupted fern, Clayton's fern. Size: 3 to 4 feet tall and wide. This fern is similar in appearance to cinnamon fern, but the pinnae are broader and pale green in color. The fertile fronds are distinctly different. They bear both sterile and fertile pinnae on the same frond. The congested, ephemeral fertile pinnae occur halfway up the frond, thus creating an "interruption" in the frond when they fall off in summer. Zones 3 to 8.

O. regalis (re-GAL-is), royal fern. Size: 4 to 6 feet tall, 3 to 5 feet wide. This distinctive fern produces congested clusters of beadlike sori at the tips of the fronds, giving the impression of a flower. The sterile pinnae are uncharacteristic and resemble leafy stems. The fronds emerge pale pink in a vase-shaped cluster. As fronds mature, the stipe turns dark and the pinnae turn deep sea green. Var. *regalis* 'Purpurascens' is a European variety with purple new growth, very dark stipes, and large, plumelike fertile pinnae. Zones 3 to 10.

How to Grow

Plant flowering ferns in consistently moist to wet, acid, humus-rich soil in sun or shade. All but interrupted fern will grow in standing water. If soil becomes dry, plants will go dormant. All *Osmunda* are slow to establish but are extremely long-lived. Large plants are difficult to transplant due to their huge, clump-forming rhizomes.

Landscape Uses

Use clumps or drifts of flowering ferns in combination with fine-textured ferns, wildflowers, and shrubs. They are perfect for greening up wet areas in combination with sensitive fern (*Onoclea sensibilis*). Plant them as an accent next to a tree or stump where the emerging fiddleheads show off

Wet to constantly moist soil is imperative for success with cinnamon ferns (*Osmunda cinnamomea*). They quickly succumb in dry soil. Plants produce their elegant vases of foliage in sun or shade, accented in spring by rusty fertile fronds.

to good advantage. Interrupted fern prefers a drier site with trilliums, celandine poppies (*Stylophorum*), Virginia bluebell (*Mertensia virginica*), and hellebores.

PACHYSANDRA

pa-ki-SAN-dra • Buxaceae, Boxwood Family

Few groundcovers are as familiar as the spurge, but there is more to the genus than this overused carpet. Pachysandras are succulent plants with leathery stems and evergreen leaves. They form large clumps or extensive groundcovers from creeping stems with succulent roots. The ragged flowers lack petals and are made up of fuzzy stamens. They are carried in dense spikes in spring or summer.

PACHYSANDRA

Common Names:
Pachysandra, spurge

Bloom Time:
Foliage plant with spring bloom

Planting Requirements:
Light to full shade

Pachysandra procumbens (pro-KUM-benz), Allegheny spurge. Size: 6 to 12 inches tall, 12 to 36 inches wide. Allegheny spurge has whorls of satiny, broad, oval

The silver-edged leaves of the variegated Japanese spurge (*Pachysandra terminalis* 'Variegata') add a bit of interest to this uninspiring but serviceable groundcover that grows everywhere, even in dry shade.

leaves with blunt terminal lobes. Unlike Japanese spurge, flowers emerge in the center of leafy clumps in early spring. New foliage emerges bright sea green mottled with pale blotches. In fall, frost brings out deep purple-blue shades in the background with silvery mottling. USDA Plant Hardiness Zones 4 (with protection) to 8.

P. stylosa (sty-LO-sa), Chinese spurge. Size: 6 to 10 inches tall, 1 to 2 feet wide. Broad, quilted black-green leaves with a glossy patina form a tight carpet of unique beauty. Hard to find but worth the effort. *P. axillaris* has narrower leaves and makes an attractive evergreen mat with time. Zones 6 to 9.

P. terminalis (ter-min-AH-lis), Japanese spurge. Size: 6 to 10 inches tall, 2 to 3 feet wide. Familiar to the point of being invisible, this ubiquitous species makes a shiny, evergreen groundcover. The trailing stems are covered with elongated, shallowly lobed leaves clustered at the stem tips.

Ragged white flowers are carried at the stem tips. Zones 4 to 9.

How to Grow

Plant in moist, humus-rich, acid soil in light to full shade. Plants spread slowly at first but form broad, rounded clumps in a few years. Divide clumps in spring before new growth emerges. They root from cuttings taken in an unconventional manner: After new growth hardens in early summer, hold a stem at ground level and yank it firmly upward. You will get a bit of the old stem as well as some new roots. Treat the stem as a cutting until it is well rooted.

Landscape Uses

Plant spurge as a groundcover in tough spots under mature shade trees, flowering trees, and shrubs such as native azaleas, along with ferns and sedges. Combine them with partridge berry (*Mitchella repens*), evergreen wild gingers (*Asarum*), Solomon's seals (*Polygonatum*), trilliums, and Allegheny foamflower (*Tiarella cordifolia*).

PAEONIA

pay-ON-ee-a • Paeoniaceae (Ranunculaceae), Peony Family

Peonies are beloved for their variety of form and color, their exceptional hardiness, and their ease of culture. Peonies have been in cultivation in China and Japan for centuries. Their popularity continues today throughout temperate gardens. Individual plants may live 100 years or more. Far too few species are grown; most garden peonies are hybrids of *Paeonia officinalis* and *P. lactiflora*. Colors range from white, cream, and yellow to pink, rose, and scarlet. Plants are classified by bloom time as early-May-blooming (April in the South), mid-May-blooming, and late-May-blooming.

PAEONIA

Common Name:
Peony

Bloom Time:
Spring and early summer bloom

Planting Requirements:
Full sun or light shade

Plants are also grouped by the shape of their flowers into four categories. Single peonies have a ring of five or more petals with a central ring of stamens (male reproductive structures). Japanese peonies have a ring of petals around a central cluster of modified stamens that are narrow and flat and bear no pollen. (Anemone-flowered peonies are similar, but the modified stamens are more petal-like.) Semidouble peonies have several rings of petals

Hybrid peonies such as *Paeonia* 'Krinkled White' take up to 3 years to reach their full flowering potential. Once established, they are long-lived and produce mounds of colorful flowers.

around visible stamens. Double peonies have many concentric rings of petals and no visible stamens.

Paeonia japonica (ja-PON-i-ka), Japanese peony. Size: 1 to 2 feet tall and wide. A woodland species with creamy white chalices in spring above gray-green leaves. The decorative seedpods split to reveal the velvety red lining with blue-black seeds. USDA Plant Hardiness Zones 4 to 9.

P. lactiflora (lak-ti-FLO-ra), Chinese peony. Size: 1½ to 3 feet tall, 2 to 3 feet wide. This late-blooming species has single white or pink flowers. Many cultivars and hybrids have been named. 'Doreen' is a midseason

rose-pink anemone. 'Duchess de Nemours' is an early white double. 'Festiva Maxima' is an early white double flecked with red. 'Gay Paree' is a midseason cerise-and-white Japanese. 'Karl Rosenfield' is a midseason, dark crimson double. 'Mons. Jules Elie' is an early rose-pink double. 'Nippon Beauty' is a late garnet-red Japanese. 'Paula Fay' is an early pink semidouble. 'Red Charm' is an early red double. 'Sara Bernhardt' is a midseason fragrant pink double. 'Sea Shell' is a midseason pink single. Zones 2 to 8.

P. mlokosewitschii (mlo-ko-sa-VICH-ee-ee), Molly the witch. Size: 2 to 3 feet tall and wide. This compact, bushy peony has creamy yellow eight-petaled, rounded flowers and blue-green leaves tinted with red in spring. Zones 5 to 8.

P. obovata (ob-o-VATE-a), woodland peony. Size: 2 to 3 feet tall and wide. A woodland species with tall stems holding sea green foliage and pink flowers above the foliage. Blooms in late spring. Zones 4 to 9.

P. officinalis (o-fis-i-NA-lis), common peony. Size: 1½ to 2 feet tall and wide. The common peony is seen most often in gardens in its fully double, shell pink form, 'Rosea Superba' (also called the Memorial Day peony). Flowers may also be single; several cultivars are readily available. 'Lobata' is a midseason, salmon-orange single. 'Mutabilis Plena' is an early- to midseason rose-pink with huge double flowers. 'Rubra Plena' is an early to midseason red double also called a Memorial Day peony. Zones 3 to 8.

P. suffruticosa (suf-froo-ti-KO-sa), tree peony. Size: 3 to 5 feet tall, 3 to 4 feet wide. Tree peonies are not trees but shrubs with woody, sparsely branching stems that grow from thick roots. The leaves and flowers are produced each season on new growth. Huge crepe paper flowers are white or rose-pink. Many cultivars of exceptional garden merit have been developed. 'Age of Gold' has fragrant semidouble flowers with visible stamens. 'Godaishu' ('Five Continents') has 10-inch semidouble pure white flowers. 'Hanadaijin' ('Minister of Flowers') has double deep purple flowers. 'Kamada-nishiki' ('Kamada Brocade') is a fragrant semidouble with lilac-purple flowers. 'Kao' ('King of Flowers') has semidouble brilliant red flowers. 'Yae-sakura' ('Cherry Two Two') has double cherry red flowers with lighter margins to the petals.

P. tenuifolia (ten-u-i-FO-lee-a), fern leaf peony. Size: 1 to 1½ feet tall, 1 to 2 feet wide. This delicate peony has finely divided, fan-shaped leaves with narrow leaflets. Ruby red spring flowers are perched on the top of the stems, surrounded by the leaves. 'Rubra Plena' has deep red double flowers. Zones 5 to 8.

Other species peonies: Wild forms are at last becoming available, and the many diverse species offer early bloom, excellent foliage, and decorative seedheads. *P. anomala* has deeply cut foliage and raspberry red flowers. *P. mascula* has many forms, most with pink to rose flowers. *P. perigrina* has quilted leaves and scarlet flowers. *P. veitchii* is compact, with cut leaves and deep rose flowers. Zones 3 to 8.

How to Grow

Peonies require moist, loamy, humus-rich soil in full sun or light shade. Plant the thick, fleshy roots of herbaceous peonies in September or October. Excavate a hole 8 to 10 inches deep in well-prepared rich soil. Place the eyes (buds for next year) no more than 2 inches below the soil surface. If fertilizer is necessary, incorporate manure or other organics into the soil below the root zone. Plant rootstocks at least 3 feet from other plants to allow for their eventual full spread. Mulch plants the first winter to

Single-flowered peonies such as glowing red *Paeonia* 'America' generally have self-supporting stems that stand up to wind and rain without staking. Double-flowered hybrids are generally top-heavy and benefit from the support of a hoop or stake.

keep them from heaving. In areas where winter temperatures dip consistently below zero and snow cover is unpredictable, an annual winter mulch is beneficial. Taller selections and most doubles usually need staking to keep their faces out of the mud. Nurseries sell circular hoops for this purpose. Peonies bloom for only 1 to 2 weeks, but by planting early, mid-, and late-season varieties you can have blooms for up to 6 weeks. In warm zones, shade from afternoon sun will prolong flowering and help keep colors from fading.

After flowering, the deep green foliage remains attractive all season. In fall, cut stems to the ground. Plants may grow undisturbed for years, but if rootstocks get overcrowded or soil gets impoverished, bloom may trail off. Lift plants in late summer, wash off soil, and cut roots into sections with four or five eyes (buds). Use a sharp knife and make clean cuts. Replant divisions into well-prepared soil. Occasionally peonies fail to bloom. The American Peony Society suggests the following reasons for poor garden performance.

- Plants not blooming size
- Planted more than 1 to 2 inches deep
- Clumps need dividing
- Buds killed by winter cold
- Buds killed by disease or insects. Botrytis, a bacterial disease, may cause buds to abort, may wilt and kill stems, or may even rot roots. Destroy badly infected plants, or spray leaves and stems with fungicide. Thrips, tiny insects that hide under leaves and in bud scales, may cause deformed stems and blasted buds. Spray with insecticidal soap every 3 days for 2 weeks.
- Plants need fertilizer. Use manure or a high-potassium fertilizer such as greensand.
- Soil is too dry; plants need evenly moist soil
- Not enough sun; plants need 6 to 8 hours of full sun

Tree peonies are equally easy to grow. Plant potted divisions in well-prepared, neutral to slightly acid, humus-rich soil in full sun or partial shade. Plants are often grafted, so be sure to plant them with the graft union 6 to 12 inches below the soil. This is especially important in cooler zones where plants should be encouraged to form their own roots. Winter protection is important north of Zone 6 to ensure that stems are not damaged. Prune plants as needed to encourage good form. If suckers arise from rootstocks, remove them. Plant woodland species in light to partial shade in humus-rich soil. They thrive for years without disturbance and in time make wide, multiflowered clumps.

Landscape Uses

Peonies are prized for their glorious flowers and excellent foliage. Plan combinations that utilize their beauty and grace throughout the season. Plant them with minor bulbs and forget-me-nots (*Myosotis*) for early spring when the ruby red shoots are just emerging. The expanding foliage will shroud declining bulb foliage. Combine flowers with spring and early-summer perennials such as Siberian iris (*Iris sibirica*), foxgloves (*Digitalis*), columbines (*Aquilegia*), cranesbills (*Geranium*), astilbes (*Astilbe* ×*arendsii* and others), and ground clematis (*Clematis recta*). In summer and fall, the dark green foliage in shrubby mounds complements fine-textured foliage and myriad colorful perennials, such as garden phlox (*Phlox paniculata*), yarrows (*Achillea*), white gaura (*Gaura lindheimeri*), baby's-breath (*Gypsophila paniculata*), and ornamental grasses. Combine woodland species with hellebores, windflowers (*Anemone*), trilliums, sedges (*Carex*), and ferns. Choose tree peonies for a shrub border or plant them with fine textures and small flowers.

PANICUM

PAH-ni-kum • Poaceae, Grass Family

The airy, beaded inflorescences of switchgrass are held above the gracefully arching foliage on thin but stiff, leafy stalks. Spring foliage may be red tinged, and in autumn plants turn rich russet. The inflorescences bear beadlike seeds that are prized for their beauty by gardeners, and for food by wildlife. Plants grow from short, fibrous-rooted crowns.

PANICUM

Common Name:
Switchgrass

Bloom Time:
Summer bloom

Planting Requirements:
Sun

Panicum virgatum (ver-GAY-tum), switchgrass. Size: 3 to 8 feet tall, 4 to 5 feet wide. This variable species with upright, densely clumping stems exploits multiple habitats in the wild, from sandy dunes to wetland margins. As a result, cultivars vary in size and form. 'Cloud Nine' grows to 7 feet with huge, diaphanous heads and gray-green leaves on stems that may flop in wind and rain. 'Dallas Blues' has blue foliage and pink flowers on 5-foot stems. 'Haense Herns' is upright with red tinged foliage. 'Northwind' has upright, 5-foot stems clothed in wide, deep green leaves. 'Prairie Sky' has the bluest foliage, but stems may flop. 'Shenandoah' reaches 4 feet with burgundy fall color. USDA Plant Hardiness Zones 3 to 9.

P. amarum (am-ARE-um), sand switchgrass. Size: 2 to 3 feet tall, 3 to 4 feet wide. A graceful, arching grass with blue-green leaves and densely branched, drooping inflorescences. 'Dewey Blue' is a beautiful selection with dusty blue foliage. Zones 5 to 9.

How to Grow

Plant in average to rich, moist soil in full sun. Plants are widely adaptable to drought and wet soil. Established plants form dense, wiry clumps that slowly creep outward. In time, the center dies out. Dig clumps, discard the dead center, and replant in fresh soil.

Landscape Uses

Use switchgrass as a specimen in the garden or in a container. Different cultivars have different forms, from strictly upright to full and blowsy. Choose the form that complements its companions. Billowing selections soften walls and provide a hazy backdrop for perennials. Upright 'Heavy Metal' makes a handsome exclamation flanking an entrance.

The strictly upright, fully flop-proof stems of 'Heavy Metal' switchgrass (*Panicum virgatum* 'Heavy Metal') add excitement to any border. The blue-gray foliage and airy plumes are sure to please.

PAPAVER

pa-PAH-ver • Papaveraceae, Poppy Family

Poppies are delightful flowers with crepe-paper petals surrounding a ring of dark stamens and a central knot that will ultimately become a seedpod. The diaphanous flowers are carried singly atop stout stems and open from nodding buds. Plants produce clumps of broadly lance-shaped, oval or lobed foliage from thick, deep taproots. Leaves have toothed margins and may be smooth and waxy or rough and hairy. The juice of the plants is milky.

PAPAVER

Common Name:
  Poppy

Bloom Time:
  Spring and early summer bloom

Planting Requirements:
  Full sun

Papaver nudicaule (new-di-KAW-lee), Iceland poppy. Size: 1 to 1½ feet tall, 1 foot wide. This short-lived perennial poppy has basal clumps of gray-green, lobed leaves and blousy pink, salmon, orange, or white flowers in spring. 'Wonderland' hybrids are available in mixed colors of 3-inch flowers. USDA Plant Hardiness Zones 2 to 7.

P. orientale (o-ree-en-TAH-lee), Oriental poppy. Size: 2 to 3 feet tall and wide. Oriental poppies are among the showiest perennials in the early summer garden. The flowers boast black spots at the bases of the petals and a central ring of fuzzy black stamens. The somewhat rank, hairy, lobed foliage disappears after flowering as plants go dormant. 'Allegro' is a compact 18-inch grower with scarlet flowers. 'Aslahan' is creamy white fading to salmon edges with showy purple blotches at the center. 'Beauty of Livermore' has deep red flowers on 3-foot stems. 'Bonfire' is a widely sold cultivar with large brilliant red flowers. 'Brilliant' is the ubiquitous cultivar with fiery red flowers. 'Degas' is a late-blooming salmon with dark spots. 'Helen Elizabeth' has pale salmon-pink unspotted flowers. 'Patty's Plum' is smoky violet-rose. 'Princess Victoria Louise' has bright salmon-pink flowers. 'Snow Queen' is pure white with prominent black spots. 'Watermelon' is watermelon pink. Zones 2 to 7.

How to Grow

Oriental poppies are tough, long-lived plants. Give them average to rich, well-drained soil in full sun. In warmer zones, afternoon shade is advisable. Once established, poppies grow to fill 2 to 3 square feet of garden space. Huge flowers are carried for several weeks, then plants begin to fade and quickly disappear altogether. Their disappearance leaves large gaps in the garden, which must be artfully filled by neighboring foliage and flowers. When temperatures moderate in late summer, plants produce a new rosette of foliage. This is the time to divide overgrown clumps, a task usually required every 5 or 6 years. Lifted clumps invariably leave behind a few broken roots, which will form new plants. To propagate, remove pencil-size pieces of roots while you are dividing clumps, and root them in moist sand. New

Oriental poppies such as *Papaver orientale* 'White King' are extremely drought- and heat-tolerant. They grow from stout taproots that enable them to store water for dry periods.

plants develop quickly and can be planted out next spring.

Landscape Uses

Poppies are bold plants that have an arresting presence when in flower but disappear soon thereafter. Plant them with fine-textured perennials such as catmints (*Nepeta*), speedwells (*Veronica*), cranesbills (*Geranium*), bowman's root (*Porteranthus trifoliatus*), bellflowers (*Campanula*), ornamental grasses, and green mounds of false indigos (*Baptisia*) or blue stars (*Amsonia*). Use spreading plants such as calamints (*Calamintha*), asters, and other bushy, late-blooming plants to fill the inevitable border gaps.

PATRINIA

pa-TRIN-ee-a • Valerianacea, Valerian Family

Patrinia has no generally accepted common name, but many have been proposed, including Elvis eyes, lemon lollapalooza, giraffe's knees, and golden lace. These underutilized perennials have upright stems with bold, pinnately divided leaves arranged in basal rosettes, with leaves reduced in size as they ascend the stems. The flowers are borne in round umbels. Plants grow from stout branching taproots.

PATRINIA

Common Name:
Patrinia

Bloom Time:
Late summer and fall bloom

Planting Requirements:
Full sun or light shade

Patrinia gibbosa (gib-BOW-sah), yellow patrinia. Size: 1 to 2 feet tall and wide. Attractive divided leaves with shiny, rounded, toothed terminal leaflets set off stems that arch outward to form a vase crowned with open clusters of yellow flowers in summer. USDA Plant Hardiness Zones 4 to 9.

P. scabiosifolia (scab-i-o-si-FO-lee-a), lemon lollapalooza. Size: 3 to 6 feet tall, 2 to 3 feet wide. A tall, stately plant with branching stems crowned with a profusion of small, yellow-flowered umbels in late summer. 'Nagoya' is a shorter selection originating in Japan. Zones 4 to 9.

P. villosa (vil-LO-sa), white patrinia. Size: 2 to 2½ feet tall, 2 feet wide. This compact, spreading species has attractive hand-shaped basal leaves and leafy stalks topped in fall with open clusters of white flowers. Zones 5 to 9.

How to Grow

Patrinias are easy to grow in average to rich, moist but well-drained soil in full sun or light shade. Once established, they are long-lived and seldom need division. They bloom from late summer through fall. One drawback is their prolific seeding. Remove flower heads as they fade, or cut bloom stalks down when most flowers have past. Foliage is attractive all season. Propagate from seed sown outdoors, from division in spring, or after flowering. Fresh flowers last for weeks when cut and brought indoors.

Landscape Uses

Choose patrinia for a border, a relaxed cottage garden, or a mass planting with shrubs along a woodland edge. Plant tall patrinias in the middle or at the back of perennial gardens with boltonia (*Boltonia asteroides*), tall asters (*Aster novae-angliae* or *A. tartaricus*), Joe-Pye weeds (*Eupatorium*), ironweeds (*Vernonia*), cannas, sunflowers (*Helianthus*), and ornamental grasses.

Mature specimens of autumn-flowering white patrinia (*Patrinia villosa*) are best placed at the front of a border. Sharply lobed leaves turn rusty red at season's end.

PENNISETUM

pen-ni-SAY-tum • Poaceae, Grass Family

Fountain grass is one of the most popular ornamental grasses. It's prized for its foxtail spikes of fuzzy flowers that are held above the rounded, fountainlike clumps of fine-textured foliage. Plants dry to an attractive russet or taupe in fall, and though flowers may shatter early, foliage still makes a show. Many selections reseed vigorously and may be invasive. Choose tender species to avoid introduction into the wild.

PENNISETUM

Common Name:
Fountain grass

Bloom Time:
Summer bloom

Planting Requirements:
Sun

Though an annual in most of the country, tender fountain grass (*Pennisetum setaceum*) can be planted in the ground or in containers and enjoyed for its elegant foxtail plumes throughout summer and fall.

Pennisetum alopecuroides (a-lo-peck-you-ROY-deez), perennial fountain grass. Size: 1 to 2½ feet tall and wide. This species forms a symmetrical vase of foliage and holds thick, fuzzy plumes above the leaf tips. 'Cassian' has golden fall color and holds its flowers well above the leaves. Less hardy (Zone 6), 'Hamelin' is compact with creamy flowers; a popular selection. 'Little Bunny' grows just 18 inches tall with slender, stiff plumes. 'Moudry' is popular for its full blackish plumes, but it reseeds vigorously and should be avoided. 'Oceanside' is a giant tender hybrid of unknown origin to 10 feet tall. USDA Plant Hardiness Zones 5 to 9.

P. orientale (o-ree-en-TAH-le), fountain grass. Size: 2 to 3 feet tall and wide. A distinctive species with elongated plumes and flowers in tiered clusters. Foliage rises just below the flowers. Plants rarely self-sow. 'Karley Rose' has rose plumes. 'Tall Tails' is a large, full-bodied selection with tan plumes to 6 feet tall. Zones 6 to 10.

P. setaceum (se-TAY-see-um), tender fountain grass. Size: 4 to 5 feet tall and wide. Noted for its rosy, long plumes held well above the vase of foliage. 'Rubrum' has red foliage and plumes. 'Burgundy Giant' is a hybrid with wide, deep red leaves and huge rosy plumes on 6-foot stems. Similar *P. villosum* has short, fuzzy white plumes on weak stems. Zones 9 to 10.

How to Grow

Fountain grass is easy to grow in average to rich, moist but well-drained soil in full sun or light shade. Plants form large clumps rapidly that keep their form well as they age. In time, the center of the clump will die out, and rejuvenation is necessary. Self-sown seedlings may be plentiful.

Landscape Uses

Pennisetum is stunning in mass plantings or lining a walkway, as well as singly as an accent. Use plants among dwarf and creeping evergreens to add height and seasonal color. In beds, surround the full crowns with low plants that won't compete for attention.

PENSTEMON

PEN-ste-mon • Scrophulariaceae, Figwort Family

Beardtongues produce slender, unbranched spikes with tiers of inflated, irregularly shaped flowers with two upper and three lower lips. Flowers vary in color from white to pink, rose, lavender, and violet. Lush rosettes of evergreen leaves form wide patches that make attractive groundcovers when the plants are not in bloom. Clumps grow from fibrous roots. Many species are cultivated, but few succeed in eastern gardens, largely because gardeners choose species native to the western mountains that cook in the heat and rot in the humidity and dampness of midwestern and eastern gardens. Many excellent eastern natives and other adaptable species are available.

PENSTEMON

Common Names:
Beardtongue, penstemon

Bloom Time:
Spring and summer bloom

Planting Requirements:
Full sun or light shade

Penstemon albidus (AL-bi-dus), white-flowered penstemon. Size: 6 to 14 inches tall and wide. This prairie native has compact flowerstalks and small white flowers with flat faces. USDA Plant Hardiness Zones 3 to 8.

P. australis (aus-TRAY-lis), southern penstemon. Size: 2½ to 3 feet tall, 1 to 2 feet wide. Southern penstemon has soft hairy leaves and stems and white to pale pink flowers with deep rose stripes. Zones 5 to 9.

P. barbatus (bar-BA-tus), common beardtongue. Size: 1½ to 3 feet tall, 1 to 2 feet wide. This stately plant has lance-shaped gray-green foliage and stout spikes of pink to carmine flowers. 'Bashful' has salmon flowers on 12- to 14-inch stems. 'Coccineus' is scarlet. 'Elfin Pink' has dark green foliage and bright pink flowers on 12-inch stems.

'Pink Beauty' has clear pink flowers on 2- to 2½-foot stems. Zones 4 to 8.

P. cobaea (ko-BYE-a), foxglove. Size: 1 to 2½ feet tall, 1 foot wide. This handsome penstemon has inflated white flowers with violet stripes borne in tight clusters on flowering stalks. Zones 5 to 9.

P. digitalis (dij-i-TAH-lis), foxglove penstemon. Size: 2½ to 5 feet tall, 1 to 2 feet wide. This tall penstemon grows in moist soil. Shiny green leaves form tufted rosettes; flowerstalks bear open clusters of somewhat inflated white flowers. 'Husker Red' has deep ruby red foliage and stems and pink flowers. 'Rachel's Dance' has purple-red leaves and deep wine-red stems. Zones 4 to 8.

P. hirsutus (her-SUIT-us), hairy beardtongue. Size: 2 to 3 feet tall, 1 to 2 feet wide. A fuzzy penstemon with purple to violet, narrow tubular flowers. 'Pygmaeus' has reddish foliage and lilac flowers on 8-inch stems. Zones 4 to 8.

P. laevigatus (le-vi-GA-tus), smooth beardtongue. Size: 2 to 3 feet tall, 1 to 2 feet wide. Similar to *P. digitalis*, but flowers are often pink and plants are more compact. Prefers drier soil. Zones 5 to 9.

P. pinifolius (pin-i-FO-lee-us), pine-leaf penstemon. Size: 1 to 2 feet tall and wide. This shrubby penstemon has multi-branched stems covered in small, needlelike leaves and crowned with tubular, scarlet flowers. 'Mercer Yellow' is an important color break. Zones 6 to 8.

P. smallii (SMALL-ee-ee), Small's beardtongue. Size: 2 to 2½ feet tall, 1 to 2 feet wide. This shrubby penstemon is covered top to bottom in rose-purple flowers for several weeks in early spring. Plants are short-lived. Zones 6 to 8.

P. strictus (STRIKT-us), porch penstemon. Size: 2 to 3 feet tall, 1 to 2 feet wide. A western native with straight spikes of showy white, pink, or lavender flowers. Leaves are mostly basal and descend in size up the stems. Zones 5 to 8.

Hybrids

Many hybrids of mixed parentage are available. Some of the most adaptable are listed. 'Blue Midnight' is deep blue-violet. 'Cerise Kissed' is vibrant raspberry with a white center. 'Firebird' has scarlet flowers in summer on 2-foot stems. 'Garnet' is deep red with a pale throat. 'Mesa' has deep vi-

olet flowers on 20-inch stems. 'Prairie Dusk' has pendant, bell-shaped purple flowers on 1½- to 2-foot stems. 'Prairie Fire' produces orange-red flowers all summer on 30-inch stems. 'Red Rocks is rose-pink and heat-tolerant. 'Sour Grapes' has inflated red-violet flowers. Zones 4 to 8.

How to Grow

Plant penstemons in sandy or loamy, humus-rich, well drained soil in full sun or light shade. Good drainage is essential for

Tough, drought-tolerant hairy beardtongue (*Penstemon hirsutus*) is perfect for a rock garden or for planting on a dry bank in full sun to light shade.

all but *P. digitalis,* which tolerates moist or even wet soils. Clumps increase by slow-creeping stems to form dense clumps. Divide clumps every 4 to 6 years to keep them vigorous. *P. smallii* and *P. cobaea* are short-lived and demand a lean, sandy soil and excellent drainage. Plants peter out after 3 years but self-sow profusely. Propagate by seed sown outdoors in fall or indoors with 4 to 6 weeks of cold-moist stratification. Seedlings develop quickly and may bloom the first year.

Landscape Uses

Penstemons are versatile plants for the perennial or rock garden. Combine their spiky forms with cranesbills (*Geranium*), spiderworts (*Tradescantia*), yarrows (*Achillea*), sundrops (*Oenothera*), lamb's ears (*Stachys*), yuccas, and ornamental grasses. Use *P. cobaea, P. hirsutus* 'Pygmaeus', *P. pinifolius,* and *P. smallii* in rock gardens where good drainage is assured.

PEROVSKIA

pe-ROF-ski-a • Lamiaceae, Mint Family

Spires of blue-violet reach for the summer sky above filigreed gray-green leaves. This tough, adaptable perennial is amazingly hardy, as it hails from the steppes of Russia. Plants are popular in public spaces and as border perennials. Actually a subshrub, perovskia has persistent woody stems in mild climates and grows from a thick, fibrous-rooted crown.

> **PEROVSKIA**
>
> **Common Name:**
> Russian sage
>
> **Bloom Time:**
> Summer bloom
>
> **Planting Requirements:**
> Full sun

Perovskia atriplicifolia (a-tri-plis-i-FO-lee-a), Russian sage. Size: 3 to 5 feet tall and wide. Russian sage is a subshrub grown as a perennial with small, gray-green, deeply toothed leaves and airy sprays of powder blue flowers on stout stems that persist where winters are mild. Plants grow from woody crowns with dense fibrous roots. Gray buds appear atop stems in early summer, and blue flowers emerge for several weeks from mid- to late summer. The dried seedheads are also attractive. 'Blue Spire' is an erect, branching selection with violet-blue flowers. 'Filigrin', a hybrid, has deeply divided, fine-textured leaves on compact, 3½-foot plants. 'Little Spire' is a dwarf only 2 feet tall, making it good for small gardens. 'Longin', possibly a hybrid, has stout, erect stems and grows 6 feet or more tall. USDA Plant Hardiness Zones 4 to 9.

How to Grow

Plant Russian sage in well-drained sandy or loamy soil in full sun. Good drainage is essential for success, especially in winter. Plants require warm summers to flower well. In cooler zones, site plants in full southern or western sun so they will perform well. After hard frost, cut the plants back to 12 inches or so. The lower, woody stems will produce next year's growth. In the North, plants often die back to the soil line but resprout from the rootstock. Plants seldom need dividing, but be sure to account for their eventual size when spacing other plants around them. Propagate by stem cuttings in early summer.

Landscape Uses

Combine Russian sage with tall or inter-mediate-size perennials at the middle or back of the border, or use it as a hedge to separate garden spaces or line a walk. Plants in the North do not grow as tall as elsewhere, so keep that in mind when choosing a spot to plant. The soft blue flowers complement pink, yellow, deeper blues, and purples. Choose yarrows (*Achillea*), garden phlox (*Phlox panicu-*

Russian sage (*Perovskia atriplici-folia*) earns its keep in the garden, from the soft, gray-green shoots of spring through the silky gray seedheads of fall. The flowers open for over a month in summer.

lata), balloon flower (*Platycodon grandi-florus*), blazing-stars (*Liatris*), and orna-mental grasses. Combine it with flaming orange Maltese cross (*Lychnis chal-cedonica*) and purple-leaved cannas for a dramatic show.

PERSICARIA

per-si-CAR-ee-a • Polygonaceae, Smartweed Family

Knotweeds are creeping plants bearing oblong shiny leaves alternating up jointed stems. The erect flower spikes, sometimes nodding at the tip, are composed of tiny, tightly packed pink flowers with no distinguishable petals. Some species have large, branched inflorescences. The mere mention of knotweed makes conservationists shudder because so many species are invasive exotics. Species included here are not invasive. They grow from stout crowns with fibrous roots. Plants in this genus were once classified as *Polygonum* or *Fallopia*.

PERSICARIA

Common Names:
 Knotweed, smartweed

Bloom Time:
 Summer and fall bloom

Planting Requirements:
 Full sun or partial shade

Persicaria affine (a-FEE-nee), Himalayan fleece flower. Size: 6 to 10 inches tall, 12 to 24 inches wide. This slow spreader has bright green leaves with prominent midveins and tight, erect spikes of rose-red flowers. 'Border Jewel' has rose-pink flowers. 'Darjeeling Red' has deep crimson-pink flowers. 'Dimity' has lighter pink flowers. USDA Plant Hardiness Zones 3 to 7.

P. amplexicaule (am-plex-e-KAUL-e), mountain fleece flower, mountain knotweed. Size: 3 to 4 feet tall and wide. Erect flower spikes composed of tiny, tightly packed rose flowers emerge from rattail buds throughout summer and fall. Plants have jointed or knotted stems to 3 feet tall with puckered, lance-shaped leaves that clasp the stems. 'Alba' is ghostly white. 'Firetail' has long, narrow cerise spikes. 'Inverleith' has brick red flowers on com-

pact plants. 'Rosea' has fat pink spikes. Zones 3 to 8.

P. bistorta (bis-TOR-ta), snakeweed. Size: 1½ to 2½ feet tall and wide. This is a stout plant with broad paddle-like foliage and dense, fat spikes of bright pink flowers held well above the foliage. 'Superbum' has huge flower spikes. Zones 3 to 8.

P. microcephala (mi-cro-ceph-AL-a) 'Red Dragon', red dragon smartweed. Size: 2 to 3 feet tall and wide. A stunning foliage plant with spear-shaped purple leaves with bicolor cream-and-dark-green chevrons at the centers. Small clusters of creamy white flowers grace the tips of zigzag stems. Zones 5 to 9.

P. polymorpha (poly-MORF-a), white dragon. Size: 4 to 6 feet tall and wide. A huge, clump-forming species with broadly lance-shaped leaves and fluffy plumes like giant astilbes in summer. Zones 4 to 9.

P. virginica (vir-GIN-i-ka), (*To-vara*), joint weed. Size: 1 to 2½ feet tall and wide. Oval leaves alternate up stems crowned with long whiplike spikes of small green flowers. An unassuming plant in the wild, but several excellent selections are worth noting. 'Lance Corporal' has obovate leaves that emerge chartreuse with a maroon chevron and darken through the season. 'Painter's Pallette' has tricolor leaves splashed with cream, green, and red. The small flowers are cerise. Zones 3 to 9.

How to Grow

Plant knotweeds in moist, humus-rich soil in full sun or partial shade. All species with the exception of *P. affine* tolerate considerable moisture. If the soil gets too dry, the leaf margins may get crispy. Knotweeds spread by slow-creeping stems that root as they go. Plants do not tolerate full sun in warm zones. Divide clumps in spring or fall to control their spread.

Cerise rattail flower spikes shoot out all summer long like flaming rockets from mountain fleece flower (*Persicaria amplexi-caule* 'Firetail'). This workhorse perennial forms large clumps in moist soil and full sun to light shade.

Landscape Uses

Plant knotweeds where you need a spreading groundcover with excellent foliage and spiky flowers. Use *P. affine* at the front of the border or along steps and walks. Choose *P. bistorta* for the moist-soil garden with Siberian and other water irises (*Iris sibirica*), astilbe (*Astilbe* ×*arendsii*), hostas, ligularias, rodgersias, ferns, sedges (*Carex*), and other foliage plants. Mountain fleece flowers excel in both foliage and flower in combination with ginger lilies (*Hedychium*), cannas, and Joe-Pye weeds (*Eupatorium*).

PHLOMIS

FLOW-mis • Lamaiaceae, Mint Family

Magnificent Mediterranean marvels for a dry garden, Phlomis have distinctive spikes of tiered whorls of hooded, tubular flowers that sit on leafy bracts. Leaf and flower together make for a handsome addition to any combination. Plants are herbaceous or woody and grow from fibrous-rooted crowns.

> **PHLOMIS**
>
> **Common Name:**
> Jerusalem sage
>
> **Bloom Time:**
> Late spring and summer bloom
>
> **Planting Requirements:**
> Sun

Phlomis cashmeriana (kash-meer-ee-AY-na), Kashmir sage. Size: 2 to 3 feet tall, 1 to 2 feet wide. Large felted basal leaves set off erect stems packed with dense tiers of soft lilac-pink flowers. Plants perform best where summer humidity is low. *P. samia* is similar, with pink flowers on 2-foot stems. USDA Plant Hardiness Zones 5 to 8.

P. fruticosa (froo-tea-KO-sa), Jerusalem sage. Size: 3 to 4 feet tall and wide. The erect, branched stems of this shrub feature fine-textured foliage and butter yellow spring flowers in tight tiers. Zones 5 to 8.

P. russeliana (ru-sell-e-AY-na), Jerusalem sage. Size: 3 to 4 feet tall and wide. Carpets of attractive, wavy gray-green leaves are good enough without erect, unbranched spikes of glossy yellow flowers. 'E. A. Bowles' is a hybrid between Jerusalem sage and the subshrub *P. fruticosa*. More delicate in overall aspect than Jerusalem sage, the soft yellow flowers are carried on 3-foot leafy stems. Zones 4 to 8.

P. tuberosa (too-ber-OH-sa), steppe sage. Size: 4 to 6 feet tall, 1 to 2 feet wide. Erect stems have well-spaced tiered clusters of rose-purple to violet flowers in summer

Jerusalem sage (*Phlomis russeliana*) blooms with the first hot days of summer but is undaunted by the heat that sends gardeners indoors to wait for the cool of evening.

over broad, quilted basal leaves. 'Amazonica' has larger, felted leaves and more dense (therefore more showy) flower clusters. Zones 4 to 9.

How to Grow

Good drainage and lots of sun are the keys to success with Jerusalem sages. These extremely tough plants seem to thrive with little water and lots of heat. They tolerate the cold of Zone 4 winters with a protective mulch or snow cover.

Landscape Uses

Though gardeners deplore hot, dry sunny spots, many showy plants prefer such conditions to the perfect, moist loam of garden books. Combine the exotic spikes of Jerusalem sages with other high-plains natives like winecups (*Callirhoe*), catmints (*Nepeta*), penstemons, and sages (*Salvia*) for a lovely blue and purple contrast. In a hot-color garden with reds and oranges, choose torch lilies (*Kniphofia*), evening primroses (*Oenothera*), marguerites (*Anthemis*), and yellow variegated yucca (*Yucca* 'Color Guard').

PHLOX

FLOX • Polemoniaceae, Phlox Family

Phlox have been grown since colonial times for their fragrance and color. They were among the first plants sent to Europe from the New World. They are beloved garden favorites among wildflower fanciers and perennial enthusiasts alike. The flowers are tubular at the base and flair at the end to form flat-faced, five-petaled flowers that open from gracefully twisted buds. Flowers may be white, pink, rose, red, violet, blue, or bicolor. The plants often form basal carpets of opposite, short-stalked foliage with ephemeral bloom stalks that wither away after seeds ripen.

PHLOX
Common Name:
Phlox
Bloom Time:
Spring and summer bloom
Planting Requirements:
Full sun to shade

Others produce tall, persistent leafy stems crowned with dense, domed heads of flowers. Plants grow from crowns with dense, fibrous white roots.

Phlox bifida (BI-fid-a), sand phlox. Size: 6 to 8 inches tall, 12 inches wide. A creeping plant with needlelike leaves and loose clusters of spring flowers with deeply notched white to lavender petals. 'Betty Blake' is lavender blue. 'Colvin's White' has pure white flowers. USDA Plant Hardiness Zones 4 to 8.

P. carolina (kare-o-LIE-na), Carolina phlox, thick leaf phlox. Size: 3 to 4 feet tall, 1 to 2 feet wide. This stout phlox has glossy, broadly lance-shaped leaves and elongated flower clusters. Flowers are pink to purple, sometimes white. 'Miss Lingard' has white flowers with pale yellow eyes and is mildew-resistant. 'Rosalinde' has vibrant deep pink flowers. Zones 4 to 9.

P. divaricata (di-var-i-KATE-a), wild blue phlox, woodland phlox. Size: 10 to 15 inches tall, 12 to 24 inches wide. This woodland species forms erect, spreading clumps of glossy, evergreen, broadly lance-shaped leaves. The flowering stems are erect and hairy, topped by an open cluster of fragrant sky blue flowers. The stalk withers after flowering. 'Clouds of Perfume' has intensely fragrant, ice blue flowers. 'Dirigo Ice' has pale blue flowers. 'Fuller's White' is a sturdy, compact plant with pure white flowers. 'Louisiana Purple' is violet-blue with a cerise eye. 'Montrose Tricolor' has medium sky blue flowers over white-edged leaves tinged pink in spring. Var. *laphamii* has periwinkle-blue flowers. Zones 3 to 9.

P. douglasii (DOUG-las-ee-ee), Douglas's phlox. Size: 4 to 8 inches tall, 12 inches wide. The creeping stems form dense mats with needlelike leaves and lavender, pink, or white flowers in one- to three-flowered clusters. 'Blue Eye' is white with a blue eye. 'Boothman's Variety' is soft violet with a deep purple eye. 'Cracker Jack' has carmine-red flowers. 'Waterloo' has violet-red flowers. Zones 3 to 8.

P. maculata (mak-u-LAY-ta), early phlox, wild sweet William. Size: 2 to 3 feet tall, 1 to 2 feet wide. Early phlox is similar to *P. carolina* but with linear foliage and

The floriferous woodland phlox (*Phlox divaricata* 'Dirigo Ice') has fragrant, sky blue flowers that last for 2 weeks in shaded gardens. Glossy, evergreen leaves make an attractive summer groundcover.

narrower flower clusters. 'Alpha' has rose-pink flowers with slightly darker eyes. 'Delta' has elongated, 1-foot heads of white flowers with deep pink eyes. 'Natascha' is a white-and-rose bicolor with a pinwheel pattern. 'Omega' has white flowers with lilac-pink eyes. Zones 3 to 9.

P. ovata (o-VAY-ta), mountain phlox. Size: 12 to 20 inches tall, 12 to 24 inches wide. This upright, spreading phlox has glossy, oval leaves and open clusters of pink or magenta flowers in late spring. 'Spring

Delight' has rose-pink flowers from late spring through early summer. Zones 4 to 8.

P. paniculata (pa-nik-u-LAY-ta), garden phlox, summer phlox. Size: 3 to 4 feet tall, 2 to 3 feet wide. Garden phlox is a popular summer perennial with huge domed clusters of fragrant magenta, pink, or white flowers and broad, lance-shaped, dull green leaves on erect, stiff stems. Hundreds of selections and hybrids have been made to increase the color range to violet, purple, rose, cerise, salmon, orange, and bicolor. Hybridizers have also endeavored to increase the mildew resistance of garden phlox by crossing them with glossy-leaved species, particularly *P. maculata*. Some of the most popular selections are listed here. (Some cultivars are hardy only to Zone 4;

The heady fragrance of border phlox (*Phlox paniculata* 'David') is familiar to generations of perennial gardeners. This large-flowered selection is extremely durable and the foliage is mildew-resistant.

check with local nurseries.) 'Becky Toe' has yellow-edged leaves and carmine flowers. 'Blue Paradise' is medium blue with a dark eye. 'Bright Eyes' has pink flowers with crimson eyes and is mildew-resistant. 'David' has huge heads of pure white flowers and shows excellent mildew resistance. 'Gold Mine' has gold-edged leaves and magenta flowers. 'Katherine' is lavender with a white eye. 'Nicky' opens violet and turns royal purple. 'Orange Perfection' is a compact (24-inch) grower with orange-salmon flowers. 'Robert Poore' has large heads of rose-purple flowers. 'Sandra' is a dwarf (18-inch) grower with scarlet flowers. 'Sir John Falstaff' has deep salmon-pink flowers with purple eyes. 'Speed Limit 45' is hot pink. 'Starfire' is an early, vibrant deep red with red-tinged foliage. 'The King' has deep purple flowers. 'Tracy's Treasure' is soft pink and mildew-resistant. Zones 3 to 8.

P. pilosa (pye-LOW-sa), prairie phlox. Size: 1 to 1½ feet tall and wide. Domed clusters of pink flowers are held on delicate stems above narrow, hairy leaves in early summer. Ssp. *ozarkana* is medium pink. 'Eco Happy Traveler' is rose-pink and floriferous. *P. amoena* is similar, with hairy, stiff leaves. 'Cabot Blue' is lavender blue. *P.* 'Chatahoochee', a hybrid of contested origin with *P. divaricata* var. *laphamii*, has linear leaves and lavender-blue flowers with violet eyes that bleed their color into the petals. *P. glaberrima* is a similar species with smooth rather than hairy leaves and larger flowers than *P. pilosa* in more open clusters. 'Morris Berd' has large heads of clear pink flowers. All species prefer sun. Zones 3 to 8.

P. stolonifera (sto-lon-IF-er-a), creeping phlox. Size: 6 to 8 inches tall, 12 to 24 inches wide. This lovely woodland phlox forms broad, dense clumps from creeping stems that root as they go. The ephemeral bloom stalks carry open clusters of magenta to pink flowers in early to mid-spring. 'Blue Ridge' has lilac-blue flowers. 'Bruce's White' has white flowers with yellow eyes. 'Pink Ridge' has mauve-pink flowers. 'Sherwood Purple' has purple-blue, fragrant flowers. 'Variegata' has pink flowers and white-edged leaves. Zones 2 to 8.

P. subulata (sub-u-LAY-ta), moss phlox. Size: 4 to 8 inches tall, 12 to 24 inches wide. The best-selling spring phlox, moss phlox is ubiquitous on slopes and banks and in rock gardens. The pink, magenta, or white flowers cover mounds of needlelike foliage and wiry stems. Bloom lasts for several weeks. 'Alexander's Wild Rose' has pink flowers. 'Candy Stripe' is a white-and-pink bicolor. 'Crimson Beauty' has deep rose-red flowers. 'Emerald Cushion Blue' has blue flowers. 'Emerald Cushion Pink' has pink flowers and is long-blooming. 'Maiden's Blush' is pink-flushed white with a red eye and is a good rebloomer. 'Milstream Daphne', a hybrid with *P. stolonifera,* is vibrant pink with a yellow eye. 'Snowflake' and 'White Delight' have pure white flowers. *P. borealis* and *P. nivalis* are additional pink-flowered ground-cover species. Zones 2 to 9.

How to Grow

The cultivated phlox can be placed into three groups based on their requirements for growth. **The woodland species,** including *P. divaricata* and *P. stolonifera*, require evenly moist, humus-rich soil in light to full shade. They form evergreen groundcovers that seldom need dividing unless they crowd other plants. Division is best done after flowering. Take cuttings in May and June. They root quickly and bloom the next season.

The low, mounding phlox include *P. amoena, P. bifida, P. douglasii, P. glaberrima, P. pilosa,* and *P. subulata.* Give them average sandy or loamy well-drained soil in full sun. Divide them in fall or take cuttings in spring or early summer.

The border phlox include *P. carolina, P. maculata, P. ovata,* and *P. paniculata.* Plant garden phlox in average to rich, moist but well-drained soil in full sun or light shade. Plants perform best where summers are cool. They often bloom for weeks on end. With careful cultivar selection, you can have garden phlox in bloom from June through September. They form multistemmed clumps that need division every 3 or 4 years in spring. Cultivars vary in their susceptibility to mildew but need abundant moisture, good air circulation, and thinning of dense clumps to keep them in peak condition. Mildew is often the greatest threat at the end of summer during hot, dry spells when plants wilt, opening leaves to infection. Spray with wettable sulfur 1 or 2 times per week when white mildew is first noticed.

Woodland species are also mildly susceptible to mildew and can be treated similarly if infection develops. Propagate plants by stem cuttings in spring and early summer. They also grow from root cuttings taken in fall and laid horizontally in moist sand.

All phlox are savored by rabbits and deer, who make it their annoying habit to mow plants to the ground on a regular basis. Use deterrent sprays or a fence rather than removing the phlox.

Landscape Uses

Choose the woodland phlox for early color in the shade or wildflower garden. Plant them with spring bulbs, hellebores, fairy wings (*Epimedium*), lungworts (*Pulmonaria*), lily-of-the-valley (*Convallaria majalis*), bellflowers (*Campanula*), leopard's bane (*Doronicum caucasicum*), bleeding hearts (*Dicentra*), Solomon's seals (*Polygonatum*), hostas, and ferns. Wildflowers such as columbine (*Aquilegia canadensis*), Virginia bluebells (*Mertensia virginica*), spring beauty (*Claytonia virginica*), Canada wild ginger (*Asarum canadense*), and Allegheny foamflower (*Tiarella cordifolia*) are also good choices. The low-mounding species are perfect for rock gardens, at the front of the border, or along walks. Plant them with basket-of-gold (*Aurinia saxatilis*), stonecrops (*Sedum*), rock cresses (*Arabis*), beardtongues (*Penstemon*), and yuccas. Border phlox are best placed in the middle or rear of the garden. Give them ample room to spread, and combine them with perennials such as irises, catmints (*Nepeta*), Joe-Pye weeds (*Eupatorium*), bee balms (*Monarda*), Shasta daisies (*Leucanthemum maximum*), astilbes, meadowsweets (*Filipendula*), cranesbills (*Geranium*), delphiniums, daylilies (*Hemerocallis*), and ornamental grasses.

PHYGELIUS

phy-GEEL-e-us • Scrophulariaceae, Figwort Family

The exotic allure of cape fuchsia is undeniable, yet the plant is little known outside the Pacific Northwest. The tall, branched stems of this South African shrub carry dozens of nodding, slender tubular flowers with flared tips. The outside color of the flower often differs from the inner color, making a sharp and showy contrast. Plants begin flowering in June and continue throughout summer and fall.

PHYGELIUS

Common Names:
Cape fuchsia, cape figwort

Bloom Time:
Summer and fall bloom

Planting Requirements:
Sun to light shade

Phygelius ×*rectus* (RECK-tus), cape fuchsia. Size: 3 to 5 feet tall, 3 to 4 feet wide. This hybrid was created by crossing *P. aequalis* with *P. capaensis*. The two species are similar, but *P. capaensis* is more open, with elongated clusters of smaller flowers all around the stem, than its showier relation with one-sided flower clusters. The hybrids share traits of both parents. 'African Queen' is salmon-orange, with a yellow throat. 'Devil's Tears' is scarlet with smaller flowers that bend outward. 'Moonraker' is a favorite, with chiffon yellow flowers. 'Winchester Fanfare' is cerise. USDA Plant Hardiness Zones 7 to 9.

How to Grow

Cape fuchsias are native to the arid mountains of South Africa, where they grow along streams with a constant source of moisture. Plants need rich, evenly moist soil but also good drainage. Plants dislike humidity. They have rather succulent stems that are damaged by extreme cold and are susceptible to rot if too wet in winter.

Shocking red-orange tubular flowers of cape fuchsia (*Phygelius* ×*rectus* 'Winchester fanfare') delight gardeners and hummingbirds where nights are cool and humidity is low. In Zone 6 and colder, plants are grown as annuals or overwintered in pots indoors.

Landscape Uses

Cape fuchsias are the stars of the summer and fall border where they are hardy. Their bright colors and long season of bloom make them indispensable for colorful combinations with asters, goldenrods (*Solidago*), sages (*Salvia*), phlox, and a host of other perennials. The nodding trumpets in airy veils are spellbinding with the stiff leaves of *Phormium* or ornamental grasses.

PHYSOSTEGIA

fie-so-STEE-gee-a • Lamiaceae, Mint Family

Obedient plant is a bit of a misnomer for this colorful, late season mint that romps through the garden. This heirloom plant has been passed around gardens for generations, no doubt because everyone had so much to share! So many cultivars abound, you can mix and match colors in all shades of pink and rose, as well as pure white. Plants grow from creeping stems with dense, fibrous roots.

> **PHYSOSTEGIA**
>
> **Common Name:**
>   Obedient plant
>
> **Bloom Time:**
>   Late summer bloom
>
> **Planting Requirements:**
>   Full sun to partial shade

Physostegia virginiana (vir-jin-ee-AH-na), obedient plant, dragon mint, false dragonhead. Size: 3 to 4 feet tall and wide. Obedient plant is a fast

The vivid pink flowers of obedient plant (*Physostegia virginiana* 'Rosy Spire') open for up to 3 weeks in late summer. Plants will bloom a month or more if faithfully deadheaded.

spreader with creeping stems and fibrous roots that seem anything but obedient. The flower stalks are covered in coarsely toothed, lance-shaped opposite leaves. The flower spikes are 1 to 1½ feet tall with four vertical rows of bilobed flowers forming a cross-shaped pattern when viewed from above. The name *obedient plant* arises from the odd tendency of the pale lilac-pink flowers to remain in any position to which they are shifted by gardeners weary of the regimented arrangement. Plants bloom in late summer, and flowering lasts well into fall. 'Eyeful Tower' is a giant to 6 feet tall. 'Miss Manners' is a white-flowered selection that for some reason does not romp. 'Pink Bouquet' has bright pink flowers on 3- to 4-foot stems. 'Summer Snow' is pure white, compact (to 3 feet), and less rampant. It blooms several weeks earlier than the other cultivars. 'Variegata' has leaves edged in creamy white and pale pink flowers. 'Vivid' has vibrant rose-pink flowers on 2- to 3-foot stems. USDA Plant Hardiness Zones 2 to 9.

How to Grow

Place obedient plants in evenly moist, humus-rich soil in full sun or partial shade. They tolerate considerable moisture and will grow pondside. The plants are heavy feeders but tend to flop in rich soil. Select a compact cultivar. Staking may still be necessary. Divide plants every 2 or 3 years to control their exuberant spread. Replant into amended soil. If divisions don't provide for your insatiable need for plants, stem cuttings root easily in early summer.

Landscape Uses

Combine obedient plant with late-summer perennials such as boltonia (*Boltonia asteroides*), ironweeds (*Vernonia*), garden phlox (*Phlox paniculata*), meadow rues (*Thalictrum*), asters, Joe-Pye weeds (*Eupatorium*), goldenrods (*Solidago*), sunflowers (*Helianthus*), cannas, and ornamental grasses.

PLATYCODON

pla-tee-KO-don • Campanulaceae, Bellflower Family

We have always loved the out-facing, starry blue-violet chalices of balloon flower, and gained a new appreciation for it seeing drifts growing wild in a flower-filled meadow at the base of Japan's Mount Fuji. Plants thrive in moist meadows in the wild but are adaptable to a wide range of garden conditions, from moist to dry.

PLATYCODON

Common Name:
Balloon flower

Bloom Time:
Summer bloom

Planting Requirements:
Full sun to light shade

Platycodon grandiflorus (grand-i-FLO-rus), balloon flower. Size: 2 to 3 feet tall, 1 to 2 feet wide. Balloon flower is a showstopper. Huge, bright blue, saucer-shaped flowers have five starry lobes that open from inflated round buds (hence the common name). Plants produce upright succulent stems covered in toothed, triangular leaves from a thick, fleshy rootstock. Flowers are borne singly on short branches off the main stems. Var. *albus* ('Albus') has white flowers. 'Apoyama' produces blue-violet flowers on 6-inch plants. Many semi-dwarf plants are sold under this name.

No matter what the size of your garden, there is a balloon flower (like the compact *Platycodon grandiflorus* 'Sentimental Blue') to fit your space. Sizes range from the 3-foot species to this diminutive cultivar only 9 inches tall.

'Double Blue' has bright blue double flowers on 2-foot plants. Fuji Series is a seed-grown strain of mixed pink, white, and blue selections on tall stems. 'Hakone Blue' has double flowers on 18-inch stems. 'Komachi' is clear blue and 1 to 2 feet tall. Var. *mariesii* ('Mariesii') has rich blue flowers on 12- to 18-inch plants. 'Misato Purple' has large blue-violet flowers. 'Shell Pink' has soft pale pink flowers on 2-foot plants. USDA Plant Hardiness Zones 3 to 8.

How to Grow

Plant balloon flowers in average to rich, well-drained soil in full sun or light shade.

Plants are tough and adaptable. New shoots are slow to emerge in spring. Take care not to dig into clumps by mistake. Plants flower for a month or more in early to midsummer. Removing spent flowers will encourage continued bloom and keep plants tidy. They seldom need division once established. If you wish to divide for propagation or transplanting, lift clumps in spring or early fall. Dig deeply to avoid damaging thick rootstocks. Plants will self-sow in the garden. Sow seeds outdoors when ripe. Plants will bloom the second year.

Landscape Uses

Combine balloon flowers with summer-blooming perennials such as yellow yarrows (*Achillea* 'Moonshine' and *A. fillipendulina*), ornamental onions (*Allium*), Mongolian aster (*Asteromoea mongolica*), calamints (*Calamintha*), purple garden sage (*Salvia nemorosa*), bee balm (*Monarda didyma*), and garden phlox (*Phlox paniculata*). Use foliage to set off the bright blue or pink flowers. Choose lamb's ears (*Stachys byzantina*), wormwoods (*Artemisia*), and ornamental grasses. The dwarf and compact varieties are well-suited to pot culture. Flowers last well as fresh cuts. Singe the stem end with a match to stop the milky sap from flowing.

PLEIOBLASTUS

plee-o-BLAS-tis • Poaceae, Grass Family

Bamboos offer refinement and elegance to the garden whether in the ground or in containers. Foliage is lance-shaped to narrowly oval, with pointed tips. The jointed stems are often branched, with gracefully arching side shoots. There are dozens of attractive bamboos, but many spread like lightning and are a lot of work to keep under control. If you want bamboo to be low maintenance, put it in a sturdy container. Plants grow from stout, creeping rhizomes with wiry, fibrous roots. Bamboos take many years to reach maturity. They bloom only once and then die.

PLEIOBLASTUS

Common Name:
Bamboo

Bloom Time:
Foliage plant

Planting Requirements:
Sun or partial shade

Pleioblastus auricomis (awe-re-KO-mis) (*viridi-striatus*), bamboo. Size: 2 to 3 feet tall, 3 to 4 feet wide. A lovely, variegated species with dense, crowded stems bearing yellow-and-green-striped broadly lance-shaped leaves. USDA Plant Hardiness Zones 5 to 9.

P. pygmaeus (pig-MY-us). Size: 1 to 1½ feet tall, 2 to 3 feet wide. This is a true dwarf with dense, narrow lance-shaped leaves born in parallel rows on both sides of the stem. Zones 5 to 9.

P. variegatus (var-e-a-GAY-tus). Size: 1 to 2½ feet tall and 2 to 3 feet wide. This attractive species has upright, narrow, white-and-green-striped leaves. Zones 5 to 9.

Other Bamboos

Fargesia nitida, fountain bamboo, is a large evergreen species with branched woody stems 5 to 14 feet tall. Side branches bear drooping, lance-shaped blades. 'Anceps' has small, attractive leaves and is heat-tolerant. Zones 4 to 9.

Sasa is a genus of shrubby bamboos with arching, wiry stems that emerge from slow-creeping rhizomes. The broadly lance-

Though it romps like most bamboos, the diminutive size of *Pleioblastus pygmaeus* makes it easier to control. Plants form a tidy, exotic-looking groundcover in sun or shade.

For a spot of bright color in the dry shade of shrubs and trees, try *Pleioblastus variegatus*. The white-and-green striated leaves form tufted clumps that spread more slowly than larger bamboos.

shaped leaves are clustered toward the tips of the stems. *S. palmata* has broad, pointed, deep green leaves to 1 foot long. *S. veitchii* is smaller and more delicate. The edges of leaves turn papery and pale in winter, giving a variegated effect. Both species prefer shade. Zones 6 to 9.

How to Grow

Plant bamboo in average to rich, moist soil in sun or partial shade, depending on species. Plants can spread very rapidly from tough, creeping rhizomes. Control can be difficult as the rhizomes are tough and often quite deep. Bamboo is invasive in some areas. Propagate by division after growth hardens.

Landscape Uses

Choose bamboo for a dramatic foliage accent in containers, in beds along fences or walls, or in the center of a lawn area. Plants make great living fences to divide spaces and provide privacy. Combine them with shrubs along the edge of a woodland or as the backdrop for a perennial border.

POLEMONIUM

po-lee-MO-nee-um • Polemoniaceae, Phlox Family

Jacob's ladders are noted for their distinctive, pinnately divided leaves with leaflets spaced as regularly as the rungs of a ladder. The flowers are carried in loose clusters atop succulent stems. They have five overlapping petals that form a cup or shallow saucer, depending on the species. The flowers are sky blue to blue-violet, rarely pink or white. Plants grow from a crown of fibrous roots.

POLEMONIUM

Common Name:
Jacob's ladder

Bloom Time:
Spring and summer bloom

Planting Requirements:
Sun or partial shade

Polemonium caeruleum (kie-RU-lee-um), Jacob's ladder. Size: 1½ to 2 feet tall and wide. This tall, early-summer-blooming species has erect stems with leaves reduced in size as they ascend toward compound clusters of nodding, deep blue flowers. Var. *album* has white flowers. 'Brise d'Anjou' has creamy yellow-edged leaves and blue flowers. 'Snow and Sapphires' has white-edged leaves and is more vigorous than other variegated selections. USDA Plant Hardiness Zones 3 to 7.

P. reptans (REP-tanz), creeping Jacob's ladder. Size: 8 to 16 inches tall and wide. This lovely wildflower produces mounds of attractive foliage and short, branching stems with open clusters of nodding, deep sky blue flowers. 'Blue Pearl' has clear blue flowers. 'Firmament' has violet-blue flowers. 'Lambrook Mauve' is an excellent hybrid with lavender-blue flowers. Zones 2 to 8.

P. yezoense (jez-o-EN-se), Jacob's ladder. Size: 2 feet tall, 1 foot wide. A new introduction with dense basal rosettes of lacy, divided leaves. 'Purple Rain' has deep purple spring leaves that fade a bit in summer and deep gentian blue flowers. Zones 6 to 8.

How to Grow

Plant Jacob's ladders in evenly moist, humus-rich soil in full sun or partial shade. In warm regions, partial shade is a must to keep plants from burning. Variegated selections seem to need more sun to flourish, but they will burn in hot afternoon sun.

Site them with care. *P. reptans* is more heat-tolerant. After flowering, cut bloom stalks to the ground and foliage will remain attractive all season. Do not remove old foliage until new growth starts in spring. Plants seldom need division. Propagate by seed sown outdoors in fall.

Landscape Uses

Choose Jacob's ladders for informal and formal gardens alike. Plant them in masses under shrubs or airy flowering trees such as shadblows (*Amelanchier*), wild camellias (*Stewartia*), and silverbells (*Halesia*). Combine them with wildflowers, hostas, ferns, and border perennials.

After the charming, mauve flowers of Jacob's ladder (*Polemonium* 'Lambrook Mauve') fade, the pinnately divided leaves make an attractive groundcover throughout summer.

POLYGONATUM

po-lig-o-NAY-tum • Convallariaceae (Liliaceae), Lily-of-the-Valley Family

The graceful arching stems of Solomon's seals are clothed in alternating, broadly oval leaves that form stair steps along the stem. The clustered, bell-shaped green flowers hang below the foliage from the nodes. Waxy, blue-black berries are produced in summer. Plants grow from thick, slow-creeping rhizomes with spidery, fibrous roots.

POLYGONATUM

Common Name:
Solomon's seal

Bloom Time:
Foliage plant with spring bloom

Planting Requirements:
Light to full shade

Polygonatum biflorum (bi-FLOR-um), smooth Solomon's seal. Size: 1 to 3 feet tall, 1 to 2 feet wide. This plant has narrowly oval, deep gray-green leaves spaced in close succession along the stem. The flowers are carried in pairs. Var. *commutatum*, great Solomon's seal, is a giant with stout stems to 7 feet, well-spaced oval leaves, and clusters of three to eight flowers. USDA Plant Hardiness Zones 3 to 9.

P. hirtum (HIRT-um), Solomon's seal. Size: 1 to 2 feet tall and wide. Leaves of this species are more leathery than other species. Flowers are in pairs or triads. 'Dwarf Form' is an excellent groundcover to 10 inches tall with thick, dark green foliage. Zones 5 to 10.

P. humile (HEW-mi-le), dwarf Solomon's seal. Size: 3 to 6 inches tall and 8 to 12 inches wide. A diminutive species with pleated, oval leaves and oversize

If you have dry shade, variegated Japanese Solomon's seal (*Polygonatum odoratum* 'Variegatum') is a must. The arching stems clothed in white-edged leaves are an elegant addition to any shaded garden.

green flowers. Plants make open clumps from creeping stems. Zones 4 to 9.

P. kingianum (king-e-AY-num), thread-leaf Solomon's seal. Size: 4 to 5 feet tall, 2 to 3 feet wide. A stunning plant with erect stems bearing tiered whorls of long, needle-like leaves with curly hairlike tips. 'Orange Flowered Form' has orange flowers tipped in yellow. *P. cirrhifolium* is similar with white flowers. Zones 5 to 9.

P. multiflorum (mul-ti-FLOR-um), Eurasian Solomon's seal. Size: 2 to 3 feet tall and wide. This species resemble *P. biflorum* but the leaves are broader and the flowers are white. *P. ×hybridum,* as crossed with the following species, is popular for its sea green, rounded leaflets on arching stems, and large greenish white flowers. Zones 4 to 7.

P. odoratum (o-dor-AH-tum), Japanese Solomon's seal. Size: 1½ to 2½ feet tall and 2 to 3 feet wide. This species has fragrant flowers and is seen in cultivation as var. *pluriflorum* (*thunbergii*) 'Variegatum'. This cultivar is larger (to 3 feet) and has broadly oval leaves edged with creamy white. Zones 3 to 9.

P. verticillatum (ver-ti-ki-LAY-tum), whorled Solomon's seal. Size: 3 to 6 feet tall, 2 to 3 feet wide. This species and the similar *P. sibiricum* and *P. curvistylum* have whorled leaves in decorative tiers up the tall stalks and greenish flowers that dangle between leaves from the nodes. Zones 5 to 9.

How to Grow

Plant Solomon's seals in moist, humus-rich soil in partial to full shade. Plants tolerate sun in the North but must have shade from any but morning sun in the South. Most species tolerate periodically dry soil. Plants spread by branching rhizomes and can be divided whenever they overgrow their position. Lift clumps in spring or fall, and replant into amended soil. To propagate, remove seeds from the pulpy fruit and sow immediately outdoors. They may take 2 years to germinate and grow slowly.

Landscape Uses

Solomon's seals are prized for the strong architectural quality of their arching stems. Combine them with bold foliage plants such as hostas, bugbanes (*Cimicifuga*), irises, ferns, and sedges (*Carex*). Plant small species with coral bells (*Heuchera*), lady's-mantle (*Alchemilla mollis*), and cranesbills (*Geranium*). Use mass plantings in combination with ferns to underplant shrubs and flowering trees. Most species tolerate dry shade under mature canopy trees.

POLYSTICHUM

po-LI-sti-kum • Dryopteridaceae, Shield Fern Family

Sword ferns produce tufted clumps of stiff, deep green fronds from creeping, crown-forming rhizomes with dense, fibrous roots. The persistent fronds were once collected for holiday decoration. Some species have spiny, hollylike pinnae that give rise to the common name.

> **POLYSTICHUM**
>
> **Common Names:**
> Holly fern, sword fern
>
> **Bloom Time:**
> Foliage plant
>
> **Planting Requirements:**
> Light to full shade

Polystichum acrostichoides (a-krow-st-KOY-deez), Christmas fern. Size: 1 to 3 feet tall and wide. Evergreen fronds are divided once and have narrow-toothed pinnae carried stiffly up the scaly stipes. Plants form an upright vase. Zones 3 to 9.

P. makinoi (mak-in-O-ee), Makino's holly fern. Size: 1 to 2 feet tall and wide. An attractive fern for moderate-size gardens with an arching vase of elegant, soft, spiny fronds. *P. ringens* is similar, but the fronds are stiffer and glossy green. Zones 4 (with protection) to 8.

P. munitum (mew-KNEE-tum), western sword fern. Size: 3 to 5 feet tall and wide. Huge clumps of deep glossy evergreen fronds form graceful vases. Once-divided fronds have long, slender pointed pinnae. Established plants are drought-tolerant. Zones 5 to 9.

P. neolobatum (ne-o-low-BAY-tum), long-eared holly fern. Size: 1 to 2 feet tall and wide. An unusual fern with narrow, stiff, glossy fronds held in an upright vase. Zones 6 to 9; trial in colder zones.

P. polyblepharum (poly-BLEPH-are-um), tassel fern. Size: 2 to 4 feet tall and wide. This robust fern forms an arching vase of stiff, glossy fronds from a creeping, crown-forming rhizome. The pinnae are sharply toothed and appear spiny. Zones 6 to 9; trial in colder zones.

P. setiferum (se-ti-FER-um), soft shield fern. Size: 2 to 4½ feet tall and wide. Soft shield fern produces delicate, billowing evergreen clumps of deeply cut, frilly fronds. Many forms have been selected for variations in the dissection of the fronds. The fronds arise in a flattened vase shape from the rhizome in the manner typical of the genus. Some forms produce plantlets along the rachis that fall to the ground to form new plants. 'Congestum Cristatum' has constricted pinnule segments on compact plants. 'Divisilobum' is a frilly selection with three to four pinnate fronds with finely divided segments. 'Plumosum Bevis' is the best form, with a broad arching vase of elegant, dissected fronds. Heat-tolerant. 'Rotundatum Cristatum' has rounded pinnae and crested frond tips. Zones 4 to 9.

P. tsus-simense (tsoos-see-MEN-see), Korean rock fern. Size: 8 to 12 inches tall and wide. This diminutive fern bears triangular to lance-shaped, deep green fronds from a creeping, crown-forming rhizome. Zoncs 6 to 9.

How to Grow

Plant sword ferns in moist, well-drained, neutral to acid, humus-rich soil in light to full shade. Plants tolerate dense shade and dry soil; if soil is moist, they tolerate considerable sun. Divide clumps in spring or fall if they get too dense.

Landscape Uses

Combine sword ferns with other ferns in foundation plantings, along walks and steps, or in woodland gardens with bulbs, wildflowers, and groundcovers. The stiff fronds remain erect until hard frost or heavy snow pushes them over.

Versatile and elegant describe Makino's holly fern (*Polystichum makinoi*), whose stiff, evergreen arching fronds fit comfortably into any garden.

PORTERANTHUS (GILLENIA)

por-ter-AN-thus • Rosaceae, Rose Family

Popular in Europe but ignored at home, this native wildflower suffers from homeland obscurity, which keeps it and many other fine native perennials out of American gardens. The clouds of white flowers in early summer endear bowman's root to all who grow it. Plants tolerate extreme drought, and the orange fall foliage adds to the plant's attributes. They grow from thick deep roots.

PORTERANTHUS (GILLENIA)

Common Names:
Indian physic, bowman's root

Bloom Time:
Late spring bloom

Planting Requirements:
Full sun to partial shade

A veritable Milky Way of tiny white stars falls to earth in late spring when the flowers of bowman's root (*Porteranthus trifoliatus*) open aloft and quivering on wiry stems.

Porteranthus trifoliatus (tri-fo-lee-A-tus), bowman's root. Size: 2 to 4 feet tall, 2 to 3 feet wide. An erect, shrublike perennial with wiry stems sparsely covered in toothed trifoliate leaves. Broad terminal clusters of four-petaled starry white or pinkish fragrant flowers smother the plant in late spring and early summer. *P. stipulatus* has ragged leaves. USDA Plant Hardiness Zones 4 to 8.

How to Grow

Plant bowman's roots in moist, rich soil in sun or partial shade. Once established, plants are quite drought-tolerant. They are native to shaded sites but will tolerate full sun in all but the hottest regions. Plants spread slowly to form tight clumps that seldom need dividing. Take stem cuttings in spring or sow seed outdoors. Germination occurs the next spring. Plants take 3 to 4 years to attain good form.

Landscape Uses

In nature, bowman's root grows in vast patches on lightly shaded hillsides in the company of red fire pinks (*Silene virginica*), pink Carolina phlox (*Phlox carolina*), and grasses. Plant them in borders with wormwoods (*Artemisia*), late tulips, and large-flowered perennials like coneflowers (*Echinacea*), daylily (*Hemerocallis*), and peonies. In less formal areas plant bowman's root with Siberian iris (*Iris sibirica*), ferns, and ornamental grasses.

POTENTILLA

po-ten-TILL-a • Rosaceae, Rose Family

Cinquefoils have tight rosettes of hairy, palmately divided or occasionally pinnately divided leaves growing from a weakly taprooted crown. The flowers have five petals arrayed around a ring of fuzzy stamens. The petals may be yellow, orange, red, or occasionally white. Flowers are grouped into open, branching clusters.

POTENTILLA

Common Name:
Cinquefoil

Bloom Time:
Summer bloom

Planting Requirements:
Full sun or light shade

Potentilla atrosanguinea (at-ro-sang-GWIN-ee-a), Himalayan cinquefoil. Size: 1 to 2 feet tall and wide. Tufts of three-parted leaves set off the open clusters of deep red flowers. 'Firedance' has salmon-red flowers on 12-inch stems. 'Gibson's Scarlet' produces brilliant red flowers all summer on 18-inch stems. 'Vulcan' has deep red double flowers on 12-inch stems. 'William Rollison' has large (1½-inch) deep orange flowers with bright yellow centers. Plants bloom all summer. USDA Plant Hardiness Zones 5 to 8.

P. nepalensis (ne-pal-EN-sis), Nepal cinquefoil. Size: 1 to 2 feet tall and wide. This bushy species has long-petioled leaves with three to five leaflets. Crimson flowers are carried above the foliage in open branching clusters. 'Miss Wilmot' is a compact grower, to 1 foot, with carmine flowers. This selection is superior to the species. 'Ron McBeath' is carmine-red. Zones 5 to 8.

P. palustris (pa-LUS-tris), marsh cinquefoil. Size: 1 to 1½ feet tall and wide. The gray-green, five-part leaves of this species are a handsome backdrop to the deep wine-red flowers. Zones 2 to 7.

P. recta (REK-ta), sulphur cinquefoil. Size: 1 to 2½ feet tall, 1 to 2 feet wide. This weedy species has rounded tufts of leaves with five to nine leaflets and erect, broad clusters of yellow flowers. Var. *warrenii* is floriferous and showy. Zones 3 to 7.

P. tridentata (tri-den-TAY-ta), wine-leaf cinquefoil. Size: 6 to 12 inches tall, 12 to 24 inches wide. The shiny, three-part deep green foliage and clustered white

Use the diminutive spring cinquefoil (*Potentilla tabernaemontani*) as a ground-cover in well-drained rock gardens or in the crevices of stone walls.

flowers make this species desirable. The leaves turn deep wine red and orange in fall. 'Minima' is only 4 to 6 inches tall. Zones 2 to 8.

How to Grow

Cinquefoils grow best in well-drained sandy or loamy soils in full sun or light shade. Most are extremely drought-tolerant once established. *P. palustris* is an exception. Give it rich, constantly to evenly moist soil. All thrive best in acid soils. All species creep slowly to form dense clumps. *P. tridentata* has woody stems that form broad mats. Plants grow best where neither winter nor summer temperatures are extreme. Some species are hardy far into the North and do not tolerate the heat of warmer zones.

Landscape Uses

Plant cinquefoils in rock gardens, in rock walls, or at the front of perennial gardens. They clamber artfully between pavers. Combine them with evening primroses (*Oenothera*), winecups (*Callirhoe*), stonecrops (*Sedum*), flax (*Linum*), speedwells (*Veronica*), baby's-breath (*Gypsophila repens*), and ornamental grasses.

PRIMULA

PRIM-yoo-la • Primulaceae, Primrose Family

Primroses are beloved spring flowers that bloom with flowering bulbs when the world is reawakening. The broad leaves rise directly from stout crowns with fibrous roots. The flowers are tubular with broad, flattened five-petaled faces. They are carried in open, branched clusters or in whorled tiers on erect stems. Most are native to cool regions, and some do not perform well in heat and high humidity.

PRIMULA

Common Names:
  Primrose, cowslip

Bloom Time:
  Spring and early summer bloom

Planting Requirements:
  Sun to partial shade

Primula auricula (aw-RIK-yoo-la), auricula primrose. Size: 2 to 8 inches tall and wide. This hardy alpine primrose has thick, bright green paddle-shaped leaves. The clustered, flat-faced, bell-shaped bright yellow flowers are produced in April and May. Many hybrid selections are named. USDA Plant Hardiness Zones 2 to 8.

P. denticulata (den-tik-ew-LAY-ta), drumstick primrose. Size: 8 to 12 inches tall and wide. The sharply toothed spatulate leaves surround a thick stalk crowned by a rounded cluster of small lilac or white flowers. Var. *alba* ('Alba') has white flowers. 'Cashmere Ruby' has wine-colored flowers.

'Ronsdorf Strain' is a seed-grown strain of mixed white, rose, purple, or lavender flowers. 'Rubin' is carmine. Zones 4 to 8.

P. elatior (e-LAY-ti-or), oxslip. Size: 10 to 12 inches tall and wide. The broad leaves are puckered or crinkled. The open, nodding flowers are soft yellow. Hybrids include 'Cowichan Hybrids' in a mix of rich colors, especially blues and purples, and 'Velvet Moon' with yellow-eyed deep maroon flowers. Zones 4 (with protection) or 5 to 7.

P. japonica (ja-PON-i-ka), Japanese primrose. Size: 1 to 2 feet tall, 1 foot wide. The broad paddle-shaped leaves have sharply toothed margins. The tiered, whorled clusters of pink, rose, or white flowers are borne in late spring and early summer. 'Album' is white. 'Millar's Crimson' has bright rose-red flowers. 'Redfield Strain' comes in mixed colors and is extremely hardy. Zones 3 to 8.

P. juliae (JEW-le-i), Caucasian primrose. Size: 2 to 3 inches tall, 6 to 8 inches wide. A diminutive species with surprisingly large flowers, to 1 inch. Quilted basal leaves hug the ground. Many hybrids fall into the Juliae group. 'Garryarde Guinevere' has soft pink flowers and maroon-tinted leaves. 'JayJay' is rose-purple. 'Wanda' has deep magenta flowers with yellow eyes. Zones 4 (with protection) to 8.

P. kisoana (key-so-AY-na), Japanese woodland primrose. Size: 3 to 8 inches tall, 12 inches wide. A heat-tolerant and easy-care species with clusters of showy magenta flowers beginning in early spring. The felted, maple-like leaves persist through summer. Plants spread by runners to form broad, open clumps. 'Alba' is white-flowered. Zones 4 to 8.

P. ×polyantha (pah-lee-ANTH-a), polyantha primrose. Size: 8 to 12 inches tall and wide. These hybrids have broad crinkled leaves and short stalks with sparse clusters of flat, broad-petaled flowers. Many selections are available in a range of solid and bicolor forms. Zones 3 to 8.

P. sieboldii (see-BOLD-ee-ee), Siebold's primrose. Size: 4 to 8 inches tall, 8 to 12 inches wide. Siebold's primrose has fuzzy heart-shaped leaves with rounded teeth and flattened white, lavender, pink, or rose flowers with notched petals. 'Barnhaven Hybrids' come in mixed colors. 'Breaking Wave' is lavender with a white picotee edge. 'Geisha Girl' is shocking pink with a touch of frost at the center. 'Ice Princess' has intricately cut lavender-blue flowers with a dark reverse. 'Mikado' is deep magenta, the darkest of all. 'Snowflake' has attractively cut white petals. Zones 4 to 8.

P. veris (VE-ris), cowslip. Size: 8 to 12 inches tall and wide. Lovely, nodding, fragrant yellow flowers are held above the elongated oval leaves of this delicate early primrose. 'Sunset Shades' are a mixture of orange, terra-cotta, and yellow. Zones 4 to 8.

P. vulgaris (vul-GAH-ris), English primrose. Size: 6 to 9 inches tall and wide. The

Modern hybrid English primroses (*Primula vulgaris* 'Barnhaven Hybrids') are easy-care plants for lightly shaded woodlands or rock gardens. The flowers come in a full range of colors from white through yellow, butterscotch, and red to blue.

For a wet site with rich soil, choose the lovely, early-summer-blooming Japanese primroses (*Primula japonica*) or one of the other species of candelabra primroses with whorled tiers of flowers on tall stalks.

wild English primrose has wrinkled, elongated, oval foliage and broad, pale yellow flowers with darker centers borne one to a stem. *P. ×variabilis* is a yellow, heat-tolerant hybrid passed around gardens for generations. Ssp. *sibthorpii* has early pink flowers with large yellow eyes. Zones 4 to 8.

Hybrids

Many hybrid selections involve *P. elatior, P. juliae, P. veris,* and *P. vulgaris.* 'Dawn Ansell' has double white flowers with frilly green collars. 'Ken Dearman' is a deep butterscotch double. 'Sunshine Suzy' is a double chiffon yellow.

How to Grow

Most primroses grow best in moist, humus-rich soil in light to partial shade. *P. japonica* and *P. denticulata* require constantly moist to boggy, humusy soil. They all are of easy culture if their simple needs are correctly met. In northern zones, winter mulch is essential, especially if snowfall is erratic. In the South, protection from hot sun and a consistent moisture supply are required. When plants get too hot or dry, they go dormant early, usually without adverse results. An organic mulch left in place will help enrich soil. Clumps increase from the central crown to form many dense rosettes. Divide overgrown clumps after flowering, and replant into amended soil. Some hybrids need regular division (every 2 years or so) to keep them vigorous. Plants are easily grown from fresh seed sown outdoors in fall or inside in early spring.

Landscape Uses

Primroses have a place in every garden. Plant clumps or drifts of plants with spring bulbs such as tulips, snowdrops (*Galanthus*), daffodils (*Narcissus*), and Spanish bluebell (*Hyacinthoides hispanica*). Early perennials such as hellebores, Virginia bluebells (*Mertensia virginica*), lungworts (*Pulmonaria*), blue garden phlox (*Phlox paniculata*), windflowers (*Anemone*), cranesbills (*Geranium*), and irises are good choices for light shade. Combine the wet-soil species with irises, hostas, ferns, forget-me-nots (*Myosotis*), lady's-mantle (*Alchemilla mollis*), and astilbe (*Astilbe ×arendsii*).

PULMONARIA

pul-mon-AIR-ee-a • Boraginaceae, Borage Family

Lungworts are early-blooming perennials with short, weakly upright stems sporting open clusters of nodding five-petaled flowers. Some species have flowers that open pink and turn to blue; others bear pink, red, or white blooms. The basal leaves emerge and expand as flowers are fading. They may be ovate with pointed tapering tips and long petioles or lance-shaped. Some are spotted and blotched with silver; others are solid green. Plants grow from stout crowns with thick, fibrous roots.

PULMONARIA

Common Names:
Lungwort, Bethlehem sage

Bloom Time:
Spring bloom

Planting Requirements:
Light to full shade

Pulmonaria angustifolia (an-gus-ti-FO-lee-a), blue lungwort. Size: 9 to 12 inches tall, 12 to 18 inches wide. Blue lungwort has deep indigo flowers and narrowly oval, bristly leaves. The plants spread by underground stems to form open clumps. 'Azurea' has vibrant gentian blue flowers. 'Johnson's Blue' has deep blue flowers. USDA Plant Hardiness Zones 2 to 8.

P. longifolia (lon-gi-FO-lee-a), long-leaved lungwort. Size: 9 to 12 inches tall, 12 to 24 inches wide. The strap-shaped pointed leaves of this species are speckled with silver-gray. The flowers open pink and change to rich blue. 'Bertram Anderson' has narrower leaves than the species. Ssp. *cevennensis* has silver-splotched leaves to 1 foot long and blue flowers. Zones 3 to 8.

P. rubra (REW-bra), red lungwort. Size: 1 to 2 feet tall and wide. This tall species has weakly upright stems and pointed oval green leaves. The coral-red flowers make this a popular plant. 'David Ward' has dramatic, white-edged leaves. 'Redstart' is an old favorite with salmon-red flowers. Zones 4 to 7.

P. saccharata (sa-ka-RAH-ta), Bethlehem sage. Size: 9 to 18 inches tall, 12 to 18 inches wide. This is the most well-known lungwort, grown for its pointed oval foliage with silver spots and clusters of pink buds that fade to blue. 'Highdown' is an excellent blue. 'Janet Fisk' has densely spotted leaves and lavender-pink flowers. 'Marjorie Fisk' has sky blue flowers and heavily marked foliage. 'Mrs. Moon' has large broad leaves and pink flowers that fade to blue. *P. officinalis* is similar. 'Sissinghurst White' is pure white with silvery leaves. Zones 3 to 8.

Hybrids

Dozens of new hybrids have been developed in recent years. Choose among

The delicate bicolor spring flowers of Bethlehem sage (*Pulmonaria saccharata* 'Leopard') are just the beginning of this plant's seasonal display. The flowers are followed by broad clumps of lush, silver-spotted foliage that persist until hard frost.

How to Grow

Lungworts are easy to grow in evenly moist, humus-rich soil in light to full shade. In cool northern zones, sun is acceptable. Plants are moderately drought-tolerant once established but may go dormant if conditions get too dry. Wilted foliage opens plants to powdery mildew infection. Divide overgrown clumps after flowering or in fall. Replant into enriched soil. An annual mulch left to decay helps enrich soil.

Landscape Uses

Lungworts are lovely spring perennials with colorful foliage and flowers. Combine them with daffodils (*Narcissus*), grape hyacinths (*Muscari*), snowdrops (*Galanthu*), and other spring bulbs in beds and borders or under flowering trees and shrubs. The tough summer foliage is an outstanding groundcover. In the perennial garden, plant them in drifts with hellebores, windflowers (*Anemone*), bleeding hearts (*Dicentra*), irises, primroses (*Primula*), and Allegheny foamflower (*Tiarella cordifolia*). Contrast the lovely summer foliage with lady's-mantle (*Alchemilla mollis*), coral bells (*Heuchera*), bergenias, Solomon's seals (*Polygonatum*), hostas, and ferns.

standouts such as 'Benediction' with medium blue flowers and excellent form, 'Cotton Cool' with elongated silver leaves and blue flowers, or 'Dark Vader' with blue-violet flowers and evenly spotted leaves. 'Majeste' has entirely silver leaves and blue flowers. 'Raspberry Ice' is like berries and cream with white-edged leaves and vibrant pink flowers. 'Raspberry Splash' has deep pink flowers and long, upright leaves. 'Trevi Fountain' has cobalt blue flowers over upright vases of heavily spotted leaves.

PULSATILLA

pul-sa-TIL-la • Ranunculaceae, Buttercup Family

The hairy foliage of pasque flowers seems appropriately clad to endure the early spring chill that dominates when these harbingers of spring open their first blooms. Starry, five-petaled flowers surrounding a central ring of fuzzy orange-yellow stamens are followed by fuzzy, plumed seedheads. Plants grow from thick, fibrous-rooted crowns.

PULSATILLA

Common Names:
  Pasque flower, prairie crocus

Bloom Time:
  Spring bloom

Planting Requirements:
  Sun

Pulsatilla patens (PAY-tenz), prairie crocus, pasque flower. Size: 3 to 8 inches tall, 8 to 12 inches wide. Prairie crocus has white or pale blue flowers and is very sensitive to wet soils. Plant only in sandy or gravelly, well-drained soil. Plants go dormant in hot weather. USDA Plant Hardiness Zones 3 to 7.

P. vulgaris (vul-GAR-is), European pasque flower. Size: 1 to 1½ feet tall and wide. Purple flowers have five starry petals above deeply cut, spidery foliage. Overall larger and more vigorous than our native species. Var. *alba* has creamy white flowers. Var. *rubra* has burgundy flowers. Zones 3 to 8.

The royal purple blooms of pasque flower (*Pulsatilla vulgaris*) open in the chilly spring breeze wrapped in a coat of soft hairs for insulation. The starry flowers open wide on sunny days and nod shyly when chilly breezes blow.

How to Grow

Plant pasque flowers in average to rich, well-drained soil in full sun or light shade. Plants do not tolerate soggy soils. Pasque flowers begin blooming just as they emerge in spring and continue for several weeks as they grow larger. Do not crowd plants or allow neighbors to flop over them, as this will encourage rot. After seed is set, plants go dormant unless conditions are cool. Clumps get quite large but seldom need division. Divide clumps after flowering or in fall. Sow seed outdoors. Self-sown seedlings are plentiful.

Landscape Uses

Pasque flowers are perfect for rock gardens with early bulbs, rock cresses (*Arabis*), basket-of-gold (*Aurinia saxatilis*), perennial candytuft (*Iberis sempervirens*), and columbines (*Aquilegia*). Use prairie crocus in wild gardens with violets (*Viola*), prairie smoke (*Geum triflorum*), penstemons, and grasses.

PUSCHKINIA

push-KIN-ee-a • Hyacinthaceae (Liliaceae), Hyacinth Family

White flowers with milky blue tracery open in early spring to the delight of gardeners. This true bulb offers an alternative to the prolifically seeding scillas. The foliage is neat and unobtrusive after the flowers fade. Use drifts as a groundcover with shrubs or in beds with daylilies and peonies that will overtop them later in the season.

PUSCHKINIA

Common Name:
Striped squill

Bloom Time:
Spring bloom

Planting Requirements:
Sun

Puschkinia scilloides var. **libanotica** (skill-LOY-deez var. lib-a-TON-i-ka), striped squill. Size: 3 to 6 inches tall and wide. A charming, early bulb of diminutive stature but big show. The starry white flowers with sky blue stripes down the center of each petal emerge before the paired leaves, which begin to unfurl as the flowerstalk elongates. Plants go dormant soon after seeds ripen in early summer. 'Alba' has white flowers. Zones 3 to 8.

How to Grow

Set the rounded, paper-coated white bulbs 2 to 3 inches below the surface of rich, evenly moist soil in a spot with full to partial shade. Plants generously self-sow and increase by offsets as well.

Landscape Uses

In time, a dozen bulbs will spread to form a lovely drift among stems of taller bulbs like daffodils and tulips, accented by the emerging pink noses of variegated Solomon's seal (*Polygonatum odoratum* 'Variegatum') and unfurling fern fronds. Use them in rock gardens or en masse under shrubs.

Striped squills (*Puschkinia scilloides* var. *libatonica*) are underused bulbs with dense white flower spikes delicately laced in blue. A pure white form is also available.

R

RANUNCULUS

rah-NUN-kew-lus • Ranunculaceae, Buttercup Family

Buttercups are bright spring plants of meadows and gardens. The shiny yellow flowers have five petal-like sepals surrounding a ring of fuzzy stamens (male reproductive structures). The flowers may be borne singly or in loose, sparse clusters on leafy stems. All produce basal rosettes of leaves that may be simple, lobed, or divided. Plants grow from fibrous rootstocks or bulbs.

RANUNCULUS

Common Name:
Buttercup

Bloom Time:
Spring bloom

Planting Requirements:
Light to partial shade

Ranunculus acris (AH-kris), common buttercup. Size: 2 to 3 feet tall, 1 to 2 feet wide. This familiar buttercup is naturalized across much of eastern North America. The basal leaves have three to seven (usually five), palmately divided leaflets. The stem leaves have three leaflets below the sparse, long-stalked flowers. 'Flore Pleno' ('Multiplex') has 1-inch double flowers. *R. aconitifolia* is similar in size but white-flowered; most commonly seen in its attractive double form called 'Flore Pleno'. USDA Plant Hardiness Zones 3 to 7.

R. asiaticus (ay-see-AH-ti-kus), Persian buttercup. Size: 1 to 2½ feet tall, 1 to 2 feet wide. This larger version of *R. acris* has thrice-divided leaves with three leaflets on each division and larger, usually double flowers. Zones 8 to 10.

R. repens (RE-penz), creeping buttercup. Size: 1 to 1½ feet tall and wide. A fast-creeping perennial with three-lobed palmate leaves and sparse stalks bearing shiny yellow flowers. 'Buttered Popcorn' has yellow varigated leaves that set off the

For a fast-spreading groundcover in a moist spot, try creeping buttercup (*Ranunculus repens* 'Flore Pleno'). Double pompon yellow flowers in spring make this plant irresistible.

flowers. 'Flore Pleno' has rounded, double flowers. Zones 3 to 8.

How to Grow

Plant buttercups in evenly moist, humus-rich soil in full sun or light shade. Plants spread rapidly by roots and self-sown seedlings and may need control. Cut bloom stalks off as flowers fade to control seeding. Divide clumps after flowering or in fall. Plants are considered invasive in some states, especially *R. ficaria*, which should not be grown even in its double forms, which spread vegetatively.

Landscape Uses

Use buttercups as groundcovers in moist soil with shrubs and small trees in combination with hostas, ferns, and other plants that can hold their own. Plants are best kept out of the formal perennial garden. Use them in containers in water gardens.

RHEUM

RAY-um • Polygonaceae, Smartweed Family

"Outrageous" and "elegant" are two of the best words to describe ornamental rhubarbs. They are grown for their tropical-looking foliage and strong, upright flower clusters. If you have the room for them, give them a try. You will not be disappointed. They are sure to jazz up any garden in the ground or in containers. Plants produce huge, succulent crowns with dense, leathery, fibrous roots.

RHEUM

Common Name:
Rhubarb

Bloom Time:
Foliage plant with early summer bloom

Planting Requirements:
Sun to partial shade

Rheum alexandrae (al-ex-AN-dri), rhubarb. Size: 3 to 4 feet tall, 2 to 3 feet wide. This curious but exceedingly handsome species is grown more for the showy chartreuse bracts than the flowers they hide. The lance-shaped, leathery leaves form attractive basal clumps. Plants require rich soil and even moisture in a sunny to partially shaded spot. USDA Plant Hardiness Zones 5 to 8.

R. palmatum (pal-MATE-um), ornamental rhubarb. Size: 4 to 7 feet tall, 3 to 5 feet wide. Huge, deeply cut leaves emerge deep purple and fade to deep green with a purple reverse in summer. The leaves of mature plants stand up to 4 feet tall, and the bloom spike may reach 7 feet. The huge spike expands to reveal many ascending to horizontal side branches studded with small, creamy white flowers.

Elegant and outrageous describe ornamental rhubarb (*Rheum palmatum*). This giant is grown for its huge, triangular clawed leaves as much as its tall, strong flower clusters. 'Atrosanguineum' has leaves tinted with bronze and the flowers are smoky cerise.

Plants take several years to mature. 'Atrosanguineum' is similar in proportions to the species, but the leaves are tinted with bronze through summer, and the flowers are smoky cerise rather than white. Plants make a dramatic display in flower. Var. *tanguticum* has leathery leaves that are less raggedly cut than the species. Zones 4 (with protection) to 8.

R. rhabarbarum (rah-BAR-ba-rum), culinary rhubarb. Size: 3 to 5 feet tall, 2 to 4 feet wide. Though grown to be eaten, culinary rhubarb is a handsome ornamental in its own right. The wavy, triangular leaves add bold texture among fine-leaved plants, and the red petioles make a dramatic show. The tall flower spikes spoil the taste but add to the show. Zones 3 to 7.

How to Grow

Grow rhubarb in humus-rich soil that stays evenly moist all season in sun to partial shade. This plant delights in a boggy spot, with the crown dry and the roots in wet soil. Rhubarbs are voracious feeders. Top-dress plants annually with compost or rotted manure to keep soil rich and light. Full sun brings out the best color in foliage, but plants grow well in partial shade, too. Where summer nights are hot, plants will decline after flowering but will resprout in late summer.

Landscape Uses

"Bodacious" best describes the enormous leaves of ornamental rhubarbs. Plants are so dramatic that they demand attention. Place them in the foreground of a garden to frame a distant view, or use them like a decorative vase or a bench. As a focal point, surround them with finer textures. For a really outrageous planting, try a battle of the bold, with rhubarb among other big leaves like elephant ears (*Colocasia*), Roger's-flowers (*Rodgersia*), hibiscus, cannas, butterburs (*Petasites*), and crinums.

RODGERSIA

ro-JERZ-ee-a • Saxifragaceae, Saxifrage Family

Bold, elegant foliage and frothy plumes of fuzzy flowers are the lure of rodgersias. These stately plants have enormous palmately lobed leaves on long stalks. Tall, densely branched spikes of small fuzzy flowers are carried above the foliage in early summer. They grow from thick, slow, creeping rhizomes with fibrous roots. Mature plants form huge crowns with dozens of eyes.

RODGERSIA
Common Names:
Rodgersia,
Roger's-flower
Bloom Time:
Foliage plant with late spring to early summer bloom
Planting Requirements:
Partial to full shade

Rodgersia aesculifolia (ee-skew-li-FO-lee-a), fingerleaf rodgersia. Size: 4 to 6 feet tall, 4 to 5 feet wide. This handsome plant has five to seven broad, crinkled leaves with abruptly tapering tips. The flowers are creamy white. USDA Plant Hardiness Zones 4 to 7; may be hardier farther north.

R. pinnata (pin-NAH-ta), featherleaf rodgersia. Size: 3 to 4 feet tall and wide; flowers small, in 2-foot clusters. Quilted leaves are palmate; tall, foamy spikes have pink flowers. 'Superba' has bronze foliage and deep rose-pink flowers. *R. sambucifolia* is similar. Zones 4 to 7.

R. podophylla (po-do-FIL-la), bronze-leaf rodgersia. Size: 2 to 3 feet tall, 3 to 4 feet wide. This attractive species has bronze foliage with ragged, blunt-tipped leaflets and white flowers. *R. henrici* is similar. Zones 4 to 7.

R. tabularis (tab-u-LAR-is), astilboides. Size: 3 to 4 feet tall and wide. Huge, ragged circular leaves like a saw blade set

this apart from other species. White flowers are carried in plumes above leaves in summer. Zones 4 to 7.

In moist or wet soils along ponds or streams, the bold foliage and airy plumes of bronze-leaf rodgersia (*Rodgersia podophylla*) create an impression of tropical luxuriance. The broccoli-like buds emerge wrapped in the rich bronzy new leaves. Fully expanded, they are like giant parasols that turn bronze again in fall.

How to Grow

Rodgersias must have constantly moist to wet, humus-rich soil in light to full shade. Plants in warm zones need considerable shade. Hot sun quickly burns foliage and destroys plants on impact. Creeping root-stocks eventually form broad clumps that can be left in place for many years. Propagate by division in fall.

Landscape Uses

Rodgersias are lovely plants for bog and water gardens. Plant them with water iris like *Iris sibirica,* Japanese primroses (*Primula japonica*), meadowsweets (*Filipendula*), globeflowers (*Trollius*), ligularias, astilbes (*Astilbe ×arendsii*), hostas, sedges (*Carex*), and ferns. They are adaptable to moist shade gardens as long as the soil does not dry out.

ROMNEYA

rom-KNEE-ya • Papaveraceae, Poppy Family

Matilija poppy hails from the arid, summer-dry regions of California and Mexico, so you know it is tough. The pity for most gardeners is that its limited hardiness and intolerance of soggy soils limits it to regions close to its native range. The luscious, white crepe-paper flowers with bright yellow stamens are stunning.

ROMNEYA

Common Name:
  Matilija poppy

Bloom Time:
  Summer bloom

Planting Requirements:
  Sun to light shade

Though it romps a bit, matilija poppy (*Romneya coulteri*) is a beautiful addition to a courtyard, border, or mixed shrub planting. Plants thrive on heat and drought.

Romneya coulteri (COLE-ter-e), matilija poppy. Size: 4 to 8 feet tall, 3 to 6 feet wide. Bright white, 5-inch crepe-paper flowers with bright yellow centers top the succulent stems of this widely stoloniferous perennial. The stems are covered in blue-green lobed leaves that make the broad clumps attractive even when it's not in flower. Plants have limited hardiness, but they are easily grown in containers. USDA Plant Hardiness Zones 8 to 10.

How to Grow

Plant in moist, well-drained sandy or gravelly soil in full sun or light shade. Plants will not tolerate poor drainage. Suckers are abundant and can be used for propagation or dug to control the plant's spread. A sheltered spot may extend hardiness a zone.

Landscape Uses

Matilija poppy easily dominates a garden. Use it as a specimen or in a mixed planting of grasses. Good companions include prickly pears (*Opuntia*), penstemons, century plants (*Agave*), and yuccas.

RUDBECKIA

rud-BEK-ee-a • Asteraceae, Aster Family

Black-eyed Susans are bright summer flowers of meadows, woods, and roadsides. The daisylike flowers have golden yellow petal-like rays and brown to green central, domed, or buttonlike disks. Plants form broad clumps from branched crowns with fibrous roots. The basal leaves are oval, occasionally lobed, and usually rough and hairy. Stem leaves are smaller.

> **RUDBECKIA**
>
> **Common Names:**
>   Black-eyed Susan,
>   coneflower
>
> **Bloom Time:**
>   Summer bloom
>
> **Planting Requirements:**
>   Full sun to light shade

Rudbeckia fulgida (FUL-ji-da), orange black-eyed Susan. Size: 1½ to 3 feet tall and wide. This popular perennial has showy, orange-yellow flowers with deep brown centers. The rough, hairy leaves are oval to broadly lance-shaped. Several varieties exist, but only one is widely available. Var. *sullivantii* is a stout grower with leafy stems and large flowers. 'Goldsturm' belongs to this variety and is a compact, floriferous seed strain with 3- to 4-inch flowers. Many plants sold under this name are seed-grown and therefore variable, but are all good garden plants. USDA Plant Hardiness Zones 3 to 9.

R. laciniata (la-sin-ee-AH-ta), ragged coneflower, green-headed coneflower. Size: 2½ to 6 feet tall, 3 to 4 feet wide. This tall, stout plant has large, three- to five-lobed basal leaves and leafy stems with three-lobed leaves. The stems are crowned by branched clusters of clear yellow flowers with drooping rays and a conical green disk. 'Golden Glow' has 3½- to 4-inch lemon yellow flowers on 3- to 5-foot stems. 'Goldquelle' ('Gold Drop') is a floriferous selection with shaggy double flowers on 3-foot stems. Zones 3 to 8.

R. maxima (MAX-e-ma), giant coneflower. Size: 4 to 6 feet tall, 2 to 3 feet wide. This striking plant has dense clumps of 2-foot, waxy, blue-green oval leaves with long stalks and stout, sparsely branching stems to 6 feet tall. The flowers have 3-inch drooping oval rays and 3- to 4-inch, dark brown conical disks. Zones 4 to 9.

R. nitida (NIT-i-da), shiny coneflower. Size: 3 to 4 feet tall, 2 to 3 feet wide. This species is similar to *R. laciniata* but has oval leaves without lobes. The rays are broader with rounded tips and the disk is dark. 'Herbstonne' ('Autumn Sun') is 5 to 7 feet tall with bright yellow flowers. Zones 4 to 9.

R. subtomentosa (sub-toe-men-TOW-sa), sweet coneflower. Size: 3 to 4 feet tall, 2 to 3 feet wide. A delicate species with 3-foot stems bearing branched clusters of clear yellow flowers with rich brown centers. Plants bloom for several weeks in mid- to late summer. The soft, hairy, fragrant oval leaves are lobed or toothed. Zones 4 to 9.

How to Grow

Plant in moist but well-drained, average to rich soil in full sun or light shade. Plants grow vigorously and need frequent division in spring to control their spread and to re-plenish the impoverished soil they leave in their wake. Every 2 or 3 years is recommended for *R. fulgida*. Divide *R. laciniata* every 3 to 5 years depending on your size constraints. Their ease of culture and foolproof hardiness have put coneflowers among the most widely grown perennials. Black-eyed Susans bloom profusely for nearly a month in mid- to late summer. Coneflowers bloom earlier, and the tall selections may need staking. If plants are

Plant the double-flowered towering 5- to 6-foot shining coneflower (*Rudbeckia nitida* 'Goldquelle') at the back of the border with ornamental grasses or in informal meadow gardens. Plants thrive in moist soil but tolerate average conditions.

floppy, cut them to the ground after flowering. Some species are attacked by red aphids that gather below the flowers. Spray with insecticidal soap.

Landscape Uses

Rudbeckias are perfect for adding bright, long-lasting color to perennial gardens. Plant them with summer flowers such as catmints (*Nepeta*), purple coneflowers (*Echinacea*), Russian sage (*Perovskia atriplicifolia*), daylilies (*Hemerocallis*), garden phlox (*Phlox paniculata*), stonecrops (*Sedum*), bee balms (*Monarda*), and ornamental grasses. Plants are excellent for informal meadow and prairie gardens, and *R. laciniata* will grow well in lightly shaded woodland gardens among ferns and wildflowers.

The bright yellow daisies of orange black-eyed Susan (*Rudbeckia fulgida*) are classic summer perennials for beds, borders, and meadow plantings. They are tough, adaptable, and even thrive in containers left outdoors in winter.

RUTA

ROO-ta • Rutaceae, Rue Family

Rue has been in cultivation for centuries for its medicinal and ornamental properties. The divided, delicately lobed, blue-gray leaves have given their name to many plants with similar foliage, including rue anemone (*Anemonella thalictroides*) and meadow rues (*Thalictrum*). A subshrub with persistent stem bases, rue has thick, fibrous roots. Sap may cause skin irritation; handle with care.

RUTA

Common Name:
Rue

Bloom Time:
Foliage plant with summer bloom

Planting Requirements:
Full sun

As with many gray-leaved plants, rue (*Ruta graveolens* 'Jackman Blue') grows best in a sandy, well-drained soil in full sun. This compact selection is one of the bluest available.

Ruta graveolens (gra-VEE-o-lenz), rue. Size: 1 to 3 feet tall, 1 to 2 feet wide. Aromatic leaves are finely dissected into many small leaflets. Leafy flowerstalks are crowned by flattened, branched clusters of small yellow flowers. Plants grow from a persistent woody base with a twisted, branched taproot. 'Blue Mound' is a wide-spreading selection with rich blue-green foliage. 'Jackman Blue' is a compact, blue-leaved variety to 16 inches tall. *Note:* Plants are poisonous and may cause a skin rash if leaves are bruised. USDA Plant Hardiness Zones 4 to 9.

How to Grow

Give rues sandy or loamy, moist but well-drained soil in full sun. Plants are easy to establish and long-lived. They grow larger and more shrubby with the years but seldom need division. Propagate by stem cuttings taken in late summer and early fall.

Landscape Uses

Rues are good plants for bordering beds, delineating herb gardens, and configuring knot gardens. In ornamental gardens, plant them with white, pale yellow, and blue flowers. Winecups (*Callirhoe*), evening primroses (*Oenothera*), yarrows (*Achillea*), baby's-breath (*Gypsophila paniculata*), balloon flower (*Platycodon grandiflorus*), bellflowers (*Campanula*), flax (*Linum*), catchflys (*Lychnis*), and pinks (*Dianthus*) are good choices.

SALVIA

SAL-vee-a • Lamiaceae, Mint Family

Sages are mounded to shrubby mints with the tubular, bilobed flowers and square stems indicative of their kinship. The flowers have inflated protruding upper lips that project over the lower ones. They are borne in tiered whorls at the tips of branching stems. Many have aromatic foliage. Leaves may be oval or broadly lance-shaped. They grow from woody crowns with fibrous roots. Species vary in hardiness from tough to extremely frost-tender. Many good garden sages are available.

SALVIA

Common Name:
Sage

Bloom Time:
Summer and fall bloom

Planting Requirements:
Full sun to light shade

Salvia argentea (ar-JEN-tee-a), silver sage. Size: 2 to 4 feet tall, 1 to 2 feet wide. Silver sage is grown for its luscious, crinkled, soft silver-gray foliage. The ragged white flowers are best removed before they open. USDA Plant Hardiness Zones 5 to 9.

S. azurea (a-ZEW-ree-a), azure sage. Size: 3 to 4 feet tall, 2 to 3 feet wide. This upright bushy sage has lance-shaped basal leaves, leafy stems, and dense terminal spikes of azure blue flowers. Var. *grandiflora* has larger flowers. *S. uliginosa,* bog sage, has a similar form, with azure-and-white bicolor flowers on 4- to 5-foot stems. Zones 4 (with protection) to 9.

S. darcyi (DAR-see-ee), Darcy sage. Size: 2 to 3 feet tall, 3 to 4 feet wide. A stunning plant with vermilion flowers held above fragrant wedge-shaped, resinous leaves. Look out hummingbirds! *S. regia* has small, kidney-shaped leaves that are mostly basal, and tall spikes, to 3 feet, of red flowers in fall. 'Jame' is a good red-orange selection. Zones 7 to 10.

S. farinacea (far-i-NA-see-a), mealycup sage. Size: 1½ to 4 feet tall, 1 to 2 feet wide. This open, loosely branching sage has narrowly oval leaves and terminal spikes of violet-blue flowers held above foliage. Grown as a popular annual in colder zones. 'Blue Bedder' has deep blue flowers on 2- to 2½-foot stems. 'Victoria' is similar but more compact (18 inches). 'Indigo Spires' is an open-crowned hybrid sage to 3 feet tall with spikes of tiered deep blue flowers. Zones 8 to 10.

S. greggii (GREG-ge-ee), autumn sage. Size: 2 to 4 feet tall and wide. A small, rounded shrub with delicate, soft, hairy leaves and terminal clusters of red flowers all season. In colder zones, plants die back partially or to the ground and do not begin blooming until early summer. 'Dark Dancer' has deep raspberry red flowers. *S. ×jamensis* is a red-flowered hybrid.

S. microphylla is similar to autumn sage but a bit less hardy. Leaf size is variable, not always small as the name would indicate. 'San Carlos Festival' is a great compact selection with deep fuchsia-pink flowers. 'Wild Watermelon' is watermelon pink. Many hybrid selections are available. 'Maraschino' has cherry red flowers. 'Raspberry Royale' has glowing raspberry flowers. 'Silke's Dream' is rich scarlet. Zones 7 to 10. (Some selections a bit less hardy.)

S. guaranitica (gar-an-IT-i-ka), blue anise sage. Size: 4 to 6 feet tall, 3 to 4 feet wide. A tall, leafy sage with deep blue flowers on stout stems. 'Argentine Skies' has soft sky blue flowers. 'Black and Blue' has deep indigo flowers with near-black calyces on compact plants to 3 feet tall. Zones 7 to 10.

S. koyamae (ko-YAM-eye), yellow sage. Size: 1 to 2 feet tall, 2 to 3 feet wide. A woodland sage with spear-shaped leaves and spikes of milky yellow flowers in late summer and fall. *S. nipponica* has a similar form but is more compact. 'Fuji Snow' has white-edged, speckled leaves. Zones 6 to 8.

S. leucantha (lew-KAN-tha), velvet sage. Size: 3 to 4 feet tall and wide. This shrubby sage has woolly stems and leaves and 10-foot spires of white flowers with purple calyces from midsummer through frost. 'Midnight' has red-violet flowers and purple calyces. 'Santa Barbara' is a compact selection, 2 feet tall and 3 to 4 feet wide. 'Anthony Parker' is a hybrid with purple-blue flowers on open plants. Zones 8 to 10.

S. nemorosa (nem-or-OH-sa), garden sage. Size: 1½ to 3½ feet tall and wide. This lovely sage is smothered in stiff spikes of violet-blue flowers for 3 to 4 weeks in early to midsummer. Triangular leaves are soft, hairy, bright green. 'Caradonna' is tall (2½ feet) with open spikes of blue-violet flowers all summer. 'Lubecca' has blue-violet flowers on tall, open spikes. 'Marcus' is a true dwarf to 8 inches with blue-violet flowers. 'Ostfriesland' ('East Friesland') has deep purple flowers on compact stems 1 to 1½ feet tall. Cultivars are sometimes listed under the similar hybrid *S. ×sylvestris*. The following selections belong here. 'Blaukonigin' ('Blue Queen') has violet flowers

Use clumps of hybrid garden sage (*Salvia ×superba*) to add upright, spiky forms to the middle or front of the border. They bloom for up to 2 months if old flower spikes are removed.

and is 1½ to 2 feet tall. 'Mainacht' ('May Night') has purple flowers and red-violet calyxes. 'Rosenkonigin' ('Rose Queen') has rose-pink flowers. 'Schneehuegal' ('Snow Hill') has white flowers. 'Viola Klose' has dark blue flowers. Zones 4 to 7.

S. officinalis (o-fis-i-NAY-lis), culinary sage. Size: 1½ to 2 feet tall, 2 to 3 feet wide. Ornamental and culinary, a semiwoody shrub with woolly, oblong leaves and somewhat insignificant blue-violet flowers. Many handsome leaf colors with compact form are available. 'Berggarten' has broad oval leaves and is quite showy with blue-violet flowers. 'Compacta' is a compact grower to 15 inches with smaller leaves. 'Icterina' has gold-and-green variegated foliage. 'Purpurescens' has gray-violet leaves. 'Tricolor' has pink, green, and white leaves. Zones 3 to 9.

S. pratensis (prah-TEN-sis), meadow sage. Size: 1 to 3 feet tall, 2 to 3 feet wide. This slender sage has bushy rosettes of oval leaves and tall, branching stems tipped with showy violet-blue flowers. Excellent cultivars are available. 'Haematodes' has showy blue-violet flowers. 'Rosea' has rose-purple flowers. *S. verticillata*, whorled sage, is a sprawling species with blue flowers atop lax spikes. 'Purple Rain' is smoky purple. 'White Rain' is white-flowered and has a more compact form, to 2 feet tall and 3 feet wide. Zones 3 to 9.

How to Grow

Plant sages in well-drained, sandy or loamy soils in full sun or light shade. They will get

The open habit of violet-blue-flowered anise sage (*Salvia guarantica*) makes it perfect for sprawling among flowering shrubs and tall perennials like sunflowers. Plants form tuberlike swellings on their roots that help them survive cold winters.

leggy and flop in too much shade. Overly rich or moist soils also encourage flopping. Most species are tough and extremely drought-tolerant. Divide plants in spring or fall if they overgrow their position. Cut plants back to the ground in fall or early spring. Tender and woody salvias should be cut back in spring only. Propagate by stem cuttings in early summer. The less hardy species can be treated as annuals in colder zones and grown each season from seed sown indoors or from overwintered cuttings. Mulching with a cover of straw or chopped leaves may improve hardiness. Woodland species need rich, evenly moist soil in some shade.

Landscape Uses

Sages are excellent additions to well-drained perennial gardens. There are so many sizes and forms that there is one for every garden situation. Combine meadow and garden sage and their hybrids with yuccas (*Yucca*), yarrows (*Achillea*), catmints (*Nepeta*), stonecrops (*Sedum*), black-eyed Susans (*Rudbeckia*), daylilies (*Hemerocallis*), tickseeds (*Coreopsis*), daisies and mums (*Chrysanthemum*), and ornamental grasses. Plant culinary sage in herb gardens or with ornamentals. In borders or prairie gardens, combine autumn sage with verbenas, winecups (*Callirhoe*), lavenders (*Lavandula*), sundrops (*Calylophus*), ornamental onions (*Allium*), asters, yuccas, and grasses. Large species such as anise sage look great with tropicals like cannas, elephant ears, and coleuses. All sages respond well to container culture. Contrast their rich colors with filamentous bronze New Zealand hairy sedge (*Carex comans* 'Bronze'), ever-blooming diascias, and bold African daisy hybrids (*Gazanias*).

SANGUINARIA

san-gwin-AY-ree-a • Papaveraceae, Poppy Family

Pristine white flowers grace moist woodlands while the trees are bare and the nights are chilly. This early blooming native wildflower is fleeting, so savor the few days when flowers are open. Plants thrive in rich woods and are easily cultivated in most garden soils. The dazzling double-flowered form is prized for its singular beauty and longer-lasting blooms.

SANGUINARIA

Common Name:
Bloodroot

Bloom Time:
Spring bloom

Planting Requirements:
Sun or shade

Sanguinaria canadensis (kan-a-DEN-sis), bloodroot. Size: 4 to 10 feet tall, 12 feet wide. Bloodroot opens its pure white stars in early spring when few other native wildflowers are stirring. Plants emerge with a single, deeply lobed leaf wrapped around the flower bud. Each flower has 8 to 11 narrow petals surrounding a cluster of yellow stamens. Plants grow from a thick creeping rhizome with bright orange juice, for which the plant is named. An extract of bloodroot is an important anti-plaque agent in some toothpastes and mouthwashes. 'Flore Pleno' ('Multiplex') is a stunning, fully double form with long-lasting flowers and huge, thick leaves. Plants must be divided every 2 or 3 years as rhizomes quickly become tangled and rot may set in, destroying plants. USDA Plant Hardiness Zones 3 to 9.

How to Grow

Plant bloodroot in moist, humus-rich soil in light to full shade. Spring sun is important, but summer shade is necessary. Unlike many bulbous plants, the leaves of bloodroot persist well into summer, but during prolonged dry spells plants may go dormant with no ill effect. Plants form dense clumps that can be divided in fall. Self-sown seedlings will appear, and plants flower in 2 or 3 years.

Landscape Uses

Combine bloodroot with wood anemone (*Anemone nemorosa*), spring beauties (*Claytonia*), merrybells (*Uvularia*), Virginia bluebells (*Mertensia virginica*), sedges (*Carex*), and ferns. Spring bulbs, hostas, and primroses (*Primula*) are also good companions. A groundcover under shrubs and flowering trees gives the illusion of snow in the spring garden for the few glorious days they are in bloom.

The gardenia-like flowers of double bloodroot (*Sanguinaria canadensis* 'Flore Pleno') last a few days longer than their single counterparts, but both are fleetingly beautiful additions to the spring garden. The lobed foliage stays attractive all summer.

SANGUISORBA

san-gwe-SOR-ba • Rosaceae, Rose Family

The tall bottlebrushes of burnet wave on stout stems clothed in handsome, pinnately divided leaves with oblong leaflets that resemble the herb salad burnet. Most are northern plants that dislike heat, but there are a few heat-tolerant species available. All make spectacular clumps with dozens of flowering stems. Plants grow from thick, fleshy-rooted crowns.

SANGUISORBA

Common Name:
Burnet

Bloom Time:
Summer bloom

Planting Requirements:
Sun to light shade

Tall wands of tightly packed, fuzzy flowers add drama to the lush, pinnately divided foliage of Canadian burnet (*Sanguisorba canadensis*). Plants need consistent moisture and cool nights to thrive.

Sanguisorba canadensis (kan-a-DEN-sis), Canadian burnet. Size: 3 to 4 feet tall, 1 to 2 feet wide. The fuzzy, white, late-summer flowers lack petals. They are tightly packed into dense spikes; hence the bottlebrush appearance. Plants form broad dense clumps at maturity. USDA Plant Hardiness Zones 2 to 8.

S. obtusa (ob-TEW-sa), Japanese burnet. Size: 3 to 4 feet tall, 2 to 3 feet wide. The pink bottlebrush flowers arch above attractive basal clumps of foliage with nearly rounded leaflets. *S. albiflora* is similar but has blue-gray foliage and white flowers on 1- to 2-foot stems. Zones 4 to 7.

S. tenuifolia (ten-yoo-i-FOL-ee-ah), narrow-leaf burnet. Size: 4 to 5 feet tall, 2 to 3 feet wide. As attractive in leaf as in flower. 1-foot leaves have narrow, glossy leaflets in full clumps. Tall stems are sparsely covered in smaller leaves and crowned with open clusters of dense flowers on long stalks. 'Alba' has white flowers. 'Purpurea' has long, drooping maroon flower clusters. *S. officinalis*, great burnet, has maroon flowers on stems to 2 feet tall. The foliage of young plants is eaten like salad burnet. Zones 4 to 8.

How to Grow

Plant burnets in evenly moist, humus-rich soil in full sun to light shade. Plants are intolerant of excessive summer heat and dry soil. Mulch to help keep soil cool and moist. They form stout clumps with age. Divide overgrown clumps in spring. Sow seed outdoors in fall. Self-sown seedlings will appear.

Landscape Uses

Plant burnet at the middle or rear of the border with phlox, monkshoods (*Aconitum*), asters, goldenrods (*Solidago*), boltonia (*Boltonia asteroides*), Joe-Pye weeds (*Eupatorium*), sneezeweeds (*Helenium*), and grasses. They grow well along streams or at the edge of ponds with ironweeds (*Vernonia*), monkeyflowers (*Mimulus*), hibiscus, sedges (*Carex*), and ferns.

SANTOLINA

san-toe-LIE-na • Asteraceae, Aster Family

Lavender cottons are familiar to knot and herb gardeners for their architectural contributions. These woody shrubs form dense, thickly branched mounds of small, white, woolly leaves. Plants grow from fibrous-rooted woody crowns. In summer, buttonlike clusters of yellow flowers are held above the leaves on naked stalks. In severe winter weather, the woody stems are easily damaged, marring the plant's form.

SANTOLINA

Common Name:
Lavender cotton

Bloom Time:
Summer bloom

Planting Requirements:
Full sun

Santolina chamaecyparissus (ka-mie-sip-a-RIS-us), lavender cotton. Size: 1 to 2 feet tall, 2 to 3 feet wide. This dense shrub has white, woolly, pinnately divided leaves and woolly flower heads with yellow flowers. 'Nana' is a dwarf form only 8 inches tall. USDA Plant Hardiness Zones 6 to 8.

S. virens (VEER-enz), green lavender cotton. Size: 1 to 2 feet tall, 2 to 3 feet wide. This species is similar to *S. chamaecyparissus* but has deep green foliage and smooth stems. Zones 6 to 8.

How to Grow

Plant lavender cottons in well-drained, sandy or loamy soil in full sun. Plants are easy to grow and quite drought-resistant. Excessive cold may kill all or part of unprotected plants grown at the edge of their range. Plants tend to fall open with age. Prune them hard after flowering to keep them bushy and full. Plants seldom need dividing. Propagate by tip cuttings taken any time during the growing season.

Landscape Uses

Lavender cottons were made for edging beds and walks and for configuring knot gardens. In the garden, plant them with other dry-soil perennials such as yarrows (*Achillea*), pinks (*Dianthus*), stonecrops (*Sedum*), and basket-of-gold (*Aurinia saxatilis*).

The tight, mounded evergreen clumps of lavender cotton (*Santolina chamaecyparissus*) are perfect for edging beds or configuring knot gardens. The plants are easily pruned to hold rigid shapes.

SAPONARIA

sap-o-NAY-ree-a • Caryophyllaceae, Pink Family

Soapworts produce masses of five-petaled pink flowers for several weeks in summer. The flowers crown leafy stems covered in opposite, oval leaves. Plants grow from fleshy runners with white roots that produce new shoots as they creep. Floppy stems often root where they touch the ground.

> **SAPONARIA**
>
> **Common Name:**
> Soapwort
>
> **Bloom Time:**
> Summer bloom
>
> **Planting Requirements:**
> Full sun or light shade

Saponaria ×lempergii (lem-PERG-ee-ee), soapwort. Size: 4 to 6 inches tall, 12 to 24 inches wide. Sprawling, leafy clumps covered with deep pink flowers

The small flowers of rock soapwort (*Saponaria ocymoides* 'Rubra Compacta') smother the creeping clumps of foliage in early summer. Use the plant as a ground-cover in rock gardens or for cascading over stone walls.

typify this stellar hybrid. 'Max Frei' is a compact grower with pink flowers. USDA Plant Hardiness Zones 4 (with protection) or 5 to 8.

S. ocymoides (o-kim-OI-deez), rock soapwort. Size: 4 to 6 inches tall, 12 to 24 inches wide. This sprawling plant is covered in small, bright pink flowers for several weeks in early summer. 'Alba' and 'Snow Tip' have white flowers. 'Splendens' has rose-pink flowers. 'Rubra Compacta' has deep rose-red flowers. Zones 3 to 7.

S. officinalis (o-fis-i-NAY-lis), bouncing bet. Size: 1 to 2½ feet tall, 2 to 3 feet wide. This tall, sprawling species has oval leaves and pale pink flowers. 'Alba Plena' has double white flowers. 'Nana' is compact with pink flowers. 'Rosea-plena' has double rose-pink flowers. Zones 2 to 8.

How to Grow

Soapworts grow in average sandy or loamy, well-drained soil in full sun or light shade. Rich soil causes them to overgrow and flop. Plants spread enthusiastically to form broad clumps. Bouncing bet is a compact grower, and any but the double form is best left to roadsides, where it proliferates. After flowering, cut plants back to encourage fresh growth. *S. ocymoides* may rebloom. Divide plants in spring or fall to control their spread. Cuttings are easy to take all summer.

Landscape Uses

Choose rock soapwort for the rock garden or for edging along walks and steps. In the border, combine soapworts with summer perennials such as wormwoods (*Artemisia*), yarrows (*Achillea*), daylilies (*Hemerocallis*), speedwells (*Veronica*), and stonecrops (*Sedum*). Let low species weave among larger perennials to tie plantings together.

SAXIFRAGA

sax-e-FRAG-a • Saxifragaceae, Saxifrage Family

Saxifrages are low cushion or groundcover plants from habitats as diverse as alpine meadows and shaded woodlands. Plants have excellent foliage, which is often the main attribute, but the small white to pink flowers carried in singly or in open, branched clusters are airy and also attractive. Plants grow from fibrous-rooted crowns.

SAXIFRAGA

Common Name:
Saxifrage

Bloom Time:
Foliage plant with spring and summer bloom

Planting Requirements:
Sun or shade

Saxifraga arendsii (ah-RENDZ-ee-ee), Arend's saxifrage. Size: 5 to 10 inches tall, 12 inches wide. An attractive evergreen groundcover with cushions of needlelike leaves and starry flowers borne singly on threadlike stems above leaves. 'Blutenteppich' ('Blood Carpet') has dark carmine flowers. Part of a series with pink, purple, and white selections. 'Flowers of Sulphur' has pale yellow flowers. 'Triumph' has large, dark red flowers. USDA Plant Hardiness Zones 5 to 7.

S. fortunei (FOR-tu-nye), Fortune's saxifrage. Size: 12 to 18 inches tall, 12 to 24 inches wide. Ragged, maple-shaped leaves form an attractive groundcover under tall, airy white flower clusters. 'Jade Dragon' has deep green leaves laced with burgundy and jade green flowers. 'Silver Velvet' has purple-bronze leaves with striking silver palmate venation. 'White Chrysanthemum' has green leaves accented by white veining and white flowers. Zones 6 to 9.

S. stolonifera (sto-lon-IF-er-a), strawberry begonia. Size: 10 to 12 inches tall, 12 to 24 inches wide. Kidney-shaped leaves with blunt teeth are silver with deep green palmate veins. White flowers are held in open clusters above basal leaves. Plants spread to form broad clumps. 'Harvest Moon' has chartreuse leaves. 'Maroon Beauty' has deep purple leaves veined in silver. 'Tricolor' has pink, silver, and green leaves. Zones 5 (with protection) or 6 to 9.

Silver-splashed leaves make the open mats of strawberry begonia (*Saxifraga stolonifera*) seem to glow in the shade of a woodland. Let them creep among taller perennials and ferns to create a lush tapestry.

S. umbrosa (um-BROS-a), saxifrage. Size: 6 to 8 inches tall, 12 inches wide. Thick, scalloped leaves form tight rosettes accented by pink flowers. 'Charles Elliot' is compact with rose flowers on red stems. 'Variegata' has yellow-splashed leaves. 'Walter Ingwersen' has bronze foliage and deep red flowers. Selections may belong in the hybrid species *S. ×urbium,* London pride. Zones 5 to 7.

How to Grow

Plant saxifrages in moist but well-drained humus-rich soil in sun or light shade. *S.* *fortunei* and *S. stolonifera* tolerate more shade. Plants spread to form tight clumps. Divide in spring or late summer to control spread or for propagation.

Landscape Uses

Cushion saxifrages are lovely in rock gardens or rock walls. Plant them with pinks (*Dianthus*), creeping phlox (*Phlox stolonifera*), rock cresses (*Arabis*), dwarf bearded iris hybrids, and yuccas. Plant fortune's saxifrage and strawberry begonias in woodlands with bulbs, wild gingers (*Asarum*), phlox, small irises, sedges (*Carex*), and ferns.

SCABIOSA

skab-ee-O-sa • Dipsacacea, Teasel Family

Pincushion flowers are old-fashioned perennials with broad, flat heads actually composed of many soft blue flowers that increase in size as they near the margins of the heads. Each head is held on a slender naked stem from a sparsely branched clump. Basal leaves are lance-shaped, and stem leaves often have three pointed leaflets. All foliage is gray-green and fuzzy. Plants grow from a fibrous-rooted crown.

SCABIOSA

Common Name:
  Pincushion flower

Bloom Time:
  Summer bloom

Planting Requirements:
  Full sun or light shade

Scabiosa caucasica (kaw-KA-si-ca), pincushion flower. Size: 1½ to 2 feet tall and wide. This species has been grown for generations, but *S. columbaria* is a better garden plant. 'Alba' has white flowers. 'Blue Perfection' has lavender-blue flowers with fringed petals. 'Fama' has 4-inch deep lavender-blue flowers on 18-inch stems. 'Isaac House Hybrids' come in mixed blues and whites. USDA Plant Hardiness Zones 3 to 7.

S. columbaria (kol-um-BAR-ee-a), pincushion flower. Size: 1 to 2½ feet tall and wide. A more compact and floriferous species with several excellent cultivars. 'Butterfly Blue' is the best blue scabiosa, with sturdy lavender-blue flowers on 20- to 24-inch stems. 'Pink Mist' is an excellent, heavily flowered pink. Zones 3 to 7.

S. ochroleuca (oak-ro-LEW-ka), yellow scabiosa. Size: 2 to 3 feet tall and wide. Lacy, soft yellow heads to 2 inches are carried on open, branching stems above the mostly basal foliage. Plants may be short-lived. Zones 5 to 7.

How to Grow

Plant pincushion flowers in well-drained sandy or loamy, humus-rich, alkaline soil in full sun or light shade. Plants in southern zones require afternoon shade to

The old-fashioned lacy flowers of pincushion flower (*Scabiosa caucasica*) are held on tall stems, making them perfect for cutting.

moderate summer temperatures. Plants form good-size clumps under ideal conditions but are sensitive to heat and excess soil moisture. Deadhead plants to prolong flowering. Divide plants in spring only if they become overcrowded. Propagate by sowing fresh seed outdoors in fall or indoors in late winter.

Landscape Uses

Pincushion flowers are best planted in groups of three or more to ensure a significant display. Combine them with asiatic lilies (*Lilium*), bee balms (*Monarda*), border phlox (*Phlox*), daylilies (*Hemerocallis*), and yarrows (*Achillea*).

SCHIZACHYRIUM

skitz-a-KEER-e-um • Poaceae, Grass Family

Native ornamental grasses have traditionally been relegated to informal meadows and prairies, but they needn't be limited. Use them in beds and borders, where their late flowers and beautiful form complement all perennials. The dense clumps of little bluestems produce wiry gray to bluish stems that sway in the breeze. In autumn, the stems turn russet and are lined by the silken seeds. Plants grow from fibrous-rooted crowns.

SCHIZACHYRIUM
Common Name:
  Little bluestem
Bloom Time:
  Fall bloom
Planting Requirements:
  Sun

Schizachyrium scoparium (sco-PARE-e-um), little bluestem. Size: 1 to 3 feet tall and wide. Little bluestem turns acres of prairies glowing bronze and glistening silver in fall. This adaptable warm-season native grass begins growth in summer, and silvery seeds are prominently displayed late in the season on burgundy or golden stalks. 'Blaze' is prized for its reddish fall color. 'The Blues' has powder blue stalks in summer. USDA Plant Hardiness Zones 3 to 9.

Andropogon gerardii (ger-ARD-ee-ee), big bluestem. Size: 4 to 6 feet tall, 2 to 4 feet wide. (Note: *Andropogon* is a closely related genus; in fact, *Schizachyrium* used to be in

Andropogen, which is why we've chosen to include *Andropogen* here, rather than create a whole new entry.) A tall, lithe grass with branched flower clusters resembling a turkey foot, which gives the plant one of its many common names. Zones 3 to 8.

A. glomeratus (glom-er-AY-tus), bushy beard grass. Size: 2 to 4 feet tall, 1 to 2 feet wide. A showy species with flowers aggregated into clublike heads at the top of leafy stems. Zones 5 to 9.

A. ternarius (ter-NAIR-e-us), split-beard broomsedge. Size: 1 to 2 feet tall and wide. This handsome grass has tufted silvery plumes lining bronze stems in fall. Zones 6 to 8.

How to Grow

Plant little bluestem in sandy or loamy, well-drained soil in full sun or light shade. Established plants have deep water-seeking roots that hold soil and bestow superior drought resistance. Plugs are inexpensive and establish quickly if planted before midfall. Trim plants back to just above the ground in spring to make way for new growth.

Landscape Uses

Bluestems add fine texture and perpetual motion to meadow gardens and perennial beds alike. In the garden, use a drift of bluestem among perennials such as butterfly weed (*Asclepias tuberosa*), Russian sage (*Perovskia atriplicifolia*), and white gaura. Use little bluestem as the matrix in meadow and prairie plantings where its low stature easily conforms with most community weed ordinances. Use taller species in drifts as accents among shorter plants.

Little bluestem (*Schizachyrium scoparium*) is most showy when the tufts of silvery seeds expand in fall, catching the slanting rays of the sun like silken webs.

SCHIZOSTYLIS

sky-zo-STY-lis, or *skitz-o-STY-lis* • Iridaceae, Iris Family

Late borders are dominated by blues, purples, and yellows, so use crimson flag for some welcome contrast. The bright flower spikes are a good foil to the rounded asters that usher autumn into the garden. Subtle pinks and even a white selection are available for those that find crimson and cerise too difficult to incorporate into their color schemes.

SCHIZOSTYLIS

Common Name:
  Crimson flag

Bloom Time:
  Summer bloom

Planting Requirements:
  Sun or light shade

Crimson flag (*Schizostylis coccineus*) blooms late in the season after most perennials have gone by. The glorious spires of starry red flowers set off fall colors such as gold and purple.

Sunset' has intense cerise flowers that glow in evening light. 'Salmon Charm' is rosy salmon. 'Sunrise' is deep pink. 'Viscountess Bing' is a softer shell pink and the latest to flower. USDA Plant Hardiness Zones 5 (with protection) to 10.

How to Grow

Plant in rich, consistently moist soil in a sunny to lightly shaded spot. Foliage emerges early in spring, and flowering starts in August and continue through October in the North, later in warmer zones. Plants form multiple crowns that can be lifted for propagation. They are easy to grow in pots in a light but rich, well-drained soil. Place containers in a sunny spot and enjoy the show. Let pots overwinter on the dry side in a cool spot.

Landscape Uses

Match crimson flag selections by color to your schemes in formal or informal gardens. Place vibrant 'Oregon Sunset' with rich lavender-purple aromatic aster (*Aster oblongifolius* 'Raydon's Favorite') or royal purple *Aster novae-angliae* 'Purple Dome'. Softer shades combine well with any asters and other late-season perennials such as autumn sage (*Salvia greggii*), goldenrods (*Solidago*), rain lilies (*Zephyranthes*), gentians (*Gentiana*), and ornamental grasses. Choose the colorful berries of viburnums, deciduous hollies, and beautyberries (*Callicarpa*) for late-season interest.

Schizostylis coccineus (kock-SIN-e-us), crimson flag. Size: 1 to 2 feet tall and wide. Brilliant sunset colors as well as the softer shades of dawn characterize this late-season bloomer. The starry, five-petaled flowers open up slender stalks reminiscent of delicate gladiola spires in late summer and fall. Plants produce abundant, swordlike leaves from slender rhizomes and multiply generously to form thick, multiflowered clumps. 'Alba' is white-flowered. 'Mrs. Hagerty' and 'November Cheer' are pure pink. 'Oregon

SCILLA

SKILL-a • Hyacinthaceae (Liliaceae), Hyacinth Family

Squills have true blue spring flowers that endear them to bulb enthusiasts and gardeners. Their early bloom makes them all the more valuable, as our winter-weary eyes are starved for color when the flowers open. A handful of bulbs quickly forms an attractive clump, and plants thrive for years with little care. Two or three linear leaves grow from true bulbs and disappear soon after flowering.

SCILLA

Common Names:
Squill, scilla

Bloom Time:
Spring bloom

Planting Requirements:
Sun

Scilla bifolia (bi-FO-lee-a), two-leaves squill. Size: 3 to 6 inches tall and wide. A diminutive species with paired leaves and short, branched stems carrying six to eight small, starry blue flowers. Var. *alba* is white-flowered. Var. *rosea* is pink-flowered. USDA Plant Hardiness Zones 4 to 8.

S. mischtschenkoana (mist-cheng-ko-AH-na), Tubergen squill. Size: 4 to 6 inches tall and wide. The light blue flowers open as they push through the ground before the three or four keeled basal leaves emerge. 'Alba' has white flowers. 'Zwanenberg' has larger flowers with deep blue stripes in the petals. Zones 4 to 7.

S. peruviana (per-oo-ve-AH-na), Cuban lily. Size: 6 to 10 inches tall, 10 to 12 inches wide. The holy grail of scillas, this tender species has domed clusters of small, starry gentian blue flowers above a rosette of keeled foliage. Var. *alba* is white-flowered. Var. *elegans* has rosy red flowers. Zones 7 (with protection) or 8 to 10.

S. siberica (si-BEER-e-ka), Siberian squill. Size: 4 to 6 inches tall and wide. The deep gentian blue flowers of Siberian squill have been enjoyed for generations. Flower

The intense blue flowers of Siberian squill (*Scilla siberica*) have been enjoyed since colonial times. Plants spread rapidly by seed, and the clumps get larger each year from natural division.

buds appear with glossy leaves. 'Alba' is white-flowered. 'Azurea' is azure blue. 'Spring Beauty' is a robust form with deepest blue flowers. Zones 2 to 7.

How to Grow

Plant scillas in moist, rich, well-drained soil in sun. They are not fussy and adapt to most garden situations. Set bulbs out in fall. Lift and divide them as foliage begins to yellow. *Scilla siberica* may self-sow to the point of being a nuisance, though an attractive one.

Landscape Uses

Use scillas wherever you need a spot of early color. Combine them with daffodils and other bulbs under flowering shrubs or in a border between perennials that will emerge later.

SCUTELLARIA

skew-te-LAIR-e-ah • Lamiaceae, Mint Family

Skullcaps are underappreciated wildflowers notable for their blue spring and summer flowers. The individual, irregular flowers have arching upper lips and broad, speckled lower lips. The hairy, opposite leaves are attractive all season and turn yellow in fall. Plants grow from fibrous-rooted crowns.

SCUTELLARIA

Common Name:
Skullcap

Bloom Time:
Spring and summer bloom

Planting Requirements:
Sun to partial shade

Scutellaria incana (in-KAY-na), hoary scullcap. Size: 3 to 4 feet tall, 1 to 2 feet wide. This tall plant has branched terminal clusters of 1-inch, deep blue flowers. The pointed, egg-shaped leaves stand out at right angles to the stem, giving the plant a rigid appearance. USDA Plant Hardiness Zones 4 to 8.

S. integrifolia (in-teg-re-FOL-e-ah), hyssop skullcap. Size: 1½ feet tall, 1 foot wide. A delicate plant with 1- to 2-inch lance-shaped leaves on erect stems crowned with open, terminal clusters of 1-inch, pale to medium blue flowers in late spring and early summer. Zones 5 to 9.

S. resinosa (rez-in-O-sa), bushy scullcap, resinous scullcap. Size: 4 to 8 inches tall, 10 to 16 inches wide. This short, shrubby plant boasts a profusion of ¾-inch, deep blue flowers for months in summer. The thick, gray-green oval leaves are decorative when the plant is out of bloom. Many tightly packed stems rise 10 inches from a woody, taprooted crown. Zones 4 to 8.

S. serrata (ser-RAY-tah), showy skullcap. Size: 1 to 2 feet tall and wide. The broad oval, toothed leaves of showy skullcap make a perfect backdrop for the dense spikes of showy, 1-inch, medium blue flowers. Plants form bushy clumps. Zones 4 to 8.

Showy skullcap (*Scutellaria serrata*), a shade-tolerant native perennial, is tough and adaptable and should be more widely grown. Tidy clumps of oval leaves are accented in late spring with short spikes of deep blue flowers.

How to Grow

Plant in average to rich, moist but well-drained soil in full sun or partial shade. Bushy skullcap demands average to lean, well-drained soil in full sun. Plants thrive on neglect and tolerate all manner of climatic abuse, including cold, heat, and wind. Set out young transplants and do not disturb established clumps. Sow seeds in January for transplants by summer.

Landscape Uses

Choose small species for rock gardens and the front of beds and borders, as well as in-formal plantings. Combine them with creeping phlox (*Phlox stolonifera*), purple prairie clover (*Dalea purpurea*), evening primroses (*Oenothera*), grasses, and cacti. Use drifts of showy scullcap along a woodland path or in a lightly shaded border with rue anemone (*Anemonella thalictroides*), Solomon's plumes (*Smilacina*), bloodroot (*Sanguinaria canadensis*), and ferns. Combine the larger species with bowman's root (*Porteranthus trifoliatus*), Indian pink (*Spigelia marilandica*), green-and-gold (*Chrysogonum virginianum*), phlox, irises, and grasses.

SEDUM

SEE-dum • Crassulaceae, Stonecrop Family

Stonecrops are drought-tolerant plants with thick, succulent, waxy leaves and fleshy, often trailing stems. The small starry flowers are borne in domed or flat clusters in spring or summer. The seedheads of many species retain their color after flowering and hold their form when dried. Plants grow from fibrous-rooted crowns or trailing stems.

SEDUM

Common Names:
Stonecrop, sedum

Bloom Time:
Spring and summer bloom

Planting Requirements:
Full sun to partial shade

Count on variegated showy stonecrop (*Sedum* 'Frosty Morn') to add a spot of light foliage and flowers to a dry, sunny spot.

Sedum aizoon (AYE-zoon), Aizoon stonecrop. Size: 12 to 15 inches tall, 12 to 24 inches wide. This sedum is an upright grower with oval, toothed leaves and flat terminal clusters of yellow flowers in early summer. USDA Plant Hardiness Zones 4 to 9.

S. album (AL-bum), white stonecrop. Size: 4 to 6 inches tall, 6 to 12 inches wide.

This creeping sedum has lance-shaped, evergreen leaves and white flowers in early summer. 'Chubby Fingers' has plump, succulent leaves. 'Coral Carpet' has dark green leaves with orange highlights in spring. 'Murale' has red winter foliage. Zones 3 to 9.

S. kamtschaticum (kamt-SHA-ti-cum), Kamschatka stonecrop. Size: 2 to 6 inches tall, 12 to 24 inches wide. This low-spreading sedum produces short, upright stems clothed in narrow, toothed green leaves and topped by open clusters of bright yellow flowers. Var. *middendorffianum* has more slender, toothed leaves. 'Variegatum' has leaves edged in creamy white. 'Weihenstephaner Gold' has dense, rich, yellow flowers. Zones 3 to 8.

S. lineare (lin-e-ARE-e) 'Variegatum', carpet sedum. Size: 6 to 9 inches tall, 12 to 24 inches wide. A new introduction with white edges, fat needlelike leaves, and yellow flowers in late spring on erect stems. Zones 6 to 9.

S. maximum (MAX-i-mum), stonecrop. Size: 1½ to 2 feet tall and wide. This upright sedum has thick oval leaves and domed clusters of creamy rose flowers. Var. *atropurpureum* 'Honeysong' has deep rose-purple leaves and darker rose flowers. Zones 3 to 8.

S. sieboldii (see-BOLD-ee-ee), October daphne. Size: 6 to 9 inches tall, 12 to 24 inches wide. Pink flowers in tightly packed, domed clusters smother the rounded leaves of this spreading species in September and October. 'Mediovariegatum' has creamy yellow leaves edged in blue-gray. 'Variegatum' has white variegated leaves. Zones 3 to 8.

S. spectabile (spek-TAB-i-lee), showy stonecrop. Size: 1 to 2 feet tall, 2 to 3 feet wide. Showy stonecrop is one of the most popular sedums. The 4- to 6-inch domed heads of pink flowers crown erect stems covered in broad, blue-green leaves. 'Atropurpureum' has deep rose-red flowers. 'Brilliant' has bright rose-pink flowers. 'Carmen' has dark carmine pink flowers. 'Iceburg' has white flowers. 'Neon' is dayglow fuchsia. 'Stardust' is silvery pink. Zones 3 to 9.

S. spurium (SPUR-ee-um), two-row sedum. Size: 2 to 6 inches tall, 12 to 24 inches wide. This sedum forms mats of wiry stems with rounded leaves crowded toward their tips. Open clusters of pink flowers are produced in summer. Winter foliage is bronze. 'Album Superbum' is white-flowered. 'Bronze Carpet' has pink flowers. 'Fulda Glow' is an improved version of 'Dragon's Blood' with red-tinted foliage and rose-red flowers. 'Tricolor' has pink, white, and green variegated leaves. Zones 3 to 8.

S. ternatum (ter-NA-tum), whorled stonecrop. Size: 2 to 6 inches tall, 12 to 24 inches wide. This low, open spreader has disproportionately large, starry white inflorescences with three long arms. 'White Waters' has larger flowers. *S. nevii* has smaller, blue-green foliage and is delicate. Zones 4 to 8.

Hybrids

Dwarf Types. 'John Creech' is 2 inches tall with showy pink flowers. 'Sunset Cloud' has scalloped blue-green leaves that are purple in winter and late-season wine-red flowers on 4- to 6-inch plants.

Tall Hybrids. 'Autumn Joy' is a stout version of *S. spectabile* with thick 2-foot stems densely covered in rounded leaves and

Plant two-row sedum (*Sedum spurium* 'Ruby Mantle') in the crevices of a stone wall where the creeping stems will cascade over the faces of the stones. This selection with dark red flowers and burgundy foliage makes an excellent groundcover in rock gardens or on dry, sunny banks.

crowned with domed, 5- to 6-inch clusters of pink flowers in late summer. 'Frosty Morn' is a shrubby sedum with white-edged leaves and pale pink flowers. 'Matrona' is perhaps the best of the large sedums, with stiff stems clothed in blue-gray leaves and terminal clusters of dusty pink flowers that dry to rich chocolate brown. 'Purple Emperor' has rich purple flowers and rose flowers on open clumps to 15 inches tall and 18 inches wide. 'Ruby Glow' and 'Bertram Anderson' have weakly upright or sprawling 12-inch stems with rounded purple-tinged leaves and ruby red flowers. 'Strawberries and Cream' has purple leaves and rosy buds that open to white flowers. 'Vera Jameson' is similar but has waxy bluish purple leaves. Most hybrids are hardy in Zones 3 to 10.

How to Grow

All sedums are tough, easy-care perennials. Plant them in average to rich well-drained soil in full sun to light shade. The low-growing species will grow in partial shade; *S. ternatum* tolerates moist, rich soil. Plants require little care once they are established except for division in spring or fall to control their spread. Cuttings root readily throughout summer.

Landscape Uses

Sedums are versatile plants for beds and borders, in rock gardens, and as ground-covers under open trees. Use the low, spreading species along paths or to cascade over walls. In rock gardens combine them with spring bulbs, bellflowers (*Campanula*), pinks (*Dianthus*), moss phlox (*Phlox subulata*), and other small plants. In beds and borders plant stonecrops with black-eyed Susans (*Rudbeckia*), coneflowers (*Echinacea*), catmints (*Nepeta*), evening primroses (*Oenothera*), yuccas, yarrows (*Achillea*), and ornamental grasses.

SENECIO

se-NEE-see-o • Asteraceae, Aster Family

Groundsels turn the woods and fields yellow with their billowing yellow flowers carried on broad clumps. Though familiar to wildflower enthusiasts, groundsels remain unknown and underutilized as garden plants. Their starry yellow flowers have straplike rays (petals) and green or yellow heads. The flowers are borne in open clusters atop loose, branching stems. Basal rosettes of semievergreen to evergreen leaves grow from fibrous-rooted crowns.

SENECIO

Common Names:
Groundsel, senecio

Bloom Time:
Spring or summer bloom

Planting Requirements:
Full sun to partial shade

Senecio adonidifolius (a-don-i-di-FO-lee-us), groundsel. Size: 12 to 18 inches tall and wide. This is a slender leafy plant with curly, pinnately divided leaves and open clusters of golden yellow flowers, each with four or five rays. USDA Plant Hardiness Zones 5 to 7.

S. aureus (ore-RE-us), golden ragwort. Size: 1½ to 2½ feet tall, 2 to 3 feet wide. Golden ragwort has basal rosettes of heart-shaped foliage and open clusters of golden yellow flowers with 8 to 10 rays each. Zones 4 to 9.

S. cineraria (sin-er-EE-a), dusty miller. Size: 1 to 2 feet tall, 1 foot wide. The ubiquitous dusty miller is popular for its pinnately lobed, silver-gray leaves. Flowers are seldom seen and are often removed in favor of foliage. Zones 8 to 10.

S. doria (DOOR-ee-a), tall groundsel. Size: 3 to 4 feet tall, 2 to 3 feet wide. This tall leafy species has upright stems covered with toothed, lance-shaped leaves and flat, broad (8- to 10-inch) clusters of bright yellow flowers. Zones 4 to 8.

S. smithii (SMITH-ee-ee), white groundsel. Size: 2 to 4 feet tall, 1 to 2 feet wide. This tall, coarse plant has large wedge-shaped hairy basal leaves and stout leafy stems with clustered white flowers. Zones 6 to 8.

How to Grow

Give groundsels average to rich, moist but well-drained soil in full sun to partial shade. *S. cineraria* needs average soil on the dry side; *S. smithii* needs rich, moist to wet soil. Both need full sun. *S. aureus* is a plant

The erect, leafy clumps of tall groundsel (*Senecio doria*) look quite undistinguished for most of the season. In late summer a dramatic show starts with starry, glowing yellow flowers in mounded clusters.

of open woods. All are of easy culture and spread readily by creeping rootstocks and self-sown seedlings. Lift clumps after flowering or in fall and replant divisions into amended soil. Grow *S. cineraria* as an annual north of Zone 8.

Landscape Uses

Groundsels are good plants for beds and borders, meadows and wild gardens, and rock gardens. Plant *S. cineraria* as an edger for beds of annuals or with perennials that complement its silvery foliage. Choose *S. aureus* for the shade garden with native wildflowers such as blue phlox (*Phlox divaricata*) and foamflower (*Tiarella cordifolia*). *S. smithii* is a good choice for the water garden. Tall *S. doria* mixes well with large perennials.

SIDALCEA

see-DAL-see-a • Malvaceae, Mallow Family

Checker-mallows grace alpine meadows and the banks of clear mountain streams of western North America. The delicate pink to rose flowers are carried in erect spikes that add height to formal gardens and meadows. Southern gardeners struggle with this and other mallows, which are best left to cooler, northern gardens.

SIDALCEA

Common Name:
Checker-mallow

Bloom Time:
Summer bloom

Planting Requirements:
Full sun to light shade

Sidalcea malviflora (mal-vi-FLO-ra), checker-mallow. Size: 2 to 4 feet tall, 2 to 3 feet wide. Checker-mallows resemble small delicate hollyhocks. They have stout stems with deeply cut, palmately lobed leaves. The 2-foot mallowlike flowers are intermingled with leaves in open spikes on the upper third of the stems. Flowers may be pink or rose. Many cultivars of mixed parentage are available in a range of colors on compact, 2-foot plants. 'Bianca' has pure white flowers. 'Brilliant' has carmine-red flowers. 'Elsie Heugh' has fringed, pale pink flowers. 'Little Princess' has frilly pink flowers on compact, 15-inch plants. 'Loveliness' is a self-supporting plant with shell pink flowers. 'Mr. Lindberg' has rosy red flowers. 'Sussex Beauty' is a tall (3- to 4-foot) plant with bright pink flowers. USDA Plant Hardiness Zones 4 to 7.

Checker-mallows (*Sidalcea malviflora*) look like miniature hollyhocks and are perfect for smaller gardens that can't accommodate the 6-foot stalks of hollyhocks.

How to Grow

Plant checker-mallows in average to rich, moist but well-drained soil in full sun or light shade. Plants increase to form large clumps from a woody rootstock with fibrous roots. Cut plants to the ground after flowering to promote fresh foliage. If plants overgrow their space or die out in the middle, lift clumps in fall and discard the old portions. Replant vigorous divisions into amended soil.

Landscape Uses

Checker-mallows are good plants for the middle or rear of the border or for meadow gardens. Plant them with coneflowers (*Echinacea*), yarrows (*Achillea*), calamints (*Calamintha*), catmints (*Nepeta*), sages (*Salvia*), Russian sage (*Perovskia atriplicifolia*), and ornamental grasses.

SILENE

si-LEE-nee • Caryophyllaceae, Pink Family

Hummingbirds love the rich, fiery-colored flowers of campion as much as gardeners do. They are a varied group of plants, with tufted basal rosettes of linear or rounded foliage and wiry to stiffly upright stalks bearing open clusters of tubular flowers with starry, five-petaled faces. Plants grow from thick, branched taproots. They may be short-lived, but self-sown seedlings are common where the plants are happy.

> **SILENE**
>
> **Common Names:**
>   Campion, pink
>
> **Bloom Time:**
>   Spring and early summer bloom
>
> **Planting Requirements:**
>   Full sun to partial shade

Silene caroliniana (kar-o-lin-ee-AH-na), Carolina pink. Size: 6 to 12 inches tall, 12 to 14 inches wide. Carolina pink has prostrate stems and clear medium pink flowers. Tufted leaves are grasslike. 'Millstream Select' has deep pink flowers. USDA Plant Hardiness Zones 5 to 8.

S. polypetala (pol-i-PET-a-la), fringed campion. Size: 4 to 6 inches tall, 6 to 12 inches wide. This tufted plant has open clusters of pink flowers with deeply incised, ragged petals. 'Longwood' is a hybrid with fringed, deep pink flowers. Zones 6 to 8.

S. regia (REE-ji-a), royal catchfly. Size: 2 to 5 feet tall, 1 to 2 feet wide. This tall catchfly has opposite stalkless leaves and 6- to 12-inch terminal clusters of fiery red flowers. Zones 5 to 8.

S. schafta (SHAF-ta), schafta pink. Size: 3 to 6 inches tall, 6 to 12 inches wide. This pink forms dense cushions of oblong leaves and few-flowered clusters of bright pink flowers. 'Splendens' has rose-pink flowers. Zones 4 to 8.

Fire pink (*Silene virginica*) is a lovely wild-flower best grown in well-drained soil of rock gardens or on dry banks in full to partial sun.

S. virginica (ver-GIN-e-ka), fire pink. Size: 1 to 1½ feet tall and wide. Plants produce a haze of brilliant red flowers on wiry stems in late spring and summer above narrow, glossy leaves. The 1-inch flowers have narrow, notched petals. Zones 4 to 8.

How to Grow

Plant pinks in average sandy or loamy soil in full sun or light shade. All species need good drainage. Sow ripe seed outdoors in fall. Seedlings develop slowly.

Landscape Uses

Campions are good plants for rock and wall gardens. *S. schafta* grows readily at the front of the border with low perennials and small ornamental grasses. *S. regia* is striking in the dry garden or in meadow and prairie plantings.

S. stellata (stel-LAY-ta), starry campion. Size: 2 to 3 feet tall, 1 to 2 feet wide. Ragged white flowers hang from tall spikes in summer above whorls of deep green, pointed leaves. Multistemmed clumps lack basal foliage common in other species. Zones 4 to 8.

SILPHIUM

SILF-ee-um • Asteraceae, Aster Family

Few plants have the panache of the towering, bold rosin-weeds. Their dramatic foliage and huge, starry flowers like refined sunflowers are sure to make a statement in any garden large enough to accommodate them. Birds love to pick the seeds from the heads in autumn. Plants produce huge crowns with thick, fleshy roots. Some species, like compass plants, have huge taproots like giant yams.

SILPHIUM

Common Names:
  Rosinweed

Bloom Time:
  Summer bloom

Planting Requirements:
  Sun

Silphium compositum (kom-POS-i-tum), oak-leaf rosinweed. Size: 3 to 5 feet tall, 1 to 1½ feet wide. This variety is grown for its large arrowhead or lobed heart-shaped basal leaves. One of the more attractive varieties has deeply lobed leaves that resemble an oak. Tall naked scapes bear open clusters of small, starry yellow daisies. USDA Plant Hardiness Zones 4 to 9.

S. dentatum (den-TAY-tum), toothed rosinweed. Size: 2 to 5 feet tall, 2 to 3 feet wide. This is one of the more diminutive members of the genus of giants, with stout stems covered in sharply toothed, narrow oval leaves. The 2-inch flowers have medium yellow rays that are widest above the middle, giving the flower a starry appearance. Zones 4 to 9.

S. integrifolium (in-teg-re-FOL-e-um), rosinweed. Size: 3 to 4 feet tall, 2 to 3 feet wide. This eye-catching species has oval or broadly lance-shaped, toothed or untoothed stalkless leaves. Showy 2-inch flowers crowd at the tops of stems in domed clusters. Zones 3 to 9.

S. laciniatum (la-sin-e-AY-tum), compass plant. Size: 4 to 8 feet tall, 3 to 4 feet wide. Stiff, bristly stalks bear chains of huge flowers that resemble fine-textured sunflowers. Narrow rays give the flower a refined look despite its size. Audacious, 3-foot, deeply lobed leaves form dense, decorative tufts not easily overlooked. Zones 4 to 9.

The tall stems of cup plant (*Silphium perfoliatum*) pierce through the center of the paired leaves, forming a small cup where birds drink. Wide heads of yellow daisies open throughout summer.

S. perfoliatum (per-fo-le-AY-tum), cup plant. Size: 4 to 6 feet tall, 3 to 4 feet wide. Tall stems pierce the center of the paired leaves, forming a small cup where birds drink. Wide heads of yellow daisies open throughout summer. Zones 3 to 9.

S. terebinthinaceum (ter-eh-bin-thin-A-see-um), prairie dock. Size: 5 to 8 feet tall, 3 to 4 feet wide. Drama is the trademark of prairie dock, whose striking 3-foot heart-shaped basal leaves erupt like rockets in open rosettes. Naked stalks bear branched clusters of 3-inch flowers. The leaves are invaluable in the garden or cut for arrangements. Zones 3 to 9.

How to Grow

Plant in moist, well-drained, humus-rich soil in full sun. Small plants you set out will quickly grow to elephantine proportions. Plants need plenty of room to spread, so space them 3 to 4 feet apart. Established clumps are deep-rooted and impossible to divide. Self-sown seedlings will appear.

Landscape Uses

Rosinweeds are among the most striking native perennials. Resist the temptation to relegate these beauties to the back of the border. Middle ground enables both foliage and flowers to show to best advantage. Some larger companions for a meadow garden include catmints (*Nepeta*), phlox, coneflowers (*Echinacea*), Culver's roots (*Veronicastrum virginicum*), spiderworts (*Tradescantia*), ironweeds (*Vernonia*), rattlesnake master (*Eryngium yuccifolium*), asters, and grasses. Place species with showy basal leaves like compass plant and oak-leaf rosinweed at the front of the bed where the leaves will show among creeping verbenas, winecups (*Callirhoe*), and phlox.

SISYRINCHIUM

sis-i-RING-key-um • Iridaceae, Iris Family

Blue-eyed grass is not a grass at all but a slender-leaved member of the iris family. Tufts of flat, grasslike foliage rise from short creeping rhizomes that branch profusely. Flower stalks resemble leaves but are crowned with open clusters of starry blue flowers with three petals and three petal-like sepals.

SISYRINCHIUM

Common Name:
 Blue-eyed grass

Bloom Time:
 Early summer bloom

Planting Requirements:
 Full sun to partial shade

Sisyrinchium angustifolium (an-gus-ti-FO-lee-um), blue-eyed grass. Size: 6 to 10 inches tall and wide. This is a delicate species with few-flowered clusters of deep steel blue flowers. 'Album' is white-flowered. 'Lucerne' has bright blue starry flowers. Hybrids such as 'Quaint and Queer' with reddish brown flowers and light blue 'California Skies' are popular. USDA Plant Hardiness Zones 3 to 9.

S. bellum (BEL-lum), California blue-eyed grass. Size: 6 to 12 inches tall and wide. This species is similar to *S. angustifolium* but is a stouter plant with large, blue-violet flowers. Zones 6 to 9.

S. striatum (stri-A-tum), Argentine blue-eyed grass. Size: 1 to 2 feet tall and wide. This lovely robust species has creamy white flowers on upright spikes. The leaves are wider (1 foot) than other species and it has showier flowers. Zones 4 to 8.

How to Grow

Plant blue-eyed grasses in moist, average to rich soil in full sun or partial shade. Plants are easy to grow and spread slowly to form thick clumps. Divide clumps after flowering to reduce their size or for propagation.

Landscape Uses

Use groups of three to five plants of blue-eyed grass in meadow plantings or as an accent in perennial gardens. Combine them with showy foliage plants such as silvery wormwoods (*Artemisia*), lamb's ears (*Stachys byzantina*), cranesbills (*Geran-*

Plant blue-eyed grass (*Sisyrinchium* 'Quaint and Queer') where the delicate red-brown flowers and fine-textured foliage can be viewed up close. Plants make a better show in groups of three or more.

ium), moss phlox (*Phlox subulata*), pinks (*Dianthus*), and fine-textured ornamental grasses.

SMILACINA

smy-la-SEE-na •Convallariaceae (Liliaceae), Lily-of-the-Valley Family

Solomon's plumes have graceful arching stems with alternate pointed oval leaves that reduce in size as they ascend the stem. Stems are crowned by single or branched clusters of starry flowers with fuzzy stamens (male reproductive structures). Plants grow from fleshy, creeping rhizomes. In fall, the plants form edible berries. Several new species from Asia such as *S. purpurea* may soon be available.

SMILACINA

Common Names:
  Solomon's plume, false Solomon's seal

Bloom Time:
  Late spring bloom

Planting Requirements:
  Light to full shade

Smilacina racemosa (ra-see-MO-sa), Solomon's plume. Size: 2 to 4 feet tall, 2 to 3 feet wide. Solomon's plume is a spectacular woodland wildflower with deep green, satiny leaves and well-branched terminal plumes of small fuzzy flowers. The globular fruit is red-and-white speckled. Native across North America, western plants are larger, to 5 feet. USDA Plant Hardiness Zones 3 to 7.

S. stellata (stel-LAY-ta), starry Solomon's plume. Size: 1 to 2 feet tall and wide. Similar to *S. racemosa* but more delicate, with oblong, gray-green leaves and 2-foot unbranched clusters of starry white flowers. The fruit has green and black stripes. Zones 2 to 7.

How to Grow

Solomon's plumes are tough, easy-to-grow plants. Give them moist, humus-rich, non-alkaline soil in light to full shade. Plants bloom more freely with some sun. They form thick clumps from their branching rhizomes. *S. stellata* spreads rapidly. Divide plants in early spring or fall for propagation or to control spread.

Solomon's plume (*Smilacina racemosa*) is a shade-tolerant native plant perfect for woodland gardens or underplanting flowering shrubs. Showy red-speckled berries follow the foamy flowers.

Landscape Uses

Use Solomon's plumes in informal plantings, in woodland gardens, or as a groundcover under trees and shrubs. Combine them with foliage plants such as hostas, sedges (*Carex*), ferns, lungworts (*Pulmonaria*), barrenworts (*Epimedium*), and purple coral bells (*Heuchera* 'Palace Purple'). Try a mass planting of *S. racemosa* on a slope to mimic a gurgling stream.

SOLIDAGO

sol-i-DAY-go • Asteraceae, Aster Family

Goldenrods flower just at a time when bloom is slacking off in the garden. Lemon yellow or golden flowers are carried in spiky, flat-topped, or plumelike clusters. Leafy stems may be smooth or hairy. Leaves are lance-shaped or (rarely) oval, often with jagged, toothed margins. Some plants are clumpers; others grow from fast-creeping rhizomes. Choose wisely based on where you position the plants in your garden.

SOLIDAGO

Common Name:
Goldenrod

Bloom Time:
Summer and fall bloom

Planting Requirements:
Full sun

Solidago caesia (SEE-zee-a), wreath goldenrod. Size: 1 to 3 feet tall, 1 to 2 feet wide. This spiky goldenrod has blue-green, linear leaves alternating up smooth wiry stems. Terminal spikes intermingle with leaves in early fall. USDA Plant Hardiness Zones 4 to 8.

S. canadensis (kan-a-DEN-sis), Canada goldenrod. Size: 2 to 5 feet tall, 2 to 3 feet wide. Canada goldenrod has showy, one-sided plume-shaped clusters of bright yellow flowers atop fuzzy, leafy stems. The toothed, lance-shaped leaves have soft, hairy undersides. Plants form large colonies from creeping rhizomes. 'Cloth of Gold' has pale yellow flowers on 18- to 24-inch stems. 'Crown of Rays' has large flaring inflorescences. *S. gigantea* is similar but with smooth leaves and stems. Zones 3 to 8.

S. flexicaulis (flex-i-CAWL-is), zigzag goldenrod. Size: 1 to 3 feet tall, 1 to 2 feet wide. Thin, wiry stems bend back and forth at the nodes of alternate, rounded leaves. Flowers are carried along the upper third of the stem. 'Variegata' has foliage splashed with gold. Zones 3 to 8.

S. juncea (JUN-ke-a), early goldenrod. Size: 2 to 3 feet tall and wide. The first goldenrod to open, in late July or August, with branched terminal flower clusters over dense vase-shaped clumps. Zones 3 to 8.

S. odora (o-DOR-a), sweet goldenrod. Size: 2 to 5 feet tall, 1 to 2 feet wide. This slender species has smooth lance-shaped, anise-scented foliage and one-sided flower clusters. Zones 3 to 9.

S. rigida (RIJ-i-da), stiff goldenrod. Size: 3 to 5 feet tall, 1 to 2 feet wide. A tall, leafy goldenrod with broad flat flower clusters, fuzzy stems, and large-leaved basal rosettes. Zones 3 to 9.

S. rugosa (rew-GO-sa), rough-stemmed goldenrod. Size: 2 to 4 feet tall and wide. This goldenrod is aptly named for its airy flower clusters with arching branches

For a fast-growing, fall-blooming ground-cover, choose spoon-leaf goldenrod (*Solidago sphacelata* 'Golden Fleece'). Plants grow in average soil in full sun or light shade.

spread over erect, leafy stems. Plants spread rapidly by runners to form broad clumps. 'Fireworks' lights up the late-season garden like a fiery explosion with linear sprays. Zones 4 to 9.

S. sempervirens (sem-per-VI-renz), seaside goldenrod. Size: 2 to 4 feet tall, 2 to 3 feet wide. A smooth goldenrod with large spatula-shaped basal leaves and lance-shaped stem leaves that reduce in size as they ascend to the one-sided plumed inflorescence. Zones 4 to 9.

S. sphacelata (sphay-see-LAY-ta), spoon-leaf goldenrod, autumn goldenrod. Size: 1 to 2 feet tall and wide. This creeping goldenrod has deep green paddle-shaped leaves and branched inflorescences like ex-

ploding yellow fireworks. 'Golden Fleece' is only 12 inches tall and is quite floriferous. Zones 4 to 9.

S. speciosa (spee-see-OH-sa), showy goldenrod. Size: 1 to 3 feet tall, 1 to 2 feet wide. Leafy, red-tinged stems are crowned by dense branched spikes in August and September. Zones 3 to 8.

S. virgaurea (vir-GAR-ee-a), European goldenrod. Size: 2 to 3 feet tall and wide. This species has branched terminal spikes of large, starry flowers. Many garden hybrids have been produced with *S. canadensis*. 'Baby Gold' is 2 to 2½ feet tall with large inflorescences. 'Golden Mosa' is 2½ feet tall with soft yellow cascading inflorescences. Zones 4 to 8.

How to Grow

Goldenrods thrive on neglect. They grow in wasteplaces, meadows, and prairies; on roadsides; and even in woodlands. Most species prefer average, moist but well-drained soil in full sun or light shade. Rich soils encourage rampant spread and flopping. *S. caesia* and *S. flexicaulis* grow in humusy woodland soil in light or partial shade. Bloom is poor in deep shade. *S. odora* and *S. sempervirens* grow in lean soil and are salt-tolerant. All species hold up well under droughty conditions. Most species increase well under cultivation and need division every 2 or 3 years. *S. canadensis*, the *S. virgaurea* hybrids, and *S. sphacelata* may need more-frequent control. Self-sown seedlings often appear.

Landscape Uses

Goldenrods are at home in formal and informal landscapes. Plant them in meadows and prairies or beds and borders. Combine them with coneflowers (*Echinacea*), black-eyed Susans (*Rudbeckia*), balloon flower (*Platycodon grandiflorus*), blazing-stars (*Liatris*), Joe-Pye weeds (*Eupatorium*), common lavender (*Lavandula angustifolia*), sages (*Salvia*), asters, and ornamental grasses. Use *S. sempervirens* in coastal gardens with other salt-tolerant species such as blanket flowers (*Gaillardia*), sea lavender (*Limonium latifolium*), and yuccas. Combine woodland species with foliage perennials and woodland asters (*Aster*), sedges (*Carex*), and ferns. Plant *S. spathulata* as a groundcover under open-canopied shrubs and trees or at the front of the perennial border.

SPIGELIA

spy-GEEL-e-ah • Loganiaceae, Logania Family

Hummingbirds prize deep red tubular flowers with yellow lips, and the blooms of Indian pink are no exception. This curiously beautiful and woefully underutilized native perennial delights gardeners and feathered visitors with late spring and summer flowers. Plants grow from tufted crowns with thick, fleshy fibrous roots.

SPIGELIA

Common Names:
Indian pink, pinkroot

Bloom Time:
Late spring bloom

Planting Requirements:
Sun or light shade

Spigelia marilandica (mar-e-LAN-dik-ah), Indian pink. Size: 1 to 2½ feet tall, 1 to 2 feet wide. Indian pink is a little-known and choice plant that deserves more attention. The unusual flowers are arrayed in an upright row on the one-sided inflorescence like tubes of brilliant red lipstick samples at a department store. Tubes open to reveal five lime green to chartreuse petals. Plants grow from fibrous-rooted crowns. Paired, glossy, deep green pointed triangular leaves carry the plant when it is out of flower. USDA Plant Hardiness Zones 4 to 9.

How to Grow

Plant in rich, moist but well-drained soil in full sun or light shade. Despite their exotic appearance, they are easy to grow. Plants form attractive, upright clumps that seldom need division. Propagate from tip cuttings taken in early summer. Only tip cuttings will root. Remove flower buds and leave the cuttings in for 4 to 6 weeks to assure thorough rooting.

Landscape Uses

Indian pinks are striking as specimen plants or in mass plantings. Use them in combination with shrubs, in borders, or along a meadow walk. Plant them with alumroots (*Heuchera*), sages (*Salvia*), phlox, bowman's root (*Porteranthus trifoliatus*), irises, gauras, and coreopsis. Use them in rock gardens with cranesbills (*Geranium*), yuccas, prairie smoke (*Geum triflorum*), and verbenas.

Few blooms offer the dynamic contrast of brilliant red and chartreuse in the same package. Indian pink (*Spigelia marilandica*) opens its bicolor blooms in midspring, followed by a second crop in summer.

STACHYS

STAY-kis • Lamiaceae, Mint Family

Though lamb's ear, the most familiar member of this genus, is known as a foliage plant, many species have beautiful flowers. Color ranges from rose and pink to white. Like all members of the mint family, betony flowers are two-lipped, with two upper and three lower lobes. They are carried in dense, tiered whorls on erect stems. All species are hairy; some have dense, soft silver hairs. Plants grow from creeping stems with fibrous roots.

STACHYS

Common Names:
  Lamb's ear, betony

Bloom Time:
  Spring and summer bloom

Planting Requirements:
  Full sun to light shade

Stachys byzantina (bi-zan-TEEN-a) (*lanata*), lamb's ear. Size: 6 to 15 inches tall, 12 to 24 inches wide. The dense, white, woolly leaves form soft mats from which equally fuzzy bloom stalks emerge. Purple flowers appear from the tangle of hairs in late spring. 'Big Ears' ('Countess Helene Von Stein') has huge, silver-green leaves and is tolerant of heat and humidity. 'Primrose Heron' has chartreuse leaves overlaid with silver fur. 'Silver Carpet' has silvery leaves. USDA Plant Hardiness Zones 4 to 8.

S. coccinea (kock-SIN-e-a), scarlet sage. Size: 1 to 2 feet tall and wide. A unique species resembling a *Salvia* with quilted triangular leaves and terminal spikes of salmon-scarlet flowers in late spring and summer. Zones 7 to 10.

S. macrantha (ma-KRANTH-a), betony. Size: 1 to 1½ feet tall, 1 to 2 feet wide. Basal rosettes of scalloped, heart-shaped leaves are punctuated with upright, leafy stalks crowned with spike-like clusters of pink flowers. Var. *robusta* ('Robusta') grows to 2 feet tall and is showier than the species. 'Alba' is white-flowered. 'Rosea' has deep rose-pink flowers. 'Superba' has magenta flowers. Zones 2 to 8.

S. officinalis (o-fis-i-NAY-lis), wood betony. Size: 1½ to 2 feet tall, 1 to 2 feet wide. This species is similar to *S. grandiflora* but has denser clusters of smaller violet flowers and narrow foliage in compact rosettes. Var. *rosea* ('Rosea') has soft rose-pink flowers. Zones 4 to 8.

The soft, woolly leaves of lamb's ear (*Stachys byzantina* 'Big Ears') create a pleasing edging for beds and borders with well-drained soil.

How to Grow

Grow lamb's ears in well-drained sandy or loamy soil in full sun or light shade. Plants do not perform well in hot, humid areas or where there is frequent summer rain. The woolly foliage traps water and is subject to rot. Good drainage is essential to success. If rot occurs, cut plants back and wait for cooler weather. They resprout in fall, and leaves often overwinter. Plant *S. grandiflora* and *S. officinalis* in average to rich, moist but well-drained soil in full sun or partial shade. All species spread well when matched to their site. Divide overgrown clumps in fall. Scarlet sage needs rich but well-drained soil and full sun.

Landscape Uses

Lamb's ears are perfect for the front of the border with ornamental onions (*Allium*), sages (*Salvia*), yuccas, stonecrops (*Sedum*), common lavender (*Lavandula angustifolia*), and ornamental grasses. Plant betony in either formal or informal landscapes with irises, goat's beards (*Aruncus*), coral bells (*Heuchera*), bergenias, lungworts (*Pulmonaria*), and hostas. Scarlet sage combines well with dwarf irises, species peonies, pinks (*Dianthus*), and small grasses. Use plants in containers where they are not hardy.

STOKESIA

STOKS-ee-a or *stow-KEYS-ee-a* • Asteracea, Aster Family

Ragged blue daisies of exceptional size and beauty grace this popular native perennial. An heirloom plant, gardeners prize the copious flowers that stand above the tidy, rich green leaves. Plants tolerate soggy soils and drought with equal poise. They grow from tufted crowns with thick, fleshy white roots.

STOKESIA

Common Name:
Stokes' aster

Bloom Time:
Summer bloom

Planting Requirements:
Full sun or light shade

Stokesia laevis (LAY-vis), Stokes' aster. Size: 12 to 24 inches tall and wide. Stoke's asters produce broad rosettes of shiny green lance-shaped leaves, each of which has a conspicuous white midvein. Branched flowerstalks rise from the center of the clump. Each stalk bears several flat flower heads with two concentric rows of ragged blue rays (petal-like structures) and fuzzy white centers. Plants grow from cordlike white roots. 'Blue Danube' has 5-foot lavender-blue flowers. 'Colorwheel' opens white and darkens to purple, giving a multicolor effect. 'Honeysong Purple' has dark violet flowers. 'Klaus Jelitto' has 4-foot deep blue flowers. 'Mary Gregory' is soft yellow. 'Omega Sky Rocket' lifts its flowers on 3- to 4-foot stems. 'Peachey' is free-blooming, with large blue-violet flowers. 'Silver Moon' has creamy white flowers. 'Wyoming' has rich blue-violet flowers. USDA Plant Hardiness Zones 5 to 9.

How to Grow

Stokes' asters are easy-to-grow, long-lived perennials. Plant them in average to rich, moist but well-drained soil in full sun or light shade. Plants form dense clumps that are easily divided in spring or fall. Divide for propagation or when plants get overcrowded. Sow ripe seed outdoors in fall or indoors after 6 weeks of cold, moist stratification. Plants bloom the second year.

Landscape Uses

Stoke's asters are dramatic in flower. Combine them with small flowers and fine-textured foliage. Plant them with verbenas, calamints (*Calamintha*), wormwoods (*Artemisia*), yarrows (*Achillea*), phlox, and ornamental grasses. In light shade, plant them with beardtongues (*Penstemon*), columbines (*Aquilegia*), irises, ferns, and hostas.

The thick, wiry roots of Stokes' aster (*Stokesia laevis*) enable these moisture-loving plants to endure periods of drought. 'Mary Gregory' produces dozens of yellow flowers and will rebloom if old stalks are removed at the base.

STYLOPHORUM

sty-LOF-or-um or *sty-low-FOR-um* • Papaveraceae, Poppy Family

Waxen, 2-inch yellow-orange flowers make wood poppies dramatic and showy woodland plants. They self-sow freely to form vast sweeps in the dappled light of a woodland or shade garden. Use them with flowering shrubs for a spectacular display. When damaged, the stems bleed sap the same color as the flowers. Plants grow from fibrous-rooted crowns.

STYLOPHORUM

Common Names:
Celandine poppy, wood poppy

Bloom Time:
Spring bloom

Planting Requirements:
Shade

Orange-flowered celandine poppy (*Stylophorum diphyllum*) opens its first flowers in early spring and continues blooming for nearly 2 months. Create a stunning combination by pairing with Virginia bluebells (*Mertensia virginica*) and ferns.

Stylophorum diphyllum (di-FILE-lum), celandine poppy. Size: 1 to 2 feet tall and wide. The celadon green leaves are as decorative as the flowers. They are deeply lobed and resemble oak leaves. The 6- to 10-inch basal leaves and the paired stem leaves are equally attractive. Flowers are borne in early to midspring. Nodding seedpods are oval. USDA Plant Hardiness Zones 4 to 8.

S. lasiocarpum (las-e-o-CARP-um), Chinese wood poppy. Size: 1 to 2 feet tall and wide. This species differs from our native in its yellow flowers and elongated leaves with toothed rather than rounded lobes. The narrow, pencil-like seedpods are held erect. Plants bloom off and on all summer. Zones 4 to 8.

How to Grow

Plant in humus-rich, evenly moist soil in light to full shade. Plants do not tolerate extremely acid soils. They may go dormant in mid-summer if conditions become hot and dry. Plants reseed freely, so you will have plenty to share with neighbors. As the ample foliage becomes yellow or crisp around the edges, cut plants to the ground to keep the garden neat.

Landscape Uses

Drifts of bright colorful wood poppies are lovely under shrubs, along woodland trails, or at the edge of a terrace garden. Combine them with Virginia bluebells (*Mertensia virginica*), woodland phlox (*Phlox divaricata*), blue-eyed Marys (*Omphalodes*), wood mint (*Meehania cordata*), and other blue flowers that complement the warm flower color. Other suitable companions include bloodroot (*Sanguinaria canadensis*), wild gingers (*Asarum*), lungworts (*Pulmonaria*), barrenworts (*Epimedium*), merrybells (*Uvularia*), sedges (*Carex*), and ferns.

SYMPHYTUM

sym-PHY-tum • Boraginaceae, Borage Family

Comfrey is a well-known medicinal herb, but it is just one of many underutilized, garden-worthy species. Ornamental species make excellent groundcovers with bold, broadly lance-shaped leaves that make enormous clumps after the flowers fade. The branched clusters of nodding white, blue, or pink flowers are carried high above the foliage in spring and early summer. Plants grow from fibrous-rooted crowns and short creeping stems.

SYMPHYTUM

Common Name:
Comfrey

Bloom Time:
Spring bloom,
summer foliage

Planting Requirements:
Sun to partial shade

Symphytum grandiflorum (grand-i-FLO-rum), large-flowered comfrey. Size: 1 foot tall, 1 to 2 feet wide. A familiar spring-blooming groundcover with broadly lance-shaped quilted leaves and clusters of nodding white flowers often flushed with blue. Foliage remains attractive all season. 'Goldsmith' has golden yellow variegation and flowers that open from pink to blue and fade toward white. 'Variegatum' has bold creamy leaf margins. 'Hidcote Blue', possibly a hybrid, has 1- to 2-foot stems of sky blue flowers. USDA Plant Hardiness Zones 3 to 8.

S. ×*uplandicum* (up-LAND-e-cum), Russian comfrey. Size: 2 to 4 feet tall and wide. Boat-size leaves (2 feet tall) are the main show, but in late spring, tall coarse stalks bear nodding, sky blue flowers. Some gardeners prefer to remove flower-stalks as they emerge. Bristly hairs on the leaves may make you itch, so wear long

Though most noteworthy for its enormous variegated leaves, Russian comfrey (*Symphytum* ×*uplandicum* 'Variegatum') has tall, stout leafy stems with clusters of nodding, bell-shaped flowers. Like many plants in the borage family, the flowers open pink and fade to light blue or white.

sleeves when tidying. 'Axminster Gold' has gorgeous gold-edged leaves. 'Variegatum' is strikingly edged with creamy white. Zones 4 to 8.

How to Grow

Comfreys appreciate rich, evenly moist soil in sun or partial shade. Established plants tolerate some drought, but the large-leaved species may brown on the margins in hot, dry conditions. Large-flowered comfrey spreads rapidly and may swamp smaller neighbors. If foliage begins to look fried, especially after flowering, cut the entire plant to the ground, and a fresh crop of leaves will soon appear. Propagate by division in early spring or before plants go dormant. Self-sown seedlings will appear.

Landscape Uses

Use comfreys as groundcovers under flowering trees or shrubs. Place bold Russian comfrey as a specimen amid ferns, fume-roots (*Corydalis*), bleeding hearts (*Dicentra*), epimediums, wild gingers (*Asarum*), and irises. A clump in a decorative urn is sensational when accented with yellow and purple pansies in spring, and verbenas in summer.

TANACETUM

tan-a-SEE-tum • Asteraceae, Aster Family

Tansy was once the sole ornamental species in this genus, but the recent breakup of the chrysanthemums has swelled its ranks, adding many garden-worthy plants of varied size and flower color. Plants share daisy flowers in clusters rather than singly as in many former mums, with the exception of the painted daisy, which bears its flowers singly. Plants grow from fibrous-rooted crowns.

TANACETUM

Common Name:
Tansy

Bloom Time:
Summer bloom

Planting Requirements:
Full sun

Tanacetum coccineum (kock-SIN-e-um), pyrethrum, painted daisy. Size: 1½ to 2 feet tall, 1 foot wide. The 3-inch deep red to rose flowers of painted daises are inexplicably scarce in American gardens. The large heads are carried singly above mostly basal leaves that are deeply cut. Plants creep slowly outward from short, fibrous-rooted crowns. Flowers are long-lasting as fresh cuts. 'James Kelway' has scarlet to crimson flowers on 1½-foot stems. 'Robinson's Crimson' has crimson flowers on 2-foot stems. USDA Plant Hardiness Zones 3 to 7.

T. corymbosum (kor-im-BO-sum), chrysanthemum. Size: 1 to 4 feet tall, 1 to 2 feet wide. A stiff, leafy perennial with dissected, mostly basal foliage and broad open clusters of 1-inch white daisies in summer. Zones 4 to 8.

T. parthenium (par-THEEN-e-um), feverfew. Size: 1 to 3 feet tall, 1 to 2 feet wide. Feverfew is an heirloom perennial with erect, bushy stems covered in bright green lobed foliage and topped with mounds of lacy white daisies. Plants bloom

Plant tansy (*Tanacetum vulgare*) in average to lean soil and full sun or it will flop. The buttonlike flowers are good for fresh cuts or for drying.

649

profusely from summer to fall. 'Aureum' has golden foliage that fades to chartreuse in summer. 'White Bobbles' has double pompon flowers. Zones 4 to 8.

T. vulgare (vul-GAR-ee), tansy. Size: 2 to 3 feet tall and wide. This rather rank and weedy perennial has stout stems clothed in deep green, ferny, pinnately divided leaves. The buttonlike heads are rich golden yellow and have no rays (petals), only the central disk flowers. All parts of the plant are strongly aromatic. The plants are naturalized from herb gardens, where they were grown for medicinal uses. Var. *crispum* is a luxuriant selection with large, more finely cut divisions. It's superior to the species as a garden plant. 'Isla Gold' emerges golden and fades to yellow by late summer. Zones 3 to 8.

How to Grow

Plant all these daisies in rich, well-drained soil in full sun. Plants tolerate sandy soil and seaside conditions. Tansies grow luxuriantly in all but the poorest soils. Plants increase quickly to form broad, dense clumps. Divide overgrown plants for size control or propagation in spring or fall. Remove spent flowers to eliminate self-sown seedlings.

Landscape Uses

Combine the richly colored flowers of painted daisies with deep blues and purples for contrast. Choose catmints (*Nepeta*), sages (*Salvia*), balloon flowers (*Platycodon*), and irises. For color harmony, choose bright pink anise hyssop (*Agastache* 'Tutti Frutti'), phlox 'Bright Eyes', cranesbills (*Geranium*), and sedums. Tansy is well suited to meadows, herb gardens, or perennial plantings. Combine all species with yarrows (*Achillea*), wormwoods (*Artemisia*), asters, sea lavender (*Limonium latifolium*), and ornamental grasses.

TELEKIA

tea-LEK-e-a • Asteraceae, Aster Family

Not another yellow daisy, you may scream! But wait, this one has unique charms. Telekia grows in sun or shade, has huge flowers to 6 inches across, and the bold foliage looks great among ferns, sedges, and other moisture-loving plants. This dramatic aristocrat deserves a second look. Plants have massive crowns with thick, fibrous roots.

TELEKIA

Common Name:
Telekia

Bloom Time:
Summer bloom

Planting Requirements:
Sun to partial shade

Telekia speciosa (spee-see-O-sa), telekia. Size: 3 to 5 feet tall and wide. Some plants were put on earth to entertain. This bold, bodacious daisy is one. Huge, toothed, triangular basal leaves nearly 2 feet long form a bold fountain of bright green. The stem leaves are smaller and intermingle with the open cluster of 2-foot, ragged yellow daisies that scream out to be noticed. Plants bloom for several weeks, and heads are attractive after the rays fall. They grow from stout, fibrous-rooted crowns. USDA Plant Hardiness Zones 2 to 8.

How to Grow

Plant in rich, evenly moist soil in sun or partial shade. These giants need 5 or more feet of bed space when they mature, so keep delicate plants out of the way. Foliage emerges early, accenting the spring garden scene. After flowers fade (as summer wears on), plants begin to look ragged, so cut them down to promote a fresh flush of fabulous foliage.

Landscape Uses

In the middle or toward the rear of a big bed, an imposing clump of telekia creates a marvelous focal point. You can also use them in mass plantings along the edge of a woodland or in a shrub border. Some big companions include Siberian iris (*Iris sibirica*), rodgersias, valerian (*Valeriana officinalis*), Joe-Pye weeds (*Eupatorium*), spikenards (*Aralia*), cow parsnips (*Heracleum*), and grasses.

Bold leaves and huge yellow daisies make telekia (*Telekia speciosa*) a dramatic addition to the summer garden when protected from hot sun by the shade of trees. Plants may decline after flowering, so cut them to the ground and a fresh foliar rosette will appear.

THALICTRUM

tha-LIK-trum • Ranunculaceae, Buttercup Family

Meadow rues are airy plants with large, dissected foliage that alternates up the stem. Each leaf consists of many small, gray-green scalloped leaflets. Stems are crowned with domed clusters of fuzzy flowers, each of which consists mainly of colorful stamens (male reproductive structures). Some species have showy sepals as well. Plants grow from fibrous rootstocks.

THALICTRUM

Common Name:
Meadow rue

Bloom Time:
Spring or summer bloom

Planting Requirements:
Sun to partial shade

Plant columbine meadow rue (*Thalictrum aquilegiifolium*) toward the center of the border where the frothy plumes contrast with bold flowers such as daylilies and iris.

Thalictrum actaeifolium (ak-tay-i-FOL-e-um), baneberry-leaf meadow rue. Size: 2 to 3 feet tall, 1 to 2 feet wide. The broad, bluntly toothed leaflets recall those of baneberry. Handsome clusters of fuzzy, pale lilac flowers open in summer. Self-sown seedlings will appear. USDA Plant Hardiness Zones 4 to 8.

T. aquilegiifolium (a-kwi-lej-i-FO-lee-um), columbine meadow rue. Size: 2 to 3 feet tall and wide. The foliage of this meadow rue has blue-gray leaflets that resemble columbines (*Aquilegia*). Each showy flower is petalless and consists of many stamens. The flower heads are 6 to 8 inches wide. 'Album' has white flowers. 'Purpureum' has violet flowers. 'Thundercloud' has deep purple flower heads. Zones 5 to 8.

T. delavayi (del-a-VAY-ee), Yunnan meadow rue. Size: 2 to 4 feet tall, 2 to 3 feet wide. This airy meadow rue has showy lilac sepals and creamy stamens. 'Hewitt's Double' has double flowers. Zones 4 to 7.

T. diffusiflorum (dif-fuse-i-FLO-rum). Size: 2 to 3 feet tall, 1 to 2 feet wide. This species may well be the showiest meadow rue, with starry flowers composed of five huge lavender sepals. Plants form open clumps of wiry, often weak stems clothed in attractive, blue-cast foliage. Though it lacks the poise of the taller species, the nickle-size flowers make the bitter pill of bad posture easier to swallow. Zones 4 to 8.

T. dioicum (die-O-i-cum), early meadow rue. Size: 1 to 3 feet tall and wide. Early meadow rue has separate male and female plants. Male plants produce candelabra-like flower clusters in spring, significant for their pendant golden stamens. Female flowers are insignificant. Good for shade. Zones 3 to 8.

T. flavum (FLA-vum) (*speciosissimum*), dusty meadow rue. Size: 3 to 5 feet tall, 2 to 3 feet wide. Dusty meadow rue is the loveliest member of the genus. The luscious foliage is gray-green and the 4-foot upright flower clusters are pale sulfur yellow. Var. *glaucum* ('Glaucum') has blue-gray foliage. 'Illuminator' has yellow mottled leaves early in the season. Zones 4 to 8.

T. ichangensis (e-chang-EN-sis) (*coreanum*), Korean meadow rue. Size: 4 to 6 inches tall, 12 inches wide. This diminutive species has charming, outfacing, shield-shaped leaves. Clouds of soft pink flowers are carried above the leaves of this floriferous species that blooms off and on throughout summer. Zones 4 to 8.

T. kiusianum (ke-you-si-AY-num), Kyosho meadow rue. Size: 2 to 6 inches tall, 12 inches wide. This plant is so tiny, if it were not for its fuzzy pink flowers, you would never think it was a meadow rue. Deep green, divided leaves form a flat below early summer flowers. Zones 4 to 8.

T. lucidum (LEW-sid-um). Size: 4 to 5 feet tall, 1 to 2 feet wide. A distinctive meadow rue with erect, conical clusters of soft yellow flowers atop self-supporting stems covered in bright green leaves with linear, unlobed leaflets quite unlike the scalloped leaflets of its kin. Plants bloom for several weeks in summer. Zones 4 to 8.

T. minus (MY-nus). Size: 4 to 6 feet tall, 2 to 3 feet wide. The dainty green leaves with nearly round leaflets are the main show, though late-summer flowers provide a green-and-white accent to the show. 'Adiantifolium' is an attractive selection with smaller, bluer foliage on dense stems. Zones 4 to 8.

T. polygamum (poly-GAM-um), tall meadow rue. Size: 4 to 8 feet tall, 2 to 3 feet wide. Plumes of creamy flowers like billowing clouds in mid- to late summer top stems covered in divided leaves with narrow, blunt-lobed leaflets. This plant deserves wider popularity. *T. dascycarpum* and *T. revolutum* are additional good natives. Zones 3 to 8.

T. rochebrunianum (roch-e-brun-i-A-num), lavender mist. Size: 4 to 6 feet tall, 2 to 3 feet wide. A tall plant with blowsy foliage and large terminal clusters of showy lilac flowers in early summer. 'Lavender Mist' is an excellent selection with large, showy flower heads. 'Elin' is a hybrid, to 10 feet, with superb, sturdy stems crowned with lavender-and-yellow bicolor flowers. Zones 4 to 7.

How to Grow

Meadow rues are easy to grow in moist, humus-rich soil in full sun or light shade. They form dense clumps with age that bear many bloom stalks. Plants seldom need division but can be lifted in fall for propagation.

Landscape Uses

Plant meadow rues at the middle or rear of the border. Their airy flowers create a charming background for larger flowers and bold foliage. Combine them with day-lilies (*Hemerocallis*), garden phlox (*Phlox paniculata*), sneezeweeds (*Helenium*), rose mallows (*Hibiscus*), and ornamental grasses. Plant *T. dioicum* in the shade garden with wildflowers, ferns, and hostas.

THERMOPSIS

ther-MOP-sis • Fabaceae, Pea Family

Bush peas are like lupines for the hot South. The terminal spikes are composed of densely packed, yellow pealike flowers. The flowers give way to narrow pods with flat seeds that are soon devoured by hungry birds. They have narrow, upright stems with alternate gray-green leaves that are fuzzy underneath. Each leaf has three oval leaflets joined to a short stalk. Plants grow from woody, fibrous-rooted crowns.

THERMOPSIS

Common Names:
Bush pea, thermopsis

Bloom Time:
Late spring bloom

Planting Requirements:
Full sun to light shade

Thermopsis lanceolata (lan-see-o-LAH-ta) (*lupinoides*), lanceleaf thermopsis. Size: 9 to 12 inches tall, 12 to 18 inches wide. This short species has small open flowers, pale yellow spikes, and unusual recurved seedpods. USDA Plant Hardiness Zones 2 to 7.

T. montana (mon-TAH-na), mountain goldenbanner. Size: 12 to 24 inches tall and wide. A rounded plant with dense spikes of lemon yellow flowers. Zones 3 to 8.

T. villosa (vil-LO-sa) (*caroliana*), Carolina bush pea. Size: 3 to 5 feet tall, 3 to 4 feet wide. This stately species has stiff stalks crowned by 8- to 12-inch dense spikelike clusters of bright lemon yellow flowers. Zones 3 to 9.

How to Grow

Plant bush peas in average to rich, moist but well-drained acid soil in full sun or light shade. In warm southern zones, partial shade is recommended. If foliage declines after flowering, cut plants back to the ground. Plants form tight erect clumps that increase in breadth each year. Division is seldom necessary. Propagate by stem cuttings taken in early summer from side shoots. Sow seed outdoors or inside after soaking for 12 to 24 hours in hot water.

Landscape Uses

Bush peas have a wide spread, so leave them plenty of room in the middle or back of the border. Combine the spiky forms with peonies (*Paeonia*), bellflowers (*Campanula*), blue stars (*Amsonia*), goat's beards (*Aruncus*), catmints (*Nepeta*), bowman's root (*Porteranthus trifoliatus*), and cranesbills (*Geranium*). Plants are also well suited to meadows and sunny wild gardens.

Carolina bush peas (*Thermopsis villosa*) are versatile native perennials valued for their lupine-like flowers and their decorative seedheads. They thrive in moist or dry soil and bloom well in sun or partial shade.

TIARELLA

tee-a-REL-a • Saxifragaceae, Saxifrage Family

Groundcovers are generally serviceable plants with limited floral prowess. Not foamflower. The fuzzy spikes of fragrant white or pink spring flowers complement the rounded to triangular evergreen leaves that form this dense, weedproof groundcover. If you are not bent on covering ground, try a clumping form, as many selections do not run.

TIARELLA

Common Name:
Foamflower

Bloom Time:
Spring bloom

Planting Requirements:
Partial to full shade

Tiarella cordifolia (kor-di-FO-lee-a), Allegheny foamflower. Size: 6 to 10 inches tall, 12 to 24 inches wide. Foamflowers are spring-blooming groundcovers with erect conical clusters of small fuzzy, fragrant, white to pale pink flowers and heart-shaped to triangular leaves with 4-inch petioles. The plants grow from fibrous-rooted crowns with central foliage rosettes and long, leafy runners. Var. *collina* (*wherryi*) produces leafy clumps with no runners and a greater profusion of flowerstalks. Leaves are also glossy green. 'Oakleaf' has green oaklike leaves. 'Cygnet' has large spidery leaves with dark veins. 'Eco Running Tapestry' is a fast-spreading groundcover with red-blotched foliage. 'Heronswood Mist' is mottled with cream and pink. 'Jeepers Creepers' is a running selection with scalloped leaves tinted with dark mottling around the veins. 'Skyrocket' is a strong clumper with lacy foliage and dense, showy flower spikes. USDA Plant Hardiness Zones 3 to 8.

Allegheny foamflower (*Tiarella cordifolia* 'Iron Butterfly') is a lush, clumping form sporting deeply lobed, black-stained leaves and dense spikes of foamy spring flowers.

How to Grow

Plant foamflowers in humus-rich, slightly acid, evenly moist soil in partial to full shade. Plants spread quickly from runners to form leafy mats. The nonrunning variety produces broad clumps with age. Divide plants in spring or fall, or remove rooted runners anytime during the growing season. Sow seed uncovered in spring.

Landscape Uses

Foamflowers make exceptional groundcovers that do double duty with lovely flowers and dense, weed-excluding foliage mats. Plant them under shrubs and trees, alone or in combination with other plants. Clumping forms add height to low plantings. In the shade garden, plants are effective with wild creeping phlox (*Phlox stolonifera*), fairy wings (*Epimedium*), wood anemone (*Anemone nemorosa*), wild columbine (*Aquilegia canadensis*), bleeding hearts (*Dicentra*), Solomon's seals (*Polygonatum*), hostas, and ferns.

TRADESCANTIA

tra-des-KANT-ee-a • Commelinaceae, Dayflower Family

Spiderworts are floriferous spring wildflowers with attractive satiny, three-petaled flowers carried in clusters atop succulent jointed stems. Flower color varies from purple, lavender, and blue to pink, rose-red and white. Each flower lasts but half a day, closing by early afternoon. The bases of the long, linear blue-green foliage encircle the joints at right angles to the stem. Plants go dormant after flowering but may reemerge in fall. They grow from thick, fleshy-rooted crowns.

> **TRADESCANTIA**
>
> **Common Name:**
> Spiderwort
>
> **Bloom Time:**
> Late spring and early summer bloom
>
> **Planting Requirements:**
> Full sun to partial shade

Tradescantia ×andersoniana (an-der-son-ee-AH-na), common spiderwort. Size: 1 to 2 feet tall and wide. This floriferous hybrid is the product of several species, including *T. virginiana*, with which it is often confused. The flowers have wide triangular petals with bright yellow stamens. 'Blue Stone' has rich, medium blue flowers. 'Concord Grape' is compact and the best purple. 'Innocence' is pure white. 'Iris Pritchard' is white with a violet-blue blush. 'James C. Weguelin' has sky blue flowers. 'Pauline' has orchid pink flowers. 'Purple Dome' has rosy purple flowers. 'Sweet Kate' ('Blue and Gold') has yellow foliage and electric blue flowers. 'Red Cloud' has maroon flowers and narrow, grasslike foliage. 'Zwanenberg Blue' has purple-blue flowers. USDA Plant Hardiness Zones 4 to 9.

T. hirsuticaulis (her-soot-i-CAWL-is), spiderwort. Size: 8 to 12 inches tall, 12 to 16 inches wide. Similar to the above but with hairy leaves and stems and showy, medium blue flowers. *T. bracteata* is also available, with dense upright foliage and medium blue flowers. Zones 4 to 9.

The flowers of common spiderwort (*Tradescantia ×andersoniana* 'Sweet Kate') open in the wee hours of morning and close by early afternoon. The glowing yellow leaves make a show even when the flowers are closed for the day.

T. ohiensis (o-HI-en-sis), Ohio spider-wort. Size: 1 to 3 feet tall, 1 to 2 feet wide. Ohio spiderwort has narrow blue-green leaves and blue, rose, or white flowers with rounded petals. Zones 3 to 9.

T. virginiana (vir-jin-ee-AH-na), Virginia spiderwort. Size: 2 to 3 feet tall, 1 to 2 feet wide. A parent of *T.* ×*andersoniana*, more delicate in form. Flowers are blue to purple. Zones 4 to 9.

How to Grow

Plant easy-care spiderworts in average to rich, moist but well-drained soil in full to light shade. Plants grow well in partial shade but do not flower as long. Plants tend to get shabby or even go dormant after flowering and are best cut to the ground. They will produce new foliage quickly where summers are cool, or by fall in warmer zones. Plants increase quickly to form dense clumps. Divide them every 2 or 3 years as they are going dormant. Self-sown seedings are often abundant.

Landscape Uses

Plant spiderworts with leafy plants that will fill the void left when they go dormant. Choose wild bleeding heart (*Dicentra eximia*), cranesbills (*Geranium*), blue stars (*Amsonia*), phlox, bowman's root (*Porteranthus trifoliatus*), catmints (*Nepeta*), lily-of-the-valley (*Convallaria majalis*), ornamental grasses, hostas, and ferns. Use them in combination with groundcovers to underplant shrubs.

TRICYRTIS

tri-SER-tis • Convallariaceae (Liliaceae), Lily-of-the-Valley Family

Toad lilies are unusual shade-loving perennials with oddly configured, upfacing funnelform flowers. Three petals and three petal-like sepals surround a raised column that sports a fuzzy, three-parted style (female reproductive structure) surrounded by purple stamens (male reproductive structures). The flowers are heavily spotted or flushed with purple. They are carried in terminal clusters or in the axils of the leaves. The leaves are broadly lance-shaped with prominent veins and clasp the stem. Plants grow from fleshy rootstocks.

TRICYRTIS

Common Name:
Toad lily

Bloom Time:
Late summer and fall bloom

Planting Requirements:
Light to partial shade

Tricyrtis formosana (for-MO-SAY-na), Formosa toad lily. Size: 1 to 2 feet tall and wide. Most plants sold today are hybrids between this species and *T. hirta*. The hybrid has erect stems to 3 feet, crowned with terminal clusters (cymes) of purple-spotted white. The true species is an erect plant to 2 feet with delicate, broadly lance-shaped leaves and open cymes. Plants sold as *T.* 'Hototogisu' are true *T. formosana*. 'Samurai' has leaves attractively edged in gold. USDA Plant Hardiness Zones 4 to 8. Plants sold as *T. formosana* 'Amethystina' are really *T. lasiocarpa*, a related species with larger flowers in branched, terminal cymes. The tepals are pale lilac, with darker spots. Zones 7 to 9.

T. hirta (HIR-ta), common toad lily. Size: 2 to 3 feet tall, 1 to 2 feet wide. This species has arching stems with purple-spotted flowers clustered in the leaf axils along the upper two-thirds of the stem and at the end of the stem. Plants bloom late in the season and may be killed by early frost in the North. 'Lilac Towers' has large, heavily spotted flowers, as does 'Miyazaki'. 'White Towers' and 'Albescens' are unspotted, pure whites. 'Alba' is white with creamy spots. 'Variegata' is a strong grower with golden-edged leaves and purple-spotted flowers, similar to 'Miyazaki Gold'. Zones 4 to 9.

T. latifolia (lah-tee-FO-lee-a), toad lily. Size: 2 to 3 feet tall and wide. This summer bloomer carries its upright yellow flowers in branched terminal clusters (cymes) above broad, clasping foliage. 'Forbidden City' is a striking selection with dark stems and outer triangular tepals each marked

Toad lilies, like the hybrid *Tricyrtis hirta ×formosana*, are unusual perennials for the shade garden. They open their curious, speckled flowers in fall, when few other woodland plants are flowering.

with a chocolate brown band across the middle. Zones 3 to 8.

T. macrantha var. *macranthopsis* (ma-KRANTH-a var. ma-KRANTH-op-sis), toad lily. Size: 2 to 4 feet tall, 1 to 2 feet wide. Decumbent stems bear broadly lance-shaped, shiny pleated leaves and gorgeous inflated yellow bells borne in the leaf axils along the upper third of the stem. Success in the garden depends on constant moisture. Zones 6 to 8.

T. macropoda (mak-row-POW-da), toad lily. Size: 2 to 3 feet tall, 1 foot wide. A handsome plant with purple-blotched white flowers with reflexed petals in terminal cymes and in the upper leaf axils. 'Yungi Temple Form' from China is a giant, to 5 feet tall, with flowers lining the stems. Zones 4 to 8.

Hybrids

'Kohaku' is derived from a cross between *T. hirta* and *T. macranthopsis*. Open, vase-shaped white flowers, heavily spotted with rich purple, face upward from the leaf axils on the upper half of the stems. 'Lemon and Lime' has golden foliage edged with green on stems under 2 feet tall. 'Lightning Strike' has gold leaves edged in dark green and lavender. 'Shining Light' has irregularly striped gold-and-green leaves with lavender flowers. 'Sinonome' has white flowers spotted with rich violet. 'Tojen' has up-right cymes of unspotted lavender-and-white flowers decorating stout stems to 2 feet tall.

How to Grow

Plant toad lilies in evenly moist, humus-rich soil in light to partial shade. They are long-lived and easy to grow. *T. formosana* spreads to form wide clumps, whereas *T. hirta* does not run. Divide them in spring for size control or propagation. Self-sown seeds will appear if the season is long enough to allow them to ripen.

Landscape Uses

Toad lilies have a subtle and unusual beauty that is best appreciated at close range. Plant them near a path in the shaded garden in the company of wildflowers, shade perennials, hostas, and ferns.

TRILLIUM

TRIL-ee-um • Trilliaceae (Liliaceae), Trillium Family

Trilliums are beloved spring wildflowers aptly named for the triads of leaves, petals, and sepals. The leaves are broadly oval and join together at the top of the stem beneath a single flower with three broad, showy petals and three green sepals. Plants grow from thick rhizomes with fleshy roots.

TRILLIUM

Common Name:
Wakerobin

Bloom Time:
Spring bloom

Planting Requirements:
Light to full shade

Trillium chloropetalum (kloor-o-PET-a-lum), giant toadshade. Size: 1 to 3 feet tall, 1 to 2 feet wide. This handsome species has red to white sessile (attached directly to the base of the plant) flowers with elongated petals that stick straight up from broad, mottled leaves. In its best forms, this is a stunning species. Native to the West Coast. *T. kurabayashii* has clear wine red flowers. USDA Plant Hardiness Zones 6 to 8.

T. cuneatum (kew-knee-AY-tum), toad trillium. Size: 1 to 2 feet tall, 1 foot wide. An attractive and curious sessile species with maroon to deep wine red flowers that smell of fruit-flavored gum. This species is often confused with the smaller *T. sessile*. Zones 4 to 8.

T. erectum (e-REK-tum), red trillium, stinking Benjamin. Size: 1 to 2 feet tall, 1 foot wide. Red trillium has deep blood red flowers that nod slightly on 1- to 4-inch stalks. They are unpleasantly scented. *T. sulcatum* has larger, outfacing flowers with broad petals. *T. vaseyi* has huge nodding flowers to 3 inches across. Zones 4 to 9.

T. flexipes (FLEX-e-peez), bent trillium. Size: 1 to 2½ feet tall, 1 foot wide. This variable species has 2-inch creamy white flowers that droop or stand erect on 1- to 4-inch stalks. Broad leaves top stems borne two or more to a clump. Zones 3 to 8.

T. grandiflorum (grand-i-FLO-rum), white trillium. Size: 1½ to 2 feet tall, 1 foot wide. White trillium has broad, snow white flowers held erect above a whorl of bright green leaves. The flowers fade to pink as they age. 'Flore-pleno' and 'Snow Bunting' have fully double flowers. *T. ovatum* is the western counterpart, with showy white petals more narrow than its cousin. Plants dislike eastern heat and humidity. Zones 3 to 9.

T. luteum (lew-TEE-um), yellow trillium. Size: 1 to 2 feet tall, 1 foot wide. A handsome sessile species with chartreuse to lemon yellow flowers that smell of lemons. Zones 4 to 8.

How to Grow

Plant trilliums in moist, humus-rich soil in shade. *T. erectum* requires a lime-free soil; other species are more adaptable. Plants emerge early in spring and bloom for 2 weeks. If the soil stays moist, foliage persists through summer. Plants may form offsets and with age can be divided. Propagation by seed is slow. Sow fresh seed outside in summer. Germination takes a year, and plants will bloom in 5 to 7 years. Many trilliums sold today are collected from the wild. Buy only nursery-propagated plants from reputable dealers.

Landscape Uses

Plant trilliums in shade gardens with wildflowers, shade perennials, sedges (*Carex*), and ferns. They are lovely planted with spring-blooming shrubs and trees.

The creamy white flowers of *Trillium chloropetalum* stand out against a full collar of rounded, mottled foliage. This West Coast native performs well in many eastern gardens but is not a plant for the hot, humid South.

TROLLIUS

TRO-lee-us • Ranunculaceae, Buttercup Family

Globeflowers are showy spring perennials with waxy bowl-shaped single or double flowers. The flowers have no petals but have orange or yellow petal-like sepals. The palmately divided leaves have five to seven incised leaflets and are carried on long stalks. Plants produce basal rosettes from thick, fleshy rootstocks.

TROLLIUS

Common Name:
 Globeflower

Bloom Time:
 Spring bloom

Planting Requirements:
 Full sun to partial shade

Trollius chinensis (chi-NEN-sis), Chinese globeflower. Size: 2 to 3 feet tall, 1 to 2 feet wide. This globeflower has five-parted leaves and tall stalks with golden yellow flowers. The flowers are more open than other species, with 1-inch erect and flattened stamens projecting from the flowers. Plants sold as *T. lederborii* belong here. 'Golden Queen' has large, single yellow flowers. USDA Plant Hardiness Zones 3 to 6.

T. ×cultorum (kul-TOR-um), hybrid globeflower. Size: 2 to 3 feet tall, 1 to 2 feet wide. This group of hybrids includes garden selections from a number of different species, especially *T. asiaticus*, *T. chinensis*, and *T. europaeus*. 'Alabaster' is creamy yellow. 'Earliest of All' has pale orange-yellow flowers early in the season. 'Golden Queen' has 2-inch tangerine flowers; may be a cultivar of *T. chinensis*. 'Lemon Queen' has lemon yellow flowers. 'Prichard's Giant' grows 3 feet tall and has bright yellow flowers. Zones 3 to 6.

Plant hybrid globeflowers such as *Trollius* 'Fireglobe' in a cool spot with moist or wet soil. Plants are intolerant of excessive heat but can dry out when dormant in summer.

T. europaeus (yoo-RO-pay-us), common globeflower. Size: 1½ to 2 feet tall and wide. Common globeflower has tufts of five-lobed leaves and erect stalks bearing one or two lemon yellow flowers. 'Superbus' is more robust and flowers more profusely. Zones 4 to 7.

How to Grow

Plant globeflowers in constantly moist to wet, humus-rich soil in light to partial shade. Plants prefer cool weather and perform best in northern zones. Clumps increase from slow creeping rootstocks. Divide plants in early spring or fall. Sow fresh seed outdoors as soon as it ripens. Stored seed has low viability.

Landscape Uses

Globeflowers produce bright spots of color in spring. Plant them in the moist-soil garden or near water's edge with irises, lady's-mantle (*Alchemilla mollis*), forget-me-nots (*Myosotis*), primroses (*Primula*), meadowsweets (*Filipendula*), ligularias, rodgersias, hostas, sedges (*Carex*), and ferns.

TULIPA

TEW-li-pa • Liliaceae, Lily Family

Tulips are classic spring flowers. Their grace is matched only by their beauty. The three petals and three petal-like sepals form the lovely flowers that are borne singly or (rarely) in threes atop naked stems. Flowers come in every color except true blue. Shades of white, pink, red, and yellow are most common. The leaves are broad and long, often with wavy margins, and may be blue-green, dark-spotted, or striped. Plants grow from true bulbs. Several species are available, but most tulips grown today are hybrids of mixed parentage.

> **TULIPA**
> **Common Name:**
>   Tulip
> **Bloom Time:**
>   Spring bloom
> **Planting Requirements:**
>   Full sun or light shade

Tulipa acuminata (a-kew-min-AH-ta), horned tulip. Size: 16 to 20 inches tall, 6 inches wide. This strange tulip has long, narrow-pointed yellow petals and slender wavy leaves. USDA Plant Hardiness Zones 5 to 8.

T. clusiana (klooz-ee-AH-na), lady tulip. Size: 10 to 12 inches tall, 6 inches wide. Lady tulips have starry flowers with rose-red stripes on the outside of white flowers. Leaves are long and slender. Zones 4 to 8.

T. praestans (PRIE-stanz), multiflowered tulip. Size: 10 to 12 inches tall, 8 inches wide. This small tulip bears one to four bright red flowers on each stem. The leaves are long and slender. Zones 4 to 8.

T. pulchella (pul-CHEL-la) (*humilis*), beautiful tulip. Size: 4 to 5 inches tall, 6 inches wide. This squat tulip has round violet flowers and strap-shaped leaves. 'Humilis' has violet-pink flowers. 'Violacea' has deep violet-purple flowers. Zones 5 to 8.

T. tarda (TAR-da), late tulip. Size: 3 to 4 inches tall, 6 inches wide. This little tulip has starry yellow flowers with white centers and straplike leaves. Zones 4 to 8.

Tulipa tarda is a diminutive early-blooming rock garden tulip that self-sows readily to form broad, handsome clumps.

Hybrids

Modern hybrids are grouped according to their flowering time, flower shape, and hybrid origin. The Royal General Bulbgrower's Association recognizes 15 divisions.

Division I. Single Early Tulips. Size: 12 to 14 inches tall. Single fragrant early flowers, usually in April and early May, later in the North. Good for bedding or forcing. Popular cultivars: 'Apricot Beauty' is rich apricot with a flush of pink. 'Beauty Queen' is shrimp pink. 'General De Wet' is flaming orange.

Division II. Double Early Tulips. Size: 10 to 12 inches tall. Double early flowers, usually in late April. Good for bedding or forcing. Popular cultivars: 'Abba' is bright red with a yellow heart. 'Peach Blossom' is rich pink suffused with white. 'Picasso 'is orange with hints of yellow and chartreuse-edged leaves.

Division III. Triumph Tulips. Size: 18 to 24 inches tall. Single midseason flowers, usually in May. Good for bedding or forcing, with strong stems and large flowers. Popular cultivars: 'Dreaming Maid' is lavender and white. 'Gavota' is rich maroon with a yellow edge. 'Princess Irene' is salmon and orange. 'Yellow Present' is soft creamy yellow.

Division IV. Darwin Hybrid Tulips. Size: 2 to 2½ feet tall. Single midseason flowers, usually in mid-May. The most popular tulips, good for bedding and cutting. Popular cultivars: 'Daydream' opens yellow and fades to soft orange. 'Ivy Floradale' ages from creamy yellow to white. 'Olympic Flame' is yellow with red flairs.

Division V. Single Late Tulips. Size: 1½ to 3 feet tall. Single late-season flowers, usually in late May. Long-stemmed and popular in the garden and for cutting. Popular cultivars: 'Blushing Lady' is elegant soft yellow-orange with a wide rose flame. 'Maureen' is ivory. 'Pink Supreme' is deep pink. 'Queen of the Night' is deep velvety maroon-black.

Division VI. Lily Flowered Tulips. Size: 2 feet tall. Single midseason flowers with reflexed, pointed petals. A good garden tulip. Popular cultivars: 'Ballade' is violet with a white edge. 'Queen of Shcba' is flaming red. 'White Elegance' is white.

Division VII. Fringed Tulips. Size: 2 feet tall. Single mid- to late-season flowers with fringed margins. Popular cultivars: 'Blue Heron' is lilac purple. 'Burgundy Lace' is deep red. 'Fringed Elegance' is soft yellow.

Division VIII. Viridiflora Tulips. Size: 20 to 22 inches tall. Single late-season flowers with green flares or stripes. Popular cultivars: 'Esperanto 'is green and red. 'Formosa' is green and yellow. 'Groenland' is green and pink. 'Spring Green' is green and cream.

Division IX. Rembrandt Tulips. Size: 18 to 20 inches tall. Single flowers with multicolored streaks, called "broken tulips." Popular cultivars: Few selections are available as the dramatic pattern is caused by a virus.

Division X. Parrot Tulips. Size: 14 to 20 inches tall. Single large late-season flowers

Lily-flowered tulips such as fiery *Tulipa* 'Queen of Sheba' bloom after most of the spring bulbs have passed. With careful planning, you can have tulips in bloom for 2 months in spring.

with wavy or incised petals on supple stalks. Popular cultivars: 'Black Parrot' is deep brown-purple. 'Bluc Parrot' is blue-purple. 'Estella Rijnveld' is red and white. 'White Parrot' is white.

Division XI. Double Late Tulips (peony-flowered). Size: 12 to 16 inches tall. Double-flowered stout tulips with large late flowers. Popular cultivars: 'Angelique' is pale rose-pink. 'Black Hero' is deep maroon. 'Mount Tacoma' is creamy white.

Division XII. Kaufmanniana Tulips. Size: 4 to 8 inches tall. Single early flowers striped or flushed on the outside, pale and solid-colored on the inside. Leaves striped with brown. Popular cultivars: *T. kaufmanniana* is creamy white flamed with rose-red. 'Hearts Delight' is rose or pale pink. 'Johann Strauss' is red and soft yellow. 'Scarlet Baby' is brilliant red.

Division XIII. Fosteriana Tulips. Size: 10 to 20 inches tall. Single early flowers elongated on leafy stems with broad leaves, often banded in brown. Favorite cultivars: *T. fosteriana* is scarlet with black spots inside. 'Pink Emperor' is a deep pink-edged yellow, inside yellow. 'Red Emperor' is vermilion with black spots. 'Sweetheart' is pale yellow with a white edge. 'White Emperor' ('Purissima') is pure white.

Division XIV. Greigii Tulips. Size: 8 to 12 inches tall. Single midseason starry flowers, leaves often lined with brown. Favorite cultivars: *T. greigii* is orange scarlet with black spots inside. 'Cape Cod' is orange and yellow. 'Easter Surprise' is buttercup yellow. 'Red Riding Hood' is scarlet.

Division XV. Miscellaneous. Species and wild forms that are not classified above, including recognizable hybrids of these species.

How to Grow

Tulips are easy to flower the first season because they are planted with the buds already developed. They are foolproof at first but often decline after the second year. Gardeners often treat them as annuals and replace them each year. This is particularly true for public displays. In the home garden, triumph, Darwin hybrid, and single late tulips are the longest-lived and most dependable. The wild tulips and species are also reliably perennial, often persisting and even increasing for many years. Tulips need ample water and food when actively growing and a reasonably dry summer dormant period. Plant them in moist but well-drained, fertile, humus-rich soil in full sun. Allow the soil to bake in summer. Plant new bulbs in fall at a depth of 8 inches at the bottom of the bulb. When bedding tulips for display, plant all bulbs at the same depth or they will bloom unevenly. Space bulbs 2 to 6 inches apart, depending on plant size at flowering. Do not remove foliage until it is fully yellow, no matter how strong the temptation, unless you are discarding the bulbs. Next years' flower production depends on the previous years' foliage.

Landscape Uses

Tulips are lovely in mass bedding schemes in single or mixed colors, combined with other spring bulbs, or planted with perennials and shrubs. Choose the species and wild tulips for rock gardens and gardens with daffodils (*Narcissus*) and early perennials such as lungworts (*Pulmonaria*), Siberian bugloss (*Brunnera macrophylla*), bleeding hearts (*Dicentra*), and columbines (*Aquilegia*).

Uvularia

yoo-view-LAH-ree-a • Convallariaceae (Liliaceae), Lily-of-the-Valley Family

Bellworts are early-spring woodland wildflowers with slender stems that pierce the blades of oblong gray-green leaves. The nodding yellow flowers have three petals and three showy sepals, each of which is twisted and curled. Mature clumps are like bamboo in overall effect. Plants grow from slender creeping rhizomes.

UVULARIA

Common Names:
  Bellwort, merrybells

Bloom Time:
  Spring bloom

Planting Requirements:
  Partial to full shade

Uvularia grandiflora (gran-di-FLO-ra), great merrybells. Size: 1 to 1½ feet tall, 2 feet wide. This is the showiest bellwort, with lemon yellow flowers and lush foliage. Plants form tight clumps with age. USDA Plant Hardiness Zones 3 to 8.

U. perfoliata (per-fo-lee-AY-ta), perfoliate bellwort. Size: 8 to 12 inches tall and wide. This is a smaller version of *U. grandiflora*, with straw yellow flowers and an open, dispersed growth pattern. Zones 4 to 8.

U. sessilifolia (ses-sil-e-FO-lee-a), wild oats. Size: 4 to 6 inches tall, 12 inches wide. A delicate groundcover with narrow, sessile leaves and small, straw-colored bells. 'Cobblewood Gold' has gold-edged leaves. 'Variegata' has cream-edged leaves. Zones 3 to 8.

After the flowers of great merrybells (*Uvularia grandiflora*) fade, the blue-green foliage resembling a bamboo forms a lush groundcover that tolerates shade and dry soil. Here, plants bloom over a carpet of spring beauty (*Claytonia virginica*).

How to Grow

Bellworts are easy to grow in moist, humus-rich soil in shade. Plants increase steadily and create a nice groundcover in time. Foliage is somewhat limp while plants are in bloom, giving the flowers prominence. As they fade, stems and leaves spread out to form excellent foliage plants. Propagate by dividing clumps in fall.

Landscape Uses

Bellworts are lovely plants for the shade garden with wildflowers, hostas, and ferns. Combine their upright form with spreading plants such as bloodroot (*Sanguinaria canadensis*), lady's-mantle (*Alchemilla mollis*), fairy wings (*Epimedium*), lungworts (*Pulmonaria*), wild gingers (*Asarum*), foamflowers (*Tiarella cordifolia*), bleeding hearts (*Dicentra*), and ferns.

VERATRUM

ver-AY-trum • Melanthiaceae (Liliaceae), Bunchflower Family

Dramatic terminal flower clusters have drooping branches adorned with densely packed starry flowers in early summer. The lush foliage is almost tropical in appearance. The accordion-pleated oval leaves may reach a foot or more in length. Leaf bases overlap one another as they ascend the 1- to 6-foot stalks. Plants grow from stout crowns with thick, fleshy roots.

Veratrum nigrum (NIGH-grum), black false hellebore. Size: 2 to 4 feet tall, 2 to 3 feet wide. This species has distinctive starry, chocolate brown flowers and broad oval leaves. USDA Plant Hardiness Zones 4 to 7.

V. viride (VIR-e-dee), Indian poke, green false hellebore. Size: 3 to 5 feet tall, 2 to 3 feet wide. A stout plant with dense trusses of sea green flowers in early summer. The lush, ribbed oval foliage covers the lower portion of the stem. In warm zones or where soil dries out, plants will go dormant. *V. album* has white flowers on compact stems. Zones 3 to 7.

How to Grow

Plant false hellebores in humus-rich, moist to wet soil in light to full shade. Plants take many years to reach blooming size. In full shade, plants are shy to bloom, and even mature plants may not bloom every year. Mature clumps have stout, deep-rooted crowns that are almost impossible to lift.

Green false hellebore (*Veratrum viride*) has a long medicinal history, but its horticultural merits are often overlooked. Celadon green flowers are packed on drooping branches of the tall, terminal flower clusters in early summer.

669

Landscape Uses

False hellebores are best suited to bog gardens, wet woods, and along streams. Combine them with skunk cabbage (*Symplocarpus foetidus*), marsh marigold (*Caltha palustris*), irises, primroses (*Primula*), rodgersias, cardinal flower (*Lobelia cardinalis*), tassel rue (*Trautvetteria carolinense*), sedges (*Carex*), and ferns. In more formal settings, the dramatic foliage is a welcome addition among fine-textured plants. On drier sites, even in rich soil, plants may go dormant after flowering, so combine them with sedges, ferns, or other foliage that will fill the void.

VERBASCUM

ver-BAS-cum • Scrophulariaceae, Figwort Family

Most people think of mulleins as roadside weeds, but many of these bold, beautiful perennials are fit for the finest borders. Mulleins have tight rosettes of oval- to wedge-shaped foliage that is quilted and soft to hairy. From the center of the rosettes rise stout leafy stalks with terminal spikes of small, five-petaled yellow or white flowers. Plants grow from stout fibrous-rooted crowns.

VERBASCUM

Common Name:
  Mullein

Bloom Time:
  Summer bloom

Planting Requirements:
  Full sun

Verbascum chaixii (SHAY-zee-ee), nettle-leaved mullein. Size: 2 to 3 feet tall, 1 to 2 feet wide. This mullein has wedge-shaped, gray-green leaves and branched, spiky clusters of yellow flowers with fuzzy purple stamens (male reproductive structures). Plants bloom for over a month in early summer. Var. *album* has white flowers with purple centers. USDA Plant Hardiness Zones 4 to 8.

V. olympicum (o-LIM-pi-cum), olympic mullein. Size: 3 to 5 feet tall, 2 to 3 feet wide. Olympic mullein is a bold plant with huge (3-foot) rosettes of oval to rounded silver-gray leaves and tall, branched spikes of yellow flowers. *V. bombyciferum* is a gray-leaved species with densely felted spikes of yellow flowers to 5 feet tall. Zones 6 to 8.

V. phoeniceum (foy-KNEE-see-um), purple mullein. Size: 20 to 24 inches tall, 12 to 24 inches wide. Open spikes of white, pink, or mauve flowers are held well above gray-green basal leaves. Many hybrid mulleins are excellent garden plants. 'Helen Johnson' has felted leaves and 20-inch spikes of copper and purple flowers. 'Jackie' has 18-inch spikes of cantaloupe orange flowers. 'Letita' has yellow spikes only 8 inches tall. 'Raspberry Ripple' has creamy pink flowers in dense 2-foot spikes.

'Summer Sorbet' has open iridescent raspberry spikes. Zones 6 to 8.

How to Grow

Plant mulleins in average, well-drained sandy or loamy soil in full sun. Good drainage is essential to success, especially for *V. chaixii*, which is a short-lived perennial. Plants seldom require dividing but are easily grown from 3-inch root cuttings taken in early spring. Self-sown seedlings will also appear.

Landscape Uses

Choose mulleins for wild gardens and meadows or plant them in the middle or rear of perennial gardens. They are valued for their lush foliage and tall spiky forms. Combine them with meadow rues (*Thalictrum*), feverfew (*Tanacetum parthenium*), wormwoods (*Artemisia*), yarrows (*Achillea*), catmints (*Nepeta*), and ornamental grasses.

All the mulleins, including nettle-leaved mullein (*Verbascum chaixii*), provide lush foliage and elongated flower spikes for the dry garden.

VERBENA

ver-BEEN-a • Verbenaceae, Vervain Family

Vervains are colorful ever-blooming perennials sporting brilliant tubular flowers with flat five-petaled faces. They are carried in flat or spikelike terminal clusters on wiry stems. The opposite leaves are oblong, usually lobed or deeply incised and dissected. Plants grow from fibrous-rooted crowns.

VERBENA

Common Names:
  Verbena, vervain

Bloom Time:
  Summer bloom

Planting Requirements:
  Full sun to light shade

Verbena bonariensis (bo-nah-ree-EN-sis), Brazilian vervain. Size: 3 to 4 feet tall, 2 to 3 feet wide. This tall verbena has open, branching stalks with sparse foliage and terminal, rounded clusters of violet flowers. The leaves are oblong and toothed. Plants reseed prolifically and may be a nuisance in warmer zones. USDA Plant Hardiness Zones 7 to 9.

V. canadensis (kan-a-DEN-sis), rose verbena. Size: 8 to 18 inches tall, 12 to 24 inches wide. Rose verbena has trailing wiry stems with sharply toothed and lobed oval leaves. The flat terminal flower clusters elongate into short spikes as the purple, rose, or white flowers open. 'Greystone

Rose verbena (*Verbena* 'Homestead Purple') is a tough drought- and salt-tolerant species that blooms for several months in spring and summer even if it is not faithfully deadheaded or pruned back.

Daphne' is pinkish lavender. Many hybrids have been introduced that vary in hardiness. 'Blue Princess' is blue-violet. 'Fiesta' is magenta. 'Homestead Purple' has rose-purple flowers. 'Hot Lips' is dayglow pink. 'Mabels Maroon' has deep wine red flowers. 'Pinwheel Princess' is lavender and white. 'Snowflurry' is white. 'Summer Blaze' is red. 'Texas Appleblossom' is rose-pink. Zones 6 to 10.

V. hastata (has-TAY-ta), blue vervain. Size: 3 to 5 feet tall, 1 to 2 feet wide. This graceful, erect verbena has long, narrow leaves and branched, candelabra-like spikes of blue flowers. Zones 3 to 8.

V. peruviana (per-oo-ve-AH-na), Peruvian verbena. Size: 6 to 12 inches tall, 12 to 24 inches wide. This verbena is similar to *V. canadensis* but is prostrate with scarlet flowers. Zones 7 to 10.

V. rigida (RIJ-i-da), rigid verbena. Size: 1 to 2 feet tall and wide. This upright verbena has oblong, toothed leaves and rounded terminal clusters of purple flowers. 'Flame' has scarlet flowers on 6-inch stems. 'Glowing Violet' has deep violet-purple flowers. 'Polaris' has pale lavender flowers. Zones 7 to 10.

V. stricta (STRIK-ta), hoary vervain. Size: 1 to 1½ feet tall and wide. This upright verbena has hairy, wedge-shaped leaves that cover branched stems. The terminal spikes bear blue-violet flowers. Zones 3 to 8.

V. tenuisecta (ten-you-i-SEK-ta), moss verbena. Size: 4 to 8 inches tall, 24 to 36 inches wide. This floriferous trailing verbena has thin, wiry stems and deeply incised and dissected foliage. Terminal clusters of deep lavender flowers elongate to short spikes. 'Edith' has pale pink flowers. 'Mystic' is lavender-blue. Zones 7 to 10.

How to Grow

Verbenas are tough, heat- and drought-tolerant perennials that bloom tirelessly during summer. Plant them in well-drained sandy or loamy soil in full sun to light shade. The creeping species spread quickly to form showy groundcovers. The clumping species increase slowly. *V. hastata* is the only verbena to grow in moist or even wet soil, but it is very adaptable to garden conditions. Plants are easily grown from stem cuttings taken anytime during the growing season. Seeds need 3 to 4 weeks of cold-moist stratification to germinate. Seedlings develop quickly.

Plant the tall Brazilian vervain (*Verbena bonariensis*) near the front of the border where you can view other plants through its airy stems. Plants are invasive in some areas; check before you plant.

Landscape Uses

Trailing verbenas are excellent weavers: Use plants to tie mixed plantings together. Let them creep among foliage plants such as yuccas, wormwoods (*Artemisia*), mulleins (*Verbascum*), and ornamental grasses. They also serve to bridge gaps between flowering perennials such as coneflowers (*Echinacea*), black-eyed Susans (*Rudbeckia*), butterfly weed (*Asclepias tuberosa*), yarrows (*Achillea*), and others. Plant upright species in mid ground for their spiky form. Airy species such as *V. bonariensis* and *V. hastata* are often positioned at the front of the border where you can view other colors through their open stems.

VERNONIA

ver-NON-ee-a • Asteraceae, Aster Family

The broad violet flower clusters of ironweeds demand attention in the summer and fall garden. Most species have many tall, stiff stems covered in deep green, lance-shaped leaves. The domed flower clusters are perfect landing pads for butterflies. The name *ironweed* presumably arises from the rust-red hairs that are prominent in the spent flower heads and on the fruits. Plants grow from woody, fibrous-rooted crowns.

VERNONIA

Common Name:
Ironweed

Bloom Time:
Late summer and fall bloom

Planting Requirements:
Full sun

Vernonia angustifolia (an-gus-te-FOL-e-ah), narrow-leaf ironweed. Size: 2 to 4 feet tall and wide. Narrow-leaf ironweed is unlike any other species. The 1-inch deep violet heads are carried in broad, open clusters on wide, shrublike clumps. The 6- to 8-inch leaves are narrowly lance-shaped and droop slightly on the stem. Zones 4 to 9.

V. fasciculata (fas-sik-yoo-LAY-ta), fascicles ironweed. Size: 3 to 4 feet tall, 2 to 3 feet wide. Compact stems have evenly spaced deep green toothed leaves and tight, upright clusters of red-violet flowers in mid- to late summer. Zones 3 to 8.

V. gigantea (ji-gan-TEA-ah) (*altissima*), tall ironweed. Size: 4 to 10 feet tall, 2 to 3 feet wide. This is the giant of the group, with dense, broad, flattened clusters of soft violet flowers in late summer and fall. Plant in rich, moist soil in full sun. USDA Plant Hardiness Zones 4 to 8.

V. noveboracensis (no-ve-bor-a-SEN-sis), New York ironweed. Size: 4 to 6 feet tall, 2 to 3 feet wide. 1-inch red-violet heads

The broad violet flower clusters of tall ironweed (*Vernonia gigantea*) demand attention in the garden.

are carried in broad, showy clusters on leafy stems. The 6- to 8-inch leaves are lance-shaped and mostly toothless. Zones 4 to 9.

How to Grow

Plant in rich, evenly moist soil in full sun or light shade. Plants are easy to grow and thrive under most garden situations. The clumps get very large in time but seldom need division. If plants are too crowded, thin stems by one-quarter in late spring. Take stem cuttings in early summer. Self-sown seedlings will appear. Leaf miners may make pale tunnels in leaves.

Landscape Uses

Ironweeds are commanding border plants. Plant them with yarrows (*Achillea*), cannas, lilies, sages (*Salvia*), and irises. They are equally well suited to meadow and prairie gardens or along the banks of ponds. Combine them with hibiscus, phlox, great blue lobelia (*Lobelia siphilitica*), Joe-Pye weeds (*Eupatorium*), turtleheads (*Chelone*), asters, goldenrods (*Solidago*), and grasses. Narrow-

Narrow-leaf ironweed (*Vernonia angustifolia*) is more like a fine-textured shrub than a perennial. The late-summer violet flowers are scattered over the entire clump.

leaf ironweed is like a rounded shrub in the border. Plant it with verbenas, yuccas, phlox, asters, goldenrods, and grasses.

VERONICA

ve-RON-e-ka • Scrophulariaceae, Figwort Family

Colorful speedwells grace the summer garden with their candelabra spikes. Trailing species bloom earlier, with brilliantly colored flowers in short spikes on creeping mats. Flowers are tubular, with flat five-petaled faces. Color varies from white to pink, rose, purple, and blue. Alternate or whorled leaves may be narrow and lance-shaped, oblong, oval, or wedge-shaped. Plants grow from fibrous-rooted crowns.

VERONICA

Common Name:
 Speedwell

Bloom Time:
 Spring and summer bloom

Planting Requirements:
 Sun to light shade

The tall stalks of *Veronica grandis* 'Blue Charm' need staking to keep them from flopping. In dry soils, plants don't grow as tall and are less susceptible to falling over in wind and rain.

Veronica alpina (al-PEEN-a), alpine speedwell. Size: 4 to 8 inches tall, 12 to 24 inches wide. This evergreen creeper has shiny oval leaves and spikes of dark blue flowers. 'Alba' has white flowers. 'Goodness Grows' is a floriferous, reblooming hybrid with deep blue flowers. USDA Plant Hardiness Zones 3 to 8.

V. austriaca (aus-tree-AK-a) (*teucrium*), Hungarian speedwell. Size: 6 to 20 inches tall, 12 to 24 inches wide. A spreading species with erect, bright blue spikes of ¼-inch flowers and oblong, toothed leaves. 'Crater Lake Blue' has ultramarine flowers. 'Royal Blue' has deep blue flowers on 12- to 15-inch stems. 'Trehane' is spreading with deep blue flowers. Zones 3 to 8.

V. gentianoides (jen-shee-un-NOY-deez), gentian speedwell. Size: 6 to 20 inches tall, 12 to 24 inches wide. An upright species with leafy stems and pyramidal spikes of ½-inch, pale sky blue flowers. 'Variegata' has leaves marked with white. Zones 4 to 8.

V. grandis (GRAN-dis). Size: 1½ to 2 feet tall, 2 to 3 feet wide. This species is often confused with *V. spicata* but has broader, shiny green leaves. Var. *holophylla* has wide, somewhat heart-shaped leaves. 'Blue Charm' ('Lavender Charm') has 6-inch spikes of rich lavender-blue flowers on bushy plants. 'Royal Candles' has navy blue flowers on compact 15- to 18-inch stems. 'Sunny Border Blue' is a sturdy, nonflopping selection with deep navy blue flowers. Zones 4 to 8.

V. incana (in-KAH-na), woolly speedwell. Size: 1 to 2 feet tall and wide. Woolly speedwell has soft, hairy, silver-gray oblong leaves and 3- to 6-inch terminal spikes of ¼-inch white, pink, or blue flowers held above mats of foliage. 'Rosea' has pink-tinged flowers. 'Wendy' has lavender-blue flowers. Some selections listed under *V. spicata* may be hybrids with this species. Zones 3 to 8.

V. longifolia (lon-gih-FOE-lee-a), long-leaf speedwell. Size: 2 to 4 feet tall, 1 to 2 feet wide. This strongly upright speedwell has opposite or whorled, lance-shaped leaves and showy, dense spikes of pale blue flowers. 'Icicle' is a good white, possibly of hybrid origin. 'Romilley Purple' has deep violet flowers on 2-foot stems. Zones 3 to 8.

V. peduncularis (pee-dunk-u-LAR-is), creeping veronica. Size: 4 to 6 inches tall, 24 to 36 inches wide. This fetching speedwell is a mat-forming profuse bloomer swamped with gentian blue flowers from earliest spring through midsummer. The rounded, glossy green leaves turn purple to bronze in winter. 'Georgia Blue' is the cultivar of choice, with gentian blue flowers. 'Waterperry' is a hybrid with ice blue flowers and round, scalloped foliage. Zones 5 to 9.

V. prostrata (pross-TRAH-tuh), harebell speedwell. Size: Size: 3 to 8 inches tall, 12 to 24 inches wide. A creeping species with oval to oblong leaves and axillary clusters of ⅓-inch blue flowers. 'Aztec Gold' and 'Buttercup' are lovely yellow-leafed selections. 'Heavenly Blue' has sapphire blue flowers. 'Loddon Blue' is deep blue. Zones 3 to 8. *V. repens* is another good groundcover, though less hardy. 'Sunshine' is a good yellow-leaf selection. Zones 7 to 9.

V. spicata (spi-KAH-ta), spike speedwell. Size: 1 to 3 feet tall, 2 to 3 feet wide. This popular speedwell has pointed flower clusters atop leafy stems. Opposite leaves are oval to oblong and covered in soft hairs. The small, two-lipped pink, blue, or white flowers are tightly packed into erect spikes. 'Barcarolle' has rose-pink flowers on 12- to 15-inch stems and gray-green leaves. 'Blue Fox' has lavender-blue flowers on 15- to 20-inch stems. 'Blue Peter' has dark blue flowers on 2-foot stems. 'Heidekind' has rose spikes on compact 6- to 8-inch stems all summer. 'Minuet' is a dwarf selection with rose-pink flowers on 1- to 1½-foot stems. 'Snow White' has branching spikes of white flowers on 1½-foot stems. Zones 3 to 8.

Veronicastrum virginicum, Culver's root, is distinguished from *Veronica* by lance-shaped leaves borne in tiered whorls. It has erect creamy white candelabra spikes on 3- to 6-foot stems. Var. *rosea* ('Rosea')

In meadows and prairies, the tall candelabras of Culver's root (*Veronicastrum virginicum*) add a touch of drama. In beds and borders, they add lift to the profile during high summer. Plants may need staking unless combined with tall neighbors to hold them up.

has pale rose-pink flowers. 'Apollo' and 'Fascination' are lilac. 'Diana' and 'Spring Dew' are excellent whites. Soft blue selections are likely to be from the Asian species, *Veronicastrum sibericum,* which has gracefully arched blue spikes. *V. sibericum* 'Pointed Fingers' is an excellent selection with deep lavender-blue flowers. Zones 4 to 8.

How to Grow

Plant speedwells in average to rich, moist but well-drained soil in full sun or light shade. Plants grow slowly to form neat, attractive clumps. To encourage continued bloom or if plants get rangy, cut back to encourage fresh growth. Divide over-grown plants in spring or fall. Take stem cuttings in late spring or early summer. Remove flower buds. *Veronicastrum* tolerates wet soil.

Landscape Uses

Plant speedwells with summer perennials that need good drainage, such as yarrows (*Achillea*), catmints (*Nepeta*), sundrops (*Oenothera*), and ornamental grasses. Their spiky forms are perfect for adding excitement to plantings. Use creeping species such as 'Georgia Blue' speedwell at the front of a border or along a walkway or wall for early color with daffodils, tulips, and other bulbs. Their foliage is attractive all summer around yuccas, irises, and other spiky plants.

VIOLA

vie-OH-la • Violaceae, Violet Family

Violets are well-loved spring beauties with distinctive, colorful blooms. Irregular flowers have two upper and three lower petals joined into a short spur at the back of the flower. The insides of the lower petals may have fuzzy beards of bright yellow markings. There are two groups of violets, which differ in their growth habits. The leaves and flowers of stemless violets arise in a clump from a creeping rhizome. Stemmed violets produce sparse basal leaves and upright stalks that bear both leaves and flowers; they grow from creeping rhizomes.

VIOLA

Common Names:
Violet, viola

Bloom Time:
Spring bloom

Planting Requirements:
Sun or shade

Viola canadensis (kan-a-DEN-sis), Canada violet. Size: 6 to 12 inches tall, 12 inches wide. This tall violet has heart-shaped leaves and ¾-inch creamy white flowers with yellow eyes and purple reverses. USDA Plant Hardiness Zones 3 to 8.

V. cornuta (core-NEW-ta), horned violet. Size: 4 to 12 inches tall, 6 to 12 inches wide. Horned violets have evergreen rosettes and sprawling, leafy stems. The 1- to 1½-inch flowers resemble pansies. Many excellent selections are available. 'Arkwright Ruby' has cherry red flowers. 'Blue Perfection' has sky blue flowers. 'Etain' is chiffon yellow with a blue picotee edge. 'Major Primrose' is rosy violet fading to white at the center of the flower. 'Painted Perfection' is rosy pink with a deep violet eye. 'Rebecca' has white flowers with purple picotee edges. 'White Perfection' has white flowers. Zones 6 to 9.

V. labradorica (lab-ruh-DOOR-ih-ka), Labrador violet. Size: 1 to 4 inches tall, 4 to 6 inches wide. This diminutive stemmed violet has deep purple flowers over deep green leaves. Var. *purpurea* has violet spring leaves that fade to deep bronzy green. Zones 3 to 8.

V. odorata (o-door-AH-ta), sweet violet. Size: 2 to 8 inches tall and wide. This stemless violet has rounded kidney-shaped leaves. The ¾-inch deep purple or blue flowers are delicately scented. 'Delores' has deep purple flowers. 'White Queen' and 'White Czar' are white-flowered. Zones 6 to 9.

The cheery flowers of horned violet (*Viola cornuta*) come in a variety of colors, including blue, purple, orange, yellow, and white. Plants bloom for several weeks in spring.

V. pedata (pe-DAY-tah), bird-foot violet, pansy violet. Size: 4 to 6 inches tall and wide. This diminutive, stemless violet has deeply lobed leaves that resemble the foot of some fanciful bird. The flat-faced, powder blue or bicolor blue-and-purple flowers open in early spring. Zones 3 to 9.

V. pubescens (pew-BES-senz), downy yellow violet. Size: 6 to 12 inches tall and wide. A stemmed species with soft, hairy, heart-shaped leaves and lemon yellow flowers. Plants form dense clumps but do not spread by runners. Zones 3 to 8.

V. sororia (sore-OR-ee-a), woolly blue violet. Size: 3 to 6 inches tall, 6 to 8 inches wide. This common native violet has hairy foliage and deep blue flowers. 'Freckles' has pale blue flowers flecked with purple. 'Priceana', the confederate violet, has white flowers with purple-blue centers. *V. cucullata* and *V. papilionaceae* are two common blue species that are a bit weedy for gardens. Zones 3 to 9.

V. striata (stry-AY-ta), cream violet. Size: 1 to 2 feet tall and wide. This stemmed species forms very dense clumps of small leaves and thin stems with creamy white flowers marked on the lower lip with purple stripes. The plants are both floriferous and prolific, and self-sown seedlings are generous. Zones 3 to 8.

How to Grow

Plant violets in moist, humus-rich soil in sun or shade. Violets grow under a wide range of soil and moisture conditions. They are prolific spreaders and make themselves at home in any garden. Control is more likely an issue than propagation, but divide plants after flowering or in fall to increase stock.

Landscape Uses

Violets form attractive groundcovers under shrubs and flowering trees. In informal gardens, plant them with bulbs, wildflowers, hostas, and early-blooming perennials. Combine woodland species like downy yellow, cream, and Canada violets with wildflowers such as trilliums, baneberries (*Actaea*), Virginia bluebells (*Mertensia virginica*), merrybells (*Uvularia*), bloodroot (*Sanguinaria canadensis*), and ferns. Plant them in a wet spot with lobelias, turtleheads (*Chelone*), marsh marigold (*Caltha palustris*), and ferns. Bird-foot violet is best used in rock gardens or on dry banks where it will not get swamped by more exuberant plants. Combine it with pinks (*Silene*), prairie smoke (*Geum triflorum*), and blue-eyed grasses (*Sisyrinchium*).

YUCCA

YUCK-a • Agavaceae (Liliaceae), Agave Family

Yuccas bring the desert to mind. They have tall, oval flower clusters and rosettes of sword-shaped, blue-green leaves. Nodding, creamy white flowers with three petals and three petal-like sepals that form a bell dangle elegantly from erect, multibranched bloom stalks that rise 5 to 15 feet above foliage. They grow from a woody crown with fleshy roots.

YUCCA

Common Names:
Yucca, Adam's needle

Bloom Time:
Late spring and early summer bloom

Planting Requirements:
Full sun to light shade

Yucca flowers nod like wax chalices from huge, branched inflorescences that shoot up from the center of the variegated rosettes of *Yucca filamentosa* 'Golden Sword' in summer.

Yucca filamentosa (fil-a-men-TOW-sa), Adam's needle, Spanish bayonet. Size: 5 to 8 feet tall, 3 to 4 feet wide. A variable species with stiff or drooping leaves from a stout rhizome that occasionally develops a short trunk. Botanists have recently lumped *Y. flaccida* and *Y. smalliana* into this species. 'Bright Edge' is a delicate selection with blue-gray leaves to 2 feet tall edged in creamy yellow. 'Color Guard' has sturdy leaves with yellow stripes down the centers that turn pink in winter. 'Golden Sword' has yellow-variegated leaves. 'Variegata' has stiff leaves with wide white margins. Zones 4 to 10.

Y. glauca (GLAW-ka), soapweed. Size: 2 to 4 feet tall, 2 to 3 feet wide. Stiff, narrow gray-green leaves to 2 feet long form dense rosettes below congested clusters of inflated, pink-tinged flowers. Zones 3 to 9.

Y. gloriosa (glor-e-OH-sa), Spanish dagger. Size: 3 to 4 feet tall and wide. A large species with stout crowns of stiff

Plant drought- and heat-tolerant *Yucca filamentosa* 'Variegata' in well-drained sandy or loamy soil as specimen plants or combined with a groundcover of self-seeding petunias.

leaves on woody trunks. Mature plants can reach 8 feet or more. 'Variegata' has yellow-edged leaves. Zones 7 to 10.

Y. rostrata (ros-STRAY-ta), beaked blue yucca. Size: 4 to 10 feet tall, 3 to 4 feet wide. This elegant species forms a nearly spherical rosette of narrow blue needles

atop a woody trunk. Old plants are multi-stemmed. Zones 5 to 10.

How to Grow

Plant yuccas in average to rich, well-drained soil in full sun or light shade. Established plants are drought- and shade-tolerant and thrive for years with little care. After flowering, the main crown dies, but basal offshoots keep clumps growing. Plants are salt-tolerant. Remove young side shoots from clumps in spring or fall.

Landscape Uses

Yuccas bring a touch of the Southwest to our gardens. Choose them as accent plants in a border, or use them massed on a bank in a seaside garden. Contrast is the key to showing off yuccas. Combine the stiff, upright foliage with mounding plants such as gauras, catmints (*Nepeta*), Mongolian aster (*Kalimeris pinnatifida*), evening primroses (*Oenothera*), sages (*Salvia*), and creeping beauties such as veronicas (*Veronica repens* and *austriacus*), winecups (*Callirhoe*), and sedums.

ZEPHYRANTHES

ze-fi-RANTH-eez • Amaryllidaceae, Amaryllis Family

Rain lilies get their name from their uncanny habit of springing into bloom soon after seasonal rains return, almost as if appearing by magic. The 2- to 3-inch flowers are carried above narrow strap-shaped to rushlike leaves that grow from true bulbs. Foliage will persist all summer if sufficient moisture is available. Plants go dormant during drought.

ZEPHYRANTHES

Common Name:
  Rain lily

Bloom Time:
  Spring, summer, or fall bloom

Planting Requirements:
  Sun to light shade

Zephyranthes atamasco (at-a-MAS-ko), rain lily, atamasco, cullowhee lily. Size: 6 to 12 inches tall and wide. A spring-blooming species with 3-inch white chalices above flat deep green foliage. USDA Plant Hardiness Zones 6 to 10. *Hymenocallis occidentalis* (a related genus), spider lily, is a showy plant with straplike leaves and clusters of fragrant spidery white flowers with six slender segments and a central, circular membrane that lies over the segments. Zones 7 to 10.

Z. candida (KAN-de-da), white rain lily. Size: 6 to 10 inches tall, 12 inches wide. White chalices resembling crocuses are carried in profusion above thin, rushlike foliage in late summer and autumn. Flowers open to showy 2-inch stars in sun. Zones 7 to 10.

Z. grandiflora (grand-i-FLO-ra), pink rain lily. Size: 8 to 10 inches tall, 12 inches wide. Starry, 3-inch deep pink flowers open over flat, grassy leaves in summer and fall. Zones 7 to 10.

Z. reginae (REG-in-ay), yellow rain lily. Size: 4 to 6 inches tall, 12 inches wide. Starry yellow flowers with a rusty reverse

Whether in a water garden or a moist perennial bed, the snowy chalices of white rain lily (*Zephyranthes candida*) are sure to raise your spirits. Plants flower in late summer and begin to bloom in the garden after a good rain.

open summer through fall above narrow leaves. *Z. citrina* and *Z. flava* are two additional yellow-flowered species. Zones 7 to 10.

Hybrids

'Big Dude' has 4-inch white flowers with pink-tipped tepals. 'Labuffarosea' is a natural hybrid with pink to white flowers. 'Sunset Strain' has coral pink flowers with a darker reverse. Zones 7 to 10.

How to Grow

Plant in rich, moist to seasonally wet, acid soil in full sun or light shade. Plants will grow in shallow water if planted in light soil. Divide bulbs after flowering if they become so congested that flowering wanes. Self-sown seedlings will appear, but seedlings develop slowly.

Landscape Uses

Rain lilies look best planted in great sweeps. Where they are happy, they will increase rapidly, so start with a dozen or so bulbs. Combine the snowy chalices with spike rushes (*Juncus*), sedges (*Carex*), flag iris (*Iris pseudacorus*), and wild hyacinth (*Camassia scilloides*). Choose cardinal flower (*Lobelia cardinalis*) and ferns for late-season interest. They add a touch of class to water gardens when grown in pots.

Suggested Reading

Landscaping

Eddison, Sydney. *The Gardener's Palette*. Chicago: Contemporary Books, 2002.

Favretti, Rudy, and Joy P. *For Every House a Garden: A Guide for Reproducing Period Gardens*. 2d ed. Hanover: University Press of New England, 1990.

Schenk, George. *The Complete Shade Gardener*. Portland: Timber Press, 2002.

Van Sweden, James, with Thomas Christopher. *Architecture in the Garden*. New York: Random House, 2002.

General Gardening

DiSabato-Aust, Tracy. *The Well-Tended Perennial Garden*. Portland: Timber Press, 1998.

Ellis, Barbara W., and Fern Marshall Bradley, eds. *The Organic Gardener's Handbook of Natural Insect and Disease Control*. Emmaus: Rodale, 1996.

Ellis, Barbara W., and Fern Marshall Bradley, eds. *Rodale's All-New Encyclopedia of Organic Gardening: The Indispensable Resource for Every Gardener*. Emmaus: Rodale, 1993.

Hogan, Sean, et al. *Flora*. Portland: Timber Press, 2003.

Lovejoy, Ann. *Organic Gardening Design School*. Emmaus: Rodale, 2001.

Tenenbaum, Frances, ed. *Taylor's Encyclopedia of Garden Plants: The Most Authoritative Guide to the Best Flowers, Trees, and Shrubs for North American Gardens*. Boston: Houghton Mifflin, 2003.

Perennials and Perennial Gardening

Armitage, Allan. *Herbaceous Perennial Plants*. 2nd ed. Champaign: Stipes Publishing, 1997.

Burrell, C. Colston. *Perennial Combinations*. Emmaus: Rodale, 1999.

Darke, Rick. *The Color Encyclopedia of Ornamental Grasses*. Portland: Timber Press, 1999.

Gerritsen, Henk, and Piet Oudolf. *Dream Plants for the Natural Garden*. Portland: Timber Press, 2000.

Harper, Pamela J. *Designing with Perennials*. Asheville: Lark Books, 2001.

Heger, Mike, et al. *Growing Perennials in Cold Climates*. Chicago: Contemporary Books, 1998.

Lloyd, Christopher. *Garden Flowers*. London: Cassell & Company, 2000.

Mickel, John. *Ferns for American Gardens*. Portland: Timber Press, 2003.

Phillips, Roger, and Martin Rix. *Perennials* 2 vols. New York: Random House, 1991.

Thomas, Graham Stuart. *Perennial Garden Plants*. Portland: Timber Press, 1990.

Herbaceous Plants for Mixed Borders

Adams, Denise. *Restoring American Gardens*. Portland: Timber Press, 2002.

Chatto, Beth. *The Green Tapestry*. New York: Collier Books, 1988.

DiSabato-Aust, Tracy. *The Well-Designed Mixed Garden*. Portland: Timber Press, 2003.

Druse, Ken. *The Natural Garden*. New York: Clarkson N. Potter, 1989.

Druse, Ken. *The Natural Shade Garden*. New York: Clarkson N. Potter, 1992.

Glattstein, Judy. *Consider the Leaf*. Portland: Timber Press, 2003.

Harper, Pamela J. *Time Tested Plants*. Portland: Timber Press, 2000.

Lacy, Allen. *The Garden in Autumn*. New York: Atlantic Monthly Press, 1990.

Lovejoy, Ann. *The American Mixed Border*. New York: Macmillan Publishing Co., 1993.

Springer, Lauren. *The Undaunted Garden*. Golden: Fulcrum Publishing, 1994.

Native Plants

Burrell, C. Colston. *A Gardener's Encyclopedia of Wildflowers*. Emmaus: Rodale, 1997.

Colina, William. *The New England Wild Flower Society Guide to Growing and Propagating Wildflowers of the United States and Canada*. Boston: Houghton Mifflin Company, 2000.

Phillips, Harry R. *Growing and Propagating Wild Flowers*. Chapel Hill: The University of North Carolina Press, 1985.

Wasowski, Sally. *Gardening with Native Plants of the South*. Dallas: Taylor Publishing Company, 1994.

Trees, Shrubs, and Vines for Mixed Borders

Dirr, Michael A. *Manual of Woody Landscape Plants: Their Identification, Ornamental Characteristics, Culture, Propagation, and Uses.* 5th ed. Champaign: Stipes Publishing Co., 1998.

Toomey, Mary. *An Illustrated Encyclopedia of Clematis.* Portland: Timber Press, 2001.

White, John. *The Illustrated Encyclopedia of Trees.* Portland: Timber Press, 2002.

Regional Gardening

Darke, Rick. *The American Woodland Garden.* Portland: Timber Press, 2002.

DeFreitas, Stan. *Complete Guide to Florida Gardening.* Rev. ed. Dallas: Taylor Publishing Co., 2002.

Hill, Lewis. *Cold-Climate Gardening.* Pownal: Storey Communications, 1987.

McKeown, Denny. *Complete Guide to Midwest Gardening.* Dallas: Taylor Publishing Co., 1985.

Rushing, Felder. *Gardening Southern Style.* Jackson: University Press of Mississippi, 1987.

Vick, Roger. *Gardening on the Prairies: A Guide to Canadian Home Gardening.* Canada: Douglas & McIntyre, 1992

Also: New Sunset Regional Guides—see your local library for your region's book.

Resources

Some nurseries offer plants that have been collected from the wild, which may contribute to the near or total extinction of a species. Make sure bulbs, wildflowers, and native plants are nursery-propagated before you buy them.

PERENNIALS AND ORNAMENTAL GRASSES

Ambergate Gardens
8730 County Road 43
Chaska, MN 55318-9358
Phone: 952-443-2248 or
     877-211-9769
www.ambergategardens.com

Andre Viette Farm & Nursery
PO Box 1109
Fishersville, VA 22939
Phone: 800-575-5538
Fax: 540-943-0782
www.inthegardenradio.com

Arrowhead Alpines
PO Box 857
1310 N. Gregory Road
Fowlerville, MI 48836
Phone: 517-223-3581
Fax: 517-223-8750
www.arrowhead-alpines.com

Bluestone Perennials
7211 Middle Ridge Road
Madison, OH 44057-3096
Phone: 800-852-5243
Fax: 440-428-7198
www.bluestoneperennials.com

Canyon Creek Nursery
3527 Dry Creek Road
Oroville, CA 95965
Phone: 530-533-2166
www.canyoncreeknursery.com

Carroll Gardens
444 East Main Street
Westminster, MD 21157-5540
Phone: 410-848-5422 or
     800-638-6334
Baltimore location: 410-876-7336
Fax: 410-857-4112
www.carrollgardens.com

Collector's Nursery
16804 NE 102nd Avenue
Battle Ground, WA 98604
Phone: 360-574-3832
Fax: 360-571-8540
www.collectorsnursery.com

Digging Dog Nursery
PO Box 471
Albion, CA 95410
Phone: 707-937-1130
Fax: 707-937-2480
www.diggingdog.com

Fairweather Gardens
PO Box 330
Greenwich, NJ 08323
Phone: 856-451-6261
Fax: 856-451-0303
www.fairweathergardens.com

Heronswood Nursery
7530 NE 288th Street
Kingston, WA 98346
360-297-4172
www.heronswood.com

Joy Creek Nursery
20300 NW Watson Road
Scappoose, OR 97056
Phone: 503-543-7474
Fax: 503-543-6933
www.joycreek.com

Klehm's Song Sparrow Perennial
     Farm
13101 East Rye Road
Avalon, WI 53505
Phone: 800-553-3715
Fax: 608-883-2257
www.klehm.com

Kurt Bluemel, Inc.
2740 Greene Lane
Baldwin, MD 21013
Phone: 410-557-7229
Fax: 410-557-9785
www.kurtbluemel.com

Milaeger's Gardens
4838 Douglas Avenue
Racine, WI 53402-2498
Phone: 800-669-9956
Fax: 262-639-1855

Park Seed Co.
1 Parkton Avenue
Greenwood, SC 29647
800-213-0076
www.parkseed.com

Plant Delights Nursery
9241 Sauls Road
Raleigh, NC 27603
Phone: 919-772-4794
Fax: 919-662-030
www.plantdelights.com

Primrose Path
Charles and Martha Oliver
921 Scottdale-Dawson Road
Scottsdale, PA 15683
Phone: 724-887-6756
Fax: 724-887-3077
www.theprimrosepath.com

Roslyn Nursery
211 Burrs Lane
Dix Hills, NY 11746
Phone: 631-643-9347
Fax: 631-427-0894
www.roslynnursery.com

Russell Graham Purveyor
    of Plants
4030 Eagle Crest Road, NW
Salem, OR 97304-9787
503-362-1135

Seneca Hill Perennials
3712 County Route 57
Oswego, NY 13126
Phone: 315-342-5915
Fax: 315-342-5573
www.senecahill.com

Singing Springs Nursery
8802 Wilkerson Road
Cedar Grove, NC 27231
Fax: 919-732-6636
www.singingspringnursery.com

Siskiyou Rare Plant Nursery
2825 Cummings Road
Medford, OR 97501
Phone: 541-772-6846
Fax: 541-772-4917
www.srpn.net

Thompson & Morgan, Inc.
PO Box 1308
Jackson, NJ 08527-0308
Phone: 800-274-7333
Fax: 888-466-4769
www.thompson-morgan.com

W. Atlee Burpee & Co.
300 Park Avenue
Warminister, PA 18974
Phone: 215-674-4900
Fax: 215-674-0838
www.burpee.com

Wayside Gardens
1 Garden Lane
Hodges, SC 29695
Phone: 800-213-0379
www.waysidegardens.com

White Flower Farm
PO Box 50
Route 63
Litchfield, CT 06759
800-503-9624
www.whiteflowerfarm.com

BULBS

Brent and Becky's Bulbs
7900 Daffodil Lane
Gloucester, VA 23061
Phone: 804-693-3966
Fax: 804-693-9436
www.brentandbeckysbulbs.com

Dutch Gardens
144 Intervale Road
Burlington, VT 05401
Phone: 800-944-2250
Toll-free fax for orders: 800-551-6712
www.dutchgardens.com

John Scheepers, Inc.
23 Tulip Drive
PO Box 638
Bantam, CT 06750
Phone: 860-567-0838
Fax: 860-567-5323
www.johnscheepers.com

K. Van Bourgondien & Sons
PO Box 1000
Babylon, NY 11702-9004
Orders: 800-552-9996
Customer service: 800-552-9916
Fax: 800-327-4268
www.kvbwholesale.com

McClure & Zimmerman
Quality Flowerbulb Brokers
108 W. Winnebago Street
PO Box 368
Friesland, WI 53935-0368
Phone: 800-883-6998
Fax: 800-374-6120
www.mzbulb.com

Nancy Wilson
6525 Briceland-Thorn Road
Garberville, CA 95542
Fax: 707-923-2407
www.asis.com/~nwilson/

Odyssey Bulbs
8984 Meadow Lane
Berrien Springs, MI 49103
Orders: 877-220-1651,
    security code 4642
Phone and fax: 269-471-4642
www.odysseybulbs.com

Vandenberg
PO Box 468
Howell, MI 48844-0468
Phone: 800-955-3813
Fax: 517-546-3429
www.internationalgarden.com/
    vandenberg

WILDFLOWERS AND NATIVE PLANTS

Fancy Fronds
PO Box 1090
Gold Bar, WA 98251
Phone: 360-793-1472
www.fancyfronds.com

High Country Gardens
2902 Rufina Street
Santa Fe, NM 87507
Phone: 800-925-9387
www.highcountrygardens.com

Munchkin Nursery
323 Woodside Drive N.W
Depauw, IN 47115-9039
Phone: 812-633-4858
www.munchkinnursery.com

Native Gardens
5737 Fisher Lane
Greenback, TN 37742
Phone and fax: 865-856-0220
www.native-gardens.com

Native Seeds, Inc.
14590 Triadelphia Mill Road
Dayton, MD 21036-1228
Phone: 301-596-9818
Fax: 301-854-3195

The Natural Garden
38W443 Highway 64
St. Charles, IL 60175
Phone: 630-584-0150
Fax: 630-584-0185
www.thenaturalgardeninc.com

Niche Gardens
1111 Dawson Road
Chapel Hill, NC 27516
Phone: 919-967-0078
Fax: 919-967-4026
www.nichegdn.com

Plants of the Southwest
Santa Fe location:
3095 Agua Fria Road
Santa Fe, NM 87507
Phone: 505-438-8888
Albuquerque location:
6680 4th Street NW
Albuquerque, NM 87107
Phone: 505-344-8830
www.plantsofthesouthwest.com

Prairie Nursery
P.O. Box 306
Westfield, WI 53964
Phone: 800-GRO-WILD (476-9453)
Fax: 608-296-2741
www.prairienursery.com

Sunlight Gardens
174 Golden Lane
Andersonville, TN 37705
Phone: 800-272-7396 or
    865-494-8237
Fax: 865-494-7086
www.sunlightgardens.com

Woodlanders, Inc.
1128 Colleton Avenue
Aiken, SC 29801
Phone: 803-648-7522
www.woodlanders.net

TOOLS, SUPPLIES, AND GARDEN ACCESSORIES

Gardener's Eden
Orders: 866-430-3336
Customer service: 800-822-1214
www.gardenerseden.com

Gardener's Supply Co.
128 Intervale Road
Burlington, VT 05401
Phone: 888-833-1412
www.gardeners.com

Gardens Alive!
5100 Schenley Place
Lawrenceburg, IN 47025
513-656-1482
Fax: 513-354-1484
www.gardensalive.com

Harmony Farm Supply
3244 Highway 116 North
Sebastopol, CA 95472
Phone: 707-823-9125
Fax: 707-823-1734
www.harmonyfarm.com

The Kinsman Company, Inc.
PO Box 428
Pipersville, PA 18947
Phone: 800-733-4146
Customer service: 800-733-4129
Fax: 215-766-5624
www.kinsmangarden.com

The Natural Gardening Co.
PO Box 750776
Petaluma, CA 94975
Phone: 707-766-9303
Fax: 707-766-9747
www.naturalgardening.com

Necessary Organics
PO Box 603
New Castle, VA 24127
Phone: 540-864-5103 or
    800-447-5354
Fax: 540-864-5186
www.agrobiologicals.com

Peaceful Valley Farm Supply
PO Box 2209
Grass Valley, CA 95945
Phone: 530-272-4769 or
    888-784-1722
www.groworganic.com

Smith & Hawken
Phone: 800-940-1170
www.smith-hawken.com

The Urban Farmer Store
San Francisco location:
2833 Vicente Street
San Francisco, CA 94114
Phone: 415-661-2204
Fax: 415-661-7826
Marin location:
653 East Blithedale
Mill Valley, CA 94941
Phone: 415-380-3840
Fax: 415-380-3848
Richmond location:
2121 San Joaquin Avenue
Richmond, CA 94804
General:
Phone: 800-753-DRIP (3747)
www.urbanfarmerstore.com

Walt Nicke Co.
PO Box 433
36 McLeod Lane
Topsfield, MA 01983
Phone: 978-887-3388

PLANT SOCIETIES

American Horticultural Society
7931 East Boulevard Drive
Alexandria, VA 22308
Phone: 703-768-5700 or
    800-777-7931
Fax: 703-768-8700

The Hardy Plant Society—
    MidAtlantic Group
1380 Warner Road
Meadowbrook, PA 19046
Phone: 215-572-0455
wilkin1380@aol.com

The Hardy Plant Society of
    Oregon
1930 NW Lovejoy Street
Portland, OR 97209-1504
Phone: 503-224-5718
Fax: 503-224-5734
www.hardyplantsociety.org

Lady Bird Johnson Wildflower
    Center
4801 La Cross Avenue
Austin, TX 78739
Information: 512-292-4100
Administration: 512-292-4200
Fax: 512-292-4627
www.wildflower.org

New England Wild Flower
    Society
180 Hemenway Road
Framingham, MA 01701
Phone: 508-877-7630 or
    508-877-3658
Fax: 508-877-6553
www.newfs.org

North American Rock Garden
    Society (NARGS)
PO Box 67
Millwood, NY 10546
www.nargs.org

Perennial Plant Association
3383 Schirtzinger Road
Hilliard, OH 43026
Phone: 614-771-8431
Fax: 614-876-5238
www.perennialplant.org

PHOTO CREDITS

INDEX

Boldface page references indicate photographs and illustrations.
Underscored references indicate tables.